Fodor's 2019

NEW YORK CITY

WELCOME TO NEW YORK CITY

From Wall Street's skyscrapers to the neon of Times Square to Central Park's leafy paths, New York City pulses with an irrepressible energy. History meets hipness in this global center of entertainment, fashion, media, and finance. World-class museums like MoMA and unforgettable icons like the Statue of Liberty beckon, but discovering the subtler strains of New York's vast ambition is equally rewarding: ethnic enclaves and shops, historic streets of dignified brownstones, and trendy bars and eateries all add to the urban buzz.

TOP REASONS TO GO

★ **Landmarks:** With towering edifices and awe-inspiring bridges, the skyline says it all.

★ **Shopping:** Whether you're in the market for top designers or inexpensive souvenirs.

★ **Food:** Dim sum to pizza and everything in between, NYC has what you're craving.

★ **Museums:** Art is it, with museums like the Guggenheim and galleries all over town.

★ **The Dazzle:** From the lights of Broadway to celebrity sightings, NYC is full of stars.

★ **Brooklyn and Elsewhere:** Cool neighborhoods and restaurants are a subway ride away.

20 ULTIMATE EXPERIENCES

New York City offers terrific experiences that should be on every traveler's list. Here are Fodor's top picks for a memorable trip.

1 See Art at the Met

NYC has some of the finest art museums in the world and the Metropolitan Museum of Art houses 5,000 years of human creativity—from the ancient Egyptian Temple of Dendur to Warhol's Mao. *(Ch. 10)*

2 Listen to an Opera

Lincoln Center is the performing arts hub for jazz, opera, and ballet and worth a visit for architecture buffs. *(Ch. 19)*

3 Take a Boat

Some of the best views of New York are from the water. From low-key and free to glamorous and expensive, there are plenty of options. *(Ch. 1)*

4 Discover Your Past

Through interactive exhibits, photographs, audio recordings, and artifacts, Ellis Island and the Statue of Liberty remind us that we are a nation of immigrants. *(Ch. 2)*

5 Eat Pizza!

You must eat at least one slice while visiting the city, and there are good pizzerias in almost every neighborhood in the five boroughs. *(Ch. 15)*

6 Walk to Brooklyn

The Brooklyn Bridge is the prettiest bridge in New York and walking across is an iconic activity and delivers some of the best views of Lower Manhattan. *(Ch. 2)*

7 Catch a Show

New York is synonymous with Broadway—the dozens of theaters in the area around Times Square are home to some of the greatest theater performances on earth. *(Ch. 19)*

8 Explore Nature

The American Museum of Natural History is the largest natural history museum in the world, with more that 30 million artifacts from the sea, land, and outer space. *(Ch. 11)*

9 Pay Your Respects

The reflecting pools at the 9/11 Memorial were built where the World Trade Center once stood and are a beautiful tribute and a somber experience. *(Ch. 2)*

10 See Downtown Art

Don't miss the downtown galleries and the acclaimed Whitney Museum of American Art, housed in a beautiful building designed by Renzo Piano. *(Ch. 6)*

11 Visit Hipsterburg

Just over the river, Williamsburg is a concentration of boutiques and vintage stores, casually chic restaurants, and perfectly Instagrammable street art. *(Ch. 13)*

12 Buy a Good Book

New York City has a surprisingly high number of awesome independent bookstores. Most of them are more than just a store, hosting author readings, and events. *(Ch. 17)*

13 View the Skyline

There's no better way to understand the scope of New York City than by a visit to the top of one of the skyscrapers that make up the iconic skyline. *(Ch. 2)*

14 Visit Central Park

Central Park is almost 850 acres of green space—from manicured lawns and beautiful stone structures to ponds and groves of trees. The park is a much appreciated oasis. *(Ch. 11)*

15 Walk the High Line

Experience world-renowned art, kooky art installations, gourmet food and drinks, views of the skyline, and above all, excellent people watching. *(Ch. 6)*

16 See the Arch

Washington Square Park is small but lively—you'll find protesters, jugglers, musicians, dog walkers, and hip NYU students lounging on their unofficial "quad." *(Ch. 5)*

17 Eat World Cuisine

Vegan Ethiopian, Yemeni flatbread, or Korean Barbecue, the city of immigrants offers food from all over the world, especially in the outer boroughs. *(Ch. 15)*

18 Laugh Along

New York is a breeding ground for comics and there's a chance to see everybody from Judah Friedlander to Samantha Bee. Enroll in the lottery for Saturday Night Live. *(Ch. 18)*

19 Enjoy the Show

Visit Coney Island and see a different side of the city. The boardwalk is a quirky, crowded, and a fun place to spend an afternoon. *(Ch. 13)*

20 Watch the Crowds

A magnificent transportation hub, Grand Central Stations Beaux-Arts main hall has a 120-foot-high blue ceiling with a sparkling mural of constellations. *(Ch. 8)*

Fodor's NEW YORK CITY 2019

Editorial: Douglas Stallings, *Editorial Director*; Margaret Kelly, Jacinta O'Halloran, *Senior Editors*; Kayla Becker, Alexis Kelly, Amanda Sadlowski, *Editors*; Teddy Minford, *Content Editor*; Rachael Roth, *Content Manager*

Design: Tina Malaney, *Design and Production Director;* Jessica Gonzalez, *Production Designer*

Photography: Jennifer Arnow, *Senior Photo Editor*

Maps: Rebecca Baer, *Senior Map Editor*; Mark Stroud (Moon Street Cartography), *Cartographers*

Production: Jennifer DePrima, *Editorial Production Manager*; Carrie Parker, *Senior Production Editor*; Elyse Rozelle, *Production Editor*

Business & Operations: Chuck Hoover, *Chief Marketing Officer*; Joy Lai, *Vice President and General Manager*; Stephen Horowitz, *Director of Business Development and Revenue Operations;* Tara McCrillis, *Director of Publishing Operations;* Eliza D. Aceves, *Content Operations Manager and Strategist*

Public Relations and Marketing: Joe Ewaskiw, *Manager;* Esther Su, *Marketing Manager*

Writers: Sarah Amandolare, Kelsy Chauvin, David Farley, Laura Itzkowitz, Josh Rogol, Kate Thorman, Caroline Trefler

Editors: Margaret Kelly, Linda Cabasin

Production Editor: Jennifer DePrima

ISBN 978-1-64097-048-9

ISSN 0736–9395

All details in this book are based on information supplied to us at press time. Always confirm information when it matters, especially if you're making a detour to visit a specific place. Fodor's expressly disclaims any liability, loss, or risk, personal or otherwise, that is incurred as a consequence of the use of any of the contents of this book.

SPECIAL SALES

This book is available at special discounts for bulk purchases for sales promotions or premiums. For more information, e-mail SpecialMarkets@fodors.com.

PRINTED IN THE UNITED STATES OF AMERICA

10 9 8 7 6 5 4 3 2 1

CONTENTS

Fodor's Features

CONTENTS

MAPS

ABOUT THIS GUIDE

Fodor's Recommendations

Everything in this guide is worth doing—we don't cover what isn't—but exceptional sights, hotels, and restaurants are recognized with additional accolades. **Fodor's**Choice★ indicates our top recommendations; and **Best Bets** call attention to notable hotels and restaurants in various categories. Care to nominate a new place? Visit Fodors.com/contact-us.

Trip Costs

We list prices wherever possible to help you budget well. Hotel and restaurant price categories from **$** to **$$$$** are noted alongside each recommendation. For hotels, we include the lowest cost of a standard double room in high season. For restaurants, we cite the average price of a main course at dinner or, if dinner isn't served, at lunch. For attractions, we always list adult admission fees; discounts are usually available for children, students, and senior citizens.

Hotels

Our local writers vet every hotel to recommend the best overnights in each price category, from budget to expensive. Unless otherwise specified, you can expect private bath, phone, and TV in your room. For expanded hotel reviews, facilities, and deals visit Fodors.com.

Top Picks

★ **Fodor's**Choice

Listings

✉ Address
📨 Branch address
☎ Telephone
📠 Fax
🌐 Website
📧 E-mail
🎟 Admission fee
🕒 Open/closed times
[M] Subway
✛ Directions or Map coordinates

Hotels & Restaurants

🏨 Hotel
🛏 Number of rooms
🍽 Meal plans
🍴 Restaurant
✍ Reservations
👔 Dress code
💳 No credit cards
[$] Price

Other

⇨ See also
☞ Take note
⛳ Golf facilities

Restaurants

Unless we state otherwise, restaurants are open for lunch and dinner daily. We mention dress code only when there's a specific requirement and reservations only when they're essential or not accepted.

Credit Cards

The hotels and restaurants in this guide typically accept credit cards. If not, we'll say so.

EUGENE FODOR

Hungarian-born Eugene Fodor (1905–91) began his travel career as an interpreter on a French cruise ship. The experience inspired him to write *On the Continent* (1936), the first guidebook to receive annual updates and discuss a country's way of life as well as its sights. Fodor later joined the U.S. Army and worked for the OSS in World War II. After the war, he kept up his intelligence work while expanding his guidebook series. During the Cold War, many guides were written by fellow agents who understood the value of insider information. Today's guides continue Fodor's legacy by providing travelers with timely coverage, insider tips, and cultural context.

EXPERIENCE NEW YORK CITY

NEW YORK CITY TODAY

The phrase "in a New York minute" exists for a reason: in this frenetic city, things really do change in a flash. With the constant ebb and flow, it can be hard to keep up. Here is just some of what New Yorkers are talking about.

Politics

As it always has, New York City remains a confluence of political ideals that lean toward the liberal side, while balancing the enormous egos and ambitions of its elected officials. In 2014, Democrat Bill de Blasio took over as mayor from Republican-turned-Independent Michael Bloomberg—the fourth-longest-serving NYC mayor in history, with 12 years in office. From the start, Mayor de Blasio faced challenges to employ his populist values and put into action his plans for economic equality across the five boroughs. He had to pick up where billionaire Bloomberg left off, attempting to rein in some of the seemingly limitless large-scale real estate development and private-public partnerships his predecessor facilitated, while still keeping more favored policies that improved public transit, schools, and parks intact. It doesn't help that de Blasio and Governor Andrew Cuomo have their own friction, leaving city and state leadership somewhat at odds with each other. But it's all a familiar song for New Yorkers, who have endured more than their fair share of political strife in both the long and short term. On the bright side, New Yorkers possess a strong survival instinct to get along with each other—it applies to politics just as much as to daily subway commutes.

Economy

A few quick positive economic indicators: New York is experiencing its biggest hotel expansion in a generation, attracting a host of new brands—from high-end boutiques to budget chains—all across the city. The city has 94 hotels in the pipeline to open through 2018 and 2019, with about half of these properties slated for the outer boroughs—a key indicator of the recent visitor trend to visit, and stay in, boroughs beyond Manhattan. And tourists keep on coming: 2016 had a record number of visitors—over 60 million, up from the previous year's 58 million, making it the seventh year in a row for tourism growth. And there's every indication that the city may exceed that number by the end of 2018.

WHAT'S NEW

There's always plenty going on in New York, but keep in mind that the opening dates of projects can change. Check before you travel.

The Pier 57 development at West 15th Street in Hudson River Park originally was a shipping terminal when it opened in 1952. Today, the pier's 12 acres are under construction with a so-called SuperPier that includes plans to introduce new retail, dining, and an elevated park and entertainment space, as well as the new Google headquarters; it's set to open in 2018.

The South Street Seaport is undergoing a $514 million makeover that includes replacing the existing complex at Pier 17 with a sleek new retail and dining complex, featuring a 60,000-square-foot landscaped rooftop. The

Battle of the Boroughs

While visitors are discovering all things Brooklyn right now, New Yorkers are steadily refocusing their trend-spotting gaze on Queens. And it's no wonder—the borough has long-standing residential communities, cheap ethnic eats, established attractions like MoMA PS1, the second-biggest Chinatown in the country, Long Island City's skyline views, and what is generally an easy subway ride to Midtown. Add less-expensive-than-Manhattan (and Brooklyn) hotel rooms and rents, the current and projected development boom, and proposed projects like the QueensWay (aka "the Queens High Line"). Keep an eye on the Bronx, too: the *New York Times* chose the South Bronx as one of the top destinations to visit in 2017. Home to Yankee Stadium, the vast New York Botanical Garden, the Bronx Zoo, and a growing number of breweries and new developments, the borough is more proof that New York City continues to morph.

The Arts

Some of the biggest movers and shakers in the New York art scene have been moving and/or shaking off dust after recent renovations, perhaps suggesting that the art world will be more focused on exhibition spaces than the exhibitions themselves. In 2015, the Whitney Museum of American Art debuted its state-of-the-art new space in the Meatpacking District, complete with terraces opening onto the High Line and stunning views of the Hudson. Meanwhile, the Metropolitan Museum of Art opened the Met Breuer in spring 2016 inside the Whitney's old digs to display its growing collection of contemporary art as it refines plans to renovate its Modern Wing. The Tenement Museum expanded its scope in late 2017, with an exhibit re-creating the life of immigrants in New York post–World War II. Looking ahead, the American Museum of Natural History is planning a six-story addition to improve navigation and add facilities for research and education, and the Lowline underground park is gaining steam; both are set to be completed in 2020.

reopening is scheduled for summer of 2018.

Coney Island's New York Aquarium is open but currently undergoing a $150 million renovation. New features will include a roof deck and a walk-through coral tunnel with sharks swimming overhead. It's set to open in 2018.

Staten Island is hoping to become a tourist destination as it redevelops its waterfront to include a mall (Empire Outlets), a giant observation wheel, an open-air pedestrian boardwalk, restaurants, and a hotel. The first spin on the Wheel is scheduled for mid-2018.

PLANNER

When to Go

New York City weather is a study in extremes. Much of winter brings bone-chilling winds and an occasional traffic-snarling snowfall, but you're just as likely to experience mild afternoons sandwiched by frigid temperatures.

In late spring and early summer, streets fill with parades and street fairs, and free outdoor performances pop up from river to river. Late August is often sweltering, sometimes bringing subway station temperatures over 100°F (thankfully most of the trains themselves have air-conditioning). This is why autumn brings palpable excitement, with colorful foliage complementing the dawn of a new cultural season. Between October and May, museums mount major exhibitions, most Broadway shows open, and opera, ballet, and concert seasons begin.

Getting Around

On Foot. The best way to explore New York is on foot. No matter what neighborhood you're headed to, you'll get a better sense of it by wandering around; you can check out the architecture, pop into cool-looking shops and cafés, and observe the walk-and-talk of the locals. And if you get lost, New Yorkers are actually very helpful with directions.

By Bike. Since Citi Bike's bike-sharing program rolled out in 2013, ridership has gradually increased and New York City's program now boasts the largest fleet of bikes in the nation—with continued expansion to new neighborhoods. The city is acclimating to this popular new mode of transportation (both with its bike lanes and attitudes), but it's still no Amsterdam—yet. Ride off-peak if possible, keep out of Midtown, wear a helmet, and stay alert at all times.

By Public Transportation. New York's subway system is a cost-effective way to get around, and it's one of few in the world that runs 24 hours a day. The subway is safe, but be smart: try to avoid riding alone (especially late at night) and stand near others on the platform or by a stairwell.

If you prefer to stay above ground, and you're not in a rush, consider taking a bus. They're particularly good at off-peak times and if you need to travel crosstown in Manhattan, plus they're all equipped with real-time GPS to track when the next bus arrives at each stop (check out the website: ⊕ *bustime.mta.info*). What a city bus lacks in speed (especially at rush hour), it makes up for in people-watching and city views.

By Taxi. If you'd rather be comfy than thrifty, hail a yellow cab. You'll also spot some apple-green "Boro Taxis" that service the outer boroughs and therefore won't make pickups south of East 96th Street or West 110th. A taxi is available if the center panel of the roof light is lit and the side panels are dark. It's helpful to give your destination address using cross streets: ask to be taken to "55th and Madison" rather than "545 Madison." Avoid trying to hail a cab between 4 and 4:30 pm, when drivers change shifts. And remember that the subway is often faster than a cab, especially when it rains or during rush hour.

E-hail Car Services. Lyft, Juno, Via, and Uber are some of the app-based car services available in Manhattan. ⇨ *For more information about getting around, check out the Travel Smart chapter.*

1

A Guide to the Grid

The map of Manhattan is, for the most part, easy to follow: north of 14th Street, streets are laid out in a numbered grid pattern. Numbered streets run east–west (crosstown), and broad avenues, most of them also numbered, run north (uptown) and south (downtown). The main exception is Broadway, which cuts across the entire length of Manhattan on a diagonal. Below 14th Street, many thoroughfares are named, not numbered, and don't follow a strict grid pattern. It's worth noting that there's a Greenwich Street and a Greenwich Avenue; there's also an East Broadway and a West Broadway, both of which run north–south, and neither of which is an extension of Broadway, leaving even locals scratching their heads.

Street Smarts

You'll look and feel less conspicuous if you replace paper maps with apps. If you have a smartphone or tablet, download a subway map app from the MTA's website to help you plan your trip (by fastest route or fewest train changes), find nearby stations, and stay up-to-date on service disruptions. Most attractions have their own apps to help you make the most of your time. Even better, download just the Fodor's NYC app for attraction overviews and suggestions of what's nearby.

New York City is safe, but it's still a city, so keep flashy jewelry out of sight on the street, and keep your extra cash and credit cards in your hotel safe.

Expect to have yourself and your possessions inspected thoroughly at museums, sports stadiums, and major attractions. There's airport-like security at tourist hot spots like the ferry for Ellis Island and the Statue of Liberty, and at the National 9/11 Memorial and Museum. Police officers reserve the right to check your bags before you pass through a subway turnstile.

We suggest politely ignoring panhandlers, people who offer to hail you a cab, and limousine and gypsy-cab drivers who (illegally) offer rides.

Opening Hours

Subways and buses run around the clock, as do plenty of restaurants. Some shops and services have longer hours than you'll find elsewhere in the United States, so you can get late-night groceries, buy souvenirs, or even get your nails done. In general, you can safely assume that most shops are open seven days a week, from about 10 to 7 or 8 Monday through Saturday, and from noon to 6 on Sunday. Bars generally close at either 2 or 4 am, though some after-hours clubs are open later.

Money-Saving Tips

If you plan to visit lots of attractions, consider buying a CityPass (⊕ *www.citypass. com*), which includes entry to six top-notch sights: the Empire State Building, the Guggenheim Museum or Top of the Rock, the American Museum of Natural History, the Metropolitan Museum of Art (including the Cloisters), Circle Line Cruises or admission to Liberty and Ellis islands, and the National 9/11 Memorial and Museum or the *Intrepid* Sea, Air & Space Museum. The $122 pass, which saves you almost half the cost of individual tickets (and time on lines), is good for nine days from first use. There's also an option for admission to three attractions.

Sign up for discount sites like Groupon, Gilt City, and LivingSocial a month before your visit to score discounts on everything from restaurants and clubs to beauty treatments and attractions.

WHAT'S WHERE

1 Lower Manhattan. This area includes the Financial District, New York Harbor, and TriBeCa. Heavy-duty landmarks anchor the southern tip of Manhattan, including Wall Street and the waterfront parks of Battery Park City. Ferry terminals dispatch boats to Staten Island, Governors Island, Ellis Island, and the Statue of Liberty. The National 9/11 Memorial and Museum, One World Trade Center, and the Brooklyn Bridge are also found here.

2 SoHo, NoLIta, Little Italy, and Chinatown. Luxe shops dominate in SoHo these days, while NoLIta, to the east, has lots of boutiques and restaurants. Little Italy is a shrinking zone of rather touristy eateries while, farther south, Chinatown teems with street vendors selling knockoff handbags and side streets with Chinese herb shops and dim-sum joints.

3 The East Village and the Lower East Side. Once a gritty neighborhood of artists and punks, the East Village is now a melting pot of NYU students, young professionals, and old-timers, but it still feels like a cohesive neighborhood. You'll find some of the best people- and pooch-watching from a bench in Tompkins Square Park. The once seedy, now trendy Lower East Side has lots of live-music clubs, indie clothing shops, and wine bars.

4 Greenwich Village and the West Village. Artists with rent-controlled apartments, out-and-proud gays, and university students still live in the Village, but because those town houses have become so expensive, residents also include wealthy media moguls, celebrities, and socialites. From 14th Street south to Houston (pronounced *how-ston* here), and from the Hudson River east to 5th Avenue, the blocks are a jumble of jazz clubs, restaurants, former speakeasies, and rainbow flags.

5 Chelsea and the Meatpacking District. With hundreds of galleries in a seven-block radius, Chelsea is still the center of the city's contemporary-art scene, even if real estate development has forced some galleries to relocate elsewhere in the city or to Brooklyn. To the south, the Meatpacking District has evolved into a swanky clubbing and restaurant scene by night and—with the High Line, the Whitney Museum of American Art, and high-end boutiques—a prime daytime destination, too.

6 Union Square, the Flatiron District, and Gramercy Park. Bustling Union Square Park hosts the city's best greenmarket. On the 14th Street edge are broad steps where break dancers and other performers busk for onlookers. Nearby, private and elegant Gramercy Park is surrounded by storied mansions and town houses of the Gramercy neighborhood.

WHAT'S WHERE

7 Midtown East, with Murray Hill. Midtown from 5th Avenue to the East River is the refined big sister of flashy Midtown West, with grand hotels, posh shopping, the Chrysler Building, and Grand Central Terminal. Murray Hill is a mix of quiet tree- and town-house-lined streets and attractions like the Empire State Building and the Morgan Library.

8 Midtown West. Head to 42nd Street to see Times Square in all its neon and mega-screen glory. Towering office buildings line Broadway up to Columbus Circle at the edge of Central Park. At Rockefeller Center are the famous ice rink and Christmas tree (in season), and nearby are swank shops like Bergdorf Goodman.

9 The Upper East Side. The Upper East Side is home to more millionaires than any other part of the city. Tucked into the stretch of 5th Avenue here is Museum Mile, including the Metropolitan Museum of Art. Madison Avenue's haute boutiques are another notable neighborhood feature.

10 The Upper West Side, with Central Park and the Cloisters. Wide sidewalks and ornate prewar buildings set the tone, and the American Museum of Natural History and Lincoln Center are big draws. Nearby is the pastoral heart of New York, Central Park, the place to come to escape the bustle of the city with its small zoo, sports fields, carousel, and even a castle. Much farther north is the Cloisters, a branch of the Metropolitan Museum of Art housing medieval works in a reconstructed monastery.

11 Harlem. A hotbed of African American and Hispanic American culture for almost a century, Harlem still sizzles. Many of the brownstone-lined blocks have been refurbished, and there are plenty of boutiques and restaurants, along with a few music venues from the 1920s and '30s that are still in full swing.

12 Brooklyn. New York's largest borough counts among its stars Prospect Park, the Brooklyn Museum, the Brooklyn Botanic Garden, and BAM (the Brooklyn Academy of Music). Its distinctive neighborhoods include Brooklyn Heights, Williamsburg, DUMBO, Park Slope, Coney Island, and Brighton Beach, among others.

13 Queens, the Bronx, and Staten Island. Queens is known for its ethnic communities and cuisine, Arthur Ashe Stadium, and Citi Field. The Bronx may be best known for Yankee Stadium, but the New York Botanical Garden and Bronx Zoo also score home runs. Staten Island's best-known feature might be the ferry, but there are reasons to stick around, including a children's museum and New York City's only historic town and farm: Historic Richmond Town.

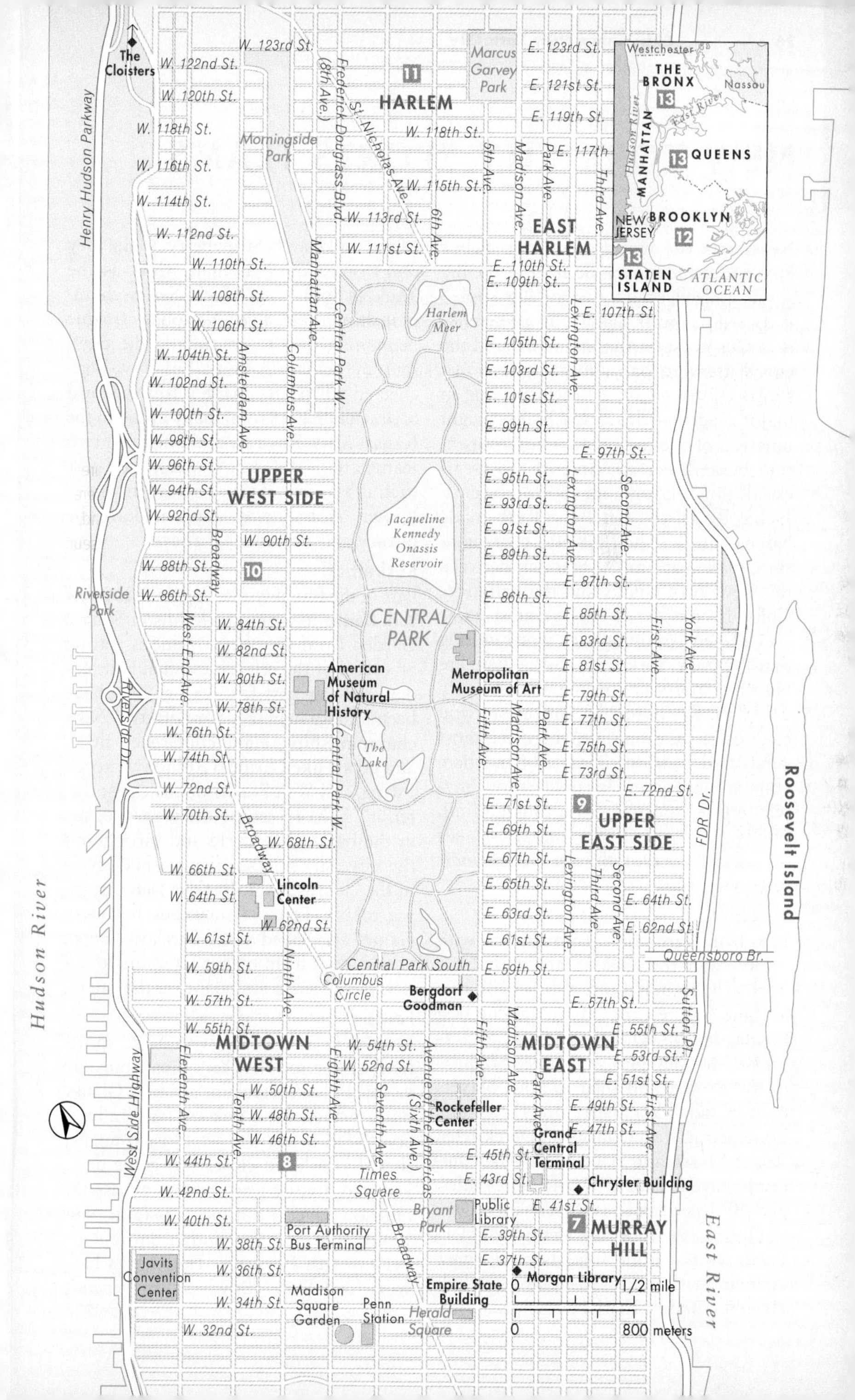

The Cloisters
Henry Hudson Parkway
W. 123rd St.
W. 122nd St.
W. 120th St.
W. 118th St.
W. 116th St.
W. 114th St.
W. 112nd St.
W. 110th St.
W. 108th St.
W. 106th St.
W. 104th St.
W. 102nd St.
W. 100th St.
W. 98th St.
W. 96th St.
W. 94th St.
W. 92nd St.
W. 90th St.
W. 88th St.
W. 86th St.
W. 84th St.
W. 82nd St.
W. 80th St.
W. 78th St.
W. 76th St.
W. 74th St.
W. 72nd St.
W. 70th St.
W. 68th St.
W. 66th St.
W. 64th St.
W. 62nd St.
W. 61st St.
W. 59th St.
W. 57th St.
W. 55th St.
W. 54th St.
W. 52nd St.
W. 50th St.
W. 48th St.
W. 46th St.
W. 44th St.
W. 42nd St.
W. 40th St.
W. 38th St.
W. 36th St.
W. 34th St.
W. 32nd St.
W. 118th St.
W. 115th St.
W. 113rd St.
W. 111st St.
Morningside Park
Frederick Douglass Blvd. (8th Ave.)
St. Nicholas Ave.
6th Ave.
Manhattan Ave.
Central Park W.
Columbus Ave.
Amsterdam Ave.
Broadway
West End Ave.
Riverside Dr.
Riverside Park
11
HARLEM
Marcus Garvey Park
E. 123rd St.
E. 121st St.
E. 119th St.
E. 117th
5th Ave.
Madison Ave.
Park Ave.
Third Ave.
EAST HARLEM
E. 110th St.
E. 109th St.
E. 107th St.
E. 105th St.
E. 103rd St.
E. 101st St.
E. 99th St.
E. 97th St.
E. 95th St.
E. 93rd St.
E. 91st St.
E. 89th St.
E. 87th St.
E. 86th St.
E. 85th St.
E. 83rd St.
E. 81st St.
E. 79th St.
E. 77th St.
E. 75th St.
E. 73rd St.
E. 72nd St.
E. 71st St.
E. 69th St.
E. 67th St.
E. 65th St.
E. 64th St.
E. 63rd St.
E. 62nd St.
E. 61st St.
E. 59th St.
E. 57th St.
E. 55th St.
E. 53rd St.
E. 51st St.
E. 49th St.
E. 47th St.
E. 45th St.
E. 43rd St.
E. 41st St.
E. 39th St.
E. 37th St.
Lexington Ave.
Second Ave.
First Ave.
York Ave.
FDR Dr.
Sutton Pl.
Harlem Meer
Jacqueline Kennedy Onassis Reservoir
CENTRAL PARK
The Lake
UPPER WEST SIDE
10
American Museum of Natural History
Metropolitan Museum of Art
Fifth Ave.
9
UPPER EAST SIDE
Roosevelt Island
Queensboro Br.
Lincoln Center
Central Park South
Columbus Circle
Ninth Ave.
Bergdorf Goodman
MIDTOWN WEST
MIDTOWN EAST
Eighth Ave.
Seventh Ave.
Avenue of the Americas (Sixth Ave.)
Eleventh Ave.
Tenth Ave.
West Side Highway
Rockefeller Center
Grand Central Terminal
8
Times Square
Chrysler Building
Bryant Park
Public Library
7
MURRAY HILL
Port Authority Bus Terminal
Javits Convention Center
Madison Square Garden
Penn Station
Herald Square
Empire State Building
Morgan Library
0 1/2 mile
0 800 meters
Hudson River
East River
Westchester
THE BRONX
13
Nassau
East River
Hudson River
MANHATTAN
QUEENS
13
NEW JERSEY
BROOKLYN
12
13
STATEN ISLAND
ATLANTIC OCEAN

NEW YORK CITY SPORTS TEAMS

No city in the world can claim such a long and storied sports heritage as the Big Apple. Indeed, even the term "Big Apple" is rooted in sports history, as a reference to 1920s horse racing in and around the city. With more than a dozen professional sports teams—many of them playing in major leagues—this town is downright fanatical about competition, not to mention being home to some of the greatest all-time players and sporting events: Jackie Robinson and Babe Ruth made baseball history; the 1958 NFL championship, played at Yankee Stadium between the New York Giants and the Baltimore Colts, is considered "the greatest game ever played" (although it's worth noting that the New York team lost). There are big-time sports happening almost every day in the five boroughs. And even if you can't catch an event live, you can almost surely find it playing in a local bar, where you may encounter fans unlike those anywhere else, sports-logo tattoos and all. *For more information about sports, see Sports and the Outdoors in Travel Smart New York City.*

Baseball

Few teams are more synonymous with a city than the **Yankees** are with New York. The team has one of baseball's best all-time win records, as well as the best regular-season win percentage (.569 as of 2017). They play at Yankee Stadium in the Bronx, and their famous players have included Yogi Berra, Joe DiMaggio, Lou Gehrig, Reggie Jackson, Derek Jeter, Roger Maris, and Babe Ruth. They currently have a total 27 World Series titles, and 40 American League pennants. Over in Queens, the **New York Mets** play at Citi Field, with a proud fan base and legacy all their own. Famous past players include Dwight Gooden, Keith Hernandez, Willie Mays, and Darryl Strawberry. While they don't boast quite as many titles as the Yankees (only two World Series championships and five National League pennants), they're considered the city's scrappy underdog, and all of New York cheered when they made it to the World Series in fall 2015 (eventually losing to the Kansas City Royals). Although the two teams are in different leagues, they play each other several times a year in what's known as a subway series, making intracity rivalry as fierce as ever.

Basketball

Part of the fun of witnessing the NBA **New York Knicks** in action at Madison Square Garden from October to June is getting an eyeful of the celebrities often in attendance. Their past few seasons may have been underwhelming, but with two NBA championships, eight conference titles, and greats like Carmelo Anthony, Patrick Ewing, and Walt Frasier on their past roster, it's hard to escape the team's legacy in the basketball world and throughout the city. Since 2012, they've had rivals in the city, with the **Brooklyn Nets** returning to NYC's most populous borough. Games are played at the Barclays Center, with former team-owner Jay-Z and other notables often in attendance at the games.

Football

Loyalty is a big thing with NYC sports fans, and some **New York Giants** fans are so loyal they even claim to bleed Giants' blue, whereas **New York Jets** fans' rallying cry "J-E-T-S Jets Jets Jets!" is so mighty that if you listen closely on game days, you can almost hear it from across the Hudson River. Both teams play in New Jersey, at MetLife Stadium, from September through February. The Giants have won four Super Bowls (most recently in 2011 against the New England Patriots) and 11 conference titles, led by such players as Eli Manning, Michael Strahan, and Lawrence Taylor. The lower-key Jets, meanwhile, are known as the city's underdog, with only one Super Bowl title (all the way back in 1968) and four division titles. They still have racked up big names like Curtis Martin, Don Maynard, and Joe Namath.

Hockey

Back in 1928, the **New York Rangers** were the first American team to win the NHL's championship Stanley Cup, and today's fans are just as eager as back then to get it back, when they play each season at Madison Square Garden. Famous players like Brian Leetch, Henrik Lundqvist, and Mark Messier have helped the team win a total of two Stanley Cups and two conference titles. Meanwhile, the **New York Islanders** relocated from their suburban Long Island stadium to Brooklyn's Barclays Center in 2015. Since they haven't won a Stanley Cup since the early 1980s, maybe Brooklyn will help them get their mojo back. Their pre-1980s glories include four Stanley Cups and five conference titles.

Soccer

Soccer fans can choose between the city's two Major League Soccer teams during its March through October season: the **New York Red Bulls** and **New York City Football Club.** Devoted Bulls fans head to the soccer-specific Red Bull Arena in Harrison, New Jersey, near Newark for games, while the New York City FC play in the hallowed baseball grounds of Yankee Stadium.

Other Sports

If you can't pick a team, consider a less contentious sport, like tennis—the **U.S. Open** brings the best in tennis to the USTA Billie Jean King National Tennis Center in Queens in late summer. You could also try to catch a matchup in smaller-scale college games, rugby, minor-league baseball, or even **Gotham Girls** roller derby. Or plan an early November trip to witness the fan favorite **NYC Marathon**, the largest marathon in the world, with more than 50,000 runners from around the globe.

SITTING IN A TV AUDIENCE

Tickets to tapings of TV shows are free but can be hard to get, especially on short notice. Most shows accept advance requests by email or phone, or online— but for the most popular shows, you might have to wait a few months. Same-day standby tickets are often available, but be prepared to wait in line for several hours, sometimes starting at 5 or 6 am, depending on how hot the show is, or the wattage of that day's celebrity guests. Remember that standby tickets do not guarantee a seat in the audience.

The Shows

The Daily Show with Trevor Noah. Jon Stewart may have moved on, but host Trevor Noah is glad to welcome you to free tapings of *The Daily Show* just like his predecessor did. Reservations can be made online only, with tickets released gradually for future shows, so check the website often to RSVP for your preferred date. Only the person whose name is on the reservation can check in, and all attendees must be at least 18. The big caveat is that a reservation doesn't guarantee entry, so get in line early. Check the website for more details. ⌧ *733 11th Ave., at 52nd St., Midtown West ⊕ www.showclix.com/ event/TheDailyShowWithTrevorNoah ☞ Free* Ⓜ *A, C, E to 50th St.*

Good Morning America. Robin Roberts, George Stephanopoulos, and Michael Strahan, et al., host this early-morning news and entertainment show. It airs live, weekdays from 7 to 9 am, and ticket requests (free but required if you want a studio tour after the show) can be made online. If you just want to be part of the outdoor audience, you can gather on the corner of West 44th Street and Broadway to participate in outdoor segments. Check the website for more information.

TIPS

■ Follow your favorite shows on social media for updates on last-minute tickets.

■ Audience members must have photo ID, and most studios do not allow shopping bags or knapsacks.

■ Wear layers: TV studios blast the air-conditioning.

■ Dress the part: most shows request business-casual attire and prefer solid, jewel-tone colors (stay away from busy patterns and all white).

■ Sitting in a TV audience can be more boring than watching the show at home. You'll have to wait intermittently while sets are changed and stars' makeup is refreshed; if your seats are in back, you may feel far from the action.

⌧ *7 Times Sq., at 44th St. and Broadway, Midtown West ⊕ www.abcnews.go.com/ GMA/part-times-square-audience/ story?id=12883468* Ⓜ *1, 2, 3, 7, N, Q, R, S, W to Times Sq.–42nd St.*

Late Night with Seth Meyers. *Saturday Night Live* alum Seth Meyers took the reins as host of *Late Night* on NBC in 2014, when former host Jimmy Fallon departed for the *Tonight Show*. Tickets are available online up to two months in advance. Same-day standby tickets are handed out at 9 am at the NBC Experience Store (49th Street entrance). Monologue-rehearsal tickets are available at the NBC Experience Store at 11:30 am. Guests must be 16 or older to be in the audience. ⌧ *30 Rockefeller Plaza, Midtown West ☎ 212/664–3056 ⊕ www.1iota.com/show/461/Late-Night-with-Seth-Meyers* Ⓜ *B, D, F, M to 47th– 50th Sts./Rockefeller Center.*

The Late Show with Stephen Colbert. After hosting the *Late Show* for 22 years, David Letterman passed the torch to former *Colbert Report* host, Stephen Colbert, in 2015. While Colbert's fictional conservative persona did not follow him to his new gig at the Ed Sullivan Theater, his loyal audience did, so expect competition for tickets. The show is usually taped daily at 5:30 pm; check the website and the show's social media for updated details and new ticket releases. You must be 16 or older to sit in the audience. ⊠ *Ed Sullivan Theater, 1697 Broadway, between 53rd and 54th Sts., Midtown West* ☎ *212/975–5853* ⊕ *colbert.1iota.com/show/536/The-Late-Show-with-Stephen-Colbert* Ⓜ *1 to 50th St.; C, E to 50th St.; B, D, E to 7th Ave.*

Live! with Kelly and Ryan Sparks fly on this morning program, which books an eclectic roster of guests. Tickets are available online about six weeks in advance. Standby tickets become available weekdays at 7 am at ABC Studios. Children under 10 are not permitted in the audience. ⊠ *7 Lincoln Sq., between W. 67th St. and Columbus Ave., Midtown West* ☎ *212/456–3054* ⊕ *www.1iota.com/Show/326/LIVE-with-Kelly–Ryan* Ⓜ *1 to 66th St.–Lincoln Center.*

Saturday Night Live. After four decades of laughs, *SNL* continues to push buttons, nurture comedic talents, and captivate audiences—all "live from New York." Standby tickets (only one per person) are distributed at 7 am on the day of the show at the West 49th Street entrance to 30 Rockefeller Plaza. You may ask for a ticket for either the dress rehearsal (8 pm) or the live show (11:30 pm). Requests for advance tickets (two per applicant) must be submitted by email only, during the month of August, to *snltickets@nbcuni.com*; recipients are determined by lottery. You must be 16 or older to sit in the audience. ⊠ *NBC Studios, 30 Rockefeller Plaza, between W. 49th and W. 50th Sts., Midtown West* ☎ *212/664–3056* ⊕ *www.nbc.com/tickets* Ⓜ *B, D, F, M to 47th–50th Sts./Rockefeller Center.*

Today. The *Today Show* doesn't have a studio audience, but if you get yourself to the corner of Rockefeller Center and West 49th Street before well before 7 am, with some posterboard and markers (fun signs always get camera time), comfortable shoes (you'll be on your feet for hours), and a smiley, fun attitude, you might get on camera. America's first morning talk-news show airs weekdays from 7 to 10 am in the glass-enclosed, ground-level NBC studio. ⊠ *Rockefeller Plaza, W. 49th St., Midtown West* ⊕ *www.today.com* Ⓜ *B, D, F, M to 47th–50th Sts./Rockefeller Center.*

The Tonight Show Starring Jimmy Fallon. In 2014, *Saturday Night Live* veteran Jimmy Fallon packed up his impressions and sketches, his roster of star friends, and his house band (the Roots) and moved from *Late Night* to the *Tonight Show,* filling the big comedic shoes of Jay Leno and Johnny Carson before him. He also moved the show back to New York, where it had resided until 1972. Visit the website to reserve free tickets; they're released during the first week of the month prior to the show. ■ TIP→ The show's Twitter feed (@FallonTonight) has up-to-date information. ⊠ *30 Rockefeller Plaza, Studio 6B, Midtown West* ☎ *212/664–3506* ⊕ *www.tonightshow.com/tickets* Ⓜ *B, D, F, M to 47th–50th Sts./Rockefeller Center.*

FREE AND CHEAP

Sometimes it seems like everything in New York costs too much, but in fact the city has tons of free or cheap things to do—you just need to know where to look for them. It's worth noting that NYC is at its most free in summer when there are many outdoor events, but you can find a "wealth" of freebies all year round.

Free Art and Museums

The $23 admission to the **American Museum of Natural History** and the $16 admission to the **Brooklyn Museum** are actually *suggested* donations. Smaller donations may get some eye-rolling from the cashier, but it's a small price to pay for access to world-famous museums. The **Museum at FIT**, "the most fashionable museum in the city" at the Fashion Institute of Technology, is home to a collection of some 50,000 garments and accessories from the 18th century to the present. It's free, off the beaten museum path, and fabulous. Another less trafficked—and free—gem, the **American Folk Art Museum,** features traditional folk art as well as contemporary works by self-taught artists. The museum's diverse collection includes everything from drawings, paintings, and ceramics to mummylike sculptures, decorative furniture, and a beautifully stitched quilt made by female slaves on a Southern plantation. **The National Museum of the American Indian (Smithsonian Institution),** in a majestic Beaux Arts building on the south side of Bowling Green in Lower Manhattan, is a small museum (by New York standards), but it offers free admission as well as free music and dance performances and an extensive permanent collection of textiles, ceremonial objects, and decorative arts. Decidedly on the beaten path, and for good reason, **MoMA** is free on Friday between 4 and 9 pm, when the $25 entry fee is waived. Arrive as close to 4 as you can, and once you get your ticket (the line is long but fast), avoid the crowds by working your way down from the fifth floor. If you want to avoid many of the crowds—and get ahead of the art game—take a gallery crawl in and out of the scores of **galleries in Chelsea** for free access to up-and-coming and superstar artists alike. Unlike major museums, galleries are rarely crowded (except for big-name, Instagram-friendly shows and some Thursdays, when galleries often host openings with free wine and cheese). You'll also find trendy art scenes in SoHo and in Brooklyn's Williamsburg and Bushwick neighborhoods.

Free Entertainment

If you don't see enough movie stars wandering around New York City, you can catch them on a big screen—under the stars—with a free summer flick. There are free screenings all across the five boroughs in summer, from Brooklyn Bridge Park to Bronx Terminal Market (⊕ *www.nycgovparks.org/events/free_summer_movies*). In Manhattan, take your blanket and picnic basket to **Bryant Park**: a tradition since 1992, watching films alfresco surrounded by tall Midtown buildings is a summertime rite of passage for New Yorkers. Be prepared to stake out a good spot on the lawn early in the day. Movie schedules are posted at ⊕ *www.bryantpark.org*.

If you prefer live entertainment, catch tango dancers and jazz musicians outside Lincoln Center at the annual, free, monthlong **Out of Doors** festival, held mid-July to early August. It includes more than 100 performances. You can also experience free music performances, film screenings, and artist conversations at Lincoln Center's **David Rubenstein Atrium**; check the online calendar ⊕ *atrium.lincolncenter.*

org before you visit. **Central Park SummerStage** is your free ticket to a variety of musical acts. There are also a few concert series in Brooklyn, most notably in Prospect Park for summer's **Celebrate Brooklyn!** festival.

Catch rising stars in music, drama, and dance at the **Juilliard School**'s free student concerts (check ⊕ *www.juilliard.edu* for a calendar of events). Free tickets are available at the Juilliard box office for theater performances; standby tickets are available an hour before the show.

One of the city's most beloved events (and the hottest free ticket in town) is **Shakespeare in the Park,** which usually features celebrities practicing their olde-English acting skills in outdoor performances in Central Park. Get in line early in the morning at the Public Theater or head to the Delacorte Theater in Central Park. There are also some free tickets available online; see ⊕ *www.shakespeareinthepark. org* for more information.

Like your theater a little less scripted? Get gratis giggles at the **Upright Citizens Brigade Theatre**'s improv comedy shows, where professional comedians, including UCB cofounder and *Saturday Night Live* alumna Amy Poehler, are sprinkled in with amateurs during the performances. Many of the shows are just $5; some are free. ⊕ *www.ucbtheatre.com.*

Another way to save your pennies for dinner is to catch a free reading at one of the city's bookstores—big (Barnes & Noble) and small (Housing Works Bookstore Café). Or you can get your fix of free words at KGB in the East Village, where authors have been reading since 1993. In Brooklyn, there are several bookstores, as well as the bars Pete's Candy Store and Franklin Park , that have reading series.

Free Rides

One of the best free rides in the city is on the **Staten Island Ferry.** A one-way trip takes 30 minutes and offers magnificent views of the Statue of Liberty, Ellis Island, and the southern tip of Manhattan—plus there's inexpensive beer and snacks. Note that you have to disembark at St. George Terminal in Staten Island before your return trip. Another cheap/sometimes-free ferry sure to (ahem) float your boat is the seven-minute ferry ride from Lower Manhattan to **Governors Island,** a 172-acre island oasis in the heart of New York Harbor. You can visit the former military base turned sculpture park and public playground daily from late May to late September to bike, picnic, wander forts, take in views of Lower Manhattan, and enjoy a variety of cultural offerings and festivals. Ferries are free on weekend mornings and $2 round-trip (for adults) on all weekday and weekend-afternoon ferries. Give your sea legs a rest and take to the sky for an almost-free aerial ride on the **Roosevelt Island Tramway.** For the price of a subway ride ($2.75), you can glide over the East River on the only commuter cable in North America and score stunning city views while you're at it. The trip takes only a few minutes (board at the East 59th Street and 2nd Avenue station) so you have plenty of time to explore Roosevelt Island and FDR Four Freedoms Park before you make the return trip.

NYC'S WATERFRONT PARKS

If Central Park makes you think, "Been there, done that," head to one of the city's many waterfront parks. Many New Yorkers are just now discovering some of these green getaways, too.

Battery Park City

Built on landfill jutting out into the Hudson River, Battery Park City is a high-rise residential neighborhood on the west side of Lower Manhattan, with the Hudson River Park promenade running along the Hudson River. There are several reasonably priced outdoor restaurants with stunning views of the Statue of Liberty. If you have kids, don't miss the excellent Teardop Park, with its long slide and its SeaGlass carousel.

Getting Here

By subway: South Battery Park: 1, R, W to Rector Place; 4, 5 to Bowling Green. North Battery Park: 1, 2, 3, A, C to Chambers Street; E to World Trade Center. By bus: M9, M20, M22.

Brooklyn Bridge Park

Over in Brooklyn, a former industrial site running along a narrow stretch of Brooklyn waterfront from Vinegar Hill to Brooklyn Heights has been turned into an 85-acre, 1.3-mile-long park featuring grassy lawns, rocky outcrops, bike paths, playgrounds, sports fields, basketball courts, and a carousel. There are picnic areas, seasonal food stands by high-profile restaurants, music and film festivals in summer, water-taxi service to Governors Island, and thousands of visitors and locals taking advantage of it all. Perhaps the best feature of this new hipster destination is one that's been here all along: the picture-postcard views of the Brooklyn and Manhattan Bridges and the Manhattan skyline.

Getting Here

By subway: A, C to High Street; F to York Street. Instead of taking the subway, you could take a water taxi (⊕ www.nywatertaxi.com) to Fulton Ferry Landing, the East River Ferry (⊕ www.nywaterway.com) to Fulton Ferry Landing, or by walking across the Brooklyn Bridge.

The East River Park

This landscaped waterfront park, stretching from Montgomery Street to 12th Street along the Manhattan side of the East River, is one of the Lower East Side's best-kept secrets, with ball fields, bike paths, tennis courts, playgrounds, gardens, and picnic areas—along with impressive views of the Brooklyn skyline and the Williamsburg Bridge. You have to cross a footbridge over the FDR Drive to get to the park.

Getting Here

By subway: J, M, Z to Essex Street; F to 2nd Avenue. By bus: M14D, M21, M22.

Governors Island

A fairly recent addition to the city's parks scene, this little island feels like a small town just 800 yards from the tip of Manhattan. Tourists love the unparalleled views of the New York Harbor and Lower Manhattan, and locals love the out-of-city experience. The 172-acre park, built in part from landfill from subway excavations, was a base for the U.S. Army and Coast Guard for almost two centuries. Until 2003, it was off-limits to the public, which could be why the 19th-century homes here are so well preserved. The island is open to the public daily from May to October, with programs including art showings, concerts, and family events. You can take a bike over on the ferry or rent one on the island. For more information, including updated ferry schedules and a calendar of activities, go to ⊕ *www.govisland.org*.

Getting Here

A $2, seven-minute ferry ride (free on weekend mornings) takes passengers to Governors Island from a dock at the restored, cast-iron Battery Maritime Building (10 South Street), near the Staten Island Ferry. Get to the ferry by subway: 1 to South Ferry; 4, 5 to Bowling Green; or R, W to Whitehall Street. By bus: M15, M20, M55.

The High Line

Once an elevated railroad track that serviced the long-ago factories along the lower west side, the High Line was converted into a linear park (like a promenade) that integrates landscaping with rail-inspired design and provides a fresh perspective on the city. Vegetation here includes 210 species of plants, trees, and shrubs intended to reflect the wild plants that flourished for decades after the tracks were abandoned in 1980. The park—30 feet above street level—is open between Gansevoort Street in the Meatpacking District and 34th Street in Midtown. Sweeping views of the Hudson River, an extended sight line of the Meatpacking District, and the Whitney Museum of American Art are the highlights. For information on tours, public programs, and a calendar of events, go to ⊕ *www. thehighline.org* or call ☎ *212/500–6035*. Note that the park is often extremely crowded, especially on afternoons and weekends.

Getting Here

The High Line is accessible at Gansevoort and every two blocks between 14th and 30th Streets, with elevator access at 14th, 16th, 23rd, 30th, and 34th Streets; no bikes are allowed. It's two blocks west of the subway station at 14th Street and 8th Avenue, served by the A, C, E, and L. You can also take the C, E to 23rd Street and walk two blocks west. The 1, 2, 3 stops at 14th Street and 7th Avenue, three blocks away. By bus: M11, M14D, M23, M34.

The Hudson River Park

This 5-mile greenway park hugs the Hudson River from 59th Street to Battery Park. Although the park has a unified design, it's divided into seven distinct sections that reflect the different Manhattan neighborhoods just across the West Side Highway. Along with refurbished piers with grass and trees, there are also attractions like the *Intrepid* Sea, Air & Space Museum at Pier 86 across from 46th Street. A few blocks south, the Circle Line and World Yacht offer boat tours of the Hudson. At Piers 96 and 40, the Downtown Boathouse (⊕ *www.downtownboathouse.org*) offers free kayaking. There's a mammoth sports center, **Chelsea Piers,** between Piers 59 and 61, and a playground, mini-golf course, and beach volleyball court at Pier 25. The park also sponsors free tours and classes, including free fishing. For a calendar of events and activities, go to ⊕ *www.hudsonriverpark. org*. North of Hudson River Park is one of Manhattan's better-known parks, **Riverside Park.**

Getting Here

Hudson River Park is on the far west side of the city, adjacent to the West Side Highway. Crosstown buses at 14th, 23rd, and 42nd Streets will get you close, but you'll still have to walk a bit. It's worth it.

NEW YORK CITY WITH KIDS

From space shuttles to vintage trains, climbing walls to climbing coasters, not to mention zoos, parks, playgrounds, kid-centric shows, and more—the city that never sleeps has plenty of ways to amuse your kids.

Museums

There's a museum for every age, interest, and attention span in New York City. Some are aimed squarely at the younger set, but you shouldn't limit yourself or your kids to "children's" museums. Most—especially the big players like MoMA, the Guggenheim, the Met, and the Whitney—offer programs to engage younger visitors (just ask at the admission desk or check online). That said, sometimes toddlers want play places designed specifically for them, like the play center and interactive exhibits created for the under-five set at the **Children's Museum of Manhattan** and the arts-and-crafts rooms and ball pit at the **Children's Museum of the Arts**. The **American Museum of Natural History** is a top choice for kids of all ages and interests, visitors and locals alike: the giant dinosaurs and the huge blue whale alone are worth the trip, as is the live Butterfly Conservatory (October through May). You'll also find an IMAX theater, ancient-culture displays, and wildlife dioramas. The space shows at the Hayden Planetarium (tickets sold separately) are a big bang with kids. Nearby, the often overlooked **DiMenna Children's History Museum**—in the New-York Historical Society—invites kids (ages eight and up) to connect to the lives of real New York children from the past through hands-on activities that include video games, cross-stitching, and interactive maps. The **Lower East Side Tenement Museum** also offers a glimpse into the lives of early New Yorkers, in this case immigrant families.

Guided tours (for ages six and up) visit restored tenement apartments where costumed "residents" bring history to life. You can also explore the history of public transit in NYC—from horsepower to the subway—at the **New York Transit Museum.** Housed in an old subway station in downtown Brooklyn, this museum has an old bus to pretend-drive, vintage subway cars, and retro ads and maps. Also in Brooklyn is the **Brooklyn Children's Museum,** which, although a trek from the subway, has great hands-on exhibits (best suited for under-eights) like an interactive greenhouse. The **Intrepid Sea, Air & Space Museum,** an aircraft carrier turned museum, houses the world's fastest jets, a Cold War–era submarine, the first space shuttle, the interactive Exploreum Hall, flight simulators, and more. When museums try to make learning fun, they often fall flat, but the **Museum of Mathematics** makes learning kaleidoscopic—and yes, fun—through interactive puzzles, games, displays, and hands-on tools like square-wheel tricycles.

Parks and Playgrounds

If you're looking for space to let off steam in Manhattan, the 843-acre **Central Park** is a good start. You can row boats on the lake, ride a carousel, explore the zoo, rent bikes, picnic, or just wander and enjoy the park's musicians, performers, and 21 playgrounds.

Head to **DUMBO** (short for Down Under the Manhattan Bridge Overpass) for family-friendly **Brooklyn Bridge Park,** a picnic-perfect waterfront park with several inventive playgrounds, Jane's Carousel, the Brooklyn Ice Cream Factory, a public swimming pool, and a variety of kid-centric music, arts, and kite-flying festivals.

If it's too hot, too cold, or the kids just want sporting time in one easy location, head to **Chelsea Piers,** between 18th and 23rd Streets along Manhattan's Hudson River. With a climbing wall, batting cages, ice-skating rinks, basketball and volleyball courts, indoor soccer fields, bowling, sailing, golf, gymnastics, and a Toddler Gym with a ball pit and slides, it's a five-block energy outlet for local and visiting kids of all ages.

Attractions

With all the screeching and honking, wild colors, and crazy behavior, New York City can feel like one big zoo, but if the kids want the real deal, there's a zoo in every borough of NYC. The **Bronx Zoo** stands out as the city's—and country's—largest metropolitan wildlife park, home to more than 4,000 animals, including endangered and threatened species. Plan to spend a whole day here so your kids don't have to choose between Congo Gorilla Forest and the Siberian cats at Tiger Mountain. Manhattan's **Central Park Zoo** is small but popular, and known to little kids as the setting for the animated *Madagascar* films. You'll find red pandas, snow leopards, a penguin house, performing sea lions, grizzly bears, and a petting zoo. You can get face-to-face with even more interesting creatures in **Coney Island,** where the whole family can enjoy a walk along Coney Island's famous boardwalk to take in the beach, Luna Park's amusement rides, the land-marked Cyclone wooden roller coaster (54-inch height requirement), minor-league baseball games at the Cyclones' stadium (MCU Park), Nathan's hot dogs, and the **New York Aquarium,** where the new *Ocean Wonders: Sharks!* exhibit is slated to open in 2018.

Shows

Once upon a time, it seemed like the only truly kid-friendly show on Broadway was *The Lion King.* These days, adults could gripe that Broadway is selling itself to the youngest bidder—but who's complaining when the shows are so adult-friendly, too. *The Lion King* is still a firm favorite with kids, but it has solid competition with the likes of *Aladdin, Matilda, Wicked,* and Off-Broadway shows like *Stomp,* the *Gazillion Bubble Show,* and *Blue Man Group.* Kids shows are popular, so it's rare to find tickets at TKTS booths; book ahead if possible. Preteens and teens who are too cool for the Disney musical experience might appreciate Sam Eaton's mind-boggling display of magic and mentalism in **The Quantum Eye,** Off-Broadway at Theatre 80 in St. Mark's Place. The **New Victory Theater** is New York City's only theater dedicated to presenting family-friendly works; tickets are affordable, and shows are entertaining, never condescending, and, yes, cool. Kids ages three–nine can partake of music, dance, comedy, storytelling, and dancing at Just Kidding at **Symphony Space,** a performing arts center on Broadway and West 95th Street that inspires and entertains with established and emerging family-friendly artists. Interacting is encouraged.

NEW YORK CITY MUSEUMS, AN OVERVIEW

From the grand institutions along Fifth Avenue's museum mile and an underground museum in a converted subway station in Brooklyn to the dramatic new Whitney Museum in the Meatpacking District, New York City is home to an almost overwhelming collection of artistic riches, so it's a good idea to plan ahead. This overview includes museums listed elsewhere in the book; check the index for full listings.

Major Museums

It's hard to create a short list of top museums in New York City, because, well, there are just so many of them. That said, ambitious art lovers will likely focus on the big five. One of the most visited museums in the world, the vast **Metropolitan Museum of Art** (known locally as "the Met," not to be confused with the Metropolitan Opera, also known as "the Met") has a collection that consists of more than 2 million works of art representing 5,000 years of history. Some of the Met's modern art collection is showcased at the Met Breuer, in the former Whitney Museum building. The **Whitney Museum of American Art** itself, which moved from its Upper East Side home to the Meatpacking District in 2015, is the city's hottest museum ticket, as much for its High Line and Hudson views as for its expansive indoor and outdoor exhibition spaces. With its world-famous dinosaur exhibits, its halls of fossils, gems, and human evolution, and its planetarium, the **American Museum of Natural History** is one of the most celebrated museums in the world. Both the **Museum of Modern Art (MoMA)** and the **Solomon R. Guggenheim Museum** are known for their incredible spaces—MoMA, a maze of glass walkways, was designed by Yoshio Taniguchi, while the nautilus-like Guggenheim is a masterwork of Frank Lloyd Wright—as

well as for their superlative collections of contemporary art and space-specific shows.

Other Top Museums

There are many other important museums in the city. The **Frick Collection**, an elegant art museum in the neoclassical mansion of industrialist Henry Clay Frick, is especially worthy of a visit. The **Morgan Library and Museum** is another mansion-museum founded on the vast and varied collections of a magnate—in this case J. P. Morgan. The **American Folk Art Museum** is dedicated to American folk art and the work of contemporary self-taught artists, while the **New Museum** is the only museum dedicated solely to contemporary art in Manhattan. There are several museums to satisfy design lovers, including the **Museum of Arts and Design**, the **Museum at FIT**, the **Skyscraper Museum**, the **Museum of Illustration and the Museum of Comic and Cartoon Art at the Society of Illustrators**, and the **Cooper Hewitt, Smithsonian Design Museum**, packed with hands-on activities for grown-ups. Speaking of lovers, the provocative, adults-only **Museum of Sex** explores the history, evolution, and cultural significance of sex, while the **Museum of American Finance** satisfies our curiosity about money and Wall Street.

New York–Specific Museums

It's appropriate that the city's oldest museum, the **New-York Historical Society**, is dedicated to the city itself. Founded in 1805, this neighbor of the American Museum of Natural History offers a unique and comprehensive overview of New York's history, as well as quirky and compelling exhibits. Other NY–centric museums include the **Museum of the City of New York**, the **Lower East Side Tenement Museum**, the **Merchant's House Museum**, the **Fraunces Tavern Museum**, the **Ellis Island Immigration Museum**, the **New York City Fire Museum**, the **National 9/11 Memorial & Museum**, and the **New York Transit Museum**.

Culturally Specific Museums

New York City is often referred to as a melting pot, which explains the profusion of culture-specific museums dedicated to sharing the broad and specific stories, struggles, and experiences of certain cultural and ethnic groups—often overlooked in mainstream museums. **El Museo del Barrio** focuses on Latin American and Caribbean art and features a popular collection of hand-carved wooden folk-art figures from Puerto Rico. The **National Museum of the American Indian (Smithsonian Institution)** explores the diversity of Native American peoples through cultural artifacts, and regular music and dance performances. The **Jewish Museum**, the **Museum of Jewish Heritage**, and the **Museum at Eldridge Street** explore Jewish culture and art, and the Jewish experience in New York. The **Asia Society and Museum**, the **Museum of Chinese in America (MOCA)**, the **Japan Society**, and the **Rubin Museum of Art** are dedicated to the art and experiences of Asian communities. Other notable ethnic- or culture-specific museums include the **Leslie-Lohman Museum of Gay and Lesbian Art**, the **Ukrainian Museum**, and the **Studio Museum in Harlem** (for artists of African descent locally, nationally, and internationally).

Museums Farther Afield

The **Brooklyn Museum** is the second-biggest museum in New York City and home to an impressive collection of European and American paintings and sculptures, an outstanding Egyptian collection, the Elizabeth A. Sackler Center for Feminist Art, and a memorial sculpture garden of salvaged architectural elements from throughout New York City. A visit to Queens means innovative and experimental art at **MoMA PS1** and the small museum and garden of the **Noguchi Museum**, dedicated to the art of Isamu Noguchi, a prominent Japanese-American sculptor. Other top museums in Queens include the **Museum of the Moving Image** and the **Queens Museum**. The enchanting **Cloisters Museum and Gardens** (an outpost of the Met museum) in Fort Tryon Park in Upper Manhattan is a bit of a trek relative to other city museums, but it's almost guaranteed that you'll find it worth the trip.

Children's Museums

Some kids' museums are fun just for the kids, like the **Children's Museum of the Arts**, the **Children's Museum of Manhattan**, and the **Brooklyn Children's Museum**, but many are fun for the entire family. Kids of all ages will appreciate the fleet of jets, the flight simulator and other hands-on activities, the space shuttle *Enterprise,* and the *Growler* submarine at the *Intrepid* **Sea, Air & Space Museum**. Other crowd-pleasers include **Madame Tussauds New York** and the **Museum of Mathematics**. The **DiMenna Children's History Museum** (at the New-York Historical Society) has interactive exhibits geared to help kids connect with children throughout New York's history.

Galleries

There are countless art galleries in Manhattan and Brooklyn worth visiting; check neighborhood chapters for specific listings. Your interest in these may vary depending on what shows are on at what times, so we also recommend checking the listings in *New York Magazine* and the *New York Times*.

GREAT ITINERARIES

It's challenging but not impossible to take in the big sights of New York City in a bite-size amount of time. Of course, with more major attractions than almost any other city on earth, New York can prove a hard town to know where to start. Here are two compact plans to sample the very best of the Big Apple, whether it's for one day or five days.

NEW YORK CITY IN 1 DAY

In one day, the best way to soak up Manhattan is to start early and mix together a bit of both downtown and Midtown. So grab New York's breakfast of champions—coffee and a bagel—and prepare yourself for the morning rush hour on the subway on your way to **Battery Park.** From this southernmost tip of the island, you'll see the **Statue of Liberty, Ellis Island,** and the **Staten Island Ferry Terminal.** Head up Broadway past **Bowling Green** and the famous *Charging Bull* statue on your way to **Wall Street.** Turn right at the 1846 Gothic Revival–style **Trinity Church** to view giant George Washington at **Federal Hall,** across from the **New York Stock Exchange.** Stroll north, then take a left on Liberty Street to the **World Trade Center** site, home to the **National 9/11 Memorial & Museum** and the 104-story **One World Trade Center.** Make your way to the top of the the latter for a bird's-eye view of Manhattan.

Take the subway uptown to spend the afternoon browsing the **Metropolitan Museum of Art** or the **Museum of Modern Art (MoMA).** Take a quick stroll through nearby **Central Park** afterward, and then take a walk downtown to 42nd Street, passing through **Times Square**—best experienced after dark. If you time it right, you may even have time to catch an 8 o'clock (7 o'clock on many weeknights) Broadway show.

NEW YORK CITY IN 5 DAYS

Five days in New York is enough to explore much of the city's culture and sights, along with a few culinary highlights. The first and most important stop is to any subway-station kiosk to buy a seven-day, unlimited-ride MetroCard for $32—it'll help you make your trip much more affordable and easier to get around the city.

Day 1: Lower Manhattan, SoHo, and Chelsea

With its four centuries of history, Lower Manhattan is a prime starting point for your trip. Kick off Day 1 with a visit to **Battery Park,** Wall Street, and **One World Trade Center,** along with a stop at the **National 9/11 Memorial & Museum.** If you get there early enough, you might have time to hop on a ferry and visit either Liberty Island, home to the **Statue of Liberty,** or **Ellis Island,** the entryway for immigrants coming to America from the late 19th century to the mid-20th century. If you're not able to visit, you'll still be able to glimpse them from Manhattan's southernmost tip.

Afterward, drift north toward Canal Street to discover **SoHo** and its unique cast-iron architecture and shops, and continue your walk even farther uptown into Chelsea (a subway ride might be in order here) to walk the **High Line** at sunset. Have dinner and then, if you're big on nightlife, explore the nearby Meatpacking District's many hopping bars and clubs to get your dance on into the wee hours of the morning.

Day 2: Grand Central, 5th Avenue, Rockefeller Center, and Times Square

Start Day 2 with breakfast at **Grand Central Terminal,** one of NYC's most majestic spaces, where you can gaze up at its ceiling's sparkling constellations and down at the throngs of commuters whizzing through. Head north on **5th Avenue** to check out **Rockefeller Center** (if it's winter, that'll include the ice-skating rink). Pop into the **NBC Experience Store** and book a tour through several classic NBC sets. On a clear day, visit the tower's observation deck for a perfect view of the **Empire State Building** and beyond.

Then make a pit stop at the **Museum of Modern Art (MoMA)** to check out one of the world's best modern art museums; must-see exhibits include Andy Warhol's soup cans and "Starry Night" by Vincent van Gogh. After you get your art fill, veer southwest toward **Times Square** to join travelers (and some locals) who converge on the "crossroads of the world" to bask in Broadway's bright lights.

Day 3: Brooklyn Bridge, Chinatown, Lower East Side, and the East Village

For Day 3, take the subway over to Brooklyn and head to **Brooklyn Bridge Park** to view the picturesque lower Manhattan skyline. There you can walk across the **Brooklyn Bridge** back to Manhattan, where you'll end up in **Chinatown**, with its many tasty eateries. Cross Canal Street and walk east past the regal **Manhattan Bridge Arch**, into the **Lower East Side**. The **Tenement Museum** is among the city's most interesting, historic experiences, so plan an hour or two there.

Then stroll north through the **East Village** and **Alphabet City,** with a break in **Tompkins Square Park** for a nice dose of people-watching. Grab a drink at one of the many bars, or treat yourself to a cannoli at an old-school Italian bakery.

Day 4: Museum Mile, Central Park, and the Upper West Side

Infuse some of NYC's best art and history into Day 4 at one of several truly great institutions along the Museum Mile on the Upper East Side. You can invest a couple of hours (or the whole day) exploring the **Metropolitan Museum of Art, Guggenheim,** and many more. You can also start (or end) your museum-hopping on the Upper West Side with the **American Museum of Natural History.** Regardless of where you start, make sure you spend a few hours checking out **Central Park** and its many points of interest, like Bethesda Terrace, the carousel, and Belvedere Castle.

As you exit the park on the west side, walk to Broadway for a taste of some of the Upper West Side's authentic delicatessen delights, and top off the evening in Harlem for a show at the historic **Apollo Theater.**

Day 5: Union Square, Washington Square Park, West Village

On Day 5, start at **Union Square,** home to a greenmarket (and seasonal holiday crafts market) and surrounded by stores big and small. Don't miss the "18 miles of books" (new and used) for sale at the Strand on Broadway, a local literary institution. Stroll down to **Washington Square Park** to hear buskers playing their hearts out and watch NYU kids hanging out between classes.

Walk toward Bleecker Street, and wander along the winding lanes of the West Village. On Christopher Street, see the historic **Stonewall Inn,** a pivotal site in the gay-rights movement, and other famous watering holes frequented by artistic luminaries throughout the decades.

NEW YORK CITY FESTIVALS

Spring

Spring means the start of baseball season with home openers, usually in the first week of April, for both of New York's Major League teams: the Yankees and the Mets.

Sakura Matsuri Cherry Blossom Festival. New Yorkers come out of hibernation en masse at the end of April to witness the extremely popular annual Sakura Matsuri Cherry Blossom Festival at the Brooklyn Botanic Garden. In addition to the blooming cherry trees, there are Taiko drumming performances, Japanese pop bands, samurai swords, martial arts, tea ceremonies, and more. ⊠ *Brooklyn Botanical Garden, 990 Washington Ave., Prospect Heights* ⊕ *www.bbg.org* ✉ *$15* Ⓜ *2, 3 to Eastern Parkway–Brooklyn Museum; 2, 3, 4, 5 to Franklin Ave.*

Tribeca Film Festival. Founded by Jane Rosenthal and Robert De Niro to contribute to the long-term recovery of Lower Manhattan after 9/11, the Tribeca Film Festival has become one of the most prominent film festivals in the world. There are upward of 250 films, more than 1,000 screenings at multiple locations including the Tribeca Film Center (TFC, 375 Greenwich St., 2nd floor), and plenty of buzz. It typically takes place mid- to late April. ⊠ *TriBeCa* ⊕ *www.tribecafilm.com.*

Summer

Free outdoor movie festivals are a huge draw in summer: choices include sci-fi movies with a view of Brooklyn Bridge Park (⊕ *www.brooklynbridgepark.org*); indie movies on city rooftops (⊕ *www.rooftopfilms.com*); and classics screened every Monday night in Midtown's Bryant Park (⊕ *www.bryantpark.org*).

Celebrate Brooklyn! Celebrate Brooklyn! is one of the city's most popular free, outdoor performing arts festivals, and *the* place to catch excellent live music in the great Brooklyn outdoors. The artists and ensembles reflect the borough's diversity, ranging from internationally acclaimed performers to up-and-coming musicians. The lineup also includes kids' shows, movies with live music, ballet, and more. Performances are rain or shine and free (suggested donation of $3), with the exception of ticketed benefit concerts, which directly support the festival. There are usually about 2,000 chairs, but many people think the best seats are on the lawn, so come early and bring a blanket. Local restaurants set up food and drink stands. ⊠ *Prospect Park Bandshell, 9th St. and Prospect Park W entrance, Park Slope* ⊕ *www.bricartsmedia.org/performing-arts/celebrate-brooklyn* ✉ *Free* Ⓜ *F, G to 7th Ave.; 2, 3 to Grand Army Plaza.*

Midsummer Night Swing. If dancing in the street is your thing, join the Midsummer Night Swing festival, an outdoor music and dance party in Lincoln Center Plaza that occurs from late June to mid-July. Take lessons with pros or just strut your natural moves on the dance floor. ⊠ *Damrosch Park, 60 Lincoln Center Plaza, Upper West Side* ⊕ *www.midsummernightswing.org* ✉ *$17–$20 or buy a pass* Ⓜ *1 to 66th St.*

Museum Mile Festival. For one day every June, thousands of locals and visitors celebrate the Museum Mile Festival when museums along 5th Avenue from 82nd Street to 105th Street open their doors for free from 6 pm to 9 pm. There's also dancing and entertainment along the street. ⊠ *Upper East Side* ⊕ *www.museummilefestival.org.*

Summer Streets. On three consecutive Saturdays every August, you can join hundreds of thousands of locals to let loose on nearly 7 miles of pedestrianized arterials for Summer Streets. From the Brooklyn Bridge to Central Park, along Park Avenue and connecting streets, New Yorkers hit the car-free streets to run, zipline, dance, experience art, or just ramble along the city's streets in a new way—all for free. ⊠ *New York* ⊕ *www.nyc.gov/summerstreets.*

Other popular summer festivals and events include Coney Island's **Mermaid Parade,** the **New York International Fringe Festival, SummerStage,** and **Shakespeare in the Park.**

Fall

Brooklyn Book Festival. The Brooklyn Book Festival is a huge, (mostly) free public event with an array of established and emerging authors, readings, panels, discussions, parties, games, and signings—all held in clubs, parks, theaters, and libraries across Brooklyn at the end of September. ⊠ *New York* ⊕ *www.brooklynbookfestival.org.*

Feast of San Gennaro. Every year, thousands of locals and visitors flock to Little Italy for the multiday Feast of San Gennaro in mid-September. This festival is a mix of religion, food, colorful parades, and live entertainment. Don't miss the cannoli-eating competition at the beginning of the festival. ⊠ *Little Italy* ⊕ *www.sangennaro.org.*

New York City Marathon. Even if you're not joining the more than 50,000 runners taking a 26.2-mile tour through New York's five boroughs on the first Sunday in November, you'll want to experience the electric atmosphere and the very best of New York with the 2 million spectators who come out to watch and cheer. ⊠ *New York* ⊕ *www.tcsnycmarathon.org.*

Other top fall events include the **Village Halloween Parade, Macy's Thanksgiving Day Parade,** and the **Rockefeller Center Tree Lighting Ceremony.**

Winter

New York Botanical Holiday Train Show. The New York Botanical Garden's Holiday Train Show is one of the city's top seasonal attractions, especially for families. It runs from the end of November to mid-January, and you'll find electric trains, more than 150 miniature replicas of city landmarks (made out of twigs and bark), and magical landscapes—all housed in a conservatory, so winter weather can't dampen your spirits. ⊠ *2900 Southern Blvd., Bronx* ☎ *718/817–8700* ⊕ *www.nybg.org* ✉ *$20–$25* Ⓜ *D, 4 to Bedford Park Blvd.; Metro-North (Harlem local line) to Botanical Garden.*

To ring in the **Lunar New Year** in January or February (the date varies), the streets of Chinatown give way to food vendors hawking traditional eats, colorful costumes and decorations, and a major parade of elaborate floats, marching bands, and dragon troupes running from Little Italy through Chinatown and Lower Manhattan. Festivities also take place in Sunset Park in Brooklyn and in the Flushing neighborhood of Queens (⊕ *www.betterchinatown.com*).

For five days each January, **Winter Jazzfest NYC** (⊕ *www.winterjazzfest.com*), happens at venues around the city. You can also sign up for a local event like the **No Pants Subway Ride** in January (⊕ *www.improveverywhere.com*).

BEST TOURS IN NEW YORK CITY

Sometimes a guided tour is the way to go, even if you usually prefer to fly solo. Tours can be a great way to investigate out-of-the-way areas, to get an insider's perspective on where locals eat and play in the city, and to learn about interesting aspects of the city's history, inhabitants, or architecture. Whether you want the classic hop-on, hop-off bus tour to get oriented in the city, or a more personal, interest-specific walk, you'll find it here. Most companies offer tours of various lengths; you can find everything from one-hour tours to full-day excursions. ■TIP→ Some of the bigger tour companies offer discounts if you book in advance online.

Boat Tours

Circle Line Sightseeing Cruise. In good weather, a Circle Line Sightseeing Cruise around Manhattan Island is one of the best ways to get oriented in the city. Popular options include the "Best of NYC" ($42), "Harbor Lights" ($39), and "Landmarks" ($36) cruises. ⊠ *Pier 83, W. 42nd St., Midtown West* ☎ *212/563-3200* ⊕ *www.circleline42.com* ✉ *From $29* Ⓜ *A, C, E to 42nd St.–Port Authority; 1, 2, 3, 7, N, Q, R, S, W to Times Sq.–42nd St.*

Manhattan By Sail. Looking for a more historical experience? Manhattan By Sail has several historic boats including an 82-foot schooner dating from the 1920s and the 158-foot-tall *Clipper City* tall ship. Public sails include themed Sunday brunch sails, a wine-tasting sail, a lobster-and-beer-lovers sail, and a jazz sail against stunning moonlit views. The cruises operate mid-April through mid-October. Reservations are advised. ⊠ *North Cove Marina at World Financial Center, Financial District* ☎ *212/619-0907* ⊕ *www.*

manhattanbysail.com ✉ *From $25* Ⓜ *A, C to Chambers St.; R, W to Cortland St.; A, C, J, Z, 2, 3, 4, 5 to Fulton St.*

Bus Tours

Big Bus New York. Like its double-decker competitors, Big Bus offers various hop-on, hop-off open-top tours of the city, but its most popular ticket is a two-day pass that includes loops that cover downtown, uptown, and Brooklyn, as well as a night tour or a sightseeing cruise, plus several city attractions. ⊠ *Ticket desk, B.B. King Blues Club & Grill, 237 W. 42nd St., Midtown West* ☎ *212/685-8687* ⊕ *www.bigbustours.com* ✉ *From $45* Ⓜ *A, C, E to 42nd St.–Port Authority; 1, 2, 3, 7, N, Q, R, S, W to Times Sq.–42nd St.*

Gray Line New York Sightseeing. Gray Line runs various hop-on, hop-off double-decker bus tours, including a downtown Manhattan loop, an upper Manhattan loop, a Brooklyn loop, and evening tours of the city. Packages include 48-hour and 72-hour options plus entrance fees to attractions. ⊠ *777 8th Ave., between 46th and 47th Sts., Midtown West* ☎ *800/669-0051* ⊕ *www.newyorksightseeing.com* ✉ *From $44* Ⓜ *A, C, E to 42nd St.–Port Authority; 1, 2, 3, 7, N, Q, R, S, W to Times Sq.–42nd St.*

Walking Tours

Big Onion Walking Tours. The wisecracking PhD candidates of Big Onion Walking Tours lead themed tours such as "Upper East Side: A Clash of Titans," "Immigrant New York," and "Gangs of New York," as well as renowned multiethnic eating tours and guided walks through neighborhoods from Harlem to the Financial District and Brooklyn. Tours run daily. ⊠ *New York* ☎ *888/606-9255* ⊕ *www.bigonion.com* ✉ *From $25.*

Like A Local Tours. Walk like a local, talk like a local, and best of all eat like a local with a highly curated tour from Like A Local. Options include the "Flatiron Food, History, and Architecture" tour, which is a lovely walk from the Flatiron District to Union Square with a lot of tasty stops, photo ops, local history, and private kitchen visits along the way. If you're looking to feel like a hip local in Brooklyn, try the "Insider Art Tour of Bushwick, Brooklyn." ⊠ *New York* ⊕ *www.likealocaltours.com* ✉ *From $50.*

The Municipal Art Society of New York. The Municipal Art Society conducts a variety of walking tours that emphasize the architecture, history, and changing faces of particular neighborhoods. Options include "Empire to Penn," "The Bronx's Urban Art," and "Storefront: the Disappearing Face of New York." The walking tour of Grand Central explores the 100-year-old terminal's architecture, history, and hidden secrets. ⊠ *Midtown West* ☎ *212/935–3960, 212/935–3960* ⊕ *www.mas.org/tours* ✉ *From $20.*

New York City Cultural Walking Tours. Alfred Pommer's walking tours cover such topics as building gargoyles, the TriBeCa Historic District, and the Upper East Side Millionaire's Mile. Check the website for more information and schedules. ⊠ *New York* ☎ *212/979–2388* ⊕ *www.nycwalk.com* ✉ *From $25.*

New York Food Tours. Options from the New York Food walking tours include "The Freakiest and Funniest Food" ($65), "Tastes of Chinatown" ($60), "Ultimate New York Food & Culture Tour" ($60), "Everything Chocolate" ($60), and an East Village food and culture tour ($75). ⊠ *New York* ☎ *347/559–0111* ⊕ *www.foodtoursofny.com* ✉ *From $60.*

Specialty Tours

Bike and Roll. From Central Park to the Brooklyn Bridge, there's a lot of ground to cover; do yourself a favor and use wheels. Bike and Roll NYC offers guided bike tours with a range of distances and levels of difficulty in Manhattan and across to Brooklyn. There's a popular tour of the waterfront parks and one of Central Park. Rates include bike rentals, helmets, and water. ⊠ *New York* ☎ *212/260–0400* ⊕ *www.bikenewyorkcity.com* ✉ *From $50.*

Boroughs of the Dead. From tours taking in haunts of the East and West Village to 19th-century true-crime tours to Manhattan's only dedicated Edgar Allan Poe walking tour, the Boroughs of the Dead two-hour tours suggest that the inhabitants of this city truly never sleep—even when they're dead. Don't wait for Halloween to explore the historical crime, gore, and paranormal activities of Manhattan and Brooklyn. No capes, costumes, or gimmicks here: just dark, haunting history. ⊠ *New York* ☎ *646/932–0680* ⊕ *boroughsofthedead.com* ✉ *From $25.*

Shop Gotham. If you're on a mission to shop till you drop, you won't want to waste time with a map. The fashion-savvy guides at Shop Gotham will save you time and money by guiding you to the best boutiques of SoHo and NoLIta and elsewhere, getting you exclusive shop discounts, and also offering styling advice. Private tours are available, too. ⊠ *New York* ☎ *212/209–3370* ⊕ *www.shopgotham.com* ✉ *From $38.*

A Slice of Brooklyn. You can manage fine without a guide to hold your hand through Rockefeller Center and past the decked-out windows of 5th Avenue, but if you're interested in experiencing a more local holiday light tradition, take A Slice of Brooklyn's bus tour to the festive (and blinding) neighborhood light scene that is Brooklyn's Dyker Heights. The tour, offered in December, introduces you to some of Brooklyn's less touristed neighborhoods. Other tours include the Original Brooklyn Pizza Tour, a bus tour of iconic Brooklyn pizza joints, and tours of quintessential Brooklyn neighborhoods. ⊠ *New York* ☎ *212/913–9917* ⊕ *www. asliceofbrooklyn.com* ✉ *From $50.*

Free Tours

Big Apple Greeter. This free volunteer-led tour service pairs visitors with knowledgeable locals who share insights and tips and cater tours to specific interests. It's like having a friend in town who squires you around and pays for his or her own lunch. Request a greeter at least three weeks before your visit by filling in the online form. ⊠ *New York* ☎ *212/669–8159* ⊕ *www.bigapplegreeter.org* ✉ *Free.*

Central Park Conservancy. The Central Park Conservancy offers free guided tours that provide an introduction to the different areas of Central Park: its woodlands, romantic vistas, Conservatory Garden, Seneca Village, and secret corners and off-the-beaten-path walks. Volunteer-led Welcome Tours meet at different points in the park, so check the website for details. Premier tours are ticketed ($15) and provide a more in-depth experience. ⊠ *New York* ☎ *212/794–6564* ⊕ *www.central-parknyc.org* ✉ *Free.*

Free Tours by Foot. The walking tours of Manhattan and Brooklyn hosted by Free Tours by Foot are technically free (you pay what you feel the tour was worth at the end). Highlights include sunset walking tours of the High Line, a Brooklyn graffiti and street art tour, and a journey through the storied past of the East Village. Reservations are required for all tours, which are about two hours. ⊠ *New York* ☎ *646/450–6831* ⊕ *www.freetours-byfoot.com* ✉ *Free (suggested donation).*

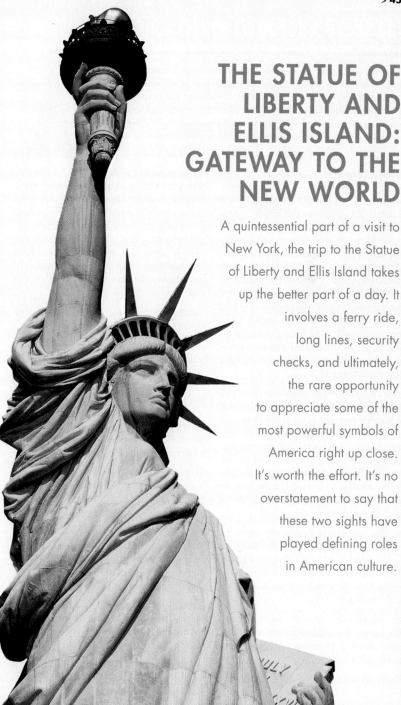

THE STATUE OF LIBERTY AND ELLIS ISLAND: GATEWAY TO THE NEW WORLD

A quintessential part of a visit to New York, the trip to the Statue of Liberty and Ellis Island takes up the better part of a day. It involves a ferry ride, long lines, security checks, and ultimately, the rare opportunity to appreciate some of the most powerful symbols of America right up close. It's worth the effort. It's no overstatement to say that these two sights have played defining roles in American culture.

THE STATUE OF LIBERTY

Impressive from the shore, the Statue of Liberty is even more majestic up close. For millions of immigrants, the first glimpse of America was Lady Liberty, growing from a vaguely defined figure on the horizon into a towering, stately colossus. Visitors approaching Liberty Island on the ferry from Battery Park may experience a similar sense of wonder as they approach. Note that at press time most of Ellis Island is still closed due to damage from Hurricane Sandy. Check www.nps.gov/elis for updates.

What's Here

The 152-foot-tall **statue** of Liberty, officially named *La Liberté éclairant le monde* ("Liberty Enlightening the World") was a gift from the people of France to the United States. It was designed by French sculptor Frédéric Auguste Bartholdi, built in France, and shipped to America where it was assembled. The statue stands atop an 89-foot-tall **pedestal** designed by American architect Richard Morris Hunt. The lines of Emma Lazarus's sonnet "The New Colossus" ("Give me your tired, your poor, your huddled masses yearning to breathe free...") are inscribed on a plaque inside the pedestal.

Inside the pedestal is an informative and entertaining **museum**. Highlights include the torch's original glass flame (the current flame is 24-karat gold and lit at night by floodlights), full-scale copper replicas of Lady Liberty's face and one of her giant feet, Bartholdi's alternative designs for the statue, and a model of the interior framework designed by Gustave Eiffel)of Eiffel Tower fame).

The **observatory platform** at the top of the pedestal is a great place for a photo op; it's 16 stories high, and you'll have all of Lower Manhattan spread out in front of you. The observatory platform is accessible via elevator if you don't want to climb the stairs.

The **crown** is the statue's highest accessible point. It's reached by stairs (154 of them; about a 20 minute journey) from the observatory platform.

Liberty Island has a pleasant outdoor café.

Know Before You Go

Buy your tickets in advance. There are a limited number of same-day standby tickets available at ferry ticket offices, where you catch the ferry but we strongly advise planning early. Once you reach the island, there are no tickets available, and without a ticket there is absolutely no admittance into the pedestal or the museum.

You have three choices when buying your ticket to the Statue of Liberty:

A. You can just buy a ferry ticket. This will get you to Liberty Island and Ellis Island but it does not get you *into* the Statue of Liberty—either the pedestal or the crown. The ferry ticket does include a self-guided audio tour of Liberty Island (there's an adult version and a kids version). Pick up your audio guide when you exit the ferry at Liberty Island.

B. You can buy your ticket with pedestal access; there is no extra charge but you should do this in advance. Pedestal access includes access to the Liberty Island Museum.

C. For crown access, plan *far* in advance, as there are only 320 spots available each day and they sell out months in advance. There is a small extra fee.

Liberty Highlights

■The surreal chance to stand next to, and be dwarfed by, the original glass torch and the copper cast of Lady Liberty's foot.

■The vistas of New York from the observatory platform.

Statue Basics

- ☎ 212/363–3200; 877/523–9849 ticket reservations
- ⊕ www.nps.gov/stli
- 🎫 Free; ferry $18 round-trip (includes Ellis Island); crown tickets $3
- ◷ Daily 9:30–5:00; extended hours in summer.

Liberty helicopters

ALTERNATIVE VIEWS

- The free Staten Island Ferry offers a great view of New York Harbor and of the Statue of Liberty from a distance (see Chapter 2).
- Webcams placed around the statue's torch allow you to see what Lady Liberty sees—wide views of the New York City skyline, the Hudson River, and ships in the harbor—from your computer or phone.
- Liberty Helicopters has sightseeing tours that fly over the crown and torch (see Chapter 1).

FAST FACT: To move the Statue of Liberty from its initial home on a Paris rooftop to its final home in the New York Harbor, the statue was broken down into 350 individual pieces and packed in 214 crates. It took four months to reassemble it.

FAST FACT: The face of Lady Liberty is actually a likeness of sculptor Frederic-Auguste Bartholdi's mother—quite a tribute.

Foundation of the pedestal to torch: 305'6"

Heel to top head: 111'6"

FAST FACT: Lady Liberty has formidable proportions. Her face is more than 8 feet tall, she has a 35-foot waistline, and she weighs 225 tons (450,000 pounds). Her crown has 7 rays, to represent the 7 continents; each is 9-feet long and weighs about 150 pounds.

ELLIS ISLAND

Chances are you'll be with a crowd of international tourists as you disembark at Ellis Island. Close your eyes and imagine the jostling crowd 100 times larger. Now imagine that your journey has lasted weeks at sea and that your day pack contains all your worldly possessions. You're hungry, tired, jobless, and homeless. This scenario just begins to set the stage for the story of the millions of immigrants who passed through Ellis Island. Between 1892 and 1924, approximately 12 million men, women, and children first set foot on U.S. soil at the Ellis Island federal immigration facility. By the time the facility closed in 1954, it had processed the ancestors of more than 40% of Americans living today. *At press time limited parts of Ellis Island have reopened after Hurricane Sandy. Visit www. nps.gov/elis/planyourvisit for updated information.

WHAT'S HERE

The island's main building, now a national monument, reopened in 1990 as the Ellis Island Immigration Museum, with more than 30 galleries of artifacts, photographs, and taped oral histories. The centerpiece of the museum is the **Registry Room** (also known as the Great Hall). It feels dignified and cavernous today, but photographs show that it took on many configurations over the years, always packed with humanity. While you're here, look out the Registry Room's tall, arched windows and try to imagine what passed through immigrants' minds as they viewed Lower Manhattan's skyline to one side and the Statue of Liberty to the other.

Along with the Registry Room, the museum includes the ground-level **Peopling of America Center,** which explores immigration to the United States before and after Ellis Island was a portal for immigrants. Graphics and poignant audio stories give firsthand accounts of the immigrants' journeys—from making the trip and arriving in the United States to their struggle and survival here. There is also the **American Family Immigration Center,** where you can search Ellis Island's records for your own ancestors, and the **American Flag of Faces,** an interactive display filled with images of immigrants submitted online (submit yours at *FlagofFaces.org*). Outside, the **American Immigrant Wall of Honor** has inscribed upon it the names of more than 600,000 immigrant Americans.

MAKING THE MOST OF YOUR VISIT

Because there's so much to take in, it's a good idea to make use of the museum's interpretive tools. Check at the visitor desk for free film tickets, ranger tour times, and special programs.

Consider starting your visit with a viewing of the free film *Island of Hope, Island of Tears.* A park ranger starts off with a short introduction, then the 25-minute film takes you through an immigrant's journey from the troubled conditions of European life (especially true for ethnic and religious minorities), to their nervous arrival at Ellis Island, and their introduction into American cities. The film is a primer into all the exhibits and will deeply enhance your experience.

The audio tour, which is included in the ticket price, is also worthwhile: it takes you through the exhibits, providing thorough, engaging commentary interspersed with recordings of immigrants recalling their experiences.

ELLIS ISLAND HIGHLIGHTS

■Surveying the Great Hall.

■The moving film *Island of Hope, Island of Tears.*

■Exploring the Peopling of America Center to gain a deeper understanding of the history of immigration in America.

■Reading the names on the American Immigrant Wall of Honor.

■Researching your own family's history.

Ellis Island Basics

📠 212/363–3200 Ellis Island; 212/561–4500 Wall of Honor information

🌐 www.nps.gov/stli

🎫 Free; ferry $18 round-trip (includes Liberty Island)

🕙 Daily 9:30–5:00; extended in summer.

IMMIGRANT HISTORY TIMELINE

Starting in the 1880s, troubled conditions throughout Europe persuaded both the poor and the persecuted to leave their family and homes to embark on what were often gruesome journeys to come to the golden shores of America.

1880s 5.7 million immigrants arrive in U.S.

1892 Federal immigration station opens on Ellis Island in January.

1901–1910 8.8 million immigrants arrive in U.S.; 6 million processed at Ellis Island.

1907 Highest number of immigrants (860,000) arrives in one year, including a record 11,747 on April 17.

1910 75% of the residents of New York, Chicago, Detroit, Cleveland, and Boston are now immigrants or children of immigrants.

1920s Federal laws set immigration quotas based on national origin.

1954 Ellis Island immigration station is closed.

New arrivals line up to have their eyes inspected.

FAST FACT: Some immigrants who passed through Ellis Island later became household names. A few include Charles Atlas (1903, Italy); Irving Berlin (1893, Russia); Frank Capra (1903, Italy); Bob Hope (1908, England); Knute Rockne (1893, Norway); and Baron Von Trapp and his family (1938, Germany).

FAST FACT: In 1897, a fire destroyed the original pine immigration structure on Ellis Island, including all immigration records dating back to 1855.

FAST FACT: The first test that immigrants had to pass was known as the "six-second medical exam." As they entered the Great Hall, they were watched by doctors; if anyone seemed disabed, their clothing was marked with chalk and they were sent for a full exam.

Four immigrants and their belongings, on a dock, look out over the water; view from behind.

PLANNING

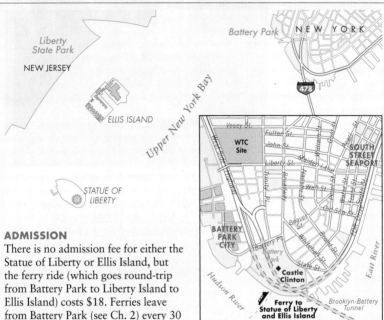

ADMISSION

There is no admission fee for either the Statue of Liberty or Ellis Island, but the ferry ride (which goes round-trip from Battery Park to Liberty Island to Ellis Island) costs $18. Ferries leave from Battery Park (see Ch. 2) every 30 to 40 minutes, depending on the time of year. There are often long lines, so arrive early, especially if you have a reserved-time ticket. (Oversize bags and backpacks aren't permitted onboard.) Reserve tickets online—you'll still have to wait in line, both to pick up the tickets (or print your tickets at home) and to board the ferry, but you'll be able to pick up a Monument Pass for access to the pedestal, the museum, and the statue's interior. There is no fee for the Monument Pass, but you cannot enter the Statue of Liberty without it.

WHERE TO CATCH THE FERRY

Broadway and Battery Pl., Lower Manhattan Ⓜ Subway: 4, 5 to Bowling Green.

PLANNING TIPS

Buy tickets in advance. This is the only way to assure that you'll have tickets to actually enter the Statue of Liberty museum and observatory platform.

Be prepared for intense security. At the ferry security check, you will need to remove your coat; at the statue, you will need to remove your coat as well as your belt, watch, and any metal accessories. At this writing, no strollers, large umbrellas, or backpacks are allowed in the statue.

Check ferry schedules in advance. Before you go, check www.statuecruises.com.

Keep in mind that even though the last entry time for the monument is at 4:30 PM, **the last ferry to the Statue of Liberty and Ellis Island is at 3:30 PM.** You need to arrive by at least 3 PM (to allow for security checks and lines) if you want to make the last ferry of the day.

LOWER
MANHATTAN

Getting Oriented

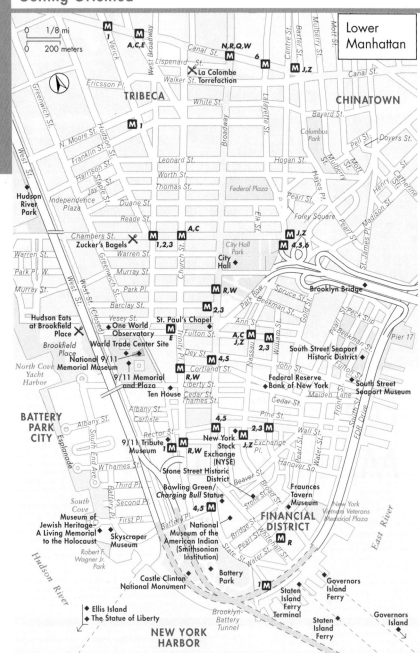

MAKING THE MOST OF YOUR TIME

Visit the Financial District during the weekend and you might feel like a lone explorer in a canyon of buildings; even on weeknights the decibel level of the neighborhood reduces significantly after about 6 pm. Weekdays, however, the sidewalks are so busy that you can expect to be jostled if you stand still too long. End your visit by watching the sunset over the Hudson River.

The sights of New York Harbor are some of the most quintessential of New York, but be prepared for long lines to go to Ellis Island and the Statue of Liberty, especially on weekends. TriBeCa is one of the quieter neighborhoods in Manhattan, being mostly residential. There are pleasant shops, restaurants, and bars, but the neighborhood tends not to be a tourist attraction unless the Tribeca Film Festival is going on.

COFFEE AND QUICK BITES

Hudson Eats at Brookfield Place. The upscale food court and terrace in the Brookfield Place complex has the best of NYC's fast and casual food options ranging from Blue Ribbon Sushi to Black Seed Bagels to Dos Toros Tacos and more. ⊠ *West St., between Vesey and Liberty Sts., Financial District* ☎ *212/978–1698* ⊕ *www.brookfieldplaceny.com* Ⓜ *E to World Trade Center; N, R, W to Cortlandt St.; A, C to Chambers St.; 2, 3 to Park Pl.; 4, 5 to Fulton St.*

La Colombe Torrefaction. In this airy space just below Canal Street, expect excellent espresso drinks and impressive latte art. Unlike other coffee shops plagued by laptops and customers clad in headphones, La Colombe does not have Wi-Fi. ⊠ *319 Church St., at Lispenard St., TriBeCa* ☎ *212/343–1515* ⊕ *www.lacolombe.com* Ⓜ *A, C, E to Canal St.*

Zucker's Bagels. This is one of the few places left in the city that still serves hand-rolled, kettle-boiled New York bagels. Coffee is from La Colombe. ⊠ *146 Chambers St., between Greenwich St. and Warren St., TriBeCa* ☎ *212/608–5844* ⊕ *www.zuckersbagels.com* Ⓜ *1, 2, 3 to Chambers St.*

TOP EXPERIENCES

Visiting the National 9/11 Memorial

2

Riding the Staten Island Ferry

Touring Ellis Island and the Statue of Liberty

Snapping a photo in front of Wall Street's bull

Strolling through Hudson River Park

BEST FOR KIDS

Castle Clinton and Battery Park

Hudson River Park

GETTING HERE

Many subway lines connect to the Financial District. Fulton Center is serviced by many different subway lines (2, 3, 4, 5, A, C, J, R, W, Z) and puts you within walking distance of the World Trade Center site, City Hall, and South Street Seaport. To get to the Brooklyn Bridge, take the 4, 5, or 6 to Brooklyn Bridge–City Hall.

For sights around New York Harbor, take the R or W to Whitehall Street, or the 4 or 5 to Bowling Green. (Note that you can also reach the Harbor area via the 1 train to South Ferry; it stops in the heart of TriBeCa, at Franklin Street, too.)

Sightseeing
★★★★★
Nightlife
★★
Dining
★★★★
Lodging
★★
Shopping
★★

Lower Manhattan, or "all the way downtown" in the parlance of New Yorkers emphatically giving directions to tourists, has long been where the action—and transaction—is. Originally the Dutch trading post called New Amsterdam (1626–47), this neighborhood is home to historic, cobblestone streets next to soaring skyscrapers. This mix of old and new, the bustle of Wall Street, and a concentration of city landmarks all lure visitors to the southern tip of Manhattan.

FINANCIAL DISTRICT

Updated
by Caroline
Trefler

Although the bustling streets thrum on weekdays with the excitement of deals being made and businesspeople rushing to work in the vast skyscrapers and financial institutions of Wall Street, the Financial District is also a good place to get a sense of Manhattan's history. Colonial-era landmarks include the Federal Hall National Memorial, on the site of the first U.S. capitol and where George Washington was inaugurated as the first president of the United States. Also here are the South Street Seaport's 19th-century brick facades and pedestrianized Stone Street, one of the city's first thoroughfares. Bounded by the East and Hudson Rivers to the east and west, respectively, and by Chambers Street and Battery Park to the north and south, the Financial District is best appreciated by getting lost in its streets.

You'll want to see what's here, but above all you'll want to see what's not, most notably in that empty gulf among skyscrapers: the World Trade Center site where two 1-acre pools represent the footprints of the fallen Twin Towers.

TOP ATTRACTIONS

FAMILY **Battery Park.** Jutting out at the southernmost point of Manhattan, tree-filled Battery Park is a respite from the narrow, winding, and (on weekdays) bustling streets of the Financial District. Even if you don't plan to stay for long, carve out a few minutes of sightseeing time to sit on a bench and take in the view, which includes the Statue of Liberty and Ellis Island. On clear days you can see all the way to Port Elizabeth's shipping cranes; to Governors Island; to hilly Staten Island in the distance; and to the old railway terminal in Liberty State Park, on the mainland in Jersey City, New Jersey. As you look away from the water and toward Lower Manhattan's skyscrapers, there's a feeling that you're at the beginning of the city, and a sense of all the possibility it possesses just a few blocks in.

The park's main structure is **Castle Clinton National Monument,** the takeoff point for ferries to the Statue of Liberty and Ellis Island. This monument was once 200 feet off the southern tip of the island and located in what was called the Southwest Battery, and was erected during the War of 1812 to defend the city. (Its sister fort, Castle Williams, sits across the water on Governors Island.) As dirt and debris from construction were dumped into the harbor, the island expanded, eventually engulfing the landmark. Later, from 1855 to 1890, it served as America's first official immigration center (Ellis Island opened in 1892).

In Battery Park are several monuments and statues, including Fritz Koenig's *The Sphere,* which for three decades stood on the plaza at the World Trade Center as a symbol of peace. Damaged but still intact after the towers collapsed, the sculpture was installed in Battery Park and will remain there indefinitely.

To the west is the **Staten Island Ferry Terminal,** and to the east is Robert F. Wagner Jr. Park, with its flat, tidy lawn and wide benches from which to view the harbor or the stream of runners and cyclists on the promenade. ⊠ *Financial District* ⊕ *www.nycgovparks.org/parks/batterypark* Ⓜ *4, 5 to Bowling Green; 1 to South Ferry.*

Fodor'sChoice ★ **Brooklyn Bridge.** "A drive-through cathedral" is how the journalist James Wolcott once described the Brooklyn Bridge, one of New York's noblest and most recognized landmarks, perhaps rivaling Walt Whitman's comment that it was "The best, most effective medicine my soul has yet partaken." The bridge stretches over the East River, connecting Manhattan and Brooklyn. A walk across its promenade—a boardwalk elevated above the roadway, shared by pedestrians and cyclists—is a quintessential New York experience, and the roughly 40-minute stroll delivers exhilarating views. If you start from Lower Manhattan, you'll end up in the heart of Brooklyn Heights (you can also take the subway to the Brooklyn side and walk back to Manhattan). It's worth noting that on evenings and weekends when the weather is nice, the narrow path gets pretty congested; it's most magical, and quietest, early in the morning. ⊠ *East River Dr., Financial District* Ⓜ *4, 5, 6 to Brooklyn Bridge–City Hall; J, Z to Chambers St.; A, C to High St. (in Brooklyn).*

National 9/11 Memorial Museum. Beside the reflecting pools on the 9/11 Memorial Plaza is the glass pavilion of the Memorial Museum. The museum descends some seven stories down to the bedrock the Twin Towers were built on, and the vast space displays a poignant, powerful collection of artifacts, memorabilia, photographs, and multimedia exhibits, as well as a gallery that takes visitors through the history of events surrounding both the 1993 and 2001 attacks. There's also a memorial wall with portraits of those who died, accompanied by recorded recitations of the names of the dead by their relatives. Giant pieces of the towers' structural steel and foundations are displayed, along with the partially destroyed Ladder Company 3 fire truck. You can also see the remnants of the "Survivors Stairs," which allowed hundreds of people to escape the buildings that fateful September day. ⊠ *180 Greenwich St., between Fulton St. and Liberty St. Walkway, Financial District* ☏ *212/266–5211* ⊕ *www.911memorial.org/museum* 🖾 *$24 (free Tues. 5–8 pm)* Ⓜ *R to Cortlandt St.; 2, 3, 4, 5, A, C, J, Z to Fulton Center; E to World Trade Center.*

New York Stock Exchange (NYSE). Unfortunately, you can't tour the stock exchange anymore—though the pace on the floor is much less frenetic than it used to be, now that technology has changed how the trading floor works. The building itself, though, at the intersection of Wall and Broad Streets, is still worth ogling. The neoclassical structure, designed by architect George B. Post, opened on April 22, 1903. It has six Corinthian columns supporting a pediment with a sculpture titled *Integrity Protecting the Works of Man,* featuring a tribute to the then-sources of American prosperity: Agriculture and Mining to the left of Integrity; Science, Industry, and Invention to the right. As an interesting aside, the Exchange was one of the world's first air-conditioned buildings. ⊠ *11 Wall St., between Broadway and Broad S., Financial District* ☏ *212/656–3000* ⊕ *www.nyse.com* Ⓜ *1 to Rector St.; R, W to Rector St.; 2, 3, 4, 5 to Wall St.; J, Z to Broad St.*

Fodor's Choice ★ **9/11 Memorial and Plaza.** Opened just in time for the 10th anniversary of 9/11, the somber Memorial was designed by Michael Arad and Peter Walker and occupies a large swath of the 16-acre World Trade Center complex, forming what's known as the Memorial Plaza. It comprises two recessed, 30-foot-tall waterfalls that occupy the giant, square footprints of where the Twin Towers once stood. Every minute, some 60,000 gallons of water cascade down the sides and then down into smaller square openings in the center of the pools. At nearly an acre in size each, they are said to be the largest man-made waterfalls in North America. Edging the Memorial pools are bronze panels inscribed with the names of the nearly 3,000 people who were killed in the attacks at the WTC site, in Flight 93's crash in Pennsylvania, and at the Pentagon, and the six people who died in the World Trade Center bombing in 1993. Because the names are arranged by affiliation rather than alphabetically, it can be difficult to locate names—visit the Memorial's website or use on-site kiosks to find the location of a particular name. Visitors are allowed to place tribute items in front of the Memorial pools as well as on the name panels. Across the plaza are benches, grassy strips, and more than 400 swamp white-oak trees harvested from within a 500-mile radius of the site, as well as from Pennsylvania and near Washington, D.C. There's also a single Callery pear tree known as the "survivor tree," which, after being nearly destroyed on September 11, 2001, was nursed, revived, and replanted here in 2010. The 9/11 Memorial is an open-access public plaza and visits are free. The National 9/11 Memorial Museum is located between the two Memorial pools. ⊠ *180 Greenwich St., between Fulton St. and*

2

Liberty St., Financial District ☎ *212/266–5211* ⊕ *www.911memorial. org* Ⓜ *R, W to Cortlandt St.; 2, 3, 4, 5, A, C, J, Z to Fulton St.; E to World Trade Center.*

9/11 Tribute Museum. This project of the September 11th Families' Association opened in 2006 with the intent of putting the events of that day into context—at the time, there was little to see beyond a big construction site. The several galleries include displays about the history and construction of Lower Manhattan; the events of September 11, 2001; the response and recovery efforts after the attacks; and first-person histories. It's a good complement to the broader mission of the separate National 9/11 Memorial and Museum. Guided walking tours by survivors and first responders take in the gallery and the memorial (not the National 9/11 Memorial Museum). ⊠ *92 Greenwich St., at Rector St., Financial District* ☎ *866/737–1184* ⊕ *www.911tributemuseum.org* 🔄 *$15 for galleries; $25 for galleries and walking tour* Ⓜ *1, R to Rector St.; 2, 3, 4, 5, A, C, J, Z to Fulton St.; E to World Trade Center.*

FAMILY **One World Observatory.** There are several thrills involved in visiting the tallest building in the Western Hemisphere, not the least of which are the spectacular views of Manhattan, Brooklyn, and New Jersey. If you time your visit around dusk, you'll get daytime views as well as sunset and sparkling evening lights. The observatory occupies the 100th, 101st, and 102nd floors of One World Trade Center, and the experience includes an exhilarating trip up in the world's fastest elevators, during which a journey through history is projected on the elevator walls. After you step out at the top, there's also a two-minute video of time-lapse images of Lower Manhattan. The ground floor has exhibits and personal stories about the building of the tower. There are several options for dining with a view, including a casual café and a fancier sit-down restaurant (reservations are recommended for the latter). Seasonal events, including Santa, are on the schedule as well. ⊠ *One World Trade Center, 285 Fulton St., between West St. and Greenwich St., Financial District* ☎ ⊕ *oneworldobservatory.com* 🔄 *$36* Ⓜ *R, W to Cortlandt St.; E to World Trade Center; 2, 3, 4, 5, A, C, J, Z to Fulton Center.*

South Street Seaport Historic District. Had this charming cobblestone corner of the city not been declared a historic district in 1977, the city's largest concentration of early-19th-century commercial buildings would have been destroyed. Today, the area is often filled with tourists, and if you've been to Boston's Quincy Market or Baltimore's Harborplace, you may feel a flash of déjà vu—the same company leased, restored, and adapted the existing buildings, resulting in a blend of quasi-authentic historic district with a slightly homogenous shopping zone.

At the intersection of Fulton and Water Streets, the gateway to the seaport, is the **Titanic Memorial Lighthouse,** a small white lighthouse that commemorates the sinking of the RMS *Titanic* in 1912. Beyond the lighthouse, Fulton Street turns into a cobblestone pedestrian mall. On the south side of Fulton is the seaport's architectural centerpiece, **Schermerhorn Row,** a redbrick terrace of Georgian- and Federal-style warehouses and countinghouses built from 1810 to 1812. Some upper floors house gallery space, and the ground floors are occupied by shops, bars, and restaurants. Cross South Street (once known as the Street of Ships) under an elevated stretch of FDR Drive to **Pier 16,** where historic ships are docked, including the *Pioneer,* a 102-foot schooner built in 1885, and the 1907 lightship *Ambrose.* The Pier 16 ticket booth provides information and sells tickets to the museum, ships, tours, and exhibits. Pier 16 also is the departure point for various seasonal cruises. (Ship tours are included in the admission to the **South Street Seaport Museum**).

To the north is **Pier 17,** previously the longtime site of the Fulton Fish Market and now a multilevel dockside shopping and dining complex that's expected to open in summer 2018 with a 60,000-square-foot landscaped rooftop. ✉ *Financial District* ☎ *212/732–8257 for event and shopping info* ⊕ *www.southstreetseaport.com* Ⓜ *2, 3, 4, 5, A, C, J, Z to Fulton Center.*

FAMILY **South Street Seaport Museum.** The history of the South Street Seaport area is outlined in the visitor center at 12 Fulton Street and in displays at the printing house around the corner (211 Water Street), but the main attractions are the the five ships docked in the harbor at Pier 16. Admission to the museum includes visits (weather permitting) on the 1907 lightship *Ambrose* and the 1885 ship *Wavertree.* There are also public sailings of the 1885 schooner *Pioneer.* The museum organizes walking tours of the area. ✉ *12 Fulton St., between Water and South Sts., Financial District* ☎ *212/748–8600* ⊕ *www.southstreetseaportmuseum. org* 🎟 *$12* Ⓜ *2, 3, 4, 5, A, C, J, Z to Fulton Center.*

Stone Street Historic District. Amid skyscrapers, the two low-rise blocks of bars and restaurants along historic Stone Street feel more like a village than the center of the financial universe. In the summer, tables spill out into the cobblestone street and the mood is convivial, especially on Thursday and Friday nights. This was Manhattan's first paved street and today the cluster of buildings along here, with South William and Pearl Streets, and Coenties Alley, make up the Stone Street Historic District. ✉ *Stone, S. William, and Pearl Sts., and Coenties Alley, Financial District* Ⓜ *R to Whitehall St.; 4,5 to Bowling Green.*

Ten House. Located just across Liberty Street from the World Trade Center site, the "Ten House" firehouse is officially known as Ladder Company 10 and Engine Company 10. On the morning of September 11, 2001, firefighters on duty here were among the first to respond to New York's terrorist attacks. The companies lost six heroes that day. The "Ten House Bravest Memorial" stands inside the firehouse to commemorate their ultimate sacrifice, and that of other Ten House heroes. Around the corner on Greenwich Street, the 56-foot long, bronze bas-relief "FDNY Memorial Wall" serves as a tribute to 343 firefighters who perished on 9/11. ✉ *124 Liberty St., at Greenwich St., Financial District* Ⓜ *2, 3, 4, 5, A, C, J, Z to Fulton St.; E to World Trade Center; N, R to Cortlandt St.*

World Trade Center Site. On September 11, 2001, terrorist hijackers steered two jets into the World Trade Center's Twin Towers, setting them ablaze and causing their collapse, killing 2,753 people and injuring countless others. The 16 acres of fenced-in rubble and debris that evolved into a construction zone known as "Ground Zero" quickly

The names of those lost on September 11th are commemorated on Memorial Plaza, at the former site of the Twin Towers.

became a memorial unto itself, a place where visitors and those who lost loved ones could mourn and reflect on what was the single-most-deadly foreign attack ever to happen on American soil. This area is now home to the 9/11 Memorial Plaza, the National 9/11 Memorial Museum, the 1,776-foot One World Trade Center, and Towers 2, 3, and 4, each designed by renowned architects, as well as the WTC Transportation Hub, known as the "Oculus," designed by Santiago Calatrava. ⊠ *Between Church and West Sts. and Vesey and Liberty Sts., Financial District* ⊕ *www.wtc.com* Ⓜ *R, W to Cortlandt St.; E to World Trade Center; 2, 3, 4, 5, A, C, J, Z to Fulton Center.*

WORTH NOTING

Bowling Green. Perhaps most recognized as the home of Arturo Di Modica's 7,000-pound, bronze *Charging Bull* statue (1989), the small plaza that is Bowling Green, at the foot of Broadway, became New York's first public park in 1733. Legend has it that before that, this was the site upon which Peter Minuit purchased the island of Manhattan from the Native Americans, in 1626, supposedly for what amounted to 24 U.S. dollars. On July 9, 1776, a few hours after citizens learned about the signing of the Declaration of Independence, rioters toppled a statue of British King George III that had occupied the spot for 11 years; much of the statue's lead was melted down into bullets. In 1783, when the occupying British forces fled the city, they defiantly hoisted a Union Jack on a greased, uncleated flagpole so it couldn't be lowered; patriot John Van Arsdale drove his own cleats into the pole to replace it with the Stars and Stripes. The copper-top subway entrance across State

Street is the original one, built in 1904–05. ⊠ *Broadway, at Whitehall St., Financial District* Ⓜ *4, 5 to Bowling Green.*

City Hall. What once marked the northernmost point of Manhattan today houses the office of the mayor, and serves as a gathering place for demonstrators and the news crews who cover their stories. This is the one of the oldest City Halls in the country, a striking (but surprisingly small) building dating back to 1803. If the history of local politics and architecture is your thing, free tours are available (sign up in advance online). Inside, highlights include the Rotunda where President Lincoln lay in state in 1865 under a soaring dome supported by 10 Corinthian columns; the Victorian-style **City Council Chamber;** and the **Governor's Room,** an elegantly preserved space with portraits of historic figures, as well as a writing table that George Washington used in 1789 when New York was the U.S. capital. ⊠ *City Hall Park, Financial District* ☎ *212/788–2656 for tour reservations* ⊕ *www1.nyc. gov/site/designcommission/public-programs/tours/city-hall.page* 🖾 *Free* ⊙ *Tours available some weekdays (reserve online or by phone)* Ⓜ *2, 3 to Park Pl.; R to City Hall; 4, 5, 6 to Brooklyn Bridge–City Hall; A, C, J, Z to Chambers St.*

Federal Reserve Bank of New York. With its imposing mix of sandstone, limestone, and ironwork, the Federal Reserve looks the way a bank ought to: strong and impregnable. The gold ingots in the subterranean vaults here are worth roughly $350 billion—reputedly a third of the world's gold reserves. Forty-five-minute tours (conducted twice a day and requiring reservations) include a visit to the gold vault, the trading desk, and "FedWorks," a multimedia exhibit center where you can track hypothetical trades. Visitors must show an officially issued photo ID, such as a driver's license or passport, and pass through scanners to enter the building. The Fed advises arriving 20 minutes before your tour to accommodate security screening. Photography is not permitted. ⊠ *33 Liberty St., between William and Nassau Sts., Financial District* ☎ *212/720–6130* ⊕ *www.newyorkfed.org* 🖾 *Free, including tours* Ⓜ *2, 3, 4, 5, A, C, J, Z to Fulton St.*

Fraunces Tavern Museum. This former tavern, where General George Washington celebrated the end of the Revolutionary War in 1783, is now a museum covering two floors above the famed restaurant and bar. ⊠ *54 Pearl St., at Broad St., Financial District* ☎ *212/425–1778* ⊕ *www.frauncestavernmuseum.org* 🖾 *$7* Ⓜ *R, W to Whitehall St.; 4, 5 to Bowling Green; 1 to South Ferry; J, Z to Broad St.*

Museum of Jewish Heritage—A Living Memorial to the Holocaust. In a granite hexagon rising 85 feet above Robert F. Wagner Jr. Park at the southern end of Battery Park City, this museum pays tribute to the 6 million Jews who perished in the Holocaust. It's one of the best such museums in the country. The museum's east wing has a theater, memorial garden, library, galleries, and café. A free audio guide, with narration by Meryl Streep and Itzhak Perlman, is available at the admissions desk. ⊠ *36 Battery Pl., Battery Park City, Financial District* ☎ *646/437–4202* ⊕ *www.mjhnyc. org* 🖾 *$12 (free Wed. and Thurs. 4–8)* ⊙ *Closed Sat. and some Jewish holidays* Ⓜ *4, 5 to Bowling Green; 1, R, W to Rector St.*

National Museum of the American Indian (Smithsonian Institution). Massive granite columns rise to a pediment topped by a double row of statues at the impressive Beaux Arts Alexander Hamilton U.S. Custom House (1907), which is home to the New York branch of this Smithsonian museum (the other branch is in Washington, D.C.). The permanent exhibit, "Infinity of Nations," is an encyclopedic survey of Native American cultures from across the continent. ✉ *1 Bowling Green, between State and Whitehall Sts., Financial District* ☏ *212/514–3700* ⊕ *www.nmai.si.edu* ✉ *Free* Ⓜ *4, 5 to Bowling Green; 1 to Rector St.; R, W to Whitehall St.; J, Z to Broad St.; 4, 5 to Wall St.*

Skyscraper Museum. Why get a crick in your neck—or worse, risk looking like a tourist—while appreciating New York City's famous skyline, when you can visit the Skyscraper Museum instead? At this small museum, you can appreciate highly detailed, hand-carved miniature wood models of Midtown and Lower Manhattan; explore the past, present, and future of the skyscraper—from New York City's Empire State Building to Dubai's Burj Khalifa (taller than the Empire State Building and Chicago's Willis Tower combined); and examine the history of the Twin Towers at the World Trade Center. The museum's exhibits continue to evolve, so expect models of current or future buildings, videos, drawings, floor plans, and talks that reveal the influence of history, real estate, and individuals on shaping city skylines. ✉ *39 Battery Pl., across from Museum of Jewish Heritage, Financial District* ☏ *212/968–1961* ⊕ *www.skyscraper.org* ✉ *$5* ☽ *Closed Mon., Tues.* Ⓜ *4, 5 to Bowling Green.*

St. Paul's Chapel. For more than a year after the 2001 World Trade Center attacks, the fence of St. Paul's Chapel served as a shrine for visitors seeking solace. People from around the world left tokens of grief and support, or signed one of the large dropcloths that hung from the fence. After serving as a 24-hour refuge where rescue and recovery workers could eat, pray, rest, and receive counseling, the chapel, which amazingly suffered no damage, reopened to the public in fall 2002. The powerful ongoing exhibit, titled "Unwavering Spirit: Hope & Healing at Ground Zero," honors the efforts of rescue workers in the months after September 11 with photos, drawings, banners, and other items sent to them as memorials. Open since 1766, St. Paul's is the oldest public building in continuous use in Manhattan. ✉ *209 Broadway, at Fulton St., Financial District* ☏ *212/602–0800* ⊕ *www. trinitywallstreet.org/about/stpaulschapel* Ⓜ *2, 3, 4, 5, A, C, J, Z to Fulton St.; E to World Trade Center.*

NEW YORK HARBOR

The southern tip of Manhattan is the key point of departure for Statue of Liberty and Ellis Island tours, which run year-round. This experience should never be dismissed as too touristy. Unlike any other, the excursion is a reminder that New York is a city of immigrants and survivors. The seasonal Governors Island ferry leaves from the Battery Maritime Building (as well as Pier 6 in Brooklyn).

Ellis Island. Between 1892 and 1924 approximately 12 million men, women, and children first set foot on U.S. soil at the Ellis Island federal immigration facility. By the time the facility closed in 1954, it had processed ancestors of more than 40% of Americans living today. The island's main building, now a national monument, is now known as the **Ellis Island National Museum of Immigration,** and it tells the story not just of Ellis Island but of immigration from the Colonial era to the present day, through numerous galleries containing artifacts, photographs, and taped oral histories. The centerpiece of the museum is the white-tile Registry Room (also known as the Great Hall). It feels dignified and cavernous today, but photographs show that it took on a multitude of configurations through the years, always packed with humanity. While you're there, check out the Registry Room's tall, arched windows and try to imagine what passed through immigrants' minds as they viewed Lower Manhattan's skyline to one side and the Statue of Liberty to the other.

Because there's so much to take in, it's a good idea to make use of the museum's interpretive tools. Check at the visitor desk for free film tickets, ranger tour times, and special programs. The audio tour (included in the price of your ferry ticket) takes you through the exhibits, providing thorough, engaging commentary interspersed with recordings of immigrants themselves recalling their experiences.

Along with the Registry Room, the museum's features include the ground-level Peopling of America Center, a major expansion to the Ellis Island Museum that explores immigration to the United States before and after Ellis Island. Interpretive graphics and poignant audio stories give first-hand accounts of the immigrant's journey—from making the trip and arriving in the United States to their struggle and survival after they arrived. There's also the American Family Immigration Center, where you can search Ellis Island's records for your own ancestors; and the American Flag of Faces, an interactive display filled with a montage of images of immigrants submitted online (submit yours at *FlagofFaces. org*). Outside is the American Immigrant Wall of Honor, which has the names of more than 600,000 immigrant Americans against the backdrop of the Manhattan skyline.

There is no admission fee for either the Statue of Liberty or Ellis Island, but the ferry ride (which goes round-trip from Battery Park to Liberty Island to Ellis Island), costs $18.50. Ferries leave from Battery Park (and from Liberty State Park in New Jersey) every 30 to 45 minutes depending on the time of year (buy your tickets online at *www.statuecruises. com*). There are often long lines, so arrive early, especially if you have a reserved-time ticket. There is an indoor-outdoor café on Ellis Island. ⊠ *Battery Park* ☎ *212/561–4588 Ellis Island, 212/561–4500 Wall of Honor information, 877/523–9849* ⊕ *www.ellisisland.org* ⊠ *Free; ferry $18.50 round-trip (includes Liberty Island).*

Governors Island. Open seasonally to the public and accessible via a short, free ferry ride, Governors Island is essentially a big, charming park that looks like a small New England town; it's popular with locals for biking by the water, summer festivals, art shows, concerts,

On a typical weekday, five ferries make roughly 110 trips back and forth between Staten Island and Manhattan, transporting about 70,000 passengers.

and family programs. The New York City Police Museum is also here. Wouter Van Twiller, a representative for the country of Holland, supposedly purchased the island for his private use, in 1637, from Native Americans for two ax heads, a string of beads, and a handful of nails. It was confiscated by the Dutch government a year later, and for the next decade its ownership switched back and forth between the Dutch and British until the Brits gained firm control of it in the 1670s. The island was officially named in 1784 for His Majesty's Governors and used by the American military until the 1960s, when the Coast Guard took it over. After their facilities were abandoned in 1995, the island was purchased by the city in 2002 and started welcoming visitors in 2003. The Governors Island ferry departs from the Battery Maritime Building and from Brooklyn's Pier 6. ⊠ *Battery Maritime Building (for Manhattan ferry), 10 South St., Battery Park* ⊕ *www.govisland.com* ⌨ *Free (including ferry)* ⊘ *Closed Nov.–Apr.* Ⓜ *1 to South Ferry; 4, 5 to Bowling Green; R, W to Whitehall St.*

Fodor's Choice ★ **Staten Island Ferry.** On weekdays, some 70,000 people ride the free ferry to Staten Island, one of the city's five boroughs, and you should be one of them. Without paying a cent, you get phenomenal views of the Lower Manhattan skyline, the Statue of Liberty, and Ellis Island during the 25-minute cruise across New York Harbor. You also pass tugboats, freighters, and cruise ships—a reminder that this is very much still a working harbor. The ferry sails every 15 to 30 minutes (24 hours a day, 365 days a year) from the Whitehall Terminal at Whitehall and South Streets, near the east end of Battery Park. You must disembark once you reach the opposite terminal, but you can just get back in line to board again if you don't plan to stay. A small concession stand on each ferry sells a few snacks and beverages (including beer). ⊠ *4 Whitehall St., Battery Park* ☎ *212/639–9675* ⊕ *www.siferry.com* 🎫 *Free* Ⓜ *1 to South Ferry; R, W to Whitehall St.; 4, 5 to Bowling Green.*

The Statue of Liberty. *See feature in Chapter 1.* ⊠ *Liberty Island, Battery Park* ☎ *212/363–3200; 877/523–9849* ⊕ *www.libertyellisfoundation.org* 🎫 *Free; ferry $18.50 round-trip (includes Ellis Island); crown tickets $3.*

TRIBECA

Tucked on the west side south of Canal Street, residential TriBeCa (the *Tri*angle *Be*low *Ca*nal Street) has a quieter vibe than most other Manhattan neighborhoods. Walk the photogenic streets, especially the stretch of Federal row houses on Harrison Street, and you'll understand why so many celebrities own apartments here. The two-block-long Staple Street, with its connecting overhead walkway, is a favorite of urban cinematographers. Although TriBeCa's money is often hidden behind grand cast-iron facades, you can get a taste of it at posh neighborhood restaurants, cocktail bars, and boutiques, or at the star-studded Tribeca Film Festival every spring.

FAMILY **Hudson River Park.** The quiet green spaces of New York City are treasured
Fodor'sChoice by locals, and one of the best is Hudson River Park, a 5-mile path from
★ Battery Place to 59th Street. This riverside stretch has been renovated into a landscaped park, incorporating the piers that jut out into the Hudson, with walking and cycling paths, a seasonal minigolf course, dog runs, and skate parks. The TriBeCa portion consists of Piers 25 and 26 and has picnic spaces, playgrounds, and a sand volleyball court. The areas adjacent to the West Village (Piers 45 and 46) and near Chelsea (Piers 63 and 64) are equally attractive, with lots of spots for leisure and recreation. To the north, beginning at 72nd Street, is Riverside Park. ⊠ *TriBeCa* ☎ *212/627–2020* ⊕ *www.hudsonriverpark.org* Ⓜ *1 to Franklin St. for TriBeCa section of the park.*

3

SOHO, NOLITA, LITTLE ITALY, AND CHINATOWN

Getting Oriented

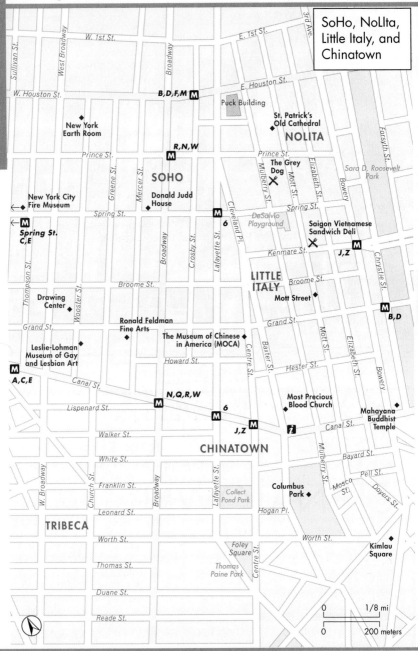

SoHo, NoLIta, Little Italy, and Chinatown

MAKING THE MOST OF YOUR TIME

If you're coming to SoHo and NoLIta to shop, there's no need to rush out the door—most shops don't open until 10 or 11 am, and many stay open until the early evening. If art is your thing, avoid Sunday since most galleries are closed. SoHo, with national chains lining its section of Broadway, is almost always a madhouse on weekend afternoons (unless it's raining), but weekdays are somewhat less frenetic. NoLIta, with less traffic, fewer chains, and more boutiques, is calmer and less crowded.

Little Italy is a small area nowadays, having lost ground to a growing Chinatown. Note that foodwise, most of the checkered-tablecloth spots in Little Italy itself are touristy, with mediocre food.

If you're visiting New York in mid-September, you'll time it right for the Feast of San Gennaro—a huge street fair in honor of the patron saint of Naples—but you'll have the company of thousands of others who enjoy exploring the many food and souvenir booths and playing games of chance. Given that few Italian Americans live in the area anymore, it's not exactly like visiting old Napoli, but it *is* a fun way to take in the sights.

Chinatown bustles with local shoppers pretty much any time of day, but there are more tourists on the weekends, when it gets so busy you may have to duck into a shop or restaurant just for a break from all the sidewalk jostling.

TOP EXPERIENCES

Browsing boutiques and people-watching in SoHo and NoLIta

Ogling the out-of-the-ordinary produce and seafood in Chinatown

Gallery-hopping in SoHo

Eating dim sum in Chinatown

Sipping a cocktail in NoLIta

GETTING HERE AND AROUND

SoHo (*South of Houston*) is bounded by Houston Street, Canal Street, 6th Avenue, and Lafayette Street. To the east, NoLIta (*North of Little Italy*) is contained by Houston, the Bowery, Kenmare, and Lafayette. Plenty of subways service the area: take the 6, C, or E to Spring Street; the N, R, or W to Prince Street; or the B, D, F, or M to Broadway–Lafayette Street. For Chinatown, farther south, take the 6, J, N, Q, R, W, or Z to Canal Street, or the B or D to Grand Street.

COFFEE AND QUICK BITES

The Grey Dog. Unpretentious and with ample seating, open early till late, and serving breakfast, brunch, lunch, dinner, baked goods, coffee, wine, and beer, the Grey Dog is perfect anytime. ⊠ *244 Mulberry St., between Prince and Spring Sts., NoLIta* ☎ *212/966-1060* ⊕ *www.thegreydog.com* Ⓜ *B, D, F, M to Broadway/Lafayette St.; N, R, W to Prince St.*

Saigon Vietnamese Sandwich Deli. Predating the *banh mi* craze by perhaps a decade, this storefront serves delicious Vietnamese sandwiches on baguettes that are crusty on the outside and soft on the inside, just as they should be. ⊠ *369 Broome St., between Mott and Elizabeth Sts., NoLIta* ☎ *212/219–8341* ⊕ *www.vietnamese-sandwich.com* ⊟ *No credit cards* Ⓜ *J, Z to Bowery; 6 to Spring St.; B, D to Grand St.*

Sightseeing
★★★
Nightlife
★★★
Dining
★★★★★
Lodging
★★★
Shopping
★★★★★

SoHo, NoLIta, Little Italy, and Chinatown are all jam-packed with humanity, all the more perfect for people-watching as you browse, nibble, and wander. Parts of SoHo and NoLIta are destinations for supertrendy shopping as well as popular chains and department stores: the boutiques are often overpriced (keep a lookout for sales) but undeniably glamorous. Little Italy and Chinatown are more about local shopping and Instagram-worthy food shops and stalls.

SOHO

Updated
by Caroline
Trefler

Once the epicenter of the New York art scene, SoHo today is now more synonymous with shopping. A bit of bohemia still exists on the cobblestone side streets, where there are charming restaurants and some of the art galleries that haven't scattered elsewhere. The main thoroughfares tend to have sidewalks lined with tables of handmade jewelry, hats, purses, and art. If you take the time to look, there's a local vibe here beneath the glitzy boutiques—like the elderly residents speaking Italian on the corners around Sullivan Street and Thompson Street, revealing the neighborhood's Italian past.

Donald Judd House. A five-story cast-iron building from 1870, 101 Spring Street was the New York home and studio of artist Donald Judd. Although the neighborhood used to be home to many single-use cast-iron buildings, this is one of the few that remain—and is a designated historic building. Judd bought it in 1968, and today, guided 90-minute tours (book in advance) explore Judd's living and working spaces and include art installations as they were arranged by Judd prior to his death in 1994. Note that climbing stairs is required. ⊠ *101 Spring St., at Mercer St., SoHo* 🕾 *212/219–2747* ⊕ *www.juddfoundation.org* 🖾 *$24* ⊘ *Closed Sun., Mon.* Ⓜ *N, R, W to Prince St.; 6 to Spring St.*

Drawing Center. At this nonprofit organization the focus is on drawings—contemporary and historical. Works shown in the three galleries

SoHo and NoLIta Architecture

There are plenty of beautiful people in SoHo and NoLIta, but tilt your eyes up, beyond the turn-of-the-20th-century cast-iron "bishop's crook" lampposts, and discover some of New York's most impressive architecture. Look down and you'll see Belgian-brick cobblestones lining some of the streets. Along Broadway and the neighboring streets of SoHo, there are "vault lights" in the sidewalk: starting in the 1850s, these glass lenses were set into sidewalks so daylight could reach basements.

The **King of Greene Street,** at 72–76 Greene, between Grand and Canal, is a five-story, Renaissance-style 1873 building with a magnificent projecting porch of Corinthian columns and pilasters. These days it's painted in high-gloss ivory. Over at 28–30 Greene Street is the **Queen of Greene Street,** a graceful 1873 cast-iron beauty that exemplifies the Second Empire style with its dormers, columns, window arches, projecting central bays, and roof.

The **Haughwout Building,** at 488–492 Broadway, north of Broome, is best known for what's no longer inside—the world's first commercial passenger elevator, invented by Elisha Graves Otis. The building's exterior is worth a look, though: nicknamed the "Parthenon of Cast Iron," the five-story, Venetian palazzo–style structure was built in 1857 to house department-store merchant E. V. Haughwout's china, silver, and glassware store. Each window is framed by Corinthian columns and rounded arches.

Built in 1904, the **Little Singer Building,** at 561 Broadway, is a masterpiece of cast-iron styling, its delicate facade covered with curlicues of wrought iron. The L-shape building's second facade is around the corner on Prince Street.

Over in Little Italy/NoLIta, the magnificent old **Police Headquarters** building at 240 Centre Street, between Broome and Grand, might be familiar from Martin Scorsese's film *Gangs of New York.* The 1909 Edwardian baroque–style structure with its striking copper dome was the headquarters of the New York City Police Department until 1973. Designed to "impress both the officer and the prisoner with the majesty of the law," it was converted into luxury condos in 1988 and is known today as the Police Building.

The 1885 Romanesque Revival **Puck Building,** at 295 Lafayette Street, on the southeast corner of Houston, is a former magazine headquarters and now a busy event space and home to REI's New York flagship store. Look for the statue of Puck just over the door: his gilding contrasts with the deep-red brick.

---

often push the envelope on what's considered drawing; many projects are commissioned by the center. ✉ *35 Wooster St., between Broome and Grand Sts., SoHo* ☎ *212/219–2166* ⊕ *www.drawingcenter.org* ✉ *$5 (free Thurs. 6–8)* ⊙ *Closed Mon., Tues.* Ⓜ *A, C, E, J, N, Q, R, W, Z, 1, 6 to Canal St.*

Leslie-Lohman Museum of Gay and Lesbian Art. Founded in 1969 in a basement on Prince Street, the foundation has its roots in the collection of its founders, Charles Leslie and Fritz Lohman, two lifelong champions

SoHo has one of the world's greatest concentrations of cast-iron buildings, created in response to fires that wiped out much of Lower Manhattan in the mid-18th century.

of LGBTQ artists. The well-curated exhibits in the spacious first-floor galleries are usually photographic (and sometimes sexually charged), though the museum's impressive archive leads to new exhibitions in various media as often as eight times a year. ⊠ *26 Wooster St., between Grand and Canal Sts., SoHo* ☎ *212/431–2609* ⊕ *www.leslielohman.org* 🎟 *Free (donations encouraged)* ☾ *Closed Mon., Tues.* Ⓜ *1, 6, A, C, E, J, N, Q, R, Z to Canal St.*

New York City Fire Museum. In the former headquarters of Engine 30, a handsome Beaux Arts building dating from 1904, retired firefighters volunteer their time in the morning and early afternoon to answer visitors' questions. The collection of firefighting tools from the 18th century to the present includes hand-pulled and horse-drawn engines, speaking trumpets, pumps, and uniforms. A memorial exhibit with photos, paintings, children's artwork, and found objects relating to the September 11, 2001, attacks is also on view—a poignant reminder and tribute to the 343 firefighters who died on 9/11. ⊠ *278 Spring St., between Hudson and Varick Sts., SoHo* ☎ *212/691–1303* ⊕ *www.nycfiremuseum.org* 🎟 *$8* Ⓜ *C, E to Spring St.; 1 to Houston St.*

New York Earth Room. Noted artist and sculptor Walter De Maria's 1977 avant-garde installation consists, quite simply, of 280,000 pounds of gently sculpted soil (22 inches deep). It fills 3,600 square feet of a second-floor gallery maintained by the Dia Art Foundation since 1980. You can't touch or walk on the dirt, nor can you take its photo, but looking at it is quite peaceful. De Maria's equally odd and impressive work, *The Broken Kilometer,* an 18.75-ton installation that consists of five columns of a total of 1,000 meter-long brass rods covering the wood floors of an open loft space, is a few blocks away (at 393 West Broadway) and is a good complement. The two installations have the same hours. ⊠ *141 Wooster St., 2nd fl., between W. Houston and Prince Sts., SoHo* ☎ *212/989–5566* ⊕ *www.diaart.org/sites/main/earthroom* 🎟 *Free* ☉ *Closed mid-June–mid-Sept.* Ⓜ *N, R, W to Prince St.; B, D, F, M to Broadway–Lafayette St.*

Ronald Feldman Fine Arts. Founded in 1971 and located in SoHo since the 1980s, this gallery represents more than 30 international contemporary artists; exhibits include contemporary painting, sculpture, installations, drawings, and prints—some are quite avant-garde. The space also hosts performances and has a large selection of Andy Warhol prints, paintings, and drawings. ⊠ *31 Mercer St., between Grand and Canal Sts., SoHo* ☎ *212/226–3232* ⊕ *www.feldmangallery.com* 🎟 *Free* ☉ *Closed Sun., Mon.* Ⓜ *1, 6, A, C, E, J, N, Q, R, W, Z to Canal St.*

NOLITA

Many locals would probably say that the spirit of old SoHo is somewhat alive in NoLIta, a charming neighborhood with an artistic spirit, independently run boutiques and restaurants, and a local vibe. The streets here are less frantic and crowded than either SoHo or Chinatown, and each block could provide hours of roaming and ducking into small shops, nursing a cappuccino at a sidewalk café, or lingering over a meal surrounded by stylish New Yorkers. This is downtown, so the prices aren't cheap, but the quality is high and the experience unique.

St. Patrick's Old Cathedral. If you've seen *The Godfather,* you've had a peek inside New York's first Roman Catholic cathedral—the interior shots of the infamous baptism scene were filmed here. Dedicated in 1815, this church lost its designation as the seat of New York's bishop when the current St. Patrick's opened uptown, in 1879. The unadorned exterior of the cathedral gives no hint of the splendors within, which include an 1868 Henry Erben pipe organ. The interior dates from the 1860s, after a large fire gutted most of the original structure. The enormous marble altar surrounded by hand-carved niches (reredos) houses an extraordinary collection of sacred statuary and other Gothic exuberance. ⊠ *273 Mulberry St., corner of Mott and Prince Sts., NoLIta* ☎ *212/226–8075* ⊕ *www.oldcathedral.org* Ⓜ *N, R, W to Prince St.; 6 to Bleecker St.*

LITTLE ITALY

Just east of Broadway, the tangle of pedestrian-friendly blocks surrounding Mulberry Street between NoLIta and bustling Canal Street are still a cheerful salute to all things Italian, although over the decades Little Italy has been whittled down by the sprawl of nearby Chinatown. There are red, green, and white street decorations on permanent display, and specialty grocers and pasta makers still dish up delights, though it's all a bit touristy these days—if it's a great Italian meal you want, you might be wise to look elsewhere. Still, Little Italy is fun to walk

The Gangs of Five Points

In the mid-19th century, the Five Points area was perhaps the city's most notorious and dangerous neighborhood. The confluence of five streets—Mulberry, Anthony (now Worth), Cross (now Park), Orange (now Baxter), and Little Water (no longer in existence)—had been built over a drainage pond that was filled in the 1820s. When buildings began to sink into the mosquito-filled muck, middleclass residents abandoned their homes. Buildings were then chopped into tiny apartments that were rented to the poorest of the poor, who at this point included newly emancipated slaves and Irish immigrants fleeing famine. Newspaper accounts at the time tell of daily robberies and other violent crimes. With corrupt political leaders like William Marcy "Boss" Tweed more concerned with lining their pockets than patrolling the streets, keeping order was left to the club-wielding hooligans portrayed in Martin Scorsese's 2002 film Gangs of New York. The neighborhood, razed in the 1880s to make way for Columbus Park, has left a lasting legacy: in the music halls where different ethnic groups grudgingly came together, the Irish jig and the African American shuffle combined to form a new type of fancy footwork called tap dancing. Today, this is the heart of Chinatown. Residents gather in Columbus Park for tai chi in the morning and rowdy board games in the afternoon.

around, and several of the classic food stores on Grand Street are worth a stop if you're after an edible souvenir, like a box of classic cannoli. For a bigger and more bustling Little Italy, head up to Arthur Avenue in the Bronx (see Chapter 14) where you'll find several good, affordable restaurants and a cornucopia of authentic Italian goods made for New Yorkers and tourists alike.

Every September, Little Italy's Mulberry Street is home to the giant Feast of San Gennaro, a busy 11-day festival that sizzles with old–New York flavors—sausages and onions included.

Most Precious Blood Church. The National Shrine of San Gennaro, a replica of the grotto at Lourdes, is the high point of Most Precious Blood Church's richly painted interior. The church becomes a focal point during the annual Feast of San Gennaro. ⊠ 109 Mulberry St., between Canal and Hester Sts., Little Italy ☎ 212/226–6427 Ⓜ 6, J, N, Q, R, W, Z to Canal St.

CHINATOWN

Chinatown is a living, breathing, anything-but-quiet enclave with vibrant streets full of food shops selling exotic produce and seafood, Chinese restaurants and bakeries, Buddhist temples, herbalists, discount massage parlors, and barbershops. A quarter of the city's Chinese residents live here, in a neighborhood that started as a seven-block area but now covers some 40-plus blocks above and below Canal Street (encroaching on what was once a thriving Little Italy). Head to **Mott Street,** south of Canal—Chinatown's main thoroughfare—where the

Some of the storefronts and signage in Chinatown are bilingual—but some are just in Chinese.

first Chinese immigrants (mostly men) settled in tenements in the late 1880s. Walk carefully, as the sidewalks can be slick from the ice underneath the eels, blue crabs, snapper, and shrimp that seem to look back at you from displays as you pass by. You can create a movable feast here with delicious soup dumplings, Peking duck, yellow custard cake, and bubble tea—each at a different place in the neighborhood. A city tourist-information kiosk (⊕ *www.explorechinatown.com*) on a traffic island where Canal, Baxter, and Walker Streets meet can help you with tours, and it also has a map that's very useful for unraveling the area's tangled and angled streets.

Columbus Park. People-watching is the thing to do in this park. Head toward the Bayard Street section, and if you swing by in the morning, you'll see men and women practicing tai chi; the afternoons bring intense games of cards and mah-jongg. In the mid-19th century the park was known as Five Points—the point where Mulberry Street, Anthony (now Worth) Street, Cross (now Park) Street, Orange (now Baxter) Street, and Little Water Street (no longer in existence) intersected—and was notoriously ruled by dangerous Irish gangs. In the 1880s a neighborhood-improvement campaign brought about the park's creation. ✉ *Chinatown* ⊕ *www.nycgovparks.org/parks/M015* Ⓜ *6, J, N, Q, R, W, Z to Canal St.*

Kimlau Square. Ten streets converge at this labyrinthine intersection crisscrossed at odd angles by pedestrian walkways. Standing on the concrete island (popular with the pigeons) is the **Kimlau Arch**, named for Ralph Kimlau, a bomber pilot who died in World War II; the arch is dedicated to all Chinese Americans who "lost their Lives in Defense of Freedom and Democracy." A statue on the square's eastern edge pays tribute to a Qing Dynasty official named Lin Zxeu, the Fujianese minister who sparked the First Opium War in 1839 by banning the drug. ⊠ *Chatham Sq., Bowery and E. Broadway, Chinatown* ⊕ *www. nycgovparks.org/parks/kimlausquare* Ⓜ *4, 5, 6 to Brooklyn Bridge–City Hall; J, Z to Chambers St.*

Mahayana Buddhist Temple. This bright and beautiful Buddhist temple is at a very busy corner, at the foot of the Manhattan Bridge Arch on the Bowery, where gilded lions guard its entrance. Inside are a 16-foot-tall Buddha seated on a lotus flower (allegedly the largest Buddha in the city), incense-burning urns, hand-painted prints, and a gift shop full of interesting items on the second floor. ⊠ *133 Canal St., at the Bowery, Chinatown* ☏ *212/925–8787* Ⓜ *B, D to Grand St.*

The Museum of Chinese in America (MOCA). Founded in 1980, this museum is dedicated to preserving and presenting the history of the Chinese people and their descendants in the United States. The current building, near the boundary between Chinatown and Little Italy (technically, many would say it's in Little Italy), was designed by Maya Lin, architect of the Vietnam Veterans Memorial in Washington, D.C. MOCA's core exhibit on Chinese American history, "With a Single Step: Stories in the Making of America," includes artworks, personal and domestic artifacts, historical documentation, and films. Chinese laundry tools, a traditional general store, and antique business signs are some of the unique objects on display. Rotating exhibits, some of which examine the sometimes turbulent relations between Asian Americans and other citizens, are on display in another gallery. MOCA sponsors workshops, neighborhood walking tours, lectures, and family events. ⊠ *215 Centre St., between Grand and Howard Sts., Chinatown* ☏ *212/619–4785* ⊕ *www.mocanyc.org* ⊠ *$10* ⊙ *Closed Mon.* Ⓜ *6, J, N, Q, R, W, Z to Canal St.*

THE EAST VILLAGE AND THE LOWER EAST SIDE

4

Getting Oriented

The East Village
and the
Lower East Side

M 4,5,6,L, N,Q,R,W

M L

M L

E. 14th St.

E. 13th St.

E. 12th St.

Broadway

Fourth Ave.

Third Ave.

Second Ave.

First Ave.

E. 11th St.

✕ Veniero's Pastry

Museum of Reclaimed Urban Space ◆→

Stuyvesant St. ◆

E. 10th St.

✕ Mudspot

E. 9th St.

Astor Place Subway Station ◆

St. Marks Place ◆

Tompkins Square Park ◆

M R,W

Astor Pl.

Astor Pl.

M 6

Fourth Ave.

Third Ave.

Taras Shevchenko Pl.

E. 7th St.

E. 6th St.

Alphabet City ◆

Lafayette St.

Ukrainian Museum ◆

EAST VILLAGE

Avenue A

Avenue B

Merchant's House Museum ◆

Cooper Square

E. 5th St.

E. 4th St.

Gt. Jones St.

E. 3rd St.

GREENWICH VILLAGE

E. 2nd St.

The Hole ◆

E. 1st St.

M 6

Bleecker St.

Il Laboratorio del Gelato ✕

M F

B,D,F,M **M**

E. Houston St.

Sperone Westwater ◆

Chrystie St.

Eldridge St.

Forsyth St.

Allen St.

Orchard St.

Ludlow St.

Essex St.

Norfolk St.

Suffolk St.

Bowery

Stanton St.

International Center of Photography ◆

Lafayette St.

New Museum ◆

LOWER EAST SIDE

◆ Krause Gallery

Prince St.

Rivington St.

Essex Street Market ◆

← SOHO

NOLITA

Tibor de Nagy Gallery ◆

M 6 Spring St.

Mulberry St.

Mott St.

Elizabeth St.

Delancey St.

M J,M,Z,F

J,Z **M**

Lower East Side Tenement Museum ◆

Broome St.

0   1/8 mile

0   200 meters

Museum at Eldridge Street ◆↓

MAKING THE MOST OF YOUR TIME

Houston Street runs east–west and neatly divides the East Village (north of Houston) and the Lower East Side (south of Houston). The eastern boundary of the East Village and Lower East Side is the East River; the western boundary is 4th Avenue and the Bowery. So many communities converge in these neighborhoods that each block can seem like a neighborhood unto itself.

The East Village lets loose on weekends, when nightlife-seekers descend on the area, filling up the bars and spilling onto the sidewalks. Weekday evenings are less frenetic, with more of a local vibe—although the term "local" around here always means a large number of students from New York University. Daytime is great for shopping in local boutiques, and brunch on weekends generally means lines for hot spots like Prune and Cafe Mogador, which fill with patrons lingering over coffee.

The Lower East Side does not tend to be an early-riser destination any day of the week. Although there's plenty to see during the day, nightfall offers a more exciting vision: blocks that were previously empty rows of pulled-down gates transform into clusters of throbbing bars. On Rivington and Stanton and their cross streets, stores, bars, and cafés buzz all week.

GETTING HERE AND AROUND

For the East Village, take the N, R, or W subway line to 8th Street–New York University (NYU), the 6 to Astor Place, or the L to 3rd Avenue. To reach Alphabet City, take the L to 1st Avenue or the F to 2nd Avenue. For the Lower East Side, head southeast from the 2nd Avenue stop on the F, or take the F, M, J, or Z to the Delancey Street–Essex Street stop.

TOP EXPERIENCES

Getting immersed in the art scene on the Lower East Side

People-watching on St. Marks Place or at Tompkins Square Park

Shopping at boutiques and vintage clothing stores

Visiting the Lower East Side Tenement Museum

COFFEE AND QUICK BITES

Il Laboratorio del Gelato. Seasonal flavors make this gelato la crème de la crème. There are 48 flavors offered each day. ⊠ *188 Ludlow St., at E. Houston St., Lower East Side* ☎ *212/343–9922* ⊕ *www.laboratoriodelgelato.com* Ⓜ *F to 2nd Ave.*

Mudspot. Stop in for take-out coffee or get a table and relax over a casual meal at this popular neighborhood spot. ⊠ *307 E. 9th St., between 1st and 2nd Aves., East Village* ☎ *212/228–9074* ⊕ *www.mudnyc.com* Ⓜ *L to 1st Ave., F to 2nd Ave.*

Veniero's Pastry. This Italian bakery has been offering cookies, coffee, and elaborate cakes and tarts since 1894—and the late hours it keeps only sweetens the deal. The fruit-topped minicheesecakes are always a good idea. ⊠ *342 E. 11th St., between 1st and 2nd Aves., East Village* ☎ *212/674–7070* ⊕ *www.venierospastry.com* Ⓜ *L to 1st Ave.*

Sightseeing
★★
Nightlife
★★★★★
Dining
★★★★★
Lodging
★★
Shopping
★★★★

Vibrant, bold, and bohemian: the streets of the East Village and the Lower East Side are some of the most electric in New York City. Both neighborhoods have a deep immigrant past, and have evolved into nighttime destinations where you can dance till dawn any day of the week. This area of downtown is tamer than it used to be (as the arrival of Whole Foods, Starbucks, and several glass-and-chrome condos attests), but a gritty edge lives on in the dive bars, sultry live music venues, and experimental restaurants. Spend time wandering the side streets, and you'll be struck by the pastiche of ethnicities whose imprints are visible in the neighborhood's shops, eateries, and, of course, people.

EAST VILLAGE

Updated
by Caroline
Trefler

Many opposites coexist peacefully in the East Village: dive bars and craft-cocktail dens, Ukrainian diners and the latest chef-driven restaurants, stylish boutiques and tattoo parlors. Famous for its nightlife, the East Village has become increasingly more upscale in recent years with St. Marks Place trading in some of its grit for a hodgepodge of students, well-earning postgrads, and international expats. At its roots, the neighborhood is a community of artists, activists, and social dissenters—and though this is still the essential vibe here, the finish is much more polished these days.

East of 1st Avenue is Alphabet City, once the city's drug haunt but now an ever more gentrified neighborhood. There is still a young, artistic (and sometimes seedy) vibe in and around Tompkins Square Park.

Keep Your Eyes Peeled

The East Village's reputation for quirkiness is evinced not only by its residents and sites but also in the many incongruous structures that somehow coexist so easily that they often go unnoticed. Keep your eyes open as you explore the streets. You never know what might turn up: There's the Hells Angels' Headquarters, for example, tucked into a residential block of 3rd Street between 1st and 2nd Avenues, surrounded by a bevy of showstopping bikes. Look up to see the giant copper statue of Vladimir Lenin that salutes the world from atop a building on Norfolk Street, just south of Houston (it was moved in 2016 from its previous home on the top of 250 Houston Street). Not far away is the shingled Cape Cod–style house perched on the apartment building at the northwest corner of Houston and 1st Avenue, one of the city's many unique rooftop retreats (it's best viewed from the east). Then there's the hidden-in-plain-sight New York Marble Cemetery (⊕ *www.marbl-ecemetery.org*), established in the 1830s on 2nd Avenue between 2nd and 3rd Streets, where thousands are interred in underground, marble-lined vaults that were thought to prevent the spread of disease in a time marked by cholera epidemics. The gardens are surrounded by 12-foot walls made of Tuckahoe marble, and entered through wrought-iron gates. It's open to the public every fourth Sunday, April through October.

TOP ATTRACTIONS

Alphabet City. The north–south avenues east of 1st Avenue, from Houston Street to 14th Street, have letters, not numbers, which gives this area its nickname: Alphabet City. Avenues A, B, and C are full of restaurants, cafés, stores, and bars that run from the low-rent and scruffy to the pricey and polished—the streets seem more mixed than in other neighborhoods downtown. Parts of Avenues A and B run along Tompkins Square Park. A close-knit Puerto Rican community makes its home around Avenue C, also called "Loisaida" (a Spanglish creation for "Lower East Side"), which is still home to many Latino shops and bodegas but also a growing number of trendy restaurants and bars. Avenue D remains a bit rough around the edges—in part because of the uninterrupted row of housing projects that run along its east side. The East River Park, farther east, provides some nice views of the Manhattan Bridge and parts of Brooklyn. To reach the park, cross Avenue D and take one of the pedestrian bridges that crosses FDR Drive at East 10th or East 5th Street, or cross the road at East Houston Street. ⊠ *East Village* Ⓜ *L to 1st Ave.; F to 2nd Ave.*

St. Marks Place. The longtime hub of the edgy East Village, St. Marks Place is the name given to idiosyncratic East 8th Street between 3rd Avenue and Avenue A. During the 1950s, beatniks Allen Ginsberg and Jack Kerouac lived and wrote in the area; the 1960s brought Bill Graham's Fillmore East (nearby, at 105 2nd Avenue), and Andy Warhol's Dom and the Electric Circus nightclub (both at Nos. 19–25), where the Velvet Underground performed. The studded, pink-haired, and shaved-head punk scene followed, and there's still a good chance of seeing some pierced rockers and teenage Goths on the block. Farther down, at No. 33, is where the punk store Manic Panic first foisted its lurid hair dyes and makeup on the world. At No. 57 stood the short-lived Club 57, a church basement that attracted such 1980s stalwarts as Keith Haring, Ann Magnuson, Klaus Nomi, Kenny Scharf, and Fab Five Freddy.

These days, there's not much cutting edge left. Some of the grungy facades lead to luxury condos, and the area has become a Little Japan, with several ramen and dumpling shops, some sake bars, and lots of young Asian students. The blocks between 2nd and 3rd Avenues can feel like a shopping arcade, crammed with body-piercing and tattoo salons, and shops selling cheap jewelry, sunglasses, incense, and wacky T-shirts. The cafés and bars from here over to Avenue A attract customers late into the night—thanks partly to lower drink prices than in other downtown neighborhoods. ⊠ *8th St., between 3rd Ave. and Ave. A, East Village* Ⓜ *6 to Astor Pl.; N, R, W to 8th St.–NYU.*

FAMILY **Tompkins Square Park.** This leafy park fills up year-round with locals partaking in picnics and drum circles, and making use of the playground and the dog run. Shady benches, a playground, and an elegant 1891 water fountain (donated by a teetotaling benefactor) are some of the park's features. There are movie screenings and music gatherings throughout the summer, a year-round farmers' market by the southwest corner on Sunday, and an annual Halloween dog-costume event. It wasn't always so rosy in the park, though: in 1988, police followed then-mayor David Dinkins's orders to evict the many homeless people who had set up makeshift homes here, and homeless rights and antigentrification activists fought back with sticks and bottles. The park was reclaimed and reopened in 1992 with a midnight curfew, still in effect today. ⊠ *From 7th to 10th St., between Aves. A and B, East Village* ⊕ *www.nycgovparks.org/parks/tompkinssquarepark* Ⓜ *6 to Astor Pl., L to 1st Ave.*

WORTH NOTING

Astor Place Subway Station. At the beginning of the 20th century, almost all of the city's Interborough Rapid Transit (IRT) subway entrances resembled the one here—an ornate cast-iron replica of a Beaux Arts kiosk marking the subway entrance for the uptown 6 train. This traffic-island entrance, which was—and still is—the stop nearest to the venerable Cooper Union college, is now on the National Register of Historic Places. Inside, plaques of beaver emblems line the tiled station walls (though they're rather grimy these days), a reference to the fur trade that contributed to John Jacob Astor's fortune. Milton Glaser, the Cooper Union graduate who originated the "I [heart] NY" logo, designed the station's murals. ⊠ *8th St. and 4th Ave., traffic island, East Village* Ⓜ *6 to Astor Pl.*

The Hole. Run by Kathy Grayson, the former director of the highly influential Deitch Projects, this contemporary-arts gallery generally hosts two simultaneous shows a month. Its artists lean more toward the up-and-coming rather than the establishment. The on-site Hole Shop carries lots of quirky zines, posters, books, and art objects. ⊠ *312 Bowery,* *between Bleecker and E. Houston Sts., East Village* ☎ *212/466–1100* ⊕ *www.theholenyc.com* ⊘ *Closed Mon., Tues.* Ⓜ *6 to Bleecker St.; B, D, F, M to Broadway–Lafayette St.*

Merchant's House Museum. Built in 1832, this redbrick house, combining Federal and Greek Revival styles, provides a glimpse into the domestic life of the period 30 years before the Civil War. Retired merchant Seabury Tredwell and his descendants lived here from 1835 until 1933. The home became a museum in 1936, with the original furnishings and architectural features preserved; family memorabilia are on display. The fourth-floor servants' bedroom, where the family's Irish servants slept and did some of their work, offers a look at the lives of Irish domestics in the mid-1800s. Guided tours are at 2 pm; there's an additional tour at 6:30 pm on Thursday. ✉ *29 E. 4th St., between the Bowery and Lafayette St., East Village* ☎ *212/777–1089* ⊕ *www.merchantshouse. org* ✉ *$15* ⊘ *Closed Tues., Wed.* Ⓜ *N, R, W to 8th St.–NYU; 6 to Astor Pl.; B, D, F, M to Broadway–Lafayette St.*

Museum of Reclaimed Urban Space. Opened in 2012, this museum of the East Village's urban activism covers key events from the 1980s to the present, during which time the city's public housing was often woefully mismanaged and hundreds of apartments lay abandoned and crumbling. Photographs and videos fill the small exhibit space inside a tenement's storefront and its basement. Squatters, community gardens, the Tompkins Square riots, and the renaissance of bicycling in the city are all given their due, as is Occupy Wall Street. Tours of community gardens, activist landmarks, and other squats, both legal and otherwise, are also run by the museum. ✉ *155 Ave. C, between 9th and 10th Sts., East Village* ☎ *973/818–8495* ⊕ *www.morusnyc.org* ✉ *$5 suggested donation; tours $20* ⊘ *Closed Mon., Wed.* Ⓜ *L to 1st Ave.*

Stuyvesant Street. This diagonal slicing through the block bounded by 2nd and 3rd Avenues and East 9th and 10th Streets is unique in Manhattan: it's the oldest street laid out precisely along an east–west axis. Among the handsome 19th-century redbrick row houses are the Federal-style **Stuyvesant-Fish House** at No. 21, built as a wedding gift for a great-great-granddaughter of the Dutch governor Peter Stuyvesant, and **Renwick Triangle,** an attractive group of Anglo-Italianate brick and brownstone residences that face Stuyvesant and East 10th Streets. ✉ *Stuyvesant St., East Village* Ⓜ *6 to Astor Pl.; N, R, W to 8th St.–NYU.*

Ukrainian Museum. From the late 19th century through the end of World War II, tens of thousands of Ukrainians made their way to New York City—and particularly to "Little Ukraine," as much of the East Village was known. This museum, which opened in 2005, examines Ukrainian Americans' dual heritage, with a permanent collection made up of folk art, fine art, and documentary materials about immigrant life. Ceramics, jewelry, hundreds of brilliantly colored Easter eggs, and an extensive collection of Ukrainian costumes and textiles are the highlights. ■ TIP➜ To continue the experience, sample a little Ukrainian food at nearby Veselka diner. ✉ *222 E. 6th St., between 2nd and 3rd Aves., East Village* ☎ *212/228–0110* ⊕ *www.ukrainianmuseum.org* ✉ *$8* ⊘ *Closed Mon., Tues.* Ⓜ *6 to Astor Pl.; N, R, W to 8th St.–NYU.*

The Tenement Museum offers a fascinating glimpse into the lives of early-20th-century immigrants.

LOWER EAST SIDE

The Lower East Side (or simply LES) is a center of all things cool: arts and nightlife, restaurants and cafés, boutiques and salons. What was once the "Gateway to America"—and home to waves of Irish, German, Jewish, Hispanic, and Chinese immigrants—is now a quickly gentrifying neighborhood where modern high-rises, the ultracontemporary New Museum, and low-key hangouts all exist in the same corner of Manhattan.

Ludlow Street and Orchard Street in particular are great for exploring the boutiques and galleries wedged between bars and small restaurants. On Friday and Saturday nights be aware that the neighborhood scene can be as raucous as in a college town, especially on Rivington and Orchard Streets.

The best time to experience the neighborhood's past is by day. The excellent Lower East Side Tenement Museum movingly captures the immigrant legacy of tough times and survival instincts. You might not find many pickles being sold from barrels anymore, but this remains a good place to nosh on delicious Jewish food like matzo-ball soup, corned beef, and knishes from Katz's Delicatessen or Russ & Daughters.

TOP ATTRACTIONS

FAMILY

Fodor's Choice

★

Lower East Side Tenement Museum. Step back in time at the partially restored 1863 tenement building at 97 Orchard Street, where guided tours take you through the preserved apartments—and lives—of several generations of immigrants who lived in the building. Themed tours run at various times each day and are limited to 15 people, so buying tickets in advance is a good idea. The "Hard Times" tour visits the homes of Natalie Gumpertz, a German-Jewish dressmaker (dating from 1878), and Adolph and Rosaria Baldizzi, Catholic immigrants from Sicily (1935). "Sweatshop Workers" visits the Levines' garment shop/apartment and the home of the Rogarshevsky family from Eastern Europe (1918). "Irish Outsiders" explores the life of the Moores, an Irish-American family living in the building in 1869. "Shop Life" looks at the various businesses operating on local streets, including a German-style bar and a kosher butcher. The "Under One Roof" exhibit explores the lives of immigrant families from Poland, China, and Puerto Rico who lived at 103 Orchard Street after World War II. ■ **TIP→ A two-hour extended experience tour with a chance for in-depth discussion is hosted daily, as are walking tours of the neighborhood; most tours don't allow kids under five.** ⊠ *103 Orchard St., at Delancey St., Lower East Side* ☎ *877/975–3786* ⊕ *www.tenement.org* ⟟ *Most tours $25* Ⓜ *B, D to Grand St.; F to Delancey St.; J, M, Z to Essex St.*

New Museum. This seven-story, 60,000-square-foot structure—a glimmering, metal-mesh-clad assemblage of off-center squares—caused a small neighborhood uproar when it was built in 2007, with some residents slow to accept the nontraditional building. Not surprisingly, given the museum's name and the building, shows are all about contemporary art. If you're visiting on the weekend, check out the seventh-floor Skyroom and its panoramic views. ■ **TIP→ Make an afternoon of it and buy a combination ticket ($27 for same-day visit; available Wed.–Sun.) with the International Center of Photography across the street.** ⊠ *235 Bowery, at Prince St., Lower East Side* ☎ *212/219–1222* ⊕ *www.newmuseum.org* ⟟ *$18 (pay-what-you-wish Thurs. 7–9)* ⊙ *Closed Mon., Tues.* Ⓜ *6 to Spring St., F to 2nd Ave.*

WORTH NOTING

Essex Street Market. There are plenty of newfangled food markets around Manhattan and Brooklyn, with outposts of well-known food purveyors, but the Essex Street Market is an old-school version. Started in 1940 as an attempt by Mayor Fiorello LaGuardia to corral street pushcarts and vendors (and thereby get them off the streets), the Essex Street Market was defined early on by the Jewish and Italian immigrants of the Lower East Side and went through several incarnations. These days there are proprietors selling meat, fish, cheeses, produce, bread, pastries, fresh juice, coffee, tacos, and more. In back is Shopsins, an eccentric restaurant with a small space and a vast menu that moved here after decades in Greenwich Village. ⊠ *120 Essex St., between Rivington and Delancey Sts., Lower East Side* ☎ *212/312–3603* ⊕ *www.essexstreetmarket.com* Ⓜ *F to Delancey St.; J, M, Z to Essex St.*

International Center of Photography. Founded in 1974 by photojournalist Cornell Capa (photographer Robert Capa's brother), this museum continues to put on exhibitions that explore the timely social and political aspects of photojournalism. While the institution has a collection of over 150,000 original prints spanning the history of photography from daguerreotypes to large-scale pigment prints, the public space here, in the first-floor and basement galleries, is devoted to temporary exhibits. There's a small gift shop and café as well. ■ **TIP→ Make an afternoon**

of it and buy a combination ticket ($27 for same-day visit; available Wed.–Sun.) with the New Museum across the street. ⊠ *250 Bowery, between E. Houston and Prince Sts., Lower East Side* ☎ *212/857–0000* ⊕ *www.icp.org* 🎫 *$14* 🕐 *Closed Mon.* Ⓜ *6 to Spring St.; F to 2nd Ave.*

Krause Gallery. Frequently changing shows of edgy contemporary work are displayed in this small two-level space established in 2004. ⊠ *149 Orchard St., between Stanton and Rivington Sts., Lower East Side* ☎ *212/777–7799* ⊕ *www.krausegallery.com* Ⓜ *F to 2nd Ave.*

Museum at Eldridge Street. The exterior of this 1887 Orthodox synagogue-turned-museum (and community space) was the first to be built by the many Eastern European Jews who settled in the Lower East Side in the late 19th century, and is a striking mix of Romanesque, Gothic, and Moorish motifs. Inside is an exceptional hand-carved ark of mahogany and walnut, a sculptured wooden balcony, jewel-tone stained-glass windows, vibrantly painted and stenciled walls, and an enormous brass chandelier. The museum can be viewed as part of an hour-long tour (starts on the hour), which begins downstairs where interactive "touch tables" teach all ages about Eldridge Street and the Lower East Side. The crowning piece of the building's decades-long restoration is a stained-glass window by artist Kiki Smith and architect Deborah Gans, which weighs 6,000 pounds and has more than 1,200 pieces of glass. ⊠ *12 Eldridge St., between Canal and Division Sts., Lower East Side* ☎ *212/219–0302* ⊕ *www.eldridgestreet.org* 🎫 *$14* 🕐 *Closed Sat.* Ⓜ *F to East Broadway; B, D to Grand St.*

Sperone Westwater. Founded in 1975 in SoHo, Sperone Westwater now finds itself a major part of the "artification" of the Lower East Side. In 2010, the gallery moved into this nine-story building, which it commissioned for itself—a vote of confidence in both its Bowery surroundings and the continued importance of its artists, who have included Bruce Nauman, William Wegman, Gerhard Richter, and a host of blue-chip minimalists. The narrow building, designed by Norman Foster, rivals the New Museum (a few doors down) for crisp poise. ⊠ *257 Bowery, between E. Houston and Stanton Sts., Lower East Side* ☎ *212/999–7337* ⊕ *www.speronewestwater.com* 🕐 *Closed Sun., Mon.* Ⓜ *6 to Spring St.; F to 2nd Ave.*

Tibor de Nagy Gallery. Started in 1950 and well-known for showing then-emerging artists such as Helen Frankenthaler, Jane Wilson, and Red Grooms, the Tibor de Nagy Gallery moved to the Lower East Side in 2017. The gallery frequently shares exhibit space with the Betty Cuningham gallery next door. ⊠ *15 Rivington St., between Bowery and Chrystie St., Lower East Side* ☎ *212/262–5050* ⊕ *www.tibordenagy. com* 🕐 *Closed Mon., Tues.* Ⓜ *F to 2nd Ave.*

GREENWICH VILLAGE AND THE WEST VILLAGE

Getting Oriented

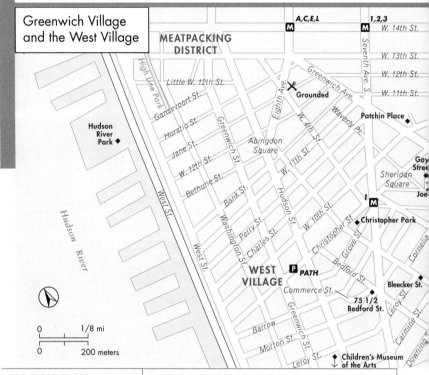

Greenwich Village and the West Village

MEATPACKING DISTRICT

Hudson River Park ◆

Hudson River

0   1/8 mi

0   200 meters

A,C,E,L   1,2,3
W. 14th St.
W. 13th St.
W. 12th St.
W. 11th St.
Patchin Place ◆
Gay Street
Sheridan Square
Joe
Christopher Park
Bleecker St.
75 1/2 Bedford St.
Commerce St.
Grounded
Abingdon Square
WEST VILLAGE   P PATH
Children's Museum of the Arts

High Line Park

Little W. 12th St.
Gansevoort St.
Horatio St.
Jane St.
W. 12th St.
Bethune St.
Bank St.
Perry St.
Charles St.
Barrow
Morton St.
Leroy St.
West St.
Washington St.
Greenwich St.
Hudson St.
Greenwich St.
W. 10th St.
W. 11th St.
W. 4th St.
Christopher St.
Grove St.
Bedford St.
Leroy St.
Carmine St.
Cornelia
Downing
Seventh Ave. S.
Eighth Ave.
Greenwich Ave.
Waverly Pl.

TOP EXPERIENCES	MAKING THE MOST OF YOUR TIME
People-watching in Washington Square Park	A visit to Washington Square Park, in the heart of Greenwich Village, is a must for people-watching and relaxing on a bench (you might also catch some live music performances). There are lots of restaurants and shops in the neighborhood, too.
Strolling and window-shopping along the picturesque streets of the West Village	
Relaxing in a café	The West Village—basically from 7th Avenue to the Hudson River—is more residential, and a bit quieter, with carefully tended, tree-lined streets that make the neighborhood a perfect place to roam, camera in hand. Everything from upscale boutiques to cheap pizza joints line Bleecker Street and Greenwich Avenue.
Walking by the water in Hudson River Park	
Eating your way down Bleecker Street	The winding streets of the West Village often seem mazelike, even to many New Yorkers, because most of the streets here are named rather than numbered, and they were established before Manhattan laid out its street-grid system back in 1811. Assume that you're going to get a little bit lost—that's part of the fun—but don't hesitate to ask for directions.

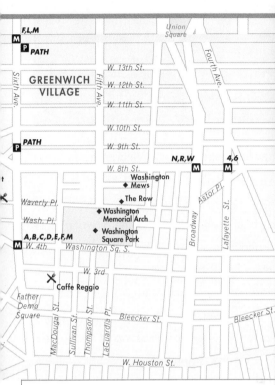

GREENWICH VILLAGE

W. 13th St.
W. 12th St.
W. 11th St.
W. 10th St.
W. 9th St.
W. 8th St.
Washington Mews
The Row
Washington Memorial Arch
Washington Square Park
Washington Sq. S.
W. 4th
W. 3rd
Caffe Reggio
Father Demo Square
Bleecker St.
W. Houston St.

F,L,M
PATH
Union Square
Fourth Ave.
N,R,W
4,6
A,B,C,D,E,F,M
Sixth Ave.
Fifth Ave.
Broadway
Lafayette St.
Astor Pl.
Waverly Pl.
Wash. Pl.
MacDougal St.
Sullivan St.
Thompson St.
LaGuardia Pl.
Bleecker St.
PATH

COFFEE AND QUICK BITES

Caffe Reggio. Usually packed, this café dates back to the 1920s, making it one of the oldest coffeehouses in the city. Do have a pastry. ⊠ *119 MacDougal St., between W. 3rd and Carmine Sts., Greenwich Village* ☎ *212/475–9557* Ⓜ *A, B, C, D, E, F, M to W. 4th St.*

Grounded. Step into this low-key spot for hot or cold brews (tea and coffee)—the specialty lattes are an excellent splurge. ⊠ *28 Jane St., between 8th and Greenwich Aves., West Village* ☎ *212/647–0943* ⊕ *www.groundedcoffee.com* Ⓜ *A, C, E to 14th St.; L to 8th Ave.; 1, 2, 3 to 14th St.*

Joe (West Village). The coffee is exquisitely prepared at this small corner café, the first of what is now a small chain. ⊠ *141 Waverly Pl., at Gay St., Greenwich Village* ☎ *212/924–6750* ⊕ *www.joenewyork.com* Ⓜ *A, B, C, D, E, F, M to W. 4th St.; 1 to Christopher St.–Sheridan Sq.*

5

GETTING HERE AND AROUND

The West 4th Street subway stop—serviced by the A, B, C, D, E, F, and M lines—puts you on the west side of Greenwich Village. Farther west, the 1 train has stops at Houston Street and at Christopher Street–Sheridan Square. The L stops at 8th Avenue, and the A, C, and E trains stop at 14th Street, which is the northern boundary of the West Village.

BEST FOR KIDS

Hudson River Park

Washington Square Park

Taking time out for pizza or dessert

Sightseeing
★★★

Nightlife
★★★★

Dining
★★★★★

Lodging
★★★★★

Shopping
★★★

★★★★

The charming, tree-lined streets of the Village are beloved by New Yorkers (whether they can afford to live there or not) for their cozy restaurants and cafés, chic cocktail bars, and inviting boutiques. Long the home of writers, artists, bohemians, and bon vivants, "the Village" is made up of Greenwich Village proper (the area surrounding Washington Square Park) and the West Village, from 7th Avenue to the Hudson River. Greenwich Village, in prime New York University (NYU) territory, has lots of young people, while the West Village is primarily residential, with lots of well-to-do couples and families and a substantial community of older gay men and some lesbians. Both sections have a relaxed, downtown vibe and a distinctly New York style in their stores, corner bars, and trendy restaurants.

GREENWICH VILLAGE

Updated
by Caroline
Trefler

Many would argue that Washington Square Park is still the beating heart of downtown, a magnet for all kinds of life. People come here to hear live music, stretch out on a picnic blanket, let the pooch loose at the dog run, or bring kids to the playground. The park anchors Greenwich Village, where you can encounter just about every variety of New Yorker, from skateboarders and students to white-collar workers on break to people who look like they've been hanging out in the park for years, playing chess and checkers at the stone tables. This is also a historic part of the neighborhood, with the grand Washington Memorial Arch looking north to two blocks of lovingly preserved Greek Revival and Federal-style town houses known as "the Row."

DID YOU KNOW?

Greenwich Village has a long bohemian history: for decades it was an enclave of artists and the counterculture, from beatniks to the antiwar movement to gay rights. Today this neighborhood is better known for its celebrity residents and sky-high housing costs.

CLOSE UP

Halloween in the Village

All things weird and wonderful, all creatures great and small, all costumes clever and fantastical: New York City has them all—and on All Hallows' Eve they strut through the streets in New York's Village Hallow-een Parade. White-sheeted ghouls seem dull compared with fishnets and leather, sequins and feathers posing and prancing along 6th Avenue in this vibrant display of vanity and insanity.

In 1974 mask-maker and puppeteer Ralph Lee paraded his puppets from house to house, visiting friends and family along the winding streets of his Greenwich Village neighborhood. His merry march quickly outgrew its origi-nal, intimate route and now, decades later, it parades up 6th Avenue, from Spring Street to 16th Street, attracting upward of 60,000 creatively costumed exhibitionists, artists, dancers, and musicians, hundreds of enormous puppets, scores of bands, and more than 2 million spectators. Anyone with a costume can join in, with no advance registration required,

although the enthusiastic interaction between participants and spectators makes it just as much fun simply to watch. It's a street event for families and singles alike (though you will be entering very dense crowds), and a joyful night unlike any other.

The parade lines up along 6th Avenue between Canal and Spring Streets from 6:30 to 8:30 pm. The walk actually starts at 7, but it takes about two hours to leave the staging area. It's best to arrive from the south to avoid the crush of participants. Get there a few hours early if possible. Costumes are usually handmade, clever, and outrageous, and revelers are happy to strike a pose. The streets are crowded along the route, with the most congestion below 14th Street. Of course, the best way to truly experi-ence the parade is to march, but if you're not feeling the face paint, it's possible to volunteer to help carry the puppets. For information, visit ⊕ *www. halloween-nyc.com.*

Bountiful doesn't even begin to describe Greenwich Village's yield of creative genius. In the late 1940s and early 1950s, abstract expression-ist painters Jackson Pollock, Lee Krasner, Mark Rothko, and Willem de Kooning congregated here, as did Beat writers Jack Kerouac, Allen Ginsberg, and Lawrence Ferlinghetti. The 1960s brought folk musicians and poets, notably Bob Dylan and Joan Baez. The area's bohemian days may be long gone, but a romantic allure still lingers along the tree-lined streets and at the back of the cafés, behind the frenetic clamor of NYU students and the polished veneer of multimillion-dollar town houses.

TOP ATTRACTIONS

Bleecker Street. Walking the stretch of Bleecker Street between 7th Avenue and Broadway provides a smattering of just about everything synonymous with Greenwich Village these days: NYU buildings, record stores, Italian cafés and food shops, pizza and takeout joints, bars and nightclubs, and funky boutiques. A lazy afternoon here may consist of sampling some of the city's best pizza, grabbing an espresso, and soak-ing up the downtown fashion scene. Foodies love the blocks between 6th and 7th Avenues for the specialty purveyors like Murray's Cheese

(No. 254). At the intersection of Bleecker and Carmine Streets is Our Lady of Pompeii Church, where Mother Cabrini, a naturalized Italian immigrant who became the first American citizen to be canonized, often prayed. West of 7th Avenue, the shops get more upscale, with fashion and home-furnishings boutiques featuring antiques, eyeglasses, handbags, shoes, and designer clothing. ⊠ *Greenwich Village* Ⓜ *A, B, C, D, E, F, M to W. 4th St.*

FAMILY

Fodor's Choice

★

Washington Square Park. NYU students, street musicians, skateboarders, jugglers, chess players, and those just watching the grand opera of it all generate a maelstrom of activity in this physical and spiritual heart of Greenwich Village. The 9¾-acre park had inauspicious beginnings as a cemetery, principally for yellow-fever victims—an estimated 10,000–22,000 bodies lie below (a headstone was even unearthed in 2009). At one time, plans to renovate the park called for the removal of the bodies, but local resistance prevented this from happening. In the early 1800s the park was a parade ground and the site of public executions; the notorious Hanging Elm still stands at the northwest corner of the square. Today that gruesome past is all but forgotten, as playgrounds attract parents with tots in tow, dogs go leash-free inside the popular dog runs, and everyone else seems drawn toward the large central fountain.

The triumphal European-style **Washington Memorial Arch** stands at the square's northern flank, marking the start of 5th Avenue. The original wood-and-papier-mâché arch, originally situated a half block north, was erected in 1889 to commemorate the 100th anniversary of George Washington's presidential inauguration. The arch was reproduced in Tuckahoe marble in 1892, and the statues—*Washington as General Accompanied by Fame and Valor* on one side, and *Washington as Statesman Accompanied by Wisdom and Justice* on the other—were added in 1916 and 1918, respectively. ⊠ *5th Ave., between Waverly Pl. and W. 4th St., Greenwich Village* Ⓜ *A, B, C, D, E, F, M to W. 4th St.*

WORTH NOTING

Gay Street. A curved, one-block lane lined with small row houses, Gay Street was probably named after an early landowner and definitely had nothing to do with gay rights. In the 1930s, this tiny thoroughfare and nearby Christopher Street became famous nationwide after Ruth McKenney began to publish somewhat zany autobiographical stories based on what happened when she and her sister moved to No. 14 from Ohio. The stories, first published in the *New Yorker*, birthed many adaptations, including the 1953 Broadway musical *Wonderful Town* (revived in 2004) and the 1942 and 1955 movies *My Sister Eileen*. ⊠ *Between Christopher St. and Waverly Pl., Greenwich Village* Ⓜ *1 to Christopher St.–Sheridan Sq.; A, B, C, D, E, F, M to W. 4th St.*

Patchin Place. This narrow, gated cul-de-sac off West 10th Street between Greenwich and 6th Avenues has 10 diminutive 1848 row houses. Around the corner on 6th Avenue is a similar dead-end street, **Milligan Place,** with five small houses completed in 1852. The houses in both quiet enclaves were originally built for waiters who worked at 5th Avenue's high-society Brevoort Hotel, long since demolished. Later

Out and On Display: George Segal's sculptures of two gay couples in Christopher Park embody LGBTQ pride in Greenwich Village.

Patchin Place residents included writers Theodore Dreiser, e. e. cummings, Jane Bowles, and Djuna Barnes. Milligan Place became popular among playwrights, including Eugene O'Neill. ⊠ *Off W. 10th St., Greenwich Village* Ⓜ *A, B, C, D, E, F, M to W. 4th St.*

The Row. Built from 1833 through 1837, this series of Greek Revival and Federal row houses along Washington Square North, between University Place and MacDougal Street, once belonged to merchants and bankers, then to writers and artists such as John Dos Passos and Edward Hopper. Many are now owned by NYU and used for housing and offices. Although the facades remain beautifully preserved, the interiors have been drastically altered over the years. ⊠ *1–13 and 19–26 Washington Sq. N, between University Pl. and MacDougal St., Greenwich Village* Ⓜ *A, B, C, D, E, F, M to W. 4th St.; N, R, W to 8th St.–NYU; 4, 6 to Astor Pl.*

Washington Mews. A rarity in Manhattan, this pretty, brick-covered street—really a glorified alley—is lined on the north side with the former mews (carriage houses) of the area's homes. Although the street is private, gated, and owned by New York University, which uses many of the buildings for clubs and offices, it's open to pedestrian traffic. ⊠ *From Washington Sq. N to 8th St., between 5th Ave. and University Pl., Greenwich Village* Ⓜ *A, B, C, D, E, F, M to W. 4th St.; N, R, W to 8th St.–NYU; 4, 6 to Astor Pl.*

CLOSE UP

Bleecker Street's Little Italy

Little Italy can be besieged by slow-moving crowds, touristy shops, and restaurant hosts hollering invitations to dine inside. Bleecker Street between 6th and 7th Avenues, on the other hand, with its crowded cafés, bakeries, pizza parlors, and old-world merchants, offers a more pleasurable, equally vital alternative to the traditional tourist traps.

For an authentic Italian bakery experience, stop by Pasticceria Rocco (No. 243) for wonderful cannoli, cream puffs, and cookies packed up, or order an espresso and linger over the treats.

Step into the past at the old-style (and now high-end) butcher shops, such as Ottomanelli & Sons (No. 285) and Faicco's Pork Store (No. 260), where locals have bought their sausage, prime beef, and custom-cut pork since 1900.

The sweet (or stinky) smell of success is nowhere more evident than at Murray's Cheese (No. 254). The original shop, opened in 1940 by Murray Greenberg (not Italian), was not much larger than the display case that stocked the stuff. Now it's a fromage-lover's emporium, with everything from imported crackers and bamboo cutting boards to a full-service sandwich counter. Samples are frequently served. Educational cheese-tasting classes are held in the upstairs classroom (sign up online in advance). Murray's has expanded to include a Cheese Bar a few doors down (No. 264).

There are also a few popular pizzerias along this strip; Kesté Pizza & Vino (No. 271) serves Neapolitan pies that some would argue rival even Da Michele in Naples. It's also the official location in the United States for the Associazione Pizzaiuoli Napoletani, whose mission is to promote pizzas made in the Neapolitan tradition, using Neapolitan products. Brick-oven favorite John's Pizzeria (No. 278) is a classic New York pizza joint—pies only, no slices!

5

WEST VILLAGE

Small curving streets, peculiar alleys, and historic town houses—it's easy to see why the tree-lined thoroughfares of the West Village (which are primarily residential) are in such high demand. A stroll here reveals charming cafés, the occasional celebrity out and about, and well-dressed children playing in the parks. Visitors come here to get a feel for local life, to daydream about living in New York. Unlike 5th Avenue or SoHo, the pace is slower, allowing shoppers to enjoy the peaceful streets and independent and designer stores. This is the place to come for unusual finds as well as global-brand goods. The West Village section of Bleecker Street is a particularly good place to indulge all sorts of shopping appetites; high-fashion foragers prowl the stretch between West 10th Street and 8th Avenue. Hudson Street and Greenwich Avenue are also prime boutique-browsing territories.

Christopher Street has long been the symbolic heart of New York's gay and lesbian community, though places like Chelsea, Hell's Kitchen, and parts of Brooklyn attract more gay and lesbian residents these days. On

Christopher Street, among the cafés and adult shops, is one of the city's most acclaimed Off-Broadway theaters, the Lucille Lortel, where major playwrights like David Mamet, Eugene Ionesco, and Edward Albee have their own sidewalk markers. Nearby, at 51–53 Christopher Street, is the site of the Stonewall Inn and the historic Stonewall riots, one of the most famous, catalyzing events in the LGBTQ civil rights movement. Across the street is a gated triangle named Christopher Park, where commemorative statues of two life-size gay and lesbian couples have posed for photos since 1992.

TOP ATTRACTIONS

Hudson River Park. ⇨ *See the listing in the TriBeCa section of Chapter 2.*

WORTH NOTING

FAMILY **Children's Museum of the Arts.** The CMA encourages children ages 1 to 15 to get creative through a variety of mediums. Along with the requisite children's museum offerings like pencils, chalk, and paint, you'll find a clay bar; a media lab with mounted cameras and a recording studio; a small slide and colorful ball pond that kids can play in; an airy exhibition space with rotating exhibits (and workshops inspired by exhibits); a permanent collection of children's art from more than 50 countries; and classes in ceramics, origami, animation, filmmaking, and more. Check the website for a busy calendar of events. ⊠ *103 Charlton St., between Hudson and Greenwich Sts., West Village* ☎ *212/274–0986* ⊕ *www. cmany.org* 🎟 *$12 or $25 for family of up to 5 people* ⊘ *Closed Tues., Wed.* Ⓜ *C, E to Spring St.; 1 to Houston St.*

Christopher Park. You might have to share a bench in this tiny park with George Segal's life-size sculptures of a lesbian couple: titled *Gay Liberation*, the white-painted bronzes were cast in 1980 but not installed until 1992. Standing next to them is a gay male couple, captured mid-chat. ⊠ *Bordered by Stonewall Pl. and W. 4th, Grove, and Christopher Sts., West Village* Ⓜ *1 to Christopher St.–Sheridan Sq.; A, B, C, D, E, F, M to W. 4th St.*

75½ Bedford Street. Rising real-estate prices inspired the construction of New York City's narrowest house—just 9½ feet wide and 32 feet deep—in 1873. Built on a lot that was originally a carriage entrance of the Isaacs-Hendricks House next door, this sliver of a building has illustrious past residents including actor John Barrymore and poet Edna St. Vincent Millay. ⊠ *75½ Bedford St., between Commerce and Morton Sts., West Village* Ⓜ *A, B, C, D, E, F, M to W. 4th St.*

CHELSEA AND THE MEATPACKING DISTRICT

Getting Oriented

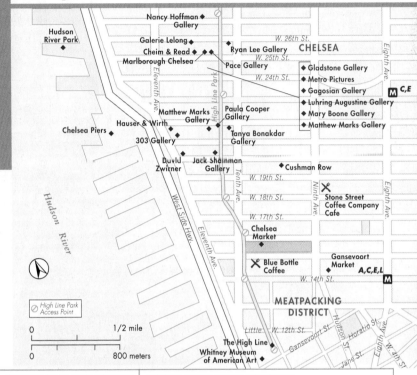

Hudson River Park

Nancy Hoffman ◆ Gallery

Galerie Lelong ◆
Cheim & Read ◆ ◆ ◆
Marlborough Chelsea

Ryan Lee Gallery   CHELSEA
W. 26th St.
W. 25th St.
Pace Gallery
W. 24th St.

◆ Gladstone Gallery
◆ Metro Pictures
◆ Gagosian Gallery   M C,E
◆ Luhring Augustine Gallery
◆ Mary Boone Gallery
◆ Matthew Marks Gallery

Matthew Marks Gallery
Hauser & Wirth
303 Gallery

Paula Cooper Gallery

Chelsea Piers ◆

Tanya Bonakdar Gallery

David Zwirner   Jack Shainman Gallery

◆ Cushman Row
W. 19th St.
W. 18th St.   ✗ Stone Street Coffee Company Cafe
W. 17th St.

Hudson River

Chelsea Market ◆

West Side Hwy

Eleventh Ave.

Tenth Ave.

Ninth Ave.

Eighth Ave.

✗ Blue Bottle Coffee

Gansevoort Market ◆   A,C,E,L   M
W. 14th St.

MEATPACKING DISTRICT
Little   W. 12th St.

The High Line ◆
Whitney Museum of American Art ◆

⊘ High Line Park Access Point

0 ————— 1/2 mile
0 ————— 800 meters

GETTING HERE AND AROUND	MAKING THE MOST OF YOUR TIME
The A, C, E, L, 1, 2, and 3 trains stop at 14th Street for both the Meatpacking District and Chelsea. The latter neighborhood is further served by the C, E, F, M, and 1 lines at 23rd Street and by the 1 train at 18th Street and 28th Street.	You can plan your visit to the High Line around food: first, work up an appetite by walking downtown along the High Line from 34th Street, and then head to Chelsea Market or any of the nearby restaurants. There are often a few seasonal food vendors on the High Line for impromptu snacking.

You can plan your visit to the High Line around food: first, work up an appetite by walking downtown along the High Line from 34th Street, and then head to Chelsea Market or any of the nearby restaurants. There are often a few seasonal food vendors on the High Line for impromptu snacking.

The High Line also pairs perfectly with a visit to the Whitney Museum, which is closed on Tuesday.

Chelsea has a dual life: typical gallery hours are Tuesday to Saturday 10–6, but at night the neighborhood changes into a party town, with bars (gay and straight) and high-profile nightclubs that don't rev up until after 11.

To truly appreciate the Meatpacking District, make a 9 pm or later dinner reservation at a hot restaurant, and then hit the bars to see the glitterati.

If shopping is your pleasure, weekdays are great; come after noon, though, or you'll find most spots shuttered.

Chelsea and the Meatpacking District

◆ Casey Kaplan
W. 27th St.
◆ Museum at FIT
W. 26th St.

Seventh Ave.
Sixth Ave.
Seventh Ave.

W. 25th St.
Madison Square Park
W. 24th St.

Madison Ave.

M W. 23rd St. **M** F,M **M** N,R,W

W. 22nd St.

W. 21st St.
Broadway

W. 20th St.
Sixth Ave.
Fifth Ave.

W. 19th St.

W. 18th St.

M W. 17th St.

◆ Rubin Museum of Art
W. 16th St.
Union Square Park

M F,M

W. 15th St.
M N,Q,R,W,4,5,6,L

✕ Donut Pub
M W. 14th St. **M** L
1,2,3

W. 13th St.

Sixth Ave.
Fifth Ave.
University Pl.

W. 12th St.

Greenwich Ave.
W. 11th St.

W. 10th St.

TOP EXPERIENCES

Gallery-hopping in Chelsea

Walking along the High Line

Exploring the Whitney Museum of American Art: the building has light-filled galleries and wonderful views from the terraces

Checking out the Meatpacking District's nightlife

Eating your way through Chelsea Market

Shopping the ultrachic boutiques in the Meatpacking District

BEST FOR KIDS

Chelsea Piers

The High Line

Hudson River Park

COFFEE AND QUICK BITES

Blue Bottle Coffee. If you're serious about coffee, this outpost of the California-based Blue Bottle is bound to make you happy with its dedication to freshness and flavor. There's a small selection of pastries and snacks as well. ⊠ *450 W. 15th St., between 9th and 10th Aves., Chelsea* ⊕ *www.bluebottlecoffee.com* Ⓜ *A, C, E to 14th St.; L to 8th Ave.*

Donut Pub. Craving a red-velvet doughnut or an old-fashioned cruller for breakfast, a midafternoon pick-me-up, or something tasty at 3 am? Pull up a stool—this superfriendly spot is open 24/7. ⊠ *203 W. 14th St., at 7th Ave., Chelsea* ☎ *212/929–0126* ⊕ *www.donutpub.com* Ⓜ *1, 2, 3, A, C, E to 14th St.; L to 8th Ave.*

Stone Street Coffee Company Cafe. There's no seating in this tiny café, but the coffee, tea, and pastries are top-notch. The hidden bar, Bathtub Gin, has it's entrance through the secret door. ⊠ *132 9th Ave., between 18th and 19th Sts., Chelsea* ☎ *646/559–1671* ⊕ *www. stonestreetcoffee.com* Ⓜ *A, C, E to 14th St.; L to 8th Ave.*

6

Sightseeing
★★★

Nightlife
★★★★★

Dining
★★★★★

Lodging
★★★

Shopping
★★★★★

Chelsea long ago usurped SoHo as the epicenter of New York contemporary art galleries, and there are literally hundreds along the streets here (often several in one building). The area has attracted art enthusiasts for many years, but the 2009 opening of the High Line above 10th Avenue gave new life to this part of the city, catalyzing new development and quickly turning the area into one of the city's most popular attractions. Momentum surged with the 2015 arrival of the Whitney Museum of American Art, which firmly established the area as a major art hub and destination.

MEATPACKING DISTRICT

Updated by Caroline Trefler

Concentrated in a few blocks of what is essentially an extension of the West Village, between the Hudson River and 9th Avenue, from Little West 12th Street to about West 17th Street, the Meatpacking District used to be the center of New York City's wholesale meat industry. There are few meat markets left in this now rather quaint cobblestone area, but it's definitely a figurative meat market at night, when the city's most fashionable denizens frequent the equally trendy restaurants and bars here. The area is also home to some of the city's swankiest retailers, including high-profile fashion designers and labels like Christian Louboutin, Diane von Furstenberg, and Tory Burch. The Whitney Museum of American Art is also here.

Fodor'sChoice ★

Whitney Museum of American Art. After four decades on the Upper East Side, the Whitney shook off its stone Marcel Breuer shell in 2015 and relocated to this light-filled, steel-and-glass Renzo Piano–designed building in the Meatpacking District. The museum welcomes visitors with a lively plaza, bold works of contemporary and modern American art, plenty of terraced outdoor spaces, and expansive windows. There are eight floors (not all open to the public), with a restaurant on the ground floor and a café on the eighth floor. The galleries house rotating exhibitions of postwar and contemporary works from the permanent collection that include artists such as Jackson Pollock, Jim Dine, Jasper Johns, Mark Rothko, Chuck Close, Cindy Sherman, and Roy Lichtenstein. Notable pieces often on view include Hopper's *Early Sunday Morning* (1930), Bellows's *Dempsey and Firpo* (1924), Alexander Calder's beloved *Circus,* and several of Georgia O'Keeffe's dazzling flower paintings. The Whitney experience is as much about the setting as the incredible artwork. The outdoor terraces on floors six, seven, and eight are connected by exterior stairs that provide a welcome reprieve from crowded galleries; the balconies also offer rotating exhibits along with stunning views of the city skyline, including the Empire State Building and One World Trade Center. Free tours of the collection and current exhibitions are offered daily; check the website for more information. After 7 pm on Friday, the price of admission is pay what you wish. ■ TIP➡ Skip the long lines and buy tickets in advance, but note that you cannot buy same-day tickets online. They must be purchased the day before and are available up to midnight. ✉ *99 Gansevoort St., between Washington St. and 10th Ave., Meatpacking District* ☎ *212/570–3600* ⊕ *www.whitney.org* ✉ *$25* ☾ *Closed Tues.* Ⓜ *A, C, E to 14th St.; L to 8th Ave.*

CHELSEA

Most of Chelsea's art galleries are found from about 20th to 27th Streets, primarily between 10th and 11th Avenues. The range of contemporary art on display includes almost every imaginable medium and style; if it's going on in the art world, it'll be in one of the 300 or so galleries here. The galleries described are just a taste of what's available. The best way to explore is to pick a gallery or two and then wander the area.

TOP ATTRACTIONS

Chelsea Market. This former Nabisco plant—where the first Oreos were baked in 1912—now houses more than 50 shops, food vendors, and sit-down restaurants. Probably the biggest draw are the food kiosks (some with counter seating) that include favorite taco spot Los Tacos No. 1, the Philadelphia-based Dizengoff hummus eatery, Amy's Bread, Fat Witch Bakery, Ninth Street Espresso, and so much more. There's also an Anthropologie store, an outpost of Pearl River Mart, a wine bar, upscale groceries, teas, spices, gift baskets, kitchen supplies, and one of New York City's last independent bookstores (Posman Books). The market's funky industrial design—a tangle of glass and metal for an awning, a factory pipe converted into an indoor waterfall—complements the eclectic assortment of shops, but the narrow space can get very crowded. A downstairs level has a few additional food stands as well as bathrooms. ■ TIP➡ There is some seating inside, but if the weather's nice, take your goodies to the High Line. ✉ *75 9th Ave., between 15th and 16th Sts., Chelsea* ☎ *212/652–2117* ⊕ *www.chelseamarket.com* Ⓜ *A, C, E to 14th St.; L to 8th Ave.*

David Zwirner. Zwirner is one of the most prominent figures in the world of contemporary art, and his several galleries around the world show multimedia work by big-name, Instagram-friendly artists including Richard Serra, Dan Flavin, Donald Judd, Jeff Koons, Gordon Matta-Clark, Yayoi Kusama, and Alice Neel. The sleek modern building on 20th Street has two floors of exhibition space, and there's a complex of buildings on West 19th Street a block away, as well as another gallery on the Upper East Side. ⊠ *537 W. 20th St., between 10th and 11th Aves., Chelsea* ☎ *212/517–8677* ⊕ *www.davidzwirner.com* ✉ *Free* ⊙ *Closed Sun., Mon.* Ⓜ *C, E to 23rd St.*

Gagosian Gallery. This internationally renowned modern gallery has two large Chelsea branches (the other is at 522 West 21st Street, between 10th and 11th Avenues) as well as two galleries on the Upper East Side and more than 10 outposts in cities around the world. Perhaps the most powerful dealer in the business, Gagosian Gallery shows works by heavy hitters such as Pablo Picasso, Jean-Michel Basquiat, Urs Fischer, Richard Serra, and pop-art icon Roy Lichtenstein, in addition to less well-known artists. ⊠ *555 W. 24th St., at 11th Ave., Chelsea* ☎ *212/741–1111* ⊕ *www.gagosian.com* ✉ *Free* ⊙ *Closed Sun., Mon.* Ⓜ *C, E to 23rd St.*

Gansevoort Market. Named after a food market that existed nearby in the 1800s, this food hall is like the younger, smaller, and lesser-known cousin of nearby tourist-mobbed Chelsea Market. About 20 stalls serve everything from upscale pizza and innovative tacos to Hawaiian poke and ice cream; there are long tables in the back. ⊠ *353 W. 14th St., between 8th and 9th Aves., Chelsea* ☎ *646/678–3231* ⊕ *www.gans-market.com* Ⓜ *A, C, E, to 14th St.; L to 8th Ave.*

Gladstone Gallery. The international roster of artists at this gallery's two large Chelsea locations includes painter Ahmed Alsoudani, sculptor Anish Kapoor, photographer Sharon Lockhart, and multimedia artists Matthew Barney and Cecilia Edefalk. The other gallery is at 530 West 21st Street, between 10th and 11th Avenues. ⊠ *515 W. 24th St., between 10th and 11th Aves., Chelsea* ☎ *212/206–9300* ⊕ *www.glad-stonegallery.com* ✉ *Free* ⊙ *Closed Sun., Mon.* Ⓜ *C, E to 23rd St.*

Hauser & Wirth. Currently occupying the former DIA:Chelsea building while its new permanent building is under construction next door, this Hauser & Wirth gallery is the opposite of its narrow town-house location on the Upper East Side. The vast space begs for sprawling exhibits and large-scale works. Emerging and established contemporary artists in the powerful Hauser & Wirth fold include Dieter Roth, Paul McCarthy, Eva Hesse, and Jason Rhoades. When the new space is finished in 2018, it's expected to have two floors of galleries, office space, and a bookstore. ⊠ *548 W. 22nd St., between 10th and 11th Aves., Chelsea* ☎ *212/790–3900* ⊕ *www.hauserwirth.com* ✉ *Free* ⊙ *Closed Sun., Mon.* Ⓜ *C, E to 23rd St.*

FAMILY

Fodor's Choice

★

The High Line. Once a railroad track carrying freight trains, this elevated space has been transformed into one of the city's top attractions—a 1½-mile landscaped "walking park," with curving walkways, picnic tables and benches, public art installations, and views of the Hudson

River and the Manhattan skyline. Running from Gansevoort Street in the Meatpacking District (at the Whitney Museum of Art) to West 34th Street, the High Line somehow manages to host about 5 million visitors a year and still feel like a wonderful retreat from the hubbub of the city. That said, the crowds can seem overwhelming when the weather is nice, so if you prefer some peaceful contemplation, visit as early in the morning as possible and avoid the lunchtime and weekend mass of humanity that can make it hard to walk along the narrow path.

One of the main draws of the High Line is the landscaping, which is carefully choreographed to be both wild and cultivated at the same time, and dotted with public art. Visitors can see many of the original plant species that grew in the rail beds, as well as shrubs, trees, grasses, and perennials chosen for their hardiness and sustainability. It's a landscape that's always changing, with each week bringing new colors, textures, and scents; you can check the website before you visit to see what's in bloom.

The Chelsea Market Passage, between 15th and 16th Streets, is accented with Spencer Finch's stained-glass art and is home to public art displays, video programs, music performances, and sit-down events.

A particularly popular feature that illustrates the High Line's greatest achievement—the ability to see the city with fresh eyes—is the 10th Avenue Square (between 16th and 17th Streets). This viewing window with stadium seating and large picture windows frames the ever-moving and -changing city below as art, encouraging viewers to linger, watch, pose, and engage with the city in a new way.

At 26th Street, you can see the changing window installations in the third-floor Ryan Lee gallery.

The best way to fully appreciate the High Line is to walk a length of the elevated park in one direction (preferably from Gansevoort Street uptown so that you can end with panoramic views of the city and Hudson River) and then make the return journey at street level, taking in the Chelsea neighborhood, and eats, below. ■ TIP➡ **Nearby Chelsea Market and Gansevoort Market are convenient places to pick up fixings for a picnic lunch.**

From April to October, starting at sunset, you can join the AAA (no, not the motor club, the Amateur Astronomers Association of New York) to view celestial bodies and stars at various points along the High Line. Check the High Line website for current details. ⊠ *10th Ave., from Gansevoort St. to 34th St., Chelsea* ☎ *212/206–9922* ⊕ *www. thehighline.org* Ⓜ *A, C, E, 1, 2, 3 to 14th St.; L to 8th Ave.; 1 to 23rd St. or 28th St.; 7 to Hudson Yards.*

Hudson River Park. ⇨ *See the listing in the TriBeCa section of Chapter 2.*

Luhring Augustine Gallery. Owners Lawrence Luhring and Roland Augustine have been working with established and emerging artists from Europe, Japan, and America since 1985. Luhring Augustine also has a Brooklyn outpost (at 25 Knickerbocker Avenue in Bushwick) for large-scale installations and long-term projects. Both spaces present fun, innovative shows. ⊠ *531 W. 24th St., between 10th and 11th Aves., Chelsea*

☏ 212/206–9100 ⊕ *www.luhringaugustine.com* ✉ *Free* ⊘ *Closed Sun., Mon. (also Sat. in summer)* Ⓜ *C, E to 23rd St.*

Marlborough Chelsea. With galleries in London, Barcelona, and Madrid, the Marlborough empire also operates two of the largest and most influential galleries in New York City. The Chelsea location (the other is on 57th Street) shows the latest work of modern artists, with a focus on sculptural forms, such as the boldly colorful paintings of Andrew Kuo. Red Grooms, Richard Estes, and Magdalena Abakanowicz are just a few of the 20th-century luminaries represented. ✉ *545 W. 25th St., between 10th and 11th Aves., Chelsea* ☏ *212/463–8634* ⊕ *www.marlboroughgallery.com* ✉ *Free* ⊘ *Closed Sun., Mon.* Ⓜ *C, E to 23rd St.*

Mary Boone Gallery. Based in SoHo in the late '70s, when the area was a hot showcase for younger artists, the Mary Boone Gallery relocated to Midtown (745 5th Avenue, near 58th Street) in 1996 and then opened this additional branch in a former garage in Chelsea in 2000. The Chelsea space allows for large-scale works and dramatic installations. Over the years, Boone has shown and represented artists including Jean-Michel Basquiat, Jeff Koons, Julian Schnabel, Ross Bleckner, and Ai Weiwei. Boone continues to show established artists such as Barbara Kruger, Pierre Bismuth, and Francesco Clemente, as well as relative newcomers such as Jacob Hashimoto and Hilary Harkness. ✉ *541 W. 24th St., between 10th and 11th Aves., Chelsea* ☏ *212/752–2929* ⊕ *www.maryboonegallery.com* ✉ *Free* ⊘ *Closed Sun., Mon.* Ⓜ *C, E to 23rd St.*

Matthew Marks Gallery. With three spaces in the area, there's always something interesting to see at Matthew Marks. Swiss artist Ugo Rondinone made his U.S. debut here, as did Andreas Gursky. Works by Luigi Ghirri, Darren Almond, Jasper Johns, Robert Adams, Nan Goldin, Ellsworth Kelly, and a cast of illustrious others are also shown here. The other two galleries are at 522 and 526 West 22nd Street. ✉ *523 W. 24th St., between 10th and 11th Aves., Chelsea* ☏ *212/243–0200* ⊕ *www.matthewmarks.com* ✉ *Free* ⊘ *Closed Sun., Mon.* Ⓜ *C, E to 23rd St.*

Fodor's Choice
★ **Museum at FIT.** What this small, three-gallery museum in the Fashion Institute of Technology (FIT) lacks in size and effects, it more than makes up for in substance and style. You may not find interactive mannequins, elaborate displays, or overcrowded galleries at the self-declared "most fashionable museum in New York City," but you will find carefully curated, fun, and interesting exhibits. The Fashion and Textile History Gallery, on the main floor, provides context with a rotating selection of historically and artistically significant objects from the museum's extensive permanent collection of more than 50,000 garments and accessories (exhibits change every six months). The real draws, though, are the special exhibitions in the lower-level gallery. Recent examples include *Expedition*, with fashion influenced by exploration of the Arctic and the sea, and *Denim: Fashion's Frontier*, an exploration of the history of denim from work wear to haute couture. Gallery FIT, also on the main floor, is dedicated to student and faculty exhibitions. ✉ *227 W. 27th St., at 7th Ave., Chelsea* ☏ *212/217–4558* ⊕ *www.fitnyc.edu/museum* ✉ *Free* ⊘ *Closed Sun., Mon.* Ⓜ *N, R to 28th St.*

Chelsea Galleries 101

Good art, bad art, edgy art, downright disturbing art—it's all here waiting to please and provoke in the contemporary art capital of the world. For the uninitiated, the concentration of nearly 300 galleries within a seven-block radius can be overwhelming, and the sometimes cool receptions on entering and the deafening silence, intimidating. Art galleries are not exactly famous for their customer service, but you don't need a degree in art appreciation to stare at a canvas or installation.

There's no required code of conduct, although most galleries are library quiet and cell phones are seriously frowned on. You won't be pressured to buy anything, either; staff will probably be doing their best to ignore you.

Galleries are generally open Tuesday through Saturday from 10 to 6. Gallery hop on a Saturday afternoon—the highest-traffic day—if you want company. You can usually find a binder with the artist's résumé, examples of previous work, and exhibit details (usually including prices) at the front desk; if not, ask. Also ask whether there's information you can take with you.

You can't see everything in one afternoon, so if you have specific interests, plan ahead. Find gallery information and current exhibit details by checking the listings in the *New Yorker* or the weekend section of the *New York Times*. Learn more about the galleries and the genres and artists they represent at ⊕ *www.artincontext.org*.

6

Pace Gallery. The impressive roster of artists represented by the Pace Gallery includes a variety of upper-echelon artists, sculptors, and photographers, such as Richard Avedon, Alexander Calder, Tara Donovan, Chuck Close, Sol LeWitt, and Robert Rauschenberg. Pace has two spaces in Chelsea, including 537 West 24th Street; a new eight-story flagship gallery is currently under construction at 540 West 25th Street. There's also a Midtown location (at 32 East 57th Street). ⊠ *510 W. 25th St., between 10th and 11th Aves., Chelsea* ☎ *212/989–4258* ⊕ *www.thepacegallery.com* ⊠ *Free* ⊗ *Closed Sun., Mon.* Ⓜ *C, E to 23rd St.*

Paula Cooper Gallery. SoHo pioneer Paula Cooper moved to Chelsea in 1996 and enlisted architect Richard Gluckman to transform a warehouse into a dramatic space with tall ceilings and handsome skylights. There are now two galleries (the other is at 521 West 21st Street) that showcase the works of artists such as Carl Andre, Sam Durant, Hans Haacke, Donald Judd, and Dan Flavin. ⊠ *534 W. 21st St., between 10th and 11th Aves., Chelsea* ☎ *212/255–1105* ⊕ *www.paulacoopergallery.com* ⊠ *Free* ⊗ *Closed Sun., Mon.* Ⓜ *C, E to 23rd St.*

Ryan Lee Gallery. The gallery occupied a street-level space nearby but made the move to this third-floor, 8,000-square-foot space in 2014 and has since found a whole new audience of millions thanks to RLWindow, which can be viewed from the High Line. RLWindow shows innovative and experimental projects by contemporary artists; recent exhibits turning heads on the High Line have included video installations from Rashaad Newsome and Rudy Burckhardt. ⊠ *515 W. 26th St., between*

10th and 11th Aves., Chelsea ☎ *212/397–0742* ⊕ *www.ryanleegallery. com* ✉ *Free* ⊘ *Closed Sun., Mon.* Ⓜ *C, E to 23rd St.*

WORTH NOTING

Casey Kaplan. While many galleries are fleeing Chelsea's high rents for less pricey and more artist-friendly neighborhoods like the Lower East Side or the Upper East Side, Casey Kaplan chose to mark its 20th anniversary in 2015 by moving just a few blocks, into a new 10,000-square-foot, two-story storefront space on West 27th Street. The Kaplan gallery represents contemporary artists from Europe and the Americas. ✉ *121 W. 27th St., between 6th and 7th Aves., Chelsea* ☎ *212/645–7335* ⊕ *www.caseykaplangallery.com* ✉ *Free* ⊘ *Closed Sun., Mon.* Ⓜ *1 to 28th St.*

Cheim & Read. Louise Bourgeois, William Eggleston, Joan Mitchell, Jenny Holzer, Donald Baechler, and Jack Pierson are among the artists represented at this prestigious gallery. ✉ *547 W. 25th St., between 10th and 11th Aves., Chelsea* ☎ *212/242–7727* ⊕ *www.cheimread.com* ✉ *Free* ⊘ *Closed Sun., Mon.* Ⓜ *C, E to 23rd St.*

FAMILY **Chelsea Piers.** This sports-and-entertainment complex along the Hudson River between 17th and 23rd Streets, a phenomenal example of adaptive reuse, is the size of four 80-story buildings laid out flat. There's pretty much every kind of sports activity going on both inside and out, including golf (check out the multitier, all-weather, outdoor driving range), sailing classes, ice-skating, rock climbing, soccer, bowling, gymnastics, and basketball. Plus there's a spa, elite sport-specific training, and a bowling alley. Chelsea Piers is the jumping-off point for some of the city's boat tours and dinner cruises. ✉ *Piers 59–62, Hudson River from 17th to 23rd Sts., entrance at 23rd St., Chelsea* ☎ *212/336–6666* ⊕ *www.chelseapiers.com* Ⓜ *C, E to 23rd St.*

Cushman Row. Built in 1840 for merchant and developer Don Alonzo Cushman, this string of redbrick beauties between 9th and 10th Avenues represents some of the country's best examples of Greek Revival row houses. Original details include small wreath-encircled attic windows, deeply recessed doorways with brownstone frames, and striking iron balustrades and fences. Note the pineapples, a traditional symbol of welcome, on top of the black iron newels in front of No. 416. ✉ *406–418 W. 20th St., between 9th and 10th Aves., Chelsea* Ⓜ *C, E to 23rd St.*

Galerie Lelong. The challenging installations at this large gallery include work by many Latin American artists. Look for art by Yoko Ono, Alfredo Jaar, Andy Goldsworthy, Cildo Meireles, Ana Mendieta, Hélio Oiticica, Nalini Malani, and Petah Coyne. ✉ *528 W. 26th St., between 10th and 11th Aves., Chelsea* ☎ *212/315–0470* ⊕ *www.galerielelong. com* ✉ *Free* ⊘ *Closed Sun., Mon.* Ⓜ *C, E to 23rd St.*

Jack Shainman Gallery. After being established in 1984 in Washington, D.C., the Jack Shainman Gallery moved to New York's East Village and then SoHo, landing in Chelsea in 1997. The original 20th Street space has been augmented by another at 524 West 24th as well as vast ex-schoolhouse space in Kinderhook, New York. The galleries all show emerging and established artists such as Nick Cave, El Anatsui, Carrie Mae Weems, Tallur L.N., and Kerry James Marshall. ✉ *513 W. 20th*

DID YOU KNOW?

If you start by Piers 63 and 64 in Chelsea, you can walk through Hudson River Park all the way to TriBeCa, getting great views of One World Trade Center on the way.

St., between 10th and 11th Aves., Chelsea ☎ *212/645–1701* ⊕ *www.jackshainman.com* ✉ *Free* ☉ *Sun., Mon.* Ⓜ *C, E to 23rd St.*

Metro Pictures. Some of the hottest talents in contemporary art are shown here, including Cindy Sherman, Olaf Breuning, Louise Lawlor, Trevor Paglen, Camille Henrot, and B. Wurtz. ✉ *519 W. 24th St., between 10th and 11th Aves., Chelsea* ☎ *212/206–7100* ⊕ *www.metropicturesgallery.com* ✉ *Free* ☉ *Closed Sun., Mon.* Ⓜ *C, E to 23rd St.*

Nancy Hoffman Gallery. Contemporary painting, sculpture, drawing, photography, and video works by an impressive array of international artists are on display in this light-filled space with high ceilings and a seasonal sculpture garden. Among the artists are Viola Frey, known for her heroic-scale ceramic male and female figures, and a strong group of young artists embarking on their first solo shows. ✉ *520 W. 27th St., between 10th and 11th Aves., Chelsea* ☎ *212/966–6676* ⊕ *www.nancyhoffmangallery.com* ✉ *Free* ☉ *Closed Sun., Mon.* Ⓜ *C, E to 23rd St.*

Rubin Museum of Art. This sleek, serene museum spread over six floors is the largest in the Western Hemisphere dedicated to the art of the Himalayas, India, and neighboring regions. The pieces shown here include paintings on cloth, metal sculptures, and textiles dating from the 2nd century onward. Many of the works from areas such as Tibet, Nepal, southwest China, and India relate to Buddhism, Hinduism, Bon, and other eastern religions. The fourth-floor Tibetan Buddhist Shrine room presents art and ritual objects as they would be in an elaborate household shrine. Temporary exhibits and a full weekly schedule of music, film, talks, and meditation events are ongoing (check the website). There's a restaurant and bar, and a gift shop on the ground floor. ✉ *150 W. 17th St., near 7th Ave., Chelsea* ☎ *212/620–5000* ⊕ *www.rmanyc.org* ✉ *$15 (free Fri. 6 pm–10 pm)* ☉ *Closed Tues.* Ⓜ *1 to 18th St.*

Tanya Bonakdar Gallery. With two floors of exhibition space, the shows here can spread out. Look for innovative modern work in a variety of media, by the likes of Olafur Eliasson, Uta Barth, Ernesto Neto, Lisa Oppenheim, and Sarah Sze, who represented the United States at the 55th Venice Biennale. ✉ *521 W. 21st St., between 10th and 11th Aves., Chelsea* ☎ *212/414–4144* ⊕ *www.tanyabonakdargallery.com* ✉ *Free* ☉ *Closed Sun., Mon.* Ⓜ *C, E to 23rd St.*

303 Gallery. International cutting-edge artists shown here include photographer Doug Aitken and installation artists Karen Kilimnik and Jane and Louise Wilson. Established in 1984, the gallery has existed in a number of locations but was one of the first to move to Chelsea in the 1990s. It's been in its current space, anchoring the first two floors and mezzanine of a new Norman Foster luxury high-rise, since 2016. ✉ *551 W. 21st St., between 10th and 11th Aves., Chelsea* ☎ *212/255–1121* ⊕ *www.303gallery.com* ✉ *Free* ☉ *Closed Sun., Mon.* Ⓜ *C, E to 23rd St.*

UNION SQUARE, THE FLATIRON DISTRICT, AND GRAMERCY PARK

Getting Oriented

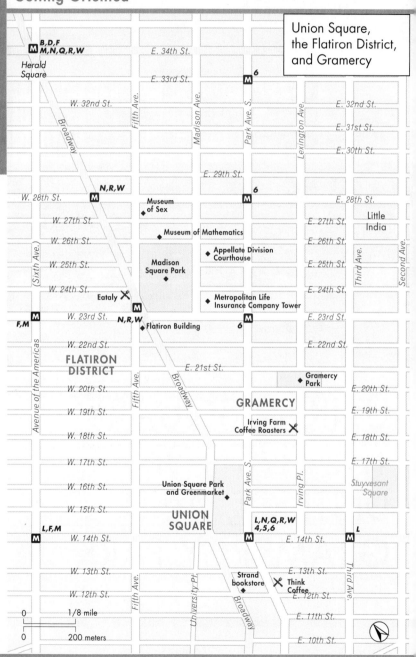

Union Square,
the Flatiron District,
and Gramercy

B,D,F
M,N,Q,R,W
Herald
Square

E. 34th St.

E. 33rd St.

6

W. 32nd St.

Fifth Ave.

Madison Ave.

Park Ave. S.

E. 32nd St.

Lexington Ave.

E. 31st St.

Broadway

E. 30th St.

E. 29th St.

N,R,W

6

W. 28th St.

E. 28th St.

(Sixth Ave.)

W. 27th St.

Museum
of Sex

Little
India

E. 27th St.

W. 26th St.

Museum of Mathematics

E. 26th St.

W. 25th St.

Appellate Division
Courthouse

Third Ave.

Second Ave.

E. 25th St.

Madison
Square Park

W. 24th St.

Eataly

Metropolitan Life
Insurance Company Tower

E. 24th St.

F,M

W. 23rd St.   N,R,W

Flatiron Building

6

E. 23rd St.

W. 22nd St.

E. 22nd St.

FLATIRON
DISTRICT

E. 21st St.

Gramercy
Park

W. 20th St.

Fifth Ave.

Broadway

E. 20th St.

W. 19th St.

GRAMERCY

E. 19th St.

Irving Farm
Coffee Roasters

W. 18th St.

Park Ave. S.

Irving Pl.

E. 18th St.

W. 17th St.

E. 17th St.

W. 16th St.

Union Square Park
and Greenmarket

Stuyvesant
Square

W. 15th St.

UNION
SQUARE

L,N,Q,R,W
4,5,6

L,F,M

L

W. 14th St.

E. 14th St.

W. 13th St.

Third Ave.

Strand
bookstore

E. 13th St.

Think
Coffee

W. 12th St.

Fifth Ave.

University Pl.

Broadway

E. 12th St.

0   1/8 mile

E. 11th St.

0   200 meters

E. 10th St.

MAKING THE MOST OF YOUR TIME

Union Square bustles, especially during the summer, with people hanging out on the steps, eating lunch, or watching street performers. Market days—Monday, Wednesday, Friday, and Saturday—are even busier.

This is definitely an area for strolling, shopping, and eating, so plan your visit around a meal—or several. Weekends get very busy, so if you prefer smaller crowds, head to this area on a weekday.

If you're planning to eat at the Shake Shack in Madison Square Park, come before noon to avoid long lines.

There are frequent (and free) art installations in Madison Square Park, and the Madison Square Eats market takes place twice a year.

COFFEE AND QUICK BITES

Eataly. There are multiple restaurants, take-out shops, cafés, and a Nutella bar, as well as a rooftop brewery, at this upscale Italian food emporium. You can also shop for all things Italian. ⊠ *200 5th Ave., at 23rd St., Flatiron District* ☎ *212/229–2560* ⊕ *www.eataly.com* Ⓜ *N, R to 23rd St.*

Irving Farm Coffee Roasters. Steps from Union Square, this busy little café (known to locals as 71 Irving) roasts its own beans and serves up good people-watching along with espresso drinks, sandwiches, muffins, and snacks. ⊠ *71 Irving Pl., between 18th and 19th Sts., Union Square* ☎ *212/995–5252* ⊕ *www.irvingfarm.com* Ⓜ *4, 5, 6, L, N, Q, R, W to 14th St.–Union Sq.*

Think Coffee. Maybe you like a little social and environmental awareness with your caffeine, or perhaps the cold-brewed iced coffees, Spanish lattes (made with condensed milk), and cool playlist are sufficient. ⊠ *123 4th Ave., between 12th and 13th Sts., Union Square* ☎ *212/614–6644* ⊕ *www.thinkcoffee.com* Ⓜ *4, 5, 6, L, N, Q, R, W to 14th St.–Union Sq.*

TOP EXPERIENCES

Strolling in Union Square Park and checking out the produce and other goodies at the greenmarket

Browsing the miles of books in the Strand bookstore

Strolling from Irving Place to Gramercy Park, and around the perimeter of this historic, private park

GETTING HERE AND AROUND

Union Square is a major subway hub, with the 4, 5, 6, L, N, Q, R, and W lines all converging here. For Madison Square Park and the Flatiron District, take the N or R train to 23rd Street (this lets you out on Broadway). The 6 stops at 23rd and 28th Streets (on Park Avenue South).

SEASONAL HIGHLIGHTS

Union Square Holiday Market. Between Thanksgiving and Christmas, this outdoor market has more than 150 vendors selling unique, often locally made products. ⊕ *www.urbanspacenyc.com*

Madison Square Eats. This monthlong pop-up food market happens twice a year (spring and fall) across the street from Madison Square Park and includes popular vendors selling Korean and Japanese-fusion food, and innovative ice cream. There's usually also a Roberta's Pizza stand. ⊕ *www.madison-squarepark.org/mad-sq-eats*

7

Sightseeing
★ ★ ★ ★ ★
Nightlife
★
Dining
★ ★ ★
Lodging
★ ★ ★
Shopping
★ ★ ★ ★

Union Square is a hub of activity and fabulous people-watching, the latter extending to the more refined neighborhoods of Gramercy and the Flatiron District. When that certain brand of New Yorker says they don't like to travel above 14th Street, they're usually thinking about Union Square as the cutoff.

UNION SQUARE

Updated
by Caroline
Trefler

The energy of Union Square reaches its peak during greenmarket days (Monday, Wednesday, Friday, and Saturday), when more than 140 regional farmers and food purveyors set up shop on the square's north and west sides to peddle everything from produce to meat and fresh fish to baked goods. The market is a great place to rub elbows with—and get elbowed by—local shoppers and chefs, and a great source for tasty souvenirs (locally produced honeys, jams, pickles, and cheeses) as well as lunch. Find a bench in the park to savor your goodies and take in the scene. Political gatherings sometimes happen here, too.

Even on a nonmarket day, Union Square regularly has vendors of all kinds, selling everything from art to jewelry to T-shirts. New York University students, nannies with their charges, visitors, and other locals gather in this open space that can at times feel more like an outdoor version of Grand Central Terminal than a park. Just south of Union Square, on Broadway at 12th Street, is the Strand, a giant institution of a bookstore that attracts book lovers from all over.

FAMILY **Union Square Park and Greenmarket.** A park, farmers' market, meeting place, and the site of rallies and demonstrations, this pocket of green space sits in the center of a bustling residential and commercial neighborhood. The name "Union" originally signified that two main roads—Broadway and 4th Avenue—crossed here. It took on a different meaning in the late 19th and early 20th centuries, when the square became a rallying spot for labor protests; many unions, as well as fringe political parties, moved their headquarters nearby.

Union Square is at its best on Monday, Wednesday, Friday, and Saturday (8–6), when the largest of the city's greenmarkets gathers farmers and food purveyors from the tristate area. Browse the stands of fruit and vegetables, flowers, plants, fresh-baked pies and breads, cheeses, cider, fish, and meat. Between Thanksgiving and Christmas, there is a popular market where artisans sell gift items and food in holiday-themed booths at the square's southwest end.

TIME OUT!

One of Union Square's intriguing features is an artwork on the face of 58–60 East 14th Street, across from the southeast corner of the park. *Metronome's* bank of cascading numbers is actually a clock that counts both time elapsed and time remaining in the day. At noon and midnight huge bursts of steam emerge.

New York University dormitories, theaters, and cavernous commercial spaces occupy the restored 19th-century commercial buildings that surround the park, along with some chain stores and restaurants. The run of diverse architectural styles on the Decker Building at 33 Union Square West is as imaginative as its former contents: this was once home to Andy Warhol's studio. The building at 17th Street and Union Square East, now a development known as 44 Union Square, was the final home of Tammany Hall, an organization famous in its day as a corrupt and powerful political machine. Statues in the park include those of George Washington, Abraham Lincoln, Mahatma Gandhi (often wreathed in flowers), and the Marquis de Lafayette (sculpted by Frederic Auguste Bartholdi, designer of the Statue of Liberty). Plaques in the sidewalk on the southeast and southwest sides chronicle the park's history from the 1600s to 1800s. ⊠ *From 14th to 17th St., between Broadway and Park Ave. S, Union Square* Ⓜ *4, 5, 6, L, N, Q, R, W to 14th St.–Union Sq.*

7

FLATIRON DISTRICT

The Flatiron District—anchored by Madison Square Park on the north and Union Square to the south—is one of the city's busiest neighborhoods, particularly along 5th Avenue and Park Avenue South. Once known as Ladies' Mile because of the fashionable row of department stores where women routinely shopped, the area is still a favorite for lady-spotting because of the number of modeling agencies and photography studios here. Lovely Madison Square Park, a pleasant green space hemmed in by some of the neighborhood's most notable architecture—from the triangular Flatiron to the dazzling, gold-pyramid-topped New York Life Building to the Metropolitan Life Tower with its elegant clock face—is the best place to savor the view. Sit and admire the scene with a burger and shake from the park's always-busy Shake Shack, or takeout from the mother (or "mamma mia") of all Italian markets, Eataly, across the street from the west side of the park.

TOP ATTRACTIONS

Flatiron Building. When completed in 1902, the oddly shaped Fuller Building, as it was originally known, caused a sensation. Architect Daniel Burnham made ingenious use of the triangular wedge of land at 23rd Street, 5th Avenue, and Broadway, employing a revolutionary steel frame that allowed for the building's 22-story, 286-foot height. Covered with a limestone-and-white-terra-cotta facade in the Italian Renaissance style, the building's shape resembled a clothing iron, hence its nickname. When it became apparent that the building generated strong winds, gawkers would loiter at 23rd Street hoping to catch sight of ladies' billowing skirts. Local traffic cops had to shoo away the male peepers—one purported origin of the phrase "23 skidoo." There is a small display of historic building and area photos in the lobby, but otherwise you have to settle for appreciating this building from the outside. ✉ *175 5th Ave., bordered by 22nd and 23rd Sts., 5th Ave., and Broadway, Flatiron District* Ⓜ *N, R, W to 23rd St.*

FAMILY **Madison Square Park.** The benches of this elegant tree-filled park afford great views of some of the city's oldest and most charming skyscrapers—the Flatiron Building, the Metropolitan Life Insurance Tower, the gold-crowned New York Life Insurance Building, and even (to the north) the Empire State Building—and serve as a perfect vantage point for people-, pigeon-, and dog-watching. Add free Wi-Fi, Shake Shack, temporary art exhibits, and free summer and fall concerts, and you realize that a bench here is certainly a special place to be. New York City's first baseball games were played in this 7-acre park in 1845 (though New Jerseyans are quick to point out that the game was actually invented across the river in Hoboken, New Jersey). On the north end of the park, an imposing 1881 statue by Augustus Saint-Gaudens memorializes Civil War naval hero Admiral David Farragut. An 1876 statue of Secretary of State William Henry Seward (the Seward of the term "Seward's Folly," coined when the United States purchased Alaska from the Russian Empire in 1867) sits in the park's southwest corner, though it's rumored that the sculptor placed a reproduction of the statesman's head on a statue of Abraham Lincoln's body. Madison Square Eats (⊕ *www.madisonsquarepark.org/mad-sq-eats)* is a popular monthlong food market that happens twice a year (spring and fall), across the street. ✉ *From 23rd to 26th St., between 5th and Madison Aves., Flatiron District* ☎ *212/520–7600* ⊕ *www.madisonsquarepark. org* Ⓜ *N, R, W to 23rd St.*

WORTH NOTING

Appellate Division Courthouse. Figures representing Wisdom and Force flank the main portal of this imposing Beaux Arts courthouse, built in 1899. The structure's purpose coincides with artistic symbolism, and there are statues of great lawmakers, including Moses, Justinian, and Confucius, lining the roof balustrade. In total, sculptures by 16 artists adorn the ornate building, a showcase of themes relating to the law. This is one of the most important appellate courts in the country: it hears more than 3,000 appeals and 6,000 motions a year, and also admits approximately 3,000 new attorneys to the bar each year. Inside the courtroom is a stunning stained-glass dome set into a gilt ceiling.

The wedge-shaped Flatiron Building got its nickname because of its resemblance to the shape of a clothes iron; its original name is the Fuller Building.

The main hall and the courtroom are open to visitors weekdays from 9 to 5. All sessions, which are generally held Tuesday to Thursday at 2 pm, are open to the public (call the main number ahead of time to be sure court is in session, or check the calendar on the website). ✉ *27 Madison Ave., entrance on 25th St., Flatiron District* ☎ *212/340–0422* ⊕ *www.courts.state.ny.us/courts/ad1* ⊘ *Closed weekends* Ⓜ *N, R, W, 6 to 23rd St.*

Metropolitan Life Insurance Company Tower. In 1909, with the addition of the 700-foot tower resembling the campanile of St. Mark's in Venice, this 1893 building became the world's tallest; it was surpassed in height a few years later (by the Woolworth Building). The building was stripped of much of its classical detail during renovations in the early 1960s but remains a prominent feature of the Midtown skyline. The clock's four faces are each three stories high, and their minute hands weigh half a ton each. If the view from the park doesn't quite cut it, you can reserve a room in the skyline itself: Marriott International and Ian Schrager now operate a luxury hotel, the New York EDITION, in the previously vacant clock-tower portion of the building. ✉ *1 Madison Ave., between 23rd and 24th Sts., Flatiron District* Ⓜ *N, R, W, 6 to 23rd St.*

FAMILY **Museum of Mathematics** (*MoMath*). There's no exact formula to get kids excited about math, but the sleek, two-floor Museum of Mathematics (MoMath)—the only cultural institution devoted to math in all of North America—comes close to finding the perfect fun-to-math ratio. Kids can ride square-wheel trikes, create human fractal trees, build virtual 3-D geometric shapes (which can be printed out on a 3-D printer

Architecture at Its Most Elaborate

Rimming **Madison Square Park** is a slice of Manhattan's most impressive skyline. In the northeast corner, the gold-top **New York Life Insurance** building was the tallest in the city when it opened in 1903. The elaborately carved beaux arts structure one block down at East 25th Street is the **Appellate Division, New York State Supreme Court,** with its main entrance tucked onto the side street. Towering over the park between East 23rd and 24th streets is another classically inspired spire, the **Metropolitan Life Insurance Tower,** which has a stunning clock face keeping time of all four sides. One of the buildings most emblematic of

New York City, the **Flatiron Building** is a limestone-and-terra-cotta vessel sailing its prowlike shape uptown from its berth on 23rd Street.

At the edge of Murray Hill, at between 33rd and 34th streets and 5th and 6th avenues, looms the inimitable **Empire State Building.** Canonized in postcards, books, and on film, the building majestically reaches toward the sky, which colorfully illuminates the night sky according to an elaborate calendar. For an excellent view of it, head one block north on 5th Avenue to the steps of the Italian-Renaissance-style **B. Altman Building,** worth a look in its own right.

for a fee), use lasers to explore cross sections of objects, solve dozens of puzzles, and generally bend their minds. The popular Robot Swarm exhibition allows kids to explore swarm robotics and interact with two dozen small (Roomba-like), glowing robots, using simple math rules. Exhibits are best suited to kids ages six and up, but preschoolers can still enjoy many interactive exhibits like the Math Square, a light-up floor programmed with math games, simulations, and patterns. ■TIP→ The museum closes at 2:30 pm the first Wednesday of every month. ⊠ *11 E. 26th St., between 5th and Madison Aves., Flatiron District* ☎ *212/542–0566* ⊕ *www.momath.org* ✉ *$16* Ⓜ *N, R, W to 28th St.*

Museum of Sex. Ponder the profound history and cultural significance of sex at this 14,000-square-foot museum while staring at vintage pornographic photos, S&M paraphernalia, antimasturbation devices from the 1800s, explicit film clips, vintage condom tins, and a collection of artwork. The Spotlight on the Permanent Collection gallery features revolving artifacts and ephemera, as well as a "Jump for Joy" bounce house (of inflated breasts) that was originally part of an exhibition called *Funland: Pleasures & Perils of the Erotic Fairground.* Other exhibits have probed such topics as desire on the Internet and the sex lives of animals. The subject matter is given serious curatorial treatment, though the gift shop is full of fun sexual kitsch. Only patrons over 18 are admitted. ⊠ *233 5th Ave., at 27th St., Flatiron District* ☎ *212/689–6337* ⊕ *www.museumofsex.com* ✉ *$17.50* Ⓜ *N, R, W to 28th St.*

GRAMERCY PARK

The haste and hullabaloo of the city calms considerably in the residential neighborhood of Gramercy Park, named for its 1831 gated garden, an early example of the city's best creative urban planning. South of the park, running north to south from 14th Street, is Irving Place, a short street honoring Washington Irving, which feels calm, green, exclusive; it has a combination of old and new eateries, stores, and architecture.

Gramercy Park. You may not be able to enter this private park (it's the only truly private park in Manhattan, and only those residing around it have keys), but a look through the bars in the wrought-iron fence that encloses it is worth your time, as is a stroll around its perimeter. The beautifully planted 2-acre park, designed by developer Samuel B. Ruggles, dates from 1831, and is flanked by grand examples of early-19th-century architecture and permeated with the character of its many celebrated occupants.

When Ruggles bought the property, it was known as Krom Moerasje ("little crooked swamp"), named by the Dutch settlers. He drained the swamp and set aside 42 lots for a park to be accessible exclusively to those who bought the surrounding lots in his planned London-style residential square. The park is still owned by residents of the buildings surrounding the square, although neighbors from the area can now buy visiting privileges. In 1966 the New York City Landmarks Preservation Commission designated Gramercy Park a historic district. Notable buildings include No. 15, a Gothic Revival brownstone with black granite trim designed by Calvert Vaux, which was once home to Samuel Tilden, governor of New York. A secret passageway to 19th Street permitted Tilden to evade his political enemies. It is now home to the National Arts Club, founded in 1898. Next door at No. 16 Gramercy Park South lived the actor Edwin Booth, perhaps most famous for being the brother of Lincoln's assassin. In 1888 he turned his Gothic-trim home into the Players Club, a clubhouse for actors and theatrical types who were not welcome in regular society. A bronze statue of Edwin Booth as Hamlet has pride of place inside the park. ■TIP➔ Alexander Calder's iconic, monumental outdoor sculpture *Janey Waney* (1969) is installed inside the park and can be viewed through the railings. ✉ *Lexington Ave. and 21st St., Gramercy* Ⓜ *4, 5, 6, L, N, Q, R, W to 14th St.–Union Sq.; 6 to 23rd St.*

MIDTOWN EAST

Getting Oriented

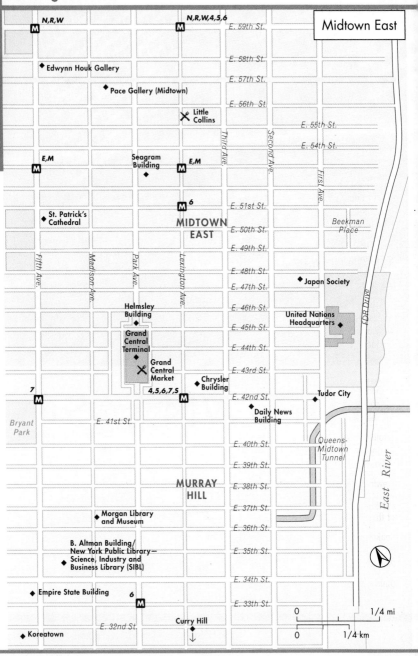

Midtown East

N,R,W

N,R,W,4,5,6

E. 59th St.

E. 58th St.

◆ Edwynn Houk Gallery

E. 57th St.

◆ Pace Gallery (Midtown)

E. 56th St.

✕ Little Collins

E. 55th St.

E. 54th St.

E,M

Seagram Building ◆

E,M

Third Ave.

Second Ave.

First Ave.

6

E. 51st St.

St. Patrick's Cathedral ◆

MIDTOWN EAST

E. 50th St.

Beekman Place

E. 49th St.

Fifth Ave.

Madison Ave.

Park Ave.

Lexington Ave.

E. 48th St.

E. 47th St.

◆ Japan Society

Helmsley Building ◆

E. 46th St.

United Nations Headquarters ◆

E. 45th St.

Grand Central Terminal ◆

E. 44th St.

✕ Grand Central Market

E. 43rd St.

◆ Chrysler Building

4,5,6,7,S

E. 42nd St.

◆ Tudor City

7

◆ Daily News Building

FDR Drive

Bryant Park

E. 41st St.

Queens-Midtown Tunnel

E. 40th St.

E. 39th St.

East River

MURRAY HILL

E. 38th St.

E. 37th St.

◆ Morgan Library and Museum

E. 36th St.

B. Altman Building/ New York Public Library— ◆ Science, Industry and Business Library (SIBL)

E. 35th St.

E. 34th St.

◆ Empire State Building

6

E. 33rd St.

0   1/4 mi

E. 32nd St.

Curry Hill ↓

0   1/4 km

◆ Koreatown

MAKING THE MOST OF YOUR TIME

The east side of Midtown is somewhat more laid-back than the west side, but there's still lots to keep you busy. Wherever you're headed, try to make sure you at least pass through Grand Central Terminal, one of New York's grandest architectural landmarks—it's a madhouse during rush hours but wonderfully slow on weekends, an ideal time to visit.

If you're planning to visit the Empire State Building when it's less crowded, aim for the morning or after sunset, when the city's evening lights are dazzling. Allow at least two hours for an observation-deck visit.

It's also worth making time for a quick trip out of the United States to visit the "international zone" of the United Nations; take a tour of the buildings and mail a postcard with a unique U.N. stamp.

TOP EXPERIENCES

Standing in the center of Grand Central Terminal's main concourse and taking in the fiber-optic map of the constellations overhead

Strolling down 5th Avenue, where some of the world's top luxury brands have flagship stores, especially around the holidays when store windows are dressed to impress

Viewing rare manuscripts at the Morgan Library

Enjoying panoramic views of the city at dusk from the top of the Empire State Building

Soaking in peace and serenity while ogling the neo-Gothic architecture, stained glass, and sculptures at iconic St. Patrick's Cathedral

Dining with locals in Koreatown and Curry Hill

GETTING HERE

To get to the east side of Midtown, take the 4, 5, 6, or 7 to Grand Central. The S, or Shuttle, travels back and forth between Grand Central and Times Square.

You can reach the Empire State Building via the B, D, F, M, N, Q, R, and W trains to 34th Street or the 6 to 33rd Street. The 6 also stops at 23rd and 28th Streets.

COFFEE AND QUICK BITES

Grand Central Market. The main level of Grand Central is home to this gourmet market, a cornucopia of food and beverage options, including Manhattan's oldest chocolatier Li-Lac Chocolates, delicious Murray's Cheese, and rich coffee by Oren's Daily Roast. ⊠ *Grand Central Terminal east entrance, Lexington Ave., at W. 43rd St., Midtown East* ⊕ *www.grand-centralterminal.com/grand-central-market/* Ⓜ *4, 5, 6, 7, S to Grand Central–42nd St.*

Little Collins. This Australian import pays as much attention to what it puts on your plate— try the avocado and feta on toast—as what it pours in your coffee mug—try the flat white (a latte without foam). ⊠ *667 Lexington Ave., near 56th St., Midtown East* ☏ *212/308–1969* ⊕ *www.littlecollinsnyc.com* Ⓜ *4, 5, 6 to 59th St.; N, Q, R to Lexington Ave./59th St.; E, M to Lexington Ave./53rd St.*

8

Sightseeing
★★★★★
Nightlife
★★
Dining
★★★★
Lodging
★★★★★
Shopping
★★★★★

Fifth Avenue is Manhattan's dividing line, marking the division of east and west sides, but the avenue itself seems to connote so much of what the city's East Side is all about. This is where some of the city's most iconic buildings are found, including the Empire State Building, in the Murray Hill neighborhood.

MIDTOWN EAST

Updated by
Kelsy Chauvin

In terms of architecture, Midtown East has some of the city's most notable gems, including the stately Chrysler Building, considered an Art Deco triumph, and the bustling Beaux Arts masterpiece, Grand Central Terminal. At night the streets here are relatively quiet, but the restaurants are filled with expense-account diners and well-heeled locals. Some of the most formal dining rooms and expensive meals in town can be found here. The blocks of 5th Avenue around 57th Street are also a designer-label paradise, home to megabrand flagships such as Louis Vuitton, Yves Saint Laurent, and Chanel, and some of the world's most famous jewelry stores, including Tiffany, Van Cleef & Arpels, and Harry Winston. New York's famous department stores like Bloomingdale's and Saks Fifth Avenue have long anchored the upscale-shopping scene.

TOP ATTRACTIONS

Chrysler Building. A monument to modernity and the mighty automotive industry, the former Chrysler headquarters wins many New Yorkers' vote for the city's most iconic and beloved skyscraper (and the world's tallest for 40 days, until the Empire State Building stole the honor). Architect William Van Alen, who designed this 1930 Art Deco masterpiece, incorporated car details into its form: American eagle gargoyles made of chromium nickel sprout from the 61st floor, resembling hood ornaments used on 1920s Chryslers; winged urns festooning the 31st floor reference the car's radiator caps. Most breathtaking is the pinnacle, with tiered crescents and spiked windows that radiate out like a magnificent steel sunburst. View it at sunset to catch the light gleaming off the tip. Even better, observe it at night, when its peak illuminates the sky. The inside is sadly off-limits, apart from the amazing time-capsule lobby replete with chrome "grillwork," intricately patterned wood elevator doors, marble walls and floors, and an enormous ceiling mural saluting transportation and human endeavor. ✉ *405 Lexington Ave., at 42nd St., Midtown East* Ⓜ *4, 5, 6, 7, S to 42nd St./Grand Central.*

Fodor's Choice **Grand Central Terminal.** Grand Central is not only the world's largest (48
★ acres and 44 platforms) and the nation's busiest railway station—nearly 750,000 commuters and subway riders use it daily—but also one of the world's most magnificent public spaces. Past the glimmering chandeliers of the waiting room is the jaw-dropping **main concourse,** 200 feet long, 120 feet wide, and 120 feet (roughly 12 stories) high, modeled after an ancient Roman public bath. In spite of it being completely cavernous, Grand Central manages to evoke a certain sense of warmth rarely found in buildings its size. Overhead, a twinkling fiber-optic map of the constellations covers the robin's-egg-blue ceiling. To admire it all with some sense of peace, avoid visiting at rush hour.

To escape the crowds, head up one of the sweeping staircases at either end, where upscale restaurants occupy the balcony spaces. Any would make an enjoyable perch from which to survey the concourse, but for a real taste of the station's early years, head beyond the western staircase to **The Campbell,** a clubby cocktail lounge housed in the restored private offices and salon of 1920s tycoon John W. Campbell. Located around and below the main concourse are fantastic shops and eateries—including the eponymous Grand Central Oyster Bar—making this one of the best, if somewhat labyrinthine, "malls" in the city.

To best admire Grand Central's exquisite Beaux Arts architecture, start with its ornate south face on East 42nd Street, modeled after a Roman triumphal arch. Crowning the facade's Corinthian columns and 75-foot-high arched windows, a graceful clock keeps time for hurried commuters. In the central window stands an 1869 bronze statue of Cornelius Vanderbilt, who built the station to house his railroad empire. Also noteworthy is the 1½-ton, cast-iron bald eagle displaying its 13-foot wingspan atop a ball near the corner of 42nd Street and Vanderbilt Avenue.

Grand Central still functions primarily as a railroad station, and its majesty was, thankfully, preserved in part by Jacqueline Kennedy Onassis's 1975 public information campaign to save it as a landmark. Underground, more than 60 ingeniously integrated railroad tracks carry trains upstate and to Connecticut via Metro-North Commuter Rail; plans to incorporate Long Island Rail Road service aim to expand the station in the next decade. The subway connects here as well. The **Municipal Art Society** (☎ *212/935–3960* ⊕ *www.mas.org/tours*) leads an official daily walking tour to explore the 1913 terminal's architecture, history, and hidden secrets. Tours begin in the main concourse at 12:30 and last 75 minutes. Tickets ($30) can be purchased in advance online (⊕ *www. docentour.com/gct*) or from the ticket booth in the main concourse. Alternatively, rent a headset ($9) and take a self-guided audio tour at your own pace (⊕ *www.grandcentralterminal.com/tours* ⊕ *www.*

8

Department stores like Saks Fifth Avenue go all out for their holiday displays come December.

grandcentralterminal.com/tours). Headsets and maps are available at GCT Tour windows on the main concourse and tours last about 45 minutes. ⊠ *Main entrance, 42nd St. and Park Ave., Midtown East* ☎ *212/935–3960* ⊕ *www.grandcentralterminal.com* Ⓜ *4, 5, 6, 7, S to Grand Central–42nd St.*

St. Patrick's Cathedral. This Gothic-style edifice—the largest Catholic cathedral in the United States, seating approximately 2,400 people—is among Manhattan's most striking churches, with its double spires topping out at 330 feet. "St. Pat's," as locals call it, holds a special place in the hearts of many New Yorkers and provides a calm and quiet refuge in the heart of buzzy Midtown, despite the throngs of tourists (the cathedral receives more than 5.5 million visitors annually).

The church dates back to 1858–79, but thanks to an extensive $177 million rehabilitation project, completed in 2015 and christened with a papal visit and mass, the cathedral no longer shows its age. The three-year renovation left no stone or detail unturned, from the stone faces of the 80-foot spires that tower above 5th Avenue to the 3,700 cleaned and glazed (for UV protection) stained-glass panels and the newly revealed skylights that had been covered with roofing for decades, down to the newly added panels of the confessional, carefully carved to match existing woodwork. The building now has a state-of-the-art sprinkler system as well as a heating and cooling system that reduces energy consumption by 30%. Highlights of this brightened and refreshed cathedral include the almost-90-year-old organ in the choir gallery with its 7,855 pipes and the famous rose window (considered stained-glass-artist Charles Connick's greatest work). Also check out the statues in the alcoves around the nave, including a modern depiction of the first American-born saint, Mother Elizabeth Ann Seton. Don't miss the ornately carved bronze double doors on your way in and out: each weighs 9,200 pounds and features sculptures of saints.

The church's *Pietà* sculpture is three times larger than the *Pietà* at St. Peter's in Rome. Daily masses are open and free to the public (check the website for schedule) with the exception of Midnight Mass on Christmas Eve, which is a ticketed event. Free guided tours are held at 10 am most days (it's best to confirm in advance), or you can download the cathedral tour app on its website for a small fee and tour at your leisure. ✉ *5th Ave., between 50th and 51st Sts., Midtown East* ☎ *212/753–2261 for rectory* ⊕ *www.saintpatrickscathedral.org* Ⓜ *E, M to 5th Ave./53rd St.*

United Nations Headquarters. Officially an "international zone" in the heart of New York City, the U.N. Headquarters is a working symbol of global cooperation. Built between 1947 and 1961, the headquarters sit on a lushly landscaped, 18-acre tract on the East River, fronted by flags of member states. The United Nations marked its 70th anniversary in 2015 with the completion of a seven-year, $2.1 billion overhaul that retained the 1950s look and feel (and in some cases, green carpet) of the complex, while incorporating state-of-the-art technology to upgrade its infrastructure, security, and energy efficiency. The only way to enter the U.N. Headquarters is with the 60-minute weekday guided tour, available in 12 languages; reservations can be made through the website, and you'll need a security pass from the visitors office at 801 1st Avenue. Arrive at least 30 minutes before the start of your tour for security screening, and if you ordered tickets online be sure to bring your printout. While the tour includes the **General Assembly,** major council chambers, and a lot of educational details, it does not cover a lot of physical ground; council chambers may be closed on any given day, and you cannot enter the Secretariat building. Also, you can no longer wander the grounds, rose garden, or riverside promenade. As you walk through the corridors of international diplomacy, you will learn about the history and work of the organization while admiring the buildings' architecture and artworks donated by member states, like the mosaic representation of Norman Rockwell's *Golden Rule*. The Security Council, the Trusteeship Council, and the Economic and Social Council are all part of the guided tour, although some may not be viewed at any given time due to closed meetings. The tour also includes exhibits on peacekeeping, nuclear nonproliferation and disarmament, and human rights. The complex's buildings (the slim, 505-foot-tall green-glass **Secretariat Building;** the much smaller, domed **General Assembly Building;** and the **Dag Hammarskjöld Library**) evoke the influential French modernist Le Corbusier (who was on the team of architects that designed the complex), and the surrounding park and plaza remain visionary. The public concourse has a visitor center with a gift shop, a bookstore, and a post office where you can mail postcards with U.N. stamps; bring your passport to add the U.N. stamp. ✉ *Visitor entrance, 1st Ave. at 46th St., Midtown East* ☎ *212/963–8687* ⊕ *visit.un.org* 🎫 *Tour $22 (plus $2 online surcharge)* ☞ *Children under 5 not admitted* Ⓜ *4, 5, 6, 7, S to Grand Central–42nd St.*

8

WORTH NOTING

Daily News Building (*The News Building*). The landmark lobby of this Art Deco tower contains an illuminated 12-foot globe that revolves beneath a black glass dome. Around it, spreading across the floor like a giant compass and literally positioning New York at the center of the world, bronze lines indicate mileage to various international destinations. Movie fans may recognize the building as the offices of the fictional newspaper *The Daily Planet* in the original *Superman* movie. On the wall behind the globe you can check out a number of meteorological gauges, which read New York City's weather—especially fun on a windy day when the meters are whipping about. The *Daily News* hasn't called this building home since 1995; only the lobby is open to the public (but that's enough). ■TIP➜ The globe was last updated in 1967 so part of the fun here is seeing how our maps have changed; note Manchuria and East and West Germany. ✉ *220 E. 42nd St., between 2nd and 3rd Aves., Midtown East* ☎ *212/687-3733* Ⓜ *4, 5, 6, 7, S to Grand Central-42nd St.*

Edwynn Houk Gallery. The impressive stable of 20th-century photographers represented and shown here includes Sally Mann, Robert Polidori, Nick Brandt, Lalla Essaydi, Annie Leibovitz, Herb Ritts, Mona Kuhn, and Elliott Erwitt. The gallery also has prints by masters Dorothea Lange and Alfred Stieglitz. ✉ *745 5th Ave., 4th fl., between 57th and 58th Sts., Midtown East* ☎ *212/750-7070* ⊕ *www.houkgallery.com* ✆ *Free* ◷ *Closed Sun., Mon.* Ⓜ *N, R, W to 5th Ave./59th St.*

Helmsley Building. This Warren & Wetmore–designed 1929 landmark was intended to match neighboring Grand Central Terminal in bearing, and it succeeded, with a gold-and-copper roof topped with an enormous lantern (originally housing a 6,000-watt light) and distinctive dual archways for traffic on Park Avenue. The building's history gets quirky. When millionaire real-estate investor Harry Helmsley purchased the building in 1977, he changed its name from the New York Central Building to the New York General Building in order to save money by replacing only two letters in the facade (only later did he rename it after himself). During a renovation the following year, however, he actually gilded the building, applying gold paint even to limestone and bronze—it was removed by a succeeding owner. In 2010, after a $100 million renovation, the Helmsley Building, no longer under Helmsley ownership (so technically 230 Park, or "the building formerly known as the Helmsley Building and informally still known as the Helmsley Building"), became the first prewar office tower to receive LEED Gold certification for energy efficiency. Despite being blocked from view from the south by the MetLife Building (originally, the Pan Am Building), the Helmsley Building remains a defining—and now "green," as opposed to gold—feature of one of the world's most lavish avenues. ✉ *230 Park Ave., between 45th and 46th Sts., Midtown East* ⊕ *helmsleybuilding. com* Ⓜ *4, 5, 6, 7, S to 42nd St./Grand Central.*

Japan Society. The stylish, serene lobby of the Japan Society underwent a 2017 renovation by renowned artist Hiroshi Sugimoto and features interior gardens with large bonsai trees and Sugimoto sculptures, all complemented by a second-floor waterfall. The 1971 building itself is a city landmark thanks to its Japanese modernist design by architect Junzo Yoshimura, and its second-floor gallery exhibits works by well-known Japanese artists. Past shows have celebrated the work of contemporary masters including Takashi Murakami, Yoko Ono, and Daido Moriyama. The society's annual performing arts season (September–June) shares works by established and emerging artists in dance, music, and theater. In July, the museum hosts an annual film festival, Japan Cuts, showcasing contemporary Japanese cinema. ⊠ *333 E. 47th St., between 1st and 2nd Aves., Midtown East* ☎ *212/832–1155* ⊕ *www. japansociety.org* ✆ *Gallery $12* ⊗ *Gallery closed Mon.* Ⓜ *4, 5, 6, 7, S to Grand Central–42nd St.; E, M to Lexington Ave./53rd St.; 6 to 51st St.*

Pace Gallery (Midtown). This leading contemporary art gallery—with two outposts in Chelsea, one in London, and other international locations—focuses on such modern and contemporary artists as Kiki Smith, Julian Schnabel, Mark Rothko, James Turrell, and Tara Donovan. ⊠ *32 E. 57th St., 2nd fl., between Park and Madison Aves., Midtown East* ☎ *212/421–3292* ⊕ *www.thepacegallery.com* ✆ *Free* ⊗ *Closed Sun., Mon.* Ⓜ *N, Q, R, W to 5th Ave./59th St.*

Seagram Building. Ludwig Mies van der Rohe, a pioneer of modernist architecture, built this boxlike bronze-and-glass tower in 1958. The austere facade belies its wit: I-beams, used to hold buildings up, here are merely attached to the surface, representing the *idea* of structural support. The Seagram Building's innovative ground-level plaza, extending out to the sidewalk, has since become a common element in urban skyscraper design, but at the time it was built, it was a radical announcement of a new, modern era of American architecture. Most visitors are distracted by more elaborate figures in the city skyline, but the Seagram is a must-visit for architecture buffs. With its two giant fountains and welcoming steps, it's also a popular lunch spot with Midtown workers. Visit late in the afternoon to avoid crowds. ⊠ *375 Park Ave., between 52nd and 53rd Sts., Midtown East* ⊕ *www.375parkavenue.com* Ⓜ *6 to 51st St.; E, M to Lexington Ave./53rd St.*

Tudor City. In 1925, prominent real-estate developer Fred F. French was among the first Americans ever to buy up a large number of buildings—more than 100, in this case, most of them tenements—and join the properties into a single, massive new complex. He designed a collection of nine apartment buildings and two parks in the "garden city" mode, which placed a building's green space not in an enclosed courtyard, but in the foreground. French also elevated the entire development 70 feet (40 stone steps) above the river and built a 39-by-50-foot "Tudor City" sign atop one of the 22-story buildings, best viewed from the eastern end of 42nd Street. The development's residential towers opened between 1927 and 1930, borrowing a marketable air of sophistication from Tudor-style stonework, stained-glass windows, and lobby-design flourishes. An official city landmark, Tudor City has been featured in numerous films, and its landmark gardens—sometimes compared to Gramercy Park, only public—remain a popular lunch spot among office workers. The neighborhood was designated a historic district in 1988. ⊠ *From 40th to 43rd St., between 1st and 2nd Aves., Midtown East* ⊕ *www.tudorcity.com* Ⓜ *4, 5, 6, 7, S to Grand Central–42nd St.*

MURRAY HILL

Murray Hill stretches roughly from 30th to 40th Street between 5th Avenue and the East River, and is a mix of high-rises, restaurants, and bars filled mostly with an affluent, postcollege crowd. The small but solid enclave of Little India (also known as "Curry Hill"), primarily around Lexington and 28th Street, is a good area for sampling authentic cuisine and shopping for traditional clothing and other goods in a handful of boutiques. Farther north, a few side streets are lined with shady trees and town houses, with some high-profile haunts, including the Morgan Library and Museum with its striking architecture and rare manuscripts. But no matter why you're here or where you're headed, New York's biggest icon, the Empire State Building, is always there to tempt your skyward gaze.

TOP ATTRACTIONS

FAMILY

Fodor'sChoice

★

Empire State Building. With a pencil-slim silhouette recognizable virtually worldwide, the Empire State Building is an Art Deco monument to progress, a symbol for New York City, and a star in some great romantic scenes, on- and off-screen. Its cinematic résumé—the building has appeared in more than 250 movies—means that it remains a fixture of popular imagination, and many visitors come to relive favorite movie scenes. You might just find yourself at the top of the building with *Elf* look-alikes or even the building's own *King Kong* impersonator.

Built in 1931 at the peak of the skyscraper craze, this 103-story limestone giant opened after a mere 13 months of construction. The framework rose at an astonishing rate of 4½ stories per week, making the Empire State Building the fastest-rising skyscraper ever built. Unfortunately, your rise to the observation deck might not be quite so record breaking.

There are three lines to get to the top of the Empire State Building: a line for tickets, a line for security, and a line for the elevators. Save time by purchasing your tickets online in advance. You can't skip the security line, but you can skip to the front of both the ticket line and the line for elevators by purchasing an Express ticket to the 86th floor ($65). ■TIP➔ If you don't want to pony up for express service, do yourself a favor and skip that last elevator line at the 80th floor by taking the stairs.

If this is your first visit, keep yourself entertained during your ascent by connecting to the building's free Wi-Fi and downloading the free ESB Observatory Experience app (available in eight languages), which offers images, maps, quizzes, and historical tidbits to supplement displays as you make your way to the top.

The 86th-floor observatory (1,050 feet high) has both a climate-controlled glass-enclosed area and an outdoor deck spanning the building's circumference. Don't be shy about going outside into the wind (even in winter) or you'll miss half the experience. Also, don't be deterred by crowds; there's an unspoken etiquette when it comes to sharing the views and backdrop, and there's plenty of city to go around. The high-powered binoculars are now free of charge (no more quarters),

The restoration and cleaning of Grand Central in the late 1990s uncovered the elaborate astronomical design on the ceiling of the main concourse.

so use them to see up to 80 miles on clear days—or or bring your own binoculars so you can get a closer look at some of the city's rooftop gardens. If it rains, the deck will be less crowded and you can view the city between the clouds or watch the rain travel sideways around the building from the shelter of the enclosed walkway.

The views of the city from the 86th-floor deck are spectacular, but the views from 16 stories up on the 102nd-floor observatory are even more so—and yet, fewer visitors make it this far. Instead of rushing back to elevator lines, ask yourself when you'll be back again, and then take the time to head up to the enclosed upper deck. The ticket for both the 86th-floor and 102nd-floor decks costs $56, but you will be rewarded with peaceful, bird's-eye views of the entire city. Also, there are fewer visitors angling for photo ops, so you can linger awhile and really soak in the city and experience.

Even if you skip the journey to the top, be sure to step into the lobby and take in the extraordinary decor and especially the ceiling, beautifully restored in 2009. The gilded gears and sweeping Art Deco lines, long hidden under a drop ceiling and decades of paint, are a romantic tribute to the machine age and part of the original vision for the building. ⊠ *350 5th Ave., at 34th St., Murray Hill* ☎ *212/736–3100, 877/692–8439* ⊕ *www.esbnyc.com* ✉ *$36; $56 for 86th-fl. and 102nd-fl. decks; $65 for express to 86th fl.* Ⓜ *B, D, F, M, N, Q, R, W to 34th St./Herald Sq.; 6 to 33rd St.*

Morgan Library and Museum. The treasures inside this museum, gathered by John Pierpont Morgan (1837–1913), one of New York's wealthiest financiers, are exceptional: medieval and Renaissance illuminated

The lights on the top of the Empire State Building often change color to support different holidays and causes.

manuscripts, old-master drawings and prints, rare books, and autographed literary and musical manuscripts. Some crowning achievements on paper include letters penned by John Keats and Thomas Jefferson; a summary of the theory of relativity in Einstein's own elegant handwriting; three Gutenberg Bibles; drawings by Dürer, Leonardo da Vinci, Rubens, Blake, and Rembrandt; the only known manuscript fragment of Milton's *Paradise Lost;* Thoreau's journals; and original manuscripts and letters by Charlotte Brontë, Jane Austen, Thomas Pynchon, and many others. Recent exhibits have included *Ernest Hemingway: Between Two Wars,* featuring notebooks, correspondence, personal items, and early drafts of short stories, and *Warhol by the Book,* an exhibition of Warhol's book projects from his early student days through his later years as a cultural icon.

The library shop is housed within an 1852 Italianate brownstone, once the home of Morgan's son, J. P. Morgan Jr. Outside on East 36th Street, the sphinx in the right-hand sculptured panel of the original library's facade is rumored to wear the face of architect Charles McKim. ⊠ *225 Madison Ave., at 36th St., Murray Hill* ☎ *212/685–0008* ⊕ *www.themorgan.org* ✉ *$20 (free Fri. 7–9)* ☾ *Closed Mon.* Ⓜ *B, D, F, M, N, Q, R, W to 34th St.–Herald Sq.; 6 to 33rd St.*

WORTH NOTING

FAMILY **B. Altman Building/New York Public Library–Science, Industry and Business Library (SIBL).** What is now a part of the New York Public Library (NYPL) began as a famous retail outpost. In 1906, department-store magnate Benjamin Altman gambled that his fashionable patrons would follow his popular store in the "Ladies' Mile" shopping district downtown up to this 5th Avenue location. His new emporium, one of the first of the grand department stores on 5th Avenue, was designed to blend in with the stately mansions nearby—note its Renaissance Revival style, limestone facade, Ionic columns, and other classical details. The building was landmarked in 1985, but the store shuttered in 1989 and stood vacant until 1996, when the NYPL moved in and formed the high-tech Science, Industry and Business Library. A 33-foot-high atrium unites the building's two floors: the lending library off the lobby and the research collections below. Downstairs, a wall of electronic ticker tapes and TVs tuned to business-news stations beams information and instructions to patrons. ⊠ *188 Madison Ave., between 34th and 35th Sts., Murray Hill* ☎ *917/275–6975* ⊕ *www.nypl.org* ☉ *Closed Sun.* Ⓜ *B, D, F, M, N, Q, R, W to 34th St.–Herald Sq.; 6 to 33rd St.*

Curry Hill. An affectionate play on the name of the neighborhood, Curry Hill is an aromatic three-block cluster of Indian restaurants and one of the city's more exciting dining destinations. There are around two dozen Indian restaurants peppered (or is it spiced?) around Lexington Avenue between 26th and 28th Streets, and while the neighborhood is popular with in-the-know New Yorkers, it is decidedly off the beaten tourist track. You'll find culinary offerings from a variety of regional cuisines, be it a filling *biryani* or a quick *chaat* (savory snack). Highlights include a *saag paneer* (spinach dish with cheese) or a flavorful tandoori at one of the neighborhood's founding restaurants, Curry in a Hurry (119 Lexington Avenue); creamy *rogan josh* (lamb curry with saffron) or *papadum* (lentil fritters) at Sahib (104 Lexington Avenue); and *kati* rolls (meat or veggie filling wrapped in flatbread) and other urban Indian street snacks at Desi Galli (101 Lexington Avenue). Don't leave the neighborhood without sampling a *dosa*, a fermented crêpe often filled with spiced potato and served with dipping sauces, and shopping the spice markets. Too full to walk? Curry Hill is a great place to score a ride as Indian cab drivers regularly stop here for food. ⊠ *Lexington Ave., between 26th and 28th Sts., Murray Hill* Ⓜ *6 to 28th St.; R, W to 23rd St.*

Koreatown. Despite sitting in the shade of the Empire State Building, and within steps of Herald Square, Koreatown (or "K-Town," as it's locally known) is not a tourist destination. In fact, it feels decidedly off the radar and insulated, as though locals wryly planted their own place to eat, drink, be merry, and get a massage—right under the noses of millions of tourists. Technically, Koreatown runs from 31st to 36th Street between 5th and 6th Avenues, though the main drag is 32nd Street between 5th and Broadway. Labeled Korea Way, this strip is home to 24/7 Korean barbecue joints, karaoke bars, and spas, all stacked on top of each other. Fill up on kimchi (spicy pickled cabbage), *kimbap* (seaweed rice), and red-bean doughnuts (delicious), try some karaoke, and then top off your Koreatown experience by stepping into a jade-igloo sauna (at Juvenex Spa, 25 West 32nd Street). Expect a big bang for your buck; you'll rub elbows with locals and get bragging rights over visitors who followed the crowds to Chinatown. ⊠ *From 31st to 36th St., between 5th and 6th Aves., Murray Hill* Ⓜ *B, D, F, M, N, Q, R, W to 34th St.–Herald Sq.; 6 to 33rd St.*

8

The Lights of the Empire State Building

At night the Empire State Building lights up the Manhattan skyline with a colorful view as awe-inspiring from a distance as the view from the top. The colors at the top of the building are changed regularly to reflect seasons, events, and holidays, so New Yorkers and visitors from around the world always have a reason to look at this icon in a new light.

The building's first light show was in November 1932, when a simple searchlight was used to spread the news that New York–born Franklin Delano Roosevelt had been elected president of the United States. Douglas Leigh, sign designer and mastermind of Times Square's kinetic billboard ads, tried to brighten up prospects at the "Empty State Building" after the Depression by negotiating with the Coca-Cola Company to occupy the top floors. He proposed that Coca-Cola could change the lights of the building to serve as a weather forecast and then publish a small guide on its bottles to decipher the colors. Coca-Cola loved this idea, but the deal fell through after the bombing at Pearl Harbor, when the U.S. government needed office space in the building.

In 1956 the revolving "freedom lights" were installed to welcome people to America; then in 1964 the top 30 floors of the building were illuminated to mark the New York World's Fair. Douglas Leigh revisited the lights in 1976, when he was made chairman of City Decor to welcome the Democratic Convention. He introduced the idea of color lighting, and so the building's tower was ablaze in red, white, and blue to welcome the convention and mark the celebration of the American Bicentennial. The color lights were a huge success, and they remained red, white, and blue for the rest of the year.

Leigh's next suggestion of tying the lights to different holidays, a variation on his weather theme for Coca-Cola, is the basic scheme still used today. In 1977 the lighting system was updated to comply with energy-conservation programs and allow for a wider range of colors. Leigh further improved this new system in 1984 by designing an automated color-changing system so vertical fluorescents in the mast could be changed.

The Empire State Building's computer-driven LED light system was installed in 2012. It can produce intensely saturated full-color light and dimmable cool white light, allowing for an astonishing and flexible range of dramatic or subtle lighting effects. The system is capable of displaying 16 million different colors that can change instantaneously.

For the lighting schedule, visit ⊕ *www. esbnyc.com.*

MIDTOWN WEST

Getting Oriented

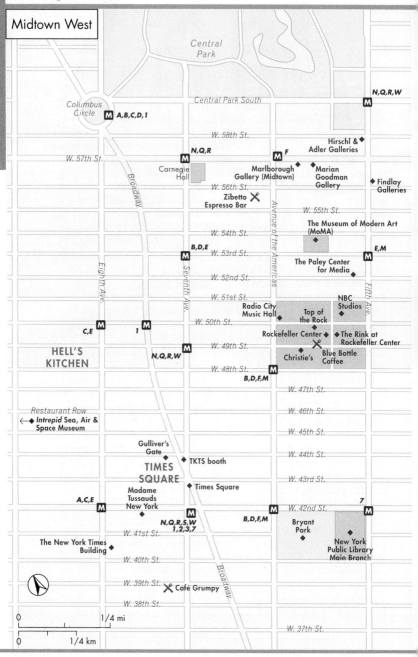

Midtown West

Central Park

Central Park South

Columbus Circle
M *A,B,C,D,1*

N,Q,R,W **M**

W. 58th St.

Hirschl & Adler Galleries ◆

N,Q,R **M**

W. 57th St.

Carnegie Hall

M *F*

Marlborough Gallery (Midtown) ◆

Marian Goodman Gallery ◆

◆ Findlay Galleries

Broadway

W. 56th St.

Zibetto Espresso Bar ✕

W. 55th St.

Avenue of the Americas

The Museum of Modern Art (MoMA) ◆

W. 54th St.

B,D,E **M** W. 53rd St.

W. 52nd St.

The Paley Center for Media ◆

E,M **M**

Eighth Ave.

Seventh Ave.

W. 51st St.

NBC Studios ◆

W. 50th St.

Radio City Music Hall ◆

Top of the Rock ◆

Fifth Ave.

C,E **M**

1 **M**

Rockefeller Center ◆ ✕

◆ The Rink at Rockefeller Center

W. 49th St.

HELL'S KITCHEN

N,Q,R,W **M**

W. 48th St.

Christie's ◆

Blue Bottle Coffee

M *B,D,F,M*

W. 47th St.

W. 46th St.

Restaurant Row

← ◆ *Intrepid* Sea, Air & Space Museum

W. 45th St.

W. 44th St.

Gulliver's Gate ◆

◆ TKTS booth

TIMES SQUARE

W. 43rd St.

◆ Times Square

Madame Tussauds New York

A,C,E **M**

M

N,Q,R,S,W 1,2,3,7

B,D,F,M **M** W. 42nd St.

7 **M**

W. 41st St.

Bryant Park ◆

New York Public Library Main Branch ◆

The New York Times Building ◆

W. 40th St.

W. 39th St. ✕ Café Grumpy

Broadway

W. 38th St.

0   1/4 mi

0   1/4 km

W. 37th St.

MAKING THE MOST OF YOUR TIME

Most people think of Times Square when they think of Midtown, but there's a lot more going on here. The Museum of Modern Art (MoMA) is one of the neighborhood's top attractions and definitely worth a visit, as is Bryant Park, a cool oasis for Midtown's workers and locals. If you have enough time, head over to 12th Avenue to visit the space shuttle *Enterprise* at the *Intrepid* Sea, Air & Space Museum.

Times Square is almost always a frenetic mass of people staring up at the lights and the giant televisions. If you're in a hurry to get somewhere, try to avoid walking—or cabbing—through here. If staying in Midtown, you can take advantage of the prime location and rise early to be first in line at landmarks, museums, or the TKTS booth for discount day-of theater tickets (⇨ *Chapter 19: Performing Arts*).

TOP EXPERIENCES

Summer film screenings at dusk in Bryant Park

Ice-skating at Rockefeller Center

Checking out the views from the Top of the Rock; opinions vary on whether the better views are from here or from the Empire State Building. Either way, if you go at night, the city spreads out below you in a mesmerizing blanket of lights.

Soaking in the art and serenity of MoMA's sculpture garden

GETTING HERE

You can get to Midtown via (almost) all the subways; many make numerous stops throughout the area. For Midtown West, the 1, 2, 3, 7, A, C, E, N, Q, R, and W serve Times Square and West 42nd Street. The S, or Shuttle, travels back and forth between Times Square and Grand Central Station. The B, D, F, and M trains serve Rockefeller Center.

COFFEE AND QUICK BITES

Blue Bottle Coffee. Known for meticulous brewing, freshly roasted organic beans (prepared in a Brooklyn roastery), and delicious treats and pastries (also rushed in fresh from Brooklyn), the Rock Center outpost of this cult California coffee favorite is the perfect, if pricey, refueling spot amid the chaos of Midtown. ⊠ *1 Rockefeller Plaza, Concourse level, Midtown West* ☎ *510/653–3394* ⊕ *www.bluebottlecoffee. com* Ⓜ *B, D, F, M to 47–50th Sts./Rockefeller Center; E, M to 5th Ave./53rd St.*

Café Grumpy. Stop by this Garment District outlet of the New York minichain and turn any sign of grumpiness into a smile with coffee roasted at the Greenpoint, Brooklyn, location. All pastries are baked at the Lower East Side branch: the black-pepper-and-cardamom banana bread is a standout. ⊠ *200 W. 39th St., between 7th and 8th Aves., Midtown West* ☎ *646/449–8747* ⊕ *www. cafegrumpy.com* Ⓜ *1, 2, 3, 7, N, Q, R, S, W to Times Sq.–42nd St.*

Zibetto Espresso Bar. You won't find any seats here, but you will find arguably the best espresso in New York. ⊠ *1385 6th Ave., at 56th St., Midtown West* ☎ *646/707-0505* ⊕ *www. zibettoespressobar.com* Ⓜ *F to 57th St.*

9

Sightseeing
★★★★★
Nightlife
★★★
Dining
★★★★★
Lodging
★★★★★
Shopping
★★★★★

Big is the buzz in Times Square, where giant TV screens, towering skyscrapers, and Broadway theaters play starring roles alongside megastores and over-the-top street performers. Love it or hate it, Times Square is the flashy and flashing heart of Midtown. A visit to New York demands a photo op in Times Square. Just don't forget that there's plenty more to see and experience around Midtown.

Updated by
Kelsy Chauvin

Luckily, you needn't go far from Times Square to get away from the crowds. Head over to 9th Avenue—also known as Hell's Kitchen (where the food is heavenly)—and calmer side streets, home to a mixed bag of locals, many of whom work in the theater industry. There are lots of eclectic restaurants, pretheater dining options, and cute boutiques for shopping. Head over to the Avenue of the Americas (6th Avenue) and discover Bryant Park's Zen green space, stretched out like a yoga mat at the back door of the New York Public Library (another refuge from Midtown madness).

You can score good seats to some of the hottest Broadway and Off-Broadway shows for half the going rate at the TKTS booth in Duffy Square at 47th Street and Broadway *(see Performing Arts)*. Although people think of Broadway as the heart of the theater scene, few theaters actually line the thoroughfare. For some of the grande dames, head west on 45th Street. There are several Broadway beauties here, including the **Booth,** the **Schoenfeld,** the **Jacobs,** the **Music Box,** and the **Imperial.** On the southern side of 45th Street there's the pedestrians-only **Shubert Alley,** distinguished by colorful posters advertising the latest hit plays and musicals, and the **Shubert Theatre,** one of Broadway's most lustrous gems. Head west along 44th Street to see the **Helen Hayes,** the **Broadhurst,** the **Majestic,** and the **St. James.**

You might be surprised to learn that Chelsea is not the only gallery hub in the city; 57th Street between 5th and 6th Avenues is home to some of the city's most prestigious galleries, including Marian Goodman, the Pace Gallery, and the Marlborough Gallery.

Bryant Park is one of the best places to bring your lunch and people-watch in the city.

TOP ATTRACTIONS

FAMILY

Fodor's Choice

★

Bryant Park. This lovely green space spread out among landmarks and skyscrapers is one of Manhattan's most popular parks. Tall London plane trees line the perimeter of the sunny central lawn, overlooking stone terraces, formal flower beds, gravel pathways, and a smattering of kiosks selling everything from cappuccinos to Belgian waffles. The garden tables scattered about fill with lunching office workers and folks enjoying the park's free Wi-Fi (signs explain how to log on). In summer you can check out free live jazz and "Broadway in Bryant Park" musical theater performances, as well as author readings. Most popular of all is the Summer Film Festival: locals leave work early to snag a spot on the lawn for the outdoor screenings each Monday at dusk. At the east side of the park, near a squatting bronze cast of Gertrude Stein, is the stylish Bryant Park Grill, which has a rooftop garden, and the adjacent open-air Bryant Park Café, open seasonally. On the south side of the park is an old-fashioned **carousel** ($3) where kids can ride fanciful rabbits and frogs instead of horses, and attend storytellings and magic shows. Big kids can play with the park's selection of lawn and tabletop games, which includes everything from boccie and Scrabble to Chinese checkers and table tennis. Come late October the park rolls out the artificial frozen **"pond"** (*Oct.–Mar., daily 8 am–10 pm; skate rental $15–$19*) for free ice-skating (bring your own padlock for the lockers). Surrounding the ice rink are the Christmas-market stalls of the **Holiday Shops,** selling handcrafted goods and local foods. ✉ *6th Ave., between 40th and 42nd Sts., Midtown West* ☎ *212/768–4242* ⊕ *www. bryantpark.org* Ⓜ *B, D, F, M to 42nd St.–Bryant Park; 7 to 5th Ave.*

FAMILY **Gulliver's Gate.** At this attraction in Times Square, "the crossroads of the world," behold miniature, detailed, sometimes animated versions of the world's major cities and sights, starting with a 1,000-square-foot scale model of the Big Apple itself (see if you can find the tiny Spiderman). From there, follow a path through the sprawling exhibit and witness 50 nations and 300 small-scale scenes—from the Eiffel Tower and Big Ben to the Taj Mahal and Machu Picchu—each built by artists and model makers native to the region represented. There are more than 100,000 tiny people throughout, plus more than 3,200 feet of railroad track; thousands of trucks, trains, boats, planes, and cars; and a fully operational mini airport where you can watch planes taking off precisely as they do in real life. Along the way, use a digital key to bring scenes to life, and watch model makers in action in the gallery. You can even step into a special 3-D modeling machine to have a scan of yourself made into a lifelike miniature souvenir—take it home, or add it to the model for all the world's travelers to see. ⊠ *216 W. 44th St., between Broadway and 8th Ave., Times Square* ☎ *212/235–2016* ⊕ *gulliversgate.com* ⊠ *$36 (discounts available online)* Ⓜ *1, 2, 3, 7, N, Q, R, S, W to Times Sq.–42nd St.; A, C, E to 42nd St.–Port Authority.*

FAMILY **Intrepid Sea, Air & Space Museum.** Manhattan's only floating museum is a historic, nonprofit, and educational institution like no other: the centerpiece is the *Intrepid*, a 900-foot-long aircraft carrier that was launched in 1943 and decommissioned in 1974. The carrier's most trying moment of service, the day it was attacked in World War II by kamikaze pilots, is recounted in a stirring multimedia presentation. On the ship's various indoor and outdoor decks is a collection of 28 aircraft, including a Lockheed A-12 spy plane and a WWII-era Avenger torpedo bomber. The interactive **Exploreum** contains hands-on exhibits where visitors can experience a flight simulator, transmit messages in Morse code, and see what it was like to live aboard the massive carrier. The space shuttle *Enterprise*—NASA's original prototype orbiter that paved the way for the space-shuttle program—is housed in a climate-controlled pavilion on the *Intrepid*'s flight deck. Surrounding exhibits share the shuttle's history and that of NASA's decades-long space-shuttle program. Docked alongside the *Intrepid* is the submarine *Growler,* the only American guided-missile submarine open to the public. *Growler* offers visitors a firsthand look at life aboard a submarine and a close-up inspection of the once "top-secret" missile command center. Also among the museum's collection is a retired British Airways Concorde, the world's fastest passenger jet. This record-breaking plane—the Concorde Alpha Delta G-BOAD—holds the record for the fastest Atlantic crossing by any Concorde. The museum provides specialized programs and resources to support those with disabilities and their families. ⊠ *Pier 86, 12th Ave. at 46th St., Midtown West* ☎ *212/245–0072, 877/957–7447* ⊕ *www. intrepidmuseum.org* ⊠ *$33; free for U.S. military/veterans* Ⓜ *A, C, E to 42nd St.–Port Authority.*

Fodor'sChoice **The Museum of Modern Art (MoMA).** Housing one of the world's finest
★ collections of modern art, the Museum of Modern Art (MoMA) is renowned for its permanent exhibits, which include masterpieces by Picasso, van Gogh, Monet, and Dalí, as well as its first-rate—and

highly buzzed about—exhibitions on modern art, photography, and film. Located minutes from Rockefeller Center, it is slowly expanding along 53rd Street to accommodate both its growing collection and audience. MoMA's current building design features a maze of glass walkways to permit art viewing from many angles; a high-end restaurant and bar, The Modern; and a cinema that offers curated international film selections and talks.

The museum spans six levels, with an impressive lineup of special exhibits on the skylighted top floor; painting and sculpture on Levels 5 and 4; architecture, design, drawings, and photography on 3; and contemporary galleries, prints, and books on Level 2. It's best to explore the museum from top to bottom, beginning with the museum's main attractions and ending on Level 1 at a favorite resting spot, the Abby Aldrich Rockefeller Sculpture Garden. Designed by Philip Johnson, it features Barnett Newman's *Broken Obelisk* (1962–69). The glass wall lets visitors look directly into the surrounding galleries from the garden, where there's also a reflecting pool and trees. Plans for an expansion into the space next door (this meant tearing down the American Folk Art Museum, which has relocated) include additional gallery space, a retractable glass wall, an expanded lobby, and the opening of its entire first floor, including the sculpture garden, as a free public space. Construction is under way, with an expected completion date in 2019. ■TIP➜ **Entrance between 4 and 8 pm on Friday is free, but expect long lines.** ✉ *11 W. 53rd St., between 5th and 6th Aves., Midtown West* ☎ *212/708–9400* ⊕ *www.moma.org* ✉ *$25* Ⓜ *E, M to 5th Ave./53rd St.; F to 57th St.; B, D, E to 7th Ave.*

Radio City Music Hall. ⇨ *See the listing in Chapter 19: Performing Arts.*

FAMILY **The Rink at Rockefeller Center.** Set in the shadow of the giant Rockefeller Center Christmas tree, the city's most iconic ice-skating rink is a quintessential experience for visitors and a longstanding tradition for many locals. Skaters swoop or stumble across the ice while crowds gather at street level to watch the spins and spills. General-admission skating is on a first-come, first-served basis, so it is best to come early, and on weekdays, to avoid crowds. First Skate tickets ($50–$65, reserved online) allow 7 am access to the rink, followed by a complimentary hot chocolate or coffee and pastry or breakfast. VIP Skate packages ($60–$150) allow guests to skate past the long lines and include skate rental, 90 minutes of ice time, and hot chocolate and cookies. Other packages include Christmas Show and VIP Skate (from $116), which covers orchestra seating for the Radio City Christmas Spectacular as well as admission to the rink, skate rental, and refreshments. The rink is a café in summer. ✉ *30 Rockefeller Plaza, between 49th and 50th Sts., Midtown West* ⊕ *www.therinkatrockcenter.com* ✉ *$25–$32; $12 skate rental* ⊙ *Closed mid-Apr.–Sept.* Ⓜ *B, D, F, M to 47th–50th Sts./ Rockefeller Center; E, M to 5th Ave./53rd St.*

Rockefeller Center. If Times Square is New York's crossroads, Rockefeller Center is its communal gathering place, where the entire world converges to snap pictures, skate on the ice rink, peek in on a taping of the *Today* show, shop, eat, and take in the monumental Art Deco structures

Ice-skating under the sculpture of Prometheus, at Rockefeller Center, is a winter ritual for many local and visiting families.

and public sculptures from the past century. Totaling more than 100 shops and 50 eateries (including Thomas Keller's Bouchon Bakery), the complex runs from 47th to 52nd Streets between 5th and 6th Avenues. Special events and huge pieces of art dominate the central plazas in spring and summer. In December an enormous twinkling tree towers above the ice-skating rink, causing huge crowds of visitors from across the country and the globe to shuffle through with necks craned and cameras flashing. The first official tree-lighting ceremony was held in 1933.

The world's most famous ice-skating rink *(The Rink at Rockefeller Center)* occupies Rockefeller Center's sunken lower plaza October through mid-April and converts to a café in summer. The gold-leaf statue of the fire-stealing Greek hero **Prometheus**—Rockefeller Center's most famous sculpture—hovers above, forming the backdrop to zillions of photos. Carved into the wall behind it, a quotation from Aeschylus reads, "Prometheus, teacher in every art, brought the fire that hath proved to mortals a means to mighty ends." The lower plaza also provides access to the marble-lined concourse underneath Rockefeller Center, which houses restaurants, a post office, and clean public restrooms—a rarity in Midtown.

Rising from the Lower Plaza's west side is the 70-story (850-foot-tall) Art Deco **GE Building,** a testament to modern urban development. Here Rockefeller commissioned and then destroyed a mural by Diego Rivera (upon learning that it featured Vladimir Lenin). He replaced it with the monumental *American Progress* by José María Sert, still on view in the lobby, flanked by additional murals by Sert and English artist Frank Brangwyn. Up on the 65th floor is the landmark **Rainbow**

CLOSE UP

Art in Rockefeller Center

The mosaics, murals, and sculptures that grace Rockefeller Center—many of them Art Deco masterpieces—were part of John D. Rockefeller Jr.'s plans. In 1932, as the steel girders on the first of the buildings soared heavenward, he put together a team of advisers to find artists who could make the project "as beautiful as possible." Some artists scoffed at the idea of decorating an office building: Picasso declined to meet with Rockefeller, and Matisse replied that busy businessmen wouldn't be in the "quiet and reflective state of mind" needed to appreciate his art. Those who agreed to contribute, including muralists Diego Rivera (from Mexico) and José María Sert (from Spain), were relatively unknown, though a group of American artists protested Rockefeller's decision to hire "alien" artists. More than 50 artists were commissioned for 200 works.

As Rockefeller Center neared completion in 1932, Rockefeller still needed a mural for the lobby of the main buildings and he wanted the subject to be grandiose: "human intelligence in control of the forces of nature." He hired Rivera. *Man at the Cross-roads*, with its depiction of massive machinery moving mankind forward, seemed exactly what Rockefeller wanted—until it was realized that a portrait of Soviet Premier Vladimir Lenin surrounded by red-kerchiefed workers occupied a space in the center. Rockefeller, who was building what was essentially a monument to capitalism, was less than thrilled. When Rivera was accused of propagandizing, he famously replied, "All art is propaganda."

Rivera refused to remove the offending portrait and, in early 1934, as Rivera was working, representatives for Rockefeller informed him that his services were no longer required. Within a half hour, tar paper had been hung over the mural. Despite negotiations to move the artwork to the Museum of Modern Art, Rockefeller was determined to get rid of the mural once and for all. Not content to have it painted over, he ordered ax-wielding workers to chip away the entire wall. He commissioned a less offensive one (by Sert) instead.

Rivera had the last word, though: he re-created the mural in the Palacio de Bellas Artes in Mexico City, adding a portrait of Rockefeller among the Champagne-swilling swells ignoring the plight of the workers.

The largest of the original artworks that remains is Lee Lawrie's 2-ton sculpture, *Atlas*. Its building also stirred up controversy, as it was said to resemble Italy's fascist dictator, Benito Mussolini. The sculpture, depicting a muscle-bound man holding up the world, drew protests in 1936. Some even derided Paul Manship's golden *Prometheus*, which soars over the ice-skating rink, when it was unveiled the same year. Both are now considered to be among the best public artworks of the 20th century.

Lawrie's sculpture *Wisdom*, over the main entrance of 20 Rockefeller Plaza, is another gem. Also look for Isamu Noguchi's stainless-steel plaque *News* over the entrance of 50 Rockefeller Plaza and Attilio Piccirilli's 2-ton glass-block panel *Youth Leading Industry* over the entrance of the International Building at 636 Fifth Avenue.

9

Room, a glittering big-band ballroom dating to 1934; it serves a showy and very expensive brunch on Sunday, and dinner and entertainment on Monday nights. Higher up, **Top of the Rock** has what many consider the finest panoramic views of the city. ⊠ *30 Rockefeller Plaza, from 47th to 52nd Sts. between 5th and 6th Aves., Midtown West* ⊕ *www. rockefellercenter.com* Ⓜ *B, D, F, M to 47th–50th Sts./Rockefeller Center; E, M to 5th Ave./53rd St.*

Times Square. Hands down, this is the most energetic part of New York City, a cacophony of flashing lights and shoulder-to-shoulder crowds that many New Yorkers studiously avoid. Originally named after the *New York Times* (whose headquarters have since relocated to 8th Avenue), the area has seen many changes since the first subway line, which included a 42nd Street station, opened in 1904. While the area was once a bastion of the city's unseemly side, today it's a vibrant, family-friendly destination with pedestrian stretches that have lined Broadway Plaza with tables, chairs, and granite benches. There's even stadium seating at the north end (above discount-theater-ticket-seller TKTS), where you can pause to take in the square's wild mix of flashing digital billboards, on-location television broadcasts, and ever-present traffic cacophony. In response to a wave of overly aggressive costumed street performers, in 2016 the city created "designated activity zones" for entertainers and vendors—leaving open plazas and "express lane" walkways. There's no longer a visitor center, but you can drop by the official NYC Information Center, a movable kiosk (usually located at West 44th Street) with maps, brochures, coupons, and a bilingual staff.

The focus of the entertainment may have shifted over the years, but showtime is still the heart of Midtown's theater scene, and there are 40 Broadway theaters nearby. Learn about Broadway's history and architecture with a one-hour walking tour ($50) by Manhattan Walking Tours (*www.manhattanwalkingtour.com*); or join the guided Broadway Walking tour (*$35; daily at 9:30; additional times offered in summer and holiday seasons; www.walkinbroadway.com*) that includes audio headsets for musical interludes, and leaves from the Actor's Chapel on West 49th Street, between Broadway and 8th Avenue. ⊠ *Broadway between 42nd and 48th Sts., Midtown West* ☎ *212/768–1560 for Times Square Alliance* ⊕ *www.timessquarenyc. org* Ⓜ *1, 2, 3, 7, N, Q, R, S, W to Times Sq.–42 St.*

Fodor's Choice
★

Top of the Rock. Rockefeller Center's multifloor observation deck, the Top of the Rock, on the 69th and 70th floors of the building, provides views that rival those from the Empire State Building (some say they're even better because the views include the Empire State Building). Arriving just before sunset affords a view of the city that morphs before your eyes into a dazzling wash of colors, with a bird's-eye view of the tops of the Empire State Building, the Citicorp Building, and the Chrysler Building, and sweeping views northward to Central Park and south to the Statue of Liberty. Timed-entry ticketing eliminates long lines. Indoor exhibits include films of Rockefeller Center's history and a model of the building. Rapid elevators lift you to the 67th-floor interior viewing area, and then an escalator leads to the outdoor deck on the 69th floor for sightseeing through nonreflective glass safety panels. Then, take another

Some of the world's most famous paintings hang in the MoMA, including Monet's *Water Lilies*.

elevator or stairs to the 70th floor for a 360-degree outdoor panorama of New York City on a deck that is only 20 feet wide and nearly 200 feet long. Especially interesting is a Plexiglas screen on the floor with footage showing Rock Center construction workers dangling on beams high above the streets; the brave can even "walk" across a beam to get a sense of what it might have been like to erect this skyscraper. A Sun & Stars ticket ($49) allows you to visit twice and see the city as it rises and sets in the same day. ⊠ *30 Rockefeller Plaza, 50th St. entrance, between 5th and 6th Aves., Midtown West* ☎ *212/698–2000* ⊕ *www. topoftherocknyc.com* ⊠ *$34* Ⓜ *B, D, F, M to 47th–50th Sts./Rockefeller Center; E, M to 5th Ave./53rd St.*

WORTH NOTING

Christie's. You could easily spend an hour or more wandering the free, museumlike galleries at the New York outpost of this famous auction house, where on any given day you find impressive works of art, estate jewelry, furniture, and other rarely displayed letters and objects of interest that are usually housed in (and most likely, soon to be returned to) private collections. One of the first items to be auctioned here, when it opened in 2000, was the "Happy Birthday" dress worn by Marilyn Monroe when she sang to President Kennedy (it sold for more than $1.2 million, in case you were wondering). Yes, the auction house has come a long way since James Christie launched his business in England by selling two chamber pots, among other household goods, in 1766. The lobby's specially commissioned abstract Sol LeWitt mural alone makes it worth visiting the 310,000-square-foot space.

Hours vary by sale, so call ahead to confirm. ⊠ *20 Rockefeller Plaza, 49th St. between 5th and 6th Aves., Midtown West* ☎ *212/636–2000* ⊕ *www.christies.com* ✉ *Free* Ⓜ *B, D, F, M to 47th–50th Sts./Rockefeller Center; E, M to 5th Ave./53rd St.*

Findlay Galleries. A 2016 merger between the well-established David Findlay Jr. Gallery and Wally Findlay Gallery led to this combined Midtown space with the same concentration of the former's contemporary and 20th-century American artists—from Whistler to Herman Cherry, Byron Brown, and David Aronson—and the latter's presentation of impressionist and postimpressionist works. ⊠ *724 5th Ave., 7th fl., between 56th and 57th Sts., Midtown West* ☎ *212/486–7660* ⊕ *www.findlaygalleries.com* ✉ *Free* ☉ *Closed Sun., also Mon. fall–spring* Ⓜ *N, Q, R, W to 5th Ave./59th St.*

Hirschl & Adler Galleries. Although this gallery has a selection of European works, it's best known for American paintings, prints, and decorative arts. The celebrated 19th- and 20th-century artists whose works are featured include Stuart Davis, Childe Hassam, and Camille Pissarro. Each year, the gallery presents up to a dozen special exhibits exploring historical themes of works culled from its collection. ⊠ *730 5th Ave., 4th fl., at 57th St., Midtown West* ☎ *212/535–8810* ⊕ *www.hirschlandadler.com* ✉ *Free* ☉ *Closed Sun.* Ⓜ *N, Q, R, W to 5th Ave./59th St.*

FAMILY **Madame Tussauds New York.** Croon with Michael Jackson, Tina Turner, and Taylor Swift, pucker up to your favorite heartthrob (be it Justin Bieber or Justin Timberlake), strike a fierce pose with fashionista Heidi Klum, or enjoy a royal chat with the Duke and Duchess of Cambridge, William and Kate. Much of the fun here comes from photo opportunities—you're encouraged to pose with and touch the more than 200 realistic replicas of the famous, infamous, and downright super. The Marvel 4D Experience includes wax likenesses of heroes like the Hulk, Captain America, Ironman, and Thor, as well as a short animated movie shown on a 360-degree screen that surrounds the viewer. Other interactive options at the museum include a karaoke café, a celebrity walk down the red carpet, and a Sports Zone where you can see how you measure up to sporting legends like Lionel Messi, Serena Williams, Derek Jeter, and Michelle Kwan. Note that closing hours vary during peak seasons, but the last tickets sold are always one hour prior. ⊠ *234 W. 42nd St., between 7th and 8th Aves., Midtown West* ☎ *866/841–3505* ⊕ *www.madame-tussauds.com* ✉ *$37 (discounts available online)* Ⓜ *1, 2, 3, 7, N, Q, R, S, W to Times Sq.–42nd St.; A, C, E to 42nd St.–Port Authority.*

Marian Goodman Gallery. Perhaps the most respected contemporary art dealer in town, the Marian Goodman Gallery has been introducing top European artists to American audiences for over 40 years. The stable of excellent contemporary artists in the Goodman fold includes Gerhard Richter, Jeff Wall, John Baldessari, William Kentridge, Chantal Akerman, and Steve McQueen. ⊠ *24 W. 57th St., between 5th and 6th Aves., Midtown West* ☎ *212/977–7160* ⊕ *www.mariangoodman.com* ✉ *Free* ☉ *Closed Sun.* Ⓜ *F to 57th St.*

Marlborough Gallery (Midtown). The gallery has an international reputation, representing modern artists such as Magdalena Abakanowicz, Beverly Pepper, and Red Grooms, architect Santiago Calatrava, and photo-realist Richard Estes. Look for sculptures by Tom Otterness, whose whimsical bronzes are found in several subway stations. A Chelsea branch specializes in contemporary art. ✉ *40 W. 57th St., between 5th and 6th Aves., Midtown West* ☎ *212/541–4900* ⊕ *www.marlboroughgallery.com* ✉ *Free* ☽ *Closed Sun.* Ⓜ *F to 57th St.*

NBC Studios. You can join the gawking crowds watching news tapings outside the NBC studios (which are housed in the Art Deco GE Building on Rockefeller Plaza), or you can get even closer to the action (without having to elbow anyone) by taking a slick behind-the-scenes tour of the legendary studios. Tours depart every 20 minutes daily, delving into the history of television and the actual recording studios of some of the network's top shows, like *Saturday Night Live, The Tonight Show Starring Jimmy Fallon,* and *NBC Nightly News.* Tours start at the Shop at NBC Studios (49th Street between 5th and 6th Avenues); advance tickets are sold online (recommended). ✉ *30 Rockefeller Plaza, between 5th and 6th Aves. at 49th St., Midtown West* ☎ *212/664–3700* ⊕ *www. thetouratnbcstudios.com* ✉ *$33* ☞ *Children under 6 not permitted* Ⓜ *B, D, F, M to 47th–50th Sts./Rockefeller Center.*

New York Public Library Main Branch. The "Library with the Lions" celebrated its centennial in 2011 as a masterpiece of Beaux Arts design and as one of the great research institutions in the world, with millions of items including books, manuscripts, photographs, maps, periodicals, and more. Expect changes, if not to the look, then to the feel, of the building as it attempts to become more welcoming and useful for its next 100 years of use. Renovation plans include the creation of more public space, a new 40th Street entrance, improved infrastructure, and expanded exhibition spaces. The major work is planned between 2018 and 2021, and the building will remain open throughout. This renovation follows upgrades including restoration of the landmarked Rose Main Reading Room's extraordinary ceilings, and expansion of state-of-the-art collections storage. The marble staircase at the library's grand 5th Avenue entrance is an excellent perch for people-watching before or after you explore the opulent interior.

The library's bronze front doors open into **Astor Hall,** which leads to special exhibit galleries and, to the left, a stunning periodicals room with wall paintings of New York publishing houses. Ascend the sweeping double staircase to a second-floor balconied corridor overlooking the hall, with panels highlighting the library's development. Continue up to the magisterial **Rose Main Reading Room**—297 feet long (almost two full north–south city blocks), 78 feet wide, and just over 51 feet high; walk through to appreciate the rows of oak tables and natural light pouring through the massive windows. Several additional third-floor galleries show rotating exhibits on print and photography. On the ground floor, visit the Children's Center to see a display of Winnie-the-Pooh and friends, the actual dolls owned by Christopher Robin that inspired A. A. Milne's beloved tales. Free hour-long tours leave Monday–Saturday at 11 and 2, and Sunday at 2 from Astor Hall. Women's

9

bathrooms are on the ground floor and third floor, and there's a men's bathroom on the third floor. ⊠ *476 5th Ave., between 40th and 42nd Sts., Midtown West* ☎ *212/930–0800 for exhibit info* ⊕ *www.nypl.org* Ⓜ *B, D, F, M to 42nd St.–Bryant Park; 7 to 5th Ave.*

The New York Times Building. Completed in 2007, this 52-story building with its distinctive, ladderlike ceramic rods is a testament to clean-lined modernism. The architect, Renzo Piano, extended the ceramic rods beyond the top of the building so that it would give the impression of dissolving into the sky. One of the skyscraper's best features—and the one that's open to the public—is the building's lobby atrium, which includes an open-air moss garden with 50-foot paper-birch trees and a wooden footbridge; a 560-screen media art installation titled *Moveable Type,* streaming a mix of the newspaper's near-real-time and archival content; and the New York flagship store of minimalist home-goods designer MUJI. You never know which famous journalists you'll spy on the coffee line in Dean & DeLuca. Unfortunately, tours are not offered. ⊠ *620 8th Ave., between 40th and 41st Sts., Midtown West* ☎ *212/984–8128* ⊕ *www.newyorktimesbuilding.com* Ⓜ *A, C, E to 42nd St.–Port Authority; 1, 2, 3, 7, N, Q, R, S, W to Times Sq.–42nd St.*

The Paley Center for Media. With an ever-changing exhibition gallery, small cinema, screening room, and a computerized catalog of more than 160,000 television and radio programs, the Paley Center for Media's New York outpost examines the constantly evolving state of media. Temporary exhibits on the first floor may showcase anything from game shows to sporting events to celebrity ensembles through photographs, recordings, and artifacts. The center also hosts special events, public seminars, lectures, and screenings that explore and celebrate the history of broadcasting. The fourth-floor library is a top draw here: if you want to see an archived awards show, news program, sitcom, or historic event, simply check into a semiprivate computer terminal, enter your search terms, and enjoy. Possibly the most entertaining part of these TV shows from yesteryear is the fact that the original commercials are still embedded in many of the programs. If ads are your thing, you can also skip the programming altogether and watch compilations of classic commercials. ⊠ *25 W. 52nd St., between 5th and 6th Aves., Midtown West* ☎ *212/621–6800* ⊕ *www.paleycenter.org* ✉ *$10 (suggested admission)* ⊙ *Closed Mon., Tues.* Ⓜ *E, M to 5th Ave./53rd St.; B, D, F, M to 47th–50th Sts./Rockefeller Center.*

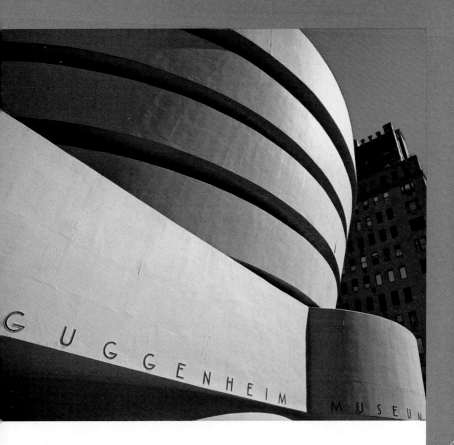

THE UPPER
EAST SIDE

10

Getting Oriented

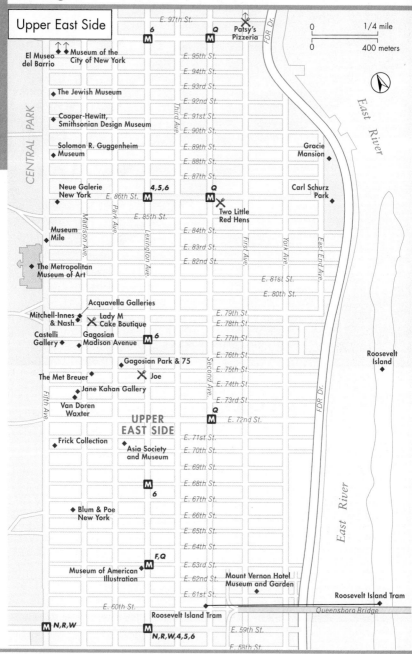

Upper East Side

E. 97th St.

Patsy's Pizzeria

FDR Dr.

0   1/4 mile
0   400 meters

East River

El Museo del Barrio

◆ Museum of the City of New York

E. 95th St.

E. 94th St.

E. 93rd St.

◆ The Jewish Museum

E. 92nd St.

◆ Cooper-Hewitt, Smithsonian Design Museum

E. 91st St.

E. 90th St.

Solomon R. Guggenheim ◆ Museum

E. 89th St.

E. 88th St.

Gracie Mansion

E. 87th St.

CENTRAL PARK

Neue Galerie New York

4,5,6

E. 86th St.

Carl Schurz Park

Q

Two Little Red Hens

E. 85th St.

Museum Mile

Madison Ave.

Park Ave.

Lexington Ave.

Third Ave.

E. 84th St.

E. 83rd St.

E. 82nd St.

First Ave.

York Ave.

East End Ave.

◆ The Metropolitan Museum of Art

E. 81st St.

E. 80th St.

Acquavella Galleries

E. 79th St.

Mitchell-Innes & Nash

Lady M Cake Boutique

E. 78th St.

Castelli Gallery ◆

Gagosian Madison Avenue

6

E. 77th St.

Second Ave.

E. 76th St.

Gagosian Park & 75

E. 75th St.

The Met Breuer ◆

Joe

E. 74th St.

Jane Kahan Gallery

E. 73rd St.

Van Doren Waxter

Q

E. 72nd St.

UPPER EAST SIDE

Fifth Ave.

Roosevelt Island

E. 71st St.

◆ Frick Collection

E. 70th St.

Asia Society and Museum

E. 69th St.

E. 68th St.

6

E. 67th St.

◆ Blum & Poe New York

E. 66th St.

E. 65th St.

E. 64th St.

F,Q

E. 63rd St.

Museum of American Illustration

E. 62nd St.

Mount Vernon Hotel Museum and Garden

E. 61st St.

Roosevelt Island Tram

East River

FDR Dr.

Roosevelt Island Tram

E. 60th St.

Roosevelt Island Tram

Queensboro Bridge

N,R,W

N,R,W,4,5,6

E. 59th St.

E. 58th St.

MAKING THE MOST OF YOUR TIME

The Upper East Side lends itself to a surprising variety of simple but distinct itineraries: exploring the landmarks on Museum Mile; languorous gallery grazing; window-shopping on Madison Avenue; or, for just-out-of-college kids, barhopping on 2nd Avenue. If it's the museums you're after, make sure to plan at least a few hours per museum—with some snack or coffee breaks. There's a lot to see, so don't plan on visiting more than one museum a day. The Upper East Side's town houses, boutiques, consignment stores, and hidden gardens are easy to miss unless you take some time to wander.

GETTING HERE

Take the Lexington Avenue 4 or 5 express train to 59th or 86th Street. The 6 local train also stops at 59th, 68th, 77th, 86th, and 96th Streets. The 2nd Avenue subway line opened in 2017 with Q train stops at 72nd, 86th, and 96th streets. From Midtown, the F and Q trains let you out at Lexington Avenue at 63rd Street, where you can transfer to the 4, 5, or 6 after a short walk (and free transfer). From the Upper West Side, take one of the crosstown buses, the M66, M72, M79, M86, or M96. You can also take the N, R, or W train to 59th Street and Lexington Avenue.

TOP EXPERIENCES

Exploring any of the world-class museums here, followed by a relaxing, restorative lunch

Gallery-hopping the UES's so-unhip-it's-now-hip art scene (plus they're free)

Window-shopping on Madison Avenue

Appreciating the views from the cable car on the ride to Four Freedoms Park on Roosevelt Island

COFFEE AND QUICK BITES

Joe (Upper East Side). One of the city's best coffee chains, Joe has the kind of quality caffeine and sweets to fuel you up and down Museum Mile (and maybe even around the park). ⊠ *1045 Lexington Ave., between 74th and 75th Sts., Upper East Side* ☎ *212/988–2500* ⊕ *www.joenewyork.com/locations/lexington* Ⓜ *6 to 77th St.*

Lady M Cake Boutique. The signature here is the Mille Crepes cake: 20 crêpes stacked together with a delicious cream filling. Thank us later. ⊠ *41 E. 78th St., at Madison Ave., Upper East Side* ☎ *212/452–2222* ⊕ *www.ladym.com* Ⓜ *6 to 77th St.*

Patsy's Pizzeria. Great coal-oven pizza and rustic, classic red-sauce dishes make this cash-only former Frank Sinatra favorite worth the trek up to 118th Street. There are panini, too. ⊠ *2287 1st Ave., at 118th St., Upper East Side* ☎ *212/534–9783* ⊕ *www.thepatsyspizza.com* ⊟ *No credit cards* Ⓜ *6 to 116th St.*

Two Little Red Hens. With first-rate coffee and delicious cupcakes, cheesecake, and cookies to match, this little bakery is a legend with locals. ⊠ *1652 2nd Ave., at 86th St., Upper East Side* ☎ *212/452–0476* ⊕ *www.twolittleredhens.com* Ⓜ *4, 5, 6, Q to 86th St.*

10

Sightseeing
★★★★
Nightlife
★
Dining
★★
Lodging
★★
Shopping
★★★★

To many New Yorkers, the Upper East Side connotes old money and high society. Alongside Central Park, between 5th and Lexington Avenues, up to East 96th Street, the trappings of wealth are everywhere apparent: posh buildings, Madison Avenue's flagship boutiques, and doormen in braided livery. It's also a key destination for visitors, because some of the most fantastic museums in the country are here.

Updated by
Joshua Rogol

There's a reason this stretch of Manhattan is called "Museum Mile": this is where you'll find the **Metropolitan Museum of Art,** the **Solomon R. Guggenheim Museum,** and the **Cooper Hewitt, Smithsonian Design Museum,** as well as a number of art galleries. For a local taste of the luxe life, catwalk down Madison Avenue for its lavish boutiques; strolling the platinum-card corridor between 60th and 82nd Street is like stepping into the pages of a glossy magazine. Many fashion houses have their flagships here and showcase their lush threads in exquisite settings.

Venture east of Lexington Avenue and encounter a less wealthy—and more diverse—Upper East Side, inhabited by couples seeking some of the last (relatively) affordable places to raise a family south of 100th Street, as well as recent college grads getting a foothold in the city (on weekend nights 2nd Avenue resembles a miles-long fraternity and sorority reunion). One neighborhood particularly worth exploring is northeast-lying Yorkville, especially between 78th and 86th Streets east of 2nd Avenue. Once a remote hamlet with a large German population, Yorkville has several remaining ethnic food shops, 19th-century row houses, and—one of the city's best-kept secrets—**Carl Schurz Park,** which make for a good half-day's exploration, as does catching a glimpse of the most striking residence there, **Gracie Mansion.**

If art galleries appeal, there are some elegant ones on the Upper East Side. In keeping with the tony surroundings, the emphasis here is on works by established masters.

TOP ATTRACTIONS

Asia Society and Museum. The Asian art collection of Mr. and Mrs. John D. Rockefeller III forms the core of this museum's holdings, which span territory from Pakistan to Java and date back to the 11th century BC, and include Hindu stone sculpture, Tibetan Buddhist paintings, Vietnamese ceramics, Han Dynasty bronzes, and Japanese woodblock prints. Founded in 1956, the society has a regular program of lectures, films, and performances, in addition to changing exhibitions of traditional and contemporary art. Trees grow in the glass-enclosed, skylighted Garden Court Café, which serves an eclectic Asian lunch menu and weekend brunch. Call ahead to reserve afternoon tea service. Admission is free Friday 6–9 pm (September to June). A free audio tour is included with admission, or you can take a free guided tour at 2 daily and 6:30 Friday. ⊠ *725 Park Ave., at 70th St., Upper East Side* ☎ *212/288–6400* ⊕ *www.asiasociety.org/ny* ⊠ *$12* ⊗ *Closed Mon.* Ⓜ *6 to 68th St.–Hunter College.*

Blum & Poe New York. This contemporary art gallery may be a relative newbie on the Upper East Side art scene (it opened in 2014), but as one of L.A.'s top art galleries, Blum & Poe was very quick to settle into its renovated town house on East 66th Street—a cozy space compared to its sprawling, 21,000-square-foot L.A. counterpart—and to establish itself in the New York art world. Past exhibits have featured artists including Hugh Scott-Douglas, Kishio Suga, Yun Hyong-Keun, and Zhu Jinshi. ⊠ *19 E. 66th St., between 5th and Madison Aves., Upper East Side* ☎ *212/249–2249* ⊕ *www.blumandpoe.com* ⊗ *Closed Sun., Mon.* Ⓜ *6 to 68th St.–Hunter College; F, Q to Lexington Ave.–63rd St.*

FAMILY **Cooper Hewitt, Smithsonian Design Museum.** Reopened in 2014 after a major three-year overhaul, the Cooper Hewitt is a slick, 21st-century museum that has taken an ornate, century-old mansion (once the residence of industrialist Andrew Carnegie) and outfitted it with the latest technologies and amenities to create a highly interactive experience. You don't just *look* at design here; you play with it, engage it, and then take it home. On arrival at the museum, visitors receive a digital pen that acts as a key to the museum's entire collection of more than 200,000 objects, everything from antique cutlery and Japanese sword fittings to robotics and animation. Museum highlights include giant touch-screen tables where visitors can summon random-yet-relevant items from the museum's collection by drawing a squiggle or a shape; the Immersion Room, where visitors can view and save their favorite wallpapers from the museum's incredible collection or create their own designs; and the Process Lab, where visitors get hands-on to solve design dilemmas and enhance everyday design objects. The focus on design and discovery extends to "SHOP," where limited-edition objects created in collaboration with contemporary designers are for sale. There is a café, and an outdoor garden is free and open to the public. Guided tours run daily at 11:30 and 1:30 on weekdays and 1 and 3 on weekends. Admission is pay-what-you-wish Saturday evening from 6 to 9. ⊠ *2 E. 91st St., at 5th Ave., Upper East Side* ☎ *212/849–8400* ⊕ *www.cooperhewitt.org* ⊠ *$18 ($16 online)* Ⓜ *4, 5, 6 to 86th St.*

10

El Museo del Barrio. *El barrio* is Spanish for "the neighborhood" and the nickname for East Harlem, a largely Spanish-speaking Puerto Rican and Dominican community; El Museo del Barrio, on the edge of this neighborhood, focuses on Latin American and Caribbean art, with some 10% of its collection concentrated on works by self-taught artists from New York, Puerto Rico, the Caribbean, and Latin America. The more than 6,500-object permanent collection includes over 400 pre-Columbian artifacts, sculpture, photography, film and video, and traditional art from all over Latin America. The collection of 360 *santos*, carved wooden folk-art figures from Puerto Rico, is popular. El Museo hosts performances, lectures, films, and cultural events, including a monthlong Día de los Muertos celebration. The museum closed in fall 2017 for upgrades of basic systems and other improvements. Las Galerias are scheduled to reopen in summer 2018, and El Teatro in fall 2018. ■ TIP→ Admission to El Museo del Barrio gains you free entrance to the neighboring Museum of the City of New York. ✉ *1230 5th Ave., between 104th and 105th Sts., Upper East Side* 📞 *212/831–7272* ⊕ *www.elmuseo.org* ✉ *$9 suggested donation* Ⓜ *6 to 103rd St.*

Fodor'sChoice
★
Frick Collection. Henry Clay Frick (1849–1919) made his fortune amid the soot and smoke of Pittsburgh, where he was a coke (a coal fuel derivative) and steel baron, but this lovely art museum, once Frick's private New York residence, is decidedly removed from soot. With an exceptional collection of works from the Renaissance through the late 19th century that includes Édouard Manet's *The Bullfight* (1864), a Chinard portrait bust (1809), three Vermeers, three Rembrandts, works by El Greco, Goya, Van Dyck, Hogarth, Degas, and Turner, as well as sculpture, decorative arts, and 18th-century French furniture, everything here is a highlight. The Portico Gallery, an enclosed portico along the building's 5th Avenue garden, houses the museum's growing collection of sculpture. An audio guide, available in several languages, is included with admission, as are the year-round temporary exhibits. The tranquil indoor garden court is a magical spot for a rest. Children under 10 are not admitted, and those ages 10–16 with an adult only. ✉ *1 E. 70th St., at 5th Ave., Upper East Side* 📞 *212/288–0700* ⊕ *www.frick.org* ✉ *$22; pay-what-you-wish Wed. 2–6* ⊘ *Closed Mon.* Ⓜ *6 to 68th St.–Hunter College.*

Gagosian Madison Avenue. If you are looking for ambitious works by the world's most acclaimed artists in a gallery that easily competes with the city's top museums, you have to visit Gagosian. Perhaps the most powerful art dealer in the world, Larry Gagosian has galleries in London, Paris, Rome, Athens, and Hong Kong, among other cities, as well as five galleries in New York (three of which are on the Upper East Side). The 980 Madison Avenue location, the contemporary art empire's headquarters, is a multifloor gallery that has shown works by big names like Warhol, Pollock, Miró, Calder, Twombly, and Hirst. Because Gagosian likes to dominate the real estate market the way he dominates the art market, he also has spaces at nearby 976 Madison Avenue, as well as at the newest uptown outpost (with a decidedly downtown feel)—a storefront space on Park Avenue and 75th Street. ✉ *980 Madison Ave., near 76th St., Upper East Side* 📞 *212/744–2313* ⊕ *www.gagosian.com* ✉ *Free* ⊘ *Closed Sun.; call ahead for hours Mon.* Ⓜ *6 to 77th St.*

Gracie Mansion. The official mayor's residence, Gracie Mansion was built in 1799 by shipping merchant Archibald Gracie, and enlarged in 1966. Nine mayors have lived here since it became the official residence in 1942, though Michael Bloomberg chose to stay in his own 79th Street town house during his three terms as mayor. He poured millions into renovations at Gracie Mansion without spending a single night there. In 2014, the polished and spruced-up mansion became home to Mayor Bill de Blasio and his family—and the renovations resumed. The "People's House"—with all its history and colorful rooms furnished over centuries and packed with American objets d'art—finally reopened its doors (and tours) to the people in late 2015. Visitors can see that the resident first family of New York City has been busy adding its personal touch to the mansion, swapping out much of the artwork to better reflect the city's diversity. The collection now includes a bill of sale for a slave, a portrait of Frederick Douglass, and Native American artifacts. Tours are offered Tuesdays and reservations must be made online; plan at least two weeks in advance, if possible. ⊠ *Carl Schurz Park, East End Ave., at 88th St., Upper East Side* ☎ *212/676–3060* ⊕ *www1.nyc.gov/gracie* ⊠ *Free* ⊙ *Closed Wed.–Mon.* Ⓜ *4, 5, 6, Q to 86th St.*

The Jewish Museum. In a Gothic-style 1908 mansion, the Jewish Museum draws on a large collection of art and ceremonial objects to explore Jewish identity and culture spanning more than 4,000 years. The two-floor permanent exhibition "Culture and Continuity: The Jewish Journey" displays nearly 800 objects complemented by interactive media. The wide-ranging collection includes a 3rd-century Roman burial plaque, 20th-century sculpture by Elie Nadelman, and contemporary art from artists such as Marc Chagall and Man Ray. Changing exhibitions are well curated and lively. Don't leave without checking out the museum's café, Russ & Daughters, an outpost of the more than a century-old Jewish appetizing shop and Lower East Side institution. ⊠ *1109 5th Ave., at 92nd St., Upper East Side* ☎ *212/423–3200* ⊕ *www.thejewishmuseum.org* ⊠ *$15 (free Sat., pay-what-you-wish Thurs. 5–8)* ⊙ *Closed Wed.* Ⓜ *6 to 96th St.*

The Met Breuer. A great addition to the Metropolitan Museum of Art's already stunning collection, the Met Breuer offers art lovers four floors of rotating exhibits focusing on modern and contemporary art from the 20th and 21st centuries. The former site of the Whitney Museum (now in the Meatpacking District), the Brutalist-style building was designed by Marcel Breuer (pronounced BROY-er) and also offers performances, art commissions, and educational programs. A ticket to the Met Breuer also includes admission to the Met a few blocks away on 5th Avenue and the Cloisters farther uptown. ⊠ *945 Madison Ave., at 75th St., Upper East Side* ☎ *212/731–1675* ⊕ *www.metmuseum.org/visit/met-breuer* ⊠ *$25 for 3-day ticket (includes the Metropolitan Museum and Met Cloisters); $25 suggested donation for New York State residents (full donation includes 3-day ticket to Metropolitan Museum and Met Cloisters)* ⊙ *Closed Mon.* Ⓜ *6 to 77th St.*

10

The Metropolitan Museum of Art. *See feature, this chapter.* ⊠ *1000 5th Ave. at 82nd St.* Ⓜ *4, 5, 6 to 86th St.* ☎ *212/535–7710* ⊕ *www.metmuseum. org* ⊠ *$25 for 3-day ticket (includes Met Breuer and Met Cloisters);*

$25 suggested donation for New York state residents (full donation includes 3-day ticket to Met Breuer and Met Cloisters).

Museum of the City of New York. The city's present, past, and future are explored through quirky, engaging exhibits on subjects such as architecture, fashion, history, and politics in a Colonial Revival building designed for the museum in the 1930s. The ongoing exhibition "New York At Its Core" explores the sweep and diverse facets of the city's 400-year history through artifacts, photography, archival film, and interactive digital experiences. Don't miss *Timescapes*, a 25-minute media projection that innovatively illustrates New York's physical expansion and population changes, or "Activist New York," an ongoing exploration of the city's history of social activism. You can also find New York–centric lectures, films, and walking tours here. In 2015, the museum completed a renovation that included an updated lobby and terrace, a redesigned gift shop, the addition of a state-of-the-art auditorium and a new café, and restored historical elements throughout the building. After touring the museum, cross the street and stroll through the Vanderbilt Gates to enter the Conservatory Garden, one of Central Park's hidden gems. ✉ *1220 5th Ave., at 103rd St., Upper East Side* 🕾 *212/534–1672* ⊕ *www.mcny.org* ✉ *$18 suggested donation* Ⓜ *6 to 103rd St.*

Neue Galerie New York. Early-20th-century German and Austrian art and design are the focus here, with works by artists Gustav Klimt, Wassily Kandinsky, Paul Klee, and Egon Schiele, as well as Josef Hoffmann and other designers from the Wiener Werkstätte, taking center stage. The Neue Galerie was founded by the late art dealer Serge Sabarsky and cosmetics heir and art collector Ronald S. Lauder. It's in a 1914 wood-and marble-floored mansion designed by Carrère and Hastings, which was once home to Mrs. Cornelius Vanderbilt III. An audio guide is included with admission. Children under 12 are not admitted, and teens 12–16 must be accompanied by an adult. **Café Sabarsky**, in an elegant, high-ceiling space on the first floor, is a destination in its own right for Viennese coffee, cakes, strudels, and Sacher tortes. ■ **TIP→ Admission is free 6–8 pm on the first Friday of the month.** ✉ *1048 5th Ave., at 86th St., Upper East Side* 🕾 *212/628–6200* ⊕ *www.neuegalerie.org* ✉ *$20* ⊙ *Closed Tues., Weds.* Ⓜ *4, 5, 6 to 86th St.*

Fodor's Choice ★ **Solomon R. Guggenheim Museum.** Frank Lloyd Wright's landmark curving, nautilus-like museum building is renowned as much for its famous architecture as for its superlative collection of art and well-curated shows. Opened in 1959, shortly after Wright's death, the Guggenheim is acclaimed as one of the greatest buildings of the 20th century. Inside, under a 96-foot-high glass dome, a ramp spirals down, past the artworks of the current exhibits (the ramp is just over a quarter-mile long). The museum has strong holdings of Wassily Kandinsky, Paul Klee, Marc Chagall, Pablo Picasso, and Robert Mapplethorpe.

Wright's design was criticized by some who believed that the distinctive building detracted from the art within, but the interior nautilus design allows artworks to be viewed from several different angles and distances. Be sure to notice not only what's in front of you but also what's across the spiral. On permanent display, the museum's Thannhauser Collection is made up primarily of works by French impressionists and postimpressionists van Gogh, Toulouse-Lautrec, Cézanne, Renoir, and Manet. Perhaps more than any other 20th-century painter, Wassily Kandinsky, one of the first "pure" abstract artists, has been closely linked to the museum's history: beginning with the acquisition of his masterpiece *Composition 8* (1923) in 1930, the collection has grown to encompass more than 150 works by the artist. The museum is pay-what-you-wish on Saturday evening from 5:45 to 7:45. Lines can be long, so arrive early. The last tickets are handed out at 7:15.

Even if you aren't planning to eat, be sure to stop at the museum's modern American restaurant, the Wright (at 88th Street), for its stunning design by Andre Kikoski. If planning to eat, note that hours are limited and prices high. ■TIP→ Escape the crowded lobby by taking the elevator to the top and working your way down the spiral. ⊠ *1071 5th Ave., between 88th and 89th Sts., Upper East Side* ☎ *212/423–3500* ⊕ *www.guggenheim.org* ⊠ *$25* ⊙ *Closed Thurs.* Ⓜ *4, 5, 6 to 86th St.*

WORTH NOTING

Acquavella Galleries. The 19th- and 20th-century museum-quality art inside this five-story, marble-floored French neoclassical mansion tends to be big name, from impressionists through pop artists, including Picasso, Lucian Freud, Jean-Michel Basquiat, James Rosenquist, and Wayne Thiebaud. ⊠ *18 E. 79th St., between 5th and Madison Aves., Upper East Side* ☎ *212/734–6300* ⊕ *www.acquavellagalleries.com* ⊠ *Free* ⊙ *Closed Sun.; Sat. by appointment* Ⓜ *6 to 77th St.*

FAMILY **Carl Schurz Park.** Facing the East River, this park, named for a German immigrant who was a prominent newspaper editor in the 19th century, is so tranquil you'd never guess you're directly above the FDR Drive. Walk along the promenade, where you can take in views of the river and the Roosevelt Island Lighthouse across the way. To the north are Randalls and Wards Islands and the RFK Bridge (aka the Triborough Bridge)—as well as the more immediate sight of locals pushing strollers, riding bikes, or walking their dogs. If you use the 86th Street entrance, you'll find yourself near the grounds of a Federal-style wood-frame house that belies the grandeur of its name: Gracie Mansion. ⊠ *From 84th to 90th St., between East End Ave. and the East River, Upper East Side* ☎ *212/459–4455* ⊕ *www.carlschurzparknyc.org* Ⓜ *4, 5, 6, Q to 86th St.*

Castelli Gallery. One of the most influential dealers of the 20th century, Leo Castelli helped foster the careers of many important artists, including one of his first discoveries, Jasper Johns. Castelli died in 1999, but the gallery continues to show works by Roy Lichtenstein, Andy Warhol, Ed Ruscha, Frank Stella, Robert Morris, and other heavy hitters. ⊠ *18 E. 77th St., between 5th and Madison Aves., Upper East Side* ☎ *212/249–4470* ⊕ *www.castelligallery.com* ⊠ *Free* ⊙ *Closed Sun., Mon.* Ⓜ *6 to 77th St.*

Jane Kahan Gallery. This welcoming gallery represents some lofty artists. In addition to tapestries by modern masters like Pablo Picasso, Joan Miró, and Alexander Calder—one of this gallery's specialties—works

Continued on page 161

THE METROPOLITAN MUSEUM OF ART

Mesmerizing carvings in the ancient Egyptian Temple of Dendur.

If the city held no other museum than the colossal Metropolitan Museum of Art, you could still occupy yourself for days roaming its labyrinthine corridors. Because the Metropolitan Museum has more than 2 million works of art representing 5,000 years of history, you're going to have to make tough choices. Looking at everything here could take a week.

Before you begin exploring the museum, check the museum's floor plan, available at all entrances, for location of the major wings and collections. Google Maps will help you find your way through the museum. The service tracks your location with a blue dot and guides you through exhibits, across floors, and to bathrooms and exits. It can even help you avoid the gift shop if you're visiting with kids!

The posted adult admission, though only a suggestion, is one that's strongly encouraged. Whatever you choose to pay, admission includes all special exhibits and same-day entrance to the Cloisters (see Chapter 12). The Met's audio guide costs an additional $7, and if you intend to stay more than an hour or so, it's worth it. The generally perceptive commentary covers museum highlights and directors' picks, with separate commentary tracks directed at kids.

If you want to avoid the crowds, visit weekday mornings. Also good are Friday and Saturday evenings, when live classical music plays from the Great Hall balcony. If the Great Hall (the main entrance) is mobbed, avoid the chaos by heading to the street-level entrance to the left of the main stairs, near 81st Street. Ticket lines and coat checks are much less ferocious here.

What to see? Check out the museum highlights on the following pages.

MUSEUM HIGHLIGHTS

Egyptian Art

A major star is the **Temple of Dendur** (circa 15 BC), in a huge atrium to itself and with a moatlike pool of water to represent its original location near the Nile. The temple was commissioned by the Roman emperor Augustus to honor the goddess Isis and the sons of a Nubian chieftain. Look for the scratched-in graffiti from 19th-century Western explorers on the inside. Egypt gave the temple as a gift to the U.S. in 1965; it would have been submerged after the construction of the Aswan High Dam.

The Egyptian collection as a whole covers 4,000 years of history, with papyrus pages from the Egyptian Book of the Dead, stone sarcophagi inscribed with hieroglyphics, and tombs. The galleries should be walked through counterclockwise from the Ancient Kingdom (2650–2150 BC), to the period under Roman rule (30 BC–400 AD). In the latter, keep an eye out for the enormous, bulbous **Sarcophagus of Horkhebil**, sculpted from basalt.

Greek and Roman Art

Today's tabloids have nothing on ancient Greece and Rome. They had it all—sex, cults, drugs, unrelenting violence, and, of course, stunning art. The recently redone Greek and Roman galleries encompass 6,000 works of art that reveal aspects of everyday life in these influential cultures.

The urnlike terracotta kraters were used by the Greeks for mixing wine and water at parties and other events. Given that, it's not surprising that most depict slightly racy scenes. Some of the most impressive can be found in the gallery covering 5th century BC.

On the mezzanine of the Roman galleries, the Etruscan bronze chariot from 650 BC depicts scenes from the life of Achilles. Notice how the simplistic Etruscan style in combination with the Greek influence evolved into the naturalistic Roman statues below.

The frescoes from a bedroom in the Villa of P. Fannius Synistor preserved by the explosion of Mt. Vesuvius in 79 AD give us a glimpse into the stylistic achievement of perspective in Roman painting.

Temple of Dendur

ART TO TAKE HOME

You don't have to pay admission to get to the mammoth gift shop on the first floor. One of the better souvenirs here is also one of the more reasonable: the Met's own **illustrated guide** to 869 of the best items in its collection ($19.95).

Engelhard Court

An artifact from ancient Greece.

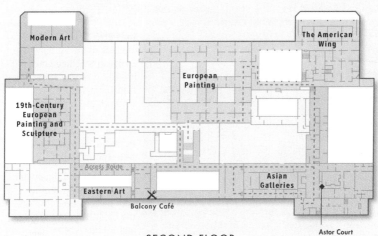

SECOND FLOOR

MEZZANINES

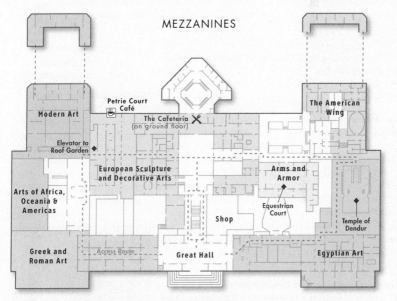

FIRST FLOOR

5th Avenue

The American Wing of the Metropolitan Museum of Art.

American Wing

After years of extensive renovations, the Met's revitalized **New American Wing Galleries for Paintings, Sculpture, and Decorative Arts** reopened in 2012 with 30,000 square feet of skylit space to showcase one of the best and largest collections of American art in the country.

There's much to see, from Colonial furniture to the works of the great masters, including John Singleton Copley, Gilbert Stuart, Thomas Cole, Frederic Edwin Church, Winslow Homer, and Thomas Eakins, among others. The highlight of the new installation is Emanuel Gottlieb Leutze's magnificent 1851 painting, *Washington Crossing the Delaware*. Hung in an immense gilded frame (recreated from an 1864 photograph of the painting), Leutze's iconic work is displayed just as it was at a fundraiser for Union soldiers in 1864—flanked by Frederic Church's *Heart of the Andes* and Albert Bierstadt's *Rocky Mountains*.

Also not to be missed are John Singer Sargent's *Madame X*, a once-scandalous portrait of a Parisian socialite; the recreation of the entrance hall of the 18th Century Van Rensselaer Manor House in Albany, New York; and the collection of portrait miniatures—detailed watercolors to be carried or gifted as tokens of love.

TIME TO EAT?
INSIDE THE MUSEUM

The **Petrie Court Café**, at the back of the 1st-floor European Sculpture Court, has waiter service. Prices range from $12 for a sandwich to $21 for organic chicken salad. Afternoon tea is served from 2:30 PM to 4:30 PM during the week. Dinner is served on weekends.

The **Great Hall Balcony Bar** is located on the second floor belcony overlooking the Great Hall. On Fridays and Saturdays, 4 PM TO 8:30 PM waiters serve appetizers and cocktails accompanied by live classical music.

The **cafeteria** on the ground floor has stations for pasta, main courses, antipasti, and sandwiches.

Looking for one of the best views in town? The **Roof Garden** (open May–Oct.) exhibits contemporary sculpture, but most people take the elevator here to have a drink or snack while checking out Central Park and the skyline.

Tiffany

Arms and Armor

The **Equestrian Court**, where the knights are mounted on armored models of horses, is one of the most dramatic rooms in the museum. For a bird's-eye view, check it out again from the balconies in the Musical Instruments collection on the second floor.

European Sculpture and Decorative Arts

Among the many sculptures in the sun-filled Petrie Court, *Ugolino and His Sons* still stands out for the despairing poses of its subjects. Ugolino, a nobleman whose family's tragic story is told in Dante's *Inferno*, was punished for treason by being left to starve to death with his grandsons and sons in a locked tower. (It's not clear if putting such a sculpture so near the Petrie Court's café is some curator's idea of a joke or not.) By the way, the redbrick and granite wall on the court's north side is the museum's original entrance.

The newly renovated Wrightsman Galleries for French Decorative Arts on the first floor displays the opulence that caused Louis the XVI to lose his head. The blindingly golden Boiserie from the Hotel de Cabris, a remnant of French 18th century Neo-classical interiors, represents the finest collection of French decorative arts in the country.

Anna Wintour Costume Center

In May 2014, after a two-year renovation, the Met's Costume Institute reopened with a newly designed 4,200-square-foot main gallery, an updated costume conservation laboratory, expanded study and storage facilities, and a new name—the Anna Wintour Costume Center. Named for the legendary *Vogue* editor-in-chief and Met Trustee (responsible for the annual Met Gala), and housing one of the most comprehensive costume collections in the world, the new Costume Center (northeast end of the museum on the ground floor) is sure to be a huge draw for fashion lovers.

European Paintings

On the second floor, the 13th- to 18th-century paintings are grouped at the top of the Great Hall's stairs.

Recently, the Met spent about $45 million to buy Duccio di Buoninsegna's *Madonna and Child,* painted circa 1300. The last remaining Duccio in private hands, this painting, the size of a piece of typewriter paper, is unimpressive at first glance. The work, though rigid, represents a revolution in Byzantine art. The humanity reflected in the baby Jesus grabbing his mother's veil changed European painting.

IN FOCUS THE METROPOLITAN MUSEUM OF ART

10

Equestrian Court (1930)

Rembrandt's masterful *Aristotle with a Bust of Homer* (1653) shows a philosopher contemplating worldly gains versus values through its play of light and use of symbols. Around Aristotle is a gold medal of Alexander the Great, one of the philosopher's students.

In the room dedicated to **Monet** you can get to all his greatest hits—poplar trees, haystacks, water lilies, and the Rouen Cathedral. The muted tones of Pissaro are followed by a room full of bright and garish colors announcing works by Gauguin, Matisse, and Van Gogh.

Vincent van Gogh,
Wheatfield with Cypresses

Islamic Galleries

In late 2011, after an eight-year renovation, the Met reopened its Islamic galleries, a suite of 15 galleries housing one of the world's premier collections of Islamic art. Now known as the "Art of the Arab Lands, Turkey, Iran, Central Asia, and Later South Asia," the collection comprises more than 12,000 works of art and traces the course of Islamic Civilization over a span of 13 centuries. Highlights include an 11-foot-high 14th century mihrab, or prayer niche, decorated with glazed ceramic tiles; the recently restored Emperor's Carpet—a 16th century Persian carpet that was presented to the Hapsburg Emperor Leopold I by Peter the Great of Russia; the Damascus Room—a Syrian Ottoman reception room decorated with poetic verses; and glass, ceramics, and metalwork from Egypt, Syria, Iraq, and Iran.

Asian Galleries

The serene **Astor Court**, which has its own skylight and pond of real-life koi (goldfish), is a model of a scholar's court garden in Soochow, China.

The Han dynasty (206 BC–220 AD) introduced the practice of sending the dead on to the afterlife with small objects to help them there. Keep an eye out for these **small clay figures**, which include farm animals (enclosed in barnyards) and dancing entertainers.

On display in a glass case in the center of an early-Chinese gallery is a complete set of 14 **bronze altar vessels**. Dating 1100 BC—800 AD, these green and slightly crusty pieces were used for worshipping ancestors. The Met displays some of its finest **Asian stoneware and porcelain** along the balcony overlooking the Great Hall.

The teak dome and minature balconies from a **Jain meeting hall** in western India were carved in the 16th century. Just about the entire surface is covered with musicians, animals, gods, and servants.

WHAT'S NEW

Under construction for two years, the front steps of the Met—one of Manhattan's most iconic meeting places—reopens in late 2014 as a European-style plaza with additional public seating, a modernized fountain, landscaping, and improved museum access. Food and ticket kiosks may be added in early 2015.

Standing eight-armed
Avalokiteshvara

by late-19th- and early-20th-century modern artists like Fernand Léger and Marc Chagall are showcased. There's also a location in the neighborhood at 330 East 59th Street. ⊠ *922 Madison Ave., 2nd fl., between 73rd and 74th Sts., Upper East Side* ☏ *212/744–1490* ⊕ *www. janekahan.com* ⊡ *Free* ⊘ *Closed Sun., Mon.; also Sat. July–Aug.* Ⓜ *6 to 77th St.*

Mitchell-Innes & Nash. This sleek spot represents the estates of Roy Lichtenstein, Alberto Burri, and Nancy Graves as well as other impressionist, modern, and contemporary masters. ⊠ *1018 Madison Ave., between 78th and 79th Sts., Upper East Side* ☏ *212/744–7400* ⊕ *www.miandn. com* ⊡ *Free* ⊘ *Closed Sun.; Mon. by appointment only* Ⓜ *6 to 77th St.*

FAMILY **Mount Vernon Hotel Museum and Garden.** Built in 1799, this former carriage house became a day hotel (a sort of country club) in 1826. Now restored and owned by the Colonial Dames of America, it provides a glimpse of the days when the city ended at 14th Street and this area was a country escape for New Yorkers. A 45-minute tour (the only way to see the museum and garden) passes through the eight rooms that display furniture and artifacts of the Federal and Empire periods. Many rooms have real artifacts such as clothes, hats, and fans that children can handle. There is a lovely adjoining garden, designed in an 18th-century style. Tours are on demand and can be geared to specific interests. Arrive at least a half hour before closing time to allow for tour. ■TIP→ Entrance is free for children under 12. ⊠ *421 E. 61st St., between York and 1st Aves., Upper East Side* ☏ *212/838–6878* ⊕ *www. mvhm.org* ⊡ *$8* ⊘ *Closed Mon.* Ⓜ *4, 5, 6 to 59th St.; N, R, W to Lexington Ave./59th St.; F, Q to Lexington Ave./63rd St.*

Museum of American Illustration. Founded in 1901, the museum of the Society of Illustrators presents its annual "Oscars," a juried international competition, from January to March. The best in children's book illustration is showcased October through December. In between are eclectic exhibitions on science fiction, fashion, politics, and history illustrations. The Society of Illustrators has also incorporated the holdings of the Museum of Comic and Cartoon Art (MoCCA) into its collections. MoCCA's collection is in its own gallery on the second floor, and there are workshops, programs, and a comic festival (MoCCA Fest). ■TIP→ Admission is free on Tuesday 5–8. ⊠ *128 E. 63rd St., between Lexington and Park Aves., Upper East Side* ☏ *212/838–2560* ⊕ *www. societyillustrators.org* ⊡ *$15* ⊘ *Closed Sun., Mon.* Ⓜ *F, Q to Lexington Ave./63rd St.; 4, 5, 6 to 59th St.; N, R, W to Lexington Ave./59th St.*

FAMILY **Roosevelt Island.** The 2-mile-long East River slice of land that parallels Manhattan from 48th to 85th Streets is now a quasi-suburb of more than 14,000 people, and the vestiges of its infamous asylums, hospitals, and prisons make this an offbeat trip for the historically curious. At its southern tip are the eerie ruins of a **Smallpox Hospital,** built in 1854 in a Gothic Revival style by the prominent architect James Renwick Jr. (Among many other works, Renwick also designed St. Patrick's Cathedral.) Neighboring the hospital ruins is **Four Freedoms Park,** a memorial to Franklin Delano Roosevelt designed by famed architect Louis I. Kahn. The monument to President Roosevelt is essentially a large,

10

open granite box with a giant bust of FDR, and a wall inscribed with the words of the wartime Four Freedoms speech. Visitors can stroll the stone walkways and the symmetrical tree-lined pebble paths that run along the manicured lawn and enjoy unique views of the United Nations and East River. Individual or group guided walking tours ($20 per person) of FDR Four Freedoms Park are available if scheduled in advance; email or call to reserve. At the island's north tip is a small park with a lighthouse built in 1872 by island convicts. The first phase of Cornell University's sustainable Tech campus opened on the island in 2017. When the project is completed, the campus will include 2 million square feet of state-of-the-art facilities. You can get to the island by subway—but why would you, when you can take the five-minute ride on the **Roosevelt Island Tramway,** the only commuter cable car in North America, which lifts you 250 feet in the air for impressive views of Queens and Manhattan? A visitor center, made from an old trolley kiosk, stands to your left as you exit the tram. Free red buses service the island. ⊠ *Tramway entrance, 2nd Ave., between 59th and 60th Sts., Upper East Side* ☎ *212/688–4836 for visitor center, 212/204–8831 Four Freedoms Park tours* ⊕ *www.fdrfourfreedomspark.org* ☞ *$2.75 (one-way subway or tram fare)* ⊗ *Four Freedoms Park closed Tues.* ☞ *Tram leaves approximately every 15 mins* Ⓜ *F to Roosevelt Island.*

Van Doren Waxter. In 2017, this gallery in a historic town house on a tree-lined street merged with its sister gallery on the Lower East Side, 11R (formerly Eleven Rivington). The combined galleries feature contemporary artists with a focus on the historical connection of their art to works by established artists. ⊠ *23 E. 73rd St., between Madison and 5th Aves., Upper East Side* ☎ *212/445–0444* ⊕ *www.vandorenwaxter.com* ☞ *Free* ⊗ *Closed Sun., Mon.* Ⓜ *6 to 77th St.*

THE UPPER WEST SIDE

Getting Oriented

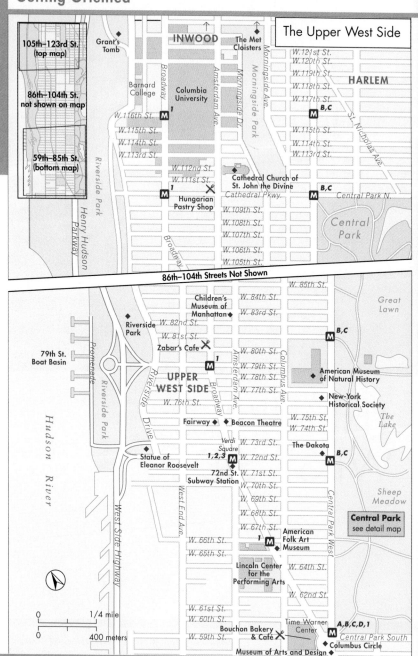

The Upper West Side

105th–123rd St. (top map)

86th–104th St. not shown on map

59th–85th St. (bottom map)

INWOOD

The Met Cloisters

Grant's Tomb

HARLEM

W. 121st St.
W. 120th St.
W. 119th St.
W. 118th St.
W. 117th St.
W. 116th St.
W. 115th St.
W. 114th St.
W. 113th St.

Barnard College

Columbia University

Morningside Dr.

Amsterdam Ave.

Morningside Park

St. Nicholas Ave.

Broadway

Riverside Park

Henry Hudson Parkway

W. 112th St.
W. 111th St.

Cathedral Church of St. John the Divine

Cathedral Pkwy.

Central Park N.

Hungarian Pastry Shop

W. 109th St.
W. 108th St.
W. 107th St.
W. 106th St.
W. 105th St.

Central Park

86th–104th Streets Not Shown

Children's Museum of Manhattan

W. 85th St.
W. 84th St.
W. 83rd St.
W. 82nd St.
W. 81st St.
W. 80th St.
W. 79th St.
W. 78th St.
W. 77th St.

Great Lawn

Riverside Park

79th St. Boat Basin

Zabar's Cafe

Amsterdam Ave.

Columbus Ave.

B,C

American Museum of Natural History

New-York Historical Society

UPPER WEST SIDE

Broadway

W. 76th St.

Fairway

Beacon Theatre

W. 75th St.
W. 74th St.

The Lake

Promenade

Riverside Drive

Hudson River

Verdi Square

W. 73rd St.
W. 72nd St.
W. 71st St.
W. 70th St.
W. 69th St.
W. 68th St.
W. 67th St.
W. 66th St.
W. 65th St.
W. 64th St.
W. 62nd St.
W. 61st St.
W. 60th St.
W. 59th St.

1,2,3

The Dakota

B,C

Statue of Eleanor Roosevelt

72nd St. Subway Station

Sheep Meadow

Central Park see detail map

West End Ave.

West Side Highway

American Folk Art Museum

Central Park West

Lincoln Center for the Performing Arts

Time Warner Center

A,B,C,D,1

Central Park South

Bouchon Bakery & Café

Columbus Circle

Museum of Arts and Design

0   1/4 mile
0   400 meters

MAKING THE MOST OF YOUR TIME

Broadway is one of the most walkable and interesting thoroughfares on the Upper West Side because of its broad sidewalks and lively mix of retail stores, restaurants, and apartment buildings. If you head north from the Lincoln Center area (around 65th Street) to about 81st Street (about 1 mile), you'll get a feel for the neighborhood's local color, particularly above 72nd Street. Up here you'll encounter residents of every conceivable age and ethnicity either shambling or sprinting; street vendors hawking used and newish books; and such beloved landmarks as the 72nd Street subway station, the Beacon Theatre, the grocery mecca Fairway (the cause of perhaps the most perpetually congested block), and Zabar's (a market and eatery that will woo all five senses—and may drain your wallet). The Upper West Side's other two main avenues—Columbus and Amsterdam—are more residential but also have myriad restaurants and shops.

If you're intrigued by the city's only Ivy League school, hop the 1 train to 116th Street and emerge smack-dab in front of illustrious Columbia University, founded in (lower) Manhattan in 1754 as King's College. Pass through its gates and up the walk to view its open central campus, surrounded by a cluster of buildings so elegant you'll understand why it's long been an iconic NYC destination.

GETTING HERE

The A, B, C, D, and 1 subway lines take you to Columbus Circle. From there, the B and C lines make local stops along Central Park. Along Broadway, the 1 train runs local, while the express 2 and 3 trains stop only at 72nd and 96th Streets.

TOP EXPERIENCES

Strolling through Riverside Park past the boat basin

Exploring Central Park

Standing below the gigantic blue whale at the American Museum of Natural History

Taking in the views, gardens, and medieval masterpieces at the Cloisters Museum and Gardens

COFFEE AND QUICK BITES

Bouchon Bakery & Café. In Columbus Circle's busy Time Warner shopping center, this take-out bakery outpost of the sit-down restaurant serves excellent sandwiches, quiches, pastries, and coffee. There are a few seats, too. ✉ *10 Columbus Circle, 3rd fl., Upper West Side* ☎ *212/823–9366* ⊕ *www.thomaskeller.com* Ⓜ *1, A, B, C, D to 59th St.–Columbus Circle.*

Hungarian Pastry Shop. Linger over a danish and bottomless cups of coffee with the Columbia kids and professors at this old-world (cash only) café and bakery. ✉ *1030 Amsterdam Ave., at 111th St., Upper West Side* ☎ *212/866–4230* Ⓜ *1 to Cathedral Pkwy.–110th St.*

Zabar's Cafe. Fast-track the Zabar's experience with a gourmet coffee and sandwich, pickled lox, or slice of cheesecake. ✉ *2245 Broadway, at 80th St., Upper West Side* ☎ *212/787–2000* ⊕ *www.zabars.com* Ⓜ *1 to 79th St.*

Sightseeing
★ ★ ★
Nightlife
★ ★
Dining
★ ★
Lodging
★
Shopping
★ ★ ★ ★

Updated by
Kelsy Chauvin

The Upper West Side is one of Manhattan's quieter, more residential neighborhoods, with wide sidewalks and a (relatively) slower pace. The Cloisters, in Inwood, houses part of the Metropolitan Museum's medieval collection.

The tree-lined side streets of the Upper West Side are lovely, with high stoops leading up to stately brownstones. Central Park, of course, is one of the main attractions here no matter the season or time of day; though locals know that Riverside Park, along the Hudson River, can be even more appealing thanks to smaller crowds.

The Upper West Side also has its share of cultural institutions, from the 16-acre **Lincoln Center** complex, to the impressive and quirky collection at the **New-York Historical Society,** to Columbus Circle's **Museum of Arts and Design** and the much-loved, soon-to-be-expanded **American Museum of Natural History.**

Most people think the area north of 106th Street and south of 125th Street on the West Side is just an extension of the Upper West Side. Technically it's Morningside Heights, largely dominated by Columbia University along with a cluster of academic, religious, and medical institutions, including Barnard College and the **Cathedral Church of St. John the Divine.**

TOP ATTRACTIONS

American Museum of Natural History. *See feature, this chapter.* ⊠ *Central Park W. at W. 79th St.* Ⓜ *B, C to 81st St./Museum of Natural History* ☎ *212/769–5100* ⊕ *www.amnh.org* ✉ *$22 suggested donation, includes admission to Rose Center for Earth and Space; $27 includes an IMAX or space show.*

Cathedral Church of St. John the Divine. The largest Gothic-style cathedral in the world, even with its towers and transepts still unfinished, this divine behemoth comfortably asserts its bulk in the country's most vertical city. As such, the cathedral has long been a global landmark, and in 2017 it was at last designated a landmark by New York City. The seat of the Episcopal diocese in New York, it acts as a sanctuary for all, giving special services that include a celebration of New York's gay and lesbian community as well as the annual Blessing of the Bikes

11

AMNH on Film

Does the inside of AMNH look familiar? It should. The museum is a popular location for movies filming in New York. In *Spider-Man 2* (2004), Peter Parker (Tobey Maguire) has yet another bad day wrestling with his secret identity while in the Rose Center. Larry (Ben Stiller) is chased through the halls by a T. rex and outsmarts a monkey in the Hall of African Mammals while working as a night security guard in *Night at the Museum* (2006). AMNH plays a role in *Night at the Museum: Battle of the Smithsonian* (2009) and *Night at the Museum: Secret of the Tomb* (2014), too. In the coming-of-age film *The Squid & the Whale* (2005), Walt Berkman (Jesse Eisenberg) comes to a revelation that he is the squid and his father is the whale in front of the Hall of Ocean Life's famous diorama. And then there's *The Devil Wears Prada* (2006), where Andrea (Anne Hathaway) wins over Miranda (Meryl Streep) by remembering the names of high-society guests while attending a benefit here.

(mid-spring), when cyclists of all faiths bring their wheels for a holy-water benediction. Built in two long spurts starting in 1892, the cathedral remains only two-thirds complete. What began as a Romanesque Byzantine–style structure under the original architects, George Heins and Christopher Grant Lafarge, shifted upon Heins's death in 1911 to French Gothic under the direction of Gothic Revival purist Ralph Adams Cram. You can spot the juxtaposition of the two medieval styles by comparing the finished Gothic arches, which are pointed, with the still-uncovered arches, which are rounded in the Byzantine style.

To get the full effect of the cathedral's size, approach it from Broadway along 112th Street (all the while doing your best to avoid the sight of the two unholy 15-story rental towers cozying up to—and obscuring—the 113th Street side of the cathedral). Above the 3-ton central bronze doors is the intricately carved **Portal of Paradise,** which depicts St. John witnessing the Transfiguration of Jesus, and 32 biblical characters. Step inside to the cavernous nave: more than 600 feet long, it holds some 5,000 worshippers, and the 162-foot-tall dome crossing could comfortably contain the Statue of Liberty (minus its pedestal). The **Great Rose Window** is the largest stained-glass window in the United States; it's made from more than 10,000 pieces of colored glass.

At the end of the nave, surrounding the altar, are seven chapels expressing the cathedral's interfaith tradition and international mission—with menorahs, Shinto vases, and dedications to various ethnic groups. The **Saint Saviour Chapel** contains a three-panel bronze altar in white gold leaf with religious scenes by artist Keith Haring (his last work before he died in 1990). Outside in the cathedral's south grounds is the eye-catching **Peace Fountain.** It depicts the struggle of good and evil in the form of the archangel Michael decapitating Satan, whose head hangs from one side. Encircling it are whimsical animals cast in bronze from pieces sculpted by children.

On the first Sunday of October, in honor of St. Francis of Assisi, the patron saint of animals, the church holds its usual Sunday service with a twist: the service is attended by men, women, children, dogs, cats, rabbits, hamsters, and the occasional horse, sheep, or ant farm. In past years upward of 3,500 New Yorkers have shown up to have their pets blessed. A procession is led by such guest animals as elephants, camels, llamas, and golden eagles. Sunday services are at 8, 9, 11, and 4. Tours including a Highlights Tour and a Vertical Tour are offered throughout the week; check the website for prices and to reserve. ✉ *1047 Amsterdam Ave., at 112th St., Upper West Side* ☎ *212/316–7540, 866/811–4111 for tour reservations* ⊕ *www.stjohndivine.org* 🎫 *$10 suggested donation; tours $12–$20* Ⓜ *1 to Cathedral Pkwy.–110th St.*

Lincoln Center for the Performing Arts. *See the listing in Chapter 19, Performing Arts.*

Fodor'sChoice **New-York Historical Society.** Manhattan's oldest (and perhaps most under-
★ the-radar) museum, founded in 1804, boasts one of the city's finest research libraries in addition to a contemporary glass facade, sleek interactive technology, a children's museum, a café, and inventive exhibitions that showcase the museum's eclectic collections and unique voice. While the permanent collection of more than 6 million pieces of art, literature, and memorabilia sheds light on America's history, art, and architecture, the special exhibitions showcase the museum's fresh—and often surprising—insight on all things New York. The transformed Henry Luce III Center for the Study of American Culture includes 100 dazzling Tiffany lamps on display; historic treasures that tell the American story from the permanent collection in a novel way; and the new Center for the Study of Women's History, with permanent and rotating exhibitions that examine and celebrate the untold stories of women who have impacted and continue to shape the American experience. The **DiMenna Children's History Museum** on the lower level invites children to become "history detectives" and explore New York's past through interactive displays, hands-on activities, and the stories of iconic New York children through the centuries. The Historical Viewfinder allows kids to see how certain New York sites have changed over time. Unlike most other children's museums, this one is geared to mature elementary and middle schoolers, not toddlers. Storico, the light-filled restaurant on the first floor (with a separate entrance), serves upscale Italian food at lunch and dinner and is open for weekend brunch; Parliament Coffee & Espresso Bar sells beverages, pastries, and light lunch fare. ✉ *170 Central Park W, at 77th St., Upper West Side* ☎ *212/873–3400* ⊕ *www.nyhistory.org* 🎫 *$21 (pay-what-you-wish Fri. 6–8 pm)* ✷ *Closed Mon.* Ⓜ *B, C to 81st St.–Museum of Natural History.*

WORTH NOTING

FAMILY **American Folk Art Museum.** After a near-death, or rather, near- *debt* experience in 2011, the American Folk Art Museum left its home of 10 years on 53rd Street (since razed and taken over by MoMA) and returned to its humble rental near Lincoln Center. Here, the focus returns to its incredible collection of contemporary self-taught artists of the 20th and 21st centuries, including the single largest collection of reclusive Chicago artist Henry Darger, known for his painstakingly detailed collage paintings of fantasy worlds. The gift shop has an impressive collection of hand-crafted items. ✉ *2 Lincoln Sq., Columbus Ave. at 66th St., Upper West Side* ☎ *212/595–9533* ⊕ *www.folkartmuseum.org* ✉ *Free* Ⓜ *1 to 66th St.–Lincoln Center; A, B, C, D to 59th St.–Columbus Circle.*

FAMILY **Children's Museum of Manhattan.** In this five-story exploratorium, children ages one–seven are invited to paint their own masterpieces, float boats down a "stream" (weather permitting), rescue animals with Dora and Diego (in an exhibition created in collaboration with Nickelodeon), and walk through giant interactive human organs to explore the connections between food, sleep, and play. Special exhibits are thoughtfully put together and fun. Seasonal programs include a Grinch Holiday workshop. Art workshops, science programs, and storytelling sessions are held daily. ■ TIP➔ Admission is free 5–8 pm on the first Friday of every month. ✉ *212 W. 83rd St., between Broadway and Amsterdam Ave., Upper West Side* ☎ *212/721–1223* ⊕ *www.cmom.org* ✉ *$14* ⊗ *Closed Mon.* Ⓜ *1 to 79th St.*

Columbus Circle. This busy traffic circle at Central Park's southwest corner anchors the Upper West Side and makes a good starting place for exploring the neighborhood if you're coming from south of 59th Street. The central 700-ton granite monument (capped by a marble statue of Christopher Columbus) serves as a popular meeting place. To some people, Columbus Circle is synonymous with the **Time Warner Center** building (☎ *212/823–6300;* ⊕ *www.theshopsatcolumbuscircle.com*) and its several floors of shops and restaurants, including the underground food hall Turnstyle (on the subway-station mezzanine)—a good spot to pick up fixings for a Central Park picnic. It's also home to the Rose Hall performing arts complex, part of Jazz at Lincoln Center. ✉ *Broadway at 58th St. to 60th St., Upper West Side* Ⓜ *1, A, B, C, D to 59 St.–Columbus Circle.*

The Dakota. One of the first residences built on the Upper West Side, the château-style Dakota (1884) remains an architectural fixture with its lovely gables, gaslights, copper turrets, and central courtyard. Celebrity residents have included Boris Karloff, Rudolf Nureyev, José Ferrer, Rosemary Clooney, Lauren Bacall, Leonard Bernstein, Gilda Radner, Yoko Ono, and Connie Chung, but none more famous than John Lennon, who in 1980 was shot and killed at the Dakota's gate by a deranged fan. Visitors are not welcome in the lobby and there are no tours of the building. Fortunately, the elaborate exterior is best admired from across the street. ✉ *1 W. 72nd St., at Central Park W, Upper West Side* Ⓜ *B, C to 72nd St.*

Grant's Tomb (*General Grant National Memorial*). Walk through upper Riverside Park and you're sure to notice this towering granite mausoleum (1897), the final resting place of Civil War general and two-term president Ulysses S. Grant and his wife, Julia Dent Grant. As the old joke goes, who's buried here? Nobody—they're *entombed* in a crypt beneath a domed rotunda, surrounded by photographs and Grant memorabilia. Once a more popular sight than the Statue of Liberty, this pillared Classical Revival edifice remains a moving tribute, regal and timeless. The words engraved on the tomb, "Let Us Have Peace,"

Continued on page 178

AMERICAN MUSEUM ^{of} NATURAL HISTORY

The largest natural history museum in the world is also one of the most impressive sights in New York. Four city blocks make up its 45 exhibition halls, which hold more than 30 million artifacts and wonders from the land, the sea, and outer space. With all those wonders, you won't be able to see everything on a single visit, but you can easily hit the highlights in half a day.

Theodore Roosevelt Memorial Hall

Before you begin, plan a route before setting out. Be sure to pick up a map when you pay your admission. The museum's four floors (and lower level) are mazelike.

Visitors can use the free AMNH Explorer app to navigate the museum. It tracks your location, has turn-by-turn directions, profiles of iconic museum objects, and tours, and guides you to bathrooms and exits. There are free companion apps to support special exhibits; check the website. The museum has devices you can borrow if you don't have an app-friendly phone.

Enter the museum at the below-street-level entrance connected to the 81st Street subway station for the shortest lines (look for the subway entrance to the left of the museum's steps). The entrance on Central Park West, where the vast steps lead up into the impressive, barrel-ceilinged Theodore Roosevelt Rotunda, is central and a good starting place for exploring.

The Rose Center for Earth and Space is attached to the museum. Enter from West 81st Street, where a path slopes down to the entrance, after which elevators and stairs descend to the ticket line on the lower level.

What to see? Check out the museum highlights on the following pages.

✉ Central Park West at W. 79th St., Upper West Side

Ⓜ Subway: B, C to 81st St.

☎ 212/769-5100

⊕ www.amnh.org

🎟 $22 suggested donation, includes admission to Rose Center for Earth and Space

🕙 Daily 10–5:45.

Left, Spectrum of Life Wall

MUSEUM HIGHLIGHTS

Left, Woolly Mammoth
Above, Tyrannosaurus rex

Dinosaurs and Mammals

An amazing assembly of dinosaur and mammal fossils covers the entire fourth floor. The organization can be hard to grasp at first, so head to the **Wallace Orientation Center,** where a short film explains how each of the Fossil Halls lead into each other. You'll want to spend at least an hour here—the highlights include a *T. rex,* an *Apatosaurus* (formerly called a *Brontosaurus*), and the *Buettneria,* which resembles a modern-day crocodile.

The specimens are not in chronological order; they're put together based on their shared characteristics. Key branching-off points—a watertight egg, a grasping hand—are highlighted in the center of rooms and surrounded by related fossil groups. Check out the touch screens here; they make a complex topic more comprehensible.

Reptiles and Amphibians

Head for the Reptiles and Amphibians Hall on the third floor to check out the Komodo Dragon lizards and a 23-foot-long python skeleton. The weirdest display is the enlarged model of the Suriname toad *Pipa pipa,* whose young hatch from the female's back. The Primates Hall carries brief but interesting comparisons between apes, monkeys, and humans. Also on the third floor is the upper gallery of the famed Akeley Hall of African Mammals.

SPECIAL SHOWS AND NEW EXHIBITS

Special exhibits, the IMAX theater, and the Space Show cost extra. The timed tickets are available in advance at the museum's Web site and are sold same day at the door. Between October and May, don't miss the warm, plant-filled Butterfly Conservatory, where blue morphos, monarchs, and other butterflies flit and feed. Ten minutes is probably enough time to enjoy it.

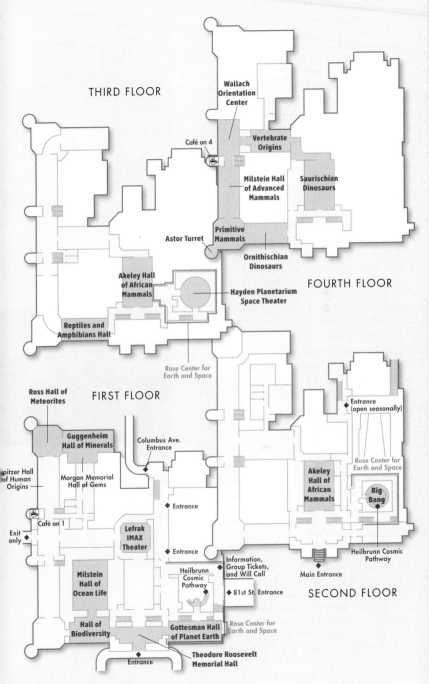

THIRD FLOOR

Wallach
Orientation
Center

Café on 4

Vertebrate
Origins

Milstein Hall
of Advanced
Mammals

Saurischian
Dinosaurs

Astor Turret

Primitive
Mammals

Ornithischian
Dinosaurs

FOURTH FLOOR

Akeley Hall
of African
Mammals

Hayden Planetarium
Space Theater

Reptiles and
Amphibians Hall

Rose Center for
Earth and Space

Ross Hall of
Meteorites

FIRST FLOOR

Entrance
(open seasonally)

Guggenheim
Hall of Minerals

Columbus Ave.
Entrance

Rose Center for
Earth and Space

pitzer Hall
of Human
Origins

Morgan Memorial
Hall of Gems

Akeley
Hall of
African
Mammals

Big
Bang

Café on 1

Entrance

Exit
only

Lefrak
IMAX
Theater

Entrance

Heilbrunn Cosmic
Pathway

Milstein
Hall of
Ocean Life

Heilbrunn
Cosmic
Pathway

Information,
Group Tickets,
and Will Call

Main Entrance

SECOND FLOOR

81st St. Entrance

Hall of
Biodiversity

Gottesman Hall
of Planet Earth

Rose Center for
Earth and Space

Entrance

Theodore Roosevelt
Memorial Hall

Theodore Roosevelt Memorial

After a $40 million renovation, the two-story Theodore Roosevelt Memorial re-opened in late 2012. It includes the restored Central Park West entrance, the Theodore Roosevelt Rotunda, and the Theodore Roosevelt Memorial Hall. Highlights are a new bronze statue of a seated Roosevelt, celebratory murals honoring the Conservation President, touch-screen timelines, and film footage. The Hall of North American Mammals was also restored as part of the memorial to Roosevelt; the hall originally opened in 1942 and many of its displays feature scenes from National Parks that were signed into being by the president.

Akeley Hall of African Mammals

Opened in 1936, this hall on the third floor, its 28 dramatically lighted dioramas is one of the most beloved parts of the museum.

The hall was the life's work of the explorer Carl Akeley, who came up with the idea for the hall, raised the funds for the expeditions, gathered specimens, and sketched landscape studies for what would become the stunning backgrounds. (The backgrounds themselves were painted by James Perry Wilson, whose works can be found throughout the museum.)

Akeley died a decade before the hall opened on an expedition in what's now Rwanda. His gravesite is near the landscape portrayed in the gorilla diorama, completed after his death as a memorial to him and his work.

Hall of Human Origins

The Spitzer Hall of Human Origins on the first floor is a comprehensive exhibit that allows visitors to draw their own conclusions about human evolution by presenting both the scientific methods and the material evidence that goes into evolutionary theory.

The exhibit then traces the evolution of our species over six million years of fossil record and spells out our ancestors' physical and intellectual advancements. Highlights include casts of our famous hairy relative "Lucy," who walked the plains of Africa over 1.8 million years ago.

Hall of Biodiversity

The small **Hall of Biodiversity** on the first floor includes a shady replica of a Central African Republic rain forest. Nearby, the **Spectrum of Life Wall** showcases 1,500 specimens and models, helping show just how weird life can get. The wall opens into the gaping Milstein Hall of Ocean Life, designed to give it an underwater glow and to show off the 94-foot model of a **blue whale** that's suspended from the ceiling.

ROSE CENTER FOR EARTH AND SPACE

The vast expanses of space and time involved in the creation of the universe can be hard to grasp even with the guiding hand of a museum, so you may want to visit the center when you're at your sharpest. The stunning glass building's centerpiece is the aluminum-clad Hayden Sphere, 87 feet in diameter. Enclosed within are the planetarium, called the Space Theater, and an audiovisual Big Bang presentation consisting of four minutes of narration by Maya Angelou, indistinct washes of color, and frightening bursts of sound. The rock-filled **Hall of Planet Earth** is particularly timely given the earthquakes and other natural disasters of recent years: one section uses a working earthquake monitor to help explain just what causes such seismic violence.

The Space Theater

At the Space Theater, the stage is the dome above you and the actors, heavenly projections. One of the world's largest virtual reality simulators, the theater uses surround sound and slight vibrations in the seats, to immerse you in scenes of planets, star clusters, and galaxies. *Dark Universe* puts Hollywood effects to shame as it explores the cosmos and just how little we know about it.

Tip: The Museum's Cosmic Discoveries app allows you to take the universe, and all its galaxies and planets, with you when you leave. The app offers images, findings, and bulletins all culled from the museum's archives and curated by the museum's astrophysicists. ⊕ *www.amnh.org/apps*

TIME TO EAT?

Inside the museum:
The main food court on the lower level serves sandwiches, pizza, hamburgers and global street food. The animal- and planet-shaped cookies are draws for kids; adults should check out the barbecue station.

The small **Café on 4**, in a turret next to the fossil halls, offers garden views and sells premade sandwiches and salads, soup, yogurt, and desserts.

The über-white **Café on 1**, tucked away beside the Hall of Human Origins, sells warm sandwiches, soup, salads, beer and wine at New York prices.

TIME TO PLAY

Nights at the museum aren't just for kids! Bust out your moonwalk and enjoy a few *cosmic*politans at the Rose Center's monthly One Step Beyond series, featuring live bands, DJs, VJs, cocktails, and dynamic visuals. Get tickets at amnh.org/plan-your-visit/one-step-beyond

TIME TO WATCH

Each October, the AMNH hosts the Margaret Mead Film & Video Festival, the longest-running premiere showcase for international documentaries in the United States. Tickets are made available one month prior to the festival, and online at www.amnh.org/mead

AMNH TALKS TO FODOR'S

Interview with Ellen V. Futter, President of the American Museum of Natural History, conducted by Michelle Delio.

If You Only Have an Hour: The American Museum of Natural History has the world's finest collection of dinosaur fossils, so a visit to the fourth-floor's Fossil Halls, where more than 600 specimens are on display, is a must. An extraordinarily high percentage of the specimens on view—85%—are real fossilized bones as opposed to casts. At most museums those percentages are reversed, so here visitors have the chance to see the real thing including T. rex, velociraptor, and triceratops.

What to Hit Next? The museum also is renowned for its habitat dioramas, which are considered among the finest examples in the world. Visits to the Akeley Hall of African Mammals, the Hall of North American Mammals, and the Sanford Hall of North American Birds provide an overview of the diorama arts—pioneered and advanced at the museum—while allowing visitors to come face-to-face with some glorious and beautiful animals depicted in their natural habitats—habitats which in many cases no longer exist in such pristine conditions.

If You're Looking to Be Starstruck: Even if you don't have time to take in a space show in the Hayden Planetarium, the Rose Center for Earth and Space has lots of fascinating exhibits describing the vast range of sizes in the cosmos; the 13-billion-year history of the universe; the nature of galaxies, stars, and planets; and the dynamic features of our own unique planet Earth—all enclosed in a facility with spectacular award-winning architecture.

Hidden gems

The museum consists of 45 exhibition halls in 25 interconnected buildings so there are gems around every corner. Some lesser-known treasures include:

Star of India: The 563-carat Star of India, the largest and most famous star sapphire in the world, is displayed in the Morgan Memorial Hall of Gems.

Rose Center for Earth and Space

ID PLEASE!

Once a year (usually in May or June—check website for details), the museum invites visitors to share rocks, teeth, shells, insects, feathers, and other curiosities with their scientists and anthropologists. Previous Identification Days have yielded rocks from the Jurassic Period, a fossilized walrus skull, and a 5,000-year-old stone spear point from Morocco. Lines can be long, but it's *so* interesting.

Black Smokers: These sulfide chimneys—collected during groundbreaking museum expeditions to the Pacific Ocean—are the only such specimens exhibited anywhere. Black smokers form around hot springs on the deep ocean floor and support a microbial community that does not live off sunlight but instead on the chemical energy of the Earth. Some of these microbes are considered the most ancient forms of life on Earth and may offer clues to the development of life here and the possibility of life elsewhere. See them in the Gottesman Hall of Planet Earth.

Spectrum of Life: The Hall of Biodiversity aims to showcase the glorious diversity of life on Earth resulting from 3.5 billion years of evolution. The impressive "Spectrum of Life" display is a 100-foot-long installation of more than 1,500 specimens and models—microorganisms and mammals, bacteria and beetles, fungi and fish. Use the computer workstations to learn more about the species depicted in each area.

Dodo: One of the museum's rarest treasures is the skeleton of a dodo bird, displayed along with other endangered or extinct species in the "Endangered Case" in the Hall of Biodiversity.

Small Dioramas: Tucked along the sides of the Hall of North American Mammals are two easy-to-miss corridors displaying a number of exquisitely rendered dioramas. In these jewel-box-like displays, some a mere 3 feet deep, you will see the smaller animals such as wolves galloping through a snowy night, a Canada lynx stalking a snowshoe hare, and a spotted skunk standing on its hands, preparing to spray a cacomistle, to name just a few of the evocative scenes.

Dinosaur Eggs: In 1993 museum scientists working in the Gobi Desert of Mongolia were the first to unearth fossilized embryos in dinosaur eggs, as well as the fossil of an adult oviraptor in a brooding posture over its nest. This discovery provided invaluable information about dinosaur gestation and revolutionized thinking about dinosaur behavior. Look for the display in the museum's Fossil Halls on the fourth floor.

Ross Terrace: In warmer months the Ross Terrace, with its fountains and cosmic theme, offers a wonderful outdoor spot for resting and reflecting, while providing a spectacular view of the Rose Center for Earth and Space.

Star of India

A diorama featuring a Komodo Dragon, the largest and most powerful lizard in the world.

MOST INTERESTING OBJECT?

What's most interesting about the American Museum of Natural History is not any single object on exhibit, but the sheer range and scope of what you can experience here. Think of it is a field guide to the natural world, the universe, and the cultures of humanity—all under one roof. The experience of visiting the museum is ultimately about awakening a sense of discovery, wonder, awe, and stewardship of this Earth we call home.

recall Grant's speech to the Republican convention upon his presidential nomination. Surrounding the memorial are the so-called "rolling benches," which are swoopy and covered with colorful mosaic tiles that bring to mind the works of architect Antoni Gaudí's Park Güell, in Barcelona. Made in the 1970s as a public art project, they are now as beloved as they are incongruous with the grand memorial they surround. ■TIP→ Stop by the visitor center (across the street from the tomb) for a 20-minute film about Grant. Note that the memorial itself is open every other hour due to staffing limitations. ⊠ *Riverside Dr. at W. 122nd St., Upper West Side* ☎ *212/666–1640* ⊕ *www.nps.gov/gegr* ⊠ *Free* ⊙ *Closed Mon., Tues.* Ⓜ *1 to 116th St.*

Museum of Arts and Design (*MAD*). Housed in a glass and glazed terra-cotta building on the rim of Columbus Circle, the Museum of Arts and Design celebrates joyful quirkiness and personal, sometimes even obsessive, artistic visions. The art is human scale here, much of it neatly housed in display cases rather than hanging on walls, with a strong focus on contemporary jewelry, glass, ceramic, fiber, wood, and mixed-media works. Be sure to exit through the gift shop with its incredible housewares, jewelry, and other artful pieces unseen anywhere else. Thursday evening is pay-what-you-wish at the museum. ⊠ *2 Columbus Circle, 59th St. at 8th Ave., Upper West Side* ☎ *212/299–7777* ⊕ *www.madmuseum.org* ⊠ *$16* ⊙ *Closed Mon.* Ⓜ *1, A, B, C, D to 59th St.–Columbus Circle.*

FAMILY **Riverside Park.** Surrounded by the culture and concrete of the Upper West Side, you might not realize that there is an expansive green space running along the Hudson River just blocks away. Riverside Park dishes out a dose of tranquility from 72nd to 156th Streets, as does the park's south extension, from about 55th to 66th Streets. The original sections of Riverside Park, designed by Frederick Law Olmsted and Calvert Vaux of Central Park fame and laid out between 1873 and 1888, have a waterfront bike and walking path. There are several access points to the park, including one at West 72nd Street and Riverside Drive (look for the statue of Eleanor Roosevelt), where you reach the waterfront path by an underpass beneath the West Side Highway. You can then head north along the Hudson River, past the 79th Street Boat Basin, where a flotilla of houseboats bobs in the water. Above it, a ramp leads to the Rotunda, home in summer to the Boat Basin Café, a dog-friendly open-air café that serves lunch and dinner in the warmer months (from about March through October). The 91st Street Garden, planted by community gardeners, explodes with flowers in most seasons and is a level up from the water: leave the riverside path near 92nd Street by taking another underpass and then heading up the path on the right. ⊠ *From 55th to 156th St., between Riverside Dr. and the Hudson River, Upper West Side* ⊕ *www.nyc-govparks.org/parks/riversidepark* Ⓜ *1, 2, 3 to 72nd St.*

CENTRAL PARK

More than 25 million people visit Central Park each year; on an average summer weekend day, a quarter of a million children and adults flood these precincts, frolicking in the 21 playgrounds and 26 ballfields, and resting on more than 9,000 benches that would span 7 miles if you lined them up. There are more than 55 monuments and sculptures in the park, and countless ways to have fun.

TOP ATTRACTIONS

FAMILY
Fodor'sChoice
★

Bethesda Fountain. Few New York views are more romantic than the one from the top of the magnificent stone staircase that leads down to the ornate, three-tiered Bethesda Fountain. The fountain, dedicated in 1873, was built to celebrate the opening of the Croton Aqueduct, which brought clean drinking water to New York City. The name Bethesda was taken from the biblical pool in Jerusalem that was supposedly given healing powers by an angel, which explains the statue *The Angel of the Waters* rising from the center. The four figures around the fountain's base symbolize Temperance, Purity, Health, and Peace. Beyond the terrace stretches the lake, filled with swans, gondolas, and amateur rowboat captains. At its western end is the Boathouse, home of an outdoor café for on-the-go snacks, and a pricier restaurant for more leisurely meals. ✉ *Mid-park at 72nd St. transverse, Central Park* Ⓜ *B, C to 72nd St.*

FAMILY
Fodor'sChoice
★

Central Park. Central Park's creators had a simple goal: to design a place where city dwellers could go to forget the city. Even though New York eventually grew far taller than the trees planted to hide it, this goal has never faltered. A combination escape hatch and exercise yard, Central Park is an urbanized Eden that gives residents and visitors alike a bite of the apple. Indeed, without the Central Park's 843 acres of meandering paths, tranquil lakes, ponds, and open meadows, New Yorkers (especially Manhattanites) might be a lot less sane.

The busy southern section of Central Park, from 59th to 72nd Street, is where most visitors get their first impression. But no matter how many people congregate around here, you can always find a spot to picnic, ponder, or just take in the foliage, especially on a sunny day. Playgrounds, lawns, jogging and biking paths, and striking buildings populate the midsection of the park, from 72nd Street to the Reservoir. You can soak up the sun, take in the public art, take pictures at Bethesda Fountain, visit the penguins at the Central Park Zoo, or join the runners huffing counterclockwise on the dirt track that surrounds the reservoir. North of the reservoir and up to 110th Street, Central Park is less crowded and feels more rugged. Not many people know about Lasker Rink & Pool in the northeast corner of the park, a swimming pool that becomes a skating rink in winter—and it's much less crowded than Wollman Rink in the southern part of the park. To find out about park events and a variety of year-round walking tours, visit the website of the Central Park Conservancy.

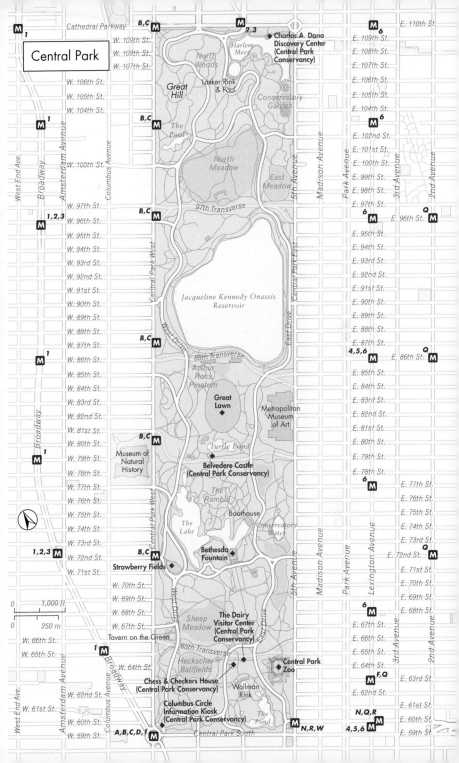

If you're taking the subway to the park's southernmost parts, then the stops at either Columbus Circle (southwest corner) or 5th Avenue/59th Street (southeast corner) are handy. If headed for points north, the B, D, A, and C subway lines travel along Central Park West (beware of local versus express stops), while the 4, 5, and 6 lines travel along Lexington Avenue, three blocks east of 5th Avenue and the park.

There are many paved pedestrian entrances into the park, from 5th Avenue, Central Park North (110th Street), Central Park West, and Central Park South (59th Street). Four roads, or transverses, cut through the park from east to west—66th, 79th, 86th, and 96th Streets. The East and West drives are both along the north–south axis; Center Drive enters the south edge of the park at 6th Avenue and connects with East Drive around 66th Street. Along the main loop, lampposts are marked with location codes that include a letter—always "E" (for east) or "W" (for west)—followed by numbers, the first two of which tell you the nearest cross street. For example, E7803 means you're near 78th Street; above 99, the initial "1" is omitted, so W0401 is near West 104th Street. Download the Central Park Conservancy's free app for a GPS-enabled map to help you navigate the park. The app also includes an audio guide, self-guided tours, and current events in the park. Central Park has one of the lowest crime rates in the city. Still, use common sense and stay within sight of other park visitors, and in general, avoid the park after dark.

If you haven't packed a picnic and you want a snack, you can usually find one of those rather tired-looking food carts selling pretzels and ice-cream sandwiches. But these days, there are often specialty-food carts around, too, mostly in the southern half of the park—your taste buds will thank you. Other reliable options include the café next to the Boathouse Restaurant (mid-park at 74th Street), or the park's branch of Le Pain Quotidien (mid-park at 69th Street). Both serve sandwiches, soup, pastries, and other satisfying on-the-go grub (and Le Pain also has free Wi-Fi). If you're looking for something a little more iconic, you can stop for brunch, lunch, or dinner at the Tavern on the Green.

As part of a park-wide restoration project named Plan for Play, all 21 playgrounds have undergone or will get an update through the 2010s. Most will see renovations to play structures, plus other improvements that will ensure each one's structural stability and ongoing maintenance for decades to come. ⊠ *Central Park* ☎ *212/794–6564 Dairy Visitor Center, 212/360–2726 for schedule of walking tours, 212/310–6600 Central Park Conservancy* ⊕ *www.centralparknyc.org* Ⓜ *A, B, C, D, 1 to Columbus Circle; N, R, W to 5th Ave.–59th St.*

FAMILY **Central Park Conservancy.** Five visitor centers—the Dairy (mid-park at 65th Street), Belvedere Castle (mid-park at 79th Street), the Chess & Checkers House (mid-park at 64th Street), the Charles A. Dana Discovery Center (at the top northeast corner of the park at 110th Street, on the shore of Harlem Meer), and the Columbus Circle Information Kiosk (southeast corner of the park at West 59th Street)—have directions, park maps, event calendars, and volunteers who can give you guidance. ⊠ *Dairy Visitor Center, 65th St. transverse, Central Park* ☎ *212/310–6600 Central Park Conservancy* ⊕ *www.centralparknyc.org.*

Many Beatles fans come to Strawberry Fields to pay their respects to John Lennon, who was murdered across the street at the Dakota apartments.

FAMILY **Central Park Zoo.** Even a leisurely visit to this small but delightful menagerie takes only about an hour (unless, of course, you fall under the spell of the zoo's adorable animals, be they the ever-friendly penguins, the spry snow leopard, or other furry/feathered residents). There are more than 130 species here, but no space for animals like zebras and giraffes to roam; the biggest specimens here are Betty and Veronica—two lovable grizzly bears who joined the zoo in 2014. Don't miss the sea lion feedings, possibly the zoo's most popular attraction, daily at 11:30, 1:30, and 3. Clustered around the central Sea Lion Pool are separate exhibits for each of the Earth's major environments: penguins and polar bears live at Polar Circle; the highlights of the open-air Temperate Territory are the chattering monkeys; and the Tropic Zone contains the flora and fauna of rain forests. The Tisch Children's Zoo (no additional ticket required) gives kids the opportunity to feed sheep, goats, cows, and pigs. The 4-D theater ($7) shows 15-minute-long family-friendly films like "Ice Age 4-D: No Time for Nuts" that feature sensory effects like wind, mist, bubbles, and scents. ⊠ *Entrance at 5th Ave. and E. 64th St., Central Park* ☎ *212/439–6500* ⊕ *www.centralparkzoo.org* ✉ *$12; $18 Total Experience (includes 4-D show)* ☞ *Children under 12 not admitted without adult* Ⓜ *6 to 68th St./Hunter College; N, R, W to 5th Ave./59th St.; F, Q to Lexington Ave./63rd St.*

FAMILY **Great Lawn.** This truly great 14-acre oval has endured billions of footsteps, thousands of ball games, hundreds of downpours, scores of concerts, and even the crush of people attending one papal Mass. Yet it's the stuff of a suburbanite's dream—perfectly tended turf (a mix of rye and Kentucky bluegrass), state-of-the-art drainage systems, automatic sprinklers, and careful horticultural monitoring. The area hums with action on weekends and most summer evenings, when its softball fields and picnicking grounds provide a much-needed outlet for city folk (and city dogs) of all ages. ⊠ *Mid-park between 81st and 85th Sts., Central Park* ⊕ *www.centralparknyc.org* Ⓜ *B, C to 81st St./ Museum of Natural History.*

Strawberry Fields. This memorial to John Lennon, who penned the classic 1967 song "Strawberry Fields Forever," is sometimes called the "international garden of peace." The curving paths, shrubs, trees, and flower beds create a deliberately informal landscape reminiscent of English parks. Every year on December 8, Beatles fans mark the anniversary of Lennon's death by gathering around the star-shape, black-and-white "Imagine" mosaic set into the pavement. Though Lennon's 1980 murder took place across the street at the Dakota apartment building, where he lived, this atmospheric tribute provides a bit of solace to all who visit. ⊠ *Just off W. 72nd St., Central Park* ⊕ *www.centralparknyc.org* Ⓜ *B, C to 72nd St.*

INWOOD

Well north of Harlem, at the very northern tip of Manhattan, Inwood is still essentially the upper Upper West Side, with Fort Tryon Park lying just to its south.

The Met Cloisters. Perched on a wooded hill in Fort Tryon Park, near Manhattan's northwestern tip, the Cloisters museum and gardens houses part of the medieval collection of the Metropolitan Museum of Art and is a scenic destination in its own right. Colonnaded walks connect authentic French and Spanish monastic cloisters, a French Romanesque chapel, a 12th-century chapter house, and a Romanesque apse. One room is devoted to the 15th- and 16th-century Unicorn Tapestries, which date to 1500—a must-see masterpiece of medieval mythology. The tomb effigies are another highlight. Two of the three enclosed gardens shelter more than 250 species of plants similar to those grown during the Middle Ages, including flowers, herbs, and medicinals; the third is an ornamental garden planted with both modern and medieval plants, providing color and fragrance from early spring until late fall. Concerts of medieval music are held here regularly (concert tickets include same-day admission to the museum). The outdoor Trie Café is open 10 to 4:15 Tuesday through Sunday, from April to October, and serves sandwiches, coffee, and snacks. ■TIP→ Admission includes entry over three consecutive days to the Metropolitan Museum of Art's main building on 82nd Street, as well as its new contemporary art outpost—the Met Breuer—on 75th Street. ⊠ *99 Margaret Corbin Dr., Fort Tryon Park, Upper West Side* ☎ *212/923–3700* ⊕ *www.metmuseum.org* ☑ *$25 for 3-day ticket (includes Metropolitan Museum and Met Breuer); $25 suggested donation for New York State residents (full donation includes 3-day ticket to Metropolitan Museum and Met Breuer)* Ⓜ *A to 190th St.*

HARLEM

Getting Oriented

Harlem

0 — 1/4 mile

0 — 400 meters

THE BRONX

MAKING THE MOST OF YOUR TIME

Harlem's simplest pleasures are free. Take time to walk the areas around Strivers' Row, Hamilton Heights, Sugar Hill, and 116th Street to see some impressive—and often fanciful—architecture. Hear the sweet sounds of a choir practice as you stroll by any of Harlem's churches (which number in the hundreds). See well-curated exhibits showcasing the work of contemporary artists of African descent at the Studio Museum in Harlem (open Thursday–Sunday), or visit the Morris-Jumel Mansion for a trip back in time to Colonial New York.

GETTING HERE AND AROUND

The 2 and 3 subway lines stop on Lenox Avenue; the 1 goes along Broadway, to the west; and the A, B, C, and D trains travel along St. Nicholas and 8th Avenues (note: the B train does not run on weekends). And yes, as the song goes, the A train is still usually "the quickest way to Harlem."

The city's north–south avenues take on different names in Harlem: 6th Avenue is called both Malcolm X Boulevard *and* Lenox Avenue; 7th Avenue is Adam Clayton Powell Jr. Boulevard (named for the influential minister and congressman); and 8th Avenue is Frederick Douglass Boulevard. West 125th Street, the major east–west street and Harlem's commercial center, is also known as Dr. Martin Luther King Jr. Boulevard.

12

TOP EXPERIENCES

Spending an evening at the iconic Apollo Theater

Visiting the Studio Museum in Harlem

Shopping at the bimonthly Sugar Hill Market

Donning your Sunday best for jazz brunch at places such as Red Rooster ⇨ *Chapter 15, Where to Eat*

COFFEE AND QUICK BITES

Levain Bakery. From coffee and cakes to breads and scones, this bakery has something for every sweet tooth. It's the cookies, however, that make it famous. ✉ *2167 Frederick Douglass Blvd., between 116th and 117th Sts., Harlem* ☎ *646/455–0952* ⊕ *www.levainbakery.com* Ⓜ *B, C to 116th St.*

Manhattanville Coffee. It may be on a quiet corner, but this coffee shop is always buzzing. The vintage-inspired space appeals to laptop-toting locals with a large communal table, tufted leather couches, and free Wi-Fi. ✉ *142 Edgecombe Ave., at 142nd St., Harlem* ☎ *646/781–9900* ⊕ *www.manhattanvillecoffee.com* Ⓜ *A, B, C, D to 145th St.; B, C to 135th St.*

Sightseeing
★ ★
Nightlife
★ ★ ★ ★
Dining
★ ★ ★
Lodging
★ ★
Shopping
★ ★

Harlem is known throughout the world as a vibrant center of African American culture, music, and life. The neighborhood invites visitors to see historic jewels such as the Apollo Theater, architecturally splendid churches, cultural magnets like the Studio Museum in Harlem, as well as an ongoing list of new and renovated sites and buildings.

Updated by
Joshua Rogol

A stroll along Harlem's 125th Street reveals the electric energy of the neighborhood, from impromptu drum circles to a bustling farmers' market to sidewalk vendors hawking bootleg DVDs, incense, and African shea butter. This east–west stretch is the heart of the neighborhood, and home to some of the best people-watching in Manhattan. Bill Clinton's New York office is at 55 West 125th Street, and the legendary Apollo Theater stands at No. 253. A large number of chains (Starbucks, Red Lobster, H&M) make it hard to distinguish 125th Street from the city's other heavily commercialized areas, but there are still a few things that set it apart: the wide number of languages spoken, the aroma of West African spices for sale, and stylish locals who take pride in their fashion.

To get a feel for Harlem, spend time visiting its past and present. On 116th Street, particularly between St. Nicholas and Lenox Avenues (Malcolm X Boulevard), you'll find some of the area's most interesting religious buildings, from ornate churches to a green-domed mosque.

Along Lenox Avenue and Frederick Douglass Boulevard between 110th and 130th Streets are chic restaurants, bars, and a few boutiques offering everything from bespoke cocktails and live music to Harlem-inspired gifts and high-end menswear.

TOP ATTRACTIONS

Apollo Theater. ⇨ *See the listing in Chapter 19, Performing Arts.*

Hamilton Heights. To envision this neighborhood's Harlem Renaissance days, walk down tree-lined Convent Avenue and cross over to **Hamilton Terrace** to see a time capsule of elegant stone row houses in mint condition. One of the neighborhood's most beautiful blocks, it's popular with film and TV crews. The **Hamilton Grange National Memorial,** founding father Alexander Hamilton's Federal-style mansion, is located at the southern end of the block, on 141st Street. Turn west and continue down Convent Avenue to see the looming Gothic spires (1905) of **City College.** Next, head east to visit **Strivers' Row.** ⊠ *Convent Ave., between 135th and 150th Sts., Harlem* Ⓜ *A, B, C, D to 145th St.*

FAMILY **Morris-Jumel Mansion.** During the Revolutionary War, General Washington used this wooden, pillared 8,500-square-foot house (1765) as his headquarters, and when he visited as president in 1790, he brought along John Quincy Adams, Thomas Jefferson, and Alexander Hamilton. Inside rooms are furnished with period decorations; upstairs, keep an eye out for the hand-painted wallpaper (original to the house) and a "commode chair," stuck in a corner of the dressing room. Outside, behind the house, is a Colonial-era marker that says it's 11 miles to New York—a reminder of what a small sliver of Manhattan the city was at that time. East of the house is the block-long Sylvan Terrace, a row of crisp two-story clapboard houses built in 1882. ⊠ *65 Jumel Terr., north of 160th St., between St. Nicholas and Edgecombe Aves., Harlem* ☎ *212/923–8008* ⊕ *www.morrisjumel.org* 🖃 *$10; guided tour $12* ⊘ *Closed Mon.* Ⓜ *C to 163rd St.*

Strivers' Row. This block of gorgeous 1890s Georgian and Italian Renaissance Revival homes earned its nickname in the 1920s from less affluent Harlemites who felt its residents were "striving" to become well-to-do. Some of the few remaining private service alleys, used when deliveries arrived via horse and cart, lie behind these houses and are visible through iron gates. Note the gatepost between Nos. 251 and 253 on 138th Street that reads, "Private Road. Walk Your Horses." These houses were built by the contractor David H. King Jr., whose works also include the base for the Statue of Liberty and the oldest parts of the Cathedral Church of St. John the Divine. When they failed to sell to whites, the properties on these blocks were sold to African American doctors, lawyers, and other professionals; composers and musicians W. C. Handy and Eubie Blake were also among the residents. If you have the time, detour a block north to see the palazzo-style group of houses designed by Stanford White, on the north side of 139th Street. ⊠ *138th and 139th Sts., between Adam Clayton Powell Jr. and Frederick Douglass Blvds., Harlem* Ⓜ *B, C to 135th St.; A, B, C, D to 145th St.*

Fodor'sChoice **Studio Museum in Harlem.** Contemporary art by African American, Carib-
★ bean, and African artists is the focus of this small museum with a light-filled sculpture garden. Three artists in residence present their works each year, and lively Uptown Fridays! in summer feature DJs, cocktails, and a fashionable crowd. The gift shop is small but packs a punch; don't miss its fantastic collection of coffee-table books. ⊠ *144 W. 125th St., between Lenox Ave. and Adam Clayton Powell Jr. Blvd., Harlem* ☎ *212/864–4500* ⊕ *www.studiomuseum.org* 🖃 *$7 suggested donation (free Sun.)* ⊘ *Closed Mon.–Wed.* Ⓜ *2, 3, A, B, C, D to 125th St.*

Fodor'sChoice **Sugar Hill Market.** This bimonthly market, held on the ground floor of
★ an art gallery's brownstone space, features a mostly consistent roster

D.I.Y. Harlem Gospel Tours

Since 2000, the popularity of Sunday gospel tours has surged. While some in the community see it as an opportunity to broaden horizons and encourage diversity, others find tours disruptive and complain that tourists take seats away from regular parishioners (churches regularly fill to capacity). If you plan on attending a service, here are some tips:

Most churches have Sunday services at 11, but you may need to arrive as much as two hours early (depending on the church) to get in. Dress nicely (no shorts, sneakers, or jeans); be as quiet as possible; do not leave in the middle of the service; and do not take photos or videos or use your cell phone. Most important, remember that parishioners do not consider the service, or themselves, tourist attractions or entertainment.

A bus tour is generally an inauthentic (and more expensive) way to experience Harlem. Explore the neighborhood and churches on your own, or join a small tour like those led by **Harlem Heritage Tours** (☎ 646/302–1575 ⊕ www.harlemheritage.com).

Their tours (starting at $39) get high marks from past clients and are run by guides who were born and raised in Harlem. Groups are no larger than 25 people.

The following are some of the uptown churches with Sunday services:

Abyssinian Baptist Church (☎ 212/862–7474 ⊕ www.abyssinian.org) is one of the few churches that does not allow tour groups. Services for visitors are held at 11:30; arrive at least two hours ahead of time. **Canaan Baptist Church of Christ** (☎ 212/866–0301 ⊕ www.cbccnyc.org) has services at 10. **Convent Avenue Baptist Church** (☎ 212/234–6767 ⊕ www.conventchurch.org) has services at 7, 8, and 11. **First Corinthian Baptist Church** (☎ 212/864–5976 ⊕ www.fcbcnyc.org) has services at 7:30, 9:30, and 11:30. **Greater Refuge Temple** (☎ 212/866–1700 ⊕ www.greaterrefugetemple.org) has services at 11 and 4. **Memorial Baptist Church** (☎ 212/663–8830 ⊕ www.mbcvisionharlem.org) has services at 10.

of Harlem-based designers. Expect to find handmade items including vegan soaps, pottery, gourmet jams, and clothing fusing modern silhouettes with colorful Ghanaian fabrics. The market's founder (who happens to have a fashion background) creates limited-edition Harlem T-shirts that make great souvenirs. The date and location of the market varies, so check the website before visiting. ⊠ *La Maison d'Art, 259 W. 132nd St., between Frederick Douglass and Adam Clayton Powell Jr. Blvds., Harlem* ⊹ *Located on the ground floor of a brownstone; look for the sandwich board on the sidewalk* ⊕ *www.sugarhillmarket.com* Ⓜ *B, C, 2, 3 to 135th St.; A, B, C, D to 125th St.*

WORTH NOTING

FAMILY **Hamilton Grange National Memorial.** Founding father Alexander Hamilton and his wife raised eight kids in this Federal-style country home, which he called his "sweet project." Once located on Hamilton's 32

The Studio Museum features contemporary art by African American, Caribbean, and African artists.

acres, the Grange, named after his father's childhood home in Scotland, has moved three times since it was built in 1802. It now stands in St. Nicholas Park and gives a lesson in Hamilton's life, from his illegitimate birth in the West Indies and his appointment as the nation's first Secretary of the Treasury to his authorship of *The Federalist Papers* and his death following a duel with Vice President Aaron Burr. The house's ground floor, formerly servants' quarters, hosts an interactive exhibit that includes a short film on Hamilton's life. Upstairs a parlor, study, dining room, and two guest rooms are open to view; note the beautiful piano, which belonged to his daughter Angelica. ✉ *414 W. 141st St., between St. Nicholas and Convent Aves., Harlem* ☎ *646/548–2310* ⊕ *www.nps.gov/hagr/index.htm* ✈ *Free* ◔ *Closed Mon., Tues.* ☞ *Self-guided tours of the furnished rooms noon–1 and 3–4 only; 30-min ranger-led tours at 10, 11, 2, and 4* Ⓜ *1 to 137th St.–City College; A, B, C, D to 145th St.*

Masjid Malcolm Shabazz (*Mosque*). Talk about religious conversions: in the mid-'60s, the Lenox Casino was transformed into this house of worship and cultural center, and given bright yellow arches and a huge, green onion dome that loudly proclaims its presence in a neighborhood of churches. Once functioning as Temple No. 7 under the Nation of Islam with a message of pro-black racism, the mosque was bombed after the assassination of Malcolm X, who had preached here. It was then rebuilt and renamed in honor of the name Malcolm took at the end of his life, El-Hajj Malik Shabazz; its philosophy now is one of inclusion. These days the Sunni congregation has a large proportion of immigrants from Senegal, many of whom live in and around 116th

Harlem's Jazz Age

It was in Harlem that Billie Holiday got her first singing job, Duke Ellington made his first recording, and Louis Armstrong was propelled to stardom. Jazz was king during the Harlem Renaissance in the 1920s and '30s, and though Chicago and New Orleans may duke it out for the "birthplace of jazz" title, New York was where jazz musicians came to be heard.

In the 1920s, socialites made the journey uptown to Harlem's Cotton Club and Connie's Inn (131st Street and 7th Avenue) to hear "black" music. Both clubs were white-owned and barred blacks from entering,

except as performers. (The rules changed years later.) Connie's introduced New Yorkers to Louis Armstrong. The Cotton Club—Harlem's most popular nightspot by far— booked such big names as Fletcher Henderson, Coleman Hawkins, Duke Ellington, Cab Calloway, and Ethel Waters. After shows ended at the paying clubs, musicians would head to after-hours establishments with black patrons, such as Small's Paradise, Minton's Playhouse (which reopened in 2013), and Basement Brownies, where they'd hammer out new riffs into the wee hours.

Street. Next door is Graceline Court, a 16-story luxury condominium building that cantilevers somewhat awkwardly over the mosque. Farther east on 116th Street is the outdoor **Malcolm Shabazz Harlem Market,** where you can find African and African-inspired jewelry, art, clothing, and fabrics. On weekends with nice weather, more vendors open. ✉ *102 W. 116th St., at Malcolm X Blvd. (Lenox Ave.), Harlem* 🕾 *212/662–2200* ⊕ *themasjidmalcolmshabazz.com* ☞ *To attend services, requests must be made in advance by writing to msmosque@aol. com* Ⓜ *2, 3 to 116th St.*

Sugar Hill. Standing on the bluff of Sugar Hill overlooking Jackie Robinson Park, outside the slightly run-down **409 Edgecombe Avenue,** you'd never guess that here resided such influential African Americans as NAACP founder W.E.B. DuBois and Supreme Court Justice Thurgood Marshall, or that farther north at **555 Edgecombe** (known as the "Triple Nickel"), writers Langston Hughes and Zora Neale Hurston and jazz musicians Duke Ellington, Count Basie, and others lived, wrote, and played. It's also here that for more than 20 years musician Marjorie Eliot has been hosting jazz concerts in her apartment, 3F, at 3:30 pm every Sunday. Farther down, at No. 345, you can't miss the **Benzinger House** with its flared mansard roof. Amid all this history, the modern-looking **Sugar Hill Children's Museum of Art & Storytelling,** at 155th Street and St. Nicholas Avenue, gathers local families for programs that encourage the creative spirit of children. ✉ *From 145th to 155th Sts., between Edgecombe and St. Nicholas Aves., Harlem* Ⓜ *A, B, C, D to 145th St.*

BROOKLYN

Getting Oriented

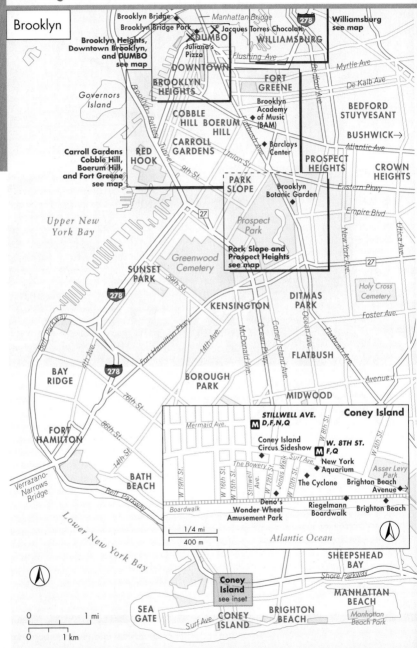

Brooklyn

Brooklyn Bridge
Brooklyn Bridge Park
Jacques Torres Chocolate

Manhattan Bridge

278

Williamsburg
see map

Brooklyn Heights,
Downtown Brooklyn,
and DUMBO
see map

DUMBO
Juliana's
Pizza

WILLIAMSBURG

Flushing Ave.

DOWNTOWN

Myrtle Ave.

De Kalb Ave.

Governors
Island

BROOKLYN
HEIGHTS

FORT
GREENE

BEDFORD
STUYVESANT

COBBLE
HILL BOERUM
HILL

Brooklyn
Academy
of Music
(BAM)

BUSHWICK→

Atlantic Ave.

Carroll Gardens
Cobble Hill,
Boerum Hill,
and Fort Greene
see map

CARROLL
GARDENS

RED
HOOK

Barclays
Center

PROSPECT
HEIGHTS

CROWN
HEIGHTS

Union St.

9th St.

Upper New
York Bay

27

PARK
SLOPE

Prospect
Park

Brooklyn
Botanic Garden

Eastern Pkwy.

Empire Blvd.

Utica Ave.

New York Ave.

Park Slope and
Prospect Heights
see map

27

Greenwood
Cemetery

Holy Cross
Cemetery

SUNSET
PARK

39th St.

DITMAS
PARK

Foster Ave.

278

KENSINGTON

14th Ave.

McDonald Ave.

Coney Island Ave.

Ocean Ave.

FLATBUSH

Elizabeth Ave.

Avenue J.

Fort Hamilton Pkwy.

BAY
RIDGE

4th Ave.

278

76th St.

BOROUGH
PARK

MIDWOOD

Belt Parkway

FORT
HAMILTON

86th St.

14th Ave.

STILLWELL AVE.
M D,F,N,Q

Coney Island

Verrazano-
Narrows
Bridge

BATH
BEACH

Mermaid Ave.

Coney Island
Circus Sideshow

W. 8th St.

W. 8TH ST.
M F,Q

New York
Aquarium

Asser Levy
Park

Belt Parkway

The Bowery

W 19th St.

W 16th St.
W 15th St.
Stillwell Ave.
Jones Walk
W 12th St.
W 10th St.

Surf Ave.

The Cyclone

Brighton Beach
Avenue →

Brighton Beach

Lower New York Bay

Boardwalk

Deno's
Wonder Wheel
Amusement Park

Riegelmann
Boardwalk

Atlantic Ocean

1/4 mi

400 m

SHEEPSHEAD
BAY

Shore Parkway

0   1 mi

0   1 km

Coney
Island
see inset

SEA
GATE

Surf Ave.

CONEY
ISLAND

BRIGHTON
BEACH

MANHATTAN
BEACH

Manhattan
Beach Park

TOP EXPERIENCES

Eating and barhopping in Williamsburg

Screaming at the top of the Cyclone roller coaster in Coney Island

Smelling the roses, and everything else, at the Brooklyn Botanic Garden

Catching a show at BAM or Barclays Center

Walking across the Brooklyn Bridge

Picnicking in Brooklyn Bridge Park

Being awestruck by architecture in Brooklyn Heights or street art in Bushwick

GETTING HERE

Brooklyn is very accessible by subway from Manhattan; check the listings for subway info. Brooklyn Heights, Downtown Brooklyn, DUMBO, and Williamsburg are the closest neighborhoods to Manhattan. Coney Island and Brighton Beach are the farthest; budget about an hour each way if you're traveling from Midtown.

MAKING THE MOST OF YOUR TIME

The best way to get to Brooklyn is by its most majestic bridge. Walking along the wooden pedestrian path of the Brooklyn Bridge—a classic New York experience—takes about 30 minutes, worth it for the panoramic views of the skylines and the harbor. On summer weekends the path is crowded, unless you go early in the morning. Exit the bridge onto Cadman Plaza on the Brooklyn side, then walk southwest to get to Brooklyn Heights, a charming neighborhood of 19th-century brownstone homes, or walk north into the hip neighborhood of DUMBO.

QUICK BITES

Jacques Torres Chocolate. French-born Torres is New York's adopted Willy Wonka. Here, he dishes out drool-worthy truffles and bonbons, and hot chocolate rich enough to make a Swiss miss blush. ⊠ *66 Water St., DUMBO* ☎ *718/875–1269* ⊕ *www.mrchocolate.com* Ⓜ *A, C to High St.; F to York St.*

Juliana's Pizza. Skip the lines at the more famed Grimaldi's and walk next door. Here you'll find what many Brooklynites think of as the "real" Grimaldi's. ⊠ *19 Old Fulton St., DUMBO* ☎ *718/596–6700* ⊕ *julianaspizza.com* Ⓜ *F to York St.*

13

Sightseeing
★★★
Nightlife
★★★★
Dining
★★★★ ★
Lodging
★ ★
Shopping
★★★

Updated
by Caroline
Trefler

Hardly Manhattan's sidekick, Brooklyn is a destination in its own right, with many diverse neighborhoods and a seemingly endless number of compelling sights and fabulous places to eat and drink and shop.

Across the East River from Manhattan, on Long Island's western edge, Brooklyn is one of New York City's five boroughs. At 71 square miles, it's more than three times the size of Manhattan, and with more than 2½ million people, if it were a city it would be the fourth largest in the United States, in terms of population. Brooklyn *was* a city until the end of the 19th century, with its own widely circulated newspaper (*The Brooklyn Eagle*), its own expansive park (Prospect Park), and its own baseball team that would eventually be called the Brooklyn Dodgers. In 1883 it also got its own bridge: the Brooklyn Bridge, which drew the attention of the entire country.

Brooklyn Heights and **DUMBO** are easily accessible from Manhattan by subway or via the Brooklyn Bridge; both neighborhoods have compelling but very different architecture (brownstones versus 19th-century warehouses), and fabulous views of Manhattan. **Carroll Gardens, Cobble Hill, Boerum Hill,** and **Fort Greene** all have plenty of lovely streets to stroll with thriving restaurant and bar scenes. The latter also has the Brooklyn Academy of Music. **Williamsburg** is the epicenter of trendsetting Brooklyn, which is overflowing into up-and-coming **Bushwick** and **East Williamsburg. Park Slope** and **Prospect Park** welcome with laid-back, family-friendly activities, while **Prospect Heights** and **Crown Heights** are home to heavy hitters like the Barclays Center, the Brooklyn Botanic Gardens, Weeksville Heritage Center, and the Brooklyn Children's Museum. **Coney Island** and **Brighton Beach** have Brooklyn's subway-accessible beaches, boardwalks, and amusement parks, including the legendary Cyclone roller coaster.

Brooklyn Is Book Country

Brooklyn has been a mecca for writers and literature since the days of *Uncle Tom's Cabin*, written by a preacher's daughter in Brooklyn Heights. Since then, writers have flocked here for the cheap rent and quiet streets. Henry Miller, Norman Mailer, Truman Capote, Arthur Miller (with Marilyn Monroe), Paul and Jane Bowles, Carson McCullers, James Purdy, and Walt Whitman created more than one masterpiece here.

Today, amid the gentrification, Brooklyn continues to lure famous and near-famous writers and musicians from all over the world.

Perhaps reflecting the plethora of writers in the neighborhood, the borough has a relatively high density of both used and new bookstores, and also several small presses, including Melville House, a publisher with a storefront.

And with all these writers so close by, it only makes sense that Brooklyn has a fabulous book festival, to boot. The Brooklyn Book Festival happens every year at Borough Hall, on the third weekend in September. Authors gather for readings and signings, and independent publishers display their wares.

BROOKLYN HEIGHTS

Brooklyn Heights is quintessential "brownstone Brooklyn." It's the oldest neighborhood in the borough, and the original village of Brooklyn; almost the entire neighborhood is part of the Brooklyn Heights Historic District. This is still very much the neighborhood of shady lanes, cobblestone streets, centuries-old row houses, and landmark buildings that Walt Whitman rhapsodized about, and the magnificent postcard views of the Manhattan skyline and the Brooklyn Bridge have inspired countless artists and photographers since. In the early to mid-20th century, Brooklyn Heights was a bohemian haven, home to such writers as Arthur Miller, Truman Capote, Henry Miller, Alfred Kazin, Carson McCullers, Paul Bowles, Marianne Moore, Norman Mailer, and W.E.B. DuBois.

The majestic **Brooklyn Bridge** has one foot in Brooklyn Heights, near DUMBO, and a walk across it either to or from Lower Manhattan is one of the classic New York experiences.

TOP ATTRACTIONS

Brooklyn Bridge. (⇨ *Chapter 2*) F to York St.; A, C to High St.

FAMILY

Fodor's Choice

★

Brooklyn Bridge Park. This sweeping feat of green urban renewal stretches from the Manhattan Bridge in DUMBO to the Brooklyn Bridge and south all the way to Pier 6, carpeting old industrial sites along the waterfront with scenic esplanades and lush meadows. The park has playgrounds, sports fields, food concessions, the wonderfully restored Jane's Carousel, and lots of grass for lounging. You can access the park at various points; just head down the hill toward the East River and you can't miss it. ⊠ *Brooklyn waterfront, Brooklyn Heights* ☏ *718/222–9939* ⊕ *www.brooklynbridgepark.org* Ⓜ *2, 3 to Clark St.; A, C to High St.; F to York St.*

FAMILY
Fodor's Choice
★

Brooklyn Heights Promenade. Strolling this mile-long path, famous for its magnificent Manhattan views, you might find it surprising to learn that its origins were purely functional: the promenade was built as a sound barrier to protect nearby brownstones from highway noise. Find a bench and take in the skyline, the Statue of Liberty, and the Brooklyn Bridge; in the evening, the lights of Manhattan sparkle across the East River. Below are the Brooklyn–Queens Expressway and Brooklyn Bridge Park. ⊠ *Between Remsen and Cranberry Sts., Brooklyn Heights* Ⓜ *2, 3 to Clark St.; A, C to High St.; R to Court St.*

Fodor's Choice
★

Brooklyn Historical Society. Four centuries' worth of art and artifacts bring Brooklyn's story to life at this marvelous space. Housed in an 1881 Queen Anne–style National Historic Landmark building, the society surveys the borough's changing identity through permanent exhibits that include interactive displays, landscape paintings, photographs, portraits of Brooklynites, and fascinating memorabilia. The gift shop features an eclectic assortment of Brooklyn-themed books and tchotchkes. Stop by the society's DUMBO outpost in the Empire Stores development at 55 Water Street for special exhibits. ⊠ *128 Pierrepont St., Brooklyn Heights* ☎ *718/222–4111* ⊕ *www.brooklynhistory.org* 🖎 *$10 suggested donation* ☉ *Closed Mon. and Tues.* Ⓜ *2, 3, 4, 5 to Borough Hall; R to Court St.; A, C, F to Jay St.–MetroTech.*

"Fruit" Streets. The quiet blocks of Pineapple, Cranberry, and Orange streets contain some of Brooklyn Heights's most picturesque brownstones and brick homes. A few homes made of wood still exist here, too, although new construction of this type has been banned in this area as a fire hazard since the mid-19th century. The wood-frame Federal-style house at 24 Middagh Street dates to the 1820s, its lane commemorating one Lady Middagh, whom we can thank for bestowing such memorable fruit-themed names on this enclave. ⊠ *Pineapple, Orange, and Cranberry Sts., Brooklyn Heights* Ⓜ *2, 3 to Clark St.; A, C to High St.*

WORTH NOTING

Brooklyn Borough Hall. Built in 1848 as Brooklyn's city hall, this Greek Revival landmark, adorned with Tuckahoe marble, is one of the borough's handsomest buildings. The statue of Justice atop its cast-iron cupola was part of the original plan but wasn't installed until 1988. Today the building serves as the office of Brooklyn's borough president and the home of the Brooklyn Tourism & Visitors Center. ⊠ *209 Joralemon St., Brooklyn Heights* ☎ *718/802–3700* ⊕ *www.explorebk. com* ☉ *Closed weekends* Ⓜ *2, 3, 4, 5 to Borough Hall; R to Court St.; A, C, F, R to Jay St.–MetroTech.*

FAMILY

New York Transit Museum. Step down into an old 1930s subway station to experience this entertaining museum's displays of vintage trains and memorabilia. You can wander through trains and turnstiles and sit behind the wheel of a former city bus (it's not only the kids who do this). Original advertising, signage, and upholstery make this feel like a trip back in time. The gift shop carries subway-line socks, decorative tile reproductions, and other fun stuff. ⊠ *Boerum Pl., Brooklyn Heights* ☎ *718/694–1600* ⊕ *www. mta.info/museum* 🖎 *$10* ☉ *Closed Mon.* Ⓜ *2, 3, 4, 5 to Borough Hall; A, C, G to Hoyt–Schermerhorn Sts.; A, C, F, R to Jay St.–MetroTech.*

Brooklyn Heights is well-known for its multitude of picturesque brownstones.

DOWNTOWN BROOKLYN

Downtown Brooklyn is modern and bustling, and other than a few notable restaurants, there isn't much to attract visitors—but it's convenient to the Brooklyn Bridge and Brooklyn Heights, and walking distance to neighborhoods like Cobble Hill, Boerum Hill, and DUMBO.

DUMBO

For sheer jaw-dropping drama, few city walks are as cinematic as strolling the DUMBO waterfront. The photogenic area pairs 19th-century warehouses and refurbished industrial buildings on cobblestone streets with rumbling trains and soaring bridges overhead. (The latter gives the district its name, an acronym of Down Under the Manhattan Bridge Overpass.) Across the East River, the glittering Manhattan skyline provides epic views and popular backdrops for wedding proposals, fashion shoots, and innumerable selfies. Major galleries and performance hubs imbue the neighborhood with artistic élan, and the adjacent Navy Yard is a booming example of Brooklyn's revitalized industrial waterfront.

An integral part of DUMBO is the Brooklyn Bridge Park, and its renovated piers and rolling green spaces. Crowds of locals and tourists alike flock to its riverfront benches and tiny beaches to sunbathe or simply to ponder the magnificence of one of the city's finest views.

DUMBO Walls. Keep an eye out under and around the Manhattan Bridge and the Brooklyn-Queens Expressway, where walls display street art by the likes of CAM, Shepard Fairey, and MOMO. The

Brooklyn Heights,
Downtown Brooklyn,
and DUMBO

0   1/4 mile

0   1/4 km

project is sponsored by the DUMBO Improvement District and Two Trees Management Co., along with the New York City Department of Transportation Urban Art Program and the Jonathan LeVine Gallery. ⊠ *DUMBO* Ⓜ *F to York St.*

Fodor's Choice **Empire Stores.** Housed in a sparkling renovation of an enormous 19th-century warehouse, this collection of shops and restaurants features a 7,000-square-foot rooftop garden with East River and Manhattan views. It's also home to a 3,200-square-foot exhibition space from the Brooklyn Historical Society that has small displays and a gift shop in a modern, industrial-chic space. Other tenants include area businesses, a luxury automobile showroom, and a West Elm store with a Brooklyn Roasting Company café. ⊠ *53–83 Water St., DUMBO* ⊕ *empirestores-dumbo.com* Ⓜ *A, C to High St.; F to Jay St.*

Smack Mellon. The transformation of an industrial boiler house into an edgy arts compound is quintessential DUMBO. This 12,000-square-foot structure now hosts large-scale, avant-garde exhibitions and runs a prestigious residency program. Don't be surprised if you pass a smartphone-clutching event planner on your way in: the 5,000-square-foot gallery here is also a popular wedding venue. ⊠ *92 Plymouth St., DUMBO* ☎ *718/834–8761* ⊕ *www.smackmellon.org* ☉ *Closed Mon. and Tues.* Ⓜ *A, C to High St.; F to York St.*

Fodor's Choice **The Stable Building.** Although the Galapagos Art Space moved to Detroit,
★ the site continues its arts legacy, housing four first-floor gallery spaces
that were previously part of the 111 Front Street gallery collective.
Minus Space shows artists specializing in "reductive abstract art"
(simple materials, precise craftsmanship, monochromatic or limited
color, repetition of shapes). United Photo Industries (UPI) shows work
by emerging photographers and those working in new photography
styles. The Klompching Gallery focuses on fine-art photography. Masters Projects represents artists working in all sorts of media, including
paint, mixed media, street art, photography, and installations. Gallery
hours vary, but weekday and Saturday afternoons are your best bet to
visit; most are closed Monday. ⊠ *16 Main St., DUMBO* Ⓜ *2, 3 to Clark
St.; A, C to High St.; F to York St.*

13

CARROLL GARDENS

Named for Charles Carroll, the only Catholic signatory of the Declaration of Independence, and the lush front gardens that line the neighborhood's brownstones, Carroll Gardens was a well-kept secret until
the 1980s. Traditionally an Italian neighborhood, many old-school
vestiges, including some that have served the area for well over a half
century, still remain. Court and Smith Streets are the backbone of
the community, and now feature a mix of top-notch restaurants and
bistros, handsome cocktail lounges and craft-beer bars, and boutiques
selling the most current styles, to go along with original mom-and-pop
bakeries and butcher shops. A recent influx of French expats makes
the neighborhood's annual Bastille Day festival and petanque (like
lawn bowling but played on sand using heavy metal balls) tournament
a high point each July.

COBBLE HILL

Cobble Hill stands out for its 19th-century architecture, leafy and compact park, and more recently, for escalating real estate prices. Dutch residents called the area Cobleshill in reference to a Revolutionary War–era
land mound, which was flattened by British soldiers to prevent strategic
use by George Washington's troops. These days, most of the 22-block
neighborhood is landmarked as Brooklyn's second-oldest district, a mix
of brick town houses, brownstones, and Victorian schoolhouses, where
only the Gothic Revival churches exceed a 50-foot height limit. Historically working-class, the neighborhood has adopted all the trappings of
haute Brooklyn, especially along busy Court Street.

BOERUM HILL

Understated elegance defines Boerum Hill, where redbrick town houses
and brownstones line quiet, tree-lined thoroughfares from 4th Avenue
to Smith Street and Schermerhorn to Baltic. The neighborhood saw an
influx of immigrants in the late 1800s, with completion of the Brooklyn
Bridge and the emergence of trolley cars, but fell into disrepair after

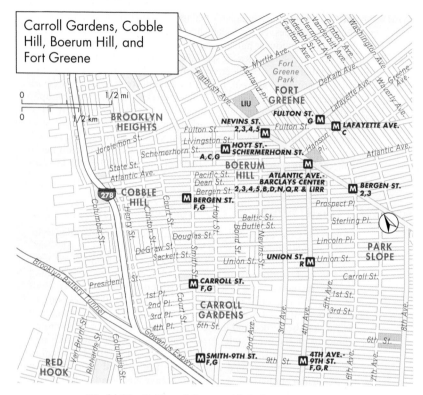

Carroll Gardens, Cobble
Hill, Boerum Hill, and
Fort Greene

World War II. Now fully gentrified, the setting is laden with beautiful cafés and plays host to Atlantic Antic, NYC's largest street festival and unofficial fall kick-off, each September. Despite its air of sophistication, Boerum Hill presents moments of levity, namely artist Susan Gardner's sparkly mosaic-covered brownstone at 108 Wyckoff Street.

FORT GREENE

Art institutions, flatteringly lit eateries, and the sort of showstopping architecture that sends real estate agents into early retirement make Fort Greene irresistible. Bookended by the Pratt Institute and the former Williamsburg Savings Bank Tower (now 1 Hanson Place)—a four-sided clock tower that was once the borough's tallest building and remains a local landmark—the neighborhood has a central location and an illustrious past. Climb the 96 steps or the grassy slopes of Fort Greene Park and you'll be greeted by vistas of the Manhattan skyline, while standing in the silhouette of the 149-foot tall Prison Ship Martyrs' Monument—dedicated to the thousands of Americans who died on British prison ships during the Revolutionary War. Everyone from Walt Whitman to Spike Lee has called these iconic streets home.

WILLIAMSBURG

These days, it's impossible to walk through North Brooklyn without encountering something new. Fabulous boutiques, vintage shops, and forward-thinking restaurants crop up constantly, lending an energy that verges on overwhelming. The neighborhood has certainly glossed itself up in recent years, evinced by pricey cocktail bars, high-rise waterfront condos, and expensive boutiques. But Williamsburg's past is also endlessly intriguing: for much of the 20th century this industrial area on the East River was home to a mix of working-class Americans. Rising Manhattan rents in the 1990s sent an influx of East Village artists and musicians onto the L train, and since then the area has rapidly, albeit creatively, gentrified. And while some side streets may appear graffitied and creepy, rest assured that there's likely to be a DIY concert-gallery space in one of those seemingly abandoned factories.

Williamsburg's 70-plus galleries are distributed randomly, with no single main drag. Plan your trip ahead of time using the online **Brooklyn Art Guide** at ⊕ *www.wagmag.org.* (You can also pick up a copy at neighborhood galleries and some cafés.) Hours vary widely, but most are open weekends (call ahead). Although serendipitous poking is the best way to sample the art, longtime gallery Pierogi is a must-see.

FAMILY **City Reliquary.** Subway tokens, Statue of Liberty figurines, antique seltzer bottles, and other artifacts you might find in a time capsule crowd the cases of this museum that celebrates New York City's past and present. Temporary exhibits here have included one about doughnut shops and another about Jewish gangsters of the Lower East Side. ⊠ *370 Metropolitan Ave.* ☎ *718/782–4842* ⊕ *www.cityreliquary.org* ✉ *$7* ☉ *Closed Mon.–Wed.* Ⓜ *L to Lorimer St.; G to Metropolitan Ave.*

Urban Oyster Tours. For a glimpse into Brooklyn's illustrious past as the nation's brewing capital (once home to 48 breweries), book a spot on the **Brewed in Brooklyn** walking tour ($65 per person). The journey starts with a tour and tasting at **Brooklyn Brewery** (79 N. 11th Street), followed by a stroll through historic Brewers Row with stops that include a 19th-century German brewery once operated by Otto Huber, lunch at Danny's Pizzeria, and, of course, a craft beer at each watering hole along the way. Other popular tour offerings include the Williamsburg Fermented Craft Beer Crawl and the Neighborhood Eats: Brownstone Brooklyn tour, which is without a doubt the best way to sample the eclectic bites of BoCoCa (Boerum Hill, Cobble Hill, Carroll Gardens) in one afternoon. ⊠ *Williamsburg* ☎ *347/618–8687* ⊕ *www.urbanoyster.com.*

BUSHWICK

Bushwick is young and cool, but also gritty and very industrial—working factories make everything from wontons to plastic bags—but it's definitely where to go if you're interested in street art: check out the Bushwick Collective and the streets surrounding it. The neighborhood also has pockets of cafés and restaurants, including Roberta's—making some of the best Neopolitan-style pizza this side of the Atlantic.

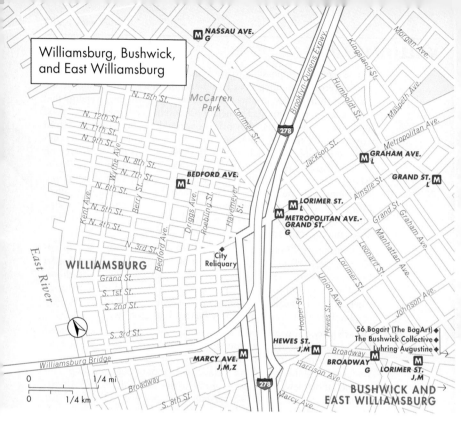

Fodor's Choice

★

The Bushwick Collective. For evidence of art's ability to transform lives, visit this colorful outdoor street-art gallery curated by Joseph Ficalora, a Bushwick native who came of age during the neighborhood's period of decline and channeled his grief over losing both of his parents into a space where street artists create temporary works of art. Pixel Pancho of Turin and Baltimore-based Gaia are among the established artists featured at this urban street-arts destination. ⊠ *Troutman St., Bushwick* ⊕ *thebushwickcollective.com* Ⓜ *L to Jefferson St.*

56 Bogart (The BogArt). Many young Bushwick galleries showcase edgy and experimental work—visiting this converted warehouse is an easy way to see a lot of art in one shot. The BogArt contains large studios and more than a dozen galleries. Standouts include Robert Henry Contemporary, Theodore:Art, David & Schweitzer Contemporary, and Fuchs Project. ■**TIP**➜ **Gallery hours vary, but the best time to visit is on Friday and weekends, when most of them are open.** ⊠ *56 Bogart St., Bushwick* ☎ *718/599–0800* ⊕ *www.56bogartstreet.com* Ⓜ *L to Morgan Ave.*

On a walk through Bushwick and East Williamsburg, you'll find plenty of dynamic local street art.

EAST WILLIAMSBURG

Industrial East Williamsburg, between Williamsburg and Bushwick, has become an enclave of street art, up-and-coming art galleries, cafés, and restaurants.

Luhring Augustine. Probably the neighborhood's most established gallery, this annex of the Chelsea original is worth a stop to see whatever show is up and to appreciate the soaring space and its cantilevered ceiling. ⊠ *25 Knickerbocker Ave.* ☎ *718/386–2746* ⊕ *www.luhringaugustine. com* ☉ *Closed Mon.–Wed. Sept.–June and Sun.–Tues. July and Aug.* Ⓜ *L to Morgan Ave.*

PARK SLOPE

Full of young families, dog walkers, double-wide strollers, and impeccably curated shops, the neighborhood that literally slopes down from Prospect Park can feel like a veritable Norman Rockwell painting. Add to all that a slew of laptop-friendly coffeehouses and turn-of-the-20th-century brownstones—remnants of the days when Park Slope had the nation's highest per-capita income—and it's no surprise that academics and writers have flocked here. Park Slope's busiest drags, 5th and 7th Avenues, present plenty of shopping and noshing opportunities. Head to the elegant, 585-acre Prospect Park for long strolls or bicycle rides past lazy meadows, shady forests, and lakes designed by Olmsted and Vaux of Central Park fame (look out for free summertime concerts). Adjacent is Brooklyn Botanic Garden, which features a variety of public

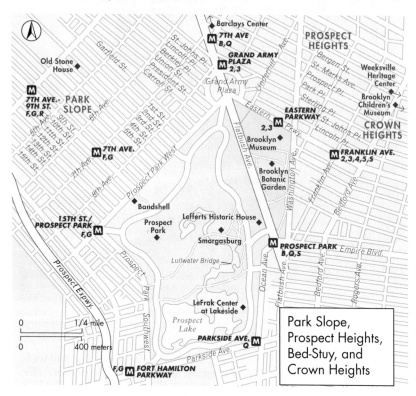

Park Slope, Prospect Heights, Bed-Stuy, and Crown Heights

classes and the springtime Cherry Blossom Festival. Also perched on the park is the Brooklyn Museum, lauded for collections of American, Egyptian, and feminist art.

TOP ATTRACTIONS

FAMILY **LeFrak Center at Lakeside.** The highlight of this 26-acre space in Prospect Park is the all-season ice- and roller-skating rink. The walkways, the esplanade near the lake, and the Music Island nature reserve are—all part of the original Olmsted and Vaux plans—make for a pleasant stroll. Themed roller-skating night takes place on Friday, April through October; in winter, the rink hosts hockey and curling clinics for all ages. The Bluestone Café offers sunny outdoor seating year-round. ⊠ *171 East Dr., Prospect Park* ☎ *718/462–0010* ⊕ *www. lakesidebrooklyn.com* 🎟 *Skating $6 weekdays, $9 weekends; rentals $6–$7* ⊙ *Rink: closed days vary by season* Ⓜ *B, Q, S to Prospect Park; Q to Parkside Ave.*

Fodor'sChoice **Smorgasburg.** More than a hundred of New York City's best and brightest
★ cooks and culinary artisans unite in Prospect Park (replacing the Brooklyn Bridge Park Pier 5 location) every Sunday to form the city's hottest foodie flea market. An offshoot of the Brooklyn Flea, this food bazaar extravaganza has launched countless culinary crazes (ramen burger, anyone?), and most vendors are small-scale, homegrown operators.

Lines can grow long and vendors can sell out as the afternoon goes on, so head over early in the day if possible. There is also an outpost on the Williamsburg waterfront (between Kent Avenue and North 7th Street) on Saturdays, as well as smaller Smorgasburgs in Queens, at Coney Island, at the South Street Seaport, and at Central Park SummerStage events. The latest addition to this grub empire is a collaboration with the Winter Flea, held weekends year-round at Industry City in Sunset Park. The larger Smorgasburgs are seasonal and generally take place from May through October, but check the website to confirm. ☒ *Breeze Hill, Prospect Park ⊕ www.brooklynflea.com* Ⓜ *Q, S to Prospect Park; F, G to 15th St.–Prospect Park.*

FAMILY
Fodor'sChoice
★
Prospect Park. Brooklyn residents are passionate about Prospect Park, and with good reason: lush green spaces, gently curved walkways, summer concerts, vivid foliage in autumn, and an all-season skating rink make it a year-round getaway. In 1859 the New York Legislature decided to develop plans for a park in the fast-growing city of Brooklyn. After landscape architects Frederick Law Olmsted and Calvert Vaux completed the park in the late 1880s, Olmsted remarked that he was prouder of Prospect Park than of any of his other works—Manhattan's Central Park included. Many critics agree that this is their most beautiful work. On weekends, those not jogging the 3.35-mile loop gravitate to the tree-ringed Long Meadow to fly kites, picnic, or play cricket, flag football, or Frisbee. The park's north entrance is at Grand Army Plaza, where the Soldiers' and Sailors' Memorial Arch (patterned on the Arc de Triomphe in Paris) honors Civil War veterans. On Saturdays year-round, a green market at the plaza throngs with shoppers.

A good way to experience the park is to walk the Long Meadow and then head to the eastern side, where you'll find the lake and most attractions, including the Lefferts Historic House, Prospect Park Audubon Center, and the LeFrak Center. The Prospect Park Carousel, built in 1912, still thrills the kids. The annual Celebrate Brooklyn! festival takes place at the Prospect Park Bandshell from early June through mid-August. The many other events include free yoga classes on the Long Meadow in summer and the Sunday Smorgaburg outdoor food market at Breeze Hill, April through October. ☒ *450 Flatbush Ave., Prospect Park* ☎ *718/965–8951* ⊕ *www.prospectpark.org* ✉ *Carousel: $2* ⊙ *Carousel: closed Mon.–Wed.* Ⓜ *2, 3 to Grand Army Plaza; F, G to 7th Ave. or 15th St.–Prospect Park; B, Q to 7th Ave.*

WORTH NOTING

FAMILY
Lefferts Historic House. A visit to this Dutch Colonial farmhouse, built in 1783 and moved from nearby Flatbush Avenue to Prospect Park in 1918, is a window into how Brooklynites lived in the 19th century, when the area was predominantly farmland. Rooms are furnished with antiques and reproductions from the 1820s, when the house was last redecorated. ☒ *452 Flatbush Ave., Prospect Park* ☎ *718/789–2822* ⊕ *www.prospectpark.org/lefferts* ✉ *$3 suggested donation* ⊙ *Closed weekdays* Ⓜ *B, Q, S to Prospect Park.*

FAMILY
Old Stone House. This reconstructed Dutch farmhouse dating to 1699, played a central role in the Battle of Brooklyn, one of the largest

The boathouse in Prospect Park, built in 1905, was one of the first buildings in New York City to be declared a historic landmark.

battles of the Revolutionary War, and survived until the 1890s. The small museum here focuses on the Revolutionary era in Brooklyn from 1776 until 1783. Art exhibits, concerts, plays, and other community events take place year-round, including a ball game to celebrate the Brooklyn Baseball Club, which started here and gave rise to the Brooklyn Dodgers. ☒ *Washington Park/J.J. Byrne Playground, 336 3rd St., Park Slope* 🕾 *718/768–3195* ⊕ *www.theoldstonehouse.org* 🖃 *$3 suggested donation* 🕙 *Closed Mon.–Thurs.* Ⓜ *R to Union St.; F, G, R to 4th Ave.–9th St.*

PROSPECT HEIGHTS

An influx of creative young professionals and impressive eats has lifted Prospect Heights out from the shadow of nearby Park Slope. Swing by Grand Army Plaza on a Saturday to hit the borough's flagship farmers' market, where cooking demos and fresh produce entice the food-loving hoards. Or gorge on everything from lobster rolls to Korean tacos at the plaza's Food Truck Rally held on select Sundays, May through October. Vanderbilt Avenue and Washington Avenue are the main drags for restaurants and bars.

FAMILY **Barclays Center.** This rust-tinted spaceship of an arena houses two sports franchises—basketball's Brooklyn Nets and ice hockey's New York Islanders—and hosts events from rock concerts to circuses. With a capacity rivaling Madison Square Garden's, Barclays also has plenty of room to offer concessions courtesy of local restaurateurs, including Williamsburg Pizza, Paisano's Burger, and Calexico. ☒ *620 Atlantic*

Ave., Prospect Heights ☎ *917/618–6100* ⊕ *www.barclayscenter.com* Ⓜ *2, 3, 4, 5, B, D, N, Q, R to Atlantic Ave.–Barclays Ctr.; G to Fulton St.; C to Lafayette Ave.; LIRR to Atlantic Terminal.*

FAMILY

Fodor's Choice

★

Brooklyn Museum. First-time visitors may well gasp at the vastness of New York's second-largest museum (after Manhattan's Metropolitan Museum of Art) and one of the largest in America at 560,000 square feet of exhibition space. The colossal beaux arts structure houses one of the best collections of Egyptian art in the world and impressive collections of African, pre-Columbian, and Native American art. It's also worth seeking out the museum's works by Georgia O'Keeffe, Winslow Homer, John Singer Sargent, George Bellows, Thomas Eakins, and Milton Avery. The museum is also well known for very contemporary, cutting-edge special exhibits. The monthly (except for September) "First Saturday" free-entry night is a neighborhood party of art, music, and dancing, with food vendors and several cash bars. ⊠ *200 Eastern Pkwy., Prospect Heights* ☎ *718/638–5000* ⊕ *www. brooklynmuseum.org* ⊇ *$16 suggested donation, $25 combo ticket with Brooklyn Botanic Garden* ☉ *Closed Mon. and Tues.* Ⓜ *2, 3 to Eastern Pkwy.–Brooklyn Museum.*

13

BED-STUY AND CROWN HEIGHTS

Crown Heights and nearby Bedford-Stuyvesant (known as Bed-Stuy) are vast and historic neighborhoods with a tumultuous past. Long since the 1991 riots that escalated tensions between the area's Hasidic and black communities, these days Crown Heights is more likely to inspire thoughts of diverse stoops and row houses, rapid gentrification, and authentic Caribbean fare. Crown Heights is also home to the Brooklyn Children's Museum and Weeksville Heritage Center.

FAMILY

Fodor's Choice

★

Brooklyn Botanic Garden. A verdant 52-acre oasis, the BBG charms with its array of "gardens within the garden," including an idyllic Japanese hill-and-pond garden, a stunning rose garden, and a Shakespeare garden. The Japanese cherry arbor turns into a breathtaking cloud of pink every spring, and the Sakura Matsuri two-day cherry blossom festival is the largest public-garden event in America. There are multiple entrances, and a variety of free garden tours are available with admission; check the website for seasonal details. ⊠ *150 Eastern Pkwy., Prospect Heights* ☎ *718/623–7200* ⊕ *www.bbg.org* ⊇ *$15* ☉ *Closed Mon. except major holidays* Ⓜ *2, 3 to Eastern Pkwy.–Brooklyn Museum; 2, 3, 4, 5 to Franklin Ave.; S to Botanic Garden; B, Q to Prospect Park.*

FAMILY

Brooklyn Children's Museum. What's red, yellow, and green, and shaped like a spaceship? The Brooklyn Children's Museum, an interactive space where kids can run, touch and play with abandon. Exhibits range from a working greenhouse to art experiences. The cornerstone is World Brooklyn, a warren of rooms dedicated to various NYC cultures that includes an Italian pizza shop, Hispanic bakery, and a replica MTA bus. ⊠ *145 Brooklyn Ave., Crown Heights* ☎ *718/735–4400* ⊕ *www.brooklynkids.org* ⊇ *$11* ☉ *Closed Mon.* Ⓜ *C to Kingston–Throop Aves.; 3 to Kingston Ave.; A, C to Nostrand Ave.*

A stroll on the boardwalk at Coney Island is a New York summer tradition.

FAMILY **Weeksville Heritage Center.** Honoring the history of the 19th-century African American community of Weeksville, one of the first communities of free blacks in New York (founded by James Weeks), this Crown Heights museum comprises an industrial-modern building by Caples Jefferson Architects, botanical gardens, and three houses that date as far back as 1838. The restored homes, along historic, gravel Hunterfly Road, are now period re-creations depicting life in the 1860s, 1900s, and 1930s. Tours ($8) are Tuesday, Thursday, and Friday at 3 pm. ✉ *158 Buffalo Ave., Crown Heights* ☎ *718/756–5250* ⊕ *www.weeksvillesociety.org* ✉ *$8 house tours; grounds free* ☉ *Closed Sat.–Mon.* Ⓜ *A, C to Utica Ave.; 3, 4 to Crown Heights–Utica Ave.*

CONEY ISLAND

Coney Island is practically synonymous with the sounds, smells, and sights of a New York City summer: hot dogs and ice cream, suntan lotion, roller coasters, excited crowds, and weathered old men fishing.

Named Konijn Eiland (Rabbit Island) by the Dutch for its wild rabbit population, the Coney Island peninsula has a boardwalk, a 2½-mile-long beach, amusement parks, and the **New York Aquarium**, which is currently undergoing a $157 million face-lift that will showcase the much-anticipated exhibit, *Ocean Wonders: Sharks!* Nathan's Famous (*1310 Surf Avenue*) is the quintessential hot dog spot.

Among the other entertainments out here are the freakish attractions at **Coney Island Circus Sideshow** and the heart-stopping plunge of the granddaddy of all roller coasters—the **Cyclone.** The Mets' minor-league baseball team, the Cyclones, plays at MCU Park, where music concerts are also held in summer. The area's banner day is during the raucous Mermaid Parade, held in June. A fireworks display lights up the sky Friday night from late June through Labor Day.

TOP ATTRACTIONS

FAMILY **The Cyclone.** This historic wooden roller coaster first thrilled riders in 1927 and it'll still make you scream. Anticipation builds as the cars slowly clack up to the first unforgettable 85-foot plunge—and the look on your face is captured in photos that you can purchase at the end of the ride. The Cyclone may not have the speed or the twists and turns of more modern rides, but that's all part of its rickety charm. It's one of two New York City landmarks in Coney Island; the other is Deno's Wonder Wheel. ✉ *Luna Park, 834 Surf Ave., Coney Island* ☎ *718/373–5862* ⊕ *www.lunaparknyc.com* ✉ *$10* ⊘ *Closed hrs vary, but are generally mid-Oct.–early May. Check website for details.* Ⓜ *F, Q to W. 8th St.–NY Aquarium; D, F, N, Q to Coney Island–Stillwell Ave.*

FAMILY **New York Aquarium.** The oldest continually operating aquarium in the
Fodor's Choice United States is run by the Wildlife Conservation Society; its mission
★ is to save wildlife and wild places worldwide through science, conservation action, and education. The aquarium occupies 14 acres of beachfront property and is home to 266 aquatic species. At the Sea Cliffs, you can watch penguins, sea lions, sea otters, and seals frolic: the best action is at feeding time. The Conservation Hall and Glovers Reef building is home to marine life from Belize, Fiji, and all over the world, including angelfish, eels, rays, and piranhas. The new *Ocean Wonders: Sharks!* exhibit will bring hundreds more species, including nurse sharks, to the aquarium. The highlight will be a coral-reef tunnel that provides 360-degree views of this underwater universe. ■TIP➔ Purchase tickets online for discounted rates. ✉ *602 Surf Ave., Coney Island* ☎ *718/265–3474* ⊕ *www.nyaquarium.com* ✉ *$12* Ⓜ *F, Q to W. 8th St.–NY Aquarium; D, F, N, Q to Coney Island–Stillwell Ave.*

FAMILY **Riegelmann Boardwalk.** Built in 1923, just one year before legendary
Fodor's Choice Totonno's Pizzeria opened its doors on nearby Neptune Avenue, this
★ famous wood-planked walkway is better known as the Coney Island Boardwalk, and in summer it seems like all of Brooklyn is out strolling along the 2½-mile stretch. The quintessential walk starts at the end of the pier in Coney Island, opposite the Parachute Jump—you can see the shoreline stretched out before you, a beautiful confluence of nature and city. From here to Brighton Beach is a little over a mile and should take about a half hour at a leisurely amble. Those modernistic, rectangular structures perched over the beach are new bathrooms and lifeguard stations. ✉ *Between W. 37th St. and Brighton 15th St., Coney Island* Ⓜ *D, F, N, Q to Coney Island–Stillwell Ave.; F, Q to W. 8th St.–NY Aquarium; B, Q to Brighton Beach; Q to Ocean Pkwy.*

WORTH NOTING

Coney Island Circus Sideshow. The cast of talented freaks and geeks who keep Coney Island's carnival tradition alive include sword swallowers, fire-eaters, knife throwers, contortionists, and Serpentina the snake dancer. Every show is an extravaganza, with 10 different acts to fascinate and impress. ⊠ *Sideshows by the Seashore, 1208 Surf Ave., Coney Island* ☎ *718/372–5159* ⊕ *www.coneyisland.com/sideshow. shtml* ⊠ *$10* ⊙ *Closed Oct.–Mar.* Ⓜ *F, Q to W. 8th St.–NY Aquarium; D, F, N, Q to Coney Island–Stillwell Ave.*

FAMILY **Deno's Wonder Wheel Amusement Park.** The star attraction at Deno's is the towering 150-foot-tall Wonder Wheel. The Ferris wheel first opened in 1920, making it the oldest ride in Coney Island, and the spectacular views from the top take in a long stretch of the shoreline. Other rides for tots here include the Dizzy Dragons, the Pony Carts, and a brightly painted carousel. ⊠ *1025 Riegelmann Boardwalk, Coney Island* ☎ *718/372–2592* ⊠ *$8* ⊙ *Closed Nov.–early Mar.; hrs vary* Ⓜ *F, Q to W. 8th St.–NY Aquarium; D, F, N, Q to Coney Island–Stillwell Ave.*

BRIGHTON BEACH

A pleasant stroll just down the boardwalk from Coney Island is Brighton Beach, named after Britain's beach resort. In the early 1900s Brighton Beach was a resort in its own right, with seaside hotels that catered to rich Manhattan families visiting for the summer. Since the 1970s and '80s Brighton Beach has been known for its 100,000 Soviet émigrés. To get to the heart of "Little Odessa" from Coney Island, walk about a mile east along the boardwalk to Brighton 1st Place, then head up to Brighton Beach Avenue. To get here from Manhattan directly, take the B or Q train to the Brighton Beach stop; the trip takes about an hour from Midtown Manhattan.

FAMILY **Brighton Beach.** Just steps from the subway, this stretch of golden sand
Fodor's Choice is the showpiece of Brooklyn's ocean-side playground. Families set up
★ beach blankets, umbrellas, and coolers, and pickup games of beach volleyball and football add to the excitement. Calm surf, a lively boardwalk, and a handful of restaurants for shade and refreshments complete the package. That spit of land in the distance is the Rockaway Peninsula, in Queens. ⊠ *Brighton Beach Ave., Brighton Beach* Ⓜ *B, Q to Brighton Beach; Q to Ocean Pkwy.*

Brighton Beach Avenue. The main thoroughfare of "Little Odessa" can feel more like Kiev than Manhattan. Cyrillic shop signs advertise everything from salted tomatoes and pickled mushrooms to Russian-language DVDs and Armani handbags. When the weather's good, local bakeries sell sweet honey cake, cheese-stuffed *vatrushki* danishes, and chocolatey rugelach from sidewalk tables. ⊠ *Brighton Beach Ave., Brighton Beach* Ⓜ *B, Q to Brighton Beach.*

QUEENS, THE BRONX, AND STATEN ISLAND

Getting Oriented

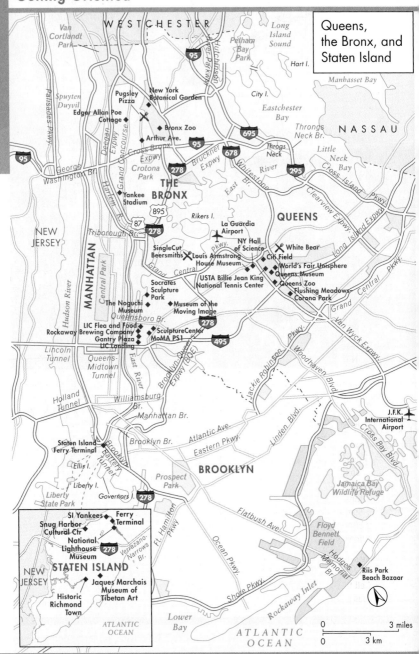

Queens,
the Bronx, and
Staten Island

MAKING THE MOST OF YOUR TIME

Queens is rich with museums, authentic ethnic cuisine, and innovative craft breweries. A day spent hopping around Long Island City and Astoria enables you to take in the MoMA PS1 contemporary art center, the Museum of the Moving Image, and the Noguchi Museum. Then jump on the 7 train and sample international dishes at neighborhood eateries in Jackson Heights or Flushing.

It's easy to spend a full day at either of the Bronx's treasures: the New York Botanical Garden or the Bronx Zoo. To visit both, start early and plan a late lunch or early dinner in the Arthur Avenue area.

GETTING HERE

Queens is served by many subway lines. To get to Astoria, take the N or W train. For Long Island City, take the E, M, G, or 7 train. To get to Jackson Heights, take the 7 train to the 74th Street–Broadway stop. You can also take the E, F, M, or R train to Jackson Heights–Roosevelt Avenue. The 7 brings you out to the attractions of Flushing Meadows Corona Park, as well as Citi Field.

The Bronx is serviced by the 1, 2, 4, 5, 6, B, and D trains. The attractions in the Bronx are spread out across the borough, though, so you need to take different lines to get where you want to go, and it's not necessarily convenient to make connections across town. The B, D, and 4 trains all go to Yankee Stadium, and the B and D continue uptown to the vicinity of Arthur Avenue. The 2 and 5 trains take you close to the Bronx Zoo and Arthur Avenue.

From the scenic (and free) Staten Island Ferry, you can catch a local bus or hop in a taxi to hit up attractions that are farther afield. Tell the driver where you're going, and ask about the return bus schedule or taxi pickup.

TOP EXPERIENCES

Sampling ethnic eats and local brews in Queens

Catching a game at Yankee Stadium or Citi Field

Taking a free ride on the Staten Island Ferry

Soaking up modern art at Long Island City museums

14

QUICK BITES

Pugsley Pizza. Dig in to delicious and piping-hot pies at this fun, family-run neighborhood favorite and hangout for nearby Fordham University students. It's been a locals' go-to for quality slices for more than 30 years. ⊠ *590 E. 191st St., Belmont* ☎ *718/365-0327* Ⓜ *4, B, D to Fordham Rd.*

SingleCut Beersmiths. Named for a body style of guitar, this craft brewery has a taproom that also serves food like empanadas, flatbread pizzas, and brats. ⊠ *19-33 37th St., Astoria* ⊹ *15-min walk from Ditmars Blvd. stop on the N, W train* ☎ *718/606-0788* ⊕ *singlecut. com* ⊘ *Closed Mon., Tues.* Ⓜ *N, W to Astoria–Ditmars Blvd.*

White Bear. The wontons at this tiny hole-in-the-wall are worth the trek to another of New York's Chinatowns, in Flushing. Order the No. 6: a dozen wontons with hot chili oil for $6. ⊠ *135-02 Roosevelt Ave., entrance on Prince St., Flushing* ☎ *718/961-2322* ⊟ *No credit cards* Ⓜ *7 to Flushing–Main St.*

Sightseeing
★ ★ ★
Nightlife
★ ★ ★
Dining
★ ★ ★ ★
Lodging
★ ★
Shopping
★ ★ ★ ★

Many tourists miss out on Queens, the Bronx, and Staten Island—the three boroughs of New York City other than the biggies for tourism, Manhattan and Brooklyn—and that's a shame. There are some noteworthy restaurants, museums, and attractions, and the subway's handful of express trains means that they're closer than you might think.

QUEENS

Updated by
Joshua Rogol

Just for the museums and restaurants alone, it's truly worth it to take a short 15-minute trip from Midtown on the 7, E, or M train to **Long Island City** or a slightly longer ride on the N, W, M, or R train to **Astoria**. In Long Island City, major art must-sees are **MoMA PS1** and the **Noguchi Museum**. No trip to Astoria—once nicknamed "Little Athens"—is complete without sampling some of the city's finest Greek and Mediterranean fare and a stop at the **Museum of the Moving Image**.

Jackson Heights boasts a diverse cornucopia of culture and cuisine and is home to one of the city's busiest Indian shopping districts. It's a wonderful place to spend an afternoon browsing shops and dining in one of the many authentic ethnic restaurants.

Top reasons to trek out to **Flushing** and **Corona** include seeing a ball game at the New York Mets' stadium, **Citi Field**, spending time at the expansive **Flushing Meadows Corona Park**, especially if you're traveling with kids, and devouring Asian dim sum in Flushing's Chinatown.

ASTORIA

Head to Astoria for authentic Greek restaurants, shops, and grocery stores. Here you can buy kalamata olives and salty sheep's (or sheep-and-goat's) milk feta from store owners who can tell you where to go for the best gyro or spanakopita (spinach pie). **Taverna Kyclades** is well known for classic Greek seafood dishes that attract diners from all five boroughs, while just a few blocks up the road, SingleCut Beersmiths

TIPS FOR QUEENS ADDRESSES

Addresses in Queens can seem confusing at first. Not only is there 30th Street and 30th Avenue, but also 30th Drive and 30th Road, all next to one another. But the system is actually logical. Sequentially numbered avenues run east to west, and sequentially numbered streets run north to south. If there are any smaller roads between avenues, they have the same number as the nearest avenue and are called roads or drives. Thus, 30th Road is one block south of 30th Avenue. Similarly, smaller side roads between streets are called places or lanes. Additionally, most addresses have two pairs of numbers, separated by a hyphen. The first pair indicates the nearest cross street, and the second gives the location on the block. If this all still seems confusing to you, there's good news: locals are used to giving directions to visitors.

14

runs free brewery tours and pours some tasty ales and lagers. Astoria, named for John Jacob Astor—America's first multimillionaire—has been the center of Greek immigrant life in New York City for more than 60 years. Today substantial numbers of Arab, Asian, Eastern European, Irish, and Latino immigrants have also joined the dwindling Greek and Italian populations that call Astoria home. The presence of the Greek community is still evident on strips along both 23rd Avenue and Ditmars Boulevard. Another busy thoroughfare is 30th Avenue, with almost every kind of food store imaginable. Astoria is also home to the nation's only museum devoted to the art, technology, and history of film, TV, and digital media. The Museum of the Moving Image has a dynamic hands-on exhibition that allows visitors to immerse themselves in the creative process of making movies and television shows.

Fodor's Choice ★ **Museum of the Moving Image.** The Museum of the Moving Image is full of Hollywood and television memorabilia, but the core exhibition, *Behind the Screen,* demonstrates how movies and TV shows are produced and shown, including stations where visitors can create their own short animation, experiment with sound effects, or view the behind-the-scenes editing process of a live Mets baseball game. A wide range of films (more than 400), from classic Hollywood to avant-garde works to foreign-festival hits, is generally shown weekend evenings and afternoons. In addition, there are other special programs including film retrospectives, lectures, and workshops. ✉ 36-01 35th Ave., at 37th St., Astoria ☎ 718/777–6888 ⊕ www.movingimage.us ⏱ $15 (free Fri. after 4) ⊘ Closed Mon., Tues. Ⓜ M, R to Steinway St.; N, W to 36th Ave.

LONG ISLAND CITY

Long Island City (LIC) is the art capital of Queens, with MoMA PS1, which presents experimental and innovative contemporary work; the Noguchi Museum, showcasing the work of Japanese American sculptor Isamu Noguchi in a large, peaceful garden and galleries; and the Socrates Sculpture Park, with large outdoor installations fronting the East River.

Food Market Mania

Queens has always ranked high for its eclectic and authentically ethnic culinary landscape, and its foodie-friendly appeal has only been bolstered in recent years by new food markets. In Long Island City, **LIC Flea & Food** (⊠ *5-25 46th Ave.* ⊕ *www.licflea.com*) runs on weekends between April and October. It features some 85 stands that range from food to handmade items, as well as a beer garden pouring Queens-brewed beers on tap from Rockaway Brewing Company, Finback Brewery, and more. The **Queens Night Market** (⊕ *www. queensnightmarket.com*) is an outdoor market held Saturday evenings, late April through October in Flushing Meadows Corona Park. It's reminiscent of Asia's popular food markets, and

you can expect to find about 100 vendors serving flavorful (and often adventurous) ethnic fare such as ceviche, Peking duck buns, Trinidadian shark sandwiches, and more. Finally, a beach trip to the Rockaways anytime between Memorial Day and Labor Day rewards visitors with the **Riis Park Beach Bazaar** (⊕ *www.riisparkbeachbazaar.com*). It features a half-dozen local food-and-drink vendors as well as rotating pop-up vendors (try organic chicken shawarma from Samesa or Sweet as Honey ice cream from Brooklyn-based Ample Hills Creamery), cultural offerings (like free weekend concerts), beach activities (volleyball, kite flying, and more), and assorted handicrafts vendors on the waterfront at Jacob Riis Park Beach.

Worth noting for art buffs, the free LIC Art Bus shuttles guests between Socrates Sculpture Park, the Noguchi Museum, SculptureCenter, and MoMA PS1 on Saturday and Sunday afternoons between May and early September. It runs every 45 minutes between 1 and 6 pm.

TOP ATTRACTIONS

Fodor's Choice
★

MoMA PS1. A pioneer in the "alternative-space" movement, PS1 rose from the ruins of an abandoned school in 1976 as a sort of community arts center for the future. MoMA PS1 focuses on the work of currently active experimental and innovative artists. Long-term installations include work by Sol LeWitt, James Turrell, and Pipilotti Rist. Every available corner of the enormous building is used; discover art not only in former classrooms-turned-galleries, but also on the rooftop, in the boiler room, and even in some bathrooms. Also inside the museum is **M. Wells Dinette,** a café designed to resemble a school classroom, with daily specials listed on the chalkboard and lunch served at your "desk." On summer Saturdays, MoMA PS1 presents "Warm Up," an outdoor dance party series that attracts a hip art-school crowd, held in the courtyard noon–9. Similarly, their "Sunday Sessions" are held on Sundays from fall through spring (hours and dates vary) in the VW Performance Dome and include various artistic installations, scholarly lectures, and special performances. ⊠ *22–25 Jackson Ave., at 46th Ave., Long Island City* ☎ *718/784–2084* ⊕ *www.momaps1.org* ✉ *$10 suggested donation (free with MoMA entrance ticket, within 14 days of visit); Warm Up $18 in advance, $20 at the door; Sunday Sessions $15; free to NYC residents* ⊘ *Closed Tues., Wed.* Ⓜ *7 to Court Sq.; E, M to Court Sq.–23rd St.; G to 21st St.*

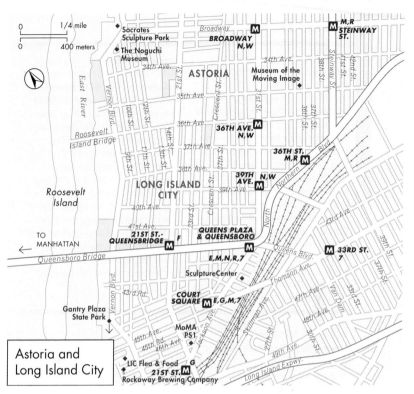

0 — 1/4 mile
0 — 400 meters

Socrates Sculpture Park
The Noguchi Museum
Broadway **BROADWAY** N,W
M,R STEINWAY ST.
34th Ave.
ASTORIA
Museum of the Moving Image
East River
35th Ave.
36th Ave. **36TH AVE.** N,W
37th Ave.
Roosevelt Island Bridge
38th Ave. **36TH ST.** M,R
LONG ISLAND CITY
39TH AVE. N,W
39th Ave.
Roosevelt Island
40th Ave.
41st Ave.
TO MANHATTAN
21ST ST.- QUEENSBRIDGE F
QUEENS PLAZA & QUEENSBORO
Queensboro Bridge
Queens Blvd.
E,M,N,R,7
33RD ST. 7
SculptureCenter
43rd Rd.
COURT SQUARE E,G,M,7
Thomson Ave.
Gantry Plaza State Park
45th Ave.
45th Rd.
46th Ave.
MoMA PS1
Jackson Ave.
Long Island Expwy.
LIC Flea & Food
21ST ST. G
Rockaway Brewing Company

Astoria and Long Island City

14

NEED A BREAK ✕**Mu Ramen.** Savory bowls of *tonkotsu* (pork-bone broth) ramen is what this cozy little shop is known for. Topped with *ton toro* (pork jowl) and drizzled with a black garlic oil, the ramen lacks only *nitamago* (a seasoned, soft-boiled egg), which can be added to any ramen on the menu. ⊠ *12-09 Jackson Ave., Long Island City* ☎ *917/868–8903* ⊕ *ramennyc.wixsite.com/popup* ⊘ *No lunch* Ⓜ *7 to Vernon Blvd.–Jackson Ave.; G to 21st St.–Van Alst Station.*

The Noguchi Museum. In 1985 the Japanese American sculptor Isamu Noguchi (1904–88) transformed this former industrial plant into a place to display his modernist and earlier works. A peaceful central garden is surrounded by galleries, and there are some 200 pieces in stone, metal, clay, and other materials on display. Temporary exhibits have examined his collaborations with others, such as industrial designer Isamu Kenmochi, architect and inventor R. Buckminster Fuller, and choreographer Martha Graham. The museum is about a mile from subway stops; check the website for complete directions. ■**TIP**➜ There are extended evening hours on the first Friday of the month, from May through September. ⊠ *9-01 33rd Rd., at Vernon Blvd., Long Island City* ☎ *718/204–7088* ⊕ *www.noguchi.org* ☝ *$10 (free 1st Fri. of month)* ⊘ *Closed Mon., Tues.* Ⓜ *N, W to Broadway.*

Queens Brewing Boom

Queens has plenty on tap for craft-beer lovers; by December 2017, a dozen of New York City's 35 (and counting) breweries called the borough home. There are currently six breweries in Long Island City alone (keep an eye on Transmitter Brewing, as a mid-2018 move to the Brooklyn Navy Yard is in the works): **Rockaway Brewing Company** (⊠ *46-01 5th St.* ⊕ *rockawaybrewco.com*); **Transmitter Brewing** (⊠ *53-02 11th St.* ⊕ *www.transmitterbrewing.com*); **Big aLICe Brewing** (⊠ *8-08 43rd Rd.* ⊕ *bigalicebrewing.com*); **LIC Beer Project** (⊠ *39-28 23rd St.* ⊕ *licbeerproject.com*); **Fifth Hammer Brewing Co.** (⊠ *10-28 46th Ave.* ⊕ *www.transmitterbrewing.com*); and **ICONYC**

Brewing Company (⊠ *45-13 34th Ave.* ⊕ *www.transmitterbrewing.com*). In Astoria, try **SingleCut Beersmiths** (⊠ *19-33 37th St.* ⊕ *www.singlecutbeer.com*); in Glendale, hit up **Finback Brewery** (⊠ *78-01 77th Ave.* ⊕ *www.finbackbrewery.com*), or in Ridgewood check out **Queens Brewery** (⊠ *1539 Covert St.* ⊕ *www.queensbrewery.com*) for an assortment of IPAs and other inventive brews. For a walking tour that includes beer, pizza, a bit of Queens brewing history, and a visit to three of Long Island City's top craft breweries, hop on the **Urban Adventures NYC Brewery Tour** (⊕ *www.queensbrewery.com*) that launched in 2017.

WORTH NOTING

Gantry Plaza State Park. Mosey down to this 12-acre waterfront park for sweeping views of Midtown Manhattan across the East River. The atmospheric stretch comes with piers, manicured lawns, Adirondack chairs and well-designed benches, and interesting relics that nod to Long Island City's industrial past, including towering, restored old gantries (once used as shipping lifts between barges and rail cars) that fringe the river and a massive Pepsi-Cola sign that once stood atop a factory here. ⊠ *4-09 47th Rd., at Center Blvd., Long Island City* ☎ *718/786–6385* ⊕ *nysparks.com/parks* 🎫 *Free* Ⓜ *7 to Vernon Blvd.–Jackson Ave.*

LIC Flea & Food. On Saturdays and Sundays between April and October, the outdoor LIC Flea & Food market welcomes visitors to peruse stands from some 85 vendors selling foodie fare and handcrafted wares. Sample snacks from many Queens-based food vendors hawking everything from ethnic eats like Filipino *lumpias* (spring rolls) to fresh-baked bundt cakes. Wash it all down at the alfresco beer garden, selling Queens-brewed beers from Rockaway Brewing Company, Finback Brewery, and more. ⊠ *5-25 46th Ave., at 5th St., Long Island City* ☎ *718/224–5863* ⊕ *www.licflea.com* ☉ *Closed weekdays and Nov.–Mar.* Ⓜ *7 to Vernon Blvd.–Jackson Ave.; G to 21st St.; E, M to Court Sq.–23rd St.*

Rockaway Brewing Company. At the epicenter of the Queens microbrew boom, this laid-back brewery offers a taproom serving up tasty hand-crafted brews (take-home growlers and cans are available), as well as free brewery tours on weekends. Evenings—though it closes at 9 or 10—and weekends are the best times to visit. ⊠ *46-01 5th St., at 46th Ave., Long Island City* ☎ *718/482–6528* ⊕ *rockawaybrewco.*

The Noguchi Museum is dedicated to the work of visionary sculptor Isamu Noguchi.

com ⊙ *Closed weekday afternoons* Ⓜ *7 to Vernon Blvd.–Jackson Ave.; G to 21st St.; E, M to Court Sq.–23rd St.*

SculptureCenter. Founded by artists in 1928 to exhibit innovative contemporary work, SculptureCenter now occupies a former trolley repair shop that was renovated by artist Maya Lin in 2002 and expanded by Andrew Berman Architect in 2014; it's not far from MoMA PS1. Indoor and outdoor exhibition spaces sometimes close between shows; call ahead before visiting. ⊠ *44-19 Purves St., at Jackson Ave., Long Island City* ☎ *718/361–1750* ⊕ *www.sculpture-center.org* ⊠ *$5 suggested donation* ⊙ *Closed Mon., Tues.* Ⓜ *7, G to Court Sq.; E, M to Court Sq.–23rd St.; N, W to Queensboro Plaza.*

FAMILY **Socrates Sculpture Park.** In 1986 local artist Mark di Suvero and other residents rallied to transform what had been an abandoned landfill and illegal dump site into this 4½-acre waterfront park devoted to public art. Today a superb view of the East River and Manhattan frames changing exhibitions of contemporary sculptures and multimedia installations. Free public programs include art workshops and an annual outdoor international film series (Wednesday evenings in July and August). ■TIP→ Socrates is open 365 days a year, but the best time to visit is during warmer months. Check online for a list of current and upcoming exhibitions. ⊠ *32-01 Vernon Blvd., at Broadway, Long Island City* ⊹ *From subway, walk about 8 blocks west on Broadway* ☎ *718/956–1819* ⊕ *www.socratessculpturepark.org* ⊠ *Free* Ⓜ *N, W to Broadway.*

JACKSON HEIGHTS

Much more than just a hub for traditional Indian delicacies, Jackson Heights resembles a giant international food court. Even in the diverse borough of Queens, it stands out for being a true multicultural neighborhood. In just a few blocks surrounding the three-way intersection of Roosevelt Avenue, 74th Street, and Broadway are shops and restaurants catering to the area's strong Tibetan, Nepalese, Bangladeshi, Colombian, Mexican, and Ecuadorian communities. Built as a planned "garden community" in the late 1910s, the area boasts many prewar apartments with elaborate block-long interior gardens as well as English-style residences. Celebs who grew up in the area include Lucy Liu and Gene Simmons. It's also the birthplace of the board game Scrabble.

QUICK BITE

✗ **Kababish.** For freshly baked *naan* (Indian-style flatbread) and grilled kebabs, pop in to this wee Jackson Heights takeout-only eatery churning out authentic Indian, Pakistani, and Bangladeshi fare. Everything is made to order, so consider calling ahead to avoid a wait. ✉ *70-64 Broadway, at 72nd St., Jackson Heights* ☎ *718/565–5131* ⊕ *www. kababish.com* Ⓜ *7 to 74th St.–Broadway; E, F, M, R to Jackson Heights–Roosevelt Ave.*

FLUSHING AND CORONA

To New Yorkers, making the trip to Flushing usually means catching a baseball game at Citi Field or hunting down the best the Far East has to offer in its vibrant Chinatown. The historic town of Flushing is a microcosm of a larger city, with a bustling downtown area, fantastic restaurants, and the bucolic Flushing Meadows Corona Park nearby. Flushing may seem like a strange name for a neighborhood, but it's an English adaption of the original (and hard-to-pronounce) Dutch name Vlissingen (the Dutch named it for a favorite port city in the Netherlands).

Next door, quiet Corona could easily be overlooked, but that would be a mistake, with attractions like the Queens Zoo, Queens Museum, and New York Hall of Science spilling over into the neighborhood from within Flushing Meadows Corona Park. Here you also find two huge legacies: the Louis Armstrong House Museum and the cooling Italian ices at neighborhood institution The Lemon Ice King of Corona.

TOP ATTRACTIONS

FAMILY

Fodor's Choice

★

Citi Field. Opened in 2009, the Mets' stadium was designed to hark back to Ebbets Field (where the Dodgers played in Brooklyn until 1957), with a brick exterior and lots of fun features for fans of all ages, from a batting cage and Wiffle-ball field to the original giant apple taken from the team's old residence, Shea Stadium. Even those who aren't Mets fans but simply love baseball should come to see the Jackie Robinson Rotunda, a soaring multistory entrance and history exhibit dedicated to the Dodgers player who shattered baseball's color barrier. While here, don't miss the chance to taste your way through the fabulous food court, Taste of the City, set behind center field (on the Field Level), where you'll find Shake Shack burgers, Blue Smoke ribs, close to 40 beer varieties at the

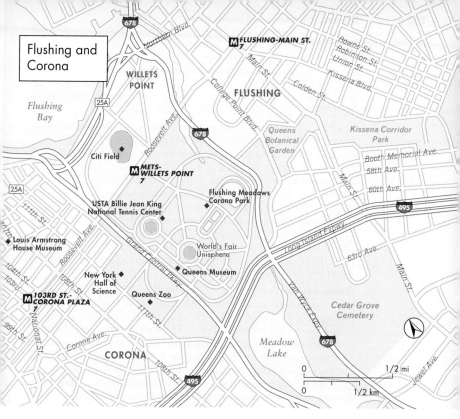

Flushing and Corona

WILLETS POINT

M FLUSHING-MAIN ST.
7

Flushing Bay

FLUSHING

Citi Field

Queens Botanical Garden

Kissena Corridor Park

M METS-WILLETS POINT
7

USTA Billie Jean King National Tennis Center

Flushing Meadows Corona Park

Louis Armstrong House Museum

World's Fair Unisphere

Queens Museum

New York Hall of Science

M 103RD ST.-CORONA PLAZA
7

Queens Zoo

Cedar Grove Cemetery

CORONA

Meadow Lake

0   1/2 mi

0   1/2 km

Big Apple Brews stand, and even mole-chicken tacos and bacon cheese fries. Still feeling nostalgic for the old Shea? Stop by the Mets Hall of Fame & Museum, or check out the plaques designating the spots where Shea's old home plate, pitching mound, and bases were in what's now parking lot D. ■TIP➜ One-hour ballpark tours ($13) are conducted rain or shine; see mets.com/tours for schedule and ticketing info. ✉ 123-01 Roosevelt Ave., at 126th St., Flushing ☎ 718/507–8499 for tickets ⊕ www.mlb.com/mets Ⓜ 7 to Mets–Willets Point.

FAMILY **Flushing Meadows Corona Park.** Standing in the lush grass of this park, you'd never imagine that it was once a swamp and dumping ground. But the gleaming Unisphere (an enormous 140-foot-high steel globe) might tip you off that this 898-acre park was also the site of two World's Fairs. Take advantage of the park's barbecue pits, seasonal boat rentals, sports fields, and big cultural festivals, but don't forget that there's an art museum, science hall, zoo, theater, carousel, indoor pool, ice-skating rink, pitch-and-putt golf and minigolf course, and even a model-airplane field. There's way too much to see here to pack into a day, so aim to hit a few primary spots, noting that while several are clustered together on the northwest side of the park, visitors should be prepared for long peaceful walks in between. ■TIP➜ The flat grounds are ideal for family biking; bike rentals are available at two locations from March to October. The park is open from 6 am to 9 pm, 365 days a year (like most city parks, it's advisable to exercise caution when visiting outside of sunlight hours). ⊠ *Between 111th St./Grand Central Pkwy. and Van Wyck Expressway/College Point Blvd., Flushing* ⊕ *www.nycgovparks.org/parks/fmcp* ☞ *Free parking available* Ⓜ *7 to 111th St. or Mets–Willets Point.*

FAMILY **New York Hall of Science.** At the northwestern edge of Flushing Meadows Corona Park, the New York Hall of Science has more than 450 hands-on exhibits that make science a playground for inquisitive minds of all ages. Climb aboard a replica of John Glenn's space capsule, throw a fastball and investigate its speed, explore Charles and Ray Eames's classic Mathematica exhibition, or check out the exhibit in the iconic Great Hall, *Connected Worlds,* which demonstrates the interconnectedness of ecosystems via animation and motion-activated displays. ⊠ *47-01 111th St., at 48th Ave., Corona* ☎ *718/699–0005* ⊕ *www.nysci.org* 🎟 *$16 (free Fri. 2–5 pm and Sun. 10–11 am)* ☞ *3-D Theater, Rocket Park Mini Golf, and Science Playground require additional fees; parking $10* Ⓜ *7 to 111th St.*

Queens Museum. Between the zoo and the Unisphere in Flushing Meadows Corona Park lies the Queens Museum. Don't miss the astonishing Panorama of the City of New York, a nearly 900,000-building model of NYC made for the 1964 World's Fair. There are also rotating exhibitions of contemporary art, a massive map of the NYC water supply system, and a permanent collection of Louis Comfort Tiffany stained glass. From fall 2018 to winter 2019, Queens International 2018 (QI 2018), a collection of contemporary cultural works curated by Queens artists, will take over the temporary exhibition spaces. There are free guided tours on Sunday afternoons. ⊠ *Flushing Meadows Corona Park, New York City Building, Corona* ✢ *From the subway, the museum is about a 15-minute walk southwest through Flushing Meadows Corona Park* ☎ *718/592–9700* ⊕ *www.queensmuseum.org* 🎟 *$8 suggested donation* ☉ *Closed Mon., Tues.* ☞ *Free (limited) parking* Ⓜ *7 to Mets–Willets Point.*

FAMILY **Queens Zoo.** Flushing Meadows Corona Park is home to the intimate Queens Zoo, dedicated to the animals of North and South America. The 11-acre facility features puma, Andean bears, Canadian lynx, and *pudu*—the world's smallest deer species. The zoo also maintains a farm with domesticated animals like sheep, goats, horses, rabbits, and more. ⊠ *53-51 111th St., at 53rd Ave., Corona* ☎ *718/271–1500* ⊕ *www.queenszoo.com* 🎟 *$8* ☞ *Last ticket sold 30 mins before closing* Ⓜ *7 to 111th St.*

USTA Billie Jean King National Tennis Center. Each year, from late August through early September, 700,000 fans come here for the U.S. Open, which claims the title of highest-attended annual sporting event in the world. The rest of the year, the 34 courts (19 outdoor and 12 indoor, all DecoTurf, plus 3 stadium courts) are open to the public for $24–$68 hourly. Make reservations up to two days in advance. ⊠ *Flushing Meadows Corona Park, Flushing* ✢ *Walk 3 mins down the ramp from the subway* ☎ *718/760–6200* ⊕ *www.ntc.usta.com* ☉ *Closed 1 month around U.S. Open* ☞ *Free (limited) parking* Ⓜ *7 to Mets–Willets Point.*

The big matches for the U.S. Open happen at Arthur Ashe Stadium, part of the USTA Billie Jean King National Tennis Center.

WORTH NOTING

Louis Armstrong House Museum. For the last 28 years of his life, the famed jazz musician lived in this modest three-story house in Corona with his wife, Lucille. Take a 40-minute guided tour (departing on the hour until 4; required), and note the difference between the rooms vividly decorated by Lucille in charming midcentury style and Louis's dark den, cluttered with phonographs and reel-to-reel tape recorders. Although photographs and family mementos throughout the house impart knowledge about Satchmo's life, it's in his den that you really begin to understand his spirit. Exclusive to the museum, guests can also tune in to intimate audio clips of Louis playing the trumpet or telling jokes on his home-recorded private tapes. The museum also hosts Armstrong-related special events and a "Hot Jazz / Cool Garden" summer concert series; check the website for details. ✉ *34-56 107th St., at 37th Ave., Corona* ☎ *718/478-8274* ⊕ *www.louisarmstronghouse.org* 🎫 *$10, includes guided house tour* ⊗ *Closed Mon.* Ⓜ *7 to 103rd St.–Corona Plaza.*

NEED A BREAK

✕ **The Lemon Ice King of Corona.** If you're looking for an authentic Queens experience, there are few as true as eating an Italian ice from The Lemon Ice King of Corona on a hot summer day. A neighborhood institution for more than 70 years, this place has dozens of flavors to dig into (just note there are no seats). ✉ *52-02 108th St., at 52nd Ave., Corona* ☎ *718/699-5133* ⊕ *www.thelemonicekingofcorona.com* Ⓜ *7 to 103rd St.-Corona Plaza Station.*

THE ROCKAWAYS

"Hitch a ride to Rockaway Beach" by taking the A train to its southernmost terminus, where the transformation of the once-neglected Rockaways (an area spanning several neighboring beach communities along the skinny Rockaway Peninsula) into a sort of Williamsburg-on-the-waterfont is fully under way. Its anti-Hamptons hipster beach scene is back on track following damage sustained during Hurricane Sandy in 2012. Throughout beach season (late May through mid-September), buzzy restaurants and beach bars (including the new Riis Park Beach Bazaar at Jacob Riis Park) draw crowds, as do the sandy shores, with plenty of water activities beyond swimming, like surfing, Jet Skiing, and even whale- and dolphin-watching cruises.

Riis Park Beach Bazaar. Launched in 2015, this outdoor fair features about a half-dozen local food-and-drink vendors. Try the organic chicken shawarma from **Samesa** or ice cream from Brooklyn-based **Ample Hills Creamery,** and check out cultural offerings (like free weekend concerts), beach activities (volleyball, kite flying, and more), and assorted handicrafts vendors on the waterfront at **Jacob Riis Park Beach.** Facilities and vendors are generally open from Memorial Day through Labor Day, with most activity unfolding on weekends. Each off-season highlights the latest restaurant-in-residence at the Art Deco pavilion, with a heated dining room and flat screens showing local sports teams. ⊠ *Jacob Riis Park, Gateway National Recreation Area, 16702 Rockaway Beach Blvd., Rockaway Park, Queens* ⊕ *www.riisparkbeachbazaar.com* ⊗ *Bazaar closed Labor Day–Memorial Day. Restaurant closed Tues. Labor Day–Memorial Day (check website for latest hours).*

NEED A BREAK

✕ **Tacoway Beach.** This small, mostly outdoor eatery is an oasis; once you're inside, it becomes hard to remember that you're actually still in New York City. For the perfect post-beach pit stop, order some Mexican-style street tacos (try the fried fish) and a cerveza, and bask in the chill surfer vibes as the sun goes down. ⊠ *302 Beach 87th St., Queens* ⊕ *www.tacowaybeach.com* ⊗ *Closed Labor Day–Memorial Day* Ⓜ *A Shuttle to Beach 90th St.*

THE BRONX

Whether you're relaxing at a ball game, indulging in fresh mozzarella and cannoli on Arthur Avenue, or scoping out exotic species at the zoo, there's plenty of fun to be had here. Named for the area's first documented European settler, Jonas Bronck, the Bronx is often the city's most misunderstood borough. Its reputation as a gritty, down-and-out place is a little outdated, and there's lots of beauty if you know where to look. There is more parkland in the Bronx than in any other borough, as well as one of the world's finest botanical collections, the largest metropolitan zoo in the country, and, of course, Yankee Stadium.

Two bronze rhinoceros statues stand at the entrance to the Keith W. Johnson Zoo Center at the Bronx Zoo. They're modeled after a rhino named Bessie, who lived at the zoo from 1923 to 1962.

TOP ATTRACTIONS

FAMILY

Fodor's Choice

★

Bronx Zoo. When it opened its gates in 1899, the Bronx Zoo had fewer than 800 animals. But today, with 265 acres and more than 10,000 animals (representing 700-plus species), it's the largest metropolitan zoo in the United States. Get up close and personal with exotic creatures in outdoor settings that re-create natural habitats; you're often separated from the animals by no more than a moat or wall of glass. Don't miss the **Congo Gorilla Forest,** a 6½-acre re-creation of a lush African rain forest with two troops of western lowland gorillas, as well as mandrills, okapis, and red river hogs. At **Tiger Mountain** an open viewing shelter lets you get incredibly close to Siberian tigers, who frolic in a pool and lounge outside (even in cold weather). As the big cats are often napping at midday, aim to visit in the morning or evening. In **Madagascar!,** the formality of the old Lion House has been replaced with a verdant re-creation of one of the most threatened natural habitats in the world. Here you see adorable lemurs and far-from-adorable hissing cockroaches.

Go on a mini-safari via the **Wild Asia Monorail,** May through October, weather permitting. As you wend your way through the forest, see Asian elephants, Indo-Chinese tigers, Indian rhinoceroses, *gaur* (the world's largest cattle), Mongolian wild horses, and several deer and antelope species. Try to visit the most popular exhibits, such as Congo Gorilla Forest, early to avoid lines later in the day. In winter the outdoor exhibitions have fewer animals on view, but there are also smaller crowds, and plenty of indoor exhibits to savor. Also note that there is an extra charge for some exhibits. If you want to see everything, you'll save money by purchasing the Total Experience ticket. ⌂ *2300 Southern Blvd., near E. 187th St., Belmont*

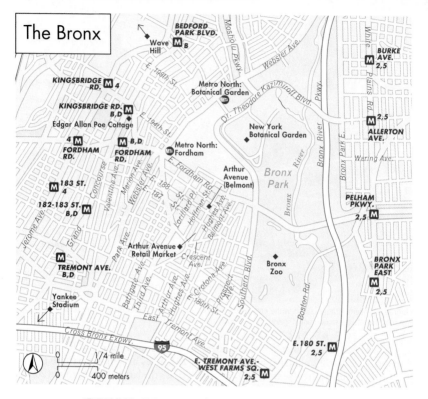

☎ 718/220–5100 ⊕ *www.bronxzoo.com* ✉ *General admission $22.95–$25.95 (extra charge for some exhibits); Total Experience $28.95–$38.95; free entry Wed. (suggested donation; some attractions extra)* ⊙ *Last entry to exhibits is 30 mins before closing; check website for seasonal discounts available when purchasing tickets online; parking $16* Ⓜ *2, 5 to Pelham Pkwy. or BxM11 express bus to Bronx River entrance.*

FAMILY

Fodor's Choice

★

New York Botanical Garden. Considered one of the leading botany centers in the world, this beautiful 250-acre garden is one of the best reasons to make a trip to the Bronx. Built around the dramatic gorge of the Bronx River, the Garden is home to lush indoor and outdoor gardens and acres of natural forest, and offers classes, concerts, and special exhibits. Be astounded by the captivating fragrance of the Peggy Rockefeller Rose Garden's 4,000 plants of more than 650 varieties; see intricate orchids that look like the stuff of science fiction; or relax outside in the leafy Thain Family Forest or indoors in the calm of the Conservatory. You can also take a jaunt through the Everett Children's Adventure Garden, a 12-acre, indoor-outdoor museum with a boulder maze, giant animal topiaries, and a plant discovery center.

The garden's roses bloom in June and September, but there's plenty to see year-round. The Victorian-style **Enid A. Haupt Conservatory** houses re-creations of misty tropical rain forests and arid African and

North American deserts, as well as exhibitions such as the annual Holiday Train Show and Orchid Show. The **All-Garden Pass** gives you access to the Conservatory, Rock Garden (Apr.–Oct.), tram tour, Everett Children's Adventure Garden, and other special exhibitions. ✉ *2900 Southern Blvd., Belmont* ☎ *718/817–8700* ⊕ *www.nybg.org* 🎫 *All-Garden Pass $20–$30. Grounds-only admission is free Sat. 9–10 and all day Wed. (available otherwise only to NYC residents for $15)* ⊗ *Closed Mon.* ☞ *Parking $15; $20 for weekends and special events* Ⓜ *B, D, 4 to Bedford Park Blvd.; then walk about 8 blocks downhill to the garden (or take the Bx26 bus). Metro-North (Harlem local line) to Botanical Garden.*

FAMILY
Fodor's Choice
★
Yankee Stadium. See one of baseball's great franchises, the "Bronx Bombers," in action at their 2009-debuted, $1.5 billion Yankee Stadium (set right across the street from the site of the original stadium, aka "the House that Ruth Built"). Tickets can be pricey, but the experience is like watching baseball in a modern-day coliseum. It's quite opulent: a traditional white frieze adorns the stadium's top; inside, limestone-and-marble hallways are lined with photos of past Yankee greats. History buffs and hard-core fans should visit the Yankees Museum (set on the main level and open till the end of the eighth inning), filled with historical team memorabilia, and Monument Park (closes 45 minutes prior to first pitch), with plaques of past Yankee legends, by center field. ■ TIP➜ **Pregame and off-season one-hour stadium tours are held on a near-daily basis year-round; visit the Yankees website for more info on times and ticketing.** ✉ *1 E. 161st St., at River Ave., Bronx* ☎ *718/293–4300* ⊕ *newyork.yankees.mlb.com* ☞ *Baseball season runs Apr.–Oct.* Ⓜ *4, B, D to 161st St.–Yankee Stadium.*

WORTH NOTING

Fodor's Choice
★
Arthur Avenue (Belmont). Manhattan's Little Italy is overrun with mediocre restaurants aimed at tourists, but Belmont (meaning "beautiful hill"), the Little Italy of the Bronx, is a real, thriving Italian-American community. Unless you have family in the area, the main reason to come here is for the food: eating it, buying it, looking at it fondly through windows, and chatting with shopkeepers so you can get recipe advice.

Nearly a century after pushcarts on Arthur Avenue catered to Italian-American workers constructing the zoo and Botanical Garden, the area teems with meat markets, bakeries, cheese makers, and shops selling kitchenware (espresso machines, pasta makers, etc.). There are debates about which store or restaurant is the "best," but thanks to generations of Italian grandmothers, most vendors here serve fresh, handmade foods.

Although the area is no longer solely Italian—many Latinos and Albanians share this neighborhood now—Italians dominate the food scene. The covered **Arthur Avenue Retail Market** is a terrific starting point. It houses some dozen vendors, including the Bronx Beer Hall. Regulars mostly shop on Saturday afternoon; many stores are shuttered on Sunday and after 5 pm. ✉ *Arthur Ave. between Crescent Ave./184th St. and 188th St., and 187th St. between Lorillard Pl. and Cambreleng Ave., Belmont* ⊕ *www.bronxlittleitaly.com* Ⓜ *4, B, D to Fordham Rd., then it's about a 15-min walk (or take Bx12 bus).*

14

✕ **Joe's Italian Deli.** Seven shops within four blocks of Arthur Avenue make fresh mozzarella daily, but Joe's is the one you don't want to miss (the trick is, they add the perfect amount of salt). The ceiling is draped with assorted house-made and imported cheeses, as well as multiple types of prosciutto and other meats. ⊠ *685 E. 187th St., at Crescent Ave., Belmont* 🖀 ⊕ *www. joesitaliandeli.com* Ⓜ *4, B, D to Fordham Rd.; walk 15 mins east.*

Edgar Allan Poe Cottage. The beloved American poet-writer's legacy is detailed at this historic house museum, tucked into a bustling section of the Bronx. The small farmhouse, dating to 1812, housed Poe; his young, ailing wife, Virginia; and his mother-in-law during his final years, from 1846 to 1849. Rooms are filled with reproduction period pieces, as well as a handful of personal effects that may have inspired the enduring poems Poe wrote here, like "Annabel Lee" and "The Bells." The surrounding green space in Poe Park lends well to the transporting back-in-time feeling of a visit here. Audio and guided tours are included with admission. ⊠ *2640 Grand Concourse, at East Kingsbridge Rd., Bronx* 🖀 *718/881–8900* ⊕ *bronxhistoricalsociety.org/poe-cottage* 🖃 *$5* ☾ *Closed Mon.–Wed.* Ⓜ *4, B, D to Kingsbridge Rd.*

Wave Hill. Drawn by views of the Hudson River and New Jersey's dramatic Palisades cliffs, 19th-century Manhattan millionaires built summer homes in the Bronx neighborhood of Riverdale. One of the most magnificent, Wave Hill, is today a 28-acre public garden and cultural center that attracts visitors from all over the world. Its themed gardens, from an aquatic garden to a shade border, are exquisite. Grand beech and oak trees tower above wide lawns, an elegant pergola overlooks the majestic river view, and benches on curving pathways provide quiet respite. Open year-round, Wave Hill House (1843) and Glyndor House (1927) host art exhibitions, Sunday concerts, wellness-minded activities, and gardening workshops. It's worth the schlep. ⊠ *649 W. 249th St., at Independence Ave., Riverdale* 🖀 *718/549–3200* ⊕ *www.wavehill. org* 🖃 *$8; Tues. and Sat., free 9–noon* ☾ *Closed Mon.* ⌨ *Parking $8, free off site* Ⓜ *1 to Van Cortlandt Park–242nd St. (free hourly shuttle service 9:10–3:10); A to Inwood–207th St., then Bx7 or Bx20 bus to W. 252nd St.; Metro-North Hudson Line to Riverdale (free hourly shuttle service 9:50–3:50).*

STATEN ISLAND

A free 25-minute ferry voyage from the southern tip of Manhattan to Staten Island provides one of the city's best views of the Statue of Liberty and the downtown Manhattan skyline. When you arrival in the St. George neighborhood, it's hard to miss the **waterfront promenade,** with its Manhattan skyline views and "Postcards" 9/11 memorial, or the Richmond County Bank Ballpark, the home of the **Staten Island Yankees** (⊕ *www.siyanks.com*), where minor leaguers in pinstripes affectionately known as "Baby Bombers" dream of one day playing in the major leagues in the Bronx. Also in St. George, the debut of the **Empire Outlets** (⊕ *www.empireoutletsnyc.com*), the city's first outlet mall, with

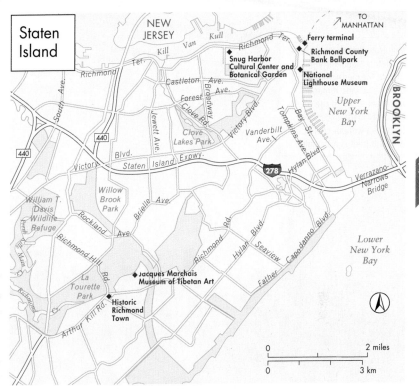

14

more than 100 planned shops, a hotel, and waterfront dining options, including an artisanal food market called Marketplace (MRKTPL), is scheduled to open by late 2018. The 630-foot-high **New York Wheel** (⊕ *newyorkwheel.com*) is a different story: disputes between the developer and intial contractor have stalled construction plans, creating an unclear future for what would be the world's tallest observation wheel. If you're near the ferry terminal Thursday through Sunday, consider stopping at Enoteca Maria (⊕ *www.enotecamaria.com*) for lunch or dinner; it serves Italian fare cooked by Italian grandmothers.

When venturing beyond the borough's northernmost tip, you will find that Staten Island is full of surprises. Along with suburban sprawl, there are wonderful small museums, including a premier collection of Tibetan art; walkable woodlands; and a historic village replicating New York's rural past. From the ferry terminal, grab an S40 bus to the **Snug Harbor Cultural Center** (less than 10 minutes) or take the S74 and combine visits to the **Jacques Marchais Museum of Tibetan Art** and **Historic Richmond Town.**

Legally part of New York City since 1898, Staten Island is in many ways a world apart. The city's most suburban borough (sometimes called the "Forgotten Borough" by locals), is geographically more separate, less populous, politically more conservative, and ethnically more homogeneous than the rest of the city.

TOP ATTRACTIONS

Jacques Marchais Museum of Tibetan Art. At the top of a hill sits this replica of a Tibetan monastery containing one of the largest collections of Tibetan and Himalayan sculpture, paintings, and artifacts outside Tibet. Meditate with visiting Buddhist monks, or just enjoy the peaceful views from the terraced garden. ⊠ *338 Lighthouse Ave., Lighthouse Hill* ☎ *718/987–3500* ⊕ *www.tibetanmuseum.org* ⊠ *$6* ☉ *Closed Mon., Tues.* Ⓜ *S74 bus to Lighthouse Ave. (35- to 45-min ride from ferry terminal) and walk uphill 15 mins; cab fare from ferry terminal is about $20.*

FAMILY

Fodor'sChoice

★

Snug Harbor Cultural Center and Botanical Garden. Once part of a retirement center for sailors, this 83-acre cultural center is now a popular spot to engage with contemporary art and historical collections. Enjoy the **Children's Museum** (*www.sichildrensmuseum.org; $8*), or take a stroll through lush gardens. (Note that all on-site attractions can be visited—and, if applicable, ticketed—independently of each other.)

Made up of 26 landmarked buildings, nine botanic gardens, 10 acres of wetlands, and a 2-acre farm, Snug Harbor is also home to a new outpost of the **Staten Island Museum** (*www.statenislandmuseum.org; $8 suggested donation*), with exhibits spanning art, history, and science; the **New York Chinese Scholar's Garden** (*$5*); as well as dance and music studios, art galleries, and residency programs. Main Hall—the oldest building on the property, dating to 1833—is home to the **Eleanor Proske Visitors Center** (*free*) and the **Newhouse Center for Contemporary Art** (*$5*), which exhibits artworks connected to Snug Harbor's history. Next door, the **Noble Maritime Collection** (*www.noblemaritime.org; suggested donation*) maintains historic collections specific to Staten Island and Snug Harbor's maritime past. ⊠ *1000 Richmond Terr., between Snug Harbor Rd. and Tysen St., Livingston* ⊹ *From the Staten Island Ferry terminal, take the S40 bus 2 miles (about 7 mins) to the Snug Harbor Rd. stop. Otherwise, grab a car service at the ferry terminal (the ride should cost about $8)* ☎ *718/448–2500* ⊕ *www.snug-harbor.org* ⊠ *Grounds and Botanical Gardens free; Chinese Scholar's Garden and Newhouse Center combo ticket $8; free parking* ☉ *Children's Museum closed Mon. Staten Island Museum closed Mon., Tues. New York Chinese Scholar's Garden closed Mon. (summer/fall); Mon., Thurs. (winter/spring). Newhouse Center closed Jan.–Mar.; Mon., Tues. (Apr.–Nov.); Mon.–Wed. (Dec.). Noble Maritime Collection closed Mon.–Wed.* ☞ *Check websites for seasonal hrs; packing a picnic is recommended.*

14

WORTH NOTING

FAMILY

Historic Richmond Town. Think of a small-scale version of Virginia's Colonial Williamsburg (the polar opposite of Brooklyn's scene-y Williamsburg), and you'll understand the appeal of Historic Richmond Town, NYC's only living-history museum. This 100-acre village, constructed from 1695 to the 19th century, was the site of Staten Island's original county seat. Fifteen of the site's 30 historic buildings are open to the public. Highlights include the Gothic Revival **Courthouse,** the one-room **General Store,** and the **Voorlezer's House,** the oldest schoolhouse in America (it served as a residence and place of worship, in addition to an elementary school). Also on-site is the **Staten Island Historical Society**

Museum, built in 1848 as the second county clerk's and surrogate's office, which now houses Staten Island artifacts plus changing exhibits about the island. There are guided tours Wednesday–Friday at 1:30 and weekends at 1:30 and 3.

You may see staff in period dress demonstrate Early American crafts and trades such as tinsmithing or basket making, though the general era meant to be re-created is 1820–1860. Check the website for special events and educational programs held throughout the year. ⊠ *441 Clarke Ave., at St. Patrick's Pl., Richmondtown ✛ Take the S74 bus (30–45 mins) or a car service (about $20) from the ferry terminal* ☎ *718/351–1611* ⊕ *www.historicrichmondtown.org* ✉ *$8 (free Fri.); free parking* ⊙ *Closed Mon., Tues.* Ⓜ *S74 bus to Richmond Rd./St. Patrick's Pl.*

National Lighthouse Museum. Just a short stroll from the ferry terminal, this museum sheds "light" on lighthouse history throughout America. It's housed in a 1912 foundry that was once part of an 18-building complex for the U.S. Lighthouse Service General Depot, which was the center of all lighthouse operations in the country from 1864 to1939. Only six structures remain, including underground vaults, an administration building where architects designed the country's lighthouses, and buildings where Fresnel lenses were assembled. Self-guided visits through the small museum take in exhibits and artifacts surrounding the history, technology, and keepers behind lighthouses, illustrating the role they collectively played in American maritime history. ⊠ *200 Promenade, at Lighthouse Point, St. George ✛ 5-min walk south of Staten Island Ferry terminal* ☎ *718/390–0040* ⊕ *lighthousemuseum. org* ✉ *$5* ⊙ *Closed Mon.*

WHERE TO EAT

EAT LIKE A LOCAL

A handful of foods are associated with New York City: apples (big ones, obviously), pizza, pastrami, hot dogs, bagels—the list of earthly delights is long and delicious. These, generally speaking, are what the locals tend to talk about.

FOOD TRUCKS

The food-truck movement is officially on. It seems there's a special truck for everything from ethnic eats to fresh-baked sweets. The southern end of Washington Square, near NYU, is a prime location, with trucks lined up serving the cuisines of Holland, Colombia, Cambodia, and Mexico, but you can find food trucks parked all over town, some with legendary followings and Twitter feeds to help you find them. Thompson Hotels, which has several properties in New York, even has a Food Truck Concierge.

PIZZA

There are few things more Big Apple than a slice of pizza, its bottom crust crispy from the coal oven. There are take-out joints for slices and sit-down restaurants that only serve pies; some are thin crust, some are thick, some even have fried dough, and everyone has a favorite. There's no question that pizza will always be synonymous with New York, but the crust is being elevated to a real art form these days. Some people say the reason the pizza here is so good is because of the excellent quality of the New York water.

SOUL FOOD IN HARLEM

Sylvia Woods, the "Queen of Soul Food" and proprietor of the eponymous Harlem restaurant, may have ascended to that great soul food restaurant in the sky, but the cuisine lives on in this historic neighborhood—in fact, more now than ever, since celeb-chef Marcus Samuelsson moved into the area, opening the Red Rooster, a global eatery that gives a big nod to soul food.

CHINESE FOOD

There's Chinese food and then there's New York's downtown Chinatown Chinese food, which some visitors might find head-scratchingly unfamiliar. That's because Chinatown boasts a diverse population from China's many regions, and menus are going to look deliciously foreign to the uninitiated. Go ahead, point and order something you've never heard of. Restaurants serving dim sum, which are basically different kinds of small fried or steamed dumplings, are popular for weekend breakfast.

BURGERS

Hamburgers will forever be a part of the Big Apple dining landscape. But it so happens that it has never been a better time to be a burger eater, and nearly every restaurant—American or not—has some kind of burger on its menu. If you're a discriminating burger lover, look for the name Pat LaFrieda, a meat purveyor par excellence. Just

don't expect to save any money; it's not unusual to see a $20 hamburger on a menu.

GASTROPUBS

The gastropub phenomenon, imported from London, began with the Spotted Pig in the West Village, and within a few years, every neighborhood had one. And why not? Blending a casual pub atmosphere with way-better-than-average pub grub is a fun and tasty combination that's hard to beat.

BANH MI SANDWICHES

The banh mi sandwich has grabbed the attention of Big Apple eaters in recent years and has not let go. This French-influenced Vietnamese sandwich consists of pork, pâté, carrots, cilantro, and jalapeño peppers stuffed into a baguette. This is a delicacy worth seeking out, so check the menus at our top Asian restaurant picks.

LOCAVORE

The focus on local food and beverages has definitely taken hold at NYC restaurants. Menus flaunt the nearby provenance of their meat and produce, whether it's from upstate New York or from the restaurant's rooftop garden. Wine lists frequently include excellent Long Island or Finger Lakes wines, as well as bourbon and other spirits brewed as close as the Brooklyn Navy Yards or the Hudson Valley.

Updated by
David Farley

Ready to take a bite out of New York? Hope you've come hungry. In a city where creativity is expressed in innumerable ways, the food scene takes center stage, with literally thousands of chances to taste what Gotham is all about. Whether lining up at street stands, gobbling down legendary deli and diner grub, or chasing a coveted reservation at the latest celebrity-chef venue, New Yorkers are a demanding yet appreciative audience.

Every neighborhood offers temptations high, low, and in between, meaning there's truly something for every taste, whim, and budget. No matter how you approach dining out here, it's hard to go wrong. Planning a day of shopping among the glittering flagship boutiques along 5th and Madison Avenues? Stop into one of the Upper East Side's storied restaurants for a repast among the "ladies who lunch." Clubbing in the Meatpacking District? Tuck into a meal at eateries as trendy as their patrons. Craving authentic ethnic? From food trucks to hidden joints, there are almost more choices than there are appetites. Recent years have also seen entire food categories, from ramen to meatballs to mac 'n' cheese, riffed upon and fetishized, and at many restaurants you find an almost religious reverence for seasonal, locally sourced cuisine.

And don't forget—New York is still home to more celebrity chefs than any other city. Your chances of running into your favorite cookbook author, Food Network celeb, or paparazzi-friendly chef are high, adding even more star wattage to a restaurant scene with an already through-the-roof glamour quotient. Newfound economic realities, however, have revived appreciation for value, meaning you can tap into wallet-friendly choices at every level of the food chain. Rest assured, this city does its part to satisfy your appetite. Ready, set, eat.

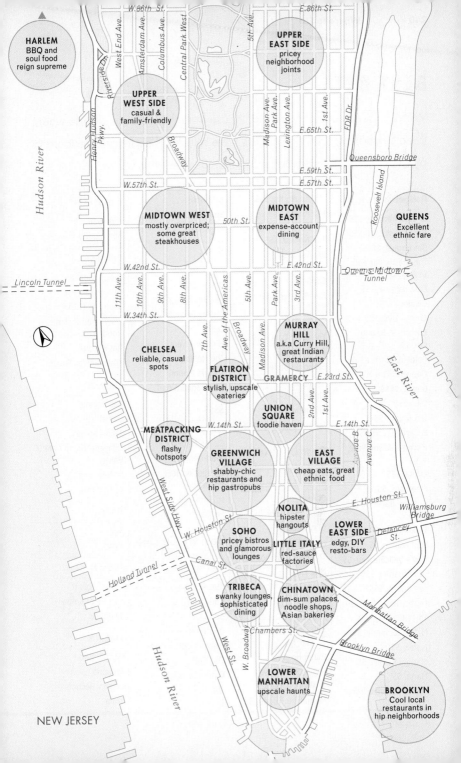

HARLEM
BBQ and soul food reign supreme

UPPER EAST SIDE
pricey neighborhood joints

UPPER WEST SIDE
casual & family-friendly

QUEENS
Excellent ethnic fare

MIDTOWN WEST
mostly overpriced; some great steakhouses

MIDTOWN EAST
expense-account dining

CHELSEA
reliable, casual spots

MURRAY HILL
a.k.a Curry Hill, great Indian restaurants

FLATIRON DISTRICT
stylish, upscale eateries

UNION SQUARE
foodie haven

MEATPACKING DISTRICT
flashy hotspots

GREENWICH VILLAGE
shabby-chic restaurants and hip gastropubs

EAST VILLAGE
cheap eats, great ethnic food

NOLITA
hipster hangouts

SOHO
pricey bistros and glamorous lounges

LITTLE ITALY
red-sauce factories

LOWER EAST SIDE
edgy, DIY resto-bars

TRIBECA
swanky lounges, sophisticated dining

CHINATOWN
dim-sum palaces, noodle shops, Asian bakeries

LOWER MANHATTAN
upscale haunts

BROOKLYN
Cool local restaurants in hip neighborhoods

Hudson River

East River

NEW JERSEY

GRAMERCY

Roosevelt Island

Lincoln Tunnel

Holland Tunnel

Queensboro Bridge

Queens-Midtown Tunnel

Williamsburg Bridge

Manhattan Bridge

Brooklyn Bridge

W. 86th St.
E. 86th St.
West End Ave.
Amsterdam Ave.
Columbus Ave.
Central Park West
5th Ave.
Riverside Dr.
Henry Hudson Pkwy.
Madison Ave.
Park Ave.
Lexington Ave.
1st Ave.
E. 65th St.
FDR Dr.
E. 59th St.
E. 57th St.
W. 57th St.
50th St.
E. 42nd St.
W. 42nd St.
11th Ave.
10th Ave.
9th Ave.
8th Ave.
7th Ave.
Ave. of the Americas
Broadway
5th Ave.
Madison Ave.
Park Ave.
3rd Ave.
2nd Ave.
1st Ave.
W. 34th St.
E. 23rd St.
W. 14th St.
E. 14th St.
Avenue A
Avenue B
Avenue C
E. Houston St.
W. Houston St.
Delancey St.
Canal St.
Chambers St.
West Side Hwy.
West St.
W. Broadway

BEST BETS

With thousands of restaurants to choose from, how do you decide where to eat? Fodor's writers and editors have selected their favorite restaurants by price, cuisine, and experience in the Best Bets lists below.

Fodor's Choice ★

al di là Trattoria, $$$
Babbo Ristorante, $$$
Bar Boulud, $$$
The Breslin Bar and Dining Room, $$$
Café Sabarsky, $$
Candle 79, $$
Charlie Bird, $$$
Clinton St. Baking Co., $$
Colonie, $$
Cosme, $$$
Daniel, $$$$
Diner, $$
Dirt Candy, $$
Edi & the Wolf, $$
Eleven Madison Park, $$$$
Estela, $$$
Freemans, $$
Gotham Bar & Grill, $$$$
Indian Accent, $$$$
Ivan Ramen, $$
Katz's Delicatessen, $$
Le Bernardin, $$$$
Le Coucou, $$$$
Legacy Records, $$$
The Little Owl, $$$
M. Wells Dinette, $$
Marea, $$$
Marlow & Sons, $$
Marta, $$
Mission Chinese Food, $$

Momofuku Ko, $$$$
Momofuku Noodle Bar, $$
The NoMad, $$$
Per Se, $$$$
Peter Luger Steakhouse, $$$$
Red Rooster Harlem, $$$
Reynard, $$$
The River Café, $$$$
Roberta's, $$
Saxon & Parole, $$
Semilla, $$$$
Shake Shack, $
SriPraPhai, $$
Sushi Nakazawa, $$$$

Best by Price

$

Burger Joint
The City Bakery
Gray's Papaya
Levain Bakery
The Meatball Shop
Mile End
Shake Shack

$$

Café Sabarsky
Candle 79
Hanoi House
Katz's Delicatessen
M. Wells Dinette
Momofuku Noodle Bar

Oda House
Somtum Der
Roberta's

$$$

ABC Kitchen
Balthazar
Bar Boulud
Legacy Records
Marea
Minetta Tavern
The NoMad
Osteria Morini
The Standard Grill

$$$$

Craft
Eleven Madison Park
Jean-Georges
L'Atelier de Joël Robuchon
Le Bernardin
Per Se

Best by Cuisine

AMERICAN

ABC Kitchen
Cookshop
Craft
Due West
Eleven Madison Park
The Grill
Gramercy Tavern
The Red Cat

BARBECUE

Fette Sau
Hill Country

CHINESE

Joe's Shanghai
Mission Chinese
Shun Lee Palace
Tasty Hand-Pulled Noodles
Tim Ho Wan
Xi'an Famous Foods

FRENCH

Bar Boulud
Daniel
Jean Georges
Lafayette Grand Café & Bakery
Le Bernardin
Le Coucou

GREEK

Kefi
Pylos

INDIAN

Indian Accent
Kati Roll Company
Tamarind

ITALIAN

Charlie Bird
Emporio
Legacy Records
Lupa

Marea
Parm
Rubirosa

JAPANESE

Ippudo
Kurumazushi
Sushi Nakazawa
Sushi of Gari
Sushi Yasuda

MEDITERRANEAN

Il Buco
The NoMad

MEXICAN

Atla
Cosme
Empellón Taqueria
La Esquina
Maya

PIZZA

Keste Pizza & Vino
Lombardi's Pizza
Pasquale Jones
Rubirosa

SEAFOOD

Grand Central Oyster
Bar & Restaurant
The John Dory
Le Bernardin
Marea
Mary's Fish Camp
Pearl Oyster Bar

SPANISH

Boqueria
Casa Mono

STEAKHOUSE

Cote
Porter House New York
Sparks Steakhouse

Best by Experience

BRUNCH

Balthazar
Bubby's
Cookshop
Harry's Café and Steak
Sarabeth's

CELEB-SPOTTING

ABC Kitchen
Balthazar
The Breslin Bar and
Dining Room
Café Boulud
Minetta Tavern
Nobu Downtown
The Standard Grill

CHILD-FRIENDLY

Bubby's
Carmine's

The City Bakery
Joe's Shanghai
Lombardi's Pizza
Odeon

GREAT VIEWS

Asiate
Marea
Michael Jordan's The
Steakhouse NYC
Per Se
Porter House New York

LATE-NIGHT DINING

Balthazar
The Breslin Bar and
Dining Room
Due West
Emporio
Minetta Tavern
The Standard Grill

15

PLANNING

CHILDREN

Although it's unusual to see children in the dining rooms of Manhattan's most elite restaurants, dining with youngsters in New York does not have to mean culinary exile. Many of the restaurants reviewed here are excellent choices for families, and are marked as such.

RESERVATIONS

It's always a good idea to plan ahead. Some renowned restaurants like Per Se, Daniel, Brooklyn Fare, and Momofuku Ko are booked weeks or even months in advance. If that's the case, you can get lucky at the last minute if you're flexible—and friendly. Most restaurants keep a few tables open for walk-ins and VIPs. Show up for dinner early (5:30) or late (after 10), and politely inquire about any last-minute vacancies or cancellations.

Occasionally, an eatery may take your credit-card number and ask you to call the day before your scheduled meal to reconfirm: don't forget or you could lose out, or possibly be charged for your oversight.

WHAT TO WEAR

New Yorkers like to dress up, and so should you. Whatever your style, dial it up a notch. Have some fun while you're at it. Pull out the clothes you've been saving for a special occasion and get glamorous. Unfair as it is, the way you look can influence how you're treated—and where you're seated. Generally speaking, jeans and a button-down shirt suffice at most table-service restaurants in the $ to $$ range. Few places require a jacket or jacket and tie, but if you have doubts, call the restaurant and ask.

TIPPING AND TAXES

In most restaurants, tip the server 15%–20%. (To figure out a 20% tip quickly, just move the decimal point one place to the left on your total and double that amount.) Tip at least $1 per drink at the bar, and $1 for each coat checked. Never tip the maître d' unless you're out to impress your guests or expect to pay another visit soon. Your restaurant bill will include a charge for a sales tax of 8.875%.

SMOKING

Smoking is prohibited in all enclosed public spaces in New York City, including restaurants and bars.

HOURS

New Yorkers seem ready to eat at any hour. Many restaurants stay open between lunch and dinner, some have late-night seating, and still others serve around the clock. Restaurants that serve breakfast often do so until noon or later. Restaurants in the East Village, Lower East Side, SoHo, TriBeCa, and Greenwich Village are likely to remain open late, whereas Midtown spots and those in the Theater and Financial districts and uptown generally close earlier. Unless otherwise noted, the restaurants listed are open daily for lunch and dinner.

PRICES

Be sure to ask the price of the daily specials recited by the waiter; the charge for specials at some restaurants is noticeably out of line with the other prices on the menu. Beware of the $10 bottle of water; ask for tap water instead, and always review your bill.

If you eat early or late, you may be able to take advantage of a prix-fixe deal not offered at peak hours. Most upscale restaurants have great lunch deals.

Credit cards are widely accepted, but many restaurants (particularly smaller ones downtown) accept only cash. If you plan to use a credit card, it's a good idea to confirm that it is acceptable when making reservations or before sitting down to eat.

WHAT IT COSTS AT DINNER			
$	$$	$$$	$$$$
RESTAURANTS under $13	$13–$24	$25–$35	over $35

Restaurant prices are the average cost of a main course at dinner or, if dinner is not served, at lunch.

15

CHECK BEFORE YOU GO

The nature of the restaurant industry means that places open and close in a New York minute. It's always a good idea to phone ahead and make sure your restaurant is still turning tables.

RESTAURANT REVIEWS

Listed alphabetically within neighborhoods. Reviews have been short-ened; for full reviews, visit Fodors.com. Use the coordinate (⊹ 1:B2) at the end of each listing to locate a property on the corresponding map at the end of the chapter.

LOWER MANHATTAN

FINANCIAL DISTRICT

The southern tip of the island, once skyscraper laden and nightlife starved, has been getting buzzier in the last few years. Exciting new bars and restaurants have opened, but the old dependable steak houses and bistros are still here.

$$$$
STEAKHOUSE
✕ **Delmonico's.** The oldest continually operating restaurant in New York City (since 1837), austere Delmonico's is steeped in cultural, political, and culinary history. Lobster Newburg and Baked Alaska were invented here—and are still served. **Known for:** the city's oldest eatery; steak; classic ambience. $ *Average main: $38* ⊠ *56 Beaver St., at William St., Financial District* ☎ *212/509–1144* ⊕ *www.delmonicosny.com* ☉ *Closed Sun. No lunch Sat.* Ⓜ *2, 3 to Wall St.; R to Whitehall St.; 4, 5 to Bowling Green; J, Z to Broad St.* ⊹ *1:D4.*

$
CAFÉ
✕ **Financier Patisserie.** On the cobblestone pedestrian street that has become the Financial District's restaurant row, this charming pâtisserie serves excellent pastries and delicious savory foods, like mushroom

bisque, salads, and hot or cold sandwiches (we have cravings for the panini pressed with prosciutto, fig jam, mascarpone, and arugula). After lunch, relax with a cappuccino and a *financier* (almond tea cake), or an elegant pastry. **Known for:** exquisite pastries; paninis; outdoor tables. [$] *Average main: $7* ✉ *62 Stone St., between Mill La. and Hanover Sq., Financial District* ☎ *212/344–5600* 🌐 *www.financierpastries.com* 🕒 *No dinner* [M] *2, 3 to Wall St.; 4, 5 to Bowling Green; J, Z to Broad St.* ⊕ *1:E4.*

$$$ STEAKHOUSE 🍴 **Harry's Café and Steak.** Its noise-dampening acoustics and maze of underground nooks combine to make Harry's Steak—the fine-dining half of the restaurant (Harry's Café is more casual, but the menu is the same)—one of the city's most intimate steak houses. Settle into a leather booth and start with a classic shrimp cocktail or the tomato trio, starring thick beefsteak slices topped with bacon and blue cheese, mozzarella and basil, and shaved onion with ranch dressing. **Known for:** prime aged porterhouse for two; dark wood-meets-leather interior; weekend brunch. [$] *Average main: $35* ✉ *1 Hanover Sq., between Stone and Pearl Sts., Financial District* ☎ *212/785–9200* 🌐 *www.harrysnyc.com* 🕒 *Closed Sun.* [M] *4, 5 to Bowling Green; 2, 3 to Wall St.; J, Z to Broad St.* ⊕ *1:E4.*

$$$$ JAPANESE 🍴 **Nobu Downtown.** At a new location in Downtown Manhattan, this sushi stalwart is as bustling and taste bud–tantalizing as ever, and New York's most famous Japanese restaurant is the downtown destination for the innovative Japanese cuisine that Nobu Matsuhisa made famous (though he's rarely in attendance these days). Dishes like fresh yellowtail sashimi with jalapeño, rock shrimp tempura, or miso-marinated Chilean sea bass continue to draw huge crowds. **Known for:** its see-and-been-seen crowd; high-quality sushi; omakase tasting menu. [$] *Average main: $39* ✉ *195 Broadway, at Fulton St., Financial District* ☎ *212/219–0500* 🌐 *www.noburestaurants.com* 🕒 *No lunch weekends* [M] *1 to Franklin St.* ⊕ *1:D3.*

$ AMERICAN 🍴 **Ulysses'.** Squeezed between skyscrapers and the towering New York Stock Exchange, Stone Street is a two-block restaurant oasis that feels more like a village than the center of the financial universe. After the market closes, Wall Streeters head to Ulysses', a popular pub with 12 beers on tap and more than 50 bottled beers. **Known for:** above-average pub grub; lively outdoor atmosphere; beer selection. [$] *Average main: $12* ✉ *95 Pearl St., near Hanover Sq., Financial District* ☎ *212/482–0400* 🌐 *www.ulyssesnyc.com* [M] *R, W to Whitehall St.; J, Z to Broad St.; 2, 3 to Wall St.* ⊕ *1:E4.*

TRIBECA

TriBeCa and its restaurants are a playground for the rich and famous. Fortunately, glamorous dining rooms in converted warehouses have been joined by more casual spots.

$$$ AUSTRIAN FAMILY 🍴 **Blaue Gans.** Chef Kurt Gutenbrunner, one of the most lauded Austrian chefs in New York, runs this sprawling brasserie like an all-day clubhouse. Pop in for a late-morning or early-afternoon snack—the coffee comes topped with *schlag,* the doughnuts filled with apricot jam—or swing by in the evening for Central European standards like sausage, schnitzel, potato dumplings, and beef goulash. **Known for:** Austrian

wine selection; above-average Central European fare; schnitzel. $ *Average main: $25* ✉ *139 Duane St., near West Broadway, TriBeCa* ☎ *212/571–8880* ◷ *Closed Sun.* Ⓜ *1, 2, 3, A, C to Chambers St.* ✛ *1:C1.*

$$ ✕ **Bubby's.** Neighborhood crowds clamoring for coffee and freshly
AMERICAN squeezed juice line up for brunch at this TriBeCa mainstay, but Bubby's
FAMILY is good for lunch and dinner, too, if you're in the mood for comfort food like mac 'n' cheese or fried chicken. The dining room is homey and cozy, with big windows; in summer, patrons sit at tables outside with their dogs. **Known for:** a true TriBeCa neighborhood spot; casual atmosphere; plenty of brunch options. $ *Average main: $18* ✉ *120 Hudson St., at N. Moore St., TriBeCa* ☎ *212/219–0666* ◉ *www.bubbys.com* Ⓜ *1 to Franklin St.* ✛ *1:C1.*

$$$ ✕ **Locanda Verde.** Run by chef Andrew Carmellini, first an acolyte of
ITALIAN Daniel Boulud, this is a consistently winning option for Italian fare in the city. The Robert De Niro–backed restaurant is warm and welcoming, with accents of brick and wood and large windows that open to the street, weather permitting, while the menu is full of inspired Italian comfort food that hits the mark. **Known for:** exquisite pasta dishes; small plates; occasional celebrity sightings. $ *Average main: $27* ✉ *377 Greenwich St., at N. Moore St., TriBeCa* ☎ *212/925-3797* ◉ *www. locandaverdenyc.com* Ⓜ *1 to Franklin St.* ✛ *1:B1.*

$$$ ✕ **Odeon.** New Yorkers change hangouts faster than they can speed-
FRENCH dial, but this spot has managed to maintain its quality and flair for
FAMILY more than 30 years. It still feels like *the* spot in TriBeCa to get a late-night bite. **Known for:** perpetually cool late-night downtown hangout; better-than-average bistro fare; wine list. $ *Average main: $28* ✉ *145 West Broadway, between Duane and Thomas Sts., TriBeCa* ☎ *212/233–0507* ◉ *www.theodeonrestaurant.com* Ⓜ *1, 2, 3, A, C to Chambers St.* ✛ *1:C1.*

$$$ ✕ **Tamarind.** Many consider Tamarind to be one of Manhattan's best
INDIAN Indian restaurants, and the elegant atmosphere makes it a different experience from many other NYC Indian eateries. Forsaking the usual brass, beads, sitar, and darkness, the dining room is full of windows and natural light. **Known for:** consistently delicious Indian fare; multiregional food; elegant setting. $ *Average main: $28* ✉ *99 Hudson St., at Franklin St., TriBeCa* ☎ *212/775–9000* ◉ *www.tamarindrestaurantsnyc.com* Ⓜ *1 to Franklin St.; A, C, E to Canal St.* ✛ *1:C1.*

SOHO, NOLITA, AND CHINATOWN

SOHO

Sure, eating in SoHo may not feel very low-key, with mostly pricey eateries full of fashionistas and the "see and be seen" crowd, but the restaurants here are worth the fight for a table.

$$$ ✕ **Balthazar.** Even with long waits and excruciating noise levels, most
FRENCH out-of-towners agree that it's worth making reservations to experience restaurateur Keith McNally's flagship, a painstakingly accurate reproduction of a Parisian brasserie with an insider New York feel. Like the decor, entrées re-create French classics: Gruyère-topped onion soup,

15

steak frites, and icy tiers of crab, oysters, and other pristine shellfish. **Known for:** lively scene; authentically Parisian ambience; brunch. Ⓢ *Average main: $28* ⊠ *80 Spring St., between Broadway and Crosby St., SoHo* ☎ *212/965–1414* ⊕ *www.balthazarny.com* Ⓜ *6 to Spring St.; N, R, W to Prince St.; B, D, F, M to Broadway–Lafayette St.* ✛ *2:E4.*

$ ✕ **Balthazar Bakery.** Follow the beguiling scent of fresh-baked bread
BAKERY to Balthazar Bakery, next door to Keith McNally's always-packed Balthazar restaurant. Choices include fresh-baked baguettes and other varieties of French breads, as well as gourmet sandwiches, soups, and memorable pastries to take out (there is no seating). **Known for:** amazingly fresh baked goods; baguettes; pastries. Ⓢ *Average main: $11* ⊠ *80 Spring St., near Crosby St., SoHo* ☎ *212/965–1785* ⊕ *www.balthazarbakery.com* ◷ *No dinner* Ⓜ *6 to Spring St.; N, R, W to Prince St.; B, D, F, M to Broadway–Lafayette St.* ✛ *2:E4.*

$$$ ✕ **Blue Ribbon.** Opened in 1992, Blue Ribbon still has a reputation not
MODERN just as an eclectic, top-notch seafood joint but also as a serious late-
AMERICAN night foodie hangout, especially for chefs. Join the genial hubbub for midnight noshing, namely the beef marrow with oxtail marmalade and renowned raw-bar platters. Trustafarians, literary types, chefs, and designers—a good-looking gang—generally fill this dark box of a room until 4 am. **Known for:** excellent seafood; late-night noshing; raw bar. Ⓢ *Average main: $33* ⊠ *97 Sullivan St., between Prince and Spring Sts., SoHo* ☎ *212/274–0404* ⊕ *www.blueribbonrestaurants.com* ◷ *No lunch* Ⓜ *C, E to Spring St.; N, R, W to Prince St.* ✛ *2:D3.*

$$$ ✕ **Blue Ribbon Sushi.** Sushi, like pizza, attracts plenty of opinionated
JAPANESE fanatics, and Blue Ribbon Sushi gets consistent raves for its überfresh sushi and sashimi. Stick to the excellent raw fish and specials here if you're a purist, or branch out and try one of the experimental rolls: the Blue Ribbon—lobster, *shiso* (Japanese basil), and black caviar—is popular. **Known for:** sceney vibe; superfresh sushi; experimental rolls. Ⓢ *Average main: $28* ⊠ *119 Sullivan St., between Prince and Spring Sts., SoHo* ☎ *212/343–0404* ⊕ *www.blueribbonrestaurants.com* Ⓜ *C, E to Spring St.; N, R, W to Prince St.* ✛ *2:D3.*

$$$ ✕ **Café Altro Paradiso.** Chef Ignacio Mattos's sequel to his much-lauded
ITALIAN Estela just northeast of here, this airy, high-ceilinged spot is a café only in name. It's a paradise of satisfying Italian fare that includes perfectly prepared (and small-portioned) pasta dishes (try the linguine with Maine lobster and chili) and hearty meat entrées like caramelized fennel-spiked pork chop. **Known for:** wine list with unusual bottles; well-done Italian fare; excellent pasta. Ⓢ *Average main: $27* ⊠ *234 Spring St. , at 6th Ave., SoHo* ☎ *646/952–0828* ⊕ *www.altroparadiso. com* ◷ *No lunch Mon.* Ⓜ *C, E to Spring St.* ✛ *2:C4.*

$$$ ✕ **The Dutch.** Perpetually packed with the see-and-be-seen crowd, chef
AMERICAN Andrew Carmellini's homage to American cuisine is really an encapsulation of recent food and dining trends. There's an excellent (and pricey) burger, a Kentucky-size bourbon collection behind the bar, greenmarket-driven comfort-food dishes like fried chicken, and unusual bacon pairings such as scallops with bacon jam. **Known for:** high-quality comfort food; notable burgers; weekend brunch. Ⓢ *Average main: $30*

⊠ *131 Sullivan St., at Prince St., SoHo* ☎ *212/677–6200* ⊕ *www.thedutchnyc.com* Ⓜ *C, E to Spring St.* ✛ *2:D3.*

$$$ ✗**Harold's Meat + Three.** Named for the type of Southern eatery where
SOUTHERN a diner picks one protein and three hearty sides, this western SoHo
spot in the Arlo SoHo hotel won't be as affordable as what you'll find
in, say, Alabama or Arkansas, but chef Harold Moore pleases with
high-quality, stick-to-your-ribs grub. Skip the appetizers and go for
the main course: choose between juicy prime rib, crispy fried chicken,
or veal meatballs, and more. **Known for:** heart attack–inducing fare;
hearty mains; choice of sides from traditional to international. Ⓢ *Average main: $26* ⊠ *Arlo SoHo, 2 Renwick St. , at Canal St., SoHo*
☎ *212/390–8484* ⊕ *www.haroldsmeatandthree.com* ✛ *2:C4.*

$$ ✗**Lucky Strike.** Whether you're lucky enough to nab a table at this
BISTRO scene-y SoHo bistro at 1 pm or 1 am, Lucky Strike always seems
like the place to be. Bedecked in classic bistro trappings—hammered-
copper stools, mirrors with menu items scrawled on them—the res-
taurant would look just as perfect in the Bastille neighborhood of
Paris as it does in this swanky part of the Big Apple. **Known for:**
classic French bistro decor; lively scene; straightforward bistro fare.
Ⓢ *Average main: $20* ⊠ *59 Grand St., between West Broadway and
Wooster St., SoHo* ☎ *212/941–0772* ⊕ *www.luckystrikeny.com* Ⓜ *1,
A, C, E to Canal St.* ✛ *2:D4.*

$$$ ✗**Lure Fishbar.** Decorated like the clubby interior of a sleek luxury liner,
SEAFOOD Lure serves oceanic fare in multiple culinary styles. From the sushi
bar, feast on options like the Lure House Roll—a shrimp tempura roll
crowned with spicy tuna and Japanese tartar sauce—or opt for creative
dishes from the kitchen, like steamed branzino with oyster mushrooms,
scallions, and ponzu sauce, or Manila clams over pancetta-studded lin-
guine. **Known for:** great SoHo location; superfresh seafood; sushi bar.
Ⓢ *Average main: $29* ⊠ *142 Mercer St., at Prince St., SoHo* ☎ *212/431–
7676* ⊕ *www.lurefishbar.com* Ⓜ *B, D, F, M to Broadway–Lafayette St.;
N, R, W to Prince St.* ✛ *2:E3.*

$$ ✗**MarieBelle.** Practically invisible from the front of the chocolate empo-
CAFÉ rium, the back entry to the Cacao Bar opens into a sweet, high-ceiling,
FAMILY 12-table hot-chocolate shop. Most people order the Aztec, European style
(that's 65% Colombian chocolate mixed with hot water—no cocoa powder here!). **Known for:** chocolate paradise; great hot and iced chocolate;
intimate spot. Ⓢ *Average main: $13* ⊠ *484 Broome St., between West
Broadway and Wooster St., SoHo* ☎ *212/925–6999* ⊕ *www.mariebelle.
com* ☾ *No dinner* Ⓜ *6 to Spring St.; A, C, E to Canal St.* ✛ *2:D4.*

$$$ ✗**The Mercer Kitchen.** Part of Alsatian superchef Jean-Georges Vongeri-
ASIAN FUSION chten's culinary empire, the celebrity-laden front room of this SoHo
spot in the Mercer Hotel is as much about scene as cuisine, which
isn't a bad thing. Dishes here look toward Asia (as is the proclivity of
Mr. Vongerichten), using simple ingredients and pairings. **Known for:**
celeb sightings; Asian-influenced, palate-pleasing haute cuisine; stellar
chef. Ⓢ *Average main: $30* ⊠ *Mercer Hotel, 99 Prince St., at Mercer
St., SoHo* ☎ *212/966–5454* ⊕ *www.themercerkitchen.com* ▭ *No credit
cards* Ⓜ *6 to Spring St.; N, R, W to Prince St.; B, D, F, M to Broad-
way–Lafayette St.* ✛ *2:E3.*

15

$$$ ITALIAN 🍴 **Osteria Morini.** Less formal than chef Michael White's other renowned Italian restaurants (like Marea in Midtown West), Osteria Morini is lively and upbeat, with communal tables at the center and a rock 'n' roll soundtrack. The food nevertheless steals the show: start with a selection of cheeses and cured meats, then move on to hearty pastas and main courses like oven-baked polenta accompanied by either sausage or mushrooms. **Known for:** the White Label burger; satisfying pastas; cheerful atmosphere. [$] *Average main: $27* ✉ *218 Lafayette St., between Spring and Broome Sts., SoHo* ☎ *212/965–8777* 🌐 *www.osteriamorini.com* [M] *6 to Spring St.* ✥ *2:E4.*

$$$ FRENCH 🍴 **Raoul's.** One of the first trendy spots in SoHo, this arty French restaurant has yet to lose its touch, either in the kitchen or atmosphere. Expect a chic bar scene—especially late at night—filled with polished PYTs and amazing photos on all available wall space, and bistro-inspired dishes, with oysters and salads to start, and pastas, fish, and meat options for mains. **Known for:** tall, juicy burgers; chic late-night scene; bistro fare. [$] *Average main: $30* ✉ *180 Prince St., between Sullivan and Thompson Sts., SoHo* ☎ *212/966–3518* 🌐 *www.raouls.com* 💳 *No credit cards* ⏲ *No lunch weekdays* [M] *C, E to Spring St.* ✥ *2:D3.*

NOLITA

In NoLIta, SoHo's trendy next-door neighborhood, the spirit of old, pre-chain-store SoHo prevails. Diminutive eateries, squeezed between up-and-coming designer boutiques, flank the narrow streets of this atmospheric neighborhood.

$ CANADIAN FAMILY 🍴 **Black Seed Bagels.** New York is known for bagels, which tend to be doughy and delicious, but the Montreal-style bagels here have a denser, sweeter dough, with "toppings" (sesame, poppy seed, salt, everything) that are more generous than on the New York bagels. The all-day menu includes sandwich options with cream cheese, smoked salmon, whitefish salad, or baked eggs. **Known for:** Montreal-style bagels; all-day menu with bagel sandwiches; classy bagel joint. [$] *Average main: $9* ✉ *170 Elizabeth St., between Kenmare and Spring Sts., NoLIta* ☎ *212/730–1950* 🌐 *www.blackseedbagels.com* [M] *6 to Spring St.* ✥ *2:F4.*

$$ MEXICAN FAMILY 🍴 **Café Habana.** The Mexican-style grilled corn, liberally sprinkled with chili powder, lime, and cotija cheese, is undoubtedly worth getting your hands dirty at this crowded, hip luncheonette. Follow up with a classic Cuban sandwich (roast pork, ham, Swiss cheese, pickles, and chipotle mayo), fish tacos, or one of the innovative salads. **Known for:** Cuban sandwiches; big-portioned Mexican fare; grilled corn. [$] *Average main: $15* ✉ *17 Prince St., at Elizabeth St., NoLIta* ☎ *212/625–2001* 🌐 *www.cafehabana.com* [M] *6 to Spring St.; N, R, W to Prince St.; J, Z to Bowery* ✥ *2:F3.*

$$ ITALIAN 🍴 **Emporio.** The brick-lined front room of this homey Roman eatery in NoLIta is a gathering spot for early-evening happy hour at the bar, where you'll find an appetizing selection of free small bites like frittata, white-bean salad, and ham-and-spinach *tramezzini* (finger sandwiches). The centerpiece of the large, skylighted back room is a wood-fired oven that turns out crisp, thin-crust pizzas topped with quality ingredients like prosciutto and buffalo mozzarella. **Known for:** thin-crust Roman-style pizza; creamy burrata cheese; ample wine selection. [$] *Average main: $23* ✉ *231 Mott St., between Prince and Spring Sts., NoLIta*

☎ *212/966–1234* ⊕ *www.emporiony.com* Ⓜ *B, D, F, M to Broadway–Lafayette St.; N, R, W to Prince St.; 6 to Bleecker St.* ✠ *2:F3.*

$$$ ✕ **Estela.** Long before Mr. and Mrs. Obama ate dinner here in 2014, this second-floor restaurant had been on the map for those in the know. Ignacio Mattos is the commander-in-chef, and his creations have a tendency to sneak up on the diner, such as the rye matzo bread under the mashed salt cod. **Known for:** hard-to-get tables; memorable and delicious menu; interesting wine list. Ⓢ *Average main: $27* ⊠ *47 E. Houston St., between Mott and Mulberry Sts., NoLIta* ☎ *212/219–7693* ⊕ *www.estelanyc.com* ⊘ *No lunch Mon.-Thurs.* Ⓜ *6 to Bleecker St.; B, D, F, M to Broadway–Lafayette St.* ✠ *2:F3.*

MEDITERRANEAN
Fodor'sChoice
★

$$ ✕ **Gato.** When an orange cat crossed celebrity-chef Bobby Flay's path while he was waiting for the real estate agent to show him this space, he decided right then to call this restaurant Gato (Spanish for cat), and a sly cat it is. Despite the name, the menu goes beyond Spain to cover large culinary swaths of the Mediterranean. **Known for:** well-known chef, Bobby Flay; Mediterranean cuisine; octopus. Ⓢ *Average main: $21* ⊠ *324 Lafayette St., at Houston St., NoLIta* ☎ *212/334–6400* ⊕ *www.gatonyc.com* ⊘ *No lunch* Ⓜ *6 to Bleecker St.; B, D, F, M to Broadway–Lafayette St.* ✠ *2:E3.*

MEDITERRANEAN

$$ ✕ **La Esquina.** Anchoring a downtown corner under a bright neon sign, La Esquina looks like nothing more than a fast-food taqueria, with cheap tacos sold to go until 2 in the morning. But "The Corner" is actually three superb south-of-the-border spots in one, with a café and brasserie. Just around the corner is the modestly priced café serving those same tacos along with more ambitious fare like chiles rellenos (stuffed peppers) and carne asada (grilled meat). **Known for:** choose-your-own-eating-adventure at one of three Mexican restaurants; reservation-only Mexican brasserie; buzzy basement scene. Ⓢ *Average main: $20* ⊠ *106 Kenmare St., between Cleveland Pl. and Lafayette St., NoLIta* ☎ *646/613–7100* ⊕ *www.esquinanyc.com* Ⓜ *6 to Spring St.* ✠ *2:E4.*

MEXICAN

$$$$ ✕ **Le Coucou.** If you heard that a Chicago-born chef was taking New York City by storm with classic Parisian fare, you might exclaim "mon Dieu!" But step into Le Coucou and you're stepping into the closest you can get to Paris without leaving the Big Apple, as chef Daniel Rose, who earned the approval of Michelin at his Paris restaurant Spring, is wowing New Yorkers with updated versions of Gallic classics. That's right: heavy sauces are back and better than ever. **Known for:** beef cheek and foie gras terrine; sweetbreads; updated French classics. Ⓢ *Average main: $40* ⊠ *138 Lafayette St., at Howard St., NoLIta* ☎ *212/271–4252* ⊕ *www.lecoucou.com* Ⓜ *6, J, N, Q, R, W, Z to Canal St.* ✠ *2:E5.*

FRENCH
Fodor'sChoice
★

$$ ✕ **Lombardi's Pizza.** Brick walls, red-and-white-checked tablecloths, and the aroma of thin-crust pies emerging from the coal oven set the mood for dining on some of the best pizza in Manhattan. Lombardi's has served pizza since 1905 (though not in the same location), and business doesn't seem to have died down one bit. **Known for:** traditional New York pizza; greaseless slices; clam pizza. Ⓢ *Average main: $18* ⊠ *32 Spring St., at Mott St., NoLIta* ☎ *212/941–7994* ⊕ *www.first-pizza.com* ▭ *No credit cards* Ⓜ *6 to Spring St.; J, Z to Bowery; N, R, W to Prince St.* ✠ *2:F4.*

PIZZA
FAMILY

15

$$ **✕ Parm.** There's more to this casual NoLIta eatery than the namesake
ITALIAN   Italian sandwich for which the budding chainlet is named. Founded
by chefs Rich Torrisi and Mario Carbone (who are behind other hits
like Dirty French, Carbone, and Torrisi Italian Specialties, right next
door), Parm has a menu that also includes large Caesar salads, baked
clams, and garlic bread. **Known for:** sloppy, tasty Italian-American
staples; plenty of parm sandwich options; good-value wine. [$] *Average
main: $13* ⌧ *248 Mulberry St., between Prince and Spring Sts., NoLIta*
☎ *212/993–7189* ⊕ *www.parmnyc.com* Ⓜ *B, D, F, M to Broadway/
Lafayette; N, R, W to Prince St.* ✛ *2:F3.*

$$$ **✕ Pasquale Jones.** The name might not necessarily scream authentic New
ITALIAN   York–Italian fare, but chef Ryan Hardy's sophomore effort (after Charlie
Bird) puts those I-talian places on the south end of Mulberry to shame.
Rather than sloppy spaghetti and meatballs and mediocre, overpriced
fare, Hardy does crispy, airy pizza and inventive Italian dishes (the
lunchtime eggs "All Amatriciana," with Ends Meat guanciale, pecorino,
and hot pepper, is a winner). **Known for:** authentic pizza; wood-oven-
baked chicken alla Romana; good wine list. [$] *Average main: $25* ⌧ *187
Mulberry St., at Kenmare St., NoLIta* ⊕ *www.pasqualejones.com* ☽ *No
lunch Mon.–Thurs.* Ⓜ *4, 6 to Spring St.* ✛ *2:E4.*

$$ **✕ Rubirosa.** Locals have shown an insatiable appetite for this exciting
ITALIAN   Italian-American eatery named for a jet-setting Dominican playboy,
so be prepared to wait for a table. The kitchen isn't trying to rein-
vent anything here; it simply serves high-quality, classic Italian dishes,
from pasta with red sauce or a fork-tender veal chop Milanese to the
thin-crust pizza. **Known for:** pizza, pizza, and pizza; quality Italian-
American food; veal chop Milanese. [$] *Average main: $19* ⌧ *235 Mul-
berry St., between Prince and Spring Sts., NoLIta* ☎ *212/965–0500*
⊕ *www.rubirosanyc.com* ⊟ *No credit cards* Ⓜ *6 to Spring St.; N, R,
W to Prince St.* ✛ *2:F3.*

$$ **✕ The Smile.** Subterranean and almost hidden, the Smile turns frowns
AMERICAN   upside down, if you like hipsters and celebrities, and, most especially,
hipster celebrities. Lounge among the fashion-conscious clientele (who
are trying oh-so-hard to not look that way) and munch on breakfast-y
items (served until 4:30 pm) like chunky granola, or go for one of the
giant sandwiches, or spaghetti with heirloom-tomato sauce. **Known
for:** celeb sightings; breakfast until 4:30 pm; comfort food. [$] *Aver-
age main: $16* ⌧ *26 Bond St., between Lafayette St. and the Bowery,
NoLIta* ☎ *646/329–5836* ⊕ *www.thesmilenyc.com* Ⓜ *B, D, F, M to
Broadway–Lafayette St.; 6 to Bleecker St.* ✛ *2:E2.*

$$ **✕ Uncle Boon's.** If you're looking for quality Thai in Manhattan, a good
THAI   choice is Uncle Boon's in NoLIta, a spot run by a husband-and-wife
chef team who originally met in the kitchen at Michelin-starred Per Se.
You won't find evidence of über-haute cuisine here, but the simple, tasty
Thai fare is very good. **Known for:** solid, high-quality Thai fare; grilled
dishes; chicken leg in yellow curry. [$] *Average main: $24* ⌧ *7 Spring St.,
near Elizabeth St., NoLIta* ☎ *646/370–6650* ⊕ *www.uncleboons.com*
☽ *No lunch* Ⓜ *J, Z to Bowery; 6 to Spring St.* ✛ *2:F3.*

CHINATOWN

Chinatown beckons adventurous diners with restaurants representing numerous regional cuisines of China, including Cantonese, Sichuan, Hunan, Fujian, Shanghai, and Hong Kong–style cooking. Malaysian and Vietnamese restaurants also have taken root here, and the neighborhood continues to grow rapidly, encroaching into what was Little Italy.

$ ╳ **Canal Street Market for Food.** The food-hall phenomenon is in full swing
INTERNATIONAL in the city. This nine-stall market (which shares space with retailers selling arts, crafts, and clothes) is heavy on the Asian food offerings, not surprisingly given its Chinatown location. **Known for:** diverse Asian offerings under one roof; dumplings and ramen; other international fare. $ *Average main: $10* ⊠ *265 Canal St., between Lafayette St. and Broadway, Chinatown* ⊕ *www.canalstreet.market* Ⓜ *4, 6 to Canal St.* ✛ *2:E5.*

$$ ╳ **456 Shanghai Cuisine.** Come to this casual Chinatown eatery for
CHINESE above-average Chinese fare, such as General Tso's chicken, pork buns, and cold sesame noodles, but do yourself a favor and order soup dumplings (*xiao long bao*) as soon as you sit down. You won't regret it: the dumplings, doughy and thin on the outside, encase morsels of crab swimming in a bold, porky broth. **Known for:** superb Shanghai soup dumplings; good Chinese fare. $ *Average main: $14* ⊠ *69 Mott St., between Canal and Bayard Sts., Chinatown* ☎ *212/964–0003* ⊟ *No credit cards* Ⓜ *6, J, N, Q, R, W, Z to Canal St.* ✛ *2:F5.*

$ ╳ **Great New York Noodletown.** Although the soups and noodles are
CHINESE unbeatable at this no-frills restaurant, what you should really order
FAMILY are the window decorations—the hanging lacquered ducks and roasted pork, listed on a simple board hung on the wall and superbly served with pungent garlic-and-ginger sauce on the side. Seasonal specialties like duck with flowering chives and salt-baked soft-shell crabs are excellent. **Known for:** Peking duck; affordable but tasty Chinese grub; late-night dining on weekends. $ *Average main: $12* ⊠ *28 Bowery, at Bayard St., Chinatown* ☎ *212/349–0923* ⊕ *www.greatnynoodletown. com* ⊟ *No credit cards* Ⓜ *6, J, N, Q, R, W, Z to Canal St.; B, D to Grand St.; F to East Broadway* ✛ *2:G5.*

$$ ╳ **Jing Fong.** On weekend mornings people pack this vast dim sum
CHINESE palace, so be prepared to wait. Once your number is called, take the
FAMILY escalator up to the carnivalesque third-floor dining room, where servers push carts crammed with tasty dim sum goodness and you are plied with delights like steamed dumplings, crispy spring rolls, barbecue pork buns, and shrimp balls. **Known for:** palatial dining room; miles of dim sum delights; busy weekend mornings. $ *Average main: $16* ⊠ *20 Elizabeth St., 2nd fl., between Bayard and Canal Sts., Chinatown* ☎ *212/964–5256* ⊕ *www.jingfongny.com* Ⓜ *6, J, N, Q, R, W, Z to Canal St.; B, D to Grand St.* ✛ *2:F5.*

$$ ╳ **Joe's Shanghai.** Joe opened his first Shanghai restaurant in Queens
CHINESE in 1995, but buoyed by the accolades showered on his steamed soup
FAMILY dumplings—filled with a rich, fragrant broth and ground pork or a pork-crabmeat mixture—several Manhattan outposts soon followed. The trick is to take a bite of the dumpling and slurp out the soup, then eat the rest. **Known for:** Shanghai soup dumplings; long menu; fast-moving line. $ *Average main: $17* ⊠ *9 Pell St., between the Bowery and*

15

Mott St., Chinatown 🕿 *212/233–8888* ⊕ *www.joeshanghairestaurants. com* Ⓜ *6, J, N, Q, R, W, Z to Canal St.; B, D to Grand St.* ✛ *2:F5.*

$$ ╳ **Mission Chinese Food.** When Oklahoma-born hipster chef Danny
CHINESE Bowien imported his wildly popular Sichuan spot from San Francis-
Fodor's Choice co's Mission District to lower Manhattan, an instant classic was born.
★ Celebrities, food writers, and foodies alike gravitate to Mission Chinese
nightly for Bowien's not-necessarily-authentic take on Sichuan cuisine,
which includes kung pao pastrami and thrice-cooked bacon. **Known
for:** hipster foodies; creative takes on "Chinese" cuisine; cocktails.
Ⓢ *Average main: $21* ✉ *171 East Broadway, between Rutgers and Jef-
ferson Sts., Chinatown* 🕿 *212/746–2986* ⊕ *www.missionchinesefood.
com* ◷ *No lunch Mon., Tues.* Ⓜ *F to East Broadway* ✛ *2:H5.*

$$ ╳ **New Malaysia.** This Malaysian restaurant, down a nondescript pas-
MALAYSIAN sageway between Bowery and Elizabeth Street, is worth the wander. The
menu is loaded with Malaysian favorites like roti flatbread with curry
and delicious red-bean and coconut-milk drinks. **Known for:** authentic Malaysian fare; good value; delicious drinks. Ⓢ *Average main: $14*
✉ *48 Bowery, near Canal St., Chinatown* 🕿 *212/964–0284* ⊕ *www.
newmalaysiarestaurant.com* Ⓜ *6, J, N, Q, R, W, Z to Canal St.; B, D
to Grand St.* ✛ *2:G5.*

$ ╳ **Tasty Hand-Pulled Noodles.** The name says it all: the open kitchen at this
CHINESE salt-of-the-earth Chinatown restaurant (located on charming, curved
Doyers Street) means you can watch the noodle-slinger in action while
awaiting your bowl of, um, tasty hand-pulled noodles. Just choose your
ingredients—beef, pork, oxtail, eel, chicken, lamb, or shrimp, among
others—and prepare to eat the most delicious bowl of noodles since
that last trip to Shanghai. The restaurant is small, so you might have to
share a table with a fellow noodle slurper. **Known for:** super-affordable
dishes; good variety of ingredients; small space. Ⓢ *Average main: $6* ✉ *1
Doyers St., at Bowery, Chinatown* 🕿 *212/791–1817* ⊕ *www.tastyhand-
pullednoodles.com* ▭ *No credit cards* Ⓜ *6, J, N, Q, R, W, Z to Canal
St.; B, D to Grand St.* ✛ *2:F6.*

$ ╳ **Vanessa's Dumpling House.** One of the best deals in Chinatown can
CHINESE be found here, with sizzling pork-and-chive dumplings (four for a
buck) and vegetarian options. The restaurant is very casual: order at
the counter and then grab a table, if you can find one. **Known for:**
ample amounts of dumplings for cheap; vegetarian choices; drawing
LES barhoppers. Ⓢ *Average main: $8* ✉ *118 Eldridge St., near Broome
St., Chinatown* 🕿 *212/625–8008* ⊕ *www.vanessasdumplinghouse.com*
Ⓜ *B, D to Grand St.* ✛ *2:G4.*

$ ╳ **Xe Lua.** A good Vietnamese restaurant in Manhattan is hard to find,
VIETNAMESE which is why you should seek out Xe Lua, in Chinatown just below
Little Italy. Quick service and the marathon-length menu should satisfy
any palate, but the real standouts are the clay-pot dishes: cooked and
served in—you guessed it—a clay pot, the pork, chicken, veggies, or
whatever you order become slightly caramelized, giving a subtle sweet-
ness to the dish. **Known for:** clay-pot dishes; pho; fast service. Ⓢ *Average main: $11* ✉ *86 Mulberry St., between Canal and Bayard Sts.,
Chinatown* 🕿 *212/577–8887* ⊕ *www.xeluarestaurantnyc.com* ▭ *No
credit cards* Ⓜ *6, J, N, Q, R, Z to Canal St.; B, D to Grand St.* ✛ *2:F5.*

GETTING CAFFEINATED IN NYC

There might be a chain coffee shop on every corner in New York City, but you won't find many locals there. The so-called "city that never sleeps" is fueled with coffee, but not just any coffee. We're a bit particular, some might say downright snobbish, about coffee, so—even if we're in a rush, which, of course, we are—we'll wait those few extra minutes for the best freshly roasted beans and pour-over brews. If you want to join discerning locals, look for outposts of Blue Bottle Coffee, Everyman Espresso, Joe Coffee, La Colombe, Ninth Street Espresso (which has locations other than 9th Street), Stumptown, and Third Rail Coffee all over Manhattan (and Brooklyn). Most spots offer the added bonus of homemade baked goods, and some also have light snacks, but don't expect that it'll be easy to find a seat.

$ CHINESE 🍴 **Xi'an Famous Foods.** Serving the very underrepresented cuisine of western China, Xi'an Famous Foods serves food like you might not have tasted before. The restaurant first made a name for itself at its original location, in the dingy basement food court of a mall in Flushing, Queens, but this spot—shinier, brighter, and cleaner—serves the same exciting fare including the spicy cumin lamb burger, which is mouthwateringly delicious. **Known for:** challenging western Chinese fare; lamb burger; good value. [$] *Average main: $10* ✉ *67 Bayard St., between Mott and Elizabeth Sts., Chinatown* ☎ *212/608–4170* 🌐 *www.xianfoods.com* 💳 *No credit cards* [M] *6, J, N, Q, R, W, Z to Canal St.; B, D to Grand St.* ✣ *2:F5.*

EAST VILLAGE AND LOWER EAST SIDE

EAST VILLAGE

Once a grungy ghetto for punk rockers and drug addicts, this neighborhood has gotten itself into shape, with great restaurants on every block—from amazing, inexpensive Asian spots to Michelin-starred destinations. St. Mark's Place is the center of New York's downtown Little Tokyo, and East 6th Street is its Indian Row.

$$ MODERN MEXICAN 🍴 **Atla.** This place has been a hit with pretty much everyone since Mexican superchef Enrique Olvera first fired up the burners here in spring 2017. A pared-down, more casual version of Olvera's hit upscale Flatiron eatery, Cosme, the 90-seat, big-windowed spot does excellent, straightfoward Mexican dishes such as chicken enchiladas as well as some decidedly not-south-of-the-border delights like white ayocote (a kind of runner bean) hummus. **Known for:** chia oatmeal; chicken soup; arctic char–stuffed avocado. [$] *Average main: $17* ✉ *371 Lafayette St., between 2nd and 3rd Sts., East Village* ☎ *646/837–6464* 🌐 *www.atlanyc.com* [M] *B, D F, M to Broadway–Lafayette St.* ✣ *2:E2.*

$$ MOROCCAN 🍴 **Cafe Mogador.** An East Village dining institution if there ever was one, Cafe Mogador is a frequent stop for locals and, for some, a hip place to be seen. Since 1983, the restaurant has been serving above-average Moroccan cuisine in a date-friendly, candlelit atmosphere. **Known for:** East Village stalwart; hummus; tagines. [$] *Average main: $16* ✉ *101*

CLOSE UP

Restaurant Chains Worth a Taste

When you're on the go or don't have time for a leisurely meal, there are several good chain restaurants and sandwich bars that have popped up around New York City. Those listed below are usually reasonably priced and the best in their category.

Dos Toros. Fresh and inexpensive tacos, burritos, and salads are the calling card at this local minichain with several locations in Manhattan and one in Brooklyn. The brothers who run the joint moved to NYC from San Francisco and were disappointed with the taqueria options here, so they took matters into their own hands. Order at the counter and grab a seat. 🌐 *www.dostoros.com.*

Le Pain Quotidien. Part bakery, part café, this Belgian chain with locations throughout the city serves fresh salads and sandwiches at lunch and is great for breakfast. You can grab a snack to go or stay and eat breakfast, lunch, or dinner with waiter service. There are more than 20 locations throughout Manhattan, including one in Central Park. 🌐 *www.lepainquotidien.com.*

Pret A Manger. This sandwich shop started in London in 1986 and opened its first American outpost in 2000. These days you can find one in various locations around NYC—there are several in Midtown, catering to the bustling lunch crowds. The sandwiches are excellent, and the salads are good, too. 🌐 *www.pret.com.*

Shake Shack. This homegrown chain has expanded across the United States and beyond, but it got its start in Madison Square Park. There are multiple locations in Manhattan and Brooklyn to enjoy burgers, hot dogs, and shakes. 🌐 *www.shakeshack.com.*

'wichcraft. Tom Colicchio may be best known these days as head judge of Bravo's *Top Chef,* but his fine-dining restaurants Craft and Craftbar are also well-known around Manhattan and beyond. At 'wichcraft, the sandwich shop he started with several partners back in 2003, the creations have his deliciously distinctive touch. 🌐 *www.wichcraftnyc.com.*

St. Marks Pl., near 2nd Ave., East Village ☎ *212/677–2226* 🌐 *www.cafemogador.com* 💳 *No credit cards* [M] *L to 1st Ave.* ✣ *2:G1.*

$ FAST FOOD FAMILY 🍴 **Crif Dogs.** Gluttony reigns at Crif Dogs, where you can indulge in creative—and delicious—hot dog creations. Try the Chihuahua, bacon wrapped and layered with avocado and sour cream, or the Tsunami, bacon wrapped with pineapple and teriyaki; there are vegetarian dogs, too. **Known for:** the "secret" bar adjacent to Crif Dogs; inventive dogs; tater tots. [$] *Average main: $6* ✉ *113 St. Marks Pl., at Ave. A, East Village* ☎ *212/614–2728* 🌐 *www.crifdogs.com* [M] *L to 1st Ave.* ✣ *3:H5.*

$$ AUSTRIAN Fodor's Choice ★ 🍴 **Edi & the Wolf.** For those who have always wanted to spend an evening in a countryside Austrian pub—and who hasn't?—but can't hop on a plane to Vienna, there's Edi & the Wolf, an outstanding restaurant deep in the section of the East Village called Alphabet City. The rustic interior (usually crammed with stylish thirtysomethings) is the perfect venue to sample dishes like honey-and-beer-accented ribs, pork-belly-laced poached eggs, and, of course, Wiener schnitzel,

which is super tender and refreshingly free of grease. **Known for:** introducing New Yorkers to Austrian cusine; Central European beers; schnitzel. [$] *Average main: $23* ✉ *102 Ave. C, at 7th St., East Village* ☎ *212/598–1040* 🌐 *www.ediandthewolf.com* 🕒 *No lunch weekdays* [M] *F to 2nd Ave., L to 1st Ave.* ✥ *2:H1.*

$ INTERNATIONAL 🍴 **Fuku.** David Chang's first location of this budding chain is almost single-handedly responsible for kicking off a fried-chicken-sandwich craze in New York City. That's because Chang's version is revelatory: the soft, unobtrusive potato bun gives way to a crispy-on-the-outside, juicy-on-the-inside chicken cutlet that is good enough to make you think you're eating this classic for the very first time. **Known for:** fried-chicken sandwich; celebrity chef; minichain. [$] *Average main: $8* ✉ *163 1st Ave., at 10th St., East Village* 🌐 *eatfuku.com* [M] *L to 1st Ave.* ✥ *3:H5.*

$$ ITALIAN 🍴 **Gnocco.** Owners Pierluigi Palazzo and Gianluca Giovannetti named their restaurant not after gnocchi but a regional Italian specialty—deep-fried dough bites served with northern Italian sliced meats like capicola, salami, and aged prosciutto. The gnocchi are certainly good, but the menu has many other options, including house-made pasta specials and pizza topped with mozzarella, truffles, and mushrooms. **Known for:** consistently good Italian food; housemade pasta; lovely back garden. [$] *Average main: $21* ✉ *337 E. 10th St., between Aves. A and B, East Village* ☎ *212/677–1913* 🌐 *www.gnocco.com* [M] *L to 1st Ave., 6 to Astor Pl.* ✥ *2:H1.*

$$ VIETNAMESE 🍴 **Hanoi House.** Most Vietnamese food in the United States is inspired by the traditions of southern Vietnam because it was largely Vietnamese from the south who left the country after the war ended in 1975. Hanoi House brings a refreshing taste of the north; the pho here, as done in Hanoi, is meatier, darker, and more flavorful, as the broth simmers in cow bones for 12 hours. **Known for:** distinctive northern Vietnamese fare; cha ca la Vong; beef pho. [$] *Average main: $18* ✉ *119 St. Marks Pl., between 1st Ave. and Ave. A, East Village* ☎ *212/995–5010* 🌐 *www.hanoihousenyc.com* 🕒 *No lunch Mon.–Sat.* [M] *L to 1st Ave.* ✥ *3:H5.*

$$ MEXICAN 🍴 **Hecho en Dumbo.** "Made in Dumbo"—referring to the restaurant's former location in Brooklyn—specializes in *antojitos,* or "little cravings," and the result is something equivalent to Mexican comfort food for the hip thirtysomethings who frequent this restaurant. Variations on the taco theme may dominate the menu, but Hecho shines with house dishes like Berkshire pork shank and roasted scallops paired with bone marrow salsa. **Known for:** comforting snacks; affordable happy hour margaritas; varieties of tacos. [$] *Average main: $17* ✉ *354 Bowery, between Great Jones and 4th Sts., East Village* ☎ *212/937–4245* 🌐 *www.hechoendumbo.com* [M] *6 to Astor Pl.; N, R, W to 8th St.–NYU* ✥ *2:F2.*

$$$ ITALIAN 🍴 **Il Buco.** The unabashed clutter of vintage kitchen gadgets and tableware harks back to Il Buco's past as an antiques store and affects a romantic country-house feel with excellent food—this is a favorite for a cozy, intimate meal. The menu focuses on meat and produce from local farms, with several excellent pasta choices, and a variety of Mediterranean tapas-like appetizers. **Known for:** intimate ambience; local produce; wine bar around corner. [$] *Average main: $29* ✉ *47 Bond St.,*

15

between the Bowery and Lafayette St., East Village ☎ *212/533–1932* 🌐 *www.ilbuco.com* ⏲ *No lunch Sun.* [M] *6 to Bleecker St.; B, D, F, M to Broadway–Lafayette St.* ⊕ *2:F2.*

$$ JAPANESE 🍴 **Ippudo.** Crowds wait hours for the ramen noodles at Ippudo, the first American branch of the Japanese chain. Loyal patrons say it's all about the rich, pork-based broth—there is a vegetarian version available but it lacks the depth of flavor. **Known for:** heaping bowls of addictive ramen; long waits; good appetizers. [$] *Average main: $17* ✉ *65 4th Ave., between 9th and 10th Sts., East Village* ☎ *212/388–0088* 🌐 *www.ippudony.com* [M] *6 to Astor Pl.; N, R, W to 8th St.–NYU* ⊕ *3:G5.*

$$$$ JAPANESE 🍴 **Jewel Bako.** Arguably the best sushi restaurant in the East Village, this tiny space gleams in a minefield of cheap, often inferior sushi houses. The futuristic bamboo tunnel of a dining room is gorgeous, but try to nab a place at the sushi bar and put yourself in the hands of sushi master Mitsunori Isoda. **Known for:** ultrafresh sushi; fixed-price menus; small space. [$] *Average main: $50* ✉ *239 E. 5th St., between 2nd and 3rd Aves., East Village* ☎ *212/979–1012* 🌐 *www.jewelbakosushi.com* ⏲ *Closed Sun. No lunch* [M] *6 to Astor Pl.; N, R, W to 8th St.–NYU* ⊕ *3:G6.*

$$$ FRENCH 🍴 **Lafayette Grand Cafe & Bakery.** Food-media darling, chef Andrew Carmellini (of Locanda Verde, Bar Primi, and the Dutch) goes Gallic here. There's no culinary trickery happening here, just straightforward and very satisfying bistro fare. **Known for:** hearty French fare; very comfortable ambience; breakfast. [$] *Average main: $25* ✉ *380 Lafayette St., at Great Jones St., East Village* ☎ *212/533–3000* 🌐 *www.lafayetteny.com* [M] *6 to Bleecker St.; B, D, F, M to Broadway–Lafayette St.; N, R, W to 8th St.–NYU* ⊕ *3:F6.*

$ MIDDLE EASTERN FAMILY 🍴 **Mamoun's Falafel.** This hole-in-the-wall institution, bustling day and night, is the place to go for speedy, hot, supercheap, and delicious Middle Eastern food. Tahini-topped pitas are packed with fresh, green-on-the-inside falafel balls. **Known for:** cheap and delicious falafel sandwiches; super-hot sauce; late-night noshing. [$] *Average main: $7* ✉ *22 St. Marks Pl., between 2nd and 3rd Aves., East Village* ☎ *212/387–7747* 🌐 *www.mamouns.com* 💳 *No credit cards* [M] *6 to Astor Pl.; N, R, W to 8th St.–NYU* ⊕ *3:G5.*

$ DELI 🍴 **Mile End.** Named for a neighborhood in Montreal where the city's famed bagel bakeries exist, Mile End has became one of the darlings of the city's fooderati since it opened in Brooklyn in 2010. The Montreal bagels are authentic, but the real reason to come here is for the impressive deli fare, including pastrami, roast beef, and smoked-meat sandwiches. **Known for:** crisp Montreal bagels; pastrami; poutine. [$] *Average main: $11* ✉ *53 Bond St., near the Bowery, East Village* ☎ *212/529–2990* 🌐 *www.mileenddeli.com* [M] *6 to Bleecker St.; B, D, F, M to Broadway–Lafayette St.* ⊕ *2:F2.*

$$ JAPANESE 🍴 **Minca.** It may have received less fanfare than some other East Village noodle bars, but the ramen at this tiny, cramped spot is among the best in the city; the fact that visiting Japanese students eat here is a good sign. Try to get a seat at the bar, where you can watch the chefs prepare your food. **Known for:** top ramen spot; spicy pork broth ramen; homemade gyoza. [$] *Average main: $15* ✉ *536 E. 5th St., between Aves. A and B,*

East Village ☎ *212/505–8001* ⊕ *www.newyorkramen.com* ▭ *No credit cards* Ⓜ *F to 2nd Ave.* ✛ *2:H2.*

$$$$ ✕ **Momofuku Ko.** At James Beard Award–winning chef David Chang's
ASIAN most formal dining option, diners sit at the bar to see Ko's chefs in
Fodor's Choice action or opt for a standalone table. The menu is prix-fixe only: 20
★ courses for $195 or an abbreviated six-course (bar only) menu for $90.
Known for: exquisite, mind-blowing prix-fixe dinners; tough to get in;
complex reservation system. Ⓢ *Average main: $195* ⊠ *8 Extra Pl., at
1st St., East Village* ☎ *212/203–095* ⊕ *www.momofuku.com* ◯ *Closed
Mon. No lunch* Ⓜ *F to 2nd Ave.* ✛ *2:F2.*

$ ✕ **Momofuku Milk Bar.** This combination bakery, ice-cream parlor, and
CAFÉ sandwich shop boasts quick-serve access to some truly psychedelic
FAMILY treats by pastry whiz Christina Tosi. Swing by for a kimchi croissant and
glass of "cereal" milk, or for treats like the curiously flavored soft-serve
ice cream (cereal milk, lemon verbena) or a "candy bar pie" (a sweet
bomb of caramel, peanut-butter nougat, and pretzels atop a chocolate-
cookie crust). **Known for:** cereal milk soft serve; addictive "crack" and
other cookies; several locations. Ⓢ *Average main: $7* ⊠ *251 E. 13th St.,
at 2nd Ave., East Village* ☎ *347/577–9504* ⊕ *www.milkbarstore.com*
Ⓜ *L to 3rd Ave.* ✛ *3:G4.*

$$ ✕ **Momofuku Noodle Bar.** Chef and owner David Chang has created a
ASIAN shrine to ramen with this stylish 70-seat restaurant. His riff on the
Fodor's Choice Japanese classic features haute ingredients like Berkshire pork, free-
★ range chicken, and organic produce—though there are plenty of other
innovative options on the menu. **Known for:** creative ramen options
from famous chef; amazing pork buns; lively ambience. Ⓢ *Average
main: $17* ⊠ *171 1st Ave., between 10th and 11th Sts., East Village*
☎ *212/777–7773* ⊕ *www.momofuku.com* Ⓜ *L to 1st Ave.* ✛ *3:H5.*

$$ ✕ **Momofuku Ssäm Bar.** This David Change restaurant is packed nightly
ASIAN with downtown diners cut from the same cloth as the pierced and tat-
tooed waitstaff and cooks. The Asian menu is constantly changing,
but the not-to-be-missed riff on the classic Chinese steamed pork bun
is almost always available. **Known for:** inventive Asian flavor combinations; always packed; rotisserie duck splurge. Ⓢ *Average main: $24*
⊠ *207 2nd Ave., at 13th St., East Village* ☎ *212/254–3500* ⊕ *www.
momofuku.com/ssam* Ⓜ *L to 1st Ave.* ✛ *3:G4.*

$$ ✕ **Motorino Pizza.** The East Village branch of the Williamsburg origi-
PIZZA nal serves up authentic Neapolitan pies made with glutinous, dough-
friendly double-zero flour and San Marzano tomatoes. You can't go
wrong with any of the signature traditional pizzas, like marinara; mar-
gherita with fresh tomatoes, mozzarella, and basil; or a pie with spicy
sopressata, sausage, and garlic. **Known for:** authentic Neapolitan pizza;
good seasonal pies; good-value lunch prix-fixe. Ⓢ *Average main: $18*
⊠ *349 E. 12th St., at 1st Ave., East Village* ☎ *212/777–2644* ⊕ *www.
motorinopizza.com* Ⓜ *L to 1st Ave.* ✛ *3:H4.*

$$ ✕ **Oda House.** Georgian cuisine isn't as well known as it should be, but
EASTERN try it once and you'll be a believer, especially at this quiet, romantic
EUROPEAN spot with large windows looking out onto the street. Start with the
khinkali (meat-and-broth-filled dumplings) and the *adjaruli khachapuri,*
a boat-shaped baked bread centered around a pool of gooey cheese and

15

a raw egg stirred in. **Known for:** Georgian cuisine and wines; adjaruli khachapuri; chakapuli (lamb stew). $ *Average main: $20* ⊠ *76 Ave. B, at 5th St., East Village* ☎ *212/353–3838* ⊕ *www.odahouse.com* ⊙ *No lunch Mon.–Thurs.* Ⓜ *L to 1st Ave.* ✛ *2:H1.*

$$$
GREEK

✕**Pylos.** The perfect setting for a relaxed dinner or an intimate special occasion, this tastefully refined, light-filled East Village restaurant emphasizes rustic cooking from all over Greece. There are delicious versions of hearty comfort-food dishes like pastitsio and moussaka on the menu, but the lighter dishes—especially fish—let the flavors shine through. **Known for:** elevated Greek fare; broad meze selection; clay-baked meat dishes. $ *Average main: $26* ⊠ *128 E. 7th St., near Ave. A, East Village* ☎ *212/473–0220* ⊕ *www.pylosrestaurant.com* ⊙ *No lunch Mon., Tues.* Ⓜ *F to 2nd Ave.; L to 1st Ave.* ✛ *3:H5.*

$$
MODERN
AMERICAN
Fodor's Choice
★

✕**Saxon & Parole.** One of the hottest spots on this burgeoning stretch of the Bowery, this eatery may be named for two 19th-century racehorses, but the food—and the good-looking crowd—is nothing you'd find in a barnyard. Settle into this cozy, sceney spot, order a cocktail, and peruse a menu loaded with the Zeitgeist dishes of New York dining: roasted bone marrow, Brussels sprouts, pork belly, chicken-liver mousse, and an overpriced but excellent burger. **Known for:** delicious, trendy food; housemade whiskey; sceney atmosphere. $ *Average main: $24* ⊠ *316 Bowery, at Bleecker St., East Village* ☎ *212/254–0350* ⊕ *www.sax-onandparole.com* ⊙ *No lunch* Ⓜ *B, D, F, M to Broadway–Lafayette St.; 6 to Bleecker St.; F to 2nd Ave.* ✛ *2:F2.*

$$
THAI

✕**Somtum Der.** New Yorkers used to venture to Queens to get good Thai food, but a handful of great Thai restaurants have opened in Manhattan in recent years, many of them hailing from Isaan, a region in northeast Thailand that emphasizes light, spicy fare. Somtum Der, originally based in Bangkok, is one of the best. **Known for:** excellent Thai food in tight quarters; green papaya salad; fried chicken. $ *Average main: $15* ⊠ *85 Ave. A, between 5th and 6th Sts., East Village* ☎ *212/260–8570* ⊕ *www.somtumder.com* ⊟ *No credit cards* Ⓜ *F to 2nd Ave.; L to 1st Ave.* ✛ *3:H6.*

$
CHINESE

✕**Tim Ho Wan.** This dim sum restaurant is best known for its original Hong Kong location being the most affordable Michelin-starred restaurant on the planet. The Big Apple outlet may or may not win any prestigious culinary awards (though you'd think it when you see the line outside), but it certainly has proven itself to be one of the best spots for dim sum in the city. **Known for:** affordable dim sum from Hong Kong; barbecue pork buns; long lines. $ *Average main: $9* ⊠ *85 4th Ave., at 10th St., East Village* ☎ *212/228–2800* ⊕ *www.timhowanusa.com* Ⓜ *4, 6 to Astor Pl.* ✛ *3:G4.*

$
CAFÉ
FAMILY

✕**Veniero's Pasticceria.** Since 1894, this bustling bakery-café has sold every kind of Italian *dolce* (sweet), from cherry-topped cookies to creamy cannoli and flaky *sfogliatelle* (shell-shape, filled pastry). Cheesecake lovers rejoice in Veniero's ricotta-based version, and in all, hungry patrons can choose from more than 150 different types of desserts. **Known for:** Old World sweets; wine list; eye-pleasing decor. $ *Average main: $6* ⊠ *342 E. 11th St., near 1st Ave., East Village* ☎ *212/674–7070* ⊕ *www.venierospastry.com* Ⓜ *6 to Astor Pl.; L to 1st Ave.* ✛ *3:H5.*

$$ EASTERN EUROPEAN FAMILY

🍴 **Veselka.** Potato pierogi are available 24 hours a day at this East Village stalwart, which opened in 1954; the name means "rainbow" in Ukrainian. The authentic Ukrainian-slash-diner food is the perfect stick-to-your-ribs ending to a night on the town—or beginning to a new day, as the restaurant serves a full array of breakfast staples. **Known for:** legendary wall-size paintings; diner food for the neighborhood; Ukrainian specialties. [$] *Average main: $13* ✉ *144 2nd Ave., at 9th St., East Village* ☎ *212/228–9682* 🌐 *www.veselka.com* [M] *6 to Astor Pl.; N, R, W to 8th St.–NYU; L to 1st Ave.* ⊕ *3:H5.*

$$ GERMAN

🍴 **Zum Schneider.** Located in Alphabet City, this garrulous Teutonic spot teaches the ABCs of beer drinking and hearty sausage eating. Grab a table outside when the weather's nice, among the young hipsters who frequent the spot, and get ready for some kraut-laden fun. **Known for:** outside drinking; meaty Teutonic grub; potato pancakes. [$] *Average main: $16* ✉ *107 Ave. C, at 7th St., East Village* ☎ *212/598–1098* 🌐 *www.zumschneider.com* 🕒 *No lunch weekdays* [M] *L to 1st Ave.; F to 2nd Ave.* ⊕ *2:H1.*

15

LOWER EAST SIDE

The Lower East Side, home to generations of immigrant newcomers, has become quite the culinary hub since 2000, with everything from molecular gastronomy to hipster Chinese cuisine. You can't walk a block without hitting a place that makes your stomach growl.

$ JAPANESE

🍴 **Bar Goto.** At this stylish bar and eatery, the high-quality cocktails have a decidedly Japanese accent to them, such as the Nippon spritz (sake, rice shochu, and tonic) and the Kyoto old-fashioned, made with rice vodka, gin matcha, and sencha. When tummy filler is called for, the bar does very good Japanese comfort food, particularly in the form of *okonomi-yaki,* savory cabbage pancakes filled with pork belly, squid, and/or smoked bacon. **Known for:** okonomi-yaki; Japanese-inspired cocktails; chicken wings. [$] *Average main: $10* ✉ *245 Eldridge St., between Stanton and E. Houston Sts., Lower East Side* ☎ *212/475–4411* 🌐 *www.bargoto.com* 🕒 *Closed Mon. No lunch* [M] *F, M to 2nd Ave.* ⊕ *2:G3.*

$$ AMERICAN Fodor's Choice ★

🍴 **Clinton St. Baking Co.** At one time this Lower East Side restaurant was *the* place to come for brunch, specifically for blueberry pancakes that many regulars professed were the best in the city, if not the whole country. But all that changed when owners Neil Kleinberg and DeDe Lahman added lunch and dinner options to the menu. **Known for:** blueberry pancakes and February pancake month; brunch; burgers. [$] *Average main: $19* ✉ *4 Clinton St., near Houston St., Lower East Side* ☎ *646/602–6263* 🌐 *www.clintonstreetbaking.com* 🕒 *No dinner Sun.* [M] *F to 2nd Ave.; J, M, Z to Essex St.* ⊕ *2:H2.*

$$ CHINESE

🍴 **Congee Village.** Don't be put off by the name—this boisterous Chinatown icon serves much more than the eponymous rice porridge. Indeed, the menu is enormous, covering an encyclopedic range of unusual Cantonese classics. **Known for:** big portions; affordable, tasty Cantonese delights; bustling scene. [$] *Average main: $15* ✉ *100 Allen St., near Delancey St., Lower East Side* ☎ *212/941–1818* 🌐 *www.congeevillagerestaurants.com* [M] *F to Delancey St.; J, M, Z to Essex St.; B, D to Grand St.* ⊕ *2:G3.*

$$ VEGETARIAN Fodor's Choice ★

🍴 **Dirt Candy.** One of the best, most inspired vegetarian restaurants outside California, Dirt Candy shines thanks to chef Amanda Cohen, who knows how to coax every bit of flavor out of vegetables so that they shine and sparkle on the plate and the palate. First-timers shouldn't ignore the jalapeño hush puppies (with maple butter) or the cauliflower curry (with a green-pea paneer). **Known for:** veggie-laden dishes that even carnivores devour; Brussels sprouts tacos; reservations needed at least a week ahead. [$] *Average main: $17* ✉ *86 Allen St., between Grand and Broome Sts., Lower East Side* ☎ *212/228–7732* 🌐 *www.dirtcandynyc.com* 🕒 *Closed Mon. No lunch* [M] *F to Delancey St.* ✣ *2:G4.*

$$$ FRENCH

🍴 **Dirty French.** Rich Torrisi and Mario Carbone, the chefs who created a small empire of Italian-American restaurants (Parm, Carbone, ZZ's Clam Bar) go Gallic at this cool Lower East Side bistro in the Ludlow Hotel. The name says it all: while the fare is French, the team takes many of the dishes on a tour of places like North Africa and Louisiana before the food lands on your table. **Known for:** oysters and fish; rotisserie meats; all-French wine list. [$] *Average main: $30* ✉ *Ludlow Hotel, 180 Ludlow St., between Houston and Stanton Sts., Lower East Side* ☎ *212/254–3000* 🌐 *www.dirtyfrench.com* [M] *F to 2nd Ave.* ✣ *2:G3.*

$ CAFÉ FAMILY

🍴 **Doughnut Plant.** If you want to know what it feels like to eat a doughnut for the first time, head to the Doughnut Plant, where the all-American junk-food staple is elevated to high art. Fresh seasonal ingredients go into these decadent treats, with real fruit and imported chocolate mixed into the batter. **Known for:** creatively flavored doughnuts; fudgy Blackout doughnuts; seasonal ingredients. [$] *Average main: $5* ✉ *379 Grand St., between Essex and Norfolk Sts., Lower East Side* ☎ *212/505–3700* 🌐 *www.doughnutplant.com* 💳 *No credit cards* [M] *F to Delancey St.; J, M, Z to Essex St.; B, D to Grand St.* ✣ *2:G4.*

$$ BRITISH

🍴 **The Fat Radish.** Years ago, the phrase "seasonal British" might have seemed puzzling, but with seasonal ingredients in vogue and British cuisine making a name for itself, this handsome, hip, and sceney Lower East Side (almost Chinatown) restaurant is worth a visit. The menu is eclectic but full of excellent choices, including a lot of kale and other en-vogue ingredients. **Known for:** good British food; fun scene; craft British brews. [$] *Average main: $22* ✉ *17 Orchard St., near Canal St., Lower East Side* ☎ *212/300–4053* 🌐 *www.thefatradishnyc.com* 🕒 *No lunch Mon.* [M] *F to East Broadway* ✣ *2:G5.*

$$ AMERICAN Fodor's Choice ★

🍴 **Freemans.** It's hard to believe now, but there was once a time when New York restaurant interiors were trying hard not to look cool, with no taxidermy or ironic tchotchkes, or lodge-ish dishes like hunters stew, potted pork, and grilled trout on the menu. But we have Freemans to thank for the change, and their equally inspired cocktails menu. **Known for:** being perpetually hip; taxidermy; down an alleyway. [$] *Average main: $22* ✉ *End of Freeman Alley, near Rivington St., Lower East Side* ☎ *212/420–0012* 🌐 *www.freemansrestaurant.com* [M] *F to 2nd Ave.; J, Z to Bowery* ✣ *2:F3.*

$$ JAPANESE Fodor's Choice ★

🍴 **Ivan Ramen.** Ivan Orkin's improbable but true story is one of the many layers that make New York City's restaurant scene so exciting, authentic, and delicious: the self-described "Jewish kid from Long Island" moved to Tokyo and became a ramen-making master, achieving near legendary status in the Japanese capital. In 2014 he opened this Lower

East Side temple to ramen and it's been packed since day one. **Known for:** ramen including mazemen; Japanese fried chicken; pork buns. [$] *Average main: $17* ✉ *25 Clinton St., between Houston and Stanton Sts., Lower East Side* ☎ *646/678–3859* 🌐 *www.ivanramen.com* [M] *F to 2nd Ave.; J, M, Z to Essex St.* ✥ *2:H3.*

$$ DELI Fodor's Choice ★ 🍴 **Katz's Delicatessen.** Everything and nothing has changed at Katz's since it first opened in 1888, when the neighborhood was dominated by Jewish immigrants. The lines still form on the weekends for giant, succulent hand-carved corned beef and pastrami sandwiches, soul-warming soups, juicy hot dogs, and crisp half-sour pickles. **Known for:** pastrami sandwiches; slice of New York culinary history; weekend lines. [$] *Average main: $17* ✉ *205 E. Houston St., at Ludlow St., Lower East Side* ☎ *212/254–2246* 🌐 *www.katzsdelicatessen.com* [M] *F to 2nd Ave.* ✥ *2:G2.*

$$ GERMAN 🍴 **Loreley Restaurant & Biergarten.** Beer gardens once dotted the New York City landscape in the way that Starbucks does now, but after World War I and Prohibition, most of these outdoor drinking spots vanished. Then in 2003 came Loreley, which kicked off a new beer-garden craze in the city that involved gaggles of hipsters nursing German craft beers while bobbing their heads to the new Radiohead album and munching on plates of sausage, meatballs, or schnitzel. **Known for:** sipping suds in the sun; German craft beers; hipster scene. [$] *Average main: $17* ✉ *7 Rivington St., near the Bowery, Lower East Side* ☎ *212/253–7077* 🌐 *www.loreleynyc.com* [M] *J, Z to Bowery; B, D to Grand St.; F to 2nd Ave.* ✥ *2:F3.*

15

$ ITALIAN FAMILY 🍴 **The Meatball Shop.** New York's first full-service meatball restaurant has a pedigree chef, a professional waitstaff, a wine list, and a hip crowd. And the meatballs, oh, the meatballs: choose beef, pork, chicken, veggie, or "special" ball options that range from chili cheese to Greek lamb and Buffalo chicken; then decide if you want them served simply as is, in sliders or a hero, as a salad, or a platter. **Known for:** delicious spheres of meat; ice-cream sandwiches; multiple locations. [$] *Average main: $12* ✉ *84 Stanton St., near Allen St., Lower East Side* ☎ *212/982–8895* 🌐 *www.themeatballshop.com* [M] *F to 2nd Ave.; J, Z to Bowery* ✥ *2:G3.*

$$ ECLECTIC FAMILY 🍴 **Shopsin's.** Don't ask for substitutions or sauce on the side at New York's most eccentric eatery, because Kenny Shopsin, owner and chef, may really toss you out or ban you for life; the attitude is part of the appeal. The eclectic menu runs to literally hundreds of items—from pumpkin pancakes to chilaquiles, and from chili cheeseburgers to lamb-curry soups. **Known for:** volatile chef-owner; long menu; mac 'n' cheese pancakes. [$] *Average main: $17* ✉ *Essex Market, 120 Essex St., near Rivington St., Lower East Side* 🌐 *www.shopsins.com* 🕓 *Closed Mon., Tues. No dinner* 💳 *No credit cards* [M] *F to Delancey St.; J, M, Z to Essex St.* ✥ *2:G3.*

$ CAFÉ FAMILY 🍴 **Sugar Sweet Sunshine.** The brainchild of two former Magnolia Bakery employees, Sugar Sweet's cupcakes are far superior; try the chocolate-almond Gooey Gooey, or the cream cheese frosting–topped pumpkin flavor. The real showstopper is swoon-inducing banana pudding, with slices of ripe fruit and crumbled Nilla wafers suspended in decadent vanilla pudding. **Known for:** great cupcakes; banana pudding cupcake.

[$] *Average main: $6* ✉ *126 Rivington St., between Essex and Norfolk Sts., Lower East Side* ☎ *212/995–1960* 🌐 *www.sugarsweetsunshine.com* [M] *F to Delancey St.; J, M, Z to Essex St.* ✥ *2:G3.*

$$ AMERICAN

🍴 **Wildair.** Named for a racehorse that had its stable on the Lower East Side in pre–Civil War days, this fantastic wine bar focuses mainly on natural wines, with ample numbers of splendid bottles from wineries in France, Spain, and even Slovenia. Wildair is the sibling of acclaimed prix-fixe wonder Contra, two doors up, but here it's more casual and the creative menu, which frequently changes, is à la carte. **Known for:** natural wines; Wagyu steak; little gem lettuce salad. [$] *Average main: $19* ✉ *142 Orchard St., between Rivington and Delancey Sts., Lower East Side* ☎ *646/964–5624* 🌐 *www.wildair.nyc* 🕒 *Closed Mon. No lunch* [M] *F to Delancy St.; J, M, Z to Essex St.* ✥ *2:G3.*

GREENWICH VILLAGE AND THE WEST VILLAGE

GREENWICH VILLAGE

Greenwich Village's bohemian days may have faded, but the romantic allure of its tiny bistros, bars, and cafés remains. Around New York University, shabby-chic eateries and take-out joints cater to students, but there is a growing number of more sophisticated dining spots, too.

$$ PIZZA FAMILY

🍴 **Arturo's.** Few guidebooks list this classic New York pizzeria, yet the jam-packed room and pleasantly smoky scent foreshadow a satisfying meal. There's a full menu of Italian classics, but pizza is the main event, and the thin-crust beauties are cooked in a coal-fired oven, to emerge sizzling with simple toppings like pepperoni, sausage, and eggplant. **Known for:** classic Big Apple pizza; wacky art on the walls; weekend waits. [$] *Average main: $21* ✉ *106 W. Houston St., near Thompson St., Greenwich Village* ☎ *212/535–4480* 🕒 *No lunch* [M] *1 to Houston St.; B, D, F, M to Broadway–Lafayette St.* ✥ *2:D3.*

$$$ ITALIAN Fodor's Choice ★

🍴 **Babbo Ristorante.** It shouldn't take more than one bite of the ethereal homemade pasta or tender barbecue squab with roast beet farrotto to understand why it's so hard to get a reservation at this casually elegant restaurant. The menu strays widely from Italian standards and hits numerous high points in dishes such as rabbit with Brussels sprouts, house-made pancetta, and carrot vinaigrette. **Known for:** palate-pleasing pastas; loud, questionable music. [$] *Average main: $31* ✉ *110 Waverly Pl., between MacDougal St. and 6th Ave., Greenwich Village* ☎ *212/777–0303* 🌐 *www.babbonyc.com* 🕒 *No lunch Sun., Mon.* [M] *A, B, C, D, E, F, M to W. 4th St.* ✥ *2:C1.*

$$$ MODERN AMERICAN

🍴 **Blue Hill.** This tasteful, sophisticated den of a restaurant—formerly a speakeasy—on a quiet side street maintains an impeccable reputation for excellence and consistency under the leadership of chef Dan Barber. Part of the slow-food, sustainable agriculture movement, Blue Hill mostly uses ingredients grown or raised within 200 miles, including the Four Season Farm at Stone Barns Center for Food and Agriculture, Barber's second culinary project in nearby Westchester County. **Known for:** pioneering farm-to-table program; lush, well-executed dishes; sophisticated setting. [$] *Average main: $33* ✉ *75 Washington Pl., between Washington Sq. W and 6th Ave., Greenwich Village*

☎ *212/539–1776* ⊕ *www.bluehillfarm.com* ⊗ *No lunch* Ⓜ *A, B, C, D, E, F, M to W. 4th St.* ✛ *2:C1.*

$$$$ ✕ **Carbone.** It seems like Mario Carbone and Rich Torrisi can do no
ITALIAN wrong, Carbone is a case in point. The achingly popular place not only sticks to the Italian-American formula that has won it (and their earlier restaurant Torrisi) acclaim, but goes further: the white-tableclothed restaurant successfully emulates the Big Apple Italian restaurants of the 1950s, with revived dishes like veal marsala, rib-eye Diana, and baked clams. **Known for:** Italian-American dishes; pricey but huge portions; retro vibe. Ⓢ *Average main: $45* ⊠ *181 Thompson St., between Bleecker and Houston Sts., Greenwich Village* ☎ *212/254–3000* ⊕ *www.carbonenewyork.com* ⊗ *No lunch weekends* Ⓜ *A, B, C, D, E, F, M to W. 4th St.* ✛ *2:D2.*

$$$ ✕ **Charlie Bird.** Packed since the day it opened in 2013, Italian-leaning
ITALIAN Charlie Bird is the brainchild of sommelier Robert Bohr, who was in
Fodor's Choice charge of wine at vino-mad Cru, and chef Ryan Hardy, who made
★ a name for himself at Little Nell in Aspen and, more recently, has been private chef for Jay-Z and Beyoncé—the restaurant has a hip-hop theme. The menu is divided into small and large plates, vegetables, a "raw" section, and pasta. **Known for:** the preferred spot for "cool kids" everywhere; hip-hop on the hi-fi; varied menu. Ⓢ *Average main: $32* ⊠ *5 King St., at 6th Ave., Greenwich Village* ☎ *212/235–7133* ⊕ *www.charliebirdnyc.com* ⊟ *No credit cards* Ⓜ *C, E to Spring St.; 1 to Houston St.* ✛ *2:C3.*

$ ✕ **Kati Roll Company.** You can think of a kati roll as a South Asian taco:
INDIAN griddled parathas stuffed with savory-spiced grilled meat, shrimp, paneer, chickpea mash, or spiced mashed potato. They're the only things sold at this tiny, popular lunch spot cheerfully festooned with Bollywood posters. **Known for:** tasty kati rolls; cheap late-night eats; long lunch lines. Ⓢ *Average main: $7* ⊠ *99 MacDougal St., near Bleecker St., Greenwich Village* ☎ *212/730–4280* ⊕ *www.thekatirollcompany. com* Ⓜ *A, B, C, D, E, F, M to W. 4th St.* ✛ *2:D2.*

$$ ✕ **Lupa.** Even the most hard-to-please connoisseurs have a soft spot for
ITALIAN Lupa, a "downscale" Roman trattoria. Rough-hewn wood, great Italian wines, and simple preparations with top-quality ingredients define the restaurant, along with the "gentle" prices for dishes such as ricotta gnocchi with sweet-sausage ragout, house-made salumi, and sardines with golden raisins and pine nuts. **Known for:** fine food without breaking the bank; good Italian wines; repeat customers. Ⓢ *Average main: $23* ⊠ *170 Thompson St., between Bleecker and Houston Sts., Greenwich Village* ☎ *212/982–5089* ⊕ *www.luparestaurant.com* Ⓜ *A, B, C, D, E, F, M to W. 4th St.* ✛ *2:D3.*

$$ ✕ **Mermaid Oyster Bar.** If you're craving a great raw bar, lobster roll, or
SEAFOOD soft-shell crab sandwich (in season), Mermaid Oyster Bar gives nearby classics Mary's Fish Camp and Pearl Oyster Bar a run for their money. Almost every dish is a winner, but the lobster bisque, the blackened striped bass, and the spicy seafood bucatini fra diavolo are all standouts. **Known for:** $1 oyster happy hour; superior seafood; excellent cocktails. Ⓢ *Average main: $23* ⊠ *79 MacDougal St., at Houston St., Greenwich*

15

Village ☎ *212/260–0100* ⊕ *www.themermaidnyc.com* ⊙ *No lunch* Ⓜ *1 to Houston St.; A, B, C, D, E, F, M to W. 4th St.* ✛ *2:D2.*

$$$
MODERN
AMERICAN
✕**Minetta Tavern.** By converting a moribund 80-year-old Italian restaurant into a cozy hot spot, restaurateur Keith McNally created yet another hit. Try early and often to score reservations, so that you can sample creations like buttery trout meunière, bone marrow on toast, expertly aged steaks, and the celebrated Black Label burger, a gorgeous assembly of meat topped with caramelized onions and an added layer of cheese. **Known for:** classic New York dining; original details and mural; tough to get a table. Ⓢ *Average main: $29* ⊠ *113 MacDougal St., between Bleecker and 3rd Sts., Greenwich Village* ☎ *212/475–3850* ⊕ *www.minettatavernny.com* ⊙ *No lunch Mon., Tues.* Ⓜ *A, B, C, D, E, F, M to W. 4th St.* ✛ *2:D2.*

$$$
JAPANESE
✕**Tokyo Record Bar.** An homage to the genre of jewel-box-size restaurant-bars in Tokyo that play vinyl while patrons sip Japanese whiskey and eat feel-good fare, this subterranean, 18-seat spot offers two seatings per night—6:30 and 8:30 pm—for a seven-course Japanese-influenced tasting menu. After 10:30 pm, an à la carte menu is offered. **Known for:** changing fixed-price menu; vintage vinyl on the hi-fi; intimate experience. Ⓢ *Average main: $30* ⊠ *127 MacDougal St., between 3rd and 4th Sts., Greenwich Village* ☎ *212/420–4777* ⊕ *www.tokyorecordbar.com* ⊙ *No lunch* Ⓜ *A, B, C, D, E, F, M to W. 4th St.* ✛ *2:D2.*

WEST VILLAGE

The West Village has mastered the art of destination restaurants that feel like neighborhood eateries. Places here are homey, yet remarkable enough to attract diners from all over the city.

$$
ISRAELI
✕**Bar Bolonat.** Chef Einat Admony, who runs the show at Taïm and Balaboosta, has devised an intriguing menu at this sleek West Village spot that serves dishes that represent the Jewish diaspora around the Mediterranean. Sit at the bar and watch the kitchen in action or dine at a two-top in the dark-hued dining room. **Known for:** Jerusalem bagel; fried olives; chickpea curry. Ⓢ *Average main: $22* ⊠ *611 Hudson St., between Jane and 12th Sts., West Village* ☎ *212/390–1545* ⊕ *www.barbolonatny.com* ⊙ *No lunch* Ⓜ *A, C, E to 14th St.; L to 8th Ave.* ✛ *3:B5.*

$$
ITALIAN
✕**Barbuto.** The specialties here are rustic Italian preparations with bright flavors, like house-made duck sausage with creamy polenta, red-wine-braised short ribs, and pasta carbonara, though the menu changes daily, depending on what's available. Chef Jonathan Waxman's acclaimed roasted chicken is usually on the menu. **Known for:** rustic fare; roasted chicken; airy, large-windowed space. Ⓢ *Average main: $22* ⊠ *775 Washington St., between Jane and 12th Sts., West Village* ☎ *212/924–9700* ⊕ *www.barbutonyc.com* Ⓜ *A, C, E to 14th St.; L to 8th Ave.; 1 to Christopher St.–Sheridan Sq.* ✛ *3:B5.*

$$$
AMERICAN
✕**Chumley's.** French writer Simone de Beauvoir visited this hidden Village gem and former famous literary hangout in the 1950s, commenting that the interior was simple yet had "something so rare in America—atmosphere." Today it still has the vibe of a former speakeasy (no sign on the door, for example), but the kitchen takes itself much more seriously these days, churning out top-notch versions of bone-marrow-spiked burgers, foie gras terrine, and harissa-laced cod. The writers

might be gone, replaced by patrons with expense accounts, but Chumley's still has that atmosphere. **Known for:** a favorite Village speakeasy; good burgers; photo-lined walls and plenty of history. $ *Average main: $30* ✉ *86 Bedford St., between Barrow and Grove Sts., West Village* ☎ *212/675–2081* ⊕ *chumleysnewyork.com* ☽ *Closed Sun. No lunch* Ⓜ *1 to Christopher St./Sheridan Sq.* ✛ *2:B2.*

$$$ ✕ **dell'anima.** Lines still snake out the door of this neighborhood
ITALIAN favorite, so it's a good idea to make a reservation. Once you're in, check out the open kitchen, where the stylish crowd converges to watch chefs prepare authentic Italian dishes with a modern twist. **Known for:** excellent Italian wine selection; pollo al diavolo; open kitchen. $ *Average main: $26* ✉ *38 8th Ave., at Jane St., West Village* ☎ *212/366–6633* ⊕ *www.dellanima.com* ☽ *No lunch weekdays* Ⓜ *1, 2, 3, A, C, E to 14th St.; L to 8th Ave.* ✛ *3:C5.*

$$ ✕ **Do Hwa.** If anyone in New York is responsible for making Korean
KOREAN food cool and user-friendly, it is the mother-daughter team behind this chic, perennially popular restaurant. Jenny Kwak and her mother, Myung Ja, serve home cooking including *kalbi jim* (braised short ribs), *bibimbop* (a spicy, mix-it-yourself vegetable-and-rice dish), and other favorites. The dishes may not be as pungent as in Koreatown but are satisfying nevertheless—in a far more sophisticated atmosphere. **Known for:** part-owner Quentin Tarantino; reliable Korean fare; lively bar area. $ *Average main: $23* ✉ *55 Carmine St., between Bedford St. and 7th Ave. S, West Village* ☎ *212/414–1224* ⊕ *www. dohwanyc.com* ☽ *No lunch Sat.–Mon.* Ⓜ *1 to Houston St.; A, B, C, D, E, F, M to W. 4th St.* ✛ *2:C2.*

$ ✕ **Dominique Ansel Kitchen.** Don't come here looking for the cronut,
BAKERY French baker Dominique Ansel's insanely popular Franken-pastry, because you won't find it (for that, head to his other bakery in SoHo). Instead, the cutting-edge baker-wizard conjures up other edible oddities such as garlic bread croissants, a French toast-like croque monsieur, and beignets sprinkled and filled with matcha powder. (The dust of these beignets explodes like a green-spewing volcano with each bite). **Known for:** not offering the cronut; inventive baked goods; outdoor tables. $ *Average main: $8* ✉ *137 7th Ave. S, between Charles St. and 10th St., West Village* ☎ *212/242–5111* ⊕ *www.dominiqueanselkitchen. com* Ⓜ *1 to Christopher St./Sheridan Sq.* ✛ *2:C1.*

$$ ✕ **Due West.** The cocktails at this handsome 65-seat, wood-clad gastro-
AMERICAN pub get as much attention and love as the feel-good food created in the kitchen. Grab a seat by the window—in summer they open up creating a refreshing al fresco ambience—and sip a Negroni or a mezcal-and-beer-laced Old Diablo while grazing on crispy chickpea fritters, pork belly tacos, and gooey hot crab dip. **Known for:** creative cocktails; late-night dining on weekends; airy ambience. $ *Average main: $16* ✉ *189 W. 10th St., between 4th and Bleecker Sts., West Village* ☎ *646/687–4609* ⊕ *www.duewestnyc.com* ☽ *No lunch* Ⓜ *1 to Christopher St.* ✛ *3:C5.*

$$ ✕ **Emily.** This beloved Brooklyn pizza and Italian-ish eatery, named for
PIZZA its pie-loving proprietor, has jumped across the East River and opened a branch on a charming block in the West Village. The specialty here is pizza, from Detroit-style grandma pies (think square instead of round,

15

thick instead of thin) to wood-fired pizzas with ingredients like clams, anchovies, and Calabrian chilies. **Known for:** different kinds of pizza; great signature burger; Brooklyn favorite. [$] *Average main: $20* ✉ *35 Downing St., at Bedford St., West Village* ☎ *917/935–6434* 🌐 *www.pizzalovesemily.com* [M] *A, B, C, D, E, F, M to W. 4th St.* ✣ *2:C3.*

$$ MEXICAN 🍴 **Empellón Taqueria.** Chef Alex Stupak worked as the wizardlike pastry chef at the now-closed wd-50, New York's introduction to molecular gastronomy, so when he left to open a taqueria, many diners wondered if they'd be served deconstructed tacos. Instead, they got simple yet well-executed fare using top-notch ingredients. **Known for:** creative takes on tacos; noted chef; margaritas. [$] *Average main: $24* ✉ *230 W. 4th St., at 10th St., West Village* ☎ *212/367–0999* 🌐 *www.empellon.com* ⏲ *No lunch* [M] *1 to Christopher St.–Sheridan Sq.* ✣ *2:B1.*

$$ ITALIAN 🍴 **Frankies 570 Spuntino.** The Frankies—that is, owners and chefs Frank Falcinelli and Frank Castronovo—have a winning formula at their West Village restaurant: serve hearty, not-necessarily-by-the-book Italian-inflected fare using local, organic, and humanely raised ingredients in a laid-back atmosphere. Most menu items change seasonally, but expect good pasta dishes. **Known for:** burrata; chicken liver crostini; friendly neighborhood spot. [$] *Average main: $20* ✉ *570 Hudson St., at 11th St., West Village* ☎ *212/924–0818* 🌐 *www.frankiesspuntino.com* [M] *A, C, E to 14th St.; L to 8th Ave.* ✣ *2:B1.*

$$ AMERICAN 🍴 **High Street on Hudson.** When this Philadelphia import opened in 2015, it received a lot of attention but not the good kind: chef Eli Kulp had been badly injured in a train accident. But eaters also soon found out that High Street was worthy of their attention for its hearty food, particularly at breakfast when the kitchen churns out deliciously messy egg-and-meat-loaded sandwiches. **Known for:** house-made spaghetti; roasted turkey sandwich; "The Bodega" breakfast sandwich. [$] *Average main: $18* ✉ *637 Hudson St., at Horatio St., West Village* ☎ *917/388–3944* 🌐 *www.highstreetonhudson.com* [M] *A, C, E to 14th St./8th Ave.* ✣ *3:B5.*

$$$ ITALIAN 🍴 **I Sodi.** In a city where you can't throw a meatball without hitting an Italian restaurant, this minimalist-design, Tuscan-focused eatery in the West Village is a real find. Spiky-haired owner Rita Sodi, a Florentine who formerly worked in the fashion industry, ensures the traditional Italian fare coming from the kitchen is satisfying and seasonal. **Known for:** high-quality seasonal Tuscan fare; good pasta; minimalist look. [$] *Average main: $27* ✉ *105 Christopher St., between Bleecker and Hudson Sts., West Village* ☎ *212/414–5774* 🌐 *www.isodinyc.com* ⏲ *No lunch* [M] *1 to Christopher St.–Sheridan Sq.* ✣ *2:B2.*

$ PIZZA FAMILY 🍴 **Joe's Pizza.** You might recognize this Greenwich Village institution from its frequent cameos in TV and film (in *Spider-Man,* Tobey Maguire's Peter Parker was a Joe's delivery boy). But it's the classic gooey New York slice, dripping melted cheese onto paper plates, that *really* makes the place famous. **Known for:** an excellent New York slice; Village classic; film cameos. [$] *Average main: $6* ✉ *7 Carmine St., near Bleecker St., West Village* ☎ *212/366–1182* 🌐 *www.joespizzanyc.com* 💳 *No credit cards* [M] *A, B, C, D, E, F, M to W. 4th St.* ✣ *2:C2.*

$$ PIZZA 🍴 **Keste Pizza & Vino.** At the back of the long, narrow Keste Pizza & Vino restaurant is a beautiful, tiled, wood-fired oven that cooks what might

be Manhattan's most authentic Neapolitan pies at 1,000° F. Blistered and chewy around the edges, the margherita pie gives way to a softer center pooled with San Marzano tomato sauce and house-made mozzarella. **Known for:** authentic Neapolitan pizza; gluten-free option; always busy. $ *Average main: $17* ⊠ *271 Bleecker St., between 6th and 7th Aves., West Village* ☎ *212/243–1500* ⊕ *www.kestepizzeria.com* Ⓜ *1 to Christopher St.–Sheridan Sq.; A, B, C, D, E, F, M to W. 4th St.* ✛ *2:C2.*

$$$
MODERN
AMERICAN
Fodor'sChoice
★

✕ **The Little Owl.** This tiny neighborhood joint, with seating for 28 people, is exceptionally eager to please—and this attitude, plus the food, is a winning combination. The menu is just as small, which actually makes it easier to decide what you want: and what you want are the pork-veal-beef-pecorino-cheese meatball "sliders," or miniburgers. **Known for:** perfect West Village neighborhood spot; sliders; beignets. $ *Average main: $25* ⊠ *90 Bedford St., at Grove St., West Village* ☎ *212/741–4695* ⊕ *www.thelittleowlnyc.com* Ⓜ *1 to Christopher St.–Sheridan Sq.; A, B, C, D, E, F, M to W. 4th St.* ✛ *3:D6.*

$$
SEAFOOD

✕ **Mary's Fish Camp.** Diners still line up down the street before the restaurant opens for dinner to get a table at this small but bustling seafood shack. The result of a split between Pearl Oyster Bar's partners, Mary's is a more intimate space, but the two have similar menus: excellent fried oysters, chowders, and, of course, the sweet lobster roll with crisp fries. **Known for:** great seafood shack; lobster rolls; friendly staff. $ *Average main: $24* ⊠ *64 Charles St., at 4th St., West Village* ☎ *646/486–2185* ⊕ *www.marysfishcamp.com* ☽ *No dinner Sun.* Ⓜ *1 to Christopher St.–Sheridan Sq.* ✛ *2:B1.*

$$
MIDDLE EASTERN

✕ **Moustache.** There's typically a crowd waiting outside for one of the copper-top tables at this casual Middle Eastern neighborhood restaurant. The focal point is the perfect pita that accompanies tasty salads like lemony chickpea and spinach, hearty lentil and bulgur, or falafel. **Known for:** reliable Middle Eastern fare; good lamb mains; perfect pita. $ *Average main: $13* ⊠ *90 Bedford St., between Barrow and Grove Sts., West Village* ☎ *212/229–2220* ⊕ *www.moustachepitza.com* Ⓜ *1 to Christopher St.–Sheridan Sq.; A, B, C, D, E, F, M to W. 4th St.* ✛ *2:B2.*

$$$
SEAFOOD

✕ **Pearl Oyster Bar.** There have been many imitators and few real competitors to this West Village seafood institution. Since 1997, Rebecca Charles has been serving arguably the best lobster roll in New York City in a no-frills space down charming, restaurant-lined Cornelia Street—and expanded next door to accommodate the throngs. **Known for:** lobster rolls; sea scallops; maybe too-speedy service. $ *Average main: $26* ⊠ *18 Cornelia St., between 4th and Bleecker Sts., West Village* ☎ *212/691–8211* ⊕ *www.pearloysterbar.com* ☽ *Closed Sun.* Ⓜ *A, B, C, D, E, F, M to W. 4th St.* ✛ *2:C2.*

$$$
CHINESE

✕ **RedFarm.** Conceived and run by Ed Schoenfeld, an expert on Chinese cuisine, and Joe Ng, known as the dumpling king of New York, this West Village restaurant specializes mostly in—you guessed it—Chinese-style dumplings. The menu focuses on dim sum—small plates and snacks (often in dumpling form)—as well as Chinese-American dishes like three-chili chicken and chicken in garlic sauce. **Known for:** dim sum; pastrami egg roll; prices that add up. $ *Average main: $30* ⊠ *529 Hudson St., between 10th and Charles Sts., West Village*

15

☎ *212/792–9700* 🌐 *www.redfarmnyc.com* ⏲ *No lunch* [M] *1 to Christopher St.–Sheridan Sq.* ✣ *2:B2.*

$$$ BRITISH 🍴 **The Spotted Pig.** Part cozy English pub, part laid-back neighborhood hangout, part gastronome's lure, the Spotted Pig showcases the impeccable food of London chef April Bloomfield. Dishes like arugula salad with radishes and Parmesan, and smoked-haddock-and-corn chowder with homemade crackers are studies in texture and flavor contrast, while the Roquefort cheeseburger is simply excellent. [$] *Average main: $27* ✉ *314 W. 11th St., at Greenwich St., West Village* ☎ *212/620–0393* 🌐 *www.thespottedpig.com* [M] *1 to Christopher St.–Sheridan Sq.; 2, 3 to 14th St.; L to 8th Ave.* ✣ *2:A1.*

$$$$ JAPANESE Fodor's Choice ★ 🍴 **Sushi Nakazawa.** It's all omakase at this acclaimed sushi spot from master Daisuke Nakazawa. Fans of the 2011 documentary *Jiro Dreams of Sushi* may remember him as the apprentice to the Tokyo-based sushi master Jiro Ono, who spent the near-entirety of the film trying to perfect the egg custard; he finally succeeded, just as he has succeeded in wooing even the most finicky New York diners. **Known for:** mind-blowing raw fish (priced to match); hard-to-get tables; Jiro Dreams of Sushi. [$] *Average main: $170* ✉ *23 Commerce St., near Bedford St., West Village* ☎ *212/924–2212* 🌐 *www.sushinakazawa.com* ⏲ *No lunch* [M] *1 to Christopher St.–Sheridan Sq.; A, B, C, D, E, F, M to W. 4th St.* ✣ *3:D6.*

$ MIDDLE EASTERN 🍴 **Taïm.** There's a real chef behind this tiny sliver of a restaurant, New York's only gourmet falafel stand. *Taïm* means "tasty" in Hebrew, and Tel Aviv transplant Einat Admony's fried chickpea balls are delicious, and available in several beguiling flavors (try them infused with spicy harissa sauce) along with a tantalizing display of à la carte salads (the carrots with Moroccan spices is a standout). There's another location in NoLIta, on Spring Street between Mott and Mulberry. **Known for:** eggplant-stuffed sabich sandwich; creative falafel; smoothies. [$] *Average main: $9* ✉ *222 Waverly Pl., near Perry St., West Village* ☎ *212/691–1287* 🌐 *www.taimfalafel.com* [M] *1, 2, 3 to 14th St.; L to 8th Ave.* ✣ *2:B1.*

$$ ITALIAN 🍴 **Via Carota.** The brainchild of chefs Jody Williams and Rita Sodi, who run Buvette and I Sodi, respectively, just a block or two away from here, Via Carota feels like the perfect West Village Italian eatery. Situated on charming Grove Street, it offers sidewalk tables (or a welcoming long bar to perch at), and consistently serves up unpretentious and above-average Italian fare. **Known for:** great neighborhood ambience; grilled octopus; pastas such as pappardelle with wild boar ragù. [$] *Average main: $20* ✉ *51 Grove St., between 7th Ave. S and Bleecker St., West Village* ☎ *212/255–1962* 🌐 *www.viacarota.com* [M] *1 to Christopher St.–Sheridan Sq.* ✣ *3:D6.*

$$$ AUSTRIAN 🍴 **Wallsé.** The modern Austrian menu at Kurt Gutenbrunner's lovely, light-filled neighborhood restaurant has a strong emphasis on Austrian tradition and urban New York attitude. It's hard to argue with such dishes as Wiener schnitzel with potato-cucumber salad and lingonberries, or venison goulash with spaetzle and Brussels sprouts, and it's often lighter than you'd think Austrian food would be. **Known for:** Wiener schnitzel; short-rib goulash; great desserts such as Sacher torte. [$] *Average main: $34* ✉ *344 W. 11th St., at Washington St., West Village* ☎ *212/352–2300* 🌐 *www.wallse.com* ⏲ *Closed Sun. No lunch* [M] *1 to Christopher St.–Sheridan Sq.; A, C, E to 14th St.; L to 8th Ave.* ✣ *3:B6.*

CHELSEA AND THE MEATPACKING DISTRICT

CHELSEA

Several big-name chefs have moved to the western part of this neighborhood in recent years, putting Chelsea on the dining map. For a tasty quick bite or a gift for your favorite foodie, stop by **Chelsea Market.**

$$$ AMERICAN 🍴 **Cookshop.** One of far-west Chelsea's first hot restaurants, Cookshop manages a casual elegance while focusing on seasonal, farm-fresh cuisine that continues to wow. Outdoor seating on 10th Avenue is quite peaceful in the evening; during the day you can survey a cross section of gallery-hoppers and shoppers. **Known for:** simple but well-executed, market-driven American cuisine; great cocktails; brunch. [$] *Average main: $26* ✉ *156 10th Ave., at 20th St., Chelsea* ☎ *212/924–4440* 🌐 *www.cookshopny.com* [M] *A, C, E to 23rd St.* ✣ *3:B3.*

$$ LATIN AMERICAN 🍴 **Coppelia.** Named for a legendary ice-cream shop in Havana, Coppelia is neither Cuban nor an ice-cream parlor. Chef Julian Medina has created a 24-hour pan-Latin diner that works on many levels—for a quick breakfast, casual lunch, or late-night bite—with a continent-size menu that emphasizes comfort food. **Known for:** 24-hour dining goodness; pan-Latin fare; pancakes. [$] *Average main: $16* ✉ *207 W. 14th St., between 7th and 8th Aves., Chelsea* ☎ *212/858–5001* 🌐 *www.coppelianyc.com* [M] *1, 2, 3, A, C, E, F, M to 14th St.; L to 8th Ave.* ✣ *3:C4.*

$ MIDDLE EASTERN 🍴 **Dizengoff.** Located inside the always bustling Chelsea Market, this Philly import might stir up the best hummus this side of the Middle Eastern hummus belt. It's utterly creamy and light, and you'll feel like you're eating chickpea puree for the very first time in your life. **Known for:** it's all about the hummus; stool seating; delicious side salads. [$] *Average main: $8* ✉ *Chelsea Market, 75 9th Ave., at 15th St., Chelsea* ☎ *646/833–7097* 🌐 *www.dizengoffhummus.com* [M] *A, C, E, L to 14th St./8th Ave.* ✣ *3:B4.*

$ INTERNATIONAL 🍴 **Gansevoort Market.** Once located on Gansevoort Street in the Meatpacking District, hence the name, this 14th Street food hall is one of the best among the recent rash of gourmet food court openings. Build up a hunger by walking the High Line and then settle in here for a worldly feast. **Known for:** Chelsea Market alternative; global cuisine; everything from pizza to Thai to ice cream. [$] *Average main: $10* ✉ *353 W. 14th St., between 8th and 9th Aves., Chelsea* ☎ *646/678–3231* 🌐 *www.gansmarket.com* [M] *A, C, E, L to 14th St./8th Ave* ✣ *3:B4.*

$$$$ FRENCH 🍴 **L'Atelier de Joël Robuchon.** This is French culinary wizard Joël Robuchon's sophomore attempt at wooing the sophisticated palates of New York diners. This time, though, he's gone downtown (though with uptown prices) and has stepped up his game with a long menu of haute-Gallic edible gifts for the taste buds. **Known for:** one of the most sophisticated dining experiences in lower Manhattan; brilliant chef; expensive tasting menu. [$] *Average main: $100* ✉ *85 10th Ave., at 15th St., Chelsea* ☎ *212/488–8885* 🌐 *www.joelrobuchonusa.com* 🕓 *No lunch* [M] *A, C, E, L to 14th St./8th Ave.* ✣ *3:A4.*

$$ CHINESE 🍴 **Legend.** Sure, there's nothing Chinese about the generic name; and the location, on a stretch of 7th Avenue in Chelsea, is flanked by forgettable eating options. But do your taste buds a favor and eat at

this affordable Sichuan spot, whose quiet opening was followed by a lot of buzz among New York's fooderati. **Known for:** high-quality, spicy Sichuan fare; great value; long menu. $ *Average main: $15* ✉ *88 7th Ave., between 15th and 16th Sts., Chelsea* ☎ *212/929–1778* ⊕ *www.legendbarrestaurant.com* Ⓜ *1, 2, 3, A, C, E, F, M to 14th St.; L to 8th Ave.* ✛ *3:D4.*

$$$ ✕ **The Red Cat.** Elegant yet unpretentious, a lovely neighborhood spot
MODERN *and* a destination restaurant, the Red Cat is a great place to chat with
AMERICAN a friend, celebrate an auspicious occasion, have a business dinner, or just enjoy an excellent meal. The American-meets-Mediterranean menu changes frequently, based on what's in season, but expect an eclectic menu of well-executed pastas, burgers, saffron-laced seafood, and meaty numbers. **Known for:** its nine-lives longevity; intimate, neighborhood vibe; special-occasion choice. $ *Average main: $27* ✉ *227 10th Ave., between 23rd and 24th Sts., Chelsea* ☎ *212/242–1122* ⊕ *www. theredcat.com* Ⓜ *C, E to 23rd St.* ✛ *3:A2.*

$$$ ✕ **Rouge Tomate.** Once an upscale vegetarian restaurant on the Upper
AMERICAN East Side, Rouge Tomate has come downtown and loosened up a bit. It now focuses on serving healthy, sustainable fare, even fish and meat, as long as it comes from an ethical source. **Known for:** sustainable fare; long, outstanding wine list; chocolate mousse with walnut foam. $ *Average main: $30* ✉ *126 W. 18th St., between 6th and 7th Aves., Chelsea* ☎ *646/395–3978* ⊕ *www.rougetomatechelsea.com* ☉ *Closed Sun., Mon. No lunch* Ⓜ *1, 2 to 18th St.* ✛ *3:D3.*

$$ ✕ **Tía Pol.** It may be sardine-can small, narrow, and dark, but that doesn't
SPANISH stop this popular tapas bar from being packed most nights. This is one of the best tapas spots in town, with a welcoming vibe, a dozen reasonably priced Spanish wines by the glass (and plenty of great bottles), and charm to spare. **Known for:** reasonably priced but high-quality tapas; patatas bravas; good Spanish wine choices. $ *Average main: $14* ✉ *205 10th Ave., between 22nd and 23rd Sts., Chelsea* ☎ *212/675–8805* ⊕ *www. tiapol.com* ☉ *No lunch Mon.* Ⓜ *C, E to 23rd St.* ✛ *3:A2.*

$$$ ✕ **Tipsy Parson.** If New York's Chelsea neighborhood were magically
SOUTHERN transported to the American South, the food might taste something like it does at this hip, Southern-accented eatery with a menu of artery-hardening delights. Named for a boozy Southern dessert, the Tipsy Parson and its menu are all about comfort in the belly and soul: fried pickles, homemade peanut butter with crackers, bourbon-laced chicken-liver mousse, and seafood potpie. **Known for:** whiskey and bourbon selection; hot fried chicken; cola-braised short ribs. $ *Average main: $25* ✉ *156 9th Ave., between 19th and 20th Sts., Chelsea* ☎ *212/620–4545* ⊕ *www. tipsyparson.com* ☉ *No lunch Mon., Tues.* Ⓜ *C, E to 23rd St.* ✛ *3:B3.*

$$ ✕ **Txikito.** The theme at this diminutive Spanish spot is *cucina vasca,*
SPANISH or Basque cuisine, one of the most exciting regions in Iberia for eating. Chef Alexandra Raij captures the moment by serving standouts like juicy lamb meatballs in a minty broth, crispy beef tongue, and an addictive crabmeat gratin. **Known for:** Basque cuisine; olive oil–poached cod; Basque wines. $ *Average main: $16* ✉ *240 9th Ave., at 25th St., Chelsea* ☎ *212/242–4730* ⊕ *www.txikitonyc.com* ☉ *No lunch* Ⓜ *C, E to 23rd St.* ✛ *3:B2.*

MEATPACKING DISTRICT

Europeans, models, actors, and the people who love them stroll the sidewalk like they're on a catwalk, going from one hot restaurant to the next in this cobblestone-laden neighborhood, which has become almost too sceney for its own good. There's plenty of great eating here—you just might have to wait awhile (or impersonate a celebrity) to get a table.

$$$$ ITALIAN 🍴 **Del Posto.** Much more formal than Babbo, the dining room at Del Posto—with its sweeping staircase, formal decor, and live music from a baby grand—has the feel of an opulent hotel lobby. This is one of the most consistently dazzling special-occasion spots in the city, and the food is stellar. **Known for:** some set menus; special-occasion Italian dining; urchin spaghetti. [$] *Average main: $65* ✉ *85 10th Ave., between 15th and 16th Sts., Meatpacking District* ☎ *212/497–8090* 🌐 *www.delposto.com* 🕓 *No lunch weekends* [M] *A, C, E to 14th St.; L to 8th Ave.* ✥ *3:A4.*

15

$$$ ITALIAN 🍴 **La Sirena.** Another Batali and Bastianich temple of Italian gastronomy, La Sirena combines excellent Italian fare with the trendy ambience of the Maritime Hotel (which houses the restaurant). The huge 200-seat space (with a long 38-seat bar) is highlighted by wavy Roman-inspired black-and-white floor tiles and globe-shaped wall lights that help keep the space relatively dim. **Known for:** huge bone-in rib eye; ravioli all'amatriciana; Italian wine list. [$] *Average main: $31* ✉ *88 9th Ave., between 16th and 17th Sts., Meatpacking District* ☎ *212/977–6096* 🌐 *www.lasirena-nyc.com* [M] *A, C, E to 14th St.* ✥ *3:B4.*

$$$ AMERICAN 🍴 **The Standard Grill.** Celebs, fashion-industry insiders, and the common folk, too, all cluster at this buzzy restaurant inside the Standard Hotel. The menu is comfort-luxe, with dishes like roast chicken for two in a cast-iron skillet and moist trout with a currant-and-pine-nut relish. **Known for:** deeply sceney; outdoor seating; comfort food until 4 am. [$] *Average main: $30* ✉ *848 Washington St., between Little W. 12th and 13th Sts., Meatpacking District* ☎ *212/645–4100* 🌐 *www.thestandardgrill.com* [M] *A, C, E to 14th St.; L to 8th Ave.* ✥ *3:B4.*

$$$ AMERICAN 🍴 **Untitled at the Whitney.** Located in the handsome Renzo Piano–designed Whitney Museum of American Art at the southern end of the High Line, restaurateur Danny Meyer's Untitled isn't necessarily the masterpiece in his collection of great restaurants, but the minimalist-design eatery is worth a look (and a bite). Chef Michael Anthony (who does double duty here and at the outstanding Gramercy Tavern) puts his usual admirable spin on deceptively simple dishes that explode with flavor. **Known for:** artsy surroundings; roasted and fried chicken; seafood cioppino. [$] *Average main: $25* ✉ *Whitney Museum of American Art, 99 Gansevoort St., at West St., Meatpacking District* ☎ *212/570–3670* 🌐 *www.untitledatthewhitney.com* [M] *A, C, E to 14th St.* ✥ *3:B5.*

UNION SQUARE WITH THE FLATIRON DISTRICT AND GRAMERCY

UNION SQUARE

Once the main spot in New York to go for protests, Union Square is now the stage for another type of communal experience: breaking bread. There is no shortage of appealing options at any price range (including picnic provisions from the wonderful greenmarket, open Monday, Wednesday, Friday, and Saturday).

$$$$
AMERICAN
Fodor'sChoice
★

✕ **Gotham Bar & Grill.** A culinary landmark, Gotham Bar & Grill is every bit as thrilling as when it opened in 1984. Celebrated chef Alfred Portale, who made the blueprint for "architectural food"—that is, towers of stacked ingredients—builds on a foundation of simple, clean flavors to create transcendent preparations: no rack of lamb is more tender, no seafood salad sweeter. **Known for:** inventing "architectural cuisine"; massive wine list; good-value prix-fixe lunch. $ *Average main: $42* ⊠ *12 E. 12th St., between 5th Ave. and University Pl., Union Square* ☎ *212/620–4020* ⊕ *www.gothambarandgrill.com* ⊗ *No lunch weekends* Ⓜ *4, 5, 6, L, N, Q, R, W to 14th St.–Union Sq.* ✢ *3:E4.*

$$
VEGETARIAN

✕ **Nix.** Chef John Fraser's "meatless Monday" menu at his Upper West Side eatery, Dovetail, spawned a good, entirely veggie restaurant downtown with a minimalist interior, lit by candles at night, that offers an intimate, sophisticated ambience. This is vegetarianism for the 21st century, and the roasted Brussels sprouts are emboldened with chestnuts and SarVecchio cheese. **Known for:** superior modern vegetarian fare; gnocchi; intimate setting. $ *Average main: $19* ⊠ *72 University Pl., between 10th and 11th Sts., Union Square* ☎ *212/498–9393* ⊕ *www.nixny.com* Ⓜ *4, 5, 6, L, N, Q, R, W to Union Sq.* ✢ *3:F5.*

$$$
MODERN
MEXICAN

✕ **Rosa Mexicano.** The idea that you can't find good south-of-the-border cuisine in the Big Apple is quickly fading, thanks in part to this Union Square restaurant (there are other locations too, including ones at Lincoln Center and TriBeCa). Although the spacious, colorfully lighted interior might tip you off that authenticity is best sought elsewhere, if you're looking for high-quality Mex-flavored fare, step right up, hombre. **Known for:** fancy lighting; potent margaritas and busy happy hour; tableside-made guac. $ *Average main: $28* ⊠ *9 E. 18th St., between 5th Ave. and Broadway, Union Square* ☎ *212/533–3350* ⊕ *www.rosamexicano.com* Ⓜ *4, 5, 6, L, N, Q, R to 14th St.–Union Sq.* ✢ *3:F3.*

$$$
MODERN
AMERICAN

✕ **Tocqueville.** Hidden just steps from busy Union Square, this refined dining oasis is a secret even to many New Yorkers. Enter through the austere reception area, past the heavy curtains and six-seat bar, and find the intimate dining area where chef and owner Marco Moreira churns out excellent Gallic-American fare. **Known for:** underrated haute fare; sea-urchin carbonara starter; jacket and tie recommended. $ *Average main: $33* ⊠ *1 E. 15th St., between 5th Ave. and Union Sq. W, Union Square* ☎ *212/647–1515* ⊕ *www.tocquevillerestaurant.com* ⊗ *No lunch Mon.* Ⓜ *4, 5, 6, L, N, Q, R to 14th St.–Union Sq.* ✢ *3:E4.*

$$$
AMERICAN

✕ **Union Square Cafe.** This popular New York culinary institution, which moved in late 2016, is still firing on all burners. Since 1985, noted restaurateur Danny Meyer's American restaurant has steadily served up unpretentious yet impressive, well-executed fare to loyal devotees, and the tradition continues in an elegant, two-floor spot a few blocks north of Union Square. **Known for:** ricotta gnocchi; the rib eye and burger; officious service. $ *Average main: $30* ✉ *101 E. 19 St., at Park Ave. S, Union Square* ☎ *212/243–4020* ⊕ *www.unionsquarecafe.com* Ⓜ *L, N, Q, R, W, 4, 5, 6 to 14th St./Union Sq.* ✛ *3:F3.*

FLATIRON DISTRICT

The popular Union Square Greenmarket has done wonders for the dining landscape in the area. Chefs, wanting to be close to the green bounty, have opened up restaurants nearby, particularly in the Flatiron District.

$$$ ✕ **ABC Kitchen.** Much more than a shopping break, Jean-Georges Vong-
AMERICAN erichten's popular restaurant, inside posh housewares emporium ABC Carpet and Home, is like a love letter to greenmarket cuisine. Underneath the exposed concrete beams, a chic crowd devours fresh, flavorful appetizers like the roasted carrot salad or pretzel-dusted calamari, and winning entrées such as roast suckling pig with smoked bacon marmalade and sea bass with chilies and herbs. **Known for:** vegetable-forward dishes; healthy power lunches; organic ingredients. $ *Average main: $29* ✉ *35 E. 18th St., between Broadway and Park Ave. S, Flatiron District* ☎ *212/475–5829* ⊕ *www.abckitchennyc.com* Ⓜ *4, 5, 6, L, N, Q, R, W to 14th St.–Union Sq.* ✛ *3:F3.*

$$$ ✕ **Aldea.** Bouley alumnus George Mendes's popular restaurant relies
PORTUGUESE on his Portuguese heritage as inspiration, which he elevates to new heights in this sleek bi-level space decorated with wood, glass, and blue accents. *Petiscos* (small bites) like cubes of crisp pork belly with apple cider reveal sophisticated cooking techniques and flavors. A delicate matsutake mushroom broth floated with a slow-poached egg is edged with a subtle brace of pine, and sea-salted cod reveals a deep, satisfying flavor strata. **Known for:** elevated Portuguese cuisine; sea-salted cod; seats at chef's counter. $ *Average main: $34* ✉ *31 W. 17th St., between 5th and 6th Aves., Flatiron District* ☎ *212/675–7223* ⊕ *www.aldeares-taurant.com* ⊙ *Closed Sun., Mon. No lunch* Ⓜ *4, 5, 6, L, N, Q, R, W to 14th St.–Union Sq.; F, M to 14th St.* ✛ *3:E3.*

$$ ✕ **Boqueria.** Perennially packed, this convivial tapas spot has leather
SPANISH banquettes lining the main room and a few seats at the bar, but if you want to make friends, opt for the communal table running down the center of the dining room—if you can get a seat. Fried quail eggs and chorizo on roasted bread are even better than they sound, and the mushroom and ham croquettes are a mainstay. **Known for:** reliable Spanish tapas in a fun atmosphere; communal table; churros. $ *Average main: $20* ✉ *53 W. 19th St., between 5th and 6th Aves., Flatiron District* ☎ *212/255–4160* ⊕ *www.boquerianyc.com* Ⓜ *1 to 18th St.; F, M to 14th St.; L to 6th Ave.; N, R, W to 23rd St.* ✛ *3:E3.*

$$$ ✕ **The Breslin Bar and Dining Room.** A sceney meatopia inside the ever-
BRITISH trendy Ace Hotel, the Breslin is not for the Lipitor crowd. English chef
Fodor'sChoice April Bloomfield, who also runs the John Dory right next door and
★ the excellent Spotted Pig in the West Village, hardens arteries with peanuts fried in pork fat, whipped lardo on pizza bianca, blood sausage accompanied by a fried duck egg, and a delicious feta-topped lamb burger. **Known for:** atery-hardening deliciousness; lamb burger;

15

cask-conditioned ales. Ⓢ *Average main: $30* ✉ *16 W. 29th St., at Broadway, Flatiron District* ☎ *212/679–1939* ⊕ *www.thebreslin.com* ☉ *No breakfast weekends* Ⓜ *N, R,W to 28th St.* ✛ *3:E1.*

$
AMERICAN
FAMILY

✕ **The City Bakery.** This self-service bakery-restaurant has the urban aesthetic to match its name. Chef and owner Maury Rubin's baked goods—giant cookies; addictively flaky, salty-sweet pretzel croissants; elegant caramel tarts—are unfailingly rich and delicious, but another major draw is the salad bar. **Known for:** hot chocolate; oversize cookies; salad bar. Ⓢ *Average main: $12* ✉ *3 W. 18th St., between 5th and 6th Aves., Flatiron District* ☎ *212/366–1414* ⊕ *www.thecitybakery. com* ☉ *No dinner* Ⓜ *4, 5, 6, L, N, Q, R, W to 14th St.–Union Sq.; F, M to 14th St.* ✛ *3:E3.*

$$$
BRITISH

✕ **The Clocktower.** Located in an actual clocktower (which also houses the New York EDITION Hotel), this Madison Square Park spot is helmed by British superchef Jason Atherton, who presides over a high-ceilinged, dark-hued dining room that feels like an adult clubhouse. Best described as elevated British tavern fare, the menu offers diners choices like the supertender red-wine-braised beef cheeks and comforting oxtail-spiked mac 'n' cheese. **Known for:** clubhouse ambience; creative cocktails; Long Island duck. Ⓢ *Average main: $33* ✉ *Metropolitan Life Insurance Co. Tower, 5 Madison Ave., 2nd fl., between 23rd and 24th Sts., Flatiron District* ☎ *212/413–4300* ⊕ *www.the-clocktowernyc.com* Ⓜ *N, R, W to 23rd St.* ✛ *3:F2.*

$$$
MEXICAN
Fodor's Choice
★

✕ **Cosme.** When Enrique Olvera, chef at Pujol, arguably Mexico's best restaurant, announced he was coming north of the border, New York foodies went loco. Olvera's haute touch to his native cuisine is magic and, coupled with the sleek design (soft lighting, minimalist decor), Cosme makes for one fine dining experience focused on small plates. **Known for:** creative small-plate Mexican fare; duck carnitas; corn tempura softshell crab. Ⓢ *Average main: $32* ✉ *35 E. 21st St., between Park Ave. and Broadway, Flatiron District* ☎ *212/913–9659* ⊕ *www. cosmenyc.com* Ⓜ *N, R, W, 6 to 23rd St.* ✛ *3:F3.*

$$$$
KOREAN
BARBECUE

✕ **Cote.** This place has blown up the staid New York steak-house formula by infusing Korean twists: that shrimp cocktail may look classic, but just wait till the hot *gochujang* hits your palate. Along with the raw meat to be grilled at your table, kimchi and *banchan* (small plates of Korean treats) arrive, adding layers of taste to your steak dinner. **Known for:** Korean-accented steak; bibimbap; Korean "bacon". Ⓢ *Average main: $45* ✉ *16 W. 22nd St., between 5th and 6th Aves., Flatiron District* ☎ *212/401–7986* ⊕ *www.cotenyc.com* Ⓜ *4, 6 to 23rd St.* ✛ *3:E3.*

$$$$
MODERN
AMERICAN

✕ **Craft.** A meal here is like a luscious choose-your-own-adventure game since every delectable dish comes à la carte. Craft is the flagship of *Top Chef* head judge Tom Colicchio's mini-empire of excellent restaurants around the country, including grab-and-go sandwich bars called 'wichcraft. Just about everything here is exceptionally prepared with little fuss, from simple yet intriguing starters (like harissa-spiked octopus) and sides (including the justly famous variety of roasted mushrooms, with oysters, trumpets, chanterelles, and hen-of-the-woods) to desserts (warm chocolate tart with buttermilk ice cream, cinnamon custard, and cashews). **Known for:** Tom Colicchio's flagship restaurant; roasted mushrooms; warm chocolate tart. $ *Average main: $40* ✉ *43 E. 19th St., between Broadway and Park Ave. S, Flatiron District* ☎ *212/780–0880* ⊕ *www.craftrestaurant.com* ⊘ *No lunch weekends* Ⓜ *4, 5, 6, L, N, Q, R, W to 14th St.–Union Sq.* ✛ *3:F3.*

$$$
ITALIAN
FAMILY

✕ **Eataly.** The cavernous Eataly, is a temple to all things Italian. Ignore the overpriced produce market by the front entrance and make a beeline for La Piazza for sandwiches made with meticulously sourced ingredients (you can eat at the stand-up tables nearby); there's also a full-service pizza and pasta restaurant, a raw bar and fish eatery, and a wine bar for quaffing glass pours and beers on tap. **Known for:** maddening crowds; Italian foods to eat or buy and bring home; rooftop birreria. $ *Average main: $25* ✉ *200 5th Ave., at 23rd St., Flatiron District* ☎ *646/398–5100* ⊕ *www.eataly.com* Ⓜ *N, R, W, 6 to 23rd St.* ✛ *3:E2.*

$$$$
MODERN
AMERICAN
Fodor'sChoice
★

✕ **Eleven Madison Park.** Luxury, precision, and creativity are the driving forces at this internationally renowned restaurant, one of the planet's best, overlooking Madison Park. Swiss-born chef Daniel Humm oversees the kitchen, concocting unexpected dishes that change often at this entirely prix-fixe eatery. **Known for:** ultimate special-occasion restaurant; constantly reinventing itself; reserve several months ahead. $ *Average main: $225* ✉ *11 Madison Ave., at 24th St., Flatiron District* ☎ *212/889–0905* ⊕ *www.elevenmadisonpark.com* ⊘ *No lunch Mon.–Thurs.* Ⓜ *N, R, W, 6 to 23rd St.* ✛ *3:F2.*

$$
BARBECUE

✕ **Hill Country.** This enormous barbecue joint is perfect for big groups and carnivorous appetites. The beef-centric Texas-sized menu features meaty ribs and exceptionally succulent slow-smoked brisket; check your diet at the door and go for the moist, fatty option. **Known for:** vast space; tasty brisket, prime rib, and pulled pork; some long lines at stations. $ *Average main: $22* ✉ *30 W. 26th St., between Broadway and 6th Ave., Flatiron District* ☎ *212/255–4544* ⊕ *www.hillcountryny.com* Ⓜ *N, R, W, 6 to 28th St.; F, M to 23rd St.* ✛ *3:E2.*

$$
SEAFOOD

✕ **The John Dory.** Chef April Bloomfield and former rock-band manager turned restaurateur Ken Friedman won taste buds and palates with gastropub Spotted Pig and the Breslin, and then turned their attention to the sea at this popular, fish-friendly spot inside the Ace Hotel. The menu is dominated by small plates—chorizo-stuffed squid, an excellent lobster roll—but focuses on crudo (raw) dishes. **Known for:** happy hour; oysters; small plates. $ *Average main: $23* ✉ *1196 Broadway, at 29th St., Flatiron District* ☎ *212/792–9000* ⊕ *www.thejohndory.com* Ⓜ *N, R, W to 28th St.* ✛ *3:E1.*

$$
AMERICAN

✕ **Made Nice.** If you balk at the price of Daniel Humm and Will Guidara's Eleven Madison Park or even The NoMad, try their fast, casual spot, likely the prototype for more to come around New York and beyond. Everything about Made Nice was designed for professionals (or visitors) who don't have an hour or two to graze: meals, such as as roasted chicken, curried cauliflower, or tuna niçoise—arrive at diners' tables within 10 minutes of ordering. **Known for:** fast-casual food from noted chef and restaurateur; braised pork and roasted Brussels sprouts; milk-and-honey soft serve. $ *Average main: $13* ✉ *8 W. 28th St., between 5th and 6th Aves., Flatiron District* ⊕ *www.madenicenyc.com* ⊘ *Closed Sun.* Ⓜ *R, W to 28th St.* ✛ *3:E2.*

15

$$$ ✕ **The NoMad.** Named for the hotel, which itself is named for the up-
MODERN and-coming neighborhood north of Madison Square Park, the NoMad
AMERICAN is brought to you by Daniel Humm and Will Guidara, the masterminds
Fodor'sChoice behind much-lauded Eleven Madison Park. The atmosphere is a blend
★ of lively and sophisticated (plush velvet chairs and drapes for the hip
young crowd), and the food is similarly vibrant yet simple: seared scal-
lops with pumpkin, juicy suckling pig with pear confit and mustard.
Known for: chic scene; whole roasted chicken for two; confit suckling
pig. $ *Average main: $35* ⊠ *NoMad Hotel, 1170 Broadway, at 28th St.,*
Flatiron District ☎ *347/472–5660* ⊕ *www.thenomadhotel.com* Ⓜ *N, R,*
W to 28th St. ✛ *3:E2.*

$ ✕ **Shake Shack.** Although there are other locations of Danny Meyer's
AMERICAN patties 'n' shakes joint around town (including Brooklyn), this is where
Fodor'sChoice it all began. Here in Madison Square Park, there's no indoor seating—
★ just snaking outdoor lines. **Known for:** burgers; shakes; outdoor seat-
ing and long lines. $ *Average main: $8* ⊠ *Madison Square Park, near*
Madison Ave. and 23rd St., Flatiron District ☎ *212/889–6600* ⊕ *www.*
shakeshack.com Ⓜ *N, R, W, 6 to 23rd St.* ✛ *3:F2.*

$$$ ✕ **Upland.** This collaboration between prolific Philly-NYC restaurateur
ITALIAN Stephen Starr and erstwhile Il Buco chef Justin Smilie tastes as if Cali-
fornia and Italy miraculously collided. Marrying organic and in-season
ingredients with Italian recipes, Upland's standouts include bucatini
alla carbonara that could pass muster with discriminating eaters in the
Eternal City or, um, the City of Angels. **Known for:** California-inspired
cuisine that New Yorkers can get behind; bucatini alla carbonara; good
wine list. $ *Average main: $27* ⊠ *345 Park Ave. S, between 25th and*
26th Sts., Flatiron District ☎ *212/686–1006* ⊕ *www.uplandnyc.com*
Ⓜ *6 to 28th St.* ✛ *3:F2.*

GRAMERCY

This leafy, high-rent neighborhood, which has an old-world, old-money
feel, is home to a few gems, tucked away down the long blocks of
brownstones. Gramercy is a great place for a stroll before dinner.

$$$$ ✕ **BLT Prime.** A masculine, vivacious space is the showcase for bold,
STEAKHOUSE appealing Franco-American cuisine. Menu specials are scrawled on a
blackboard, and although there are poultry, veal, and lamb dishes on
the menu—from lemon-rosemary chicken to a lamb T-bone—steaks
are the main event. **Known for:** 28-day dry-aged porterhouse; steaks
of all kinds; masculine space. $ *Average main: $40* ⊠ *111 E. 22nd*
St., between Lexington and Park Aves., Gramercy ☎ *212/995–8500*
⊕ *www.bltprime.com* ☾ *No lunch* Ⓜ *N, R, 6 to 23rd St.* ✛ *3:F2.*

$$ ✕ **Casa Mono.** Andy Nusser put in his time cooking Italian at Babbo
SPANISH before an obsession with Spain landed him his own acclaimed Iberian
niche. Though most menu items are delectably shareable, of particu-
lar note are all things seared *à la plancha* (grilled on a metal plate),
including blistered peppers and garlic-kissed mushrooms. **Known for:**
high-quality, authentic Spanish tapas; adventurous cuts of meat; wine-
and-ham-bar annex next door. $ *Average main: $21* ⊠ *52 Irving Pl., at*
17th St., Gramercy ☎ *212/253–2773* ⊕ *www.casamononyc.com* Ⓜ *4,*
5, 6, L, N, Q, R, W to 14th St.–Union Sq. ✛ *3:G3.*

$$$$ ✕**Gramercy Tavern.** Danny Meyer's intensely popular restaurant tops
AMERICAN many a New Yorker's list of favorite dining spots. In front, the first-
come, first-served tavern has a lighter menu along with great craft beers
and cocktails, while the more formal dining room has a seasonal, prix-
fixe American menu. **Known for:** impeccable service; seasonal American fare; craft beers in tavern. ⓢ *Average main: $38* ⊠ *42 E. 20th
St., between Broadway and Park Ave. S, Gramercy* ☏ *212/477–0777*
⊕ *www.gramercytavern.com* Ⓜ *N, R, W, 6 to 23rd St.* ✛ *3:F3.*

$$$ ✕**Maialino.** Named for its signature dish—suckling pig—the perpetually
ROMAN packed restaurant in the Gramercy Park Hotel is what it might look
like if Manhattan and Rome collided: fashionable people eating in an
Eternal City ambience. If you haven't been to the Italian capital in a
while, there's plenty to reintroduce your taste buds to *la dolce vita.*
Try the excellent fried artichokes, spaghetti alla carbonara (made with
guanciale, or pig cheek, just like in Rome), or the sausage-studded
pasta dish *lumaconi alla Norcia.* **Known for:** Roman fare in Gramercy;
roasted suckling pig; spicy tripe. ⓢ *Average main: $28* ⊠ *2 Lexington
Ave., at 21st St., Gramercy* ☏ *212/777–2410* ⊕ *www.maialinonyc.com*
Ⓜ *6 to 23rd St.* ✛ *3:G3.*

$$$ ✕**Nur.** From Israeli celeb chef Meir Adoni (who runs restaurants in
MIDDLE EASTERN Tel Aviv), Nur covers a lot of ground, serving up whatever is deli-
cious from Morocco to Yemen and everywhere in between. Start with
Palestinian tartare—raw beef sprinkled with favas and pine nuts—or
the sweet-meets-savory date doughnut (a Moroccan fritter called a
sfenj). **Known for:** wide-ranging Middle Eastern menu; Palestinian
tartare; Hills of Jerusalem dessert. ⓢ *Average main: $35* ⊠ *34 E. 20th
St., between Broadway and Park Ave. S, Gramercy* ☏ *212/505–3420*
⊕ *www.nurnyc.com* ☾ *No lunch* Ⓜ *6 to 23rd St.* ✛ *3:F3.*

MIDTOWN EAST WITH MURRAY HILL

MIDTOWN EAST
Midtown East's streets are relatively quiet at night and on weekends,
but during the week, the restaurants are filled with expense-account diners celebrating their successes. Indeed, some of the most formal dining
rooms and most expensive meals in town can be found here.

$$$$ ✕**Agern.** Set in a vast room in Grand Central that was once hidden to
SCANDINAVIAN the general public, Agern is the domain of Claus Meyer, most famous
for being a cofounder of Copenhagen's highly influential Noma. Here
Icelandic chef Gunnar Gislasen mines New York for high-quality ingre-
dients, turning them into palate-pleasing dishes such as a tender apple-
glazed pork belly and poached lobster. **Known for:** Noma in New York;
prix-fixe menus; superb ingredients. ⓢ *Average main: $70* ⊠ *Grand
Central Terminal, 89 E. 42nd St., between Vanderbilt and Park Aves.,
Midtown East* ☏ *646/568–4018* ⊕ *www.agernrestaurant.com* ☾ *Closed
Sun. No lunch Sat.* Ⓜ *4, 5, 6, 7, S to Grand Central/42nd St.* ✛ *4:F4.*

$$$$ ✕**Aquavit and Aquavit Café.** This elegant and refined Scandinavian restau-
SCANDINAVIAN rant has seen a transition in the kitchen these last few years, going from
Marcus Samuelsson to Marcus Jernmark to the steady hands of Emma
Bengtsson. Prix-fixe options include a ten-course meal, a six-course

15

seasonal affair, and a three-course dinner. **Known for:** full-flavored, inventive Scandinavian cuisine; housemade aquavit; modern Scandinavian design. [$] *Average main: $105* ✉ *65 E. 55th St., between Madison and Park Aves., Midtown East* ☎ *212/307–7311* 🌐 *www.aquavit.org* ⏲ *Closed Sun. No lunch Sat.* [M] *E, M to 5th Ave./53rd St.* ✥ *4:F2.*

$$$$ STEAKHOUSE 🍴 **BLT Steak.** Chef Laurent Tourondel may no longer be involved with his namesake steak house, but this classy space, decked out in beige with resin-top black tables, still draws crowds. The no-muss, no-fuss menu with a variety of steaks and other options is nonetheless large, and so are the portions of starters such as supple crab cakes with celery-infused mayonnaise and ruby tuna tartare with avocado and soy-lime dressing. **Known for:** complimentary Gruyère cheese puffs; thick steaks; grilled lobster. [$] *Average main: $37* ✉ *106 E. 57th St., between Lexington and Park Aves., Midtown East* ☎ *212/752–7470* 🌐 *www.bltsteak.com* ⏲ *No lunch weekends* [M] *4, 5, 6, N, R, W to 59th St./Lexington Ave.* ✥ *4:F1.*

$$$ SEAFOOD 🍴 **Grand Central Oyster Bar & Restaurant.** Deep in the belly of Grand Central Station, the vast Oyster Bar has been a worthy seafood destination since 1913. Sit at the counter for the fried oyster po'boy or to slurp an assortment of bracingly fresh oysters before a steaming bowl of clam chowder, washed down with an ice-cold beer. **Known for:** all things oyster; straightforward seafood options; gleaming, tiled subterranean space. [$] *Average main: $30* ✉ *Grand Central Terminal, dining concourse, 42nd St. at Vanderbilt Ave., Midtown East* ☎ *212/490–6650* 🌐 *www.oysterbarny.com* ⏲ *Closed Sun.* [M] *4, 5, 6, 7, S to Grand Central–42nd St.* ✥ *4:F4.*

$$$$ AMERICAN 🍴 **The Grill.** The erstwhile occupant, the Four Seasons, may have gone to restaurant heaven, but after a meal at this sceney, upscale eatery in the sharp, clean Philip Johnson interior, you'll quickly forget the number of seasons there were. Chefs Rich Torrisi and Mario Carbone (Dirty French, Parm, Carbone) took over in 2017 (they also run the adjacent restaurant, the Pool Room) and have created an instant classic, one that both updates the American food and relies on the space's rich history. **Known for:** gorgeous interior; steak and anchovy tartare; prime rib trolley service. [$] *Average main: $70* ✉ *99 E. 52nd St., between Park and Lexington Aves., Midtown East* ☎ *212/375–9001* 🌐 *www.thegrillnewyork.com* ⏲ *Closed Sun. No lunch Sat.* 👔 *Jacket required* [M] *E, M to Lexington Ave./53rd St.; 6 to 51st St.* ✥ *4:F2.*

$$$$ JAPANESE 🍴 **Kurumazushi.** Only a small sign in Japanese indicates the location of this extraordinary restaurant that serves sushi and sashimi exclusively; among the selections are hard-to-find fish imported directly from Japan. Bypass the tables, sit at the sushi bar, and put yourself in the hands of Toshihiro Uezu, the chef and owner. **Known for:** longtime spot for high-quality sushi; attentive staff; impressively expensive. [$] *Average main: $175* ✉ *7 E. 47th St., 2nd fl., between 5th and Madison Aves., Midtown East* ☎ *212/317–2802* 🌐 *www.kurumazushi.com* ⏲ *Closed Sun.* [M] *4, 5, 6, 7, S to Grand Central–42nd St.* ✥ *4:E3.*

$$$ STEAKHOUSE 🍴 **Michael Jordan's The Steakhouse NYC.** The handsomely appointed dining space in Grand Central Terminal, hung with gracious filigree chandeliers, overlooks one of the most famous (and beautiful) interiors in America. Start with the stack of soft, toasted bread soldiers in a

pool of hot Gorgonzola fondue or the pristine oysters, either making a great prelude to a prime dry-aged rib eye. **Known for:** an interior worthy of high-quality meat; oysters; good sides. $ *Average main: $35* ⊠ *Grand Central Terminal, West Balcony, 23 Vanderbilt Ave., between 43rd and 44th Sts., Midtown East* 🕾 *212/655–2300* ⊕ *www. michaeljordansnyc.com* ☾ *No lunch weekends* Ⓜ *4, 5, 6, 7, S to Grand Central–42nd St.* ✛ *4:F4.*

$$
AMERICAN
✕ **P. J. Clarke's.** This East Side institution has been dispensing great burgers and beer since 1884. Despite renovations and several owners over the years, the original location (there are offshoots in Lincoln Square and Chelsea) maintains the beveled-glass and scuffed-wood look of an old-time saloon. **Known for:** the Cadillac burger; old-time saloon; after-work mobs on weekdays. $ *Average main: $19* ⊠ *915 3rd Ave., at 55th St., Midtown East* 🕾 *212/317–1616* ⊕ *www. pjclarkes.com* Ⓜ *E, M to 5th Ave./53rd St.; N, R, W to Lexington Ave./59th St.; 4, 5, 6 to 59th St.* ✛ *4:G2.*

$$$
CHINESE
✕ **Shun Lee Palace.** If you want inexpensive Cantonese food without pretension, head to Chinatown; if you prefer to be pampered and don't mind spending a lot of money, then this is the place, which has been elegantly serving classic Chinese fare since 1971. Supposedly the dish orange beef was first made here, and indeed, it's worth a sample, but there's so much more. **Known for:** high-price Chinese food; orange beef; Beijing duck. $ *Average main: $29* ⊠ *155 E. 55th St., between Lexington and 3rd Aves., Midtown East* 🕾 *212/371–8844* ⊕ *www.shunleepalace.net* Ⓜ *N, R, W to Lexington Ave./59th St.; 4, 5, 6 to 59th St.* ✛ *4:G2.*

$$$$
STEAKHOUSE
✕ **Sparks Steakhouse.** Bring a wad of cash to this famed steak house, where magnums of wines that cost more than most people earn in a week festoon the large dining rooms. Tasty, fresh seafood is given more than fair play on the menu, and the extra-thick lamb and veal chops are also noteworthy—but Sparks is really about dry-aged steak. **Known for:** dry-aged steak; classic sides; the spot where, in 1985, members of the Gambino crime family were gunned down. $ *Average main: $42* ⊠ *210 E. 46th St., between 2nd and 3rd Aves., Midtown East* 🕾 *212/687–4855* ⊕ *www.sparkssteakhouse.com* ☾ *Closed Sun. No lunch Sat.* Ⓜ *4, 5, 6, 7, S to Grand Central–42nd St.* ✛ *4:G4.*

$$$
JAPANESE
✕ **Sushi Yasuda.** Devotees mourned the return of namesake chef Naomichi Yasuda to Japan, but things are in able hands with his handpicked successor, Mitsuru Tamura. Whether using fish flown in daily from Japan or the creamiest sea urchin, the chef makes sushi so fresh and delicate it melts in your mouth. **Known for:** attractive bar; high-quality raw fish; stylish interior. $ *Average main: $35* ⊠ *204 E. 43rd St., between 2nd and 3rd Aves., Midtown East* 🕾 *212/972–1001* ⊕ *www.sushiyasuda.com* ☾ *Closed Sun. No lunch Sat.* Ⓜ *4, 5, 6, 7, S to Grand Central–42nd St.* ✛ *4:G4.*

MURRAY HILL
This area has a residential feel with plenty of bistros perfect for a casual meal. Lexington Avenue's "Curry Hill" section between 27th and 29th Streets is home to Indian spice shops, cafés, and restaurants.

15

$$ ITALIAN Fodor's Choice ★ 🍴 **Marta.** The excellent cracker-thin crust of the Roman-style pizzas at Marta are a refreshing break from the thicker crust of the Neapolitan pizzas that have overtaken Manhattan in recent years, and we have beloved restaurateur Danny Meyer to thank for it. The high-ceiling dining room belies the casual fare, but the menu is a love letter to salt-of-the-earth Roman food. **Known for:** one of the few places in New York serving Roman-style pizza; buzzy room; Roman dishes. [$] *Average main: $20* ✉ *Redbury Hotel, 29 E. 29th St., at Madison Ave., Murray Hill* ☎ *212/651–3800* 🌐 *www.martamanhattan.com* [M] *6 to 28th St.* ✥ *3:F1.*

$$ DELI 🍴 **2nd Ave Deli.** It may no longer be on 2nd Avenue, but the most recent incarnation of this East Village institution—about a mile uptown, in Midtown—still delivers on its longtime traditional matzo ball soup, overstuffed three-decker sandwiches filled with house-cured pastrami, and other old-world specialties. Hot open-face sandwiches, like juicy beef brisket, are served with gravy and french fries. **Known for:** classic deli fare served into wee hours; matzo ball soup; brisket and pastrami. [$] *Average main: $23* ✉ *162 E. 33rd St., between Lexington and 3rd Aves., Murray Hill* ☎ *212/689–9000* 🌐 *www.2ndavedeli.com* [M] *6 to 33rd St.* ✥ *4:G6.*

$$ ITALIAN 🍴 **Tali.** The very first *Top Chef* champ, Harold Dieterle, has gone gluten-free at this restaurant with its adjacent dessert spot, Tali Dolce. At Tali, the Italian-leaning menu is a dream come true for the gluten intolerant (and the people who love them): hamburgers, pizza, plenty of pastas, and sandwiches are all gluten-free and prepared by a master chef. **Known for:** delicious gluten-free menu; array of gluten-free desserts; noted chef. [$] *Average main: $15* ✉ *77 Lexington Ave., at 26th St., Murray Hill* ☎ *212/245–5560* 🌐 *www.talirestaurant.com* [M] *6 to 23rd St.* ✥ *3:G2.*

MIDTOWN WEST

It's true that tourist traps abound on Broadway, but fortunately you needn't head far from Times Square to score a stellar meal. Just move away from the bright lights and unrelenting foot traffic that clogs the area. On calmer side streets and in adjoining Hell's Kitchen there are excellent dining options for budget travelers and expense-account diners alike. Some of the best steak houses and Italian restaurants are here, and many eateries offer budget pretheater dinners and prix-fixe lunch menus to draw in new business.

$$$$ MODERN AMERICAN 🍴 **Aureole.** An island of fine modern American dining just a stone's throw from bustling Times Square, Aureole is the second act of a New York classic from Charlie Palmer and his executive chef, Gabriele Carpentiere. The dining room (prix-fixe menus only), with its abundance of flowers, is the place to hobnob with expense-account diners and pretheater revelers. **Known for:** refined dining; prix-fixe menu; barroom with à la carte choices. [$] *Average main: $96* ✉ *135 W. 42nd St., between Broadway and 6th Ave., Midtown West* ☎ *212/319–1660* 🌐 *www.charliepalmer.com* ⏲ *Closed Sun. No lunch Sat.* [M] *B, D, F, M to 42nd St.–Bryant Park; 1, 2, 3, 7, N, Q, R, S, W to Times Sq.–42nd St.* ✥ *4:D4.*

$$$ ✕**Benoit.** Who needs to go to Paris when the world's most famous
FRENCH French chef, Alain Ducasse, can come to you? The interior of Ducasse's
imported Right Bank bistro—cozy red-velour banquettes and wall
lamps illuminating each table—is plucked straight from the City of
Light, and so is the menu, which doesn't reinvent anything as much
as it replicates. **Known for:** classic Parisian bistro fare; famous chef;
roasted veal loin. Ⓢ *Average main: $29* ⊠ *60 W. 55th St., between 5th
and 6th Aves., Midtown West* ☎ *646/943–7373* ⊕ *www.benoitny.com*
🚫 *No credit cards* Ⓜ *N, R, W to 5th Ave./59th St.; F to 57th St.* ✛ *4:D2.*

$$$ ✕**Brasserie Ruhlmann.** In a plush 120-seat dining room with just enough
BISTRO Art Deco touches to harmonize with its Rockefeller Center setting, sub-
lime French bistro cookery is on display. The room has a refined air, but
the staff is so friendly that the place could never be stuffy. **Known for:**
bistro fare and raw bar; poached branzino; steak au poivre. Ⓢ *Average
main: $30* ⊠ *45 Rockefeller Plaza, 50th St. between 5th and 6th Aves.,
Midtown West* ☎ *212/974–2020* ⊕ *www.brasserieruhlmann.com* ☉ *No
dinner Sun.* Ⓜ *B, D, F, M to 47th–50th Sts./Rockefeller Center; E, M to
5th Ave./53rd St.* ✛ *4:D3.*

$ ✕**Burger Joint.** What's a college burger bar, done up in particleboard
BURGER and rec-room design straight out of *Happy Days,* doing inside a five-
star Midtown hotel? This tongue-in-cheek lunch spot with great burgers, hidden behind a heavy red-velvet curtain in the Parker New York
hotel, does such boisterous midweek business that lines often snake
through the lobby (which means you're best off coming at noon or
earlier). **Known for:** not-so-secret spot for great burgers; long lines;
in hotel. Ⓢ *Average main: $9* ⊠ *Parker Hotel NYC, 119 W. 56th St.,
between 6th and 7th Aves., Midtown West* ☎ *212/708–7414* ⊕ *www.
burgerjointny.com* 🚫 *No credit cards* Ⓜ *N, Q, R, W to 57th St.–7th
Ave.; F to 57th St.* ✛ *4:D1.*

$$$ ✕**Carmine's.** Savvy New Yorkers line up early for the affordable family-
ITALIAN style Italian meals at this large, busy Midtown eatery. Family photos
FAMILY line the walls, and there's a convivial feeling amid all the Times Square
hubbub. **Known for:** good-value Italian fare; veal parmigiana; penne
alla vodka. Ⓢ *Average main: $25* ⊠ *200 W. 44th St., between Broadway
and 8th Ave., Midtown West* ☎ *212/221–3800* ⊕ *www.carminesnyc.
com* Ⓜ *A, C, E to 42nd St.–Port Authority; 1, 2, 3, 7, N, Q, R, S, W to
Times Sq.–42nd St.* ✛ *4:C4.*

$$ ✕**Danji.** Helmed by talented chef Hooni Kim, this diminutive Hell's
KOREAN Kitchen Korean spot stands out among the rows of restaurants that
attract theatergoing tourists to the neighborhood. That's because Kim's
take on Korean cuisine is inventive and inspired. **Known for:** Korean
fire chicken wings; bulgogi beef sliders; great lunch option. Ⓢ *Average
main: $21* ⊠ *346 W. 52nd St., between 8th and 9th Aves., Midtown
West* ☎ *212/586–2880* ⊕ *www.danjinyc.com* Ⓜ *C, E to 50th St.* ✛ *4:B2.*

$$$ ✕**db Bistro Moderne.** Daniel Boulud's "casual bistro" (it's neither,
FRENCH actually) consists of two elegantly appointed dining rooms. The
menu features classic dishes like Nantucket Bay scallops or hanger
steak exquisitely prepared—as well as the trendsetting (and pricey)
"db" hamburger stuffed with braised short ribs, foie gras, and
black truffles, credited with kick-starting the gourmet burger trend.

Known for: db burger; steak frites; worth the price. [$] *Average main: $33* ✉ *55 W. 44th St., between 5th and 6th Aves., Midtown West* ☎ *212/391–2400* 🌐 *www.dbbistro.com* [M] *B, D, F, M to 42nd St.–Bryant Park; 7 to 5th Ave.* ✥ *4:D4.*

$$ AMERICAN FAMILY 🍴 **Ellen's Stardust Diner.** If you haven't had enough Broadway singing and dancing, you'll get a kick out of Ellen's, a retro, 1950s-style diner, complete with a singing waitstaff. The menu focuses on all-American classics like meat loaf and chicken potpie, and the waiters and waitresses serenading you on roller skates have the talent to prove this restaurant is right on Broadway. **Known for:** midcentury food; star-spangled fun; good for families. [$] *Average main: $20* ✉ *1650 Broadway, at 51st St., Midtown West* ☎ *212/956–5151* 🌐 *www.ellensstardustdiner.com* [M] *1 to 50th St.; B, D, E to 7th Ave.* ✥ *4:C3.*

$$$ SEAFOOD 🍴 **Esca.** The name is Italian for "bait," and this restaurant lures diners in with delectable crudo preparations—such as tilefish with orange and Sardinian oil or pink snapper with a sprinkle of crunchy red clay salt. It then hooks them with entrées like whole, salt-crusted branzino, sea bass for two, or bucatini pasta with spicy baby octopus. **Known for:** elevated, fresh seaside Italian fare; daily-changing menu; exciting wine list. [$] *Average main: $35* ✉ *402 W. 43rd St., at 9th Ave., Midtown West* ☎ *212/564–7272* 🌐 *www.esca-nyc.com* 🕒 *No lunch Sun.* [M] *A, C, E to 42nd St.–Port Authority* ✥ *4:A4.*

$$ BURGER 🍴 **Five Napkin Burger.** This perennially packed Hell's Kitchen burger place and brasserie has been a magnet for burger lovers since day one. Though there are many menu distractions—deep-fried pickles and warm artichoke dip, to name a couple—the main attractions are the juicy burgers, like the original 10-ounce chuck with a tangle of onions, Gruyère cheese, and rosemary aioli. **Known for:** all manner of messy burgers; deep-fried pickles; milk shakes. [$] *Average main: $17* ✉ *630 9th Ave., at 45th St., Midtown West* ☎ *212/757–2277* 🌐 *www.5napkinburger.com* [M] *A, C, E to 42nd St.–Port Authority* ✥ *4:B4.*

$$$$ FRENCH 🍴 **Gabriel Kreuther.** Chef Gabriel Kreuther rose to NYC culinary prominence when he made The Modern (the eatery inside MoMa) one of *the* places for fine dining in the city. After leaving, in 2006 he fired up the burners at this eponymous place across from Bryant Park that, refreshingly, still sends out of the kitchen extremely haute prix-fixe fare, influenced by Kreuther's native Alsace. **Known for:** sturgeon and sauerkraut tart; smoked eel veloute; haute dining at haute prix-fixe price, but lunch is cheaper. [$] *Average main: $155* ✉ *41 W. 42nd St., between 5th and 6th Aves., Midtown West* ☎ *212/257–5826* 🌐 *www.gknyc.com* 🕒 *Closed Sun.* [M] *B, D, F, M to 42nd St./Bryant Park* ✥ *4:D4.*

$$$$ MODERN INDIAN Fodor's Choice ★ 🍴 **Indian Accent.** It didn't take long after chef Manish Mehrotra opened Indian Accent in New Delhi in 2009 that buzz about it being the best resaurant in India began. In 2016, he opened an outlet in a New York; it also didn't take long for buzz to circulate that this was the Big Apple's best Indian eatery, as chef Mehrotra extracts as much flavor out of his ingredients as possible. **Known for:** outstanding prix-fixe Indian dining; stuffed breads; ghee roast lamb. [$] *Average main: $75* ✉ *123 W. 56th St., between 6th and 7th Aves., Midtown West* ☎ *212/842–8070* 🌐 *www.indianaccent.com* 🕒 *No lunch Sun.* [M] *F to 57th St.* ✥ *4:D2.*

$$$
AMERICAN
✕ **L'Adresse.** This Russian import first opened up in NYC as Coffeemania, one of a chain of Moscow eateries that began as coffee-fueled spots. After landing in New York, it evolved into a full-fledged restaurant and changed its name, calling itself L'Adresse: American Bistro and serving taste bud–tingling international fare. **Known for:** lobster and uni carbonara; halvah latte; truffle burger. Ⓢ *Average main: $30* ✉ *1065 6th Ave., at 40th St., Midtown West* ☎ *212/221–2510* ⊕ *www.ladressenyc.com* ☽ *No dinner Sun.* Ⓜ *B, D, F, M to 42nd St./Bryant Park* ✛ *4:D5.*

$$$$
MODERN
AMERICAN
✕ **The Lambs Club.** Restaurateur Geoffrey Zakarian's opulent supper club on the ground floor of the Chatwal Hotel has superb Art Deco detailing, blood-red leather banquettes, and a roaring fireplace. The food is typical Zakarian, meaning new American cuisine with luxe touches in dishes like veal sweetbreads with peppered jus and grilled Treviso lettuce, or seared scallops with porcini and Indian-spiced sauce. **Known for:** famous former private-club patrons like Charlie Chaplin and John Wayne; great breakfasts; clubby vibe. Ⓢ *Average main: $36* ✉ *132 W. 44th St., between 6th Ave. and Broadway, Midtown West* ☎ *212/997–5262* ⊕ *www.thelambsclub.com* Ⓜ *1, 2, 3, 7, N, Q, R, S, W to Times Sq.–42nd St.; B, D, F, M to 47th–50th Sts./Rockefeller Center* ✛ *4:D4.*

$$$$
SEAFOOD
Fodor's Choice
★
✕ **Le Bernardin.** Owner Maguy LeCoze presides over the teak-panel dining room at this trendsetting French seafood restaurant, and chef and partner Eric Ripert works magic with anything that swims—preferring at times not to cook it at all. Deceptively simple dishes such as poached lobster in rich coconut-ginger soup or crispy spiced black bass in a Peking duck bouillon are typical of his style. **Known for:** one of the best seafood spots in the country; prix-fixe only; great wine list. Ⓢ *Average main: $155* ✉ *155 W. 51st St., between 6th and 7th Aves., Midtown West* ☎ *212/554–1515* ⊕ *www.le-bernardin.com* ☽ *Closed Sun. No lunch Sat.* 🏛 *Jacket required* Ⓜ *1 to 50th St.; N, Q, R to 49th St.; B, D, E to 7th Ave.* ✛ *4:C2.*

$$
BAKERY
✕ **Le Pain Quotidien.** This casual international Belgian chain brings its homeland ingredients with it, treating New Yorkers to crusty organic breads, jams, chocolate, and other specialty products. You can grab a snack to go or stay and eat breakfast, lunch, or dinner at wooden communal or private tables with waiter service. **Known for:** fresh bread; open-face sandwiches; salads. Ⓢ *Average main: $14* ✉ *1271 6th Ave., at 50th St., Midtown West* ☎ *646/462–4165* ⊕ *www.lepainquotidien.com* Ⓜ *B, D, F, M to 47th–50th Sts./Rockefeller Center; N, Q, R to 49th St.; 1 to 50th St.* ✛ *4:D3.*

$$$
ITALIAN
Fodor's Choice
★
✕ **Legacy Records.** Named for the space's erstwhile occupant, Legacy Recording Studios (where everyone from Jimi Hendrix to Jay-Z recorded), this Italian eatery inside Henry Hall, part of the new Hudson Yards megaproject, is made up of a culinary dream team: chef Ryan Hardy (Charlie Bird, Pasquale Jones), Arvid Rosengren, voted in 2016 as "best sommelier in the world" (by the Association de la Sommellerie), and Jeff Bell, lauded mixologist from PDT, behind the cocktail list. Hardy focuses on the cuisine of northern Italy, specifically the coastal regions, such as Liguria and Veneto (with a few nods to Friuli-Venezia Giulia). **Known for:** risotto; creative cocktails; hip scene. Ⓢ *Average main: $30* ✉ *517 W. 38th St., between 10th and 11th Aves.,*

15

Midtown West ☎ No phone ⊕ www.legacyrecordsnyc.com Ⓜ 7 to 34th St./Hudson Yards ✛ 4:A5.

$$$ ✕ **Lugo Cucina Italiana.** The area around Madison Square Garden is a
ITALIAN restaurant wasteland with the rare sparkling exception of Lugo Cucina
Italiana, founded by an Italian menswear line. Locals rejoiced at the
introduction of this spacious Italian "brasserie," serving comfort food
with a dolce-vita twist all day long. **Known for:** Italian comfort food
and house-made pastas; gnocchi with crab; meatballs. Ⓢ *Average main:
$25 ⊠ 1 Penn Plaza, 33rd St. and 8th Ave., Midtown West ☎ 212/760–
2700 ⊕ www.lugocaffe.com ⊗ Closed weekends Ⓜ 1, 2, 3, A, C, E to
34th St.–Penn Station ✛ 4:C6.*

$$$ ✕ **Marea.** Large picture windows in the dining room look out to expan-
SEAFOOD sive views of Central Park South at this upscale, seafood-centric Italian
Fodor's Choice eatery. No expense is spared in importing the very best of the ocean's
★ bounty, beginning with crudo dishes—think scallops with orange, wild
fennel, and arugula—that are becoming the restaurant's signature.
Known for: grilled octopus; memorable seafood pastas; baked branzino
for two. Ⓢ *Average main: $28 ⊠ 240 Central Park S, between Broad-
way and 7th Ave., Midtown West ☎ 212/582–5100 ⊕ www.marea-nyc.
com Ⓜ 1, A, B, C, D to 59th St.–Columbus Circle ✛ 4:B1.*

$$$ ✕ **Marseille.** With great food and a convenient location near several
MEDITERRANEAN Broadway theaters, Marseille is perpetually packed. The Mediterra-
nean creations are continually impressive, including the bouillabaisse,
the signature dish of the region for which the restaurant is named—a
mélange of mussels, shrimp, and whitefish in a fragrant broth, topped
with a garlicky crouton and served with rouille on the side. **Known for:**
three-course dinner; bouillabaisse and steak frites; beignets. Ⓢ *Average
main: $25 ⊠ 630 9th Ave., at 44th St., Midtown West ☎ 212/333–2323
⊕ www.marseillenyc.com Ⓜ A, C, E to 42nd St.–Port Authority ✛ 4:B4.*

$$$ ✕ **Oceana.** Entering this restaurant is like walking into the dressy state-
SEAFOOD room of a modern luxury ocean liner, a perfect setting for some of
the most vivid and delicious seafood in town, served with skill and
confidence by chef Ben Pollinger. Floor-to-ceiling windows look out
north and west, and the arrestingly designed raw bar backed with
Mediterranean-hue ceramics serves stunningly fresh choices including
gorgeous oysters. **Known for:** grilled whole fish; raw oyster selection;
foie gras and lobster. Ⓢ *Average main: $35 ⊠ 120 W. 49th St., at 6th
Ave., Midtown West ☎ 212/759–5941 ⊕ www.oceanarestaurant.com
⊗ No breakfast or lunch weekends Ⓜ B, D, F, M to 47th–50th Sts./
Rockefeller Center ✛ 4:D3.*

$$$ ✕ **Plataforma Churrascaria Rodizio.** This sprawling, boisterous Brazilian
BRAZILIAN shrine to meat, with its all-you-can-eat, prix-fixe menu, is best experi-
enced with a group of ravenous friends. Start with a trip to the fabulous
salad bar, piled with vegetables, meats, and cheeses—but remember,
there's about to be a parade of all manner of grilled meats and poultry,
from pork ribs to chicken hearts, delivered to the table on long skew-
ers. **Known for:** all-you-can-eat meat; salad bar; good for group meals.
Ⓢ *Average main: $35 ⊠ 316 W. 49th St., between 8th and 9th Aves.,
Midtown West ☎ 212/245–0505 ⊕ www.plataformaonline.com Ⓜ C,
E to 50th St. ✛ 4:B3.*

$$ ✕**Plaza Food Hall by Todd English.** At the Plaza Food Hall in the base-
ECLECTIC ment of the Plaza Hotel, celeb-chef Todd English oversees a series of
minirestaurants, each with its own counter and seating ideal for a quick
snack or a full-fledged meal. Entry is a little confusing: though the place
is made up of individual food concepts, you are seated by a hostess at
any available counter and then, once settled, you can get up and sur-
vey your choices before sitting down and ordering from your waiter.
Known for: lobster sliders; duck confit quesadilla; varied, affordable
lunch choices. $ *Average main: $18* ✉ *Plaza Hotel, 1 W. 59th St., at 5th
Ave., Midtown West* ☎ *212/986–9260* ⊕ *www.theplazany.com/dining/
foodhall* Ⓜ *N, R, W to 5th Ave./59th St.* ✛ *4:E1.*

$$$$ ✕**Quality Meats.** The handsome design at this steak house is inspired by
STEAKHOUSE classic New York City butcher shops in its use of warm wood, stainless
steel, and white marble. Sit at the bar to peruse the extensive menu of
wines and single-malt scotches, or sip a classic martini; then retire to
the dining room for memorable fare like the chunky crab cake, seared
scallops, and sophisticated riffs on steak-house classics like beef Wel-
lington. **Known for:** grilled bacon, peanut butter, and jalapeño; dry-aged
porterhouse; East Side short rib for two. $ *Average main: $37* ✉ *57
W. 58th St., near 6th Ave., Midtown West* ☎ *212/371–7777* ⊕ *www.
qualitymeatsnyc.com* ✪ *No lunch weekends* Ⓜ *F to 57th St.; N, R, W
to 5th Ave./59th St.* ✛ *4:D1.*

$$ ✕**Toloache.** The bi-level eatery at this bustling Mexican cantina just off
MEXICAN Broadway has a festive vibe, with several seating options: bar, balcony,
main dining room, and ceviche bar. Foodies flock here for three types
of guacamole (traditional, fruited, and spicy), well-executed ceviches,
and Mexico City–style tacos with Negra Modelo–braised brisket, and
quesadillas with black truffle and *huitlacoche* (a corn fungus known
as the "Mexican truffle"). **Known for:** quesadilla with huitlacoche;
grasshopper tacos; broad tequila selection. $ *Average main: $21* ✉ *251
W. 50th St., near 8th Ave., Midtown West* ☎ *212/581–1818* ⊕ *www.
toloachenyc.com* Ⓜ *1, C, E to 50th St.; N, Q, R, W to 49th St.* ✛ *4:B3.*

$$$$ ✕**'21' Club.** Tradition's the thing at this town-house landmark, a
AMERICAN former speakeasy that opened in 1929. Chef Sylvain Delpique tries
to satisfy everyone with standards like the famous '21' burger and
Dover sole with brown butter, as well as more modern dishes, such
as sautéed pork belly, but the food is almost secondary to the restaurant's storied past. **Known for:** storied past; appearance in many
movies; exclusivity; no jeans or sneakers allowed. $ *Average main:
$42* ✉ *21 W. 52nd St., between 5th and 6th Aves., Midtown West*
☎ *212/582–7200* ⊕ *www.21club.com* ✪ *Closed Sun. No lunch Sat.*
🏛 *Jacket required* Ⓜ *E, M to 5th Ave./53rd St.; B, D, F, M to 47th–
50th Sts./Rockefeller Center* ✛ *4:D2.*

$$$$ ✕**Uncle Jack's Steakhouse.** Surpassing even its celebrated flagship restau-
STEAKHOUSE rant in Bayside, Queens, Uncle Jack's soars directly into the pantheon
of the best steak houses in Manhattan. The space is vast and gorgeously
appointed, and service is swift and focused. **Known for:** large lobsters;
"Yabba Dabba Doo for Two"; Big Jack burger. $ *Average main: $69*
✉ *440 9th Ave., between 34th and 35th Sts., Midtown West* ☎ *212/244–
0005* ⊕ *www.unclejacks.com* Ⓜ *A, C, E to 34th St.–Penn Station* ✛ *4:B6.*

15

UPPER EAST SIDE

Long viewed as an enclave of the privileged, the Upper East Side has plenty of elegant, pricey eateries that serve the society "ladies who lunch" and bankers looking forward to a steak and single-malt scotch at the end of the day. However, visitors to Museum Mile and 5th Avenue shopping areas need not be put off. Whether you're looking to celebrate a special occasion or just want to grab a quick bite, there is something here for almost any budget.

$$$$
FRENCH

✗ **Café Boulud.** Manhattan's "who's who" in business, politics, and the art world come to hobnob at Daniel Boulud's café-in-name-only, where the food and service are top-notch. The menu is divided into four parts: under La Tradition are classic French dishes such as roasted duck breast Montmorency with cherry chutney, green Swiss chard, and baby turnips, or guinea hen terrine. **Known for:** elegant UES dining; chic bar scene; both French and international cuisine. Ⓢ *Average main: $44* ✉ *Surrey Hotel, 20 E. 76th St., between 5th and Madison Aves., Upper East Side* ☎ *212/772–2600* ⊕ *www.cafe-boulud.com* Ⓜ *6 to 77th St.* ✛ *5:F3.*

$$
AUSTRIAN
Fodor'sChoice
★

✗ **Café Sabarsky.** In the Neue Galerie, this stately coffeehouse is meant to duplicate the Viennese café experience and does a good job of it, with Art Deco furnishings, a selection of daily newspapers, and cases filled with cakes, strudels, and Sacher tortes. Museumgoers and locals love to linger here over coffee—so much so that it's sometimes a challenge to find a seat (there's a slightly less aesthetically pleasing outpost of the café in the basement). **Known for:** a slice of Vienna (and Sacher torte) on the UES; hearty Austrian food at night; coffee and pastries. Ⓢ *Average main: $19* ✉ *Neue Galerie, 1048 5th Ave., near 86th St., Upper East Side* ☎ *212/240–9557* ⊕ *www.neuegalerie.org* ⊘ *Closed Tues. No dinner Mon. and Wed.* Ⓜ *4, 5, 6 to 86th St.* ✛ *6:E6.*

$$
VEGETARIAN
Fodor'sChoice
★

✗ **Candle 79.** This vegan eatery, in an elegant, bi-level space done in warm, autumnal tones, is far from a health-food stereotype. Appetizers like rice balls with tempeh bacon may sound like hippie throwbacks, but taste more like well-executed trattoria fare. **Known for:** vegan fare delicious for all eaters; organic wines; seitan piccata. Ⓢ *Average main: $22* ✉ *154 E. 79th St., at Lexington Ave., Upper East Side* ☎ *212/537–7179* ⊕ *www.candle79.com* Ⓜ *6 to 77th St.* ✛ *5:G2.*

$$
MEXICAN

✗ **Cascabel Taqueria.** Wrestling-theme design sets a whimsical backdrop at this reasonably priced Mexican restaurant, where the tacos are inventive but don't veer too far from the comfort-food norm. The Camaron scatters plump roasted shrimp among fresh oregano, garlic oil, and black beans, while the beef tongue is slow braised, then topped with spring onion and serrano chilies. **Known for:** good tacos and lunchtime sandwiches; two-for-one drinks for weekday happy hours; outdoor tables. Ⓢ *Average main: $13* ✉ *1538 2nd Ave., between 80th and 81st Sts., Upper East Side* ☎ *212/717–8226* ⊕ *www.cascabeltaqueria.com* Ⓜ *Q to 72nd St; 6 to 77th St.* ✛ *5:H2.*

$$$
AMERICAN

✗ **Central Park Boathouse Restaurant.** There are plenty of pushcarts dispensing hot dogs and sodas, but if you're looking to soak up Central Park's magical ambience in an elegant setting, head for the Central Park Boathouse, which overlooks the gondola lake. There you can relax on the outdoor deck with a glass of wine and a cheese plate, or go for a more formal meal inside the restaurant. **Known for:** one of the city's most placid dining experiences; outdoor deck; crowded in summer. $ *Average main: $30* ✉ *E. 72nd St., at Park Dr. N, Upper East Side* ☎ *212/517–2233* ⊕ *www.thecentralparkboathouse.com* ☾ *No dinner Dec.–Mar.* Ⓜ *6 to 77th St.* ✛ *5:E3.*

$$$$
FRENCH
Fodor'sChoice
★

✕ **Daniel.** Celebrity-chef Daniel Boulud has created one of the most elegant dining experiences in Manhattan. The prix-fixe menu (there are à la carte selections in the elegant lounge and bar) is predominantly French, with such modern classics as turbot on Himalayan salt with an ale-and-gingerbread sauce, and a duo of dry-aged Black Angus beef featuring tender red-wine-braised short ribs and seared rib eye with black trumpet mushrooms and Gorgonzola cream. **Known for:** incredible service; elegant atmsophere; special-occasion haute fare. $ *Average main: $125* ✉ *60 E. 65th St., between Madison and Park Aves., Upper East Side* ☎ *212/288–0033* ⊕ *www.danielnyc.com* ☾ *Closed Sun. No lunch* 🎩 *Jacket required* Ⓜ *6 to 68th St.–Hunter College* ✛ *5:F5.*

$
PHILIPPINE

✕ **Flip Sigi.** If the Philippines and Mexico collided over Manhattan, it might look and taste a lot like this 13-seat Filipino taqueria. Chef Jordan Andino had fun creating (and naming) his menu items, including Bi-Curious tacos and an egg-and-sausage Plan B-Rito. **Known for:** lively Filipino taqueria; cleverly named dishes like Plan B-Rito and F.U.C. Me; Filipino cocktails and beer. $ *Average main: $9* ✉ *1752 2nd Ave., between 91st and 92nd Sts., Upper East Side* ☎ *646/559–1280* ⊕ *www.flipsigi.com* Ⓜ *Q to 86th St.* ✛ *6:H5.*

$$
DINER
FAMILY

✕ **Lexington Candy Shop.** Established in 1925, this corner luncheonette still sports 1940s-era milk-shake mixers, coffee urns, and a soda fountain. Enjoy the epic collection of Coca-Cola memorabilia along with fresh-made sodas, burgers, classic sandwiches, and breakfast all day. **Known for:** old-school everything; Coca-Cola items; neighborhood institution. $ *Average main: $15* ✉ *1226 Lexington Ave., at 83rd St., Upper East Side* ☎ *212/288–0057* ⊕ *www.lexingtoncandyshop.net* Ⓜ *4, 5, 6 to 86th St.* ✛ *5:G1.*

$$$
MEXICAN

✕ **Maya.** The upscale-hacienda appearance of this justifiably popular restaurant showcases some of the best Mexican food in the city, courtesy of pioneering Mexican chef Richard Sandoval. Begin with a fresh mango mojito, then tuck into delicious roasted corn soup with huitlacoche dumplings, stuffed poblano peppers, and a smoky filet mignon taco with jalapeño *escabeche* (a marinade). **Known for:** bottomless-margarita weekend brunch; bacon guac; excellent Mexican food. $ *Average main: $26* ✉ *1191 1st Ave., between 64th and 65th Sts., Upper East Side* ☎ *212/585–1818* ⊕ *www.eatmaya.com* ☾ *No lunch* Ⓜ *F, Q to Lexington Ave./63rd St.* ✛ *5:H5.*

$$$$
FRENCH

✕ **Rotisserie Georgette.** Georgette Farkas, who spent 17 years as chef Daniel Boulud's marketing and PR person, has branched out on her own and become the queen of rotisserie chicken. This elegant spot with an altarlike rotisserie in the back of the room might spin the best fowl in the city. **Known for:** foie gras–stuffed chicken; roasted octopus; rotisserie duck. $ *Average main: $40* ✉ *14 E. 60th St., between 5th and Madison Aves., Upper East Side* ☎ *212/390–8060* ⊕ *www.*

15

rotisserieg.com ⏲ *No lunch Sun.* [M] *4, 5, 6 to 59th St.; N, Q, R to 5th Ave./59th St.* ✣ *5:F6.*

$$$ JAPANESE 🍴 **Sushi of Gari.** Options at this popular sushi restaurant range from the ordinary (California roll) to the exotic, such as tuna with creamy tofu sauce, miso-marinated cod, or Japanese yellowtail with jalapeño. Japanese noodles (udon or soba) and meat dishes such as teriyaki and *negimaki* (scallions rolled in thinly sliced beef) are well prepared. Some of the inventive nonsushi items on the menu are worth a try, especially the fried cream-cheese dumplings. **Known for:** sushi with creative sauces and combos; fried cream-cheese dumplings; multiple locations. [$] *Average main: $26* ✉ *402 E. 78th St., at 1st Ave., Upper East Side* ☎ *212/517–5340* 🌐 *www.sushiofgari.com* ⏲ *Closed Mon. No lunch* [M] *6 to 77th St.; Q to 72nd St.* ✣ *5:H2.*

UPPER WEST SIDE

The area around Lincoln Center is a fine-dining hub; as you head north you'll find a mix of casual and sophisticated neighborhood spots.

$$$$ ASIAN 🍴 **Asiate.** The unparalleled view of Central Park is reason enough to visit Asiate's pristine dining room, perched on the 35th floor of the Time Warner Center in the Mandarin Oriental Hotel. The kitchen turns out contemporary dishes with an Asian influence, pairing unlikely ingredients: think foie gras and hazelnut brittle, or branzino and truffles. **Known for:** park view; noted wine list; prix-fixe menus. [$] *Average main: $100* ✉ *Mandarin Oriental Hotel, 80 Columbus Circle, 35th fl., at 60th St., Upper West Side* ☎ *212/805–8881* 🌐 *www.mandarinoriental.com* [M] *1, A, B, C, D to 59th St.–Columbus Circle* ✣ *5:C6.*

$$$ FRENCH Fodor's Choice ★ 🍴 **Bar Boulud.** Acclaimed French chef Daniel Boulud, known for upscale New York City eateries Daniel and Café Boulud, shows diners his more casual side with this lively contemporary bistro and wine bar. The menu emphasizes charcuterie, including terrines and pâtés designed by Parisian charcutier Gilles Verot, who relocated just to work with Boulud, as well as traditional French bistro dishes like steak frites and *poulet rôti à l'ail* (roast chicken with garlic mashed potatoes). **Known for:** great charcuterie; bistro classics; three-course pretheater menu. [$] *Average main: $30* ✉ *1900 Broadway, between 63rd and 64th Sts., Upper West Side* ☎ *212/595–0303* 🌐 *www.barboulud.com* [M] *1 to 66th St.–Lincoln Center; 1, A, B, C, D to 59th St.–Columbus Circle* ✣ *5:B5.*

$$ AMERICAN 🍴 **Barney Greengrass.** At this Upper West Side landmark, brusque waiters send out stellar smoked salmon, sturgeon, and whitefish to a happy crowd packed to the gills at small Formica tables. Split a fish platter with bagels, cream cheese, and other fixings, or get your velvety nova scrambled with eggs and buttery caramelized onions. **Known for:** smoked fish; chopped liver; gruff servers; less crowded on weekdays. [$] *Average main: $19* ✉ *541 Amsterdam Ave., between 86th and 87th Sts., Upper West Side* ☎ *212/724–4707* 🌐 *www.barneygreengrass.com* ⏲ *Closed Mon. No dinner* 💳 *No credit cards* [M] *1, B, C to 86th St.* ✣ *6:B6.*

$$ CAFÉ 🍴 **Bouchon Bakery.** Never mind that you're in the middle of a shopping mall—soups and sandwiches don't get much more luxurious than at

acclaimed chef Thomas Keller's low-key lunch spot (one floor down from his extravagant flagship, Per Se); it draws long lines for good reason. Fork-and-knife open-face tartines, like the tuna niçoise, are delicious. **Known for:** chicken soup; croque madame; desserts from bakery window. [$] *Average main: $18* ✉ *Time Warner Center, 10 Columbus Circle, 3rd fl., between 58th and 59th Sts., Upper West Side* ☎ *212/823–9366* 🌐 *www.bouchonbakery.com* 🕑 *No dinner* [M] *1, A, B, C, D to 59th St.–Columbus Circle* ✥ *5:C6.*

$$ FRENCH 🍴 **Café Luxembourg.** The old soul of the Lincoln Center neighborhood seems to inhabit the tiled and mirrored walls of this lively, cramped restaurant, where West End Avenue regulars—including lots of on-air talent from nearby ABC News—are greeted with kisses, and musicians and audience members pack the room after a concert. The bar's always hopping, and the menu includes classics like steak tartare and lobster roll. **Known for:** quintessential UWS bistro; busy bar; after-concert scene. [$] *Average main: $24* ✉ *200 W. 70th St., between Amsterdam and West End Aves., Upper West Side* ☎ *212/873–7411* 🌐 *www.cafe-luxembourg.com* [M] *1, 2, 3, B, C to 72nd St.* ✥ *5:A4.*

15

$$$ ITALIAN FAMILY 🍴 **Carmine's Upper West Side.** Set on a nondescript block of Broadway, this branch of the Italian mainstay is a favorite for families celebrating special occasions, pre-prom groups of teens, and plain-old folks. They come for the tried-and-true items like fried calamari, linguine with white clam sauce, chicken parmigiana, and veal saltimbocca, all served in mountainous portions. **Known for:** best red-sauce joint on UWS; cheerful scene; antipasti table. [$] *Average main: $25* ✉ *2450 Broadway, between 90th and 91st Sts., Upper West Side* ☎ *212/362–2200* 🌐 *www.carminesnyc.com* [M] *1, 2, 3 to 96th St.* ✥ *6:A6.*

$$$$ AMERICAN 🍴 **Dovetail.** Inside Dovetail, chef and owner John Fraser's subdued town-house restaurant, cream-color walls and maple panels create a warm, soothing atmosphere. The menu, which changes daily based on seasonal and available ingredients, features refined but hearty dishes. **Known for:** one of the few UWS restaurants that brings the rest of New York here to eat; seasonal menus; prix-fixe menus, with à la carte choices at the bar. [$] *Average main: $41* ✉ *103 W. 77th St., at Columbus Ave., Upper West Side* ☎ *212/362–3800* 🌐 *www.dovetailnyc.com* 🕑 *No lunch* [M] *1 to 79th St.; B, C to 81st St.–Museum of Natural History* ✥ *5:B2.*

$$ CAFÉ 🍴 **Fairway Market Café.** Fairway is a neighborhood institution, living up to its reputation for great prices on gourmet products—and shopping-cart jockeying down the narrow aisles. Upstairs, though, is the respite of Fairway Market Café, a large, brick-walled room with windows overlooking Broadway, that has pastry and coffee to go, but also a dining area with a full menu of fairly priced entrées from omelets and burgers to pizzas and steaks. **Known for:** beloved supermarket; good-value option; steak. [$] *Average main: $24* ✉ *2127 Broadway, between 74th and 75th Sts., Upper West Side* ☎ *212/595–1888* 🌐 *www.fairway-market.com* [M] *1, 2, 3 to 72nd St.* ✥ *5:A3.*

$ FAST FOOD 🍴 **Gray's Papaya.** It's a stand-up, take-out dive. And yes, limos do sometimes stop here for these legendary hot dogs—they are delicious, and quite the economical meal. **Known for:** fast, affordable Big Apple bites; hot dogs; breakfast sandwich. [$] *Average main: $5* ✉ *2090 Broadway,* *at 72nd St., Upper West Side* ☎ *212/799–0243* 🌐 *www.grayspapayanyc.com* 💳 *No credit cards* [M] *1, 2, 3 to 72nd St.* ✥ *5:B4.*

$$$$ FRENCH 🍴 **Jean-Georges.** This culinary temple in the Trump International Hotel and Towers focuses wholly on chef célèbre Jean-Georges Vongerichten's spectacular creations. The chef may now have restaurants sprinkled around the globe, but this is where you want to be, as some dishes on the prix-fixe-only menu approach the limits of the taste universe, like foie-gras brûlée with spiced fig jam and ice-wine reduction. **Known for:** masterful haute cuisine; yellowfin tuna ribbons; sesame crab toast. [$] *Average main: $125* ✉ *1 Central Park W, at 60th St., Upper West Side* ☎ *212/299–3900* 🌐 *www.jean-georges.com* 🧥 *Jacket required* [M] *1, A, B, C, D to 59th St.–Columbus Circle* ✥ *5:C6.*

$$ GREEK 🍴 **Kefi.** At Michael Psilakis's Upper West Side eatery—a giant hommage to his grandmother's Greek cooking—it's not hard to achieve the euphoric state known in Greek as *kefi*. Among the mezes, the meatballs with roasted garlic, olives, and tomato stand out; and the flavorful roast chicken with potatoes, red peppers, garlic, and thyme makes for a winning entrée. Béchamel-rich Kefi mac 'n' cheese is irresistible. **Known for:** grilled octopus; meatball meze; braised rabbit. [$] *Average main: $19* ✉ *505 Columbus Ave., between 84th and 85th Sts., Upper West Side* ☎ *212/873–0200* 🌐 *michaelpsilakis.com/kefi/* [M] *1, B, C to 86th St.* ✥ *5:B1.*

$ BAKERY FAMILY 🍴 **Levain Bakery.** Completely unpretentious and utterly delicious, Levain Bakery's cookies are rich and hefty (they clock in at 6 ounces each). Choose from the chocolate-chip walnut, dark-chocolate chocolate chip, dark-chocolate peanut-butter chip, or oatmeal raisin: batches are baked fresh daily and taste best when they're warm and melty right out of the oven. **Known for:** huge cookies; flavored breads; muffins and scones. [$] *Average main: $9* ✉ *167 W. 74th St., near Amsterdam Ave., Upper West Side* ☎ *212/874–6080* 🌐 *www.levainbakery.com* 🕒 *No dinner* [M] *1, 2, 3 to 72nd St.* ✥ *5:B3.*

$$$ BISTRO FAMILY 🍴 **Nice Matin.** If the Upper West Side and the French Riviera collided, it might look a little bit like Nice Matin. This is a longtime neighborhood favorite, particularly in warm-weather months, when regulars plant themselves at sidewalk tables and gawk at passersby while munching on Gallic fare like monkfish in sweet potato puree, garlicky mussels, and, of course, steak frites. **Known for:** moules frites; Nice burger; lengthy wine list. [$] *Average main: $25* ✉ *201 W. 79th St., at Amsterdam Ave., Upper West Side* ☎ *212/873–6423* 🌐 *www.nicematinnyc.com* 💳 *No credit cards* [M] *1 to 79th St.* ✥ *5:A2.*

$$$$ AMERICAN Fodor's Choice ★ 🍴 **Per Se.** The New York interpretation of what many consider one of America's finest restaurant (the Napa Valley's French Laundry), Per Se is chef Thomas Keller's Broadway stage—set in a large, understated dining room with great views of Central Park. Keller embraces seasonality and a witty playfulness, and some of his dishes are world-renowned, such as the tiny cones of tuna tartare topped with crème fraîche, and the "oysters and pearls"—tiny mollusks in a creamy custard with tapioca. **Known for:** reservations needed months ahead; "oysters and pearls"; duck foie gras. [$] *Average main: $340* ✉ *Time Warner Center, 10 Columbus Circle, 4th fl., at 60th St., Upper West Side* ☎ *212/823–9335*

⊕ *www.perseny.com* ⊗ *No lunch Mon.–Thurs.* 🏛 *Jacket required* Ⓜ *1, A, B, C, D to 59th St.–Columbus Circle* ✛ *5:C6.*

$$$$ ✕ **Porter House New York.** With clubby interiors by Jeffrey Beers and an
STEAKHOUSE   adjoining lounge area, Porter House is helmed by veteran chef Michael
Lomonaco. Filling the meat-and-potatoes slot in the Time Warner Center's upscale "Restaurant Collection," this masculine throwback highlights American wines and pedigreed supersize meat. **Known for:** filet mignon tartare; roasted bone marrow; côte de boeuf. Ⓢ *Average main: $47* ✉ *Time Warner Center, 10 Columbus Circle, 4th fl., at 60th St., Upper West Side* ☎ *212/823–9500* ⊕ *www.porterhousenewyork.com* Ⓜ *1, A, B, C, D to 59th St.–Columbus Circle* ✛ *5:C6.*

$$ ✕ **Sarabeth's.** Lining up for brunch here is as much an Upper West Side
AMERICAN   tradition as taking a sunny Sunday afternoon stroll in nearby Riverside
Park. Locals love the bric-a-brac-filled restaurant for sweet morningtime dishes like lemon ricotta pancakes and comforting dinners. **Known for:** the UWS place to brunch; afternoon tea with great baked goods; multiple locations. Ⓢ *Average main: $19* ✉ *423 Amsterdam Ave., at 80th St., Upper West Side* ☎ *212/496–6280* ⊕ *www.sarabeth.com* Ⓜ *1 to 79th St.* ✛ *5:B2.*

$$ ✕ **White Gold Butchers.** Walk into this UWS spot from chef April Bloom-
AMERICAN   field (the Spotted Pig, the Breslin) during the day and you'll see an
explosion of meat for sale from behind the counter, though this is no ordinary butcher shop. There's a light breakfast and lunch menu (heavy on the sandwiches) but come nightfall, the 38-seat space transforms into a carnivore-friendly restaurant serving the deliciously meaty food that made Bloomfield famous. **Known for:** porchetta; beef tartare; roast beef sandwich. Ⓢ *Average main: $17* ✉ *375 Amsterdam Ave., at 78th St., Upper West Side* ☎ *212/362–8731* ⊕ *www.whitegoldbutchers.com* Ⓜ *1, 2 to 79th St.* ✛ *5:B2.*

HARLEM

Harlem culinary renaissance? Yes, indeed. This historic northern neighborhood has seen an infusion of fantastic restaurants since 2010. There are still the standby Southern and soul-food restaurants but also newer arrivals, making your journey northward even more worthwhile.

$$$ ✕ **Red Rooster Harlem.** Marcus Samuelsson, who earned his celebrity
AMERICAN   chefdom at Aquavit in Midtown for his take on Ethiopian-accented
Fodor's Choice Scandinavian cuisine (fusing the food of his birthplace with that of
★   where he grew up), moved to Harlem in 2010, where he has created a
culinary hot spot for the ages. The comfort-food menu reflects the ethnic diversity that is modern-day New York City, from plantain-loaded oxtail to fried chicken. **Known for:** Sunday brunch with gospel music; fried chicken; ribs. Ⓢ *Average main: $26* ✉ *310 Lenox Ave., between 125th and 126th Sts., Harlem* ☎ *212/792–9001* ⊕ *www.redroosterharlem.com* Ⓜ *2, 3 to 125th St.* ✛ *6:D1.*

$$$$ ✕ **Sushi Inoue.** At this eponymous eatery from chef Shinichi Inoue (who
SUSHI   earned a Michelin star at Sushi Azabu in TriBeCa), little details lurk: he
makes two types of rice (one for heavier fish and one for lighter), just as he makes a lighter and a heavier soy sauce. And the chef hand-grates

15

real wasabi for the sushi and sashimi this place is devoted to exclusively. **Known for:** superfresh sushi and sashimi; omakase options; exquisite attention to details. ⓢ *Average main: $100* ✉ *381 Lenox Ave., at W. 129th St., Harlem* ☎ *646/766–0555* ⊕ *www.sushiinoue.com* ⊗ *Closed Mon. No lunch* Ⓜ *2, 3 to 125th St.* ✚ *6:D1.*

$$
SOUTHERN
FAMILY

✕ **Sylvia's.** A Harlem mainstay, Sylvia's has been serving soul-food favorites like smothered chicken, barbecue ribs, collard greens, and mashed potatoes to a dedicated crowd of locals, tourists, and college students since 1962. Owner Sylvia Woods may have passed on in 2012, but her restaurant and signature sauces, jarred and sold online and in the restaurant, are more popular than ever. **Known for:** Sunday gospel brunch; smothered chicken; cornmeal-dusted cafish. ⓢ *Average main: $24* ✉ *328 Lenox Ave., near 127th St., Harlem* ☎ *212/996–0660* ⊕ *www.sylviasrestaurant.com* Ⓜ *2, 3 to 125th St.* ✚ *6:D1.*

BROOKLYN

BROOKLYN HEIGHTS

Brooklyn may be the place to eat these days, but Brooklyn Heights has always been more pleasing to the eye than to the taste buds.

$$
MODERN
AMERICAN
Fodor's Choice
★

✕ **Colonie.** The key to this perpetually popular restaurant's success lies in its use of ultrafresh ingredients, sourced from local purveyors and presented with style in an upscale-casual space that honors its neighborhood's historical roots. There's always an oyster special, along with a selection of small plates. **Known for:** locally sourced ingredients; daily oyster special; open kitchen. ⓢ *Average main: $20* ✉ *127 Atlantic Ave., Brooklyn Heights* ☎ *718/855–7500* ⊕ *www.colonienyc.com* ⊗ *No lunch weekdays* Ⓜ *2, 3, 4, 5 to Borough Hall; R to Court St.* ✚ *7:A4.*

$$$$
MODERN
AMERICAN
Fodor's Choice
★

✕ **The River Café.** A deservedly popular special-occasion destination, this waterfront institution complements its exquisite Brooklyn Bridge views with memorable top-shelf cuisine served by an unfailingly attentive staff. Lobster, lamb, duck, and strip steak are among the staples of the prix-fixe menu ($130 for dinner, $47 for Saturday lunch, $60 for Sunday brunch). **Known for:** unforgettable location; top-shelf cuisine; refined atmosphere. ⓢ *Average main: $130* ✉ *1 Water St., Brooklyn Heights* ☎ *718/522–5200* ⊕ *www.therivercafe.com* ⊗ *No breakfast weekends, no lunch Sun.–Fri., no brunch Mon.–Sat.* Ⓜ *2, 3 to Clark St.; A, C to High St.; F to York St.* ✚ *7:B2.*

DOWNTOWN BROOKLYN

Filled with neoclassical courthouse buildings and glass skyscrapers, there isn't much reason to come to downtown Brooklyn—unless, of course, you managed to nab a reservation at the borough's only three-Michelin-starred restaurant, Brooklyn Fare.

$$$$
ECLECTIC

✕ **Chef's Table at Brooklyn Fare.** Should you manage to snag a seat at Brooklyn's only Michelin three-star restaurant, you're in for an exceptional culinary experience. Chef Cesar Ramirez prepares more than a dozen courses of French- and Japanese-influenced raw and cooked seafood small plates. **Known for:** French and Japanese small plates; Michelin three-star rating; extremely high set-price menu. ⓢ *Average main: $330* ✉ *200 Schermerhorn St., Downtown Brooklyn*

☎ *718/243–0050* ⊕ *www.brooklynfare.com/pages/chefs-table* ⊗ *Closed Sun. and Mon.* Ⓜ *2, 3 to Hoyt St.; 2, 3, 4, 5 to Nevins St.; A, C, G to Hoyt–Schermerhorn Sts.; B, Q, R to DeKalb Ave.* ✛ *7:B4.*

$$ ✕ **Junior's.** Famous for its thick slices of cheesecake, Junior's has been the DINER quintessential Brooklyn diner since 1950. Classic cheeseburgers loom-FAMILY ing over little cups of coleslaw and thick french fries are first-rate, as are the sweet-potato latkes and pretty much all the breakfast offerings. **Known for:** cheesecake; diner classics; quintessential Brooklyn. Ⓢ *Average main: $15* ✉ *386 Flatbush Ave., Downtown Brooklyn* ☎ *718/852–5257* ⊕ *www.juniorscheesecake.com* Ⓜ *2, 3, 4, 5 to Nevins St.; B, Q, R to DeKalb Ave.; A, C, G to Hoyt–Schermerhorn Sts.* ✛ *7:C4.*

DUMBO

Once upon a time, the primary reason for a hungry person to come to DUMBO was to eat pizza at Grimaldi's. The past few years have seen the growing gentrification of these loft-strewn cobblestone streets, though, today sprinkled with toothsome eateries and cute boutiques. Now that the Brooklyn waterfront has been fully developed you can walk off your meal on a romantic stroll.

$$ ✕ **Gran Eléctrica.** Few restaurants are equally suited to neighborhood MEXICAN families and trendy twentysomethings, but Gran Eléctrica's street-FAMILY food-centric Mexican menu pleases all palates. In addition to multire-gional tacos and small plates (try the chipotle-scented meatballs known as *albóndigas de Juana*), the buzzy, stylish space has an impressive tequila list and pours balanced cocktails. **Known for:** multiregional Mexican dishes; balanced cocktails and diverse tequilas; buzzy space that's family-friendly. Ⓢ *Average main: $14* ✉ *5 Front St., DUMBO* ☎ *718/852–2700* ⊕ *www.granelectrica.com* ⊗ *No lunch weekdays* Ⓜ *A, C to High St.; F to York St.* ✛ *7:B3.*

$$ ✕ **Juliana's.** This bright, bustling spot is the locals' favorite for clas-PIZZA sic white and margherita pizzas, homemade soups, and Brooklyn Ice FAMILY Cream Factory desserts. The lines aren't half as long as at Brooklyn pioneer Patsy Grimaldi's neighboring eponymous institution—and since Patsy himself has severed ties with Grimaldi's, Juliana's is arguably the most authentic pie on the block. **Known for:** authentic Brooklyn pizza; family-friendly dining; crowds. Ⓢ *Average main: $20* ✉ *19 Old Fulton St., DUMBO* ☎ *718/596–6700* ⊕ *www.julianaspizza.com* Ⓜ *2, 3 to Clark St.; A, C to High St.; F to York St.* ✛ *7:B3.*

$$$ ✕ **Vinegar Hill House.** Outfitted with candlelit tables and a twinkling MODERN rear patio, this romantic destination is well worth the sloping walk up AMERICAN from the waterfront. Seasonal menus include inventive New American fare and crowd-pleasing brunch dishes; wait times can be considerable, but the cozy bar pours potent cocktails, local beer, and wine by the glass. **Known for:** romantic space with a twinkling backyard; seasonal, sustainably sourced New American dishes; weekend brunch. Ⓢ *Average main: $25* ✉ *72 Hudson Ave., DUMBO* ☎ *718/522–1018* ⊕ *www. vinegarhillhouse.com* ⊗ *No lunch* Ⓜ *F to York St.* ✛ *7:C2.*

CARROLL GARDENS

Carroll Gardens has standout restaurants, which lure even those Man-hattanites who might be loathe to cross the river.

15

$$ ✕**Buttermilk Channel.** This Southern-accented new American bistro
AMERICAN draws epic brunch lines and a legion of neighborhood families (the
Clown Sundae is legendary among Carroll Gardens kids). But when day
turns to night, Buttermilk Channel transforms into a surprisingly seri-
ous restaurant with an excellent, mostly American wine list. **Known for:**
fried pork chop or chicken with cheddar waffles; three-course Monday-
night prix fixe; unusual ingredient combinations. Ⓢ *Average main: $23*
✉ *524 Court St., Carroll Gardens* ☎ *718/852–8490* ⊕ *www.buttermilk-
channelnyc.com* Ⓜ *F, G to Smith–9th Sts.* ✛ *7:A5.*

$$ ✕**Frankies Spuntino 457.** A longtime favorite culinary pioneer in Carroll
ITALIAN Gardens, Frank Castronovo and Frank Falcinelli's Italian-American
restaurant has atmosphere to spare between the backyard and former
blacksmith stable. Choose from the well-conceived menu's shareable
salads (many with vegetables roasted or marinated with the Frankies'
own Sicilian olive oil), handmade pastas like the cavatelli with hot
sausage and browned sage butter, meatballs, and crusty sandwiches
that ask to be shared. **Known for:** outdoor dining; menu options for
all kinds of eaters; less than warm staff. Ⓢ *Average main: $20* ✉ *457
Court St., Carroll Gardens* ☎ *718/403–0033* ⊕ *www.frankiesspuntino.
com* Ⓜ *F, G to Carroll St. or Smith–9th Sts.* ✛ *7:A5.*

$$ ✕**Nightingale 9.** Though it's named after an old Brooklyn telephone code,
ASIAN FUSION Nightingale 9 takes its culinary inspiration from "long distance": Asia.
Dishes are reimagined with Chef Rob Newton's Arkansas childhood in
mind, resulting in plates like grilled Mississippi catfish served cha ca style
or duck salad with collard greens, sweet potato, chili, and basil. **Known for:**
$10 pho bowls on Sunday; crispy spring rolls; the bar's cocktails. Ⓢ *Aver-
age main: $17* ✉ *329 Smith St., Carroll Gardens* ☎ *347/689–4699* ⊕ *www.
nightingale9.com* ◷ *Closed Mon. No lunch* Ⓜ *F, G to Carroll St.* ✛ *7:B5.*

$$$ ✕**Prime Meats.** Steak, sausages, and serious Prohibition-era cocktails: it's
STEAKHOUSE a winning combination for Frank Castronovo and Frank Falcinelli, who
opened this Frankies offshoot as a tribute to turn-of-the-20th-century
wood-paneled dining rooms. Try a chilled iceberg-lettuce salad with May-
tag blue cheese and a Vesper or dry martini to start, followed by a grilled
heritage pork chop or perhaps an order of steak frites—though there are
many other options, including three kinds of German-style house-made
sausages. **Known for:** meat dishes in large portions; extensive brunch menu.
Ⓢ *Average main: $26* ✉ *465 Court St., Carroll Gardens* ☎ *718/254–0327*
⊕ *www.frankspm.com* Ⓜ *F, G to Carroll St. or Smith–9th Sts.* ✛ *7:A5.*

WILLIAMSBURG

Still probably the hippest, happening-est neighborhood in the five boroughs, Williamsburg is also one of the hottest destinations on the culinary landscape. You'll find plenty of decadent twists on farm-to-table
cuisine, dressed-up comfort-food classics, and killer cocktails.

$$ ✕**Diner.** The word "diner" might evoke a greasy spoon, but this trend-
AMERICAN setting restaurant under the Williamsburg Bridge is nothing of the sort.
Fodor's Choice Andrew Tarlow—the godfather of Brooklyn's farm-to-table culinary
★ renaissance—opened it in 1999 and launched an entire movement.
Known for: trailblazing restaurateur; farm-to-table fare; intimate
space in a vintage dining car. Ⓢ *Average main: $21* ✉ *85 Broadway,*

Williamsburg ☎ *718/486–3077* ⊕ *www.dinernyc.com* Ⓜ *J, M, Z to Marcy Ave.* ✛ *7:D2.*

$$
BARBECUE

✕ **Fette Sau.** It might seem odd to go to a former auto-body repair shop to feast on meat, but the funky building and courtyard are just the right setting for the serious barbecue served here. A huge wood-and-gas smoker delivers brisket, sausages, ribs, and even duck—all ordered by the pound. **Known for:** Southern-style barbecue; excellent whiskey list; no reservations. $ *Average main: $13* ✉ *354 Metropolitan Ave., Williamsburg* ☎ *718/963–3404* ⊕ *www.fettesaubbq.com* ☾ *No lunch Mon.* Ⓜ *L to Lorimer St.; G to Metropolitan Ave.* ✛ *7:E2.*

$$
FRENCH

✕ **Le Barricou.** The team behind nearby Maison Premiere operates this Parisian-style brasserie serving escargots, coq au vin, and other French bistro classics. Diners sit at rustic wooden tables, and the walls are collaged with vintage French newspapers. **Known for:** French bistro classics; popular brunch spot; old-world atmosphere. $ *Average main: $18* ✉ *533 Grand St., Williamsburg* ☎ *718/782–7372* ⊕ *www.lebarricouny. com* Ⓜ *L to Lorimer St.; G to Metropolitan Ave.* ✛ *7:E2.*

$$
AMERICAN
Fodor's Choice
★

✕ **Marlow & Sons.** With its green-and-white-striped awning, you might easily mistake this buzzy bistro for an old-timey grocery store, but this is a wood-paneled dining room packed nightly with foodies for remarkable locavore cuisine. Part of the Andrew Tarlow empire, Marlow & Sons serves food that sounds simple until you take that first bite. **Known for:** pioneering restaurateur; inspired locavore fare; vintage grocery store–inspired design. $ *Average main: $23* ✉ *81 Broadway, Williamsburg* ☎ *718/384–1441* ⊕ *www.marlowandsons.com* Ⓜ *J, M, Z to Marcy Ave.* ✛ *7:D2.*

$$$$
STEAKHOUSE
Fodor's Choice
★

✕ **Peter Luger Steak House.** Steak lovers come to Peter Luger for the exquisite dry-aged meat and the casual atmosphere. You can order individual steaks, but the porterhouse is highly recommended and served only for two, three, or four people. **Known for:** excellent steak; historic Brooklyn ambience; no credit cards. $ *Average main: $50* ✉ *178 Broadway, Williamsburg* ☎ *718/387–7400* ⊕ *www.peterluger.com* ▭ *No credit cards* Ⓜ *J, M, Z to Marcy Ave.* ✛ *7:D2.*

$$
SOUTHERN

✕ **Pies 'N' Thighs.** Opened by three Diner alums, this little restaurant takes its moniker seriously, serving famously delicious fried chicken and pies made with organic and local ingredients. Perched on chairs from an elementary school, diners enjoy Southern-style meals that come with a protein (catfish and pulled pork for those who don't want chicken) and two sides (grits, mac 'n' cheese, and biscuits are favorites). **Known for:** fried chicken and pies; fun, casual vibe; good value. $ *Average main: $15* ✉ *166 S. 4th St., Williamsburg* ☎ *347/529–6090* ⊕ *www. piesnthighs.com* Ⓜ *J, M, Z to Marcy Ave.* ✛ *7:D2.*

$$$
MODERN
AMERICAN
Fodor's Choice
★

✕ **Reynard.** The largest of Andrew Tarlow's Williamsburg restaurants (which include Diner and Marlow & Sons), Reynard has all the hallmarks of a Tarlow venture. Farm-to-table fare highlights the season's freshest ingredients, and everything is made in-house, even the granola. **Known for:** pioneering restaurateur; farm-to-table fare; urban-rustic digs in the Wythe Hotel. $ *Average main: $26* ✉ *Wythe Hotel, 80 Wythe Ave., Williamsburg* ☎ *718/460–8004* ⊕ *www.reynardnyc.com* Ⓜ *L to Bedford Ave.* ✛ *7:D1.*

15

$$$$ AMERICAN Fodor's Choice ★ 🍴 **Semilla.** If dining has become a lot like theater then consider this Off-Off-Broadway sensation in Williamsburg to be about as entertaining on the taste buds as they come. The director, or, um, chef here is Jose Ramirez-Ruiz and he subverts the dominant dining paradigm by pushing vegetables out to the center stage, and putting meat on the sidelines as supporting cast. **Known for:** seasonal dining; menu changes nightly; intimate atmosphere. [$] *Average main: $85* ✉ *160 Havemeyer St., No. 5, Williamsburg* ☎ *718/782–3474* 🌐 *www.semillabk.com* ⏲ *Closed Sun. and Mon.* [M] *J, M, Z to Marcy Ave.* ✢ *7:D2.*

$$ STEAKHOUSE 🍴 **St. Anselm.** This modest spot grills high-quality meat and fish, all sustainably and ethically sourced, and at very reasonable prices. The sides, ordered à la carte, deserve special attention: The spinach gratin is dependably hearty, and the seasonal special of delicata squash with manchego (cheese from sheep's milk) is divine. **Known for:** grilled meat and fish; casual vibe; no reservations. [$] *Average main: $19* ✉ *355 Metropolitan Ave., Williamsburg* ☎ *718/384–5054* 🌐 *www.stanselm.net* ⏲ *No lunch weekdays* [M] *L to Lorimer St.; G to Metropolitan Ave.* ✢ *7:E1.*

BUSHWICK

The big draw in Bushwick is Roberta's. The neighborhood is still pretty industrial, but there are new restaurants and bars out here creating a scene.

$ ETHIOPIAN 🍴 **Bunna Cafe.** The best way to sample the diverse flavors, many quite spicy, of Ethiopian cuisine at this stellar restaurant are the combination platters—for one or to share—though you can also order individual dishes. If the delicious, seasonal *duba wot* (spiced pumpkin) is available, definitely include it in your platter. **Known for:** shareable plates; traditional Ethiopian coffee ceremony and teas; live music events featuring Ethiopian artists. [$] *Average main: $11* ✉ *1084 Flushing Ave., Bushwick* ☎ *347/295–2227* 🌐 *bunnaethiopia.net* [M] *L to Morgan Ave.* ✢ *7:G2.*

$$ PIZZA Fodor's Choice ★ 🍴 **Roberta's.** A neighborhood groundbreaker since it opened in 2008, this restaurant in a former garage is a must-visit, especially for pizza connoisseurs. The menu emphasizes hyperlocal ingredients—there's a rooftop garden—and the wood-fired pizzas have innovative combinations of toppings like fennel, pork sausage, and pistachio. **Known for:** award-winning, nationally recognized pizza; seasonal patio with outdoor tiki bar; impressive beverage menu includes curated coffee program. [$] *Average main: $17* ✉ *261 Moore St., Bushwick* ☎ *718/417–1118* 🌐 *www.robertaspizza.com* [M] *L to Morgan Ave.* ✢ *7:F2.*

FORT GREENE

Fort Greene has become one of the most desirable neighborhoods in Brooklyn, the lovely brownstone apartments attracting young professionals and many of the borough's established writers and artists. It's also a garden of culinary delights with restaurants leading the locavore farm-to-table movement. And who knows? Maybe even a famous director or author will be sitting at the table next to you.

$$$ ITALIAN 🍴 **Roman's.** Part of an all-star Brooklyn restaurant group that includes Williamsburg favorites Diner and Marlow & Sons, this seasonally focused eatery has an Italian accent. Menus change daily and include

farm-fresh fare like wintry fennel salads or pork meatballs *in brodo,* or delicacies like artichoke-studded house-made spaghetti in summer. **Known for:** seasonal menu; hip scene; great for special occasions. [$] *Average main: $26* ✉ *243 DeKalb Ave., Fort Greene* ☎ *718/622–5300* 🌐 *www.romansnyc.com* 🕓 *No lunch* [M] *C to Lafayette Ave.; G to Clinton–Washington Aves.* ✣ *7:D4.*

$$ AMERICAN 🍴 **Walter's.** A sister restaurant to Williamsburg's Walter Foods, this buzzy bistro has a menu of upscale comfort food, a comely crowd, and rosy-hued lighting that gives the space a glamorous vibe. Stop in for a cocktail after a day in Fort Greene Park, or come for a heartier repast courtesy of Walter's raw bar, satisfying main dishes (fried chicken with garlic mashed potatoes is a winner), and market-fresh veggie sides. **Known for:** fun bar scene; upscale comfort food; great cocktails. [$] *Average main: $20* ✉ *166 DeKalb Ave., Fort Greene* ☎ *718/488–7800* 🌐 *www.walterfoods.com/walters* [M] *B, Q, R to DeKalb Ave.; C to Lafayette Ave.; G to Fulton St.* ✣ *7:C4.*

15

PARK SLOPE

Park Slope's reputation precedes it: this handsome, gay-friendly family neighborhood also happens to be a great place to fill the tummy. Restaurant-crammed 5th Avenue is not for the indecisive; there's everything from Mexican to Italian to Thai, and it's all quite good.

$$$ ITALIAN Fodor's Choice ★ 🍴 **al di là Trattoria.** Roughly translated as "the great beyond," al di là has been consistently packed since it opened in 1998, and it's easy to understand why: perfectly prepared dishes from northern Italy in a cozy atmosphere. The warm farro salad with seasonal ingredients and goat cheese is perfectly al dente; the hand-pinched ravioli are delicious; and meatier entrées like braised rabbit, pork loin scaloppine, and charcoal-grilled young Bo Bo chicken are highlights. **Known for:** knowledgeable servers; ragus; not taking reservations. [$] *Average main: $26* ✉ *248 5th Ave., Park Slope* ☎ *718/783–4565* 🌐 *www.aldilatrattoria.com* [M] *R to Union St.* ✣ *7:C5.*

$$ ASIAN FUSION 🍴 **Talde.** *Top Chef* alumnus Dale Talde throws bold flavors into Asian-American comfort foods at this casual restaurant where seating at the chef's counter and antique mahogany carvings add touches of showbiz. Favorite dishes include Korean fried chicken with a kimchi-yogurt sauce cooled by sliced grapes, fried oyster and bacon pad thai, and pretzel pork and chive dumplings. **Known for:** unusual flavor pairings; piecemeal service style. [$] *Average main: $24* ✉ *369 7th Ave., Park Slope* ☎ *347/916–0031* 🌐 *www.taldebrooklyn.com* [M] *F, G to 7th Ave.* ✣ *7:C6.*

PROSPECT HEIGHTS

Once referred to as the "new Park Slope," the neighborhood on the other side of Flatbush has come into its own. Leafy, brownstone-laden streets are increasingly filled with great restaurants.

$$ JAPANESE 🍴 **Chuko.** A small, reliably tasty menu of signature ramen headlines this Prospect Heights institution for noodle bowls, buns, gyoza, beer, and sake. Long waits for a table have (slightly) abated since the operation moved in 2016 to this (slightly) larger location offering 20 more seats, but expect crowds, especially during winter months. **Known for:** ramen; very popular; lines. [$] *Average main: $14* ✉ *565*

Vanderbilt Ave., Prospect Heights ☎ *718/576–6701* ⊕ *www.barchuko.com* Ⓜ *2, 3 to Bergen St.; A, C to Clinton–Washington Aves.; B, Q to 7th Ave.* ✛ *7:D5.*

CONEY ISLAND

It's no longer an island, but this amusement park on the sea is salt-of-the-earth paradise. Think pizza and hot dogs and calorie-laden carnival fare. If you're in town during July 4, a Big Apple must-see is the annual Nathan's Famous hot-dog-eating contest where hundreds of people gather to watch "professional" eaters scarf down tubular meat.

$$
PIZZA
FAMILY

✕ **Totonno's Pizzeria Napolitana.** Thin-crust pies judiciously topped with fresh mozzarella and tangy, homemade tomato sauce, then baked in a coal oven—at Totonno's you're not just eating pizza, you're biting into a slice of New York history. Not much has changed since Anthony (Totonno) Pero first opened the pizzeria, in 1924, right after the subways started running to Coney Island—the restaurant is at the same location and run by the same family, who use ingredients and techniques that have been handed down through four generations. **Known for:** legendary New York pizza; family-run; historic location. Ⓢ *Average main: $17* ✉ *1524 Neptune Ave., Coney Island* ☎ *718/372–8606* ⊕ *www.totonnosconeyisland.com* ☉ *Closed Mon.–Wed.* ▭ *No credit cards* Ⓜ *D, F, N, Q to Coney Island–Stillwell Ave.* ✛ *7:G6.*

BRIGHTON BEACH

The subway trains that shuttle people out to this beachside neighborhood could be nicknamed the "time machine" because strolling the wide boardwalk along the sea feels like you've dropped into another time and space. Odessa in the 1980s comes to mind. After all, it was around that time when a mass migration of Russian immigrants settled in Brighton Beach. Today you'll hear more Slavic than English and you'll most certainly be tempted by the vodka and highly entertaining Russian restaurants that line the boardwalk.

$
ASIAN

✕ **Kashkar Cafe.** Uyghur cuisine, from the Chinese region of Xinjiang, is the focus of the menu at this postage-stamp-size café. Standouts include *naryn* (lamb dumplings), *samsa* (empanada-like lamb pies), pickles, vinegary salads, and clay-oven-baked bread. **Known for:** Uyghur and Uzbek cuisine; large portions; colorful restaurant. Ⓢ *Average main: $6* ✉ *1141 Brighton Beach Ave., Brighton Beach* ☎ *718/743–3832* ⊕ *www.kashkarcafe.com* Ⓜ *B, Q to Brighton Beach* ✛ *7:H6.*

$$
RUSSIAN

✕ **Tatiana Restaurant and Night Club.** There are two prime times at Tatiana's: day and night. Sitting at a boardwalk table on a summer afternoon, enjoying the breezes and the views of the Atlantic while eating lunch alfresco, is a quintessential Brighton Beach experience. **Known for:** Ukrainian favorites; indoor seating or outdoor along the boardwalk; weekend floor shows. Ⓢ *Average main: $22* ✉ *3152 Brighton 6th St. (or enter from boardwalk), Brighton Beach* ☎ *718/891–5151* ⊕ *www.tatianarestaurant.com* Ⓜ *B, Q to Brighton Beach* ✛ *7:H6.*

QUEENS

ASTORIA

After you're finished with the sights, why head back to Manhattan? End your day with dinner at one of Astoria's legendary Greek restaurants (on or near Broadway), or venture to the Middle Eastern restaurants farther out on Steinway Street.

$$ ✗ **Taverna Kyclades.** The current powerhouse of Hellenic eats in the
GREEK neighborhood, Taverna Kyclades serves Greek classics at a higher level than you might expect, given the simple decor and unassuming location. Fried calamari and grilled octopus make appearances at rock-bottom prices, despite their obvious quality, as do more out-of-the-ordinary dishes like "caviar dip" and swordfish kebabs. **Known for:** most authentic Greek fare this side of the Acropolis; lamb chops; no reservations taken. $ *Average main: $18* ✉ *33-07 Ditmars Blvd., Astoria* ☎ *718/545-8666* ⊕ *www.tavernakyclades.com* Ⓜ *N, W to Astoria–Ditmars Blvd.* ✛ *7:F1.*

FLUSHING

Manhattan may be known for its fine four-star restaurants, but food lovers know there's one train to take to some of the best eats in the city. The 7 snakes its way through the middle of Queens, and conveniently through some of the best dining neighborhoods in New York. At the end of the line is Flushing, home to the second-largest Chinatown in the United States. (First is San Francisco's.) Wide streets have few tourists and many interesting stores and restaurants, making the long trip worth it. A couple of tips: bring cash, because not many of these restaurants accept credit cards, and be prepared to encounter language difficulties, as English speakers are in the minority. In Manhattan, catch the 7 train at Times Square or Grand Central Terminal.

$ ✗ **Spicy and Tasty.** Flushing is crammed with quality salt-of-the-earth
CHINESE Chinese eateries, but Spicy and Tasty is the place to go for standout Chinese, particularly if you're a first-timer to the neighborhood. The restaurant lives up to its name with numbing Sichuan peppercorns and slicks of red chili oil. **Known for:** spicy, authentic Sichuan fare; tea-smoked duck; weekday lunch special. $ *Average main: $10* ✉ *39-07 Prince St., at 39th Ave., Flushing* ☎ *718/359-1601* ⊕ *www.spicyandtasty.com* ▭ *No credit cards* Ⓜ *7 to Flushing–Main St.* ✛ *7:H1.*

LONG ISLAND CITY

Long Island City began attracting more visitors when MoMA PS1 opened in the 1970s, and today it's getting more popular thanks to its hip but down-to-earth eateries and awesome views of the Manhattan skyline.

$$ ✗ **Casa Enrique.** Come for the tacos, stay for the margaritas: that's
MEXICAN what a lot of local Long Island City folks do at this popular Mexican standout. The chef is from Chiapas but expect pan-Mexican fare, with tacos crammed with slow-cooked beef tongue or unctuously rich chorizo, among other meat options. **Known for:** margaritas; meatballs; mole. $ *Average main: $17* ✉ *5-48 49th Ave., between Vernon Blvd. and 5th St., Long Island City* ☎ *347/448-6040* ⊕ *www.*

15

henrinyc.com/casa-enrique ⊘ *No lunch weekdays* Ⓜ *7 to Vernon Blvd./Jackson Ave.* ✛ *7:F1.*

$$
CANADIAN
Fodor's Choice
★
✕**M. Wells Dinette.** French-Canadian chef Hugue Dufour churns out the culinary art at his restaurant at MoMA PS1. The menu changes depending on the season, but diners might find dishes like veal cheek stroganoff with thick bucatini; bone marrow and escargot; or bacon-spiked potato and mussel soup. **Known for:** creative yet hearty Canadian fare; maple pie; currently closes at 6. Ⓢ *Average main: $20* ⊠ *MoMA PS1, 22–25 Jackson Ave., at 46th Ave., Long Island City* ☎ *718/786–1800* ⊕ *www. momaps1.org/about/mwells* ⊘ *No dinner. Closed Tues., Wed.* Ⓜ *7, G to Court Sq.; E, M to Court Sq.–23rd St.* ✛ *7:F1.*

$$$$
STEAKHOUSE
✕**M. Wells Steakhouse.** From the team that made Long Island City a dining destination with M. Wells Dinette inside MoMA PS1 comes this mecca devoted to meat. **Known for:** steak including grass-fed rib eye; venison T-bone; French onion soup. Ⓢ *Average main: $42* ⊠ *43-15 Crescent St., Long Island City* ☎ *718/786–9060* ⊕ *www.magasinwells. com* ⊘ *Closed Mon., Tues. No lunch* Ⓜ *7, N, W to Queensboro Plaza; E, M, R to Queens Plaza* ✛ *7:F1.*

JACKSON HEIGHTS

One of the most ethnically diverse parts of New York City, Jackson Heights is home to a United Nations of cuisine: from outstanding Indian and Pakistani places to surprisingly excellent taco carts. Most recently, Tibetans and Nepalese have been moving into the neighborhood, setting up small shops selling juicy meat-filled *momos* (dumplings) and other Himalayan treats.

$
TIBETAN
✕**Phayul.** Step through the doorway with the Himalayan eyebrow-threading sign above it, head up the twisting and turning stairway, then enter through a beaded curtain and you'll find yourself something of a delicious culinary anomaly: Tibetan-Sichuan cuisine. The traditional momos (Tibetan dumplings stuffed with meat) are worth trying, but the most exciting fare here lies in the fusion of the two cultures, like spicy blood sausage or tofu in a fiery chili sauce. **Known for:** momos; blood sausage; yak-cheese soup. Ⓢ *Average main: $10* ⊠ *37-65 74th St., Jackson Heights* ☎ *718/424–1869* ⊟ *No credit cards* Ⓜ *7 to 74th St.–Broadway; E, F, M, R to Jackson Heights–Roosevelt Ave.* ✛ *7:F1.*

WOODSIDE

It has long been said that to get great Thai food in the Big Apple, you have to go to Queens. While the Thai dining landscape has improved in other parts of the city, Woodside is still its epicenter. But to associate Woodside with only Thai cuisine is underselling it; you'll find a variety of ethnic eateries here, including Ecuadorian and Italian.

$$
THAI
Fodor's Choice
★
✕**SriPraPhai.** The main reason foodies flock to Woodside is to go to SriPraPhai (pronounced "See-PRA-pie"), widely considered the best Thai restaurant in New York. Don't be overwhelmed by the huge menu—it's hard to go wrong—just make sure you order the crispy watercress salad, *larb* (ground pork salad with mint and lime juice), sautéed chicken with cashews and pineapple, *kao-soy* (curried egg noodles), and/or roasted-duck green curry. **Known for:** top Thai in the Big Apple; lengthy

menu; spicy fare. $ *Average main: $14* ✉ *64-13 39th Ave., Woodside* ☎ *718/899–9599* ⊕ *www.sripraphairestaurant.com* ⊟ *No credit cards* ⊗ *Closed Wed.* Ⓜ *7 to 69th St.* ✛ *7:H1.*

THE BRONX

People don't really wander into this borough—as they do into Brooklyn and even Queens, hoping to stumble on some gem of an ethnic eatery—but the Bronx actually has a lot going for it, if you know where to look. Dotted throughout the borough are some great Mexican taquerias, African eateries, and old-school Italian joints. Skip Manhattan's Little Italy and head to the Bronx's Arthur Avenue for a real red-sauce treat; it's a much more authentic Italian-American neighborhood and a great place to carb-load.

$$ ✕ **Antonio's Trattoria.** Antonio's bills itself as "an Italian restaurant serv-
ITALIAN ing simple food," but it's underselling itself. This is fantastic salt-of-the-earth Italian fare at its best: start with the mini-meatballs wading in a marinara sauce and move on to baked clams, house-made ravioli, fettuccine carbonara, or excellent pizza, baked in a brick oven in the Neapolitan manner. **Known for:** classic Bronx red-sauce joint; brick-oven pizza; house-made ravioli. $ *Average main: $22* ✉ *2370 Belmont Ave., Belmont* ☎ *718/733–6630* ⊕ *www.antoniostrattoria.com* Ⓜ *B, D to 182nd–183rd Sts.*

$$ ✕ **Zero Otto Nove.** Though insiders who can get a table swear by Rao's
ITALIAN on 114th Street in Manhattan, Zero Otto Nove chugs along as one of the best Italian restaurants north of 96th Street. The draw is a menu that nicely balances authentic Italian fare with good Italian-American classics; you might try a wood-oven-fired pizza, perfectly chewy and loaded with buffalo mozzarella. **Known for:** pizza; pastas including mafalde e ceci; whole roasted branzino; gets very busy. $ *Average main: $17* ✉ *2357 Arthur Ave., Belmont* ☎ *718/220–1027* ⊕ *www.roberto089.com* ⊗ *Closed Mon.* Ⓜ *B, D to 182nd–183rd Sts.*

STATEN ISLAND

There's not much reason for tourists to spend time in New York's often-forgotten fifth borough, but if you made your way here on the free ferry from Whitehall Terminal and want to explore, you'll find plenty of homespun, no-frills eateries, including some of the best pizza in the city.

$$ **Denino's Pizzeria & Tavern.** Arguably the best pizzeria in the borough,
ITALIAN Denino's has been run by the same Sicilian family for more than 75
FAMILY years. Baking thin-crust pizzas in their current location since 1937, this Staten Island institution is worth the trip from St. George (half an hour by bus; 15-minute drive). **Known for:** legit Staten Island pizza; local institution. $ *Average main: $17* ✉ *524 Port Richmond Ave., Staten Island* ☎ *718/442–9401* ⊕ *www.deninos.com* ⊟ *No credit cards* Ⓜ *S44 or S94 bus from Staten Island Ferry Terminal (30 mins).*

15

$$ ITALIAN 🍴 **Enoteca Maria.** Just a short walk from the Manhattan–Staten Island ferry, Enoteca Maria may look, smell, and seem like an ordinary Italian eatery, but scratch beneath the ragu and you'll find something very interesting going on. The restaurant does not just employ one chef but a dozen or so, all Italian nonne, or grandmas, each one hailing from a different region in Italy and cooking regional dishes on different nights. **Known for:** rotating cadre of Italian grandmas in the kitchen; regional Italian fare; Italian wines. [$] *Average main: $15* ✉ *27 Hyatt St., at Central Ave., St. George* ☎ *718/447–2777* 🌐 *www.enotecamaria.com* 🕒 *Closed Mon.–Wed.* [M] *Ferry to Staten Island.*

NEW YORK CITY DINING AND LODGING ATLAS

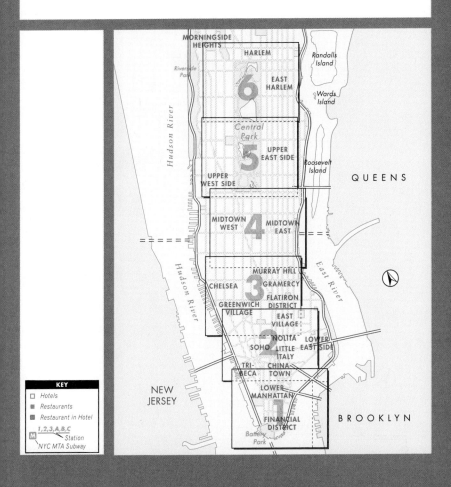

MORNINGSIDE HEIGHTS

HARLEM

Randalls Island

Riverside Park

EAST HARLEM

Wards Island

6

Hudson River

Central Park

5

UPPER EAST SIDE

Roosevelt Island

UPPER WEST SIDE

QUEENS

MIDTOWN WEST

4

MIDTOWN EAST

Hudson River

East River

MURRAY HILL

CHELSEA

GRAMERCY

3

FLATIRON DISTRICT

GREENWICH VILLAGE

EAST VILLAGE

2

NOLITA

LOWER EAST SIDE

SOHO

LITTLE ITALY

TRI-BECA

CHINA-TOWN

NEW JERSEY

LOWER MANHATTAN

1

BROOKLYN

FINANCIAL DISTRICT

Battery Park

KEY
- ☐ Hotels
- ■ Restaurants
- ■ Restaurant in Hotel

M 1,2,3,A,B,C Station
NYC MTA Subway

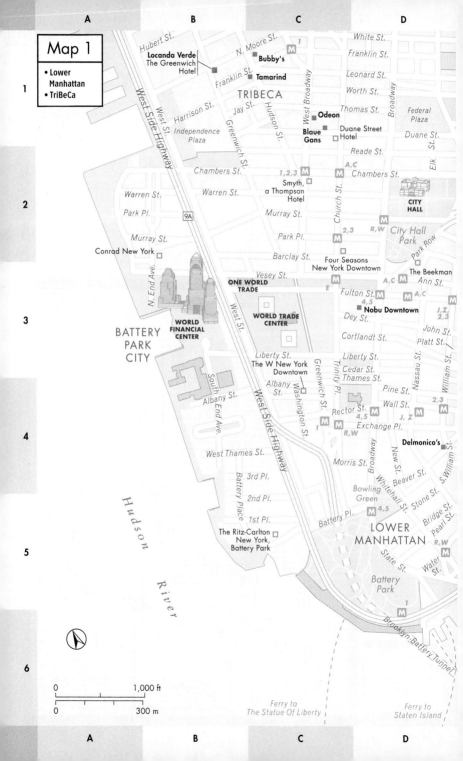

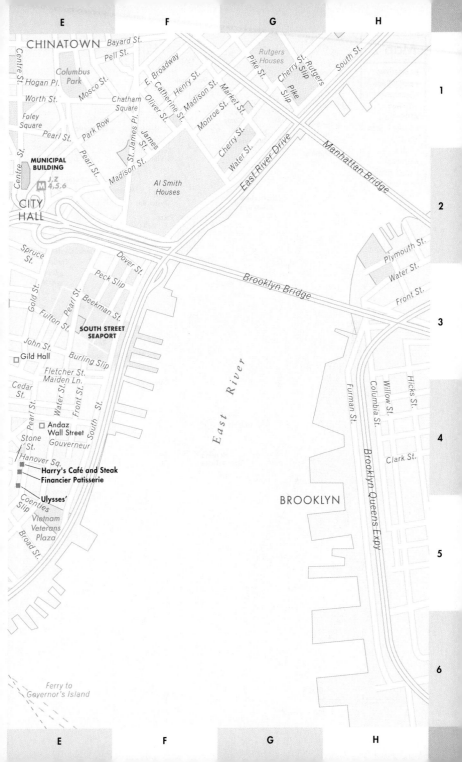

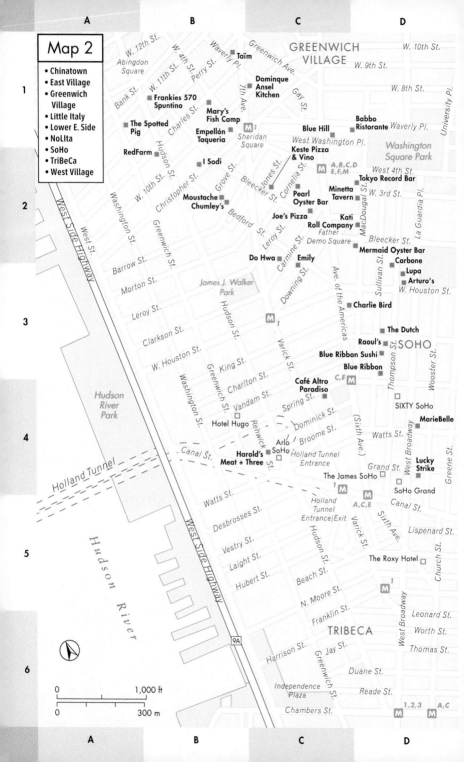

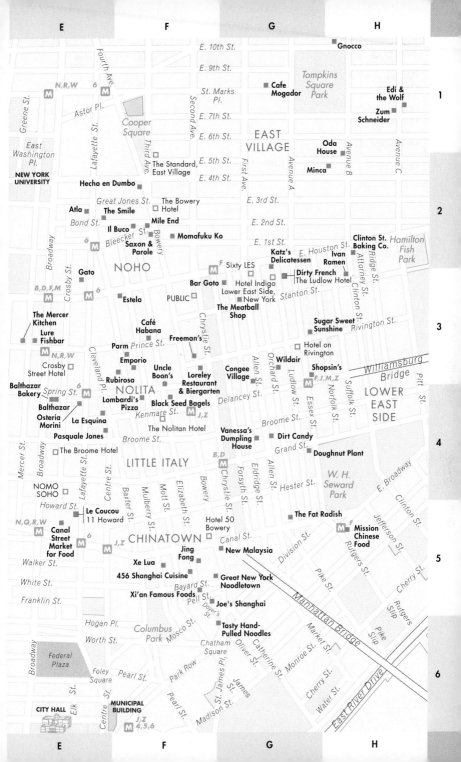

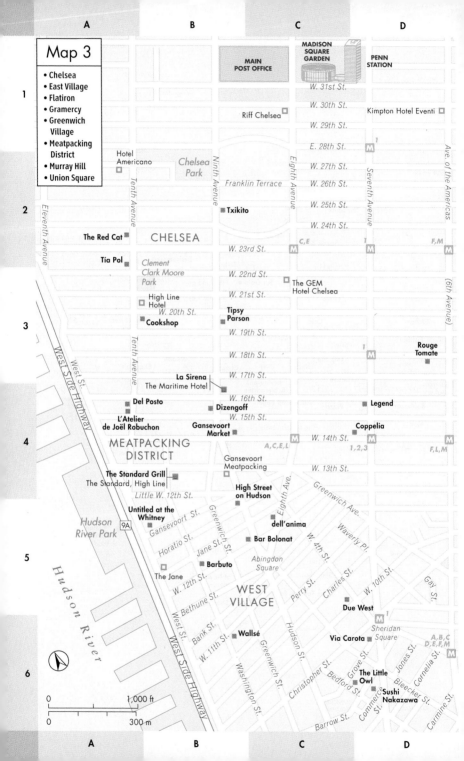

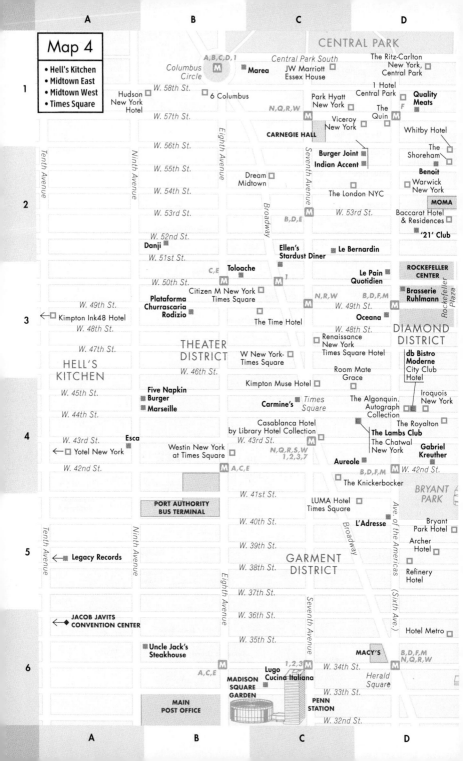

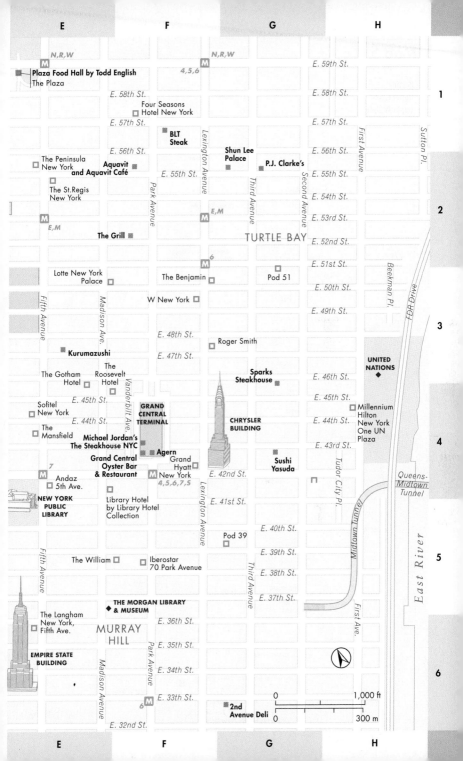

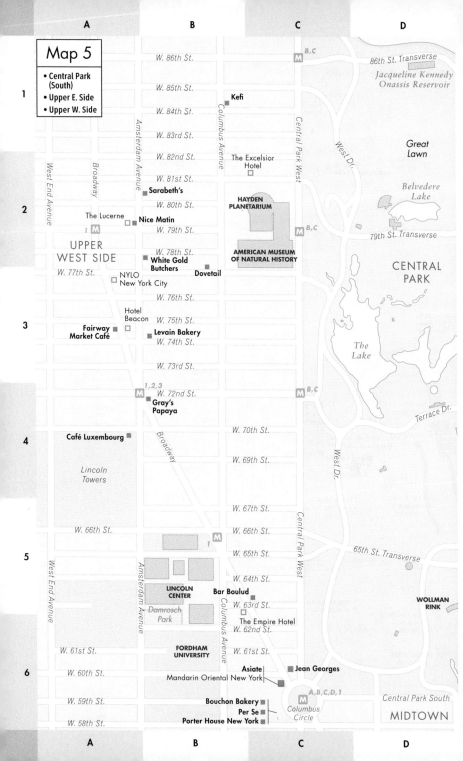

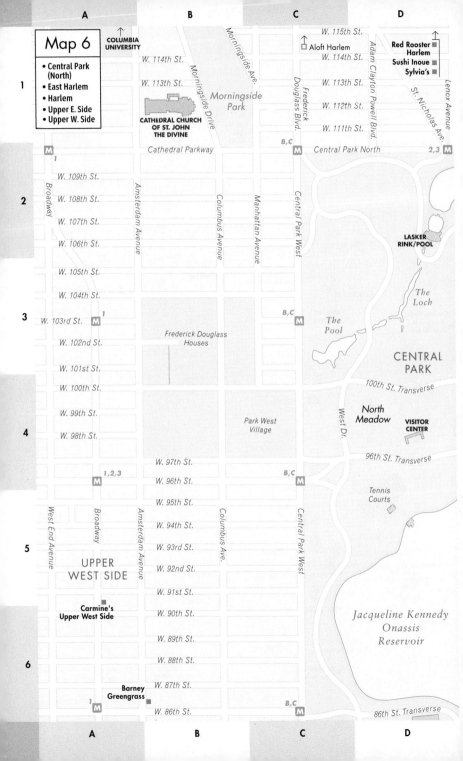

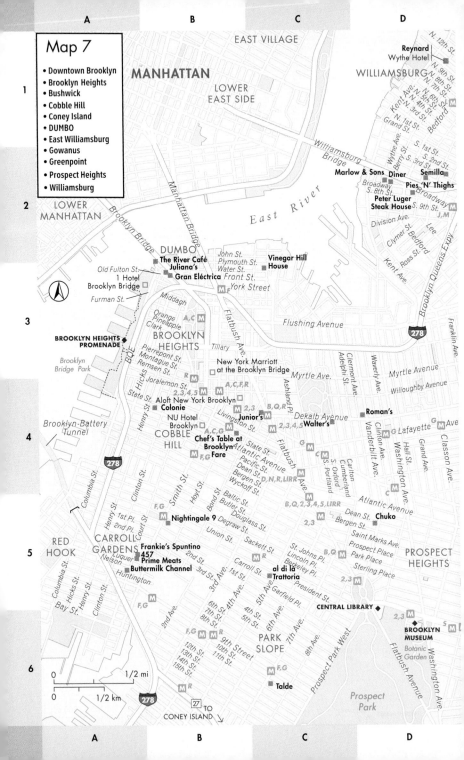

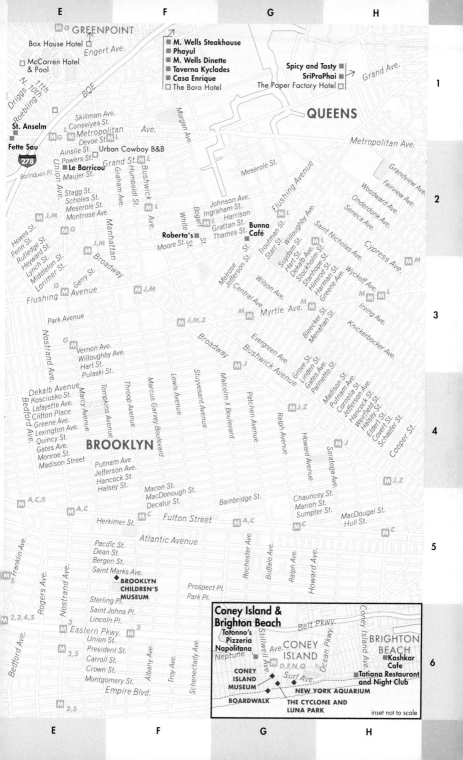

E   F   G   H

GREENPOINT

Box House Hotel

Engert Ave.

McCarren Hotel
& Pool

■ M. Wells Steakhouse
■ Phayul
■ M. Wells Dinette
■ Taverna Kyclades
■ Casa Enrique
□ The Boro Hotel

Spicy and Tasty ■
SriPraPhai ■
The Paper Factory Hotel □

Grand Ave.

BQE

Skillman Ave.
Conselyea St.
Metropolitan
Devoe St.
Ainslie St.   Urban Cowboy B&B
Powers St.

St. Anselm

Fette Sau

278

Borinquen Pl.

Le Barricou

Grand St.

Maujer St.

Stagg St.
Scholes St.
Meserole St.
Montrose Ave.

Hewes St.
Penn St.
Rutledge St.
Heyward St.
Lynch St.
Middleton St.
Lorimer St.

Flushing

Park Avenue

Nostrand Ave.

Vernon Ave.
Willoughby Ave.
Hart St.
Pulaski St.

Dekalb Avenue
Kosciusko St.
Lafayette Ave.
Clifton Place
Greene Ave.
Lexington Ave.
Quincy St.
Gates Ave.
Monroe St.
Madison Street

BROOKLYN

Putnam Ave.
Jefferson Ave.
Hancock St.
Halsey St.

Macon St.
MacDonough St.
Decatur St.

Herkimer St.

Fulton Street

Atlantic Avenue

Pacific St.
Dean St.
Bergen St.
Saint Marks Ave.

BROOKLYN
CHILDREN'S
MUSEUM

Sterling Pl.

Saint Johns Pl.
Lincoln Pl.

Eastern Pkwy.

Union St.

President St.

Carroll St.

Crown St.

Montgomery St.

Empire Blvd.

Franklin Ave.

Rogers Ave.

Nostrand Avenue

Bedford Ave.

QUEENS

Metropolitan Ave.

Grandview Ave.
Fairview Ave.
Woodward Ave.
Onderdonk Ave.
Seneca Ave.

Cypress Ave.

Meserole St.

Morgan Ave.

Flushing Avenue

Johnson Ave.
Ingraham St.
Harrison
Grattan St.
Thames St.

Roberta's ■

Moore St.

White St.

Bogart St.

Bunna
Café ■

Melrose St.
Jefferson St.

Troutman St.
Starr St.
Suydam St.
Hart St.

Willoughby Ave.
Saint Nicholas Ave.

Dekalb Ave.
Stockholm St.
Stanhope St.
Himrod St.
Harman St.
Greene Ave.

Wyckoff Ave.

Irving Ave.

Central Ave.

Wilson Ave.

Myrtle Ave.

Broadway

Evergreen Ave.

Bushwick Avenue

Bleecker St.
Menahan St.

Grove St.
Linden St.
Gates Ave.
Palmetto St.

Knickerbocker Ave.

Madison St.
Putnam Ave.
Cornelia St.
Jefferson Ave.
Hancock St.
Weirfield St.
Halsey St.
Eldert St.
Covert St.
Schaefer St.

Cooper St.

Lewis Avenue

Stuyvesant Avenue

Malcolm X Boulevard

Patchen Avenue

Ralph Avenue

Howard Avenue

Saratoga Ave.

Chauncey St.
Marion St.
Sumpter St.

MacDougal St.
Hull St.

Bainbridge St.

Rochester Ave.

Buffalo Ave.

Ralph Ave.

Howard Ave.

Prospect Pl.
Park Pl.

Coney Island &
Brighton Beach

Totonno's
Pizzeria
Napolitana
Neptune Ave.

Belt Pkwy.

Stillwell Ave.

CONEY
ISLAND

D,F,N,Q

Surf Ave.

Ocean Pkwy.

Coney Island Ave.

BRIGHTON
BEACH

Kashkar
Cafe ■

Tatiana Restaurant
and Night Club ■

CONEY
ISLAND
MUSEUM

BOARDWALK

NEW YORK AQUARIUM

THE CYCLONE AND
LUNA PARK

inset not to scale

Albany Ave.

Troy Ave.

Schenectady Ave.

Marcus Garvey Boulevard

Throop Avenue

Tompkins Avenue

Marcy Avenue

Broadway

Manhattan Avenue

Graham Avenue

Humboldt St.

Bushwick Ave.

Driggs
N. 11th
10th
Roebling

Union Ave.

E   F   G   H

1

2

3

4

5

6

WHERE TO STAY

Updated by
Laura Itzkowitz

There are more hotel rooms than ever in New York City, as exciting new properties continue to open their doors not only in Manhattan but in Brooklyn and the outer boroughs as well. But does that mean that New York is cheap? Well, we wouldn't say *cheap*, but you can still find some deals, especially if you're not set on a specific property or neighborhood, and if you don't mind a few extra minutes of commuting time.

Hotels continue to slash rates based on market sensitivity—especially if you and all of those other Internet-savvy shoppers are willing to wait until the last minute. That said, if you want to stay in a specific place and the rate seems reasonable, book it—it's just as likely to go up, especially during peak seasons (spring and fall).

How to choose? The first thing to consider is location *(Check out our "Where Should I Stay?" chart)*. Many New York City visitors insist on staying in the hectic Midtown area—and options are improving there—but other neighborhoods are often just as convenient. Less touristy areas, such as Gramercy, the Lower East Side, the Upper West Side—even Brooklyn—provide a more realistic sense of New York life, too.

Also consider timing: the least expensive months to book rooms in the city are January and February. If you're flexible on dates, ask the reservationist if there's a cheaper time to stay during your preferred traveling month—that way you can avoid peak dates, like Fashion Week and the New York City Marathon. Be sure to ask about possible weekend packages that could include a third night free. (The Financial District in particular can be a discount gold mine on weekends.)

Another source of bargains? Chain hotels. Many have moved into the city and charge reasonable room rates. In addition to favorites like the Sheraton, Hilton, and Hyatt brands, there are Best Westerns, Days Inns, and Comfort Inns. These rates aren't as low as you find outside Manhattan, but they're certainly getting closer.

WHERE SHOULD I STAY?

	Neighborhood Vibe	Pros	Cons
Lower Manhattan	Mostly skyscraper hotels in an area that buzzes with activity during week-day hours, but can be eerily quiet at night.	Low crime area; easy subway access to uptown sights; great walking paths along the water-front and in Battery Park.	Construction and congestion near World Trade Center site; limited choice of restaurants and shopping.
SoHo, NoLIta, and Chinatown (with Little Italy)	Swanky, high-end hotels with hip restaurants and lounges patronized by New Yorkers and travelers alike.	Scores of upscale clothing boutiques and art galler-ies nearby; safe area for meandering walks; easy subway access.	Not budget-friendly; streets are crowded on weekends; few major sites nearby.
East Village and the Lower East Side	The epicenter of edgy New York, great for trav-elers looking to party.	Great low-cost options for young generation. Great restaurants and indepen-dent boutiques.	One of the least subway-accessible Manhattan 'hoods; expect late-night noise.
Greenwich Vil-lage and the West Village	Hotels in this part of town are few and far between. The ones that are here are small and boutiquey.	Easy subway access to anywhere in town; great shopping, dining, and drinking venues.	Winding streets can be tough to navigate; most hotels are on the pricey side.
Chelsea and the Meatpack-ing District	More hotels are open-ing in one of the city's trendiest restaurant and nightlife areas.	"See and be seen"; lots of great shopping and art galleries.	This is a trendy and pricey neighborhood for hotels. Most hotel bars are a real scene.
Union Square, Flatiron District, and Gramercy	A relatively quiet residen-tial area.	Patches of calm respite from the hustle and bustle of downtown and Midtown; low crime area.	Limited subway access as you move east; Gramercy may be too quiet for some.
Midtown East and West, and Murray Hill	Mostly big-name hotel chains and luxury busi-ness suites around Times Square; lots of tourists.	Near Broadway theaters; budget options are avail-able in chain hotels and indies alike.	Streets are often packed with pedestrians; area around Port Authority is gritty. Murray Hill is pretty quiet.
Upper East Side	Well-heeled residential neighborhood near many museums.	Removed from Midtown hustle; near tourist attrac-tions like some museums and Central Park.	Quiet streets after 9 pm; few budget dining options; limited subways (just the 6 and Q lines).
Upper West Side	Hotels in a residential neighborhood near Cen-tral Park, Lincoln Center, and some museums.	Lovely tree-lined streets; laid-back neighborhood eateries.	Weekend trains can be slow; most hotels are on the pricey side.
Brooklyn	Brooklyn has a bit of everything so it depends on where you end up. Williamsburg is all about hipsters, while other neighborhoods are quite residential.	Generally smaller boutique-style hotels with personalized service and character; some rates are worth traveling for. Plus, a whole new borough to explore.	If you're out late in Man-hattan, it'll be a subway or a relatively pricey taxi back to Brooklyn.

16

PLANNING

NEED A RESERVATION?

Hotel reservations are a necessity when planning your trip to New York. Competition for clients also means properties must undergo frequent improvements, especially during July and August, so when booking, ask about any renovations, lest you get a room within earshot of noisy construction, or temporarily (and inconveniently) without amenities such as room service or spa access.

SERVICES

Unless otherwise noted, all hotels listed have private baths, central heating, air-conditioning, and private phones. Many now have wireless Internet (Wi-Fi) available, though it's not always free. Most large hotels have video or high-speed checkout capability, and many can arrange babysitting. Pools are a rarity, but most properties have gyms or health clubs, and sometimes full-scale spas; hotels without facilities usually have arrangements for guests at nearby gyms, sometimes for a fee.

FAMILY TRAVEL

New York has gone to great lengths to attract family vacationers, and hotels have followed the family-friendly trend. Some properties provide such diversions as Web TV and in-room video games. Most full-service Manhattan hotels provide roll-away beds, babysitting, and stroller rental, but be sure to make these arrangements when booking, not when you arrive.

DOES SIZE MATTER?

If room size is important to you, ask how many square feet a room has, not just if it's big. A hotel room in New York is considered large if it's 500 square feet. Very large rooms are 600 square feet. To stay anywhere larger, book a multiroom suite. Small rooms are a tight 150 to 200 square feet, sometimes less.

PRICES

There's no denying that New York City hotels are expensive, but rates run the full range. For high-end hotels like the Mandarin Oriental at Central Park, prices start at $795 a night for a standard room in high season, which runs from September through December. At the lower end of the spending spectrum, a bunk at the Jane starts at $99 for a single. But don't be put off by the prices printed here—many hotels slash their rates significantly for promotions and Web-only deals.

Prices in the reviews are the lowest cost of a standard double room in high season.

WHAT IT COSTS			
	$	$$	$$$	$$$$
FOR TWO PEOPLE	under $300	$300–$449	$450–$600	over $600

Prices are for a standard double room, excluding 14.75% city and state taxes.

HOTEL REVIEWS

Listed alphabetically within neighborhoods. Please visit Fodors.com for expanded reviews. Use the coordinate (⊹ 1:B2) at the end of each listing to locate a property on the corresponding map preceding this chapter.

LOWER MANHATTAN

FINANCIAL DISTRICT

$
HOTEL
Andaz Wall Street. If space is a priority, head to the southern tip of Manhattan: this sleek hotel has generous rooms with large windows, oak floors, and extra-large bathrooms. **Pros:** free Wi-Fi, bikes, snacks, and nonalcoholic beverages; excellent, intuitive lighting controls; good value. **Cons:** limited choice for restaurants and nightlife in the neighborhood; in-house restaurant not open every day; location is a bit far from many major sites. $ *Rooms from: $299* ⊠ *75 Wall St., Financial District* ☎ *212/590–1234* ⊕ *wallstreet.andaz.hyatt.com* ↻ *253 rooms* ⦿*No meals* Ⓜ *2, 3 to Wall St.* ⊹ *1:E4.*

$$$$
HOTEL
Fodor'sChoice
★
The Beekman. After sitting abandoned for many years, this historic late-19th-century downtown office building was reborn as a chic hotel that channels Old New York, with a clubby lobby bar and two restaurants by award-winning chef Tom Colicchio and restaurateur Keith McNally. **Pros:** gorgeous design with notable atrium and lots of character; excellent restaurants and bar; fantastic concierge team. **Cons:** service a bit inconsistent; limited dining and nightlife options nearby; pricey. $ *Rooms from: $699* ⊠ *123 Nassau St., Financial District* ☎ *212/233–2300* ⊕ *www.thebeekman.com* ↻ *287 rooms* ⦿*No meals* Ⓜ *2, 3, 4, 5, A, C, J, Z to Fulton St.* ⊹ *1:D2.*

$
HOTEL
FAMILY
Conrad New York. A pleasant surprise in a quiet Battery Park City location, this hotel has many coveted amenities: significant square footage, a breezy rooftop bar, and access to green space in nearby Hudson River Park. **Pros:** spacious rooms with separate living space; very family-friendly; near movie theater and restaurants. **Cons:** daily fee for Wi-Fi; removed from Midtown attractions; fee for valet and self-parking. $ *Rooms from: $291* ⊠ *102 North End Ave., between Vesey and Murray Sts., Financial District* ☎ *212/945–0100* ⊕ *www.conradnewyork.com* ↻ *463 suites* ⦿*No meals* Ⓜ *1, 2, 3, A, C to Chambers St.; E to World Trade Center* ⊹ *1:B3.*

$$$
HOTEL
Gild Hall. Elegant, cozy, and charming, this boutique sleep from Thompson Hotels offers good design and good value. **Pros:** central Financial District location; eye-popping lobby; stylish room design. **Cons:** small rooms for the price; untraditional location; scant dining options nearby. $ *Rooms from: $499* ⊠ *15 Gold St., at Platt St., Financial District* ☎ *212/232–7700* ⊕ *www.thompsonhotels.com* ↻ *130 rooms* ⦿*No meals* Ⓜ *2, 3, 4, 5, A, C, J, Z to Fulton St.* ⊹ *1:E3.*

$$$
HOTEL
FAMILY
The Ritz-Carlton New York, Battery Park. The hotel provides the classic Ritz-Carlton luxury experience—you are greeted by at least one staffer each time you walk into the lobby—and the large rooms look out to sweeping views of the New York harbor. **Pros:** excellent service; pet- and kid-friendly; Statue of Liberty views. **Cons:** removed from Midtown tourist sights; limited nighttime activities; few neighborhood options

16

for dining and entertainment. $ *Rooms from: $525* ✉ *2 West St., at Battery Park, Financial District* ☎ *212/344–0800* 🌐 *www.ritzcarlton.com/batterypark* 🛏 *298 rooms* 🍴 *No meals* [M] *1, R, W to Rector St.; 4, 5 to Bowling Green* ⊕ *1:C5.*

$ HOTEL 🏨 **The W New York Downtown.** In the heart of the Financial District, this W outpost juxtaposes the neighborhood's gritty feel with sleek surfaces and minimalist style. **Pros:** near popular tourist attractions; restaurant offers some surprisingly affordable fare; modern workout room. **Cons:** no bathtubs in any rooms; not family-friendly; fee for Wi-Fi in rooms. $ *Rooms from: $250* ✉ *8 Albany St., Financial District* ☎ *646/826–8600* 🌐 *www.wnewyorkdowntown.com* 🛏 *217 rooms* 🍴 *No meals* [M] *1, R, W to Rector St.; 4, 5 to Wall St.* ⊕ *1:C4.*

TRIBECA

$ HOTEL 🏨 **Duane Street Hotel.** Amid TriBeCa's historic warehouses and trendy art galleries sits this boutique hotel, a fashionable addition to the neighborhood. **Pros:** good value for the area; complimentary bikes provided; stylish rooms. **Cons:** off-site gym; no 24-hour room service; rooms are on the small side. $ *Rooms from: $250* ✉ *130 Duane St., TriBeCa* ☎ *212/964–4600* 🌐 *www.duanestreethotel.com* 🛏 *43 rooms* 🍴 *No meals* [M] *1, 2, 3, A, C to Chambers St.* ⊕ *1:C1.*

$$$ HOTEL 🏨 **Four Seasons New York Downtown.** Hotly anticipated, this new property by the Four Seasons is a luxurious haven near the World Trade Center, with a sleek residential-inspired design, a 75-foot indoor pool, an indulgent spa, and a restaurant by celebrity chef Wolfgang Puck. **Pros:** sleek design; excellent pool, spa, and gym; convenient (for downtown) location. **Cons:** expensive; limited dining and nightlife options nearby; far from uptown sites and museums. $ *Rooms from: $559* ✉ *27 Barclay St., TriBeCa* ☎ *646/880–1999* 🌐 *www.fourseasons.com/newyorkdowntown* 🛏 *161 rooms* 🍴 *No meals* [M] *A, C to Chambers St.; 2, 3 to Park Pl.* ⊕ *1:C2.*

$$$$ HOTEL Fodor's Choice ★ 🏨 **The Greenwich Hotel.** This understated, inviting hotel manages to fly under the radar even though Robert De Niro is an owner and Andrew Carmellini's rustic Italian restaurant, Locanda Verde, is a local favorite. **Pros:** fabulous restaurant (also available for room service); gorgeous pool; excellent service; luxurious bathrooms. **Cons:** some plumbing noise; high prices; the location isn't for everyone. $ *Rooms from: $625* ✉ *377 Greenwich St., TriBeCa* ☎ *212/941–8900* 🌐 *www.thegreenwichhotel.com* 🛏 *88 rooms* 🍴 *No meals* [M] *1 to Franklin St.* ⊕ *1:B1.*

$$ HOTEL 🏨 **The Roxy Hotel.** Formerly the Tribeca Grand, the Roxy is a fresh downtown property with an emphasis on art, music, and culture. **Pros:** great dining and bar scene with live jazz; vinyl record player upon request; complimentary tickets to the Roxy Cinema. **Cons:** rooms get noise from restaurant below; bathrooms have slightly cold design; a bit sceney for some. $ *Rooms from: $395* ✉ *2 6th Ave., between Walker and White Sts., TriBeCa* ☎ *212/519–6000* 🌐 *www.roxyhotelnyc.com* 🛏 *201 rooms* 🍴 *No meals* [M] *A, C, E to Canal St.* ⊕ *2:D5.*

$$ HOTEL 🏨 **Smyth, a Thompson Hotel.** Located almost on top of a convenient subway stop, this thoroughly modern hotel with an inviting lobby perfect for lounging makes TriBeCa a welcoming landing spot for visitors. **Pros:** great service; good restaurant; excellent subway access. **Cons:** Wi-Fi

not free; only a frosted-glass partition divides bathroom from sleeping area; bathrooms could have better lighting. $ *Rooms from: $375* ⌧ *85 West Broadway, between Chambers and Warren Sts., TriBeCa* ☎ *212/587–7000* ⊕ *www.thompsonhotels.com* ⤳ *100 rooms* ⦿| *No meals* Ⓜ *1, 2, 3, A, C to Chambers St.* ✛ *1:C2.*

SOHO, NOLITA, AND CHINATOWN

SOHO

$ ⛨ **Arlo SoHo.** Affordable rates, a prime location, sleek design, a popular
HOTEL restaurant and bar, and fitness classes make up for the tiny rooms at this microhotel by the new Arlo brand, which caters largely to millennials who'd rather spend time exploring the city than holed up in their rooms. **Pros:** supersleek design; great value for the prime SoHo location; programming like vinyl hour, meditation, and fitness classes. **Cons:** tiny rooms; glass-enclosed bathrooms lack privacy; no in-room minibar. $ *Rooms from: $199* ⌧ *231 Hudson St., SoHo* ☎ *212/806–7000* ⊕ *www.arlohotels.com* ⤳ *325 rooms* ⦿| *No meals* Ⓜ *1 to Canal St.; C, E to Spring St.* ✛ *2:C4.*

$$ ⛨ **The Broome Hotel.** A Federal-style building from 1825 has been trans-
HOTEL formed into this boutique property full of local character; it was the former home of an artists' commune in the 1980s. **Pros:** excellent location for SoHo's shopping and dining; free continental breakfast served on charming patio; good value for the neighborhood. **Cons:** no full-service restaurant on-site; small rooms; inconsistent service. $ *Rooms from: $359* ⌧ *431 Broome St., SoHo* ☎ *212/431–2929* ⊕ *www.thebroomenyc.com* ⤳ *14 rooms* ⦿| *Breakfast* Ⓜ *6 to Spring St.* ✛ *2:E4.*

$$$$ ⛨ **Crosby Street Hotel.** This whimsical boutique hotel, the first branch of
HOTEL a U.K. chain to open in the United States, has an eclectic design with
Fodor'sChoice colorful furnishings handpicked by co-owner Kit Kemp. **Pros:** unique,
★ fun design, and LEED certified; big, bright rooms; great bar. **Cons:** small gym; expensive; no pool or spa. $ *Rooms from: $695* ⌧ *79 Crosby St., between Prince and Spring Sts., SoHo* ☎ *212/226–6400* ⊕ *www.firmdalehotels.com* ⤳ *86 rooms* ⦿| *No meals* Ⓜ *6 to Spring St.; N, R, W to Prince St.; B, D, F, M to Broadway–Lafayette St.* ✛ *2:E3.*

$$ ⛨ **11 Howard.** One of the city's sleekest new hotels, 11 Howard made
HOTEL a splash with a design that melds midcentury modern furniture and Scandinavian minimalism, as well as with its highly acclaimed restaurant, Le Coucou. **Pros:** destination restaurant hailed among New York's best; midcentury meets Scandinavian minimalist design; a portion of the money from direct bookings goes to charity. **Cons:** fee for pets; some guests complain about street noise; standard rooms are small. $ *Rooms from: $389* ⌧ *11 Howard St., SoHo* ☎ *212/235–1111* ⊕ *11howard. com* ⤳ *213 rooms* ⦿| *No meals* Ⓜ *N, Q, R, W, 6 to Canal St* ✛ *2:E5.*

$ ⛨ **Hotel Hugo.** Those who dream of coming home to a SoHo loft will be
HOTEL drawn to this stylish property inspired by the neighborhood's industrial-chic residences. **Pros:** great location for walks along the Hudson River; stylish on-site dining and drinking options; rooftop with multiple spaces and fantastic views. **Cons:** space in rooms is tight; not in the prime heart of SoHo, but on the edge of it; fitness center is in a windowless basement room. $ *Rooms from: $299* ⌧ *525 Greenwich St., SoHo*

16

☎ *212/608–4848* 🌐 *www.hotelhugony.com* 🛏 *122 rooms* 🍴 *No meals* [M] *1 to Houston St.* ✥ *2:B4.*

$$ HOTEL FAMILY Fodor's Choice ★ 🏨 **The James SoHo.** This hotel on the edge of SoHo never sacrifices comfort for style, so it's no wonder there's a high percentage of return customers: creative types, businesspeople, fashionistas, and anyone else with deep pockets. **Pros:** stellar service; fabulous views from tall windows; cool SoHo location. **Cons:** rooftop bar is expensive; bathrooms offer little privacy; noise from the bar can be bothersome. [$] *Rooms from: $429* ✉ *27 Grand St., between Thompson St. and 6th Ave., SoHo* ☎ *212/465–2000* 🌐 *www.jameshotels.com/new-york/soho* 🛏 *114 rooms* 🍴 *No meals* [M] *1, A, C, E to Canal St.* ✥ *2:D4.*

$$ HOTEL Fodor's Choice ★ 🏨 **NOMO SOHO.** Snazzy, fairy-tale-inspired style and a chic SoHo vibe make this property a winner for anyone looking for a decadent downtown New York experience. **Pros:** stylish rooms; friendly to electronics addicts; fabulous views from floor-to-ceiling windows. **Cons:** elevators can be slow; standard rooms are on the small side; inconsistent service. [$] *Rooms from: $300* ✉ *9 Crosby St., SoHo* ☎ *844/735–3355* 🌐 *www.nomosoho.com* 🛏 *264 rooms* 🍴 *No meals* [M] *6, J, N, Q, R, W, Z to Canal St.* ✥ *2:E4.*

$$$ HOTEL 🏨 **SIXTY SoHo.** Formerly SoHo icon 60 Thompson, this stylish renovated and rebranded hotel has a fabulous rooftop lounge, Above SIXTY SoHo, that remains a warm-weather haven for the well dressed, with sweeping skyline views. **Pros:** central to SoHo nightlife; good dining and drinking options on-site; some rooms have balconies. **Cons:** not family-oriented; no pets allowed; rooftop bar can get crowded. [$] *Rooms from: $555* ✉ *60 Thompson St., between Broome and Spring Sts., SoHo* ☎ *877/431–0400* 🌐 *www.sixtyhotels.com/soho* 🛏 *97 rooms* 🍴 *No meals* [M] *C, E to Spring St.* ✥ *2:D4.*

$$ HOTEL 🏨 **SoHo Grand.** Once pioneering, now expensive, and with a vaguely creative vibe—the SoHo Grand defines what SoHo is today, and as new properties crowd the field, the Grand's low-key sophistication stands out. **Pros:** fashionable, laid-back sophistication; great service; surprisingly discreet setting; diverse eating and drinking options. **Cons:** closer to Canal Street than prime SoHo; rooms on small side; rather pricey. [$] *Rooms from: $425* ✉ *310 West Broadway, at Grand St., SoHo* ☎ *212/965–3000* 🌐 *www.sohogrand.com* 🛏 *353 rooms* 🍴 *No meals* [M] *1, 2, 3, A, C, E to Canal St.* ✥ *2:D4.*

NOLITA

$$ HOTEL 🏨 **The Nolitan Hotel.** The cool Nolitan combines a hip, slightly gritty feel with some luxe touches, but don't expect a lot of space to spread out. **Pros:** cool vibe; fun location convenient to lower Manhattan and Brooklyn; fabulous views from rooftop and some rooms. **Cons:** smallish rooms; gym access five-minute walk away; some street noise. [$] *Rooms from: $300* ✉ *30 Kenmare St., NoLIta* ☎ *212/925–2555* 🌐 *www.nolitanhotel.com* 🛏 *57 rooms* 🍴 *No meals* [M] *J, Z to Bowery; 6 to Spring St.* ✥ *2:F4.*

CHINATOWN

$ HOTEL **Hotel 50 Bowery.** San Francisco–based hotel company Joie de Vivre's New York debut brings a full-service hotel with modern rooms featuring street-art-style paintings; an Asian-fusion restaurant (Rice & Gold), rooftop bar (the Crown), and speakeasy (the Green Lady), all by *Top Chef* alum Dale Talde; and a permanent exhibition curated by the nearby Museum of Chinese in America to a neighborhood lacking in quality accommodations. **Pros:** rooms on higher floors have great views; double-paned windows mean no street noise; destination dining and rooftop bar. **Cons:** basement gym with no windows; limited subway access nearby; far from most tourist sites. [$] *Rooms from: $299 ✉ 50 Bowery, Chinatown ☎ 212/508–8000 🌐 www.50bowery.com 🛏 229 rooms 🍴 No meals [M] B, D to Grand St. ✥ 2:F5.*

EAST VILLAGE AND THE LOWER EAST SIDE

EAST VILLAGE

$$$ HOTEL Fodor's Choice ★ **The Bowery Hotel.** Warmed by rich tapestries and fireplaces, the Bowery Hotel is like an English hunting lodge in Manhattan—and there's no shortage of Brits, who flock to the property. **Pros:** quirky, fun location; happening bar and lobby-lounge area; celebrity sightings; interesting views. **Cons:** gritty neighbors; rooms lack luxe touches expected at this price; too sceney for some. [$] *Rooms from: $525 ✉ 335 Bowery, at 3rd St., East Village ☎ 212/505–9100 🌐 www.theboweryhotel.com 🛏 135 rooms 🍴 No meals [M] F to 2nd Ave.; 6 to Bleecker St. ✥ 2:F2.*

$$ HOTEL **The Standard, East Village.** In the low-rise East Village, this gigantic, 21-story glass-and-steel hotel building that soars above everything around, providing gorgeous views through floor-to-ceiling windows, was never going to pass under the radar—and that's guaranteed now that the scene-making Standard brand has taken over. **Pros:** stylish, sunny rooms with great views; central location for downtown exploring; near hip restaurants and bars. **Cons:** architecture out of character with area; rooms on the small side; no on-site gym or spa. [$] *Rooms from: $305 ✉ 25 Cooper Sq., between 5th and 6th Sts., East Village ☎ 212/475–5700 🌐 www.standardhotels.com 🛏 145 rooms 🍴 No meals [M] 6 to Astor Pl.; R, W to 8th St.–NYU ✥ 2:F2.*

LOWER EAST SIDE

$$$ HOTEL **Hotel Indigo Lower East Side, New York.** Smack in the center of a dynamic neighborhood, this hotel offers a fantastic launching pad for restaurants, nightlife, and people-watching, though it will be hard to beat the sweeping city views from the 14th-floor lobby's large windows. **Pros:** local flavor with emphasis on art; rooftop swimming pool; sleek dining and drinking options. **Cons:** street noise is common in this all-night neighborhood; expensive for the area; far from tourist attractions. [$] *Rooms from: $499 ✉ 171 Ludlow St., Lower East Side ☎ 212/237–1776 🌐 www.hotelindigolowereastside.com 🛏 294 rooms 🍴 No meals [M] F to 2nd Ave.; J, M, Z to Essex St. ✥ 2:G3.*

$$ HOTEL **Hotel on Rivington.** A pioneer when it opened back in 2004, this glass-walled hotel on the Lower East Side is still a great choice if you want to be in the thick of the neighborhood's dining and nightlife scene. **Pros:** cool

16

location and vibe; huge windows with wonderful New York views; many rooms have balconies; seriously luxurious bathrooms. **Cons:** feels clubby on weekends; isolated from some subway lines; a bit pricey. Ⓢ *Rooms from: $395* ✉ *107 Rivington St., between Ludlow and Essex Sts., Lower East Side* ☎ *212/475–2600* ⊕ *www.hotelonrivington.com* ⤳ *108 rooms* ⦿ *No meals* Ⓜ *F to Delancey St.; J, M, Z to Essex St.* ✛ *2:G3.*

$ | ⁛ **The Ludlow Hotel.** A stylish creation from hotelier Sean MacPherson,
HOTEL | this hotel embodies the effortless cool attitude of the Lower East Side, from its cozy lounge with limestone fireplace to the romantic trellis-covered garden. **Pros:** hot restaurant and bar scene; some rooms have terraces and great views; gorgeous bathrooms. **Cons:** lounge and court-yard can get crowded; rooms are small; might be too sceney for some. Ⓢ *Rooms from: $295* ✉ *180 Ludlow St., Lower East Side* ☎ *212/432– 1818* ⊕ *www.ludlowhotel.com* ⤳ *175 rooms* ⦿ *No meals* Ⓜ *F to 2nd Ave.; J, M, Z to Essex St.* ✛ *2:G3.*

$ | ⁛ **PUBLIC.** Ian Schrager's latest and buzziest new hotel brings the Lower
HOTEL | East Side the sleek modern design, state-of-the-art technology, destina-tion dining, and hot bar scene that define every property he touches. **Pros:** sleek design; restaurant by Jean-Georges Vongerichten; white-hot nightlife scene. **Cons:** rooms are small, even by NYC standards; noisy heat and a/c; not all rooms have great views. Ⓢ *Rooms from: $200* ✉ *215 Chrystie St., Lower East Side* ☎ *212/735–6000* ⊕ *www. publichotels.com* ⤳ *367 rooms* ⦿ *No meals* Ⓜ *F to 2nd Ave.* ✛ *2:F3.*

$$$ | ⁛ **Sixty LES.** This hotel is a great embodiment of the neighborhood
HOTEL | inhabitants: hip, but friendly when you get to know it. **Pros:** in the heart of downtown scene; great views from suites; hip rooftop bar and pool. **Cons:** occasionally snobby staff; rooms are stylish but dark; some guests complain about noise. Ⓢ *Rooms from: $465* ✉ *190 Allen St., between Houston and Stanton Sts., Lower East Side* ☎ *877/460–8888* ⊕ *www.sixtyhotels.com/lowereastside* ⤳ *141 rooms* ⦿ *No meals* Ⓜ *F to Delancey St.; J, M, Z to Essex St.* ✛ *2:G3.*

GREENWICH VILLAGE AND THE WEST VILLAGE

GREENWICH VILLAGE

$$ | ⁛ **The Marlton.** Built in 1900 and once home to Jack Kerouac, this hotel
HOTEL | has been renovated into a stylish boutique property with a residential feel. **Pros:** fresh property with luxurious touches; spacious lobby with coffee bar; great Greenwich Village location. **Cons:** very small rooms; no work desks; no room service. Ⓢ *Rooms from: $395* ✉ *5 W. 8th St., Greenwich Village* ☎ *212/321–0100* ⊕ *www.marltonhotel.com* ⤳ *107 rooms* ⦿ *Breakfast* Ⓜ *A, B, C, D, E, F, M to W. 4th St.* ✛ *3:E5.*

$$ | ⁛ **Walker Hotel.** Among the ghosts of the literary salons and speakeasies
HOTEL | of Greenwich Village is the Walker, a boutique property on a tree-lined street with an Art Deco sensibility, where gas lamps and an inconspicuous facade blend the new hotel with the old character of the neighborhood. **Pros:** delivers a true Greenwich Village experience; cozy fireplaces; quiet neighborhood location. **Cons:** small rooms; no connecting rooms; thin walls. Ⓢ *Rooms from: $345* ✉ *52 W. 13th St., between 5th and 6th Aves., Greenwich Village* ☎ *212/375–1300* ⊕ *www.walkerhotel.com* ⤳ *113 rooms* ⦿ *No meals* Ⓜ *1, 2, 3, F, M to 14th St.; L to 6th Ave.* ✛ *3:E4.*

$ HOTEL 🏨 **Washington Square Hotel.** Since 1902, this low-key hotel in Greenwich Village has hosted famous people (Ernest Hemingway, the Rolling Stones, and Bob Dylan all stayed here), and today it is popular with visiting New York University parents thanks to its location near Washington Square Park. **Pros:** park-side location; lots of historic character; great hotel bar. **Cons:** NYU students everywhere in the neighborhood; rooms are small; interior rooms don't get much light. [$] *Rooms from: $246* ✉ *103 Waverly Pl., at MacDougal St., Greenwich Village* ☎ *212/777–9515* 🌐 *www.washingtonsquarehotel.com* 🛏 *152 rooms* 🍴 *Breakfast* [M] *A, B, C, D, E, F, M to W. 4th St.* ⊕ *3:E5.*

WEST VILLAGE

$ HOTEL 🏨 **The Jane.** To some, the Jane is impossibly chic; to others, the tiny rooms with single beds and a shared unisex bathroom down the hall are reminiscent of Sing Sing. **Pros:** extraordinary value for the neighborhood; hot bar scene; gorgeous decor in lounge; great branch of weekend-brunch favorite Café Gitane; convenient neighborhood for downtown sightseeing. **Cons:** impossibly tiny standard rooms; some rooms have shared bathrooms; noise from the bar. [$] *Rooms from: $99* ✉ *113 Jane St., at West St., West Village* ☎ *212/924–6700* 🌐 *www.thejanenyc.com* 🛏 *171 rooms* 🍴 *No meals* [M] *A, C, E to 14th St.; L to 8th Ave.* ⊕ *3:B5.*

16

CHELSEA AND THE MEATPACKING DISTRICT

CHELSEA

$ HOTEL 🏨 **The GEM Hotel Chelsea.** At this stylish, well-priced boutique hotel, the modern rooms are small but designed to make the most of limited space. **Pros:** great Chelsea location near galleries and restaurants; close to several subway lines; in-room coffeemakers. **Cons:** gym and business center, both on the lower level, feel like a work in progress; rooms may be too small for some; no restaurant or room service. [$] *Rooms from: $260* ✉ *300 W. 22nd St., Chelsea* ☎ *212/675–1911* 🌐 *www.thegemhotel.com* 🛏 *81 rooms* 🍴 *No meals* [M] *1, C, E to 23rd St.* ⊕ *3:C3.*

$$ HOTEL Fodor's Choice ★ 🏨 **High Line Hotel.** A late-19th-century, redbrick, Gothic-style building on the landscaped grounds of a former seminary was transformed into this lovely hotel, full of original architectural details like stained-glass windows and pine floors. **Pros:** historic property with garden and lots of character; gorgeous design from top to bottom; close to the High Line; quality coffee bar in the lobby. **Cons:** doesn't have the best subway access; outdoor restaurant only open from May to October; no gym on-site. [$] *Rooms from: $395* ✉ *180 10th Ave., at 20th St., Chelsea* ☎ *212/929–3888* 🌐 *www.thehighlinehotel.com* 🛏 *60 rooms* 🍴 *No meals* [M] *C, E to 23rd St.* ⊕ *3:A3.*

$$$ HOTEL 🏨 **Hotel Americano.** This boutique property, which overlooks the High Line, captures the artistic and stylish spirit of Chelsea. **Pros:** year-round rooftop pool and bar; views overlooking the High Line; near the thriving gallery scene in Chelsea. **Cons:** low beds; bathrooms lack privacy; some furniture is form over function. [$] *Rooms from: $480* ✉ *518 W. 27th St., between 10th and 11th Aves., Chelsea* ☎ *212/216–0000* 🌐 *www.hotel-americano.com* 🛏 *56 rooms* 🍴 *No meals* [M] *C, E to 23rd St.* ⊕ *3:A1.*

$ HOTEL FAMILY

Kimpton Hotel Eventi. This hotel adds a touch of style just below Penn Station in an area desperately in need of new lodging options, with spacious guest rooms, comfortable beds, oversize bathrooms, and floor-to-ceiling windows. **Pros:** complimentary happy hour and morning coffee; relaxing spa; nice gym and bikes available to borrow. **Cons:** crowded lobby; few nightlife and dining options nearby; located in a forlorn part of Chelsea. [$] *Rooms from: $209* ✉ *851 6th Ave., at 30th St., Chelsea* ☎ *212/564–4567* 🌐 *www.hoteleventi.com* 🛏 *292 rooms* 🍴 *No meals* [M] *N, R, W to 28th St.* ✣ *3:D1.*

$$ HOTEL

The Maritime Hotel. The Maritime's white-ceramic tower, the former HQ for the National Maritime Union, was the first luxury hotel to be opened in the Chelsea gallery district, and the property still feels a bit nautical: the small rooms resemble modern ship cabins, with burnished teak paneling, sea-blue drapes and bed accents, and 5-foot "portholes" that face the Hudson River skyline. **Pros:** fun rooms with big porthole windows; great location near Chelsea Market and the Chelsea galleries; trendy restaurant. **Cons:** street noise; small rooms; no gym or spa. [$] *Rooms from: $395* ✉ *363 W. 16th St., at 9th Ave., Chelsea* ☎ *212/242–4300* 🌐 *www.themaritimehotel.com* 🛏 *126 rooms* 🍴 *Breakfast* [M] *A, C, E to 14th St.; L to 8th Ave.* ✣ *3:B4.*

$ HOTEL

Riff Chelsea. Formerly the Chelsea Star, this hotel has a rich music history (Madonna crashed here in the '80s) and a creative spirit, from the rock-star-inspired rooms to the ground-floor art gallery. **Pros:** central location near Penn Station; good value option; fresh, bold decor. **Cons:** some rooms have shared bathrooms; no elevator; no full-service restaurant. [$] *Rooms from: $149* ✉ *300 W. 30th St., at 8th Ave., Chelsea* ☎ *212/244–7827* 🌐 *www.riffhotels.com* 🛏 *43 rooms* 🍴 *No meals* [M] *1, 2, 3, A, C, E to 34th St.–Penn Station* ✣ *3:C1.*

MEATPACKING DISTRICT

$$ HOTEL

Gansevoort Meatpacking. Though the nearby Standard, High Line has stolen some of its thunder, there's still plenty to draw guests to this chic Meatpacking District pioneer, starting with the sleek rooms that overlook the city or the Hudson River and the rooftop deck with a 45-foot heated pool. **Pros:** rooftop pool; wonderful art collection; great location for restaurants and shopping. **Cons:** location can seem too trendy, especially at night; service can be slipshod; guests might encounter disturbances from ongoing renovation in 2018. [$] *Rooms from: $425* ✉ *18 9th Ave., at 13th St., Meatpacking District* ☎ *212/206–6700* 🌐 *www.gansevoorthotelgroup.com* 🛏 *163 rooms* 🍴 *No meals* [M] *A, C, E to 14th St.; L to 8th Ave.* ✣ *3:B4.*

$$ HOTEL Fodor's Choice ★

The Standard, High Line. This modern architectural statement on the West Side is still one of New York's hottest hotels, with the High Line running underneath it, a lobby full of glamorous types, an authentic beer garden (open year-round; dig the Ping-Pong tables), and the 18th-floor nightclub that is one of the toughest doors in town. **Pros:** beautiful building with sweeping views; beautiful people; impressive restaurant space. **Cons:** noisy at night; tight rooms; can be too sceney. [$] *Rooms from: $395* ✉ *848 Washington St., between 13th and Little W. 12th Sts., Meatpacking District* ☎ *212/645–4646* 🌐 *www.standardhotels.com* 🛏 *388 rooms* 🍴 *No meals* [M] *A, C, E to 14th St.; L to 8th Ave.* ✣ *3:B4.*

UNION SQUARE, FLATIRON DISTRICT, AND GRAMERCY

UNION SQUARE

$$ **Hyatt Union Square New York.** Experiencing a bit of "real" New York
HOTEL (and getting away from Midtown) is easy at this Hyatt just south of
Fodor'sChoice Union Square in a newly built tower with a restaurant, Library of
★ Distilled Spirits lounge, an on-site gym, and bikes to borrow. **Pros:**
convenient and vibrant location; buzzy dining and drinking outlets;
complimentary bikes available. **Cons:** feels a bit corporate; some stan-
dard rooms are small; high-traffic area. $ *Rooms from: $399* ✉ *134
4th Ave., Union Square* ☎ *212/253–1234* ⊕ *www.unionsquare.hyatt.
com* ⤶ *178 rooms* ⦿|*No meals* Ⓜ *4, 5, 6, L, N, Q, R, W to 14th
St.–Union Sq.* ✛ *3:F4.*

$$ **W New York Union Square.** The W chain's iconic New York City prop-
HOTEL erty continues to attract a mix of trendsetters and tourists, thanks to its
downtown location and funky style. **Pros:** landmark building in fashionable location; great restaurant; 24-hour room service. **Cons:** noisy
lobby; daily fee for Wi-Fi; small gym. $ *Rooms from: $325* ✉ *201 Park
Ave. S, at 17th St., Union Square* ☎ *212/253–9119* ⊕ *www.wnewyor-
kunionsquare.com* ⤶ *270 rooms* ⦿|*No meals* Ⓜ *4, 5, 6, L, N, Q, R,
W to 14th St.–Union Sq.* ✛ *3:F3.*

FLATIRON DISTRICT

$$ **Ace Hotel New York.** The Ace is not your ordinary boutique hotel;
HOTEL the lively lobby melds Ivy League library with curiosity cabinet—taxi-
Fodor'sChoice dermy, mosaic tile floors, wooden bookcases, antique sofas—while the
★ staff wear custom Levi's and Converse sneakers. **Pros:** in-house destina-
tion restaurants; supercool but friendly vibe; unfussy yet stylish. **Cons:**
dark lobby; caters to a young crowd; may be too sceney for some.
$ *Rooms from: $339* ✉ *20 W. 29th St., at Broadway, Flatiron District*
☎ *212/679–2222* ⊕ *www.acehotel.com/newyork* ⤶ *285 rooms* ⦿|*No
meals* Ⓜ *N, R, W to 28th St.* ✛ *3:E1.*

$ **Arlo NoMad.** Aimed at travelers who spend more time out and about
HOTEL than in their rooms, this microhotel opened in 2016 with a major
emphasis on stylish and functional social spaces, including *Top Chef*
alum Dale Talde's restaurant, Massoni, and a rooftop bar with unbeat-
able views of the Empire State Building. **Pros:** rooms feature smart,
space-saving design; great restaurant and rooftop bar; complimentary
bikes. **Cons:** tiny rooms may seem claustrophobic; no in-room minibars;
self-check-in isn't for everyone. $ *Rooms from: $199* ✉ *11 E. 31st
St., Flatiron District* ☎ *212/806–7000* ⊕ *www.arlohotels.com* ⤶ *249
rooms* ⦿|*No meals* Ⓜ *6 to 33rd St; B, D, F, M, N, Q, R, W to 34th
St.–Herald Sq.* ✛ *3:E1.*

$$ **Hotel Giraffe by Library Hotel Collection.** A consistent property with
HOTEL friendly service, large rooms, and lots of repeat customers (particu-
larly business travelers), Hotel Giraffe pleases with nice extras such
as a complimentary nightly wine-and-cheese reception. **Pros:** rooftop
terrace for guests; quiet hotel; nice extras like free breakfast and coffee all day. **Cons:** street noise near lower levels; no full-service restaurant; no gym on-site. $ *Rooms from: $449* ✉ *365 Park Ave. S, at 26th*

16

St., Flatiron District ☎ *212/685–7700* 🌐 *www.hotelgiraffe.com* 🛏 *72 rooms* 🍴 *Breakfast* [M] *6 to 28th St.* ✥ *3:F2.*

$$ HOTEL **James New York - NoMad.** The latest outpost of the hip hotel brand that became a phenomenon in SoHo, the James NoMad brings another stylish option to an emerging neighborhood. **Pros:** sleek design; iPads available on loan in the James Club; hit Italian restaurant Scarpetta. **Cons:** some rooms have views of brick walls; inconsistent service; street noise can be bothersome. [$] *Rooms from: $389* ✉ *22 E. 29th St., Flatiron District* ☎ *212/532–4100* 🌐 *www.jameshotels.com/new-york/nomad* 🛏 *344 rooms* 🍴 *No meals* [M] *R, W to 28th St; 6 to 28th St.* ✥ *3:F1.*

$ HOTEL **Life Hotel.** In the former headquarters of *Life* magazine designed by legendary Beaux Arts architecture firm Carrère & Hastings, this boutique hotel channels the building's past with reclaimed wood paneling, a restaurant named after the magazine's founder (Henry Luce), and a speakeasy where staffers imbibed during Prohibition. **Pros:** historic building with lots of character; great restaurant and speakeasy; some suites have great Empire State Building views. **Cons:** some rooms are tiny and lack views; no real lobby (street entrance opens onto the restaurant); noisy a/c units. [$] *Rooms from: $250* ✉ *19 W. 31st St., Flatiron District* ☎ *212/615–9900* 🌐 *www.lifehotel.com* 🛏 *98 rooms* 🍴 *No meals* [M] *B, D, F, M, N, Q, R, W to 34th St./Herald Sq.* ✥ *3:E1.*

$$ HOTEL **MADE Hotel.** Found in the centrally located NoMad neighborhood, MADE takes everything people love about the designer boutique hotel trend (hip design, rooftop bar, buzzy restaurant) and doubles down on the luxury and comfort. **Pros:** cool design; great rooftop bar and restaurant; friendly staff. **Cons:** little storage space; scant in-room amenities (no fridge or iron); some rooms have peek-a-boo bathrooms that lack privacy. [$] *Rooms from: $395* ✉ *44 W. 29th St., Flatiron District* ☎ *212/213–4429* 🌐 *madehotels.com* 🛏 *108 rooms* 🍴 *No meals* [M] *R, W to 28th St.* ✥ *3:E1.*

$$ HOTEL Fodor's Choice ★ **The New York EDITION.** The landmarked clock tower (built in 1909 for Metropolitan Life) overlooking Madison Square Park is now an übersleek bolthole masterminded by renowned hotelier Ian Schrager, with neutral-toned rooms, a luxurious lobby bar, and a Michelin-starred restaurant by British chef Jason Atheron. **Pros:** luxe modern design in a landmarked building; destination restaurant; upscale amenities by Le Labo, plus Beats bluetooth speakers. **Cons:** expensive; limited nightlife options in the neighborhood; might be too sceney for some. [$] *Rooms from: $400* ✉ *5 Madison Ave., at 24th St., Flatiron District* ☎ *212/413–4200* 🌐 *www.editionhotels.com/new-york* 🛏 *273 rooms* 🍴 *No meals* [M] *R, W to 23rd St.* ✥ *3:F2.*

$$$ HOTEL Fodor's Choice ★ **The NoMad Hotel.** Named for the emerging "North of Madison" (that is, Madison Square Park) neighborhood in which it's located, this upscale-bohemian property features a gorgeous design by Jacques Garcia, a restaurant by award-winning chef Daniel Humm of Eleven Madison Park fame, and a destination cocktail bar. **Pros:** 24-hour room service; quality, trendy on-site dining and drinking; central location. **Cons:** exposed bathtubs lack privacy; pricey; the bar gets crowded. [$] *Rooms from: $550* ✉ *1170 Broadway, at 28th St., Flatiron District* ☎ *212/796–1500* 🌐 *www.thenomadhotel.com* 🛏 *168 rooms* 🍴 *No meals* [M] *R, W to 28th St.* ✥ *3:E2.*

$ HOTEL **Park South Hotel.** In this beautifully transformed 1906 office building, now part of Joie de Vivre hotels, guest rooms feel smartly contemporary, though they've retained some period details; the modernized lobby is a comfortable place to lounge; and four restaurants and bars by restaurateurs Tim and Nancy Cushman include the upscale Japanese restaurant o ya and Covina. **Pros:** fantastic restaurants and bars; upgraded rooms and lobby; good value. **Cons:** some noisy rooms; small rooms and bathrooms; no room service. [$] *Rooms from: $189* ✉ *124 E. 28th St., between Lexington and Park Aves., Flatiron District* ☎ *212/448–0888* 🌐 *www.parksouthhotel.com* 🛏 *131 rooms* 🍴 *No meals* [M] *6 to 28th St.* ⊕ *3:F2.*

$ HOTEL **The Redbury.** Convenient to the action without being smack in the middle of it is the Redbury, a stylish hotel with three Roman-inspired dining venues by acclaimed restaurateur Danny Meyer on the ground floor, including the pizzeria Marta (reserve ahead) and wine bar Vini e Fritti. **Pros:** trendy but not over-the-top; three excellent dining and drinking venues; good value. **Cons:** sceney restaurant can be loud and crowd the lobby; lower floors lack views and can feel a bit basement-y; neighborhood a bit dull. [$] *Rooms from: $259* ✉ *29 E. 29th St., between Park and Madison Aves., Flatiron District* ☎ *212/689–1900* 🌐 *www.theredbury.com/newyork* 🛏 *257 rooms* 🍴 *No meals* [M] *6 to 28th St.* ⊕ *3:F1.*

$ HOTEL **The Roger.** A colorful choice in a rather plain neighborhood, the Roger continues to have a following among repeat visitors to New York. **Pros:** colorful room decor; friendly service; good value. **Cons:** no room service; tiny bathrooms; no free in-room coffee or tea. [$] *Rooms from: $191* ✉ *131 Madison Ave., at 31st St., Flatiron District* ☎ *212/448–7000* 🌐 *www.therogernewyork.com* 🛏 *192 rooms* 🍴 *No meals* [M] *6 to 33rd St.* ⊕ *3:F1.*

GRAMERCY

$ HOTEL **Carlton Arms.** Europeans and students know about the chipper, winning attitude of this friendly, no-frills hotel, where the rooms are painted by artists on a rotating basis. **Pros:** rock-bottom prices; friendly attitude; quieter residential location. **Cons:** no elevator; many rooms have shared baths; no TVs or phones in the rooms. [$] *Rooms from: $130* ✉ *160 E. 25th St., at 3rd Ave., Gramercy* ☎ *212/684–8337, 212/679–0680 for reservations* 🌐 *www.carltonarms.com* 🛏 *54 rooms* 🍴 *No meals* [M] *6 to 23rd St.* ⊕ *3:G2.*

$ HOTEL Fodor's Choice ★ **Freehand New York.** The New York location of this hip hostel-hotel hybrid combines a chic, homey design by Roman and Williams, four restaurants and bars (including Middle Eastern spot Studio and an outpost of Miami's award-winning Broken Shaker on the roof), and accommodations from shared bunk rooms to a two-bedroom penthouse suite. **Pros:** destination dining and drinking; great value; fun, social vibe. **Cons:** rooms and suites are on the small side; no bathtubs in any rooms; bunk rooms are a set price regardless of number of occupants. [$] *Rooms from: $129* ✉ *23 Lexington Ave., between 23rd and 24th Sts., Gramercy* ☎ *212/475–1920* 🌐 *www.freehandhotels.com* 🛏 *395 rooms* 🍴 *No meals* [M] *6 to 23rd St.* ⊕ *3:G2.*

$$$ HOTEL Fodor's Choice ★

🏨 **Gramercy Park Hotel.** A completely over-the-top, bold design, an impressive art collection, and Danny Meyer's Roman trattoria Maialino make this luxury boutique property—and celebrity magnet—stand out. **Pros:** trendy bar scene; opulent rooms; great restaurant; park-side location. **Cons:** inconsistent service; expensive bar; might be too sceney for some. [$] *Rooms from: $450* ✉ *2 Lexington Ave., at Gramercy Park, Gramercy* ☎ *212/920–3300* 🌐 *www.gramercyparkhotel.com* 🛏 *190 rooms* 🍴 *No meals* [M] *6 to 23rd St.* ✣ *3:G3.*

$$ HOTEL Fodor's Choice ★

🏨 **The Inn at Irving Place.** Fantasies of Old New York—Manhattan straight from the pages of Edith Wharton and Henry James, an era of genteel brick town houses and Tiffany lamps—spring to life at this discreet, romantic inn. **Pros:** romantic and charming; big rooms; excellent breakfast and tea service. **Cons:** rooms show some wear; some street noise; no elevator and lots of stairs. [$] *Rooms from: $445* ✉ *56 Irving Pl., between 17th and 18th Sts., Gramercy* ☎ *212/533–4600* 🌐 *www.innatirving.com* 🛏 *8 rooms* 🍴 *Breakfast* [M] *4, 5, 6, L, N, Q, R, W to 14th St.–Union Sq.* ✣ *3:G3.*

$$ HOTEL

🏨 **Marcel at Gramercy.** The chic, affordable Marcel gives guests both style and substance in a prime location; for example, the small lobby feels a bit like a swanky nightclub but is still comfortable for lounging. **Pros:** outdoor patio has spectacular views of the city; good value; great location. **Cons:** elevators are slow; some rooms are tight on space; decor not to everyone's taste. [$] *Rooms from: $309* ✉ *201 E. 24th St., Gramercy* ☎ *212/696–3800* 🌐 *www.themarcelatgramercy.com* 🛏 *136 rooms* 🍴 *No meals* [M] *6 to 23rd St.* ✣ *3:G2.*

MIDTOWN EAST AND MURRAY HILL

MIDTOWN EAST

$$$ HOTEL

🏨 **Andaz 5th Avenue.** The serene and spacious rooms at this chic, modern property evoke that coveted New York loft feel, with floor-to-ceiling windows that look out over 5th Avenue and the New York Public Library. **Pros:** spacious and stylish; suites have outdoor space; good dining and drinking options. **Cons:** pricey; busy location might not suit all guests; no closets mean little storage space. [$] *Rooms from: $499* ✉ *485 5th Ave., at 41st St., Midtown East* ☎ *212/601–1234* 🌐 *andaz.hyatt.com* 🛏 *184 rooms* 🍴 *No meals* [M] *4, 5, 6, 7, S to Grand Central–42nd St.* ✣ *4:E4.*

$$ HOTEL FAMILY

🏨 **The Benjamin.** NYC is often called the city that never sleeps, but if a good night's rest is essential for your visit, the Benjamin may be your choice accommodation—with a menu of 12 pillows to choose from (including buckwheat, water, and Swedish memory varieties), white-noise machines, and 500-thread-count sheets, they've got it covered. **Pros:** sleep-friendly; kitchenettes in big rooms; gracious staff. **Cons:** decor a bit generic; boring views; dull neighborhood after dark. [$] *Rooms from: $349* ✉ *125 E. 50th St., at Lexington Ave., Midtown East* ☎ *212/715–2500* 🌐 *www.thebenjamin.com* 🛏 *209 rooms* 🍴 *No meals* [M] *6 to 51st St.; E, M to Lexington Ave./53rd St.* ✣ *4:F3.*

$$$$ HOTEL

🏨 **Four Seasons Hotel New York.** For better or worse, Four Seasons Hotel New York remains the blueprint for what a Manhattan luxury hotel should be, with stellar service, an imposing lobby done in marble and blond wood, and a well-connected concierge who can get reservations for most of New York's hot tables. **Pros:** spacious and comfortable rooms; perfect concierge and staff service; cocktails in Ty Bar. **Cons:** very pricey; confusing room controls; some furniture could use updating. $ *Rooms from: $995* ✉ *57 E. 57th St., between Park and Madison Aves., Midtown East* ☎ *212/758–5700* ⊕ *www.fourseasons.com/newyork* ⤳ *368 suites* ⦿| *No meals* Ⓜ *4, 5, 6 to 59th St.; N, R, W to Lexington Ave./59th St.* ✛ *4:F1.*

$$ 🖳 **The Gotham Hotel.** This sleek hotel has a lot going for it, but a clincher
HOTEL is that every room has outdoor space. **Pros:** welcoming staff; central location; every room has a balcony. **Cons:** no on-site gym; some balconies are tiny; valet parking is expensive. $ *Rooms from: $350* ✉ *16 E. 46 St., between 5th and Madison Aves., Midtown East* ☎ *212/490–8500* ⊕ *www.thegothamhotelny.com* ⤳ *66 rooms* ⦿| *No meals* Ⓜ *B, D, F, M to 47th–50th Sts./Rockefeller Center; 4, 5, 6, 7, S to Grand Central–42nd St.* ✛ *4:E4.*

$$ 🖳 **Grand Hyatt New York.** Conveniently located near Grand Central, this
HOTEL historic hotel (originally built as the Commodore in 1919) is now a sleek and modern central hub. **Pros:** comfy beds; light-filled gym on a high floor; refreshing modern design; large, well-planned rooms. **Cons:** no in-room minibar; lacking in character; located in a high-traffic area. $ *Rooms from: $429* ✉ *109 E. 42nd St., between Park and Lexington Aves., Midtown East* ☎ *212/883–1234* ⊕ *newyork.grand.hyatt.com* ⤳ *1,341 rooms* ⦿| *No meals* Ⓜ *4, 5, 6, 7, S to Grand Central–42nd St.* ✛ *4:F4.*

$$$ 🖳 **The Langham, New York, Fifth Avenue.** Setting new standards for luxury,
HOTEL this towering, limestone-clad 5th Avenue hotel (formerly the Setai Fifth Avenue) is an opulent crash pad for wealthy overseas tourists, captains of industry on long-term stays, and anyone in need of some serious pampering. **Pros:** attentive service; gorgeous spa; quality dining. **Cons:** street noise reported by guests on lower floors; pricey; high-traffic location. $ *Rooms from: $595* ✉ *400 5th Ave., Midtown East* ☎ *212/695–4005* ⊕ *www.langhamhotels.com/newyork* ⤳ *234 rooms* ⦿| *No meals* Ⓜ *B, D, F, M, N, Q, R, W to 34th St.–Herald Sq.* ✛ *4:E6.*

$$ 🖳 **Library Hotel by Library Hotel Collection.** Bookishly handsome, this
HOTEL stately landmark brownstone, built in 1900, is inspired by the nearby
Fodor's Choice New York Public Library—each of its 10 floors is dedicated to one of
★ the 10 categories of the Dewey Decimal System and is stocked with art and books relevant to subtopics such as erotica, astronomy, or biography—let your interests guide your room choice. **Pros:** fun rooftop bar; access to best-selling e-books via app; complimentary wine and cheese. **Cons:** no full-service restaurant; no gym on-site; no rooms with two double beds. $ *Rooms from: $399* ✉ *299 Madison Ave., at 41st St., Midtown East* ☎ *212/983–4500, 212/983–4500* ⊕ *www.libraryhotel.com* ⤳ *60 rooms* ⦿| *Breakfast* Ⓜ *4, 5, 6, 7, S to Grand Central–42nd St.* ✛ *4:E4.*

$$$ 🖳 **Lotte New York Palace.** From the moment you enter the gilded gates
HOTEL of these connected mansions, originally built in the 1880s by railroad baron Henry Villard, you know you're somewhere special; there's a

16

reason this is called the Palace. **Pros:** luxury house car service; great service; unmatched views of St. Patrick's Cathedral. **Cons:** high prices; harried staff; expensive Wi-Fi. [$] *Rooms from: $450* ✉ *455 Madison Ave., at 50th St., Midtown East* ☎ *212/888–7000* 🌐 *www.lottenypalace.com* 🛏 *909 rooms* 🍴 *No meals* [M] *6 to 51st St.; E, M to Lexington Ave./53rd St.* ✥ *4:E3.*

$ HOTEL 🏨 **Millennium Hilton New York One UN Plaza.** In a sky-high tower near the landmark United Nations building, this branch of the Hilton starts on the 28th floor and has fabulous views—ask for a room facing west, toward Manhattan's skyline. **Pros:** unbeatable East River and city views; good value; great front-door and bell staff. **Cons:** a far walk to the subway; pricey Internet access; corporate vibe. [$] *Rooms from: $299* ✉ *1 United Nations Plaza, 44th St. and 1st Ave., Midtown East* ☎ *212/758–1234* 🌐 *www3.hilton.com* 🛏 *439 rooms* 🍴 *No meals* [M] *4, 5, 6, 7, S to Grand Central–42nd St.* ✥ *4:H4.*

$$$$ HOTEL Fodor's Choice ★ 🏨 **The Peninsula New York.** Stepping through the Peninsula's Beaux Arts facade onto the grand staircase overhung with a monumental chandelier, you know you're in for a glitzy treat. **Pros:** brilliant service; fabulous rooms with convenient controls; unforgettable rooftop bar. **Cons:** expensive; high-traffic area, especially on weekends; limited dining options nearby. [$] *Rooms from: $1,195* ✉ *700 5th Ave., at 55th St., Midtown East* ☎ *212/956–2888* 🌐 *www.peninsula.com/newyork* 🛏 *235 rooms* 🍴 *No meals* [M] *E, M to 5th Ave./53rd St.* ✥ *4:E2.*

$ HOTEL 🏨 **Pod 51.** If cramped quarters don't bother you, this is one of the best deals in town, with rooms that borrow space-saving ideas from mass transit, including sink consoles like those in an airplane restroom and built-in shelves under the beds. **Pros:** great prices; fun design; buzzy on-site dining and drinking. **Cons:** not for claustrophobes; many rooms share baths; no gym. [$] *Rooms from: $179* ✉ *230 E. 51st St., between 2nd and 3rd Aves., Midtown East* ☎ *844/763–7666* 🌐 *www.thepodhotel.com* 🛏 *345 rooms (189 with private bath)* 🍴 *No meals* [M] *6 to 51st St.; E, M to Lexington Ave./53rd St.* ✥ *4:G2.*

$ HOTEL 🏨 **Roger Smith.** This quirky choice is one of the better affordable stays in the city; the art-filled rooms, matched by the murals in the lobby, are homey and comfortable. **Pros:** good location near Grand Central; intimate atmosphere; free yogurt and granola 24/7. **Cons:** street noise; small bathrooms; feels a bit dated. [$] *Rooms from: $297* ✉ *501 Lexington Ave., between 47th and 48th Sts., Midtown East* ☎ *212/755–1400* 🌐 *www.rogersmith.com* 🛏 *130 rooms* 🍴 *No meals* [M] *6 to 51st St.; E, M to Lexington Ave./53rd St.* ✥ *4:F3.*

$ HOTEL 🏨 **The Roosevelt Hotel.** Named after Teddy, not Franklin, this Midtown icon just steps from Grand Central has an ornate lobby with cushy couches and an old-school bar detailed in heavy wood that makes the place feel like it's from another time, and it is—the property dates from 1924. **Pros:** great public areas; big bathrooms; comfortable rooftop lounge. **Cons:** dated design; limited in-room amenities; no pool or spa. [$] *Rooms from: $199* ✉ *45 E. 45th St., at Madison Ave., Midtown East* ☎ *212/661–9600* 🌐 *www.theroosevelthotel.com* 🛏 *1,015 rooms* 🍴 *No meals* [M] *4, 5, 6, 7, S to Grand Central–42nd St.* ✥ *4:F4.*

$$$$
HOTEL
Fodor's Choice
★
🏨 **The St. Regis New York.** World-class from head to toe, this 5th Avenue Beaux Arts landmark comes as close to flawless as any hotel in New York, with tech-savvy rooms, historic touches, and the iconic King Cole Bar. Butlers have been catering to the whims of each and every guest since the St. Regis first opened its doors in 1904, a touch no other New York hotel can match. **Pros:** classic NYC favorite; rooms combine true luxury with helpful technology; easy-access butler service; superb in-house dining; prestigious location. **Cons:** expensive; too serious for families seeking fun; standard rooms don't have soaking tubs. ⓢ *Rooms from: $995* ✉ *2 E. 55th St., at 5th Ave., Midtown East* ☎ *212/753–4500* ⊕ *www.stregisnewyork.com* ⇥ *171 rooms* ⦿ *No meals* Ⓜ *E, M to 5th Ave./53rd St.* ✛ *4:E2.*

$
HOTEL
🏨 **W New York.** A hopping bar and sunken lounge in the reception area, funky decor touches like window boxes filled with grass, and guest rooms that hew to the classic brand formula—they're small but they look good—make this a quintessential W property. **Pros:** central location; great-looking rooms; Bliss Spa in hotel. **Cons:** thin walls; small rooms; inconsistent service. ⓢ *Rooms from: $239* ✉ *541 Lexington Ave., between 49th and 50th Sts., Midtown East* ☎ *212/755–1200* ⊕ *www.wnewyork.com* ⇥ *696 rooms* ⦿ *No meals* Ⓜ *6 to 51st St.; E, M to Lexington Ave./53rd St.* ✛ *4:F3.*

16

MURRAY HILL

$
HOTEL
🏨 **Iberostar 70 Park Avenue.** A Midtown business-traveler favorite, the lobby and rooms here are infused with a soft color palette and modern furniture. **Pros:** some rooms have Empire State Building views; polite service; simple rooms and hotel layout. **Cons:** small rooms; design and art might not suit all tastes; some bathrooms are especially cramped. ⓢ *Rooms from: $180* ✉ *70 Park Ave., at 38th St., Murray Hill* ☎ *212/973–2400, 800/707–2752* ⊕ *www.iberostar.com* ⇥ *205 rooms* ⦿ *No meals* Ⓜ *4, 5, 6, 7, S to Grand Central–42nd St.* ✛ *4:F5.*

$$$
HOTEL
🏨 **Marmara Park Avenue.** A popular pick for extended-stay travelers, this sleek property impresses with large rooms complete with conveniences of home, like wet bars or fully equipped kitchens. **Pros:** lots of amenities in rooms; serene lap pool, sauna, and steam room; many suites have private terraces. **Cons:** neighborhood isn't the most exciting; limited subway access nearby; pricey. ⓢ *Rooms from: $500* ✉ *114 E. 32nd St., Murray Hill* ☎ *212/603–9000* ⊕ *park.marmaranyc.com* ⇥ *128 rooms* ⦿ *No meals* Ⓜ *6 to 33rd St.* ✛ *3:F1.*

$
HOTEL
🏨 **Pod 39.** The cheap and cheerful sibling of Pod 51 (on 51st Street) has tight quarters and trendy amenities, including a rooftop bar and ground-floor restaurant by famed chef April Bloomfield. **Pros:** quality taco and cocktail spot; big rooftop with gorgeous views; lobby lounge with Ping-Pong table. **Cons:** tight quarters; buzzy lobby and restaurant might not suit all guests; no gym or pool. ⓢ *Rooms from: $229* ✉ *145 E. 39th St, between Lexington and 3rd Aves., Murray Hill* ☎ *844/763–7666* ⊕ *www.thepodhotel.com* ⇥ *366 rooms* ⦿ *No meals* Ⓜ *4, 5, 6, 7, S to Grand Central–42nd St.* ✛ *4:G5.*

$$
HOTEL
🏨 **The William.** What was once two connected brownstones home to a social club for Williams College is now a modern, extended-stay hotel with an outpost of the fabulous speakeasy-style cocktail bar Raines

Law Room. **Pros:** convenient fully equipped kitchens; central location near Grand Central; good eating and drinking options. **Cons:** color and design may be too bright and modern for some guests; no gym or spa on-site; limited restaurants and nightlife in the neighborhood. $ *Rooms from: $350* ⊠ *24 E. 39th St., between Park and Madison Aves., Murray Hill* ☎ *646/922–8600* ⊕ *www.thewilliamnyc.com* ⇨ *33 rooms* ᴏᴵ *No meals* Ⓜ *4, 5, 6, 7, S to Grand Central–42nd St* ✛ *4:F5.*

MIDTOWN WEST

$ 🏨 **The Algonquin, Autograph Collection.** One of Manhattan's most historic
HOTEL properties, the Algonquin is a landmark of literary history—think oak paneling and pillars in the lobby—but with modernized rooms and contemporary comforts. **Pros:** historic character in spades; friendly, knowledgeable staff; hotel cat keeps guests company. **Cons:** some small rooms; might feel a bit old-fashioned to some; no gym on-site. $ *Rooms from: $289* ⊠ *59 W. 44th St., between 5th and 6th Aves., Midtown West* ☎ *212/840–6800* ⊕ *www.algonquinhotel.com* ⇨ *181 rooms* ᴏᴵ *No meals* Ⓜ *7 to 5th Ave.; B, D, F, M to 42nd St.–Bryant Park* ✛ *4:D4.*

$$ 🏨 **Archer Hotel.** Rooftop bar Skyglass, with its killer view of the Empire
HOTEL State Building, is the star of this quirky new-build property just south of Bryant Park with a subtly industrial-inspired look that nods to the neighborhood's past. **Pros:** rooftop bar; whimsical design and ambience; reasonably priced for Manhattan. **Cons:** small rooms; lack of amenities including gym or spa; convenient but unglamorous location. $ *Rooms from: $449* ⊠ *45 W. 38th St., Midtown West* ☎ *855/437–9100* ⊕ *www.archerhotel.com* ⇨ *180 rooms* ᴏᴵ *No meals* Ⓜ *B, D, F, M, 7 to 42nd St.–Bryant Park* ✛ *4:D5.*

$$$$ 🏨 **Baccarat Hotel & Residences.** This polished property provides pure
HOTEL luxury at every corner, from the emphasis on quality service to the glamorous, flower-filled salon and bar where all the drinks are served in Baccarat glassware. **Pros:** glamorous dining and drinking options; all rooms are stocked with Baccarat glassware; serene swimming pool and La Mer spa. **Cons:** very expensive; no coffee machine in standard rooms; inconsistent service. $ *Rooms from: $1,000* ⊠ *28 W. 53rd St., Midtown West* ☎ *212/790–8800* ⊕ *www.baccarathotels.com* ⇨ *114 rooms* ᴏᴵ *No meals* Ⓜ *E, M to 5th Ave./53rd St.* ✛ *4:D2.*

$$ 🏨 **Bryant Park Hotel.** A city landmark that towers over the New York
HOTEL Public Library and Bryant Park, this sleek hotel is still a Midtown hot spot. **Pros:** gorgeous building; fashionable crowd and setting; across from pretty Bryant Park. **Cons:** expensive; not kid-friendly; limited dining and nightlife in the area. $ *Rooms from: $395* ⊠ *40 W. 40th St., between 5th and 6th Aves., Midtown West* ☎ *212/869–0100* ⊕ *www.bryantparkhotel.com* ⇨ *128 rooms* ᴏᴵ *No meals* Ⓜ *B, D, F, M to 42nd St.–Bryant Park; 7 to 5th Ave.* ✛ *4:D5.*

$$ 🏨 **Casablanca Hotel by Library Hotel Collection.** A favorite for the com-
HOTEL fortable rooms and great location, the Casablanca evokes the sultry Mediterranean with its colors and decor. **Pros:** great access to the Theater District; free continental breakfast and evening wine-and-cheese reception; access to best-selling e-books via app. **Cons:** exercise facilities at nearby New York Sports Club, not on premises; heavy tourist

foot traffic; no full-service restaurant. $ *Rooms from: $369* ✉ *147 W. 43rd St., Midtown West* ☎ *212/869–1212* ⊕ *www.casablancahotel.com* 📭 *45 rooms* ⦿*Breakfast* Ⓜ *1, 2, 3, 7, N, Q, R, S, W to Times Sq.– 42nd St.* ✛ *4:C4.*

$$$ 🏨 **The Chatwal New York.** A lavishly refurbished reincarnation of a classic
HOTEL Manhattan theater club, the Chatwal delivers a stylish, luxury experi-
Fodor'sChoice ence with a matching price tag. **Pros:** gorgeous lobby; state-of-the-art
★ room controls and amenities; quality dining, bar, and spa. **Cons:** some
visitors may find the price too high for the Times Square location; tiny
pool barely big enough to swim laps in; breakfast not included in rate.
$ *Rooms from: $545* ✉ *130 W. 44th St., between Broadway and 6th Ave., Midtown West* ☎ *212/764–6200* ⊕ *www.thechatwalny.com* 📭 *76 rooms* ⦿*No meals* Ⓜ *B, D, F, M, 7 to 42nd St.–Bryant Park; 1, 2, 3, 7, N, Q, R, S, W to Times Sq.–42nd St.* ✛ *4:D4.*

$ 🏨 **CitizenM New York Times Square.** A stylish property with a refreshing
HOTEL attitude in Midtown, this hotel is all about giving you everything you
need and nothing you don't really require. **Pros:** all-season rooftop bar;
cozy lobby full of books and magazines; 20th-floor gym with great
views. **Cons:** rooms are tight on space; high-traffic area; streamlined
service (no bellboys, self check-in) isn't for everyone. $ *Rooms from: $225* ✉ *218 W. 50th St., Midtown West* ☎ *212/461–3638* ⊕ *www.citizenm.com* 📭 *230 rooms* ⦿*No meals* Ⓜ *1, C, E to 50th St.; N, R, W to 49th St.* ✛ *4:C3.*

$$$ 🏨 **City Club Hotel.** Ocean liner–inspired rooms at the City Club are brisk,
HOTEL bright, and masculine: they're also about the same size as a room on a
cruise ship, which means tight quarters, matey, no matter how much
you enjoy sharing space with Jonathan Adler ceramics. **Pros:** convenient Midtown location; great restaurant; personal service. **Cons:** no
gym; tiny lobby; small rooms. $ *Rooms from: $489* ✉ *55 W. 44th St., between 5th and 6th Aves., Midtown West* ☎ *212/921–5500* ⊕ *www. cityclubhotel.com* 📭 *65 rooms* ⦿*No meals* Ⓜ *B, D, F, M to 42nd St.–Bryant Park; 7 to 5th Ave.* ✛ *4:D4.*

$$ 🏨 **Dream Midtown.** Part hotel, part Kafkaesque dream, this Midtown
HOTEL spot specializes in style over comfort but is still quite livable, despite
some over-the-top design features—and noise from the scenesters
headed to the rooftop bar. **Pros:** PHD Terrace penthouse bar; large
spa; up-to-the-minute electronics. **Cons:** small rooms; spotty service;
might be too sceney for some. $ *Rooms from: $429* ✉ *210 W. 55th St., at Broadway, Midtown West* ☎ *212/247–2000* ⊕ *www.dreamhotels.com/midtown* 📭 *219 rooms* ⦿*No meals* Ⓜ *N, Q, R, W to 57th St.–7th Ave.* ✛ *4:C2.*

$ 🏨 **Hotel Metro.** In the heart of Herald Square (and with a rooftop view of
HOTEL Macy's), Hotel Metro has the convenience of location matched with the
comfort of a family-run establishment. **Pros:** complimentary coffee and
tea 24/7; renovated exercise room has flat-screen TVs; rooftop has views
of the Empire State Building. **Cons:** noise seeps in from outside; rooms
are tasteful but spartan; high-traffic area. $ *Rooms from: $294* ✉ *45 W. 35th St., between 5th and 6th Aves., Midtown West* ☎ *212/947–2500* ⊕ *www.hotelmetronyc.com* 📭 *183 rooms* ⦿*No meals* Ⓜ *B, D, F, M, N, Q, R, W to 34th St.–Herald Sq.* ✛ *4:D6.*

16

$ **Hudson New York Hotel.** Fashionistas and other modish folks who
HOTEL like to keep an eye on their budget are drawn to this stylish, affordable
hotel with its fabulous lobby (resembling a set from *A Midsummer
Night's Dream*), several bars and lounges perfect for people-watching,
and contemporary art that's an escape from the usual hotel design.
Pros: fabulous, elegant bar; gorgeous Francesco Clemente fresco in
lobby; breathtaking Sky Terrace. **Cons:** staff can be condescending; tiny
rooms; overpriced cocktails. $ *Rooms from: $250* ✉ *356 W. 58th St.,
between 8th and 9th Aves., Midtown West* ☎ *212/554-6000* ⊕ *www.
hudsonhotel.com* ↪ *878 rooms* ♭○┤ *No meals* Ⓜ *1, A, B, C, D to 59th
St.–Columbus Circle* ✛ *4:B1.*

$$$ **Iroquois New York.** Once the home of James Dean (he lived here for
HOTEL two years in the 1950s), the Iroquois is a historic hotel dating back to
1899, with a semi-secret cocktail bar that's one of the best in the neigh-
borhood. **Pros:** fantastic cocktail bar; 24-hour fitness center with Finn-
ish sauna; complimentary coffee and tea in lobby. **Cons:** room decor is
dated; most rooms are poorly lit; no rollaway beds available. $ *Rooms
from: $550* ✉ *49 W. 44th St., Midtown West* ☎ *212/840-3080* ⊕ *www.
iroquoisny.com* ↪ *117 rooms* ♭○┤ *No meals* Ⓜ *B, D, F, M to 42nd St./
Bryant Park; 7 to 5th Ave.* ✛ *4:D4.*

$$ **JW Marriott Essex House.** With Central Park views and an Art Deco
HOTEL masterpiece of a lobby, the JW Marriott Essex House is a comfortable
Midtown hotel full of character. **Pros:** great service; amazing views
and easy access to Central Park; impressive restaurant. **Cons:** overly
complex room gadgetry; expensive bar; traffic clogs up the area during
peak hours. $ *Rooms from: $406* ✉ *160 Central Park S., between 6th
and 7th Aves., Midtown West* ☎ *212/247-0300* ⊕ *www.marriott.com*
↪ *426 rooms* ♭○┤ *No meals* Ⓜ *N, Q, R, W to 57th St.–7th Ave.; F to
57th St.* ✛ *4:C1.*

$$ **Kimpton Ink48 Hotel.** If you want to be near Midtown but don't mind
HOTEL being a bit removed from the hustle and bustle, this hotel renovated in
FAMILY 2016 is a great option. **Pros:** friendly staff; great city skyline views; large
rooms; beautiful rooftop. **Cons:** out-of-the-way location; lobby can feel
overly quiet; street noise in lower-floor rooms. $ *Rooms from: $399*
✉ *653 11th Ave., at 48th St., Midtown West* ☎ *212/757-0088* ⊕ *www.
ink48.com* ↪ *222 rooms* ♭○┤ *No meals* Ⓜ *C, E to 50th St.* ✛ *4:A3.*

$$ **Kimpton Muse Hotel.** Surrealist prints and busts of Thalia, the muse
HOTEL of comedy, adorn the lobby of this polished property, a good pick for
guests looking for a Midtown boutique-hotel experience. **Pros:** contemporary interiors; bike rentals and in-room yoga mats available;
complimentary morning coffee and tea and evening wine reception.
Cons: street noise; small gym; many room views are underwhelming. $ *Rooms from: $399* ✉ *130 W. 46th St., between 6th and 7th
Aves., Midtown West* ☎ *212/485-2400* ⊕ *www.themusehotel.com*
↪ *200 rooms* ♭○┤ *No meals* Ⓜ *B, D, F, M to 47th–50th Sts./Rock-
efeller Center* ✛ *4:C4.*

$$$ **The Knickerbocker.** An oasis of elegant, urban sophistication in the
HOTEL heart of Times Square, the Knickerbocker is a soothing counterpoint
to the mass of people, lights, and excitement that converge nearby at
the crossroads of Broadway and 42nd Street. **Pros:** in Times Square

but aesthetically apart from it; spacious gym; fabulous rooftop bar. **Cons:** nearby dining isn't that exciting; small lobby; fee for Wi-Fi. $ *Rooms from: $500* ⊠ *6 Times Sq., entrance on 42nd St., east of Broadway, Midtown West* ☎ *212/204–4980* ⊕ *www.theknicker-bocker.com* ⌐ *330 rooms* ⦿| *No meals* Ⓜ *1, 2, 3, 7, N, Q, R, S, W to Times Sq.–42nd St.* ✛ *4:C4.*

$$$$ Ⓣ **The London NYC.** Stylish and sophisticated, the London NYC merges
HOTEL   the flair of both its namesake cities in spacious, tech-savvy suites that
Fodor'sChoice   are some of the largest in New York, starting at 500 square feet. **Pros:**
★   posh atmosphere without prissiness; great fitness club; generously sized rooms. **Cons:** no bathtubs in most rooms; expensive dining options; no spa. $ *Rooms from: $699* ⊠ *151 W. 54th St., between 6th and 7th Aves., Midtown West* ☎ *212/307–5000* ⊕ *www.thelondonnyc.com* ⌐ *562 suites* ⦿| *No meals* Ⓜ *B, D, E to 7th Ave.; N, Q, R, W to 57th St.–7th Ave.* ✛ *4:C2.*

$$ Ⓣ **LUMA Hotel Times Square.** Housed in a new glass building, the LUMA
HOTEL   offers streamlined contemporary design, a restaurant by James Beard Award–winning chef Jose Garces, and an intimate experience in the heart of busy Midtown Manhattan. **Pros:** great restaurant by an award-winning chef; tech-friendly amenities include plentiful USB ports and a delivery robot; simple, functional design. **Cons:** extremely high-traffic area; no gym on-site; small lobby offers little space for lounging. $ *Rooms from: $399* ⊠ *120 W. 41st St., between 6th Ave. and Broadway, Midtown West* ☎ *888/559–5862* ⊕ *www.lumahotels. com* ⌐ *130 rooms* ⦿| *No meals* Ⓜ *N, Q, R, S, W, 1, 2, 3, 7 to Times Sq.–42nd St.* ✛ *4:D5.*

$$$$ Ⓣ **Mandarin Oriental, New York.** The Mandarin's commitment to excess
HOTEL   is evident in the lobby, on the 35th floor of the Time Warner Cen-
Fodor'sChoice   ter, where dramatic floor-to-ceiling windows look out over Columbus
★   Circle and Central Park. **Pros:** fantastic views from rooms, lounges, and pool; destination-worthy cocktails and dining by acclaimed chef Grant Achatz; expansive suites. **Cons:** Trump hotel blocks some park views; expensive; mall-like surroundings. $ *Rooms from: $795* ⊠ *80 Columbus Circle, at 60th St., Midtown West* ☎ *212/805–8800* ⊕ *www. mandarinoriental.com/newyork* ⌐ *198 rooms* ⦿| *No meals* Ⓜ *1, A, B, C, D to 59th St.–Columbus Circle* ✛ *5:C6.*

$$ Ⓣ **The Mansfield.** Built in 1904 as lodging for distinguished bachelors,
HOTEL   this small, clubby property has an Edwardian sensibility that shows in details like the working fireplace in the lounge, the lobby's coffered ceiling, and a marble-and-cast-iron staircase. **Pros:** great bar; business center; 24-hour gym. **Cons:** tiny rooms and bathrooms; air-conditioners are window units; poor lighting in rooms. $ *Rooms from: $319* ⊠ *12 W. 44th St., between 5th and 6th Aves., Midtown West* ☎ *212/277–8700* ⊕ *www.mansfieldhotel.com* ⌐ *126 rooms* ⦿| *No meals* Ⓜ *B, D, F, M to 42nd St.–Bryant Park; 7 to 5th Ave.* ✛ *4:E4.*

$$$ Ⓣ **1 Hotel Central Park.** A commitment to next-level eco-friendly policies
HOTEL   is evident in the smallest details at this hotel, from in-room chalkboards (instead of notepads) to triple-filtered water straight from the taps that eliminates the need for bottled water. **Pros:** committed to green policies; each room has a living wall at the entrance; cozy window seats with

16

great city views; surprisingly quiet. **Cons:** some service inconsistencies; rooms are on the small side; no spa. [$] *Rooms from: $450* ✉ *1414 Avenue of the Americas, at 58th St., Midtown West* ☎ *212/703–2001* 🌐 *1hotels.com/central-park* 🛏 *229 rooms* 🍴 *No meals* [M] *F to 57th St; N, R, W to 5th Ave./59th St.* ✥ *4:D1.*

$$$$ HOTEL Fodor's Choice ★ 🏨 **Park Hyatt New York.** Occupying the first 25 floors of a towering Midtown skyscraper, this luxury property is the flagship of the global Park Hyatt brand and features one of the best spas in the city. **Pros:** large guest rooms; luxurious furnishings; one of the city's best spas. **Cons:** disappointing views from guest rooms; street noise audible on lower floors; expensive. [$] *Rooms from: $795* ✉ *153 W. 57th St., between 6th and 7th Aves., Midtown West* ☎ *646/774–1234* 🌐 *www.parkhyattnewyork.com* 🛏 *210 rooms* 🍴 *No meals* [M] *N, Q, R, W to 57th St.–7th Ave.* ✥ *4:C1.*

$$$$ HOTEL Fodor's Choice ★ 🏨 **The Plaza.** Eloise's adopted home on the corner of Central Park, this landmark property is one of New York's most storied hotels, hosting all manner of dignitaries, moneymakers, and royalty. **Pros:** historic property; lavish rooms, especially the renovated suites in the Legacy Collection; luxurious Guerlain spa. **Cons:** rooms aren't that big for the money; very expensive; fee for Wi-Fi. [$] *Rooms from: $895* ✉ *768 5th Ave., at Central Park, Midtown West* ☎ *212/759–3000* 🌐 *www.theplazany.com* 🛏 *282 rooms* 🍴 *No meals* [M] *N, R, W to 5th Ave./59th St.* ✥ *4:E1.*

$$$ HOTEL 🏨 **The Quin.** This luxury hotel just south of Central Park once housed artists like Marc Chagall and Georgia O'Keeffe, and it still has an emphasis on contemporary art. **Pros:** bright fitness center; spacious rooms; close to neighborhood destinations like Carnegie Hall. **Cons:** 57th Street location might be too busy for some; $100 per night charge for dogs; no pool or spa. [$] *Rooms from: $489* ✉ *101 W. 57th St., at 6th Ave., Midtown West* ☎ *877/234–7033* 🌐 *www.thequinhotel.com* 🛏 *208 rooms* 🍴 *No meals* [M] *N, R, W to 5th Ave.–59th St.; F to 57th St.* ✥ *4:D1.*

$ HOTEL Fodor's Choice ★ 🏨 **Refinery Hotel.** Set in a former hat factory, this hotel has a gorgeous year-round rooftop with Empire State Building views, impressively spacious rooms, and several buzzing bars and restaurants. **Pros:** lots of character and lovely, detailed design; rooftop lounge with great views; excellent bars and restaurant. **Cons:** limited dining and nightlife options nearby; the lobby gets crowded with people waiting to access the rooftop; service can be a bit inconsistent. [$] *Rooms from: $299* ✉ *63 W. 38th St., between 5th and 6th Aves., Midtown West* ☎ *646/664–0310* 🌐 *www.refineryhotelnewyork.com* 🛏 *197 rooms* 🍴 *No meals* [M] *B, D, F, M, 7 to 42nd St.–Bryant Park* ✥ *4:D5.*

$$$ HOTEL 🏨 **Renaissance New York Times Square Hotel.** After a shift from all-business to a more design-centric approach, the Renaissance is enjoying a renaissance of its own. **Pros:** contemporary design; latest in-room technology; comfortable beds. **Cons:** rooms can be a bit noisy; high-traffic area; Wi-Fi isn't free. [$] *Rooms from: $539* ✉ *714 7th Ave., between 47th and 48th Sts., Midtown West* ☎ *212/765–7676* 🌐 *www.renaissancehotels.com* 🛏 *305 rooms* 🍴 *No meals* [M] *N, R, W to 49th St.; 1 to 50th St.; B, D, F, M to 47th–50th Sts./Rockefeller Center* ✥ *4:C3.*

$$$$ HOTEL FAMILY Fodor's Choice ★ **The Ritz-Carlton New York, Central Park.** It's all about the park views here, though the above-and-beyond service, accommodating to a fault, makes this renowned property popular with celebs and other demanding guests able to pay the price. **Pros:** great concierge; personalized service; stellar location; park views. **Cons:** pricey; limited common areas; some may find it a bit staid. [$] *Rooms from: $995* ✉ *50 Central Park S, at 6th Ave., Midtown West* ☎ *212/308–9100* 🌐 *www.ritzcarlton.com/centralpark* 🛏 *259 rooms* 🍴 *No meals* [M] *F to 57th St.; N, R, W to 5th Ave./59th St.* ✥ *4:D1.*

$ HOTEL FAMILY **Room Mate Grace.** A favorite of European visitors and business travelers who work in fashion and entertainment, Grace delivers high-design lodgings on a budget. **Pros:** cool swimming pool lounge; friendly, helpful staff; nice design on a budget. **Cons:** small rooms; little in-room privacy (no door separating shower from main room); high-traffic area. [$] *Rooms from: $229* ✉ *125 W. 45th St., between 6th and 7th Aves., Midtown West* ☎ *212/380–2707* 🌐 *www.roommatehotels.com* 🛏 *139 rooms* 🍴 *No meals* [M] *B, D, F, M to 47th–50th Sts./Rockefeller Center* ✥ *4:D4.*

$$ HOTEL **The Royalton.** Back in the 1990s, the Royalton's lobby bar was one of the prime meeting spots for local A-listers, and a redesign has attracted a new generation of movers and shakers—be prepared to run the gauntlet of the buzzing lounge before reaching your room—but the helpful staff have ensured a smooth transition. **Pros:** hip lobby scene; luxurious beds and bathrooms; helpful service. **Cons:** dark hallways; lighting verges on eye-strainingly dim; fee for Wi-Fi. [$] *Rooms from: $399* ✉ *44 W. 44th St., between 5th and 6th Aves., Midtown West* ☎ *212/869–4400* 🌐 *www.royaltonhotel.com* 🛏 *175 rooms* 🍴 *No meals* [M] *B, D, F, M to 42nd St.–Bryant Park; 7 to 5th Ave.* ✥ *4:D4.*

$ HOTEL **The Shoreham.** In a neighborhood packed with generic hotels, the Shoreham sports a welcome dose of style, along with proximity to Midtown's attractions. **Pros:** tech-friendly rooms; pet-friendly attitude; stylish decor. **Cons:** not designed for families; limited space; fee for in-room Wi-Fi. [$] *Rooms from: $179* ✉ *33 W. 55th St., between 5th and 6th Aves., Midtown West* ☎ *212/247–6700* 🌐 *www.shorehamhotel.com* 🛏 *177 rooms* 🍴 *No meals* [M] *E, M to 5th Ave./53rd St.; F to 57th St.* ✥ *4:D2.*

$$ HOTEL FAMILY **6 Columbus.** This boutique-style hotel in the shadow of the towering Time Warner Center has the vibe and amenities of downtown lodging with a convenient Midtown location. **Pros:** convenient location; fun in-hotel restaurant; reasonably priced for neighborhood; family-friendly. **Cons:** rooms on lower floors facing 58th Street can be noisy; no gym on-site; some tiny rooms lack desks. [$] *Rooms from: $325* ✉ *308 W. 58th St., between 8th and 9th Aves., Midtown West* ☎ *877/626–5862* 🌐 *www.sixtyhotels.com/6columbus* 🛏 *88 rooms* 🍴 *No meals* [M] *1, A, B, C, D to 59th St.–Columbus Circle* ✥ *4:B1.*

$ HOTEL **Sofitel New York.** With bilingual signage throughout the hotel, plenty of velvet in the lobby, and European modern design in the rooms—think blond wood and fresh flowers—the Sofitel brings a Gallic flair to Midtown West. **Pros:** central location; great beds; some suites with terraces and views. **Cons:** room views vary; no spa or pool; high-traffic area. $ *Rooms from: $299* ✉ *45 W. 44th St., between 5th and 6th Aves., Midtown West* ☎ *212/354–8844* 🌐 *www.sofitel-new-york.com* 🛏 *398 rooms* 🍴 *No meals* [M] *B, D, F, M to 42nd St.–Bryant Park; 7 to 5th Ave.* ✥ *4:E4.*

$$$ HOTEL 🏨 **The Time Hotel.** One of the neighborhood's first boutique hotels, this spot near the din of Times Square is a contemporary retreat with a futuristic glass elevator that transports guests to the second-floor lobby and beyond. **Pros:** popular Serafina restaurant downstairs; surprisingly quiet for Times Square location; good turndown service. **Cons:** service is inconsistent; location isn't for everyone; a bit pricey for the area. $ *Rooms from: $459* ✉ *224 W. 49th St., between Broadway and 8th Ave., Midtown West* ☎ *212/246–5252, 877/846–3692* 🌐 *www.thetimeny.com* 🛏 *167 rooms* 🍴 *No meals* [M] *1, C, E to 50th St.; N, Q, R to 49th St.* ✥ *4:C3.*

$$ HOTEL 🏨 **Viceroy New York.** Handsome and finely tailored, this hotel has functional, tech-focused rooms and lots of amenities, including a well-equipped fitness center and plunge pool, a rooftop bar with park views, and a welcoming ground-floor restaurant, Kingside. **Pros:** comfortable, quiet library with "cartender" mixing drinks in late afternoon; generous rooftop space with views of Central Park; appealing restaurant. **Cons:** small, crowded lobby; busy 57th Street location might not suit all guests; Wi-Fi is only complimentary for direct bookings. $ *Rooms from: $399* ✉ *120 W. 57th St., Midtown West* ☎ *212/830–8000* 🌐 *www.viceroyhotelsandresorts.com/newyork* 🛏 *237 rooms* 🍴 *No meals* [M] *N, Q, R, W to 57th St.–7th Ave.; F to 57th St.* ✥ *4:D1.*

$ HOTEL 🏨 **W New York - Times Square.** Although it opened back in 2001, the W Times Square still stands out in the craziness of Times Square, thanks to its iconic, 57-story exterior—if you want to be in the thick of the action, this is a fun place to stay. **Pros:** bustling nightlife and happy-hour scene; sleek rooms; 24-hour room service. **Cons:** if you want quiet, head elsewhere; no bathtubs in the smaller rooms; extra fees for Wi-Fi, pets, and parking. $ *Rooms from: $230* ✉ *1567 Broadway, at 47th St., Midtown West* ☎ *855/516–1093* 🌐 *www.wnewyorktimessquare.com* 🛏 *509 rooms* 🍴 *No meals* [M] *1, 2, 3, 7, A, C, E, N, Q, R, W to Times Sq.–42th St.* ✥ *4:C3.*

$$ HOTEL 🏨 **Warwick New York.** Built by William Randolph Hearst in 1926 for his mistress, Hollywood actress Marion Davies, this grande dame has hosted many from Tinseltown since then, including Cary Grant in the Presidential Suite for 12 years. **Pros:** excellent restaurant and bar; historic property with character; spacious suites. **Cons:** some rooms could use a refresh; no a/c in the hallways; some rooms have views of an airshaft. $ *Rooms from: $399* ✉ *65 W. 54th St., at 6th Ave., Midtown West* ☎ *212/247–2700, 800/223–4099* 🌐 *www.warwickhotels.com/new-york* 🛏 *426 rooms* 🍴 *No meals* [M] *F to 57th St.; B, D, E to 7th Ave.* ✥ *4:D2.*

$$ HOTEL 🏨 **Westin New York at Times Square.** This giant Midtown hotel has all the amenities and service you expect from a reliable brand, at fairly reasonable prices. **Pros:** central for Midtown attractions; big rooms; great gym. **Cons:** congested area near Port Authority; not the best location for prime dining and nightlife; Wi-Fi isn't free. $ *Rooms from:*

$329 ⊠ 270 W. 43rd St., at 8th Ave., Midtown West ☎ *212/201–2700* ⊕ *www.westinny.com* ☞ *873 rooms* ❑ *No meals* Ⓜ *A, C, E to 42nd St.–Port Authority* ✦ *4:B4.*

$$$$ ⬚ **Whitby Hotel.** Like all Firmdale Hotels, this new (opened in 2017)
HOTEL boutique property combines owner Kit Kemp's eclectic design sensibility—rooms feature exotic fabrics, and an eye-catching installation made of baskets crowns the bar—excellent dining options including English-style afternoon tea, and attentive service. **Pros:** sophisticated design; excellent afternoon tea; state-of-the-art screening room. **Cons:** expensive; no pool or spa; rooms lack coffeemakers. Ⓢ *Rooms from: $795 ⊠ 18 W. 56th St., Midtown West* ☎ *212/586–5656* ⊕ *www.firmdalehotels.com* ☞ *86 rooms* ❑ *No meals* Ⓜ *F to 57th St.* ✦ *4:D2.*

$ ⬚ **Yotel New York.** Look beyond the gimmicks (a luggage-storing robot,
HOTEL the futuristic white design scheme) and discover one of New York's best-run, most functional lodgings—and at a great price, too. **Pros:** great value; large common outdoor space; access to West Side piers and Javits Center. **Cons:** rooms may be small for some; limited luggage storage and hanging space; 10th Avenue is a bit remote. Ⓢ *Rooms from: $119 ⊠ 570 10th Ave., at 42nd St., Midtown West* ☎ *646/449–7700* ⊕ *www.yotelnewyork.com* ☞ *713 rooms* ❑ *No meals* Ⓜ *A, C, E to 42nd St.–Port Authority* ✦ *4:A4.*

16

UPPER EAST SIDE

$$$$ ⬚ **The Carlyle, A Rosewood Hotel.** On the well-heeled corner of Madison
HOTEL Avenue and 76th Street, the Carlyle fuses venerable elegance and Man-
Fodor's Choice hattan swank, and calls for the aplomb of entering a Chanel boutique:
★ walk in chin high, wallet out, and ready to impress (and be impressed).
Pros: perhaps NYC's best Central Park views; refined service; delightful dining and bar options; chic shopping in neighborhood; great bathtubs. **Cons:** removed from touristy Manhattan; stuffy vibe may not work for families; every room is different, limiting consistency. Ⓢ *Rooms from: $725 ⊠ 35 E. 76th St., between Madison and Park Aves., Upper East Side* ☎ *212/744–1600* ⊕ *www.thecarlyle.com* ☞ *190 rooms* ❑ *No meals* Ⓜ *6 to 77th St.* ✦ *5:F3.*

$ ⬚ **The Franklin.** This nine-story town house is a boutique gem in a decid-
HOTEL edly residential neighborhood, with small but well-appointed rooms and name-brand knickknacks (including Bulgari toiletries), iHome stations, free Wi-Fi, and Frette linens. **Pros:** neighborhood-y location; generous breakfast included in the price; Bulgari toiletries in bathrooms. **Cons:** far from many tourist sights except Museum Mile; small rooms; no full-service restaurant on-site. Ⓢ *Rooms from: $279 ⊠ 164 E. 87th St., between Lexington and 3rd Aves., Upper East Side* ☎ *212/369–1000, 800/607–4009* ⊕ *www.franklinhotel.com* ☞ *50 rooms* ❑ *Breakfast* Ⓜ *4, 5, 6 to 86th St.* ✦ *6:G6.*

$$$$ ⬚ **Hôtel Plaza Athénée.** Positioned unobtrusively by Central Park on the
HOTEL Upper East Side, the Plaza Athénée (now related in name only to its Parisian cousin) makes stellar service a priority, with a personal sit-down check-in off to the side of the lobby, and extravagant in-room dining service with an old-world feel: white tablecloths, candles, and flowers are part of the deal. **Pros:** discerning service; fabulous hotel bar;

Old World vibe. **Cons:** lobby can feel dark; may feel stuffy to some; expensive. [$] *Rooms from: $999* ✉ *37 E. 64th St., at Madison Ave., Upper East Side* ☎ *212/734–9100* 🌐 *www.plaza-athenee.com* 🛏 *143 rooms* 🍴 *No meals* [M] *6 to 68th St.–Hunter College; F, Q to Lexington Ave./63rd St.* ✣ *5:F5.*

$$$ HOTEL 🏨 **Loews Regency Hotel.** Snazzy and spacious, this Park Avenue hotel has state-of-the-art technology, a 10,000-square-foot spa, and bright, tastefully appointed rooms with notably comfortable beds. **Pros:** friendly and helpful staff; appealing, buzzy bar and restaurant; huge spa and fitness center. **Cons:** expensive; limited dining and nightlife options nearby; design feels a bit generic. [$] *Rooms from: $599* ✉ *540 Park Ave., at 61st St., Upper East Side* ☎ *212/759–4100* 🌐 *www.loewshotels.com/regency-hotel* 🛏 *379 rooms* 🍴 *No meals* [M] *4, 5, 6, N, R, W to Lexington Ave./59th St.* ✣ *5:F6.*

$$$$ HOTEL 🏨 **The Lowell.** Steps from Madison Avenue shopping and the Museum Mile, this old-money refuge on a leafy residential block was built as an upscale apartment hotel in the 1920s and still delivers genteel sophistication and pampering service in an unbeatable location. **Pros:** great location; service with a personal touch; charming decor; some suites with wood-burning fireplaces. **Cons:** cramped lobby; expensive; no gym or spa. [$] *Rooms from: $855* ✉ *28 E. 63rd St., between Madison and Park Aves., Upper East Side* ☎ *212/838–1400, 212/838–1400* 🌐 *www.lowellhotel.com* 🛏 *74 rooms* 🍴 *No meals* [M] *F, Q to Lexington Ave./63rd St.* ✣ *5:F6.*

$$$$ HOTEL Fodor's Choice ★ 🏨 **The Mark.** The perfect combo of uptown panache and downtown chic, the Mark has striped marble floors, opulently appointed rooms, and a restaurant by renowned chef Jean-Georges Vongerichten. **Pros:** hip design; cavernous closet space; great service; scene-making restaurant and bar. **Cons:** expensive; limited dining and nightlife options in neighborhood; rooms on lower floors don't have good views. [$] *Rooms from: $725* ✉ *25 E. 77th St., at Madison Ave., Upper East Side* ☎ *212/744–4300* 🌐 *www.themarkhotel.com* 🛏 *105 rooms* 🍴 *No meals* [M] *6 to 77th St.* ✣ *5:F2.*

$$$$ HOTEL 🏨 **The Pierre, a Taj Hotel.** This iconic grande dame across from Central Park has played host to aristocrats and Hollywood actors, but it prides itself on treating all its guests like royalty. **Pros:** oozes historic charm; great dining and drinking options; excellent location across from Central Park. **Cons:** no full-service spa; staffed elevators can be slow; standard rooms are on the small side. [$] *Rooms from: $675* ✉ *2 E. 61st St., Upper East Side* ☎ *212/838–8000* 🌐 *www.thepierreny.com* 🛏 *149 rooms* 🍴 *No meals* [M] *N, R, W to 5th Ave./59th St.* ✣ *5:E6.*

UPPER WEST SIDE

$$$ HOTEL 🏨 **The Empire Hotel.** In a prime Upper West Side spot, the sophisticated Empire Hotel attracts locals for views from the rooftop pool and lounge area underneath the hotel's iconic red neon sign, while guests appreciate the rooms, which are a comfortable and chic escape from the bustle of the city. **Pros:** great location next to Lincoln Center and blocks from Central Park; beautiful rooftop pool and bar; nice turndown service. **Cons:** rooftop bar brings foot traffic through hotel lobby, plus noise

CLOSE UP

Lodging Alternatives

APARTMENT RENTALS VS. SUITE HOTELS

For your trip to New York, you may want a little more space than the city's typically tiny hotel rooms provide. Some travelers consider apartment rentals, but there are many good reasons to stick to hotel suites instead. Why? First, apartment rentals of less than 30 days—with some very limited exceptions—are illegal in New York City, though Airbnb's attempts to change the New York State housing laws continue. Furthermore, apartment-rental scams are an issue. In some published reports, potential guests have arrived to find that the apartment they rented does not exist, or that they are paying for an illegal sublet. In some cases, travelers have lost their deposit or their prepaid rent (never wire money to an account).

Suite hotels and bed-and-breakfasts with apartmentlike accommodations are always a good option, but if you want a short-term apartment rental, consider one of the legal providers, and be sure to read reviews of individual apartments for firsthand feedback from fellow travelers.

Suite hotels like the **Conrad New York** and **The London NYC**—in Manhattan—as well as the **Box House Hotel,** in Brooklyn, are definitely on the spacious side. **The Affinia** hotel group (🌐 *www.Affinia.com*) has many suites as well. The **Milburn Hotel** (🌐 *www.milburnhotel.com*) is one of the more popular independent budget options.

BED-AND-BREAKFASTS

B&Bs booked through a service may be either hosted (you're the guest in someone's quarters) or unhosted (you have full use of someone's vacated apartment, including kitchen privileges). Reservation services:

Bed and Breakfast Network of New York. ✉ *Midtown West* ☎ *212/645–8134, 888/707–4626* 🌐 *www.bedandbreakfastnetwork.com* 💳 *No credit cards.*

City Lights Bed and Breakfast. ☎ *212/737–7049* 🌐 *citylightsnewyork.com* 💳 *No credit cards.*

to some rooms; some rooms could use a refresh; bathrooms are nicely designed but tiny; very small pool. [$] *Rooms from: $499* ✉ *44 W. 63rd St., at Columbus Ave., Upper West Side* ☎ *212/265–7400* 🌐 *www.empirehotelnyc.com* 🛏 *422 rooms* 🍴 *No meals* [M] *1, A, B, C, D to 59th St.–Columbus Circle* ✥ *5:B5.*

$ HOTEL 🏨 **The Excelsior Hotel.** Directly across the street from the American Museum of Natural History, this well-kept, old-school spot is comfortable but has occasionally inconsistent staff. **Pros:** excellent neighborhood-y Upper West Side location near Central Park; near foodie mecca Zabar's and popular burger joint Shake Shack; tranquil environment. **Cons:** spotty front-desk staff; rooms are inconsistent; Wi-Fi is not free. [$] *Rooms from: $179* ✉ *45 W. 81st St., between Central Park W and Columbus Ave., Upper West Side* ☎ *212/362–9200* 🌐 *www.excelsiorhotelny.com* 🛏 *216 rooms* 🍴 *No meals* [M] *B, C to 81st St.–Museum of Natural History* ✥ *5:C2.*

$$$ HOTEL FAMILY **Hotel Beacon.** A neighborhood favorite for a reason, this Upper West Side hotel is three blocks from Central Park, 10 blocks from Lincoln Center, and steps from great gourmet grocery stores—Zabar's, Fairway, and Citarella. **Pros:** kitchenettes in all rooms; great UWS location; great service. **Cons:** though comfortable and spacious (at a cost), rooms won't win any design awards; limited nightlife in the area; no room service. [$] *Rooms from: $559* ✉ *2130 Broadway, at 75th St., Upper West Side* ☎ *212/787–1100* 🌐 *www.beaconhotel.com* 🛏 *278 rooms* 🍴 *No meals* [M] *1, 2, 3 to 72nd St.* ✥ *5:A3.*

$$ HOTEL FAMILY **The Lucerne.** Service is the strong suit at this landmark-facade hotel, whose exterior has more pizzazz than the predictable guest rooms decorated with dark-wood reproduction furniture and chintz bedspreads. **Pros:** close to Central Park and American Museum of Natural History; near good shopping and food shops; great gym. **Cons:** inconsistent room size; some guests report uncomfortable pillows; few nightlife options in neighborhood. [$] *Rooms from: $309* ✉ *201 W. 79th St., at Amsterdam Ave., Upper West Side* ☎ *212/875–1000, 800/492–8122* 🌐 *www.thelucernehotel.com* 🛏 *202 rooms* 🍴 *No meals* [M] *1 to 79th St.* ✥ *5:A2.*

$$ HOTEL **NYLO New York City.** Bringing modern style to the sometimes stodgy Upper West Side, this hotel nods to the jazz era—think raucous bar, decadent living room with a fireplace, and tempting restaurants. **Pros:** short walk from Central Park; quiet, safe location; excellent dining and drinking options; rooms with terraces and dynamite views. **Cons:** lobby might be too hectic for some; Upper West Side location removed from some attractions; fee for pets. [$] *Rooms from: $389* ✉ *2178 Broadway, at 77th St., Upper West Side* ☎ *212/362–1100* 🌐 *www.nylohotelnyc.com* 🛏 *291 rooms* 🍴 *No meals* [M] *1 to 79th St.* ✥ *5:A3.*

HARLEM

$ HOTEL **Aloft Harlem.** A reasonably priced option in an increasingly popular area of Harlem (Marcus Samuelsson's hot Red Rooster restaurant is nearby), this branch of the Aloft chain delivers with cheerful service and a fun atmosphere. **Pros:** good room size for the price; convenient to subways; ever-increasing local shopping and dining options. **Cons:** rooms have minimal space for hanging clothes; rooms get some street noise; far from main tourist attractions. [$] *Rooms from: $219* ✉ *2296 Frederick Douglass Blvd., between 123th and 124th Sts., Harlem* ☎ *212/749–4000* 🌐 *www.alofharlem.com* 🛏 *124 rooms* 🍴 *No meals* [M] *A, B, C, D to 125th St.* ✥ *6:C1.*

BROOKLYN

DOWNTOWN BROOKLYN

$ HOTEL FAMILY **Aloft New York Brooklyn.** A funky boutique chain operation in the heart of Downtown Brooklyn, Aloft is a lively yet comfortable space. **Pros:** easy subway access; reasonable prices; guests have access to the adjacent Sheraton's indoor swimming pool and room service. **Cons:** neighborhood can be noisy; no on-site restaurant; small closets. [$] *Rooms from: $180* ✉ *216 Duffield St., Downtown Brooklyn* ☎ *718/256–3833* *www.aloft-hotels.starwoodhotels.com* *176 rooms* *No meals* *2, 3 to Hoyt St.; A, C, F, N, R to Jay St.–MetroTech* *7:B4.*

$ HOTEL FAMILY **New York Marriott at the Brooklyn Bridge.** The rooms at this well-situated hotel are classic Marriott—large and enhanced by high ceilings, massaging showerheads, and other nice touches. **Pros:** near some of Brooklyn's hipper neighborhoods; traditional full-service hotel; good subway access. **Cons:** on a busy downtown street; Wi-Fi isn't free; design feels a bit cookie cutter. *Rooms from: $299* *333 Adams St., Downtown Brooklyn* *718/246–7000* *www.marriott.com* *667 rooms* *No meals* *2, 3, 4, 5 to Borough Hall; A, C, F, N, R to Jay St.–Metro Tech* *7:B3.*

BOERUM HILL

$$ HOTEL **NU Hotel Brooklyn.** The hip-yet-affordable NU, on one of Brooklyn's main nightlife and shopping streets, is perfect for visitors seeking a perch near the best of the borough. **Pros:** great Brooklyn launching pad; knowledgeable staff; 24-hour fitness center. **Cons:** subway or cab ride to anything in Manhattan; bar area can be a little too quiet; limited in-room amenities. *Rooms from: $399* *85 Smith St., Downtown Brooklyn* *718/852–8585* *www.nuhotelbrooklyn.com* *93 rooms* *Breakfast* *F, G to Bergen St.; A, C, G to Hoyt–Schermerhorn Sts.* *7:B4.*

16

DUMBO

$$$ HOTEL Fodor's Choice ★ **1 Hotel Brooklyn Bridge.** An ecofriendly ethos underscores this hip, beautifully designed outpost of the 1 Hotels fleet, including details such as headboards in many guest rooms made from upcycled corrugated steel; a living wall punctuates the tiered, buzzy lobby filled with low-slung leather sofas. **Pros:** beautifully designed and environmentally conscious; near Brooklyn Bridge Park; hip, trendy scene. **Cons:** east-facing rooms overlook busy thoroughfare; hotel guests have priority to rooftop bar on weekdays; uneven service. *Rooms from: $479* *60 Furman St., DUMBO* *877/803–1111* *1hotels.com/brooklyn-bridge* *194 rooms* *No meals* *7:B3.*

GREENPOINT

$$ HOTEL **Box House Hotel.** Adventurous travelers are drawn to this all-suites hotel, formerly a door factory, in industrial northern Greenpoint, where suites feel like stylish New York City apartments, with kitchens, living rooms, and homey touches like shelves lined with books (some also have terraces). **Pros:** exciting, developing neighborhood; huge suites with kitchens and living rooms; free neighborhood transportation. **Cons:** functional bathrooms not particularly luxurious; no black-out curtains; isolated location in industrial area isn't for everyone. *Rooms from: $349* *77 Box St., Greenpoint* *646/396–0251* *www.theboxhousehotel.com* *56 suites* *No meals* *G to Greenpoint Ave* *7:E1.*

WILLIAMSBURG

$ HOTEL **Hotel Le Jolie.** This no-frills favorite has excellent service and is convenient not only to Williamsburg's arts, culture, and dining scenes but also to the subway and the Brooklyn-Queens Expressway, the latter handy should you want to get into Manhattan via car. **Pros:** good value; free parking on a first-come, first-served basis; convenient part of Brooklyn.

Cons: proximity to highway can mean noise; can feel remote even though near to subways; not hip or trendy. $ *Rooms from: $249* ⊠ *235 Meeker Ave., Williamsburg* ☎ *718/625–2100* ⊕ *www.hotellejolie.com* ↩ *52 rooms* ⦿| *Breakfast* Ⓜ *L to Lorimer St.; G to Metropolitan Ave.* ✛ *7:E1.*

$ ⛶ **McCarren Hotel and Pool.** With funky design details like an underfoot, glass-encased river in the lobby (plus a fireplace), and a plum location overlooking McCarren Park, this hotel sizzles with scenester savvy. **Pros:** high hip factor; quality rooftop restaurant-bar; close to main thoroughfare Bedford Avenue. **Cons:** potential for noise from concerts in McCarren Park; some room details like lighting controls could be more user-friendly; the pool gets crowded in summer. $ *Rooms from: $295* ⊠ *160 N. 12th St., Williamsburg* ☎ *718/218–7500* ⊕ *www.mccarrenhotel.com* ↩ *64 rooms* ⦿| *No meals* Ⓜ *L to Bedford Ave.* ✛ *7:E1.*

HOTEL

$ ⛶ **Urban Cowboy B&B.** Williamsburg's only B&B, which occupies a renovated 100-year-old town house, combines the neighborhood's renegade spirit with an eye for design. **Pros:** beautiful design with personal touches; backyard Jacuzzi; personable staff. **Cons:** most rooms share a bathroom; a bit far from Williamsburg's main attractions; it can get a bit noisy. $ *Rooms from: $250* ⊠ *111 Powers St., Williamsburg* ☎ *347/840–0525* ⊕ *www.urbancowboybnb.com* ↩ *5 rooms* ⦿| *Breakfast* Ⓜ *L to Lorimer St.; G to Metropolitan Ave.* ✛ *7:E2.*

B&B/INN
Fodor's Choice
★

$$ ⛶ **Wythe Hotel.** A former cooperage on the Brooklyn waterfront has found new life as the Wythe Hotel, a stunner for its Manhattan-skyline views, locally sourced design touches and amenities, and supercool restaurant (Reynard) and bar (Ides). **Pros:** unique building history; Brooklyn-based design and environmentally friendly products; fabulous views from rooms or rooftop bar; destination-worthy restaurant. **Cons:** somewhat removed from the subway; no room service; the rooftop bar gets crowded. $ *Rooms from: $300* ⊠ *80 Wythe Ave., at N 11th St., Brooklyn* ☎ *718/460–8001* ⊕ *www.wythehotel.com* ↩ *72 rooms* ⦿| *No meals* Ⓜ *L to Bedford Ave.* ✛ *7:D1.*

HOTEL
Fodor's Choice
★

QUEENS

$ ⛶ **The Boro Hotel.** This industrial-chic property in Queens (just two subway stops from Manhattan) has spacious rooms, balconies with skyline views, and downright huge bathrooms. **Pros:** sleek design; fantastic views of Manhattan skyline; rooftop bar with lounge chairs. **Cons:** isolated location; limited dining and drinking venues nearby; rooftop bar is closed in winter. $ *Rooms from: $179* ⊠ *38-28 27th St., Long Island City* ☎ *718/433–1375* ⊕ *www.borohotel.com* ↩ *108 rooms* ⦿| *No meals* Ⓜ *N, W, 7 to Queensboro Plaza; E, M, R to Queens Plaza* ✛ *7:F1.*

HOTEL

$ ⛶ **The Paper Factory Hotel.** Space, style, access to intriguing local neighborhoods, and seriously good value—this paper factory turned chic hotel provides many reasons to stay in Queens. **Pros:** excellent value; one-minute walk to subway; stylish rooms and restaurant; generous space. **Cons:** some street noise reaches rooms; neighborhood feels a bit remote; Wi-Fi connection can be unreliable. $ *Rooms from: $199* ⊠ *37-06 36th St., Astoria* ☎ *718/392–7200* ⊕ *www.paperfactoryhotel.com* ↩ *123 rooms* ⦿| *No meals* Ⓜ *M, R to 36th St.* ✛ *7:H1.*

HOTEL
FAMILY

SHOPPING

Updated by
Kate Thorman

The Big Apple is one of the best shopping destinations in the world, rivaled perhaps only by London, Paris, and Tokyo. Its compact size, convenient subway system, and plentiful cabs (or Uber or Lyft rides) make it easy to navigate with plenty of bags in tow. But what it really comes down to is the staggering number and variety of stores. If you can't find it in New York, it probably doesn't exist.

If you like elegant flagships and money is no object, head to Midtown, where you'll find international megabrands like Louis Vuitton, Yves Saint Laurent, and Gucci, as well as famed department stores Bergdorf Goodman and Barneys. Nearby Madison Avenue has couture from Carolina Herrera and Vera Wang, and 5th Avenue is lined with famous jewelry stores such as Tiffany, Van Cleef & Arpels, and Harry Winston. This is also the neighborhood to indulge in bespoke goods, such as handmade shoes from John Lobb. If you like designer pieces but can't afford them, don't despair—there are plenty of upscale consignment shops around the city where you can find last season's Chanel suit or a vintage YSL jacket.

The small, independent shops that once lined SoHo have largely been displaced by the likes of J.Crew and UNIQLO, but if you want to hit the chains, this is a great place to do it, because the neighborhood also provides high-quality people-watching and superb lunches. Poke around on the side streets and in nearby NoLIta for outposts of smaller local and foreign designers and, if you're craving some of old SoHo's artistic spirit, don't discount the street vendors' stalls, which sell handmade jewelry and simple cotton dresses.

The East Village and Lower East Side are hotbeds of creativity and quirky coolness, with little boutiques selling everything from retro furniture to industrial-inspired jewelry. They're tucked among bars and old tenement buildings. The Meatpacking District is another great shopping destination to find chic designer stores like Diane von Furstenberg and rag & bone along with independently owned boutiques. And if you jaunt over to Brooklyn, you'll discover that some of the city's hippest designers are hanging out at boutiques just across the East River.

LOWER MANHATTAN

FINANCIAL DISTRICT
Known primarily as the home of Wall Street, the Financial District isn't the best place for browsing.

BARGAIN SHOPPING

Fodor's Choice ★ **Century 21.** For many New Yorkers this downtown fixture remains the mother lode of discount shopping. Seven floors are crammed with everything from Marc Jacobs shoes and half-price cashmere sweaters to Donna Karan sheets, though you have to sift through racks and fight crowds to find the gems. Best bets for men are shoes and designer briefs; the full floor of designer women's wear can yield some dazzling finds. Don't miss the children's section either, for brands like Ralph Lauren and Diesel. ■TIP➔ **If you're on the Upper West Side or in Downtown Brooklyn, you can check out more discount shopping at the other two locations, at Broadway and 66th or at City Point, respectively.** ⊠ *22 Cortlandt St., between Broadway and Church St., Financial District* ☎ *212/227–9092* ⊕ *www.c21stores.com* Ⓜ *R, W to Cortlandt St.*

CLOTHING
Kamakura Shirts. Located amid the high-rise office buildings of the Financial District, it's only appropriate that the high-end Brookfield Place shopping center would be home to the second U.S. outpost of boutique Japanese shirtmakers Kamakura Shirts. Known for impeccable service and timeless style, the designer offers both made-to-measure and ready-to-wear men's dress shirts, as well as custom ties. ⊠ *Brookfield Place, 225 Liberty St., between South End Ave. and West St., Financial District* ☎ *212/619–2484* ⊕ *www.kamakurashirts.com* Ⓜ *R, W to Cortlandt St.; 2, 3, 4, 5, A, C, J, Z to Fulton St.*

GIFTS AND SOUVENIRS
City Store. The official store of NYC sells anything and everything having to do with the city, from books and pamphlets to fun gifts. Pick up NYPD T-shirts, taxicab medallions, garbage truck toys, and dish towels silk-screened with the skyline. The store shuts at 5 pm on weekdays and is closed weekends. ⊠ *1 Centre St., at Chambers St., Financial District* ☎ *212/386–0007* ⊕ *a856-citystore.nyc.gov* Ⓜ *4, 5, 6 to Brooklyn Bridge–City Hall.*

TRIBECA
Known for its multimillion-dollar lofts and celebrity residents, TriBeCa is home to some of the most interesting boutiques in the city, though most are geared toward deep pockets, especially the design and clothing stores. Specialty shops such as Korin or J.Crew Men's Shop at the Liquor Store are worth a visit.

BEAUTY
ONDA Beauty. Part spa, part natural beauty boutique, this airy little shop has high standards for sourcing its products. From Ursa Major face wash to Rahua shampoo, only the highest quality—nontoxic, ethical,

17

Deals and Steals

Everyone loves a bargain—including a temporary New Yorker. Scoring a good deal is a rite of passage, and the city is home to everything from low-cost department stores like Century 21 to the outstanding sample sales scattered throughout the city.

If a seasonal sale makes New Yorkers' eyes gleam, a sample sale throws them into a frenzy. With so many designer flagships and corporate headquarters in town, merchandise fallout periodically leads to tremendous deals. Although technically the term "sample sale" refers to stock that's a sample design, show model, leftover, or already discounted item, the term is now also used for sales of current-season goods. Location adds a bit of an illicit thrill to the event: sales are held in hotels, warehouses, offices, or loft spaces, where items both incredible and unfortunate jam a motley assortment of racks, tables, and bins. Generally, there is a makeshift communal dressing room, but mirrors are scarce. Veteran sample-sale shoppers come prepared for wriggling in the aisles; some wear tank tops with tights or leggings for modest quick changes. Two rules of thumb: grab first and inspect later,

and call in advance to find out what methods of payment are accepted. The legendary Barneys Warehouse Sale, once the ultimate sample-sale experience, has become less reliable in recent years (it wasn't held in 2015, and it moved to Williamsburg from Chelsea in September 2016), but is still worth a visit if it's on—which is a good reminder to check on specific sales before you go.

Indeed, many of the department store sample sales have faded out in recent years, replaced by major discounts after the winter holiday season. Meanwhile, New York–based designers like Steven Alan and Leanne Marshall consistently hold sample sales up to twice a year, usually in early summer and early winter.

How to find out about these events? The level of publicity and regularity of sales vary. The print and online versions of *New York* magazine are always worth checking for sample-sale tip-offs, as are regular bulletins on **Racked** (⊕ *www.racked.com*) and **Time Out New York** (⊕ *www.timeout. com/newyork*). If you're interested in specific designers, call their shops and inquire—you may get lucky.

organic, all-natural—products make it onto the shelves. If you want to try any spa treatments (including facials and Reiki), be sure to book in advance. Naomi Watts and other high-profile locals are fans. ✉ *117 West Broadway, between Duane and Reade Sts., TriBeCa* ☎ *917/370–4744* ⊕ *ondabeauty.com* Ⓜ *1, 2, 3 to Chambers St.*

CLOTHING

Issey Miyake. This flagship, designed by Frank Gehry, attracts a non-fashion crowd who come just to gawk at his undulating, 25-foot-high titanium sculpture, *The Tornado*. Miyake's signature style has clothes that are sleek and slim fitting, and made from polyester or ultra-high-tech textiles. This flagship carries the entire runway collection, as well as Pleats Please and Issey Miyake Fete. It's closed on Sunday. ✉ *119*

Hudson St., at N. Moore St., TriBeCa ☎ *212/226–0100* ⊕ *www.tribe-caisseymiyake.com* Ⓜ *1 to Franklin St.; A, C, E to Canal St.*

J.Crew Men's Shop at the Liquor Store. It would be easy to walk right past this place and think it's a bar rather than an outpost of J.Crew for men, both because of the well-preserved, watering hole exterior and because it's filled with manly knickknacks like old Jack Kerouac books and vintage photographs. Some of the best finds are the limited-edition suits and cashmere sweaters, as well as non–J.Crew items like Barbour jackets and Ray-Bans. ⊠ *235 West Broadway, at White St., TriBeCa* ☎ *212/226–5476* ⊕ *www.jcrew.com* Ⓜ *1 to Franklin St.; A, C, E to Canal St.*

La Garçonne. The popular online shop has a brick-and-mortar space to display its well-edited collection of clean-lined designer duds in monochromatic hues—unlike the Web store, though, this one only carries women's clothes. Brands like Alexander Wang, Rachel Comey, and Isabel Marant are perennial favorites. The minimalist, loftlike space also sells some home decor and beauty products. ⊠ *465 Greenwich St., between Watts and Desbrosses Sts., TriBeCa* ☎ *646/553–3303* ⊕ *www.lagarconne.com* Ⓜ *1 to Canal St.*

Nili Lotan. This Israeli-born designer worked for Ralph Lauren and Nautica before launching her own collection for women. Nili Lotan is known for her knitwear, drapey coats, and love of solid colors. Her whitewashed retail space also sells rare books. ⊠ *188 Duane St., between Greenwich and Hudson Sts., TriBeCa* ☎ *212/219–8794* ⊕ *www.nililotan.com* Ⓜ *1, 2, 3 to Chambers St.*

Steven Alan. The TriBeCa flagship of this beloved NYC designer known for his signature casual, cool sportswear is the place to come if your preferred uniform is a cashmere beanie, untucked plaid shirt, and skinny jeans. The rustic space stocks clothing for men and women and sells its own line of clothing alongside a curated collection of other designers like Demylee and Rains, as well as beauty products and home accessories. ⊠ *103 Franklin St., between West Broadway and Church St., TriBeCa* ☎ *212/343–0692* ⊕ *www.stevenalan.com* Ⓜ *1 to Franklin St.*

HOME DECOR

Korin. If you're serious about cooking, head to this specialty knife store in TriBeCa. Previously only open to the trade, it is one of the best places to shop for top-quality knives and tableware imported from Japan. It's closed Sunday. ⊠ *57 Warren St., between West Broadway and Church St., TriBeCa* ☎ *212/587–7021* ⊕ *www.korin.com* Ⓜ *1, 2, 3 to Chambers St.*

SHOES, HANDBAGS, AND LEATHER GOODS

Fodor's Choice
★
Shinola. Proudly based in Detroit, this World War II–era shoe polish brand has been relaunched as a company that builds handcrafted watches, bicycles, leather goods, journals, and pet accessories. Shinola's TriBeCa flagship store also sells American-made products from other brands, such as Filson. ⊠ *177 Franklin St., between Greenwich and Hudson Sts., TriBeCa* ☎ *917/728–3000* ⊕ *www.shinola.com* Ⓜ *1 to Franklin St.; A, C, E to Canal St.*

17

CLOSE UP

Street Vendor Shopping

If you're looking for original or repro-duced artwork, the two areas to visit for street vendors are the stretch of 5th Avenue in front of the Metropoli-tan Museum of Art (roughly between 81st and 82nd Streets) and the SoHo area of West Broadway, between Houston and Broome Streets. In both areas, dozens of artists sell original paintings, drawings, and photographs (some lovely, some lurid), as well as photo reproductions of famous New York scenes (the Chrysler Building, South Street Seaport). Prices can start as low as $15, but be sure to haggle.

The east–west streets in SoHo are an excellent place to look for

handmade crafts: Spring and Prince Streets, especially, are jammed with tables full of beaded jewelry, tooled leather belts, cotton sundresses, and homemade hats and purses. These streets are also great places to find deals on art books; several vendors have titles featuring the work of artists from Diego Rivera to Annie Leibovitz, all for about 20% less than you pay at a chain. It's best to know which books you want ahead of time, though; street vendors wrap theirs in clear plastic, and can get testy if you unwrap them but don't wind up buying.

SOHO AND NOLITA

SOHO

Head to SoHo for both the cheap and the hyperchic. The narrow side-walks get very busy, especially on weekends, but this is a fun "see-and-be-seen" neighborhood. There are plenty of familiar high-fashion names like Prada, Chanel, and Louis Vuitton, as well as less expensive chains like Banana Republic and Sephora, which have made land grabs on Broadway. But you can still hit a few clothing and housewares bou-tiques not found elsewhere in this country. The hottest shopping area runs west from Broadway over to 6th Avenue, between West Houston and Grand Streets. Don't overlook a couple of streets east of Broadway, too: Crosby and Lafayette have a handful of intriguing shops.

BEAUTY

Fodor'sChoice
★ **Birchbox.** Cult favorite beauty-subscription service Birchbox has a retail space in SoHo where you can stock up on best-selling products that range from $5 to $200 and include everything from lip balm and styl-ish mugs to curling irons, headphones, and fragrance. There's a BYOB (Build Your Own Birchbox) section, where users create their own box full of samples. The store also has a separate floor set aside for makeup, hair, and nail services, as well as men's offerings. ⊠ *433 West Broad-way, between Spring and Prince Sts., SoHo* ☎ *646/589–8500* ⊕ *www.birchbox.com* Ⓜ *N, R, W to Prince St.*

MiN. If the selection of grooming products at Duane Reade isn't arti-sanal or exotic enough for you, head to MiN. This wood-paneled shop is decidedly masculine in flavor, with leather couches and exposed-brick walls, though the products appeal to all. Shop for unusual scents from Santa Maria Novella and L'Artisan Parfumeur, shaving products from

Luxe shops line the streets of SoHo.

Old Bond Street, quirkier items like mustache wax, or the brand's own signature line of fragrances and candles. ⊠ *117 Crosby St., between Prince and Houston Sts., SoHo* ☎ *212/206–6366* ⊕ *min.com* Ⓜ *N, R, W to Prince St.; B, D, F, M to Broadway–Lafayette St.*

BOOKS AND STATIONERY

Fodor's Choice
★
Housing Works Bookstore Cafe. Operated by a nonprofit that puts all proceeds toward combating AIDS and homelessness, this New York institution has an impressive collection of used and donated books. Its café is a popular spot for laptop-toting creatives, and literary and cultural events are held here almost nightly; a full calendar is available on the store's website. ⊠ *126 Crosby St., between Prince and Houston Sts., SoHo* ☎ *212/334–3324* ⊕ *www.housingworks.org/locations/bookstore-cafe* Ⓜ *B, D, F, M to Broadway–Lafayette St.; N, R, W to Prince St.*

CHILDREN'S CLOTHING

FAMILY **Les Petits Chapelais.** Designed and made in France, these clothes for kids (from newborn up to age 12) are cute and stylish but also practical. Corduroy outfits have details like embroidered flowers and contrasting cuffs, and soft, fleecy jackets are reversible. There's also a line of sailor-inspired clothes. ⊠ *146 Sullivan St., between Houston and Prince Sts., SoHo* ☎ *212/625–1023* ⊕ *lespetitschapelais-nyc.com* Ⓜ *C, E to Spring St.*

CLOTHING

& Other Stories. The first U.S. outpost of this popular shop owned by Swedish megastore H&M focuses on midrange clothes and bold twists on staples designed in Paris and Stockholm. Come here to browse chunky sweaters, pointy-toed flats, and printed coats. Don't miss the designer collaborations and beauty section. ✉ *575 Broadway, between Houston and Prince Sts., SoHo* ☎ *646/767–3063* ⊕ *www.stories.com/ us* Ⓜ *N, R, W to Prince St.; B, D, F, M to Broadway–Lafayette St.*

A Bathing Ape. Known simply as BAPE to devotees, this exclusive label has a cult following in its native Tokyo. At first it may be hard to see what the fuss is about. A small selection of camouflage gear and limited-edition T-shirts for men, women, and children is placed throughout the minimalist space; the real scene stealers are the flashy retro-style sneakers in neon colors. ✉ *91 Greene St., between Prince and Spring Sts., SoHo* ☎ *212/925–0222* ⊕ *www.bape.com* Ⓜ *N, R, W to Prince St.; B, D, F, M to Broadway–Lafayette St.*

Agent Provocateur. If Victoria's Secret is too tame for you, try this British lingerie shop, which has a naughty twist. Showpieces include boned corsets, lace sets with contrast-color trim, bottoms tied with satin ribbons, and a few fetish-type leather ensembles. A great selection of stockings is complemented by the garter belts to secure them. ✉ *133 Mercer St., between Prince and Spring Sts., SoHo* ☎ *212/343–7370* ⊕ *www.agentprovocateur.com* Ⓜ *N, R, W to Prince St.; B, D, F, M to Broadway–Lafayette St.*

Alexander Wang. *Vogue* darling Alexander Wang's flagship boutique is as unfussy and cool as his clothes. In between browsing for perfectly slouchy tank tops, sheath dresses, or edgy ankle boots, shoppers should check out the rotating display of luxe objects tucked inside the store's cage, which has included furry punching bags and marbleized surfboards. ✉ *103 Grand St., between Greene and Mercer Sts., SoHo* ☎ *212/977–9683* ⊕ *www.alexanderwang.com* Ⓜ *6, J, N, Q, R, W, Z to Canal St.*

American Two Shot. This boutique sells a carefully edited mix of contemporary designs for men and women, including clothing from Samantha Pleet, Lazy Oaf, and Nanushka, as well as rare vintage finds. The displays are fun and witty (you might see a voodoo doll). The space also functions as an art gallery and sometimes hosts events. The shop recently launched its own clothing line, which is made in L.A. ✉ *135 Grand St., between Crosby and Lafayette Sts., SoHo* ☎ *212/925–3403* ⊕ *www.americantwoshot.com* Ⓜ *6, J, N, Q, R, W, Z to Canal St.*

Anna Sui. The violet-and-black salon, with its Victorian rock-chick vibe, is the ideal setting for Sui's bohemian and rocker-influenced designs and colorful beauty products. ✉ *484 Broome St., between West Broadway and Wooster St., SoHo* ☎ *212/941–8406* ⊕ *www.annasui.com* Ⓜ *C, E to Spring St.; A, C, E to Canal St.*

The Apartment by The Line. Imagine stepping into the most understatedly hip SoHo loft and discovering that everything is, in fact, for sale. This online concept store has always focused on craftspeople and the stories behind its highly curated collections, and its first New York brick-and-mortar outpost lets you experience that firsthand. The fashions are mostly for women—think Altuzarra dresses and Pologeorgis coats—but there are also luxe beauty products, furnishings and artwork sourced from around the world, and an extensive jewelry selection. ✉ *76 Greene St., 3rd fl., between Spring and Broome Sts., SoHo* ☎ *917/460–7196* ⊕ *theline.com* Ⓜ *R, W to Prince St.*

A.P.C. This hip French boutique sells deceptively simple clothes in an equally understated setting. Choose from sharply cut gabardine and corduroy suits to dark denim jeans and jackets. For women, best bets include striped sweaters and skinny jeans. ⊠ *131 Mercer St., between Prince and Spring Sts., SoHo* ☎ *212/966–9685* ⊕ *usonline.apc.fr* Ⓜ *6 to Spring St.; N, R, W to Prince St.; B, D, F, M to Broadway–Lafayette St.*

COS. With COS's monochrome palette, clean lines, and structured styles meant to last, it's hard to believe that this minimalist fashion brand is owned by H&M. Stock up on wardrobe essentials like black dresses, white button-ups, and wool blazers. The leather shoes, handbags, and other accessories are equally elegant. ⊠ *129 Spring St., between Wooster and Greene Sts., SoHo* ☎ *212/389–1247* ⊕ *www.cosstores.com* Ⓜ *R, W to Prince St.*

Etro. This Italian fashion house is known for its trademark paisleys and bold patterns, which cover everything from suits and dresses to lustrous pillows. Etro's downtown location combines the best of Italy with a SoHo loft, with high tin ceilings, brightly colored rugs, and industrial lighting. ⊠ *89 Greene St., at Spring St., SoHo* ☎ *646/329–6929* ⊕ *www. etro.com* Ⓜ *N, R, W to Prince St.; B, D, F, M to Broadway–Lafayette St.*

45R. Cult-favorite Japanese denim brand 45rpm's New York outpost may be pricey, but fans love the label for its attention to detail, like hand-dyed denim woven on antique looms. The T-shirts are particularly stylish, the non-denim women's wear is ethereal and cozy, and the men's shirts and blazers are elegantly tailored. ⊠ *169 Mercer St., between Houston and Prince Sts., SoHo* ☎ *917/237–0045* ⊕ *www.rby45rpm. com* Ⓜ *N, R, W to Prince St.*

Fodor's Choice ★ **Isabel Marant.** If you're after that casually glamorous Parisian vibe, look no further than Isabel Marant. Long a favorite of globe-trotting fashionistas, the French designer opened her first U.S. retail store in the heart of SoHo. The tailored jackets, shorts, and flirty dresses are eclectic and sophisticated, with textured, deeply hued fabrics. ⊠ *469 Broome St., at Greene St., SoHo* ☎ *212/219–2284* ⊕ *www.isabelmarant.com* Ⓜ *N, R, W to Prince St.; A, C, E to Canal St.*

Kirna Zabête. Think of this space as a mini department store for some of the biggest names in fashion, including Alexander Wang, Azzedine Alaïa, Mansur Gavriel, and Ulla Johnson. The multilevel store has a fun, pop art–inspired design, complete with neon signs suggesting that shoppers "leave looking lovely" and that "life is short, buy the shoes." ⊠ *477 Broome St., between Greene and Wooster Sts., SoHo* ☎ *212/941–9656* ⊕ *www.kirnazabete.com* Ⓜ *N, R, W to Prince St.; A, C, E to Canal St.*

Maison Kitsuné. This decades-old French fashion and music label made its stateside debut in this airy, sun-washed boutique for mens- and women's-wear classics with a stylish Gallic twist, ranging from cardigans and loafers to blazers and dresses. ⊠ *248 Lafayette St., between Prince and Spring Sts., SoHo* ☎ *646/858–2709* ⊕ *www.kitsune.fr* Ⓜ *N, R, W to Prince St.; 6 to Spring St.*

Marc Jacobs. The designer's only NYC boutique, this sleek, high-ceilinged shop showcases Marc Jacobs's crisply tailored clothing for men and women in luxurious fabrics: silk, cashmere, wool bouclé,

17

and tweeds ranging from the demure to the flamboyant. The details, though—oversize buttons, circular patch pockets, and military-style grommet belts—add a sartorial wink. The shoe and accessories selections are not to be missed. ⊠ *113 Prince St., between Wooster and Greene Sts., SoHo* ☎ *212/343–1490* ⊕ *www.marcjacobs.com* Ⓜ *N, R, W to Prince St.; B, D, F, M to Broadway–Lafayette St.*

Marni. If you're a fan of the boho-chic look, stock up on creative director Francesco Risso's brightly colored clothes at the Italian designer's SoHo outpost. The collection features dresses and jackets in quirky prints, and many of the silhouettes are vintage inspired. Accessories are also eye-popping. ⊠ *161 Mercer St., between W. Houston and Prince Sts., SoHo* ☎ *212/343–3912* ⊕ *www.marni.com* Ⓜ *N, R, W to Prince St.; B, D, F, M to Broadway–Lafayette St.*

Michael Kors. The designer keeps rolling out boutiques around the city, but this flagship, opened in 2015, is the biggest and most impressive yet. A three-story temple to Kors' clean-lined, classic clothing and accessories, the store is the first to dedicate a whole level to menswear, and even has its own signature suit design. ⊠ *520 Broadway, between Broome and Spring Sts., SoHo* ☎ *212/336–4501* ⊕ *www.michaelkors.com* Ⓜ *6 to Spring St.; N, R, W to Prince St.*

Miu Miu. Prada front woman Miuccia Prada established a secondary line (bearing her childhood nickname, Miu Miu) to showcase her more experimental ideas. Look for Prada-esque styles in more daring colors and cuts, such as high-waist skirts with scalloped edges, Peter Pan–collar dresses in bold patterns, and pastel-hued pumps. ⊠ *100 Prince St., between Mercer and Greene Sts., SoHo* ☎ *212/334–5156* ⊕ *www. miumiu.com* Ⓜ *N, R, W to Prince St.*

Moncler. Many New Yorkers swear by Moncler coats to keep them warm but still stylish throughout the winter. This store was the Italian brand's first foray into New York, though there's now another location in Midtown. The knee-length puffer is a firm favorite, but there are stylish ski jackets and accessories, along with pieces created in collaboration with designers like Giambattista Valli and KITH. ⊠ *90 Prince St., between Mercer St. and Broadway, SoHo* ☎ *646/350–3620* ⊕ *www.moncler.com* Ⓜ *N, R, W to Prince St.*

Fodor's Choice ★ **Opening Ceremony.** Just like Colette in Paris, Opening Ceremony bills itself as a concept store, which means you never know what you'll find. The owners are constantly globe-trotting to soak up the work of foreign designers and bring back the best clothing, products, and vintage items to showcase in their store. Hong Kong, Japan, Brazil, and the United Kingdom have all been represented. The 35 Howard address includes shoes, kids' clothes, books, and women's wear, while 33 Howard, next door, is dedicated to menswear. Both spaces also double as galleries for modern art and installations. ⊠ *35 Howard St., between Broadway and Crosby St., SoHo* ☎ *212/219–2688* ⊕ *www.openingceremony.us* Ⓜ *6, J, N, Q, R, W, Z to Canal St.*

Paul Smith. Fans love Paul Smith for his classic-with-a-twist clothes, and this 5,000-square-foot flagship is a temple to his design ethos and inspirations. Victorian mahogany cases complement the dandyish British styles they hold. Embroidered vests; brightly striped socks, scarves, and shirts; and tongue-in-cheek cuff links are all signature Paul Smith looks, along with classic suits and outerwear for men and women. Shoppers also find furniture and a selection of photography books and ephemera. ⊠ *142 Greene St., between Houston and Prince Sts., SoHo* 🕾 *646/613–3060* ⊕ *www.paulsmith.co.uk* Ⓜ *N, R, W to Prince St.; B, D, F, M to Broadway–Lafayette St.*

Prada. This ultramodern flagship space, designed by Rem Koolhaas, incorporates so many technological innovations that it was written up in *Popular Science.* Dressing rooms' glass walls turn opaque at the touch of a button, and instead of mirrors, shoppers can check themselves out in large video panels. Menswear, women's clothing, the Prada Sport line, shoes, and luxe accessories fill the multilevel store. ⊠ *575 Broadway, at Prince St., SoHo* 🕾 *212/334–8888* ⊕ *www.prada.com* Ⓜ *N, R, W to Prince St.; B, D, F, M to Broadway–Lafayette St.*

Fodor's Choice ★ **Reformation.** Cool girls from Olivia Munn to Taylor Swift love this eco-friendly fashion brand from Los Angeles whose flirty, vintage-inspired dresses and two-piece outfits are made with recycled, leftover, or otherwise sustainable fabrics. This flagship store has the largest selection, but there are also locations on Bond Street and on the Lower East Side. ⊠ *23 Howard St., between Lafayette and Crosby Sts., SoHo* 🕾 *855/756–0560* ⊕ *www.thereformation.com* Ⓜ *J, N, Q, R, W, Z, 6 to Canal St.*

Reiss. Think of Reiss as the Banana Republic of Britain—a go-to place for casual-but-tailored clothes at a relatively gentle price. Kate Middleton is a loyal customer. Standouts for women include cowl-neck sweater dresses and A-line skirts. Men's wool combat trousers are complemented by shrunken blazers, military-inspired peacoats, and trim leather jackets. ⊠ *387 West Broadway, between Spring and Broome Sts., SoHo* 🕾 *212/925–5707* ⊕ *www.reissonline.com* Ⓜ *N, R, W to Prince St.; C, E to Spring St.*

Saint Laurent Paris. When Anthony Vaccarello took over the fabled French house, he used Yves Saint Laurent's most classic designs as his palette. And so the same goes for the brand's downtown flagship, its high ceilings, marble walls, and monochromatic aesthetic designed by Vaccarello's predecessor. Browse the designer's elegant women's wear and polished menswear, and don't miss the sleek shoes and structured handbags. ⊠ *80 Greene St., between Spring and Broome Sts., SoHo* 🕾 *212/431–3240* ⊕ *www.ysl.com* Ⓜ *N, R, W to Prince St.; 6 to Spring St.*

Saturdays Surf NYC. Who knew New York had a surfing scene? This almost painfully cool boutique brought the culture to the heart of SoHo with its boards, men's clothing, surf-focused fine art, and other hipster accessories. The shop also has a La Colombe coffee counter in the front and a quiet garden in the back. ⊠ *31 Crosby St., between Grand and Broome Sts., SoHo* 🕾 *212/966–7875* ⊕ *www.saturdaysnyc.com* Ⓜ *6, J, N, Q, W, Z to Canal St.; 6 to Spring St.*

Sean. This French-pedigreed shop carries classic, understated menswear imported from Europe at reasonable prices. Linen and corduroy painter's coats are best sellers, along with V-neck sweaters and a respectable collection of slim-cut suits. ⊠ *181 Prince St., between Sullivan and*

17

Thompson Sts., SoHo ☎ *212/598–5980* ⊕ *www.seanstore.com* Ⓜ *N, R, W to Prince St.; C, E to Spring St.*

7 for All Mankind. Whether you're hunting for superskinny, high-waisted, or boot-cut jeans in a dark or distressed finish, this temple to denim has it all. The jeans for men and women are a firm celebrity favorite (Cameron Diaz is a fan), but be warned: although they are guaranteed to make your derriere look good, they don't come cheap. You'll also find stylish and sexy dresses here, plus sweaters and jackets for men and women. ✉ *394 West Broadway, between Broome and Spring Sts., SoHo* ☎ *212/226–8615* ⊕ *www.7forallmankind.com* Ⓜ *C, E to Spring St.*

Stella McCartney. McCartney's flagship store has a luxe look, thanks to parquet flooring and touches of gold found in the Art Deco sculptures and clothing racks. Her main collection, done mostly in gauzy, muted colors, is on the top floor, while children's, Adidas by Stella McCartney, and lingerie are on the lower level. In keeping with McCartney's vegetarianism, fur and leather are verboten. ✉ *112 Greene St., between Spring and Prince Sts., SoHo* ☎ *212/255–1556* ⊕ *www.stellamccartney.com* Ⓜ *N, R, W to Prince St.; B, D, F, M to Broadway–Lafayette St.*

3X1. In this huge denim shop, which doubles as a factory, customers can watch 3x1 jeans being made. The walls of the pristine white space are lined with an assortment of more than 600 varieties of selvedge denim. Those looking for a bespoke pair start by selecting the perfect denim. Jeans are hand-cut and sewn by the in-house seamstresses, who work in a glass-enclosed space. Shoppers can also buy off-the-rack jeans, with hems tailored on the spot (starting at $195). ✉ *15 Mercer St., between Grand and Howard Sts., SoHo* ☎ *212/391–6969* ⊕ *www.3x1.us* Ⓜ *6, J, N, Q, R, W, Z to Canal St.*

Fodor's Choice ★ **The Webster.** When the French stylist behind this beloved luxury concept store from Miami decided to open an outpost in New York, she renovated a six-floor, landmarked building and injected some of the original store's signature Art Deco sensibilities. Clothes and displays are arranged not by their brands but rather by the store's stylists. Look for designers like Gaetano Pesce and The Row, and keep in mind that even the furniture is for sale. ✉ *29 Greene St., between Grand and Canal Sts., SoHo* ☎ *212/226–1260* ⊕ *thewebster.us* Ⓜ *J, N, Q, R, W, Z, 6 to Canal St.*

Fodor's Choice ★ **What Goes Around Comes Around.** Professional stylists and celebrities flock here to dig up pristine vintage items like Levi's and Azzedine Alaïa dresses, as well as Hermès scarves and Chanel jewelry. The vintage rock tees (think Black Sabbath, Mötley Crüe) are great finds but can set you back an eye-watering $300–$600. ✉ *351 West Broadway, between Broome and Grand Sts., SoHo* ☎ *212/343–1225* ⊕ *www.whatgoesaroundnyc.com* Ⓜ *6, J, N, Q, R, W, Z to Canal St.*

Woolrich. In a nod to this brand's almost 200-year history, Woolrich's first retail space is decorated with vintage shearing tools and catalogs from the original Pennsylvania mill. The space is cozy, thanks to throw rugs and industrial-style lighting, and the full Woolrich product line is sold here, from sweaters to blankets and thick winter coats. ✉ *125 Wooster St., between Prince and Spring Sts., SoHo* ☎ *646/371–9968* ⊕ *www.woolrich.com* Ⓜ *N, R, W to Prince St.*

CRAFTS

Purl Soho. Anyone with a crafty bent will fall in love with this colorful paradise of top-quality knitting and sewing supplies, gorgeous craft books, and much, much more. Prices aren't cheap, but the salespeople are extra friendly and knowledgeable. It's worth a browse even if you're not planning to buy anything. ⊠ *459 Broome St., between Mercer and Green Sts., SoHo* ☎ *212/420–8796* ⊕ *www.purlsoho.com* Ⓜ *6 to Spring St.; A, C, E, J, N, Q, R, W, Z, 6 to Canal St.*

FOOD AND TREATS

Harney & Sons. Fancy a cuppa? Harney & Sons produces more than 250 varieties of loose tea, which can be sampled at its store and tea salon in SoHo. The design is sleek and dramatic, with a 24-foot-long tasting bar and floor-to-ceiling shelves stocked with tea. Shoppers find classic brews like English breakfast and oolong, along with interesting herbals (ginger and licorice, or mint verbena). Enjoy a cup with a scone or other light fare, available at the tea salon. ⊠ *433 Broome St., between Broadway and Crosby St., SoHo* ☎ *212/933–4853* ⊕ *www.harney.com* Ⓜ *6 to Spring St.; A, C, E, J, N, Q, R, W, Z, 6 to Canal St.*

Jacques Torres Chocolates. Visit the café and shop here and be literally surrounded by chocolate. The glass-walled downtown space also houses the renowned French chocolatier's chocolate factory, so you can watch the goodies being made while sipping a richly spiced cocoa or nibbling on a Java Junkie bar. Signature taste: the "wicked" chocolate, laced with cinnamon and chili pepper. Serious chocolate lovers should also check out Torres's 5,000-square-foot chocolate museum, which offers tours Wednesday through Sunday and holds chocolate-making classes. ⊠ *350 Hudson St., at King St., SoHo* ☎ *212/414–2450* ⊕ *www.mrchocolate. com* Ⓜ *1 to Houston St.*

MarieBelle. The handmade chocolates here are nothing less than works of art. Square truffles and bonbons—in flavors like Earl Grey, cappuccino, passion fruit, and saffron—are painted with edible dyes (cocoa butter dyed with natural coloring) so each resembles a miniature painting. Relax in the elegant Cacao Bar and Tea Salon while sipping an Aztec hot chocolate, made from rich cacao. ⊠ *484 Broome St., between West Broadway and Wooster St., SoHo* ☎ *212/226–8901* ⊕ *www.mariebelle. com* Ⓜ *N, R, W to Prince St.; C, E to Spring St.*

Vosges Haut-Chocolat. This chandeliered salon lined with apothecary shelves takes a global approach to chocolate. Many of the creations are travel inspired: the Budapest bonbons combine dark chocolate and Hungarian paprika, while the Japanese-influenced Black Pearls contain wasabi. Don't miss the best-selling chocolate-bacon bars. ⊠ *132 Spring St., between Wooster and Greene Sts., SoHo* ☎ *212/625–2929* ⊕ *www. vosgeschocolate.com* Ⓜ *N, R, W to Prince St.*

HOME DECOR

Canal Street Market. Some of New York's most interesting designers, artists, and food vendors fill this new market hall. Browse minimalist and functional homewares at Leibal's nook, all-natural skincare products at Smoothie Beauty, and independent magazines at Office's newsstand. Apart from the anchor vendors, the rest of the stalls rotate, so you never

17

know what gems you'll find. ⊠ *265 Canal St., between Broadway and Lafayette St., SoHo* ☎ *646/694–1655* ⊕ *canalstreet.market* Ⓜ *J, N, Q, R, W, Z, 6 to Canal St.*

de Vera. Owner Federico de Vera crisscrosses the globe searching for unique decorative products, so shoppers never know what might turn up here in his airy, gallery-like space. Venetian glass vases, Thai Buddhas, and antique rose-cut diamond rings are typical finds. It's closed Sunday and Monday. ⊠ *1 Crosby St., at Howard St., SoHo* ☎ *212/625–0838* ⊕ *www.deveraobjects.com* Ⓜ *6, J, N, Q, R, W, Z to Canal St.*

Matter. Beautifully curated, this store appeals to fans of sleek, modern furniture—if money is no object. How about the iconic Tank armchair by Alvar Aalto for a cool $5,900? Or a brass-and-marble pendant lamp by Fort Standard for $5,200? Even if your budget is limited, Matter is worth a visit for inspiration. ⊠ *405 Broome St., between Centre and Lafayette Sts., SoHo* ☎ *212/343–2600* ⊕ *www.mattermatters.com* Ⓜ *6 to Spring St.*

Michele Varian. This stylish textile designer's shop is a temple to independent designers and artists, featuring a curated collection of everything from furniture to jewelry to kids' toys. Many of the pieces are by local designers, but the boutique also regularly hosts pop-up shops for out-of-town brands. ⊠ *27 Howard St., at Crosby St., SoHo* ☎ *212/343–0033* ⊕ *www.michelevarian.com* Ⓜ *6, J, N, Q, R, W, Z to Canal St.*

JEWELRY AND ACCESSORIES

Alexis Bittar. Born in Brooklyn, the designer got his start selling his first jewelry line, made from Depression-era glass, on a corner in SoHo. Now, Bittar counts A-list celebs and fashion editors among his fans. He makes clean-line, big-statement jewelry from vermeil, colored Lucite, pearls, and vintage glass. The store mirrors this aesthetic with a mix of old and new, like antique-white Victorian-era lion's-claw tables and Plexiglas walls. ⊠ *465 Broome St., between Mercer and Greene Sts., SoHo* ☎ *212/625–8340* ⊕ *www.alexisbittar.com* Ⓜ *N, R, W to Prince St.; 6, J, N, Q, R, W, Z to Canal St.*

Aurélie Bidermann. The New York boutique of this French jeweler is all white with pops of color, and includes a mural commissioned from a street artist. Bidermann's signature look is bold and inspired by her travels and nature. Look out for lace filigree gold cuffs, large turquoise necklaces, and drop earrings in the shape of gingko leaves. ⊠ *265 Lafayette St., between Prince and Spring Sts., SoHo* ☎ *212/335–0604* ⊕ *www.aureliebidermann.com* Ⓜ *N, R, W Prince St.; 6 to Spring St.*

Broken English. At the NYC outpost of this L.A. favorite, owner Laura Freedman sells a well-edited selection of jewelry from designers including Anita Ko and Atelier Zobel. Expect delicate and whimsical pieces, from diamond-encrusted ear cuffs to geometric rings. ⊠ *56 Crosby St., between Spring and Broome Sts., SoHo* ☎ *212/219–1264* ⊕ *www.brokenenglishjewelry.com* Ⓜ *6 to Spring St.*

Dinosaur Designs. The jewelry and housewares designs at this Australian-owned brand are inspired by nature and organic shapes. Resin is used to craft jewelry and vases in bold colors like hot pink and orange. Don't miss the striking tableware. ⊠ *21 Crosby St., between Grand and*

Howard Sts., SoHo ☎ *212/680–3523* ⊕ *www.dinosaurdesigns.com* Ⓜ *6, J, N, Q, R, W, Z, to Canal St.*

SHOES, HANDBAGS, AND LEATHER GOODS

Camper. Urbanites love this Spanish footwear company for its funky but comfortable shoes. The flagship store has an unusual pagoda-style roof, and inside the store, there's a vertical garden. All the slip-ons and lace-ups here have generously rounded toes and a springy feel. ✉ *110 Prince St., at Greene St., SoHo* ☎ *212/343–4220* ⊕ *www.camper.com* Ⓜ *N, R, W to Prince St.; B, D, F, M to Broadway–Lafayette St.*

The Frye Company. There's an old western feel at this 6,000-square-foot mecca to boots, thanks to the exposed brick walls and reclaimed barn doors. Boots can be tattooed—or hot stamped—with your initials while you wait in the lounge. In addition to Frye's famed boots, shoppers can also pick from flats, oxfords, clogs, and mules. ✉ *113 Spring St., between Mercer and Greene Sts., SoHo* ☎ *212/226–3793* ⊕ *www. thefryecompany.com* Ⓜ *N, R, W to Prince St.; B, D, F, M to Broadway–Lafayette St.*

Longchamp. Their Le Pliage foldable nylon bags may have become a preppy staple, but don't think this label is stuffy—or all about nylon. There's a wide selection of leather handbags as well as wallets, belts, and shoes, and the brand often collaborates with renowned artists. The distinctive store was designed by celebrity architect Thomas Heatherwick. ✉ *132 Spring St., between Wooster and Greene Sts., SoHo* ☎ *212/343–7444* ⊕ *www.longchamp.com* Ⓜ *N, R, W to Prince St.*

NOLITA

NoLIta ("North of Little Italy") is a shopping mecca, thanks to the abundance of boutiques that range from quirky to elegant. Like SoHo, NoLIta has changed from an understated, locals-only area to a crowded weekend magnet, as much about people-watching as shopping. Still, unlike those of its SoHo neighbor, these stores remain largely independent. Running along the parallel north–south spines of Elizabeth, Mott, and Mulberry Streets, between Houston and Kenmare Streets, NoLIta's boutiques tend to be small and, as real estate costs dictate, somewhat pricey.

BEAUTY

Le Labo. If you're bored with the perfume stock at department stores, come to this tiny boutique with a rustic, industrial vibe and resident mixologist who helps create your ideal perfume. After you choose your favorite scents, the perfume is mixed and a personalized label created for your bottle. ✉ *233 Elizabeth St., between Prince and Houston Sts., NoLIta* ☎ *212/219–2230* ⊕ *www.lelabofragrances.com* Ⓜ *B, D, F, M to Broadway–Lafayette St.*

Fodor's Choice
★

Santa Maria Novella. A heavy, iron-barred door leads to a hushed, scented inner sanctum of beauty products. This location is one of only two U.S. outposts for the 600-year-old Florentine company that makes intriguingly archaic colognes, creams, and soaps such as Dental Elixir and rose rice powder according to both traditional and modern recipes. Everything is packaged in bottles and jars with antique-style apothecary labels. There's also a wide selection of fragrances. ✉ *285 Lafayette St., between Houston* *and Prince Sts., NoLIta* ☎ *212/271–0884* ⊕ *buy.smnovella.com* Ⓜ *N, R, W to Prince St.; B, D, F, M to Broadway–Lafayette St.*

BOOKS AND STATIONERY

Fodor's Choice ★ **McNally Jackson.** A bibliophile's dream, this cozy independent bookstore in a bright, two-story space has hardwood floors, a café, and plenty of chairs for lounging and curling up with a book. More than 50,000 books are stocked, and the literary section is organized geographically. Author events are held almost nightly, and budding authors can self-print their tomes on a device called the Espresso Book Machine. ⊠ *52 Prince St., between Lafayette and Mulberry Sts., NoLIta* ☎ *212/274–1160* ⊕ *www. mcnallyjackson.com* Ⓜ *N, R, W to Prince St.; 6 to Spring St.*

CLOTHING

Creatures of Comfort. Owner Jade Lai has brought her popular L.A. outpost to New York at this open, airy boutique that racks cool clothes from emerging designers alongside products from around the world. Most of the colors are muted, and brands carried include Acne, Band of Outsiders, and the house label, Creatures of Comfort. There's also a small selection of shoes, as well as under-the-radar beauty products, such as Rodin hand cream. ⊠ *205 Mulberry St., between Spring and Kenmare Sts., NoLIta* ☎ *212/925–1005* ⊕ *www.creaturesofcomfort. us* Ⓜ *6 to Spring St.*

Duncan Quinn. Described as "Savile Row meets Rock 'n' Roll" by *GQ*, this designer provides full bespoke and ready-to-wear services for everything from chalk-stripe suits to cuff links and croquet shirts, all in a shop not much bigger than its silk pocket squares. Off-the-rack shirts are handmade in Italy, but if you want to splurge, get fitted for a shirt with mother-of-pearl buttons. ⊠ *70–80 Kenmare St., between Mott and Mulberry Sts., NoLIta* ☎ *212/226–7030* ⊕ *www.duncanquinn.com* Ⓜ *6 to Spring St.; J, Z to Bowery.*

Fodor's Choice ★ **Everlane.** A cult-favorite online brand has finally brought its transparently made (the company discloses fully where and how the products are made), high-quality basics for both men and women to a brick-and-mortar store. With its whitewashed walls, skylights, and electronic checkout, the boutique mimics the website experience, with the added bonus that you can try on those cashmere sweaters and silk shirts. The space regularly hosts panels, community events, and photography installations about Everlane's factories. ⊠ *28 Prince St., between Mott and Elizabeth Sts., NoLIta* ⊕ *www.everlane.com* Ⓜ *N, R, W to Prince St.; 6 to Spring St.; B, D, F, M to Broadway–Lafayette St.*

GROUPE. Formerly the longtime SoHo fashion staple Seize sur Vingt, this thoroughly modern boutique for men and women incorporates three different in-house design brands and an art gallery, touting itself as an "integrated fashion collective." You can still splurge on Seize sur Vingt's exquisitely tailored shirts and suits, both tailored off the rack or created bespoke from a mind-boggling array of fabrics (linen, broadcloth oxford, flannel). The other brands fill out your wardrobe, with sweaters, sneakers, women's wear, and more also available. ⊠ *198 Bowery, between Prince and Spring Sts., NoLIta* ☎ *212/625–1620* ⊕ *www. groupe.nyc* Ⓜ *6 to Spring St.*

INA. The clothing at this couture consignment store harks back only one or two seasons, and in some cases, the items have never been worn. Browse through the racks to spot gems from Lanvin, Chanel, and Alexander McQueen. There are multiple locations around the city; this outpost carries offerings for women, while men's clothes are offered at the location next door. ✉ *21 Prince St., between Elizabeth and Mott Sts., NoLIta* ☎ *212/334–9048* ⊕ *www.inanyc.com* Ⓜ *6 to Spring St.; B, D, F, M to Broadway–Lafayette St.*

Jay Kos. There aren't too many boutiques where the owner sometimes whips up a snack for customers in the boutique's custom kitchen, but this menswear designer—famous for dressing Diddy and Johnny Depp—wanted his boutique to have a homey feel. The clothes veer toward the fabulous: suede shoes, linen suits, and cashmere sweaters, which are displayed in armoires. ✉ *293 Mott St., at Houston St., NoLIta* ☎ *212/319–2770* ⊕ *www.jaykos.com* Ⓜ *B, D, F, M to Broadway–Lafayette St.*

Malia Mills. Swimsuit-fit fanatics have met their match with this designer—especially those gals who are different sizes on top and bottom (bikini tops go up to size F). Flattering bikini tops and bottoms are sold separately and in almost every imaginable style, ranging from sexy to retro looks. There's a collection of one-pieces as well. ✉ *199 Mulberry St., between Spring and Kenmare Sts., NoLIta* ☎ *212/625–2311* ⊕ *www.maliamills.com* Ⓜ *6 to Spring St.*

Oak. Most of the clothing here comes in black or leather, and the store carries high-end designers in addition to its own line for both men and women. Come here for skinny jeans, oversize sweaters, bomber jackets, and vintage fur and leather finds. ✉ *28 Bond St., between Lafayette St. and Bowery, NoLIta* ☎ *646/682–7899* ⊕ *www.oaknyc. com* Ⓜ *6 to Bleecker St.*

Sézane. In a setting inspired by the high ceilings, floor-to-ceiling windows, and parquet floors of Parisian apartments and brasseries, this cult French brand's first U.S. store brings its signature French-girl chic to New York. In addition to the small permanent collection (called *La Liste*), limited-edition seasonal releases ensure that the in-store stock changes regularly. Coffee and treats from nearby Maman are available, and events are held regularly. ✉ *254 Elizabeth St., between Prince and E. Houston Sts., NoLIta* ☎ *917/261–6190* ⊕ *www.sezane.com* Ⓜ *B, D, F, M to Broadway–Lafayette St.*

Thomas Sires. Aimed at chic downtown moms but frequented by anyone who daydreams of Moroccan bazaars and Mexican beaches, this jet set–inspired lifestyle boutique curates breezy women's wear, whimsical kids' clothes, and colorful accessories and home design pieces sourced from the owner's travels around the world. There's a small selection of kids' toys, and plenty of easy gift ideas, like pom-pom–adorned pouches and scented candles. ✉ *243 Elizabeth St., between Prince and E. Houston Sts., NoLIta* ☎ *646/692–4472* ⊕ *thomassires.com* Ⓜ *B, D, F, M to Broadway–Lafayette St.; 6 to Spring St.*

Warm. If you want to feel the love, come to this little boutique owned by lifelong surfers Winnie Beattie and her husband Rob Magnotta.

17

Everything has a sunny, beachy vibe, from leather sandals, bikinis, and bleached sweaters to handblown glass vases. There's also a collection of children's books, indie magazines, housewares, and menswear. ⊠ *181 Mott St., between Kenmare and Broome Sts., NoLIta* ☎ *212/925–1200* ⊕ *www.warmny.com* Ⓜ *6 to Spring St.*

GIFTS AND SOUVENIRS

Bulletin Broads. From portraits of Michelle Obama and "Nevertheless, She Persisted" mugs to necklaces reading "Nasty Woman" and greeting cards with Beyoncé lyrics, this millennial-pink boutique is your one-stop shop for feminist products. The women-run business rents out its shelves to female entrepreneurs whose wares have previously only been available on the Internet, and donates 10% of its profits to Planned Parenthood of NYC. The store regularly hosts events, many centered around activism. There are also locations in the Flatiron District and Williamsburg. ⊠ *27 Prince St., between Mott and Elizabeth Sts., NoLIta* ☎ *646/928–0213* ⊕ *bulletin.co* Ⓜ *N, R, W to Prince St.; 6 to Spring St.; B, D, F, M to Broadway–Lafayette St.*

JEWELRY AND ACCESSORIES

Erica Weiner. The eponymous designer specializes in vintage-inspired jewelry and antiques: delicate Art Deco earrings, vintage lockets, and necklaces fashioned from antique charms. The Erica Weiner collection includes pieces under $200. ⊠ *173 Elizabeth St., between Kenmare and Spring Sts., NoLIta* ☎ *212/334–6383* ⊕ *www.ericaweiner.com* Ⓜ *6 to Spring St.; J, Z to Bowery.*

Me&Ro. Minimalist, Eastern styling has gained these designers a cult following. The Indian-inspired, hand-finished gold bangles, earrings, and necklaces are covered in delicate jewels. Although the fine jewelry is expensive, small sterling silver pendants start at around $170. ⊠ *241 Elizabeth St., between Houston and Prince Sts., NoLIta* ☎ *917/237–9215* ⊕ *www.meandrojewelry.com* Ⓜ *6 to Spring St.; F to 2nd Ave.*

SHOES, HANDBAGS, AND LEATHER GOODS

Clare V. L.A.-based designer Clare Vivier's first New York store displays her signature simple-but-elegant leather fold-over clutches in every size and color, as well as understated totes and duffels. There is a line of men's accessories, plus iPad cases, sunglasses, and other sundries. ⊠ *239 Elizabeth St., between Houston and Prince Sts., NoLIta* ☎ *646/484–5757* ⊕ *www.clairev.com* Ⓜ *N, R, W to Prince St.; 6 to Spring St.; F to 2nd Ave.*

High Way. The bags here marry form and function. Totes and messenger bags come in durable leather and nylon, and some handbags have a wealth of inner pockets. ⊠ *238 Mott St., between Prince and Spring Sts., NoLIta* ☎ *212/966–4388* ⊕ *www.highwaybuzz.com* Ⓜ *6 to Spring St.; N, R, W to Prince St.*

John Fluevog Shoes. The inventor of the "Angel" sole (protects against water, acid, and "Satan"), Fluevog designs chunky, funky shoes and boots for men and women that are popular with rock stars and those who want to look like them. ⊠ *250 Mulberry St., at Prince St., NoLIta* ☎ *212/431–4484* ⊕ *www.fluevog.com* Ⓜ *N, R, W to Prince St.; 6 to Spring St.*

Manhattan Portage/Token. Although messenger bags are now ubiquitous, pay homage to the store that started it all. Super durable, the bags come in waxed canvas as well as nylon, and the line has expanded to include totes, duffels, and travel bags, all in unadorned, simple styles. ⊠ *258 Elizabeth St., between Houston and Prince Sts., NoLIta* ☎ *212/226–9655* ⊕ *www.manhattanportage.com* Ⓜ *N, R, W to Prince St.; F to 2nd Ave.*

EAST VILLAGE AND LOWER EAST SIDE

EAST VILLAGE

The East Village is a fabulous hunting ground for independent boutiques and jam-packed vintage stores.

ANTIQUES AND COLLECTIBLES

Lost City Arts. This sprawling shop is one of the best places to shop for 20th-century design furniture, lighting, and accessories. Lost City can also help you relive the Machine Age with an in-house, retro-modern line of furniture. ⊠ *18 Cooper Sq., at E. 5th St., East Village* ☎ *212/375–0500* ⊕ *www.lostcityarts.com* Ⓜ *6 to Astor Pl.*

BEAUTY

Bond No. 9. Created by the same fragrance team as Creed, this line of scents is intended to evoke the New York City experience, with a scent for every neighborhood: Central Park, a men's fragrance, is woodsy and "green," and Park Avenue is discreet but not too sweet. This flagship also carries candles and body creams. ⊠ *9 Bond St., between Lafayette St. and Broadway, East Village* ☎ *212/228–1732* ⊕ *www.bondno9.com* Ⓜ *6 to Bleecker St.*

Kiehl's Since 1851. At this favored haunt of top models and stylists (and the brand's flagship), white-smocked assistants help you choose between the lotions and potions, all of which are packaged in simple-looking bottles and jars. Some of the products, such as the Ultra Facial Cream, Creme with Silk Groom hairstyling aid, and superrich Creme de Corps, have attained near-cult status among fans. ⊠ *109 3rd Ave., at 13th St., East Village* ☎ *212/677–3171* ⊕ *www.kiehls.com* Ⓜ *L to 3rd Ave.*

CLOTHING

Cloak & Dagger. Come here if you like refined but on-trend looks. The racks are lined with pieces from cult-favorite women's wear designers like Samantha Pleet and Sessun, as well as accessories from the likes of A Peace Treaty and Illesteva, all hand-picked by owner and designer Brookelynn Starnes. ⊠ *334 E. 9th St., between 1st and 2nd Aves., East Village* ☎ *212/673–0500* ⊕ *www.cloakanddaggernyc.com* Ⓜ *6 to Astor Pl.; L to 1st Ave.*

John Varvatos. This menswear designer has long been inspired by rock 'n' roll. His ad campaigns have starred the likes of Franz Ferdinand and Green Day, so it's fitting that he transformed the former CBGB club into his New York flagship. The space is dotted with vintage pianos, guitars, and vinyl records. And the clothes? The jeans, leather pants, and suede shoes give you rock-star cred, but there are also classic, understated styles for the corporate set. ⊠ *315 Bowery, between E. 1st and 2nd Sts., East Village* ☎ *212/358–0315* ⊕ *www.johnvarvatos.com* Ⓜ *6 to Bleecker St.; F to 2nd Ave.*

17

Resurrection. If you're serious about vintage—and have deep pockets—Resurrection stocks a treasure trove of pristine pieces from Chanel, Gucci, Halston, Alaïa, and YSL among others. Kate Moss and Chloë Sevigny are fans, and designers like Marc Jacobs and Anna Sui have sought inspiration among the racks. ✉ *45 Great Jones St., between Bowery and Lafayette St., East Village* ☎ *212/625–1374* ⊕ *www.resurrectionvintage.com* Ⓜ *6 to Bleecker St.*

Fodor's Choice **Tokio 7.** Even fashion designers like Alexander Wang have been known
★ to pop into this high-end consignment store to browse. Racks are loaded with goodies from A-list designers such as Gucci, Stella McCartney, Diane von Furstenberg, and Phillip Lim, and the inventory changes almost daily. ✉ *83 E. 7th St., between 1st and 2nd Aves., East Village* ☎ *212/353–8443* ⊕ *www.tokio7.net* Ⓜ *6 to Astor Pl.*

Trash and Vaudeville. This punk mecca is famous for dressing stars like Debbie Harry and the Ramones back in the '70s, and its rock 'n' roll vibe lives on, albeit two blocks from its original location on St. Marks Place. Goths, punks, and pro wrestlers shop here for bondage-inspired pants and skirts, as well as vinyl corsets and mini kilts. ✉ *96 E. 7th St., between 1st Ave. and Ave. A, East Village* ☎ *212/982–3590* ⊕ *www. trashandvaudeville.com* Ⓜ *6 to Astor Pl.; L to 1st Ave.*

HOME DECOR
White Trash. Looking for a midcentury modern Danish desk? This is your place. Owner Stuart Zamsky crams his store with surprisingly affordable pieces that are mostly from the '40s through '70s, including tables, lamps, and chairs. Quirkier pieces include paper mobiles from the '70s, old fondue sets, and antique medical-office cabinets. ✉ *304 E. 5th St., between 1st and 2nd Aves., East Village* ☎ *212/598–5956* ⊕ *www.whitetrashnyc.com* Ⓜ *6 to Astor Pl.; F to 2nd Ave.*

JEWELRY AND ACCESSORIES
Verameat. All the jewelry here is handmade in New York City, and none of it is typical. Design motifs include wrenches, Big Macs, and grenades. Tilda Swinton is a fan. ✉ *315 E. 9th St., between 1st and 2nd Aves., East Village* ☎ *212/388–9045* ⊕ *www.verameat.com* Ⓜ *6 to Astor Pl.; R, W to 8th St.–NYU.*

SHOES, HANDBAGS, AND LEATHER GOODS
The Sabah House. Crammed with art, plants, midcentury furnishings, and decorative pieces picked up around the world, this cozy little boutique on a residential block sells one thing: handmade leather shoes based on a traditional Turkish style. Updated for modern sensibilities and made by Turkish artisans using centuries-old shoemaking methods, sabahs come in a wide range of colors—from classic black to a whimsical pink suede—but only one style. The shoes are famously comfortable and known to last years. Colors change seasonally, and children's sizes are available in some colors. ✉ *211 E. 12th St., between 2nd and 3rd Aves., East Village* ☎ *646/864–0790* ⊕ *www.sabah.am* Ⓜ *L to 3rd Ave.; 6 to Astor Pl.*

TOYS

FAMILY **Dinosaur Hill.** Forget about Elmo and Barbie. This little shop is crammed with quirky gifts for kids like hand puppets and marionettes from Asia, telescopes, and wooden rattles. Don't miss the unusual instruments, such as a cedar kalimba. ⊠ *306 E. 9th St., between 1st and 2nd Aves., East Village* ☎ *212/473–5850* ⊕ *www.dinosaurhill.com* Ⓜ *6 to Astor Pl.; R, W to 8th St.–NYU.*

WINE

Fodor'sChoice **Astor Wines & Spirits.** Stock up on wine, spirits, and sake at this beautiful
★ shop; it often has the bottle you can't find anywhere else. To unwind and learn more about food and wine, there's a wine library and a kitchen for cooking classes. ⊠ *399 Lafayette St., at E. 4th St., East Village* ☎ *212/674–7500* ⊕ *www.astorwines.com* Ⓜ *6 to Astor Pl.; R, W to 8th St.–NYU.*

LOWER EAST SIDE

Head to the Lower East Side for excellent vintage finds and edgy looks. Once home to multitudes of Eastern European immigrants and crumbling tenement buildings, the Lower East Side has transformed from New York's bargain-hunting ground into a hotbed for indie design that includes everything from clothing to furniture. Ludlow and Orchard Streets are the main drags for boutiques, bars, and hip restaurants. Head here if you want to revamp your look with a trendier style. For the full scope of this area, prowl from Allen to Essex Streets, and south of Houston Street down to Broome.

CLOTHING

Assembly New York. What started as a minimalist menswear boutique became a minimalist menswear designer, then added a minimalist women's wear line, and is now a surprisingly spacious shop full of architectural clothing and accessories from a range of international, independent designers. ⊠ *170 Ludlow St., between Stanton and E. Houston Sts., Lower East Side* ☎ *212/253–5393* ⊕ *www.assembly-newyork.com* Ⓜ *F to 2nd Ave.*

Frankie. A trendy concept store by the same team behind the now-shuttered Lower East Side favorite Pixie Market, the Frankie Shop caters to fashion-conscious women with its clean-lined, modern styles in understated hues from international designers. Best of all, the upscale-casual clothes, trendy boots, and both decor and fashion accessories look more expensive than they are. ⊠ *100 Stanton St., between Ludlow and Orchard Sts., Lower East Side* ☎ *212/253–0953* ⊕ *www.thefrankie-shop.com* Ⓜ *F to 2nd Ave.*

Fodor'sChoice **Maryam Nassir Zadeh.** A well-chosen collection of clothes, accessories,
★ and objects from some of the most exciting independent designers in the world is the draw at this minimalist, industrial-chic boutique. Try on mismatched shoes from Jacquemus or a hot-pink blazer from Eckaus Latta. Zadeh's own line is also available, and she sometimes stocks flea-market finds from her travels. ⊠ *123 Norfolk St., between Rivington and Delancey Sts., Lower East Side* ☎ *212/673–6405* ⊕ *mnzstore.com* Ⓜ *J, M, Z to Essex St.; F to Delancey St.*

17

The Rising States. An unassuming boutique from a lifelong fashion fan stocks an edited collection of ultrahip pieces for ladies—think quirky dresses, tailored pants, loose tops, and colorful heels and boots—by mostly local designers (like Samantha Pleet and Miranda Bennett) who often drop by the shop. ⊠ *168 Ludlow St., between Stanton and E. Houston Sts., Lower East Side* ☎ *646/649–2410* ⊕ *www.therising-statesnyc.com* Ⓜ *F to 2nd Ave.*

SHOES, HANDBAGS, AND LEATHER GOODS

Altman Luggage. Having trouble fitting all your purchases into your bag? Altman sells top-of-the-line luggage from Rimowa, Samsonite, and Tumi at discount prices. A selection of watches and cosmetic bags are also for sale. ⊠ *135 Orchard St., between Delancey and Rivington Sts., Lower East Side* ☎ *212/254–7275* ⊕ *www.altmanluggage.com* Ⓜ *J, M, Z to Essex St.; F to Delancey St.*

GREENWICH VILLAGE AND WEST VILLAGE

GREENWICH VILLAGE

The Beats were born and raised in the Village, but the poets and artists have long been replaced by New York University buildings and apartments with sky-high rent. Still, if you know where to look, there are charmingly offbeat stores worth exploring here that retain the flavor of the glory days.

BEAUTY

C. O. Bigelow. Founded in 1838, this is the oldest apothecary-pharmacy in the United States; Mark Twain used to fill prescriptions here. They still fill prescriptions, but the real reason to come is for the hard-to-find brands like Klorane shampoo and Elgydium toothpaste. Bigelow also has its own line of products, including green-tea lip balm and quince hand lotion. ⊠ *414 6th Ave., between 8th and 9th Sts., Greenwich Village* ☎ *212/533–2700* ⊕ *www.bigelowchemists.com* Ⓜ *A, B, C, D, E, F, M to W. 4th St.*

BOOKS AND STATIONERY

Fodor's Choice ★ **Goods for the Study.** Lovers of organization, writing, and beautiful things flock to this stationery store from the team behind McNally Jackson bookstore. In addition to a better-than-average selection of normal paper store products—greeting cards from independent artists, notebooks of handmade paper, office supplies from acclaimed designers, hundreds of pens sourced from around the world—the shop also carries art prints from its sister store, Picture Room. ⊠ *50 W. 8th St., between 6th Ave. and MacDougal St., Greenwich Village* ☎ *212/674–4400* ⊕ *goodsforthestudy.mcnallyjacksonstore.com* Ⓜ *A, B, C, D, E, F, M to W. 4th St.; R, W to 8th St.–NYU.*

CLOTHING

La Petite Coquette. Everything at this lingerie boutique is unabashedly sexy, and the helpful staff can find the perfect fit. The store's own line of corsets, camisoles, and other underpinnings comes in a range of colors. ⊠ *51 University Pl., between E. 9th and 10th Sts., Greenwich Village* ☎ *212/473–2478* ⊕ *www.thelittleflirt.com* Ⓜ *R, W to 8th St.–NYU.*

WEST VILLAGE

One of the most picturesque neighborhoods in New York, the West Village is filled with charming boutiques, restaurants, and bars—many of which have retained their vintage charm thanks to exposed brick walls and pressed tin ceilings. Stroll around, get lost on a cobblestone street, and finish a day of shopping with a drink at a cozy bar.

Bleecker Street is a particularly good place to indulge all sorts of shopping appetites. Foodies love the blocks between 6th and 7th Avenues for the specialty purveyors like Murray's Cheese (⊠ *254 Bleecker St.*). Fashion fans forage along the stretch between West 10th Street and 8th Avenue. Hudson Street and Greenwich Avenue are also prime boutique-browsing territory. Christopher Street, true to its connection with the LGBTQ community, has a handful of shops sporting rainbow flags.

ANTIQUES AND COLLECTIBLES

Kaas Glassworks. From the outside in, this shop is oh-so-charming, an old-fashioned sign and sandwich board welcoming shoppers and passersby. The specialty here is decoupage that has been turned into quirky trays and paperweights. Owner Carol Kaas uses antique prints, vintage postcards, historical maps, and ephemera in her work, and customizes decoupage trays from wedding invitations, photos, baby announcements, or other paper keepsakes. ⊠ *117 Perry St., between Greenwich and Hudson Sts., West Village* ☎ *212/366–0322* ⊕ *www.kaas.com* Ⓜ *1 to Christopher St.–Sheridan Sq.*

BEAUTY

Aedes Perfumery. Arguably the best place to buy fragrance in Manhattan, this boutique's super-knowledgeable staff helps shoppers find the perfect scent. High-end (and predominantly European) brands like L'Artisan Parfumeur and Astier de Villatte are stocked, along with luxurious skincare products, pricey candles, and room diffusers. The shop's signature gift wrap is as beautiful as what's inside the box. ⊠ *7 Greenwich Ave., at Christopher St., West Village* ☎ *212/206–8674* ⊕ *www.aedes.com* Ⓜ *1 to Christopher St.–Sheridan Sq.*

CAP Beauty. This is a one-stop shop for natural skin care and wellness products, which means that everything it stocks is 100% free from synthetic ingredients. Brands carried include May Lindstrom, Tata Harper, and Rahua. CAP also does spa treatments, facials, and acupuncture. ⊠ *238 W. 10th St., between Hudson and Bleecker Sts., West Village* ☎ *212/227–1088* ⊕ *www.capbeauty.com* Ⓜ *1 to Christopher St.–Sheridan Sq.*

Jo Malone. Crisp black-and-white decor sets a serene backdrop for sampling tangy scents like lime blossom and mandarin, or Earl Grey and cucumber. Fragrances can be worn alone or layered. The U.S. flagship for the British brand also offers complimentary hand massages (by appointment) and has a sampling bar for creating a bespoke scent. ⊠ *330 Bleecker St., at Christopher St., West Village* ☎ *212/242–1454* ⊕ *www.jomalone.com* Ⓜ *1 to Christopher St.–Sheridan Sq.*

17

BOOKS AND STATIONERY

bookbook. Crammed with the latest new releases, this small, independent bookstore also carries a thoughtful assortment of general nonfiction, travel guidebooks, and children's books. But when the weather cooperates, the real focus here is the carefully selected sale tables that spill out onto the sidewalk, with deals on everything from Graham Greene to Chuck Palahniuk. ⊠ *266 Bleecker St., between 6th and 7th Aves., West Village* ☎ *212/807–8655* ⊕ *www.bookbooknyc.com* Ⓜ *1 to Christopher St.–Sheridan Sq.; A, B, C, D, E, F, M to W. 4th St.*

Idlewild Books. Named for the pre-1960s JFK Airport, this travel-inspired bookstore is one of the last of its kind in America. They stock guidebooks, novels, and children's books grouped by destination, and also run foreign-language classes, ranging from Arabic to German. If those chairs look familiar, it may be because you huddled in one during a layover at the American Airlines terminal. ⊠ *170 7th Ave. S., at Perry St., West Village* ☎ *212/414–8888* ⊕ *www.idlewildbooks.com* Ⓜ *1 to Christopher St.–Sheridan Sq.*

Fodor'sChoice ★ **Three Lives & Company.** One of the city's best book selections is displayed on the tables and counters of this bookshop, which highlights the latest literary fiction and serious nonfiction, classics, quirky gift books, and gorgeously illustrated tomes. The staff members' literary knowledge is formidable, so don't be afraid to ask for their own picks. ⊠ *154 W. 10th St., at Waverly Pl., West Village* ☎ *212/741–2069* ⊕ *www. threelives.com* Ⓜ *1 to Christopher St.–Sheridan Sq.; A, B, C, D, E, F, M to W. 4th St.*

CLOTHING

Cynthia Rowley. The flirty, whimsical dresses at this boutique are perfect for cocktail parties. To complete the look, throw on some of the designer's colorful pumps and sharply tailored coats. ⊠ *394 Bleecker St., between Perry and W. 11th Sts., West Village* ☎ *212/242–3803* ⊕ *www.cynthiarowley.com* Ⓜ *1 to Christopher St.–Sheridan Sq.*

Hotoveli. This unprepossessing nook stocks some of the most elegant (and expensive) designers in the world, ranging from Lanvin to Yohji Yamamoto. If you have to ask how much an item costs, don't try it on. In addition to this location carrying clothes for both men and women, there's a women's wear–only boutique a couple of blocks away on Bleecker. ⊠ *271 W. 4th St., between W. 11th and Perry Sts., West Village* ☎ *212/206–7722* ⊕ *www.hotoveli.com* Ⓜ *1 to Christopher St.–Sheridan Sq.*

Khirma New York. A former magazine editor now designs an elegant line of handbags, clutches, and accessories that are favorites among stars like Blake Lively and J.Lo. She uses luxury materials, including python, alligator, crocodile, and stingray skins. ⊠ *102 Charles St., between Hudson and Bleecker Sts., West Village* ☎ *646/529–1408* ⊕ *www.khirma. com* Ⓜ *1 to Christopher St.–Sheridan Sq.*

Personnel of New York. "Lifestyle boutique" is an overused term, but it is the best way to describe this indie favorite, which specializes in men's and women's clothing from New York and L.A. designers. The boutique also stocks unusual home goods, such as bottle openers by

Japanese designer Tadanori Baba and soap from Juniper Ridge. ⊠ *9 Greenwich Ave., between Christopher and W. 10th Sts., West Village* ☎ *212/924–0604* ⊕ *www.personnelofnewyork.com* Ⓜ *1 to Christopher St.–Sheridan Sq.; A, B, C, D, E, F, M to W. 4th St.*

Screaming Mimi's. Browse through racks bulging with vintage finds from the 1920s through '90s. Retro wear includes everything from dresses to soccer shirts and prom dresses. Although most of the nondesigner finds are affordable, Screaming Mimi's also carries vintage designer duds from Valentino, Chloé, and Gaultier. ⊠ *240 W. 14th St., between 7th and 8th Ave., West Village* ☎ *212/677–6464* ⊕ *www.screamingmimis. com* Ⓜ *1, 2, 3, A, C, E to 14th St.; L to 8th Ave.*

FOOD AND TREATS

Li-Lac Chocolates. Feeding the Village's sweet tooth since 1923, Li-Lac indulges shoppers with its almond bark and coconut clusters as well as such specialty items as chocolate-molded Statues of Liberty. The coconut rolls and chocolate-covered graham crackers tempt even the most stubborn dieter. To see how the small-batch chocolates are made, visit Li-Lac's Brooklyn factory. ⊠ *40 8th Ave., at Jane St., West Village* ☎ *212/924– 2280* ⊕ *www.li-lacchocolates.com* Ⓜ *A, C, E to 14th St.; L to 8th Ave.*

Sockerbit. Who knew Scandinavians were obsessed with candy—but there's much more than Swedish fish at this gleaming white candy emporium that stocks hard candies, gummies, licorice, and chocolate. Have fun pronouncing the names of treats like Bumlingar Jordgubb and Zoo Klubba. ⊠ *89 Christopher St., between Bleecker and W. 4th Sts., West Village* ☎ *212/206–8170* ⊕ *www.sockerbit.com* Ⓜ *1 to Christopher St.–Sheridan Sq.*

JEWELRY AND ACCESSORIES

Ten Thousand Things. You might find yourself wishing for 10,000 things from the showcases in this elegant boutique, which recently moved to the West Village from its old TriBeCa haunt. Designs run from delicate gold and silver chains to long Peruvian opal earrings. Many shapes are abstract reflections of natural forms, like twigs or seedpods. Prices start around $180 but quickly rise. ⊠ *237 W. 13th St., between 7th and Greenwich Aves., West Village* ☎ *212/352–1333* ⊕ *www.tenthousandthingsnyc.com* Ⓜ *1, 2, 3, A, C, E to 14th St.; L to 8th Ave.*

SHOES, HANDBAGS, AND LEATHER GOODS

Flight 001. Frequent flyers can one-stop shop at this travel-themed store that puts a creative spin on everyday accessories. Shop for bright luggage tags, passport holders, satin sleep masks, and innovative storage for everything from shoes to toiletries. ⊠ *96 Greenwich Ave., between 12th and 13th Sts., West Village* ☎ *212/989–0001* ⊕ *www.flight001. com* Ⓜ *1, 2, 3, A, C, E to 14th St.; L to 8th Ave.*

Leffot. Simple and understated, this store focuses on one thing: selling top-quality men's shoes. Owner Steven Taffel, who previously worked at Prada, has stocked his shop with selections from John Lobb, Church's, and Edward Green. These shoes are meant to last a lifetime, and many have a price tag to match. Bespoke footwear is also available. ⊠ *10 Christopher St., at Gay St., West Village* ☎ *212/989–4577* ⊕ *www.leffot.com* Ⓜ *1 to Christopher St.–Sheridan Sq.; A, B, C, D, E, F, M to W. 4th St.*

CHELSEA AND THE MEATPACKING DISTRICT

CHELSEA

Chelsea offers one-stop shopping for some of the biggest retail brands, as well as quirky local boutiques.

BOOKS AND STATIONERY

FAMILY

Fodor'sChoice

★

Books of Wonder. Readers young and old delight in Manhattan's oldest and largest independent children's bookstore. The friendly, knowledgeable staff can help select gifts for all reading levels. Don't miss the extensive Oz section, plus the collection of old, rare, and collectible children's books and original children's book art. ⊠ *18 W. 18th St., between 5th and 6th Aves., Chelsea* ☎ *212/989–3270* ⊕ *www.booksofwonder.com* Ⓜ *F, M to 14th St.; L to 6th Ave.*

Posman Books. Come here for the outstanding selection of contemporary and classic books across genres. Don't miss the cheeky and serious high-quality greeting cards. Look for a second location at 30 Rockefeller Plaza in Midtown West. ⊠ *Chelsea Market, 75 9th Ave., between 15th and 16th Sts., Chelsea* ☎ *212/627–0304* ⊕ *www.posmanbooks.com* Ⓜ *A, C, E to 14th St.; L to 8th Ave.*

CLOTHING

Comme des Garçons. The designs in this swoopy, gold-adorned space consistently push the fashion envelope with brash patterns, unlikely juxtapositions (tulle and neoprene), and cuts that are meant to be thought-provoking, not flattering. Architecture students come just for the interior design. ⊠ *520 W. 22nd St., between 10th and 11th Aves., Chelsea* ☎ *212/604–9200* ⊕ *www.comme-des-garcons.com* Ⓜ *C, E to 23rd St.*

New York Vintage. Stylists to the stars, TV costumers, and the deep-pocketed descend upon this boutique to browse racks of prime vintage clothing. Everything is high-end, so don't expect any bargains. Take your pick from Yves Saint Laurent, Madame Grès, and Thierry Mugler items. There's a good selection of handbags and stilettos, too. ⊠ *117 W. 25th St., between 6th and 7th Aves., Chelsea* ☎ *212/647–1107* ⊕ *www. newyorkvintage.com* Ⓜ *F, M to 23rd St.*

HOME DECOR

Room & Board. Fans of streamlined, midcentury modern furniture ascend to heaven here. This location—set in a landmark 1902 building that was once the warehouse of the Siegel Cooper Company—is stocked with sleek sofas, beds, and children's furniture as well as accessories like rugs and lamps, 90% of which are made in America. Design aficionados can choose from iconic pieces like seating cubes from Frank Gehry and Eames molded plywood chairs, or items from up-and-coming designers. ⊠ *236 W. 18th St., between 7th and 8th Aves., Chelsea* ☎ *212/204–7384* ⊕ *www.roomandboard.com* Ⓜ *1 to 18th St.; 1, 2, 3, A, C, E to 14th St.; L to 8th Ave.*

Fodor'sChoice

★

Story. Launched by former consultant Rachel Shechtman, Story is a concept store with a twist. Every few weeks, it partners with a new sponsor to develop a retail "story," like a magazine spread, which ranges from wearable tech to "home for the holidays." Pop by often to admire the artful displays, and you never know what will be for sale, from chocolates to clothing to books. Story also hosts events such as talks with TED speakers. ⊠ *144 10th Ave., at 19th St., Chelsea* ☎ *212/242–4853* ⊕ *www.thisisstory.com* Ⓜ *A, C, E to 14th St.; L to 8th Ave.*

MUSIC STORES AND MEDIA

Jazz Record Center. If you're seeking rare or out-of-print jazz recordings, this is your one-stop shop. Long-lost Ellingtons and other rare pressings come to light here; the jazz-record specialist also stocks books, collectibles, DVDs, posters, CDs, and LPs. ⊠ *236 W. 26th St., 8th fl., between 7th and 8th Aves., Chelsea* ☎ *212/675–4480* ⊕ *www.jazzrecordcenter. com* Ⓜ *1 to 28th St.*

MEATPACKING DISTRICT

For nearly a century, the industrial western edge of downtown Manhattan was defined by slaughterhouses and meatpacking plants, blood-splattered cobblestone streets, and men lugging carcasses into warehouses before dawn.

But in the late 1990s, the area bounded by 14th Street, Gansevoort Street, Hudson Street, and 11th Avenue speedily transformed into another kind of meat market. Many of the old warehouses now house ultrachic shops, nightclubs, and restaurants packed with angular fashionistas. Jeffrey, a pint-sized department store, was an early arrival, followed by bigger brands such as Diane von Furstenberg and a few lofty furniture stores. Despite the influx of a few chains—albeit stylish ones like Scoop—eclectic boutiques keep popping up. The one thing that's hard to find here is a bargain.

CLOTHING

Diane von Furstenberg. At this light-filled New York flagship, try on the iconic DVF wrap dress in myriad patterns. The blouses, shorts, and skirts are equally feminine. ⊠ *874 Washington St., at 14th St., Meatpacking District* ☎ *646/486–4800* ⊕ *www.dvf.com* Ⓜ *A, C, E to 14th St.; L to 8th Ave.*

Jeffrey. The Meatpacking District really arrived when this Atlanta-based mini Barneys opened its doors. You can find an incredible array of designer shoes—Valentino and red-soled Christian Louboutins are some of the best sellers—plus top labels such as Yves Saint Laurent and Lanvin for both men and women. ⊠ *449 W. 14th St., between 9th and 10th Aves., Meatpacking District* ☎ *212/206–1272* ⊕ *www.jeffreynewyork. com* Ⓜ *A, C, E to 14th St.; L to 8th Ave.*

Rebecca Taylor. This designer is known for her soft, feminine work, which runs the gamut from sexy to understated, all with a slightly vintage flair. Taylor's downtown location is a serene, spacious environment for browsing racks of silky shirtdresses, embroidered tunics, and ruffled overcoats. Her shoes, handbags, and jewelry are equally romantic. ⊠ *34 Gansevoort St., between Greenwich and Hudson Sts., Meatpacking District* ☎ *212/243–2600* ⊕ *www.rebeccataylor.com* Ⓜ *A, C, E to 14th St.; L to 8th Ave.*

Trina Turk. Make a beeline to this boutique if you like glowing, happy colors and 1970's-influenced clothing. The shop, designed by Jonathan Adler, showcases Turk's ready-to-wear clothing in a bright, airy setting. Swimwear is a standout, and menswear is also sold here. ⊠ *67 Gansevoort St., between*

17

Washington and Greenwich Sts., Meatpacking District ☎ *212/206–7383*
⊕ *www.trinaturk.com* Ⓜ *A, C, E to 14th St.; L to 8th Ave.*

UNION SQUARE AND THE FLATIRON DISTRICT

UNION SQUARE

The several blocks around Union Square—which itself is home to the city's best greenmarket, as well as a holiday market leading up to Christmas—just south of the Flatiron District, has large retail chains such as J.Crew, Banana Republic, and Anthropologie.

BEAUTY

Fresh. Long a beauty favorite, with ingredients that are good enough to eat (think brown sugar, soy, and black tea), the Fresh flagship has an apothecary-inspired look, with beautifully packaged soaps displayed like pastries in a glass case. Pull up a seat at the communal Kitchen Table to try out a new product. ✉ *872 Broadway, at 18th St., Union Square* ☎ *212/477–1100* ⊕ *www.fresh.com* Ⓜ *4, 5, 6, L, N, Q, R, W to 14th St.–Union Sq.*

BOOKS AND STATIONERY

Fodor's Choice
★
Strand. Opened in 1927 and still run by the same family, this monstrous book emporium—home to 2 million volumes, or "18 Miles of Books"—is a symbol of a bygone era, a mecca for serious bibliophiles, and a local institution. The store has survived the Great Depression, World War II, and competition from Barnes & Noble and the Kindle. The stock includes new and secondhand books, plus thousands of collector's items and merchandise. A separate rare-book room is on the third floor (it closes at 6:15 daily). The basement has discounted, barely touched review copies of new books, organized by author. If you're looking for souvenirs, visit the New York section of the bookstore for New York–centric literature, poetry, and cookbooks, as well as T-shirts and totes. Visitors should also check the Strand's events calendar and try to attend an author or artist event. ✉ *828 Broadway, at 12th St., Union Square* ☎ *212/473–1452* ⊕ *www.strandbooks.com* Ⓜ *4, 5, 6, L, N, Q, R, W to 14th St.–Union Sq.*

CLOTHING

Beacon's Closet. A simple space, the Big Apple outpost of Brooklyn favorite Beacon's Closet is lit by multiple chandeliers and has a wide selection of gently used modern and vintage clothes. Comb through the racks and you might find pieces from Christian Dior, Marc Jacobs, or AllSaints, as well as stylish items from under-the-radar labels. ✉ *10 W. 13th St., between 5th and 6th Aves., Union Square* ☎ *917/261–4863* ⊕ *www.beaconscloset.com* Ⓜ *4, 5, 6, L, N, Q, R, W to 14th St.–Union Sq.*

Fodor's Choice
★
Journelle. This chic, New York–based boutique was started by two women who believed that sexy, pretty lingerie should be everyday wear—and comfortable, too. The staff is approachable and helpful. There are now a handful of stores around the city, including in SoHo and on the Upper East Side. ✉ *14 E. 17th St., between Broadway and 5th Ave., Union Square* ☎ *212/255–7800* ⊕ *www.journelle.com* Ⓜ *4, 5, 6, L, N, Q, R, W to 14th St.–Union Sq.*

FOOD AND WINE

Union Square Wine & Spirits. Tastings are easy at this well-stocked store, thanks to Enomatic machines. These card-operated contraptions let you sample dozens of wines. If machines don't do it for you, generous tastings are held most Fridays and Saturdays. ⊠ *140 4th Ave., at 13th St., Union Square* ☎ *212/675–8100* ⊕ *www.unionsquarewines.com* Ⓜ *4, 5, 6, L, N, Q, R, W to 14th St.–Union Sq.*

HOME DECOR

Fodor's Choice ★ **ABC Carpet & Home.** If you love eclectic luxury home goods from around the world, this is your place. Spread over 10 floors is a superb selection of rugs, antiques, textiles, furniture, and bedding, including sleek sofas and Balinese daybeds. The ground floor is a wonderland of silk pillows and jewelry, the mezzanine level is completely wellness-focused, and the basement level stocks artisanal and imported foodstuffs alongside beautiful pieces to serve them on. To refuel, there are two in-house restaurants from Jean-Georges Vongerichten. More rugs and carpets are unrolled across the street at 881 Broadway. ⊠ *888 Broadway, at 19th St., Union Square* ☎ *212/473–3000* ⊕ *www.abchome.com* Ⓜ *4, 5, 6, L, N, Q, R, W to 14th St.–Union Sq.*

JEWELRY AND ACCESSORIES

Beads of Paradise. At what is not your ordinary bead store, the baubles are sourced from around the world. Shoppers can choose silver from Bali and Mexico and ancient glass beads from China, along with semiprecious stones. Sign up for a class to learn how to put it all together. The store also has a wide range of other trinkets from around the world, including Buddha figurines from Thailand, Madonna candles from Mexico, and Ganesha-printed hangings from India. ⊠ *16 E. 17th St., between 5th Ave. and Broadway, Union Square* ☎ *212/620–0642* ⊕ *www.beadsofparadis-enyc.com* Ⓜ *4, 5, 6, L, N, Q, R, W to 14th St.–Union Sq.*

17

TOYS

FAMILY **Kidding Around.** This independent shop is piled high with old-fashioned wooden toys, sturdy musical instruments, classic kids' books, and plenty of arts-and-crafts materials. The costume racks are rich with dress-up potential. ⊠ *60 W. 15th St., between 5th and 6th Aves., Union Square* ☎ *212/645–6337* ⊕ *www.kiddingaroundtoys.com* Ⓜ *F, M to 14th St.; L to 6th Ave.; 4, 5, 6, L, N, Q, R, W to 14th St.–Union Sq.*

FLATIRON DISTRICT

The Flatiron District, north of Union Square, stretches from about 17th Street up to 29th Street, and between 6th Avenue and Lexington. This is one of the buzziest areas in New York, brimming with both large and small stores. Come here if you want to shop the big chains minus the Midtown tourist crowds.

CAMERAS AND ELECTRONICS

Sony Square NYC. Located on the ground floor of Sony headquarters, this sprawling space is more a showroom of themed, rotating installations to showcase the latest Sony electronics than it is a store. Take new Playstation games for a spin, experience the latest VR products, preview unreleased products, and even borrow top-of-the-line cameras and lenses to test around the city. The space also hosts events with celebrities and industry experts. ⊠ *25 Madison Ave., at 25th St., Flatiron District* ☎ *212/833–8800* ⊕ *www.sony.com/square-nyc* Ⓜ *R, W, 6 to 23rd St.*

CHILDREN'S CLOTHING

FAMILY **Space Kiddets.** The funky (Elvis-print rompers, CBGB onesies) mixes with the old-school (retro cowboy-print pants, brightly colored clogs, Bruce Lee T-shirts) and the high-end (Lili Gaufrette, Kenzo, Boo Foo Woo from Japan) at this casual, trendsetting store. ⊠ *26 E. 22nd St., between Broadway and Park Ave., Flatiron District* ☎ *212/420–9878* ⊕ *www.spacekiddets.com* Ⓜ *6, R, W to 23rd St.*

CLOTHING

Anthropologie. This popular women's clothing and home accessories chain epitomizes bohemian chic. Stock up on flowing dresses, floral-printed blouses, and ruffled skirts, and find pastel- and jewel-toned bedspreads and dishware. Don't miss out on the collection of luxe skincare and beauty products. ⊠ *85 5th Ave., at 16th St., Flatiron District* ☎ *212/627–5885* ⊕ *www.anthropologie.com* Ⓜ *4, 5, 6, L, N, Q, R, W to 14th St.–Union Sq.*

Madewell. A J.Crew spinoff, Madewell is ideal for casual women's staples like jeans, T-shirts, and sweaters with a vintage look. The two-story Manhattan flagship has a quirky, homespun design; merchandise is displayed on everything from old mill tables to meat hooks. Don't miss the shoe shop and home-goods collection. ⊠ *115 5th Ave., at 19th St., Flatiron District* ☎ *212/228–5172* ⊕ *www.madewell.com* Ⓜ *4, 5, 6, L, N, Q, R, W to 14th St.–Union Sq.*

FOOD AND TREATS

Fodor's Choice
★ **Eataly.** This sprawling Italian grocery, originally from Torino, has the best selection of imported foodstuffs in the city, as well as a variety of cafés and restaurants, set between the aisles and meat and cheese counters. Up on the roof, there's also a house brewery and beer garden. ⊠ *200 5th Ave., at 24th St., Flatiron District* ☎ *212/229–2560* ⊕ *www. eataly.com* Ⓜ *R, W, 6 to 23rd St.*

HOME DECOR

Fodor's Choice
★ **Fishs Eddy.** The dishes, china, and glassware for resale come from all walks of crockery life, including corporate dining rooms and failed restaurants, so you never know what you might find. Fishs Eddy also sells its own lines of dishes and kitchenware, which have both classic and whimsical looks. ■ TIP➔ **The shop is a great place to pick up New York-themed gifts, such as mugs and trays.** ⊠ *889 Broadway, at 19th St., Flatiron District* ☎ *212/420–9020* ⊕ *www.fishseddy.com* Ⓜ *4, 5, 6, L, N, Q, R, W to 14th St.–Union Sq.*

Marimekko. If you love bright, cheerful patterns, make a beeline to the Marimekko flagship. This 4,000-square-foot store is primarily white, so the colorful merchandise pops. Everything from pot holders and shower curtains to coats and dresses is available here in the Finnish brand's bold signature prints. If you're feeling crafty, pick up a few yards of fabric to create something of your own. ⊠ *200 5th Ave., between 23rd and 24th Sts., Flatiron District* ☎ *212/843–9121* ⊕ *www.marimekko.com* Ⓜ *R, W, 6 to 23rd St.*

Holiday Markets

Between Thanksgiving and Christmas, holiday markets—rows of wooden stalls, many with red-and-white-stripe awnings—spring up around town. The gifts and goods vary from year to year, but there are some perennial offerings: colorful handmade knitwear and jewelry; fragrant soaps, candles, and lotions with hand-lettered labels; glittery Christmas ornaments of every stripe; and New York–themed gift items.

While the holiday market in Grand Central Terminal's Vanderbilt Hall is indoors, most vendors set up outside. There's one every year at Columbus Circle, near the southwest entrance to Central Park, and another at Bryant Park, behind the New York City Public Library. The largest and most popular, however, is at the south end of Union Square, where you can go from the greenmarket to the stalls, just like the downtowners who meet in the afternoon or after work to look for unique or last-minute gifts.

WINE

Bottlerocket Wine & Spirit. Fun and approachable, this shop puts a new spin on wine shopping. Vintages are organized by quirky factors like their compatibility with Chinese takeout and whom they'd best suit as gifts (ranging from "Third Date" to "The Boss"). A kids' play nook and doggie area make the space extra welcoming. ⊠ *5 W. 19th St., between 5th and 6th Aves., Flatiron District* ☎ *212/929–2323* ⊕ *www. bottlerocket.com* Ⓜ *4, 5, 6, L, N, Q, R, W to 14th St.–Union Sq.*

MIDTOWN EAST

If money is no object, put on your best shopping shoes and most glamorous sunglasses and head to Midtown East. Some of the world's most luxurious brands—from Gucci to Christian Dior—have their flagship stores along 5th Avenue. All the stores *on* 5th Avenue are included in Midtown East, although some might be on the west side of the street and have West in their address.

ANTIQUES AND COLLECTIBLES

A La Vieille Russie. Antiques dealers since 1851, this shop specializes in European and Russian decorative arts, jewelry, and paintings. Behold bibelots by Fabergé and others, enameled or encrusted with jewels. If money is no object, there are also antique diamond necklaces and pieces of china once owned by Russian nobility. The shop is closed on weekends. ⊠ *745 5th Ave., 4th fl., between 57th and 58th Sts., Midtown East* ☎ *212/752–1727* ⊕ *www.alvr.com* Ⓜ *N, R, W to 5th Ave./59th St.*

The Chinese Porcelain Company. Though the name of this prestigious shop indicates one of its specialties, its stock covers more ground, ranging from lacquerware to Khmer sculpture, as well as work by contemporary Chinese artists. ⊠ *232 E. 59th St., 5th fl., between 2nd and 3rd Aves., Midtown East* ☎ *212/838–7744* ⊕ *www.chineseporcelaincompany. com/* Ⓜ *4, 5, 6 to 59th St.; N, R, W to Lexington Ave./59th St.*

17

Leo Kaplan Ltd. The impeccable items here include Art Nouveau glass and pottery, porcelain from 18th-century England, antique and modern paperweights, and Russian art. ✉ *114 E. 57th St., between Park and Lexington Aves., Midtown East* ☎ *212/355–7212* ⊕ *www.leokaplan. com* Ⓜ *4, 5, 6 to 59th St.; N, R, W to Lexington Ave./59th St.*

Newel. The huge collection here spans the Renaissance through the 20th century and includes nonfurniture finds, from figureheads to bell jars, that make for prime conversation pieces. Newel is a major supplier of antiques for Broadway shows and luxury department store windows. It's closed on weekends. ✉ *306 E. 61st St., 3rd fl., between 2nd Ave. and Ed Koch Queensboro Bridge Exit, Midtown East* ☎ *212/758–1970* ⊕ *www.newel.com* Ⓜ *4, 5, 6 to 59th St.; N, R, W to Lexington Ave./59th St.*

BOOKS AND STATIONERY

Argosy Bookstore. Family owned since 1925, Argosy is a charmingly old-fashioned place to browse for both bargain and priceless books. The shop keeps a scholarly stock of rare books and autographs. It's also a great place to find low-price maps and prints for gifts. ✉ *116 E. 59th St., between Park and Lexington Aves., Midtown East* ☎ *212/753–4455* ⊕ *www.argosybooks.com* Ⓜ *4, 5, 6 to 59th St.; N, R, W to Lexington Ave./59th St.*

CAMERAS AND ELECTRONICS

Apple Store. New York's flagship Apple Store features a 32-foot-high glass cube that appears to float over its subterranean entrance—or, at least, it normally does, though the store is under renovation until late 2018 (and is being supplemented by an adjacent temporary flagship until then). The Apple-obsessed will be happy to know this location is open 24/7, holidays included. Make an appointment (well in advance) at the Genius Bar if you need tech help. There's also an Apple Store location in SoHo, in a converted historic post office building, as well as a handful of other branches around the city, including on the Upper West Side, on West 14th Street, and in Grand Central Station. ✉ *767 5th Ave., at 59th St., Midtown East* ☎ *212/336–1440* ⊕ *www.apple. com* Ⓜ *N, R, W to 5th Ave./59th St.*

CLOTHING

BCBG Max Azria. The brand's initials are short for "bon chic, bon genre," which means stylish sportswear and embellished, embroidered evening dresses here. The collection ranges from leather pants to maxi dresses. ✉ *461 5th Ave., at 40th St., Midtown East* ☎ *212/991–9777* ⊕ *www. bcbg.com* Ⓜ *B, D, F, M to 42nd St.–Bryant Park.*

Brooks Brothers. The clothes at this classic American haberdasher are, as ever, traditional, comfortable, and fairly priced. Summer seersucker, navy-blue blazers, and the peerless oxford shirts have been staples for generations; the women's and boys' selections have variations thereon. Get scanned by a digital tailor for precisely measured custom shirts or suits; an appointment is recommended. ✉ *346 Madison Ave., at 44th St., Midtown East* ☎ *212/682–8800* ⊕ *www.brooksbrothers.com* Ⓜ *4, 5, 6, 7, S to Grand Central–42nd. St.*

Burberry. This six-story glass-and-stone flagship is a temple to all things plaid and British. The iconic trench coat can be made to measure here, and the signature plaid can be found on bikinis, scarves, and wallets. For children, there are mini versions of quilted jackets and cozy sweaters. ⊠ *9 E. 57th St., between 5th and Madison Aves., Midtown East* ☎ *212/407-7100* ⊕ *us.burberry.com* Ⓜ *N, R, W to 5th Ave./59th St.*

Chanel. The Midtown flagship at 15 East 57th Street has often been compared to a Chanel suit—slim, elegant, timeless, and decorated in the signature black-and-white colors. While that suit has some tailoring done—the store is being expanded to seven floors from two—the boutique has temporarily (to 2019, at least) relocated down the block, with all its classics in tow. Come here for the iconic suits and quilted handbags, along with other pillars of Chanel style: chic little black dresses, evening gowns, and yards of pearls. There's also a cosmetics area where you can stock up on the famed scents and nail polish. ⊠ *5 E. 57th St., between 5th and Madison Aves., Midtown East* ☎ *212/355–5050* ⊕ *www.chanel.com* Ⓜ *N, R, W to 5th Ave./59th St.; F to 57th St.*

Dior. Very white and very glossy, this space sets a serene background to showcase the luxe ready-to-wear collection along with handbags and accessories. If you're not in the market for an investment gown or fine jewelry, peruse the latest status bag. The Dior menswear boutique is next door; the cigarette-thin suits are often snapped up by women. ⊠ *21 E. 57th St., between 5th and Madison Aves., Midtown East* ☎ *212/931–2950* ⊕ *www.dior.com* Ⓜ *N, R, W to 5th Ave./59th St.; F to 57th St.*

Dover Street Market. The New York location is the only U.S. outpost of Rei Kawakubo's Dover Street Market (the others are in London, Tokyo, Singapore, and Beijing). It's basically a multilevel fashion emporium: each floor has mini boutiques from brands including Prada, Alaïa, and Alexander Wang, alongside lesser-known designers. The seven-story building is worth a look just for the people-watching. The in-house Rose Bakery is the perfect spot to refuel with an espresso or berry tart. ⊠ *160 Lexington Ave., at 30th St., Midtown East* ☎ *646/837–7750* ⊕ *newyork.doverstreetmarket.com* Ⓜ *6 to 28th St.*

Dunhill. If you're stumped on what to buy the man in your life, head to Dunhill. The menswear from the London designer is exquisitely tailored, and the accessories, like wallets and cuff links, are somewhat affordable. The walk-in humidor stores top-quality tobacco and cigars. ⊠ *545 Madison Ave., at 55th St., Midtown East* ☎ *212/753–9292* ⊕ *www.dunhill.com* Ⓜ *E, M to 5th Ave./53rd St.*

Massimo Dutti. Owned by Zara, this brand is that more ubiquitous one's older, more sophisticated sibling. The three-story space specializes in sleek basics that are perfect for work or the weekends, such as blazers, trench coats, and silky sweaters. ⊠ *689 5th Ave., between 54th and 55th Sts., Midtown East* ☎ *212/371–2555* ⊕ *www.massimodutti.com* Ⓜ *E, M to 5th Ave./53rd St.*

UNIQLO. At 89,000 square feet, this location is the biggest UNIQLO in the world (in New York, there are also branches in SoHo and near Herald Square and Brooklyn's Barclays Center). Shoppers can scoop up staples such as sweaters, skinny jeans, and button-down shirts in a

17

rainbow of colors. Don't miss the limited-edition collaborations with big-name designers and stylists. The Heattech clothing range is always a big hit. Weekday mornings are the best time to avoid long lines for the dressing rooms. ⊠ *666 5th Ave., at 53rd St., Midtown East* ☎ *877/486–4756* ⊕ *www.uniqlo.com* Ⓜ *E, M to 5th Ave./53rd St.*

Versace. The architecture here, with its marble floor and glittering chandeliers, provides the perfect backdrop for the outrageous designs and colors of Versace clothes. The brand's housewares and bedding collection are also available here. ⊠ *647 5th Ave., between 51st and 52nd Sts., Midtown East* ☎ *212/317–0224* ⊕ *www.versace.com* Ⓜ *E, M to 5th Ave./53rd St.*

Zara. This massive store is one of Zara's biggest in the United States and the place to come for affordable, stylish fashion. New merchandise arrives twice a week and ranges from classics like blazers to edgier skinny trousers. There are also two lounge areas, in case you need a shopping break. ⊠ *666 5th Ave., between 52nd and 53rd Sts., Midtown East* ☎ *212/765–0477* ⊕ *www.zara.com* Ⓜ *E, M to 5th Ave./53rd St.*

DEPARTMENT STORES

Bergdorf Goodman. The ultimate shopping destination, this luxury department store offers ladies (and gentlemen) who lunch designer clothes, a stellar shoe department, and top-notch service. The fifth floor is where to go for contemporary lines. The range of products in the beauty department is unparalleled, and shoppers can complete their look with highlights at the in-house John Barrett salon. If you need to refuel, grab a bite at the seventh-floor BG Restaurant, with Central Park views, or a quick bite at the beauty-level Good Dish. ⊠ *754 5th Ave., between 57th and 58th Sts., Midtown East* ☎ *212/753–7300* ⊕ *www.bergdorfgoodman.com* Ⓜ *N, R, W to 5th Ave./59th. St.*

Fodor's Choice ★ **Bloomingdale's.** Only a few stores in New York occupy an entire city block; the uptown branch of this New York institution is one of them. The main floor is a crazy, glittery maze of mirrored cosmetic counters and perfume-spraying salespeople. Once you get past this dizzying scene, you can find good buys on designer clothes, bedding, and housewares. ⊠ *1000 3rd Ave., main entrance at 59th St. and Lexington Ave., Midtown East* ☎ *212/705–2000* ⊕ *bloomingdales.com* Ⓜ *4, 5, 6 to 59th St.; N, R, W to Lexington Ave./59th St.*

Henri Bendel. Behind the graceful Lalique windows, discover a world of luxe accessories, all from Henri Bendel's own collection. Work your way through two floors of jewelry, scarves, handbags, and sunglasses. If you really want to pamper yourself, visit Frédéric Fekkai's hair salon on the fourth floor. ⊠ *712 5th Ave., between 55th and 56th Sts., Midtown East* ☎ *212/247–1100* ⊕ *www.henribendel.com* Ⓜ *E, M to 5th Ave./53rd St.; F to 57th St.*

Lord & Taylor. It's not your mother's Lord & Taylor: the department store has been working hard to attract a younger, hipper crowd, and shoppers find classic brands like Coach and Ralph Lauren along with jeans from 7 for All Mankind and tops by Trina Turk. Be sure to visit the lovely ground-floor beauty department. The store isn't nearly as crowded as competitor Macy's; however, the building was sold to WeWork in 2017, and Lord & Taylor will be shrinking starting in 2019. ⊠ *424 5th Ave.,* *between 38th and 39th Sts., Midtown East* ☏ *212/391–3344* ⊕ *www. lordandtaylor.com* Ⓜ *B, D, F, M to 42nd St.–Bryant Park.*

Saks Fifth Avenue. This iconic store has been upping its fashion stakes and revamping its résumé by adding more contemporary designer lines, such as Proenza Schouler and Victoria Beckham. The department store now has a designer sneaker shop, as well as an enormous Christian Louboutin shop-within-a-shop. The ground-floor beauty department stocks everything from the classics to the edgy. ✉ *611 5th Ave., between 49th and 50th Sts., Midtown East* ☏ *212/753–4000* ⊕ *www.saksfifthavenue.com* Ⓜ *E, M to 5th Ave./53rd St.; B, D, F, M to 47–50th Sts./Rockefeller Center.*

GIFTS AND SOUVENIRS

New York City Transit Museum Gallery Annex & Store. Located in the symbolic heart of New York City's transit system, this museum store features an eclectic array of merchandise all linked to the MTA (Metropolitan Transportation Authority), from straphanger ties to earrings made from old subway tokens. ✉ *Grand Central Terminal, Vanderbilt Pl. and 42nd St., Shuttle Passage, Midtown East* ☏ *212/878–0106* ⊕ *www.nytransit-museumstore.com* Ⓜ *4, 5, 6, 7, S to Grand Central–42nd St.*

HOME DECOR

Armani Casa. In keeping with the Armani aesthetic, the minimalist furniture and housewares here have a subdued color scheme (gold, gray, cream, and black). Big-ticket items include luxuriously upholstered sofas and sleek coffee tables. The desk accessories and throw pillows are equally understated. ✉ *Decoration & Design Building, 979 3rd Ave., Suite 1424, between 58th and 59th Sts., Midtown East* ☏ *212/334–1271* ⊕ *www.armanicasa.com* Ⓜ *4, 5, 6 to 59th St.; N, R, W to Lexington Ave./59th St.*

17

JEWELRY AND ACCESSORIES

Bulgari. With a recently redesigned, jewel-encrusted flagship on 5th Avenue, this Italian company is certainly not shy about its name, which encircles gems, watch faces, and an ever-growing accessories line. There are ornate, weighty rings and other pieces mixing gold with stainless steel, porcelain, and the brand's signature cabochon multicolored sapphires. Wedding and engagement rings are slightly more subdued. ✉ *730 5th Ave., at 57th St., Midtown East* ☏ *212/315–9000* ⊕ *www. bulgari.com* Ⓜ *N, R, W to 5th Ave./59th St.; F to 57th St.*

Cartier. Established in 1914, this legendary French jeweler and firm favorite among royals and celebrities is the place to come for exquisite engagement rings, luxury watches, or cuff links. Cartier's iconic designs include the panther motif, the Trinity ring, and Tank watches. ✉ *767 5th Ave., between 58th and 59th Sts., Midtown East* ☏ *212/457–3202* ⊕ *www.cartier.com* Ⓜ *N, R, W to 5th Ave./59th St.*

H. Stern. Sleek designs pose in an equally modern 5th Avenue setting; smooth cabochon-cut stones, most from South America, glow in pale wooden display cases. The designers make notable use of semiprecious stones such as citrine, tourmaline, and topaz. ✉ *645 5th Ave., between 51st and 52nd Sts., Midtown East* ☏ *800/747–8376* ⊕ *www.hstern.net* Ⓜ *E, M to 5th Ave./53rd St.*

Harry Winston. These jewels regularly adorn celebs at the Oscars, and you need an A-list bank account to shop here. The ice-clear diamonds are of impeccable quality and set in everything from emerald-cut solitaire rings to wreath necklaces resembling strings of flowers. No wonder the jeweler was immortalized in the song "Diamonds Are a Girl's Best Friend." Note that the jeweler's flagship is due to reopen after renovations by late 2018; in case the reopening is delayed, find the temporary flagship at 701 5th Avenue, at 55th Street. ⊠ *718 5th Ave., at 56th St., Midtown East* ☎ *212/399–1000* ⊕ *www.harrywinston.com* Ⓜ *F to 57th St.; N, R, W to 5th Ave./59th St.; E, M to 5th Ave./53rd St.*

Mikimoto. The Japanese originator of the cultured pearl, Mikimoto presents a glowing display of high-luster pearls. Besides the creamy strands from their own pearl farms, check out diamond-and-pearl earrings, bracelets, and rings. ⊠ *730 5th Ave., between 56th and 57th Sts., Midtown East* ☎ *212/457–4600* ⊕ *www.mikimotoamerica.com* Ⓜ *F to 57th St.; N, R, W to 5th Ave./59th St.*

Tiffany & Co. It's hard to think of a more iconic New York jewelry store than Tiffany, along with its unmistakable blue box. Daydream among the displays of platinum-and-diamond bracelets and massive engagement rings, but head to the sterling-silver floor for more affordable baubles. The Tiffany T line is streamlined and modern. ⊠ *727 5th Ave., at 57th St., Midtown East* ☎ *212/755–8000* ⊕ *www.tiffany.com* Ⓜ *N, R, W to 5th Ave./59th St.; F to 57th St.*

Van Cleef & Arpels. This French jewelry company is considerably more low-key than many of its blingy neighbors, in both design and marketing ethos (you won't see them opening a store in your average mall). Their best-known design is the cloverleaf Alhambra, which can be found on rings, necklaces, and earrings. ⊠ *744 5th Ave., at 57th St., Midtown East* ☎ *212/896–9284* ⊕ *www.vancleefarpels.com* Ⓜ *N, R, W to 5th Ave./59th St.; F to 57th St.*

SHOES, HANDBAGS, AND LEATHER GOODS

Bottega Veneta. The signature crosshatch weave graces leather handbags, slouchy satchels, and shoes; the especially satisfying brown shades extend from fawn to deep chocolate. The stylish men's and women's ready-to-wear collection is also sold here. ⊠ *650 Madison Ave., between 59th and 60th Sts., Midtown East* ☎ *212/371–5511* ⊕ *www.bottegaveneta.com* Ⓜ *4, 5, 6 to 59th St.; N, R, W to Lexington Ave./59th St.*

Cole Haan. This brand is known for its comfortable but stylish footwear—many shoes have Nike Air cushioning in the heel. Everything from sandals to boots and pumps is available. ⊠ *Rockefeller Center, 620 5th Ave., between 49th and 50th Sts., Midtown East* ☎ *212/765–9747* ⊕ *www.colehaan.com* Ⓜ *B, D, F, M to 47–50th Sts./Rockefeller Center.*

Fendi. Once known for its furs, Fendi is now synonymous with decadent handbags, and its Madison Avenue flagship is a temple to them. The purses are beaded, embroidered, and fantastically embellished within an inch of their lives. Buttery soft leathers, ladylike evening dresses, structured handbags, and other accessories are also available. ⊠ *598 Madison Ave., between 57th and 58th Sts., Midtown East* ☎ *212/897–2244* ⊕ *www.fendi.com* Ⓜ *N, R, W to 5th Ave./59th St.*

Fratelli Rossetti. Don't come here expecting sexy, skyscraper stilettos, or any overly trendy looks: this Italian leather-goods company excels at classic shoes. Riding boots are among the most popular items, but there are also pumps, loafers, and slouchy ankle boots. Men can choose from oxfords and boots. There's also a line of leather handbags. ⊠ *625 Madison Ave., between 58th and 59th Sts., Midtown East* ☎ *212/888–5107* ⊕ *www.fratellirossetti.com* Ⓜ *N, R, W to 5th Ave./59th St.; 4, 5, 6 to 59th St.*

Louis Vuitton. In the mammoth 57th Street flagship, shoppers get their fill of LV-emblazoned handbags and accessories, as well as the more subtle Damier check pattern and colorful striated leathers. The clothes and shoes here are devastatingly chic. ⊠ *1 E. 57th St., at 5th Ave., Midtown East* ☎ *212/758–8877* ⊕ *www.louisvuitton.com* Ⓜ *N, R, W to 5th Ave./59th St.*

Salvatore Ferragamo. Elegance and restraint typify these designs, from patent leather ballet flats to weekender ankle boots. The company has reworked some of its women's styles from previous decades, like the girlish Audrey (as in Hepburn) ballet flat, released seasonally for limited runs. Don't miss the silk ties for men. ⊠ *655 5th Ave., at 52nd St., Midtown East* ☎ *212/759–3822* ⊕ *www.ferragamo.com* Ⓜ *E, M to 5th Ave./53rd St.*

Stuart Weitzman. The broad range of shoe styles, from wing tips to strappy sandals, is enhanced by an even wider range of sizes and widths. Bridal shoes are hugely popular, if pricey. ⊠ *625 Madison Ave., between 58th and 59th Sts., Midtown East* ☎ *212/750–2555* ⊕ *www.stuart-weitzman.com* Ⓜ *N, R, W to 5th Ave./59th St.; 4, 5, 6 to 59th St.*

17

MIDTOWN WEST

Stretching west from ritzy 5th Avenue, Midtown West covers everything from Herald Square to Times Square, and plenty in between. In other words, whether you're window-shopping or have money to burn, you'll no doubt find something to strike your fancy, from high-end designers to major retail brands.

CAMERAS AND ELECTRONICS

Fodor's Choice ★ **B&H Photo & Video.** Low prices, good customer service, and a liberal return policy make this well-stocked emporium a favorite with pros and amateurs alike looking for audio and video equipment, new cameras, or laptops. Be sure to leave a few extra minutes for the checkout procedure; also, keep in mind that the store is closed Saturday. B&H is also known for its ceiling-height conveyor-belt system to move packages. ⊠ *420 9th Ave., between 33rd and 34th Sts., Midtown West* ☎ *212/239–7765* ⊕ *www.bhphotovideo.com* Ⓜ *1, 2, 3, A, C, E to 34th St.–Penn Station.*

CLOTHING

Forever 21. The pounding music, plethora of jeggings, and graffiti-covered NYC taxicabs parked inside appeal to tween shoppers. But even if you are older than 21, there's still reason to shop here. This location, clocking in at a whopping 90,000 square feet and perched right on Times Square, is crammed with supertrendy clothes that won't break the bank, such as slouchy sweaters, shirtdresses, and poofy skirts. Menswear and children's clothes are also sold here, and the jewelry is surprisingly well-done. There are several other locations in Manhattan, including Union Square and Herald Square. ✉ *1540 Broadway, between 45th and 46th Sts., Midtown West* ☎ *212/302–0594* ⊕ *www. forever21.com* Ⓜ *N, R, W to 49th St.; 1, 2, 3, N, Q, R, S, W, 7 to Times Square/42nd St.*

Gap. Gap may be as ubiquitous as Starbucks, but it is still a go-to place for classic denim, khakis, and sweaters in a rainbow of colors, as well as on-trend capsule collections from top designers. This Herald Square flagship also carries GapBody, GapMaternity, GapKids, and babyGap. ✉ *60 W. 34th St., at Broadway, Midtown West* ☎ *212/760–1268* ⊕ *www.gap.com* Ⓜ *B, D, F, M, N, Q, R, W to 34th St.–Herald Sq.*

Norma Kamali. A fashion fixture from the 1980s, Norma Kamali has a thoroughly modern, though still '80s-influenced, line. Her luminously white store carries graphic bathing suits, Grecian-style draped dresses, and her signature poofy "sleeping-bag coats." The in-house Wellness Café sells olive oil–based beauty products. Note that the store is closed Sunday. ✉ *11 W. 56th St., between 5th and 6th Aves., Midtown West* ☎ *212/957–9797* ⊕ *www.normakamali.com* Ⓜ *N, R, W to 5th Ave./59th St.; F to 57th St.*

DEPARTMENT STORES

Macy's. The store's massive, iconic flagship emerged in 2016 from a multiyear renovation that includes a glossier, grander look with acres of marble and new video screens. On both the cosmetics and clothing floors, the focus has been shifted to prestige brands like Gucci and Kate Spade. With over 1 million square feet of retail space at your feet, it's easy to spend an entire day shopping here. ✉ *Herald Square, 151 W. 34th St., between Broadway and 7th Ave., Midtown West* ☎ *212/695–4400* ⊕ *www.macys.com* Ⓜ *B, D, F, M, N, Q, R, W to 34th St.–Herald Sq.*

FOOD AND TREATS

Kee's Chocolates. Owner Kee Ling Tong whips up delicious truffles and macarons with unusual, Asian-inspired flavors. Try the ginger peach and rosewater lychee macarons, or truffles flavored with lemongrass mint and tamarind. ✉ *315 W. 39th St., between 8th and 9th Aves., Midtown West* ☎ *212/967–8088* ⊕ *www.keeschocolates.com* Ⓜ *A, C, E to 42nd St.–Port Authority; 1, 2, 3, 7, N, Q, R, S, W to Times Sq.–42nd St.*

Morrell. This high-end, sprawling wine shop also includes a wine bar and auction division. Come by for a free tasting or, if money is no object, head to the rare-wine vault. More than 100 fine wines are available by the glass at the store's café. ✉ *1 Rockefeller Plaza, at 49th St., Midtown West* ☎ *212/688–9370* ⊕ *morrellwine.com* Ⓜ *B, D, F, M to 47th–50th Sts./Rockefeller Center.*

HOME DECOR

Muji. If you're into simple, chic, and cheap style, Muji has you covered. The name of this Japanese import translates to "no brand," and indeed, you don't find logos plastered on the housewares or clothes. Instead, the hallmark is a streamlined, minimalist design. The whole range of goods, from milky porcelain teapots to wooden toys, is invariably user-friendly. ⊠ *620 8th Ave., at 40th St., Midtown West* ☏ *212/382–2300* ⊕ *www. muji.us* Ⓜ *A, C, E to 42nd St.–Port Authority; 1, 2, 3, 7, N, Q, R, S, W to Times Square–42nd St.*

JEWELRY AND ACCESSORIES

Skagen. Brave the crowds in Times Square to head to Skagen's flagship, which sells watches, handbags, and leather accessories inspired by Danish design. Many of the timepieces and satchels have a unisex design and are logo-free. ⊠ *1585 Broadway, between 47th and 48th Sts., Midtown West* ☏ *845/384–1221* ⊕ *www.skagen.com* Ⓜ *N, R, W to 49th St.*

MUSEUM STORES

Museum of Arts and Design Store. This well-edited gift shop stocks crafts like beautiful handmade tableware, unusual jewelry, and rugs, often tied into ongoing exhibits. It's a great place to stock up on gifts. ⊠ *2 Columbus Circle, at 8th Ave., Midtown West* ☏ *212/299–7700* ⊕ *thestore. madmuseum.org* Ⓜ *1, A, B, C, D to 59th St.–Columbus Circle.*

Fodor's Choice
★

Museum of Modern Art Design and Book Store. MoMA's in-house shop stocks a huge selection of art reproductions and impressive coffee-table books about painting, sculpture, film, and photography. Across the street is the **MoMA Design Store,** where you can find Charles and Ray Eames furniture reproductions, vases designed by Alvar Aalto, and lots of clever toys. ⊠ *11 W. 53rd St., between 5th and 6th Aves., Midtown West* ☏ *212/708–9700* ⊕ *store.moma.org* Ⓜ *E, M to 5th Ave./53rd St.*

17

PERFORMING ARTS MEMORABILIA

Drama Book Shop. If you're looking for a script, be it a lesser-known Russian translation or Broadway hit, chances are you can find it here. The range of books spans film, music, dance, TV, and biographies. The shop also hosts Q&A's with leading playwrights. ⊠ *250 W. 40th St., between 7th and 8th Aves., Midtown West* ☏ *212/944–0595* ⊕ *www. dramabookshop.com* Ⓜ *A, C, E to 42nd St.–Port Authority; 1, 2, 3, 7, N, Q, R, S, W to Times Sq.–42nd St.*

One Shubert Alley. This was the first store to sell Broadway merchandise outside of a theater. Today, souvenir posters, tees, and other knick-knacks memorializing past and present Broadway hits still reign at this Theater District shop next to the Booth Theatre. ⊠ *222 W. 45th St., between 7th and 8th Aves., Midtown West* ☏ *212/944–4133* Ⓜ *1, 2, 3, 7, N, Q, R, S, W to Times Sq.–42nd St.*

Triton Gallery. Theatrical posters both large and small are available, and the selection is democratic, with everything from Marlene Dietrich's *Blue Angel* to recent Broadway shows like *Hamilton* represented. ⊠ *The Film Center, 690 8th Ave., 6th fl., between 43rd and 44th Sts., Midtown West* ☏ *212/765–2472* ⊕ *www.tritongallery.com* Ⓜ *A, C, E to 42nd St.–Port Authority.*

SHOES, HANDBAGS, AND LEATHER GOODS

Manolo Blahnik. These sexy status shoes are some of the most expensive on the market. The signature look is a pointy toe with a high, delicate heel, but there are also ballet flats, loafers and oxfords, and over-the-knee dominatrix boots that cost upward of $1,000. Pray for a sale. ⊠ *31*

Outlet Shopping in NYC

Traditionally, dedicated bargain shoppers from around the world have devoted a day of their New York City trips to taking the bus to Woodbury Common Premium Outlets, an hour north of the city. But, as of 2018, this time-honored pilgrimage will become unnecessary, when Empire Outlets opens on Staten Island.

Located on the waterfront, the outlets are next to the Staten Island Ferry Terminal, which has a 20-minute free ferry that travels between downtown Manhattan and Staten Island. The outlets will be home to Staten Island's first gourmet-food hall, the Marketplace at Empire Outlets, as well as dozens of premium outlets and a luxury hotel.

W. 54th St., between 5th and 6th Aves., Midtown West ☎ *212/582–3007* ⊕ *www.manoloblahnik.com* Ⓜ *E, M to 5th Ave./53rd St.*

TOYS

FAMILY **American Girl Place.** Grade-school kids are crazy for American Girl dolls, whose lines range from historically accurate characters to contemporary girls with all the accompanying clothes and accessories. Bring your doll to the brand-new New York flagship for a doll hairdressing salon and spa, doll hospital café, Dress Like Your Doll shop, design-your-own-doll station, and more. ⊠ *75 Rockefeller Plaza, between 51st and 52nd Sts., Midtown West* ☎ *877/247–5223* ⊕ *www.americangirl.com* Ⓜ *B, D, F, M to 47th–50th Sts./Rockefeller Center.*

THE UPPER EAST SIDE

This well-heeled neighborhood is known for its antiques shops and high-end designers, such as Carolina Herrera, Oscar de la Renta, and Tom Ford. Shops are primarily sprinkled along Madison Avenue.

ANTIQUES AND COLLECTIBLES

Florian Papp. Established in 1900, this store has an unassailable reputation among knowledgeable collectors. Expect to find American and European antiques and paintings from the 18th to 20th centuries. Gilt mirrors, chandeliers, and mahogany tables abound. ⊠ *962 Madison Ave., between 75th and 76th Sts., Upper East Side* ☎ *212/288–6770* ⊕ *www.florianpapp.com* Ⓜ *6 to 77th St.*

Keno Auctions. Leigh Keno of *Antiques Roadshow* fame presides over this auction house, which specializes in Americana. As expected, he has a good eye and an interesting inventory; he's sold silver sauceboats from Paul Revere, masterpiece paintings, and Chippendale furniture. ⊠ *127 E. 69th St., between Park and Lexington Aves., Upper East Side* ☎ *212/734–2381* ⊕ *www.kenoauctions.com* Ⓜ *6 to 68th St.–Hunter College.*

BEAUTY

NARS. Women adore NARS for its iconic products such as Jungle Red lipstick and multiuse makeup sticks. The NARS flagship has glossy white walls and a red counter, and stocks the full NARS makeup range as well as a collection of "François' Favorite Things," which includes books, films, and photographs that have served as inspiration. ⊠ *971 Madison Ave., between 75th and 76th Sts., Upper East Side* ☎ *212/861–2945* ⊕ *www.narscosmetics.com* Ⓜ *6 to 77th St.*

CHILDREN'S CLOTHING

FAMILY

Fodor'sChoice

★

Bonpoint. Celebrities love this French children's boutique for the beautiful designs and impeccable workmanship—think pony-hair baby booties, hand-embroidered jumpers, and cashmere onesies. The flagship has a loftlike design with whimsical touches, such as a large indoor tree and a cloud sculpture. ⊠ *805 Madison Ave., between 67th and 68th Sts., Upper East Side* ☎ *212/879–0900* ⊕ *www.bonpoint.com* Ⓜ *6 to 68th St.–Hunter College.*

FAMILY

Infinity. Prep-school girls and their mothers giggle and gossip over the tween clothes (with more than a few moms picking up T-shirts and jeans for themselves) with Les Tout Petits dresses, Juicy Couture jeans, and tees emblazoned with Justin Bieber. ⊠ *1116 Madison Ave., at 83rd St., Upper East Side* ☎ *212/734–0077* Ⓜ *4, 5, 6 to 86th St.*

CLOTHING

Alexander McQueen. The New York flagship of this iconic fashion house is full of rich details, like intricately patterned floors, and tiny architectural details meant to draw the eye, such as feathers in the molding. Now under the helm of Sarah Burton, the designer sells both menswear and women's wear, in styles that lean towards edgy gothic. ⊠ *747 Madison Ave., between 64th and 65th Sts., Upper East Side* ☎ *212/645–1797* ⊕ *www.alexandermcqueen.com* Ⓜ *6 to 68th St.–Hunter College; F, Q to Lexington Ave.–63rd St.*

Balenciaga. This sleek new flagship on Madison Avenue is a manifestation of recently installed creative director Demna Gvasalia's fresh vision for the iconic French fashion house. Minimalist and warehouse-inspired, the boutique lets Gvasalia's clever, colorful designs—asymmetrical jackets, oversize shirts, those infamous Ikea-inspired bags—take center stage and forgoes the typical stuffiness of most Upper East Side high-fashion shops. ⊠ *840 Madison Ave., between 69th and 70th Sts., Upper East Side* ☎ *212/328–1671* ⊕ *www.balenciaga.com* Ⓜ *6 to 68th St.–Hunter College.*

Barbour. The signature look here is the British company's waxed-cotton and quilted jackets, available for men and women. The quilted jackets, tweeds, moleskin pants, lamb's-wool sweaters, and tattersall shirts invariably call up images of country rambles. ⊠ *1047 Madison Ave., at 80th St., Upper East Side* ☎ *212/570–2600* ⊕ *www.barbour.com* Ⓜ *6 to 77th St.*

Belstaff. Nearly a century old, this British brand specializes in motorcycle gear that has quite the pedigree—both Che Guevara and Steve McQueen have worn Belstaff. The relaunched company has expanded its collection to include luxury basics for men and women, including peacoats,

17

waxed jackets, and leather skirts. ✉ *814 Madison Ave., between E. 68th and 69th Sts., Upper East Side* ☎ *212/897–1880* ⊕ *www.belstaff.com* Ⓜ *6 to 68th St.–Hunter College.*

Bra Smyth. Chic and sexy underthings in soft cottons and silks line the shelves of this longtime uptown staple. In addition to the selection of bridal-ready white bustiers and custom-fit swimsuits (made in bra-cup sizes), the store is best known for its knowledgeable staff, many of whom can give tips on proper fit and size you up on sight. Cup sizes run from AA to J. ✉ *905 Madison Ave., at 73rd St., Upper East Side* ☎ *212/772–9400* Ⓜ *6 to 68th St.–Hunter College.*

Calvin Klein 205W39NYC. Though the namesake designer has bowed out, the label keeps channeling his particular style. Under the leadership of creative director Raf Simons, this new line reimagines the designer's luxury ready-to-wear line and showcases it in the brand's flagship store alongside art installations. Inspired by classic Americana, clothing for both men and women tends to be soft around the edges, with dashes of both whimsy and timelessness. There are also shoes, accessories, and fragrances. ✉ *654 Madison Ave., at 60th St., Upper East Side* ☎ *212/292–9000* ⊕ *www.calvinklein.com* Ⓜ *4, 5, 6 to 59th St.; N, R, W to Lexington Ave./59th St.*

Carolina Herrera. A favorite of the high-society set (and A-list celebs), Herrera's designs are ladylike and elegant. Her suits, gowns, and cocktail dresses in luxurious fabrics make for timeless silhouettes. The New York flagship also carries her bridal collection. ✉ *954 Madison Ave., at 75th St., Upper East Side* ☎ *212/249–6552* ⊕ *www.carolinaherrera. com* Ⓜ *6 to 77th St.*

Christopher Fischer. Featherweight cashmere sweaters, wraps, and throws in every hue, from Easter-egg pastels to rich jewel tones, have made Fischer the darling of the men and women of the preppy set. His shop also carries leather accessories, housewares, and baby clothes. ✉ *1225 Madison Ave., between 88th and 89th Sts., Upper East Side* ☎ *212/831– 8880* ⊕ *www.christopherfischer.com* Ⓜ *4, 5, 6 to 86th St.*

Kate Spade. The Kate Spade flagship is in a pretty uptown town house, so it feels like shopping in a well-appointed home—albeit one with oversize chandeliers and glamorous custom rugs. The nearly 8,000-square-foot space contains every Kate Spade product, from clothing to shoes and beauty. ✉ *789 Madison Ave., between 66th and 67th Sts., Upper East Side* ☎ *212/988–0259* ⊕ *www.katespade. com* Ⓜ *6 to 68th St.–Hunter College.*

La Perla. If money is no object, shop here for some of the sexiest underthings around. The collection includes lace sets, corsets, and exquisite bridal lingerie. ✉ *803 Madison Ave., between 67th and 68th Sts., Upper East Side* ☎ *212/570–0050* ⊕ *www.laperla.com* Ⓜ *6 to 68th St.–Hunter College.*

Lanvin. This French label has been around since 1889 and is the oldest French fashion house still in existence. With Bouchra Jarrar at the helm, Lanvin's signature look is understatedly elegant; think tailored dresses, wide-leg pants, and ruffled blouses. This elegant town house was the first U.S. outpost. The interior design itself is a showstopper;

the three-story space oozes old money and glamour with its Art Deco chandeliers and soothing gray walls. And the clothes? Just as slinky. ✉ *815 Madison Ave., between 68th and 69th Sts., Upper East Side* ☎ *646/439–0380* ⊕ *www.lanvin.com* Ⓜ *6 to 68th St.–Hunter College.*

Fodor's Choice **Ludivine.** Make a beeline for this store if you love French designers.
★ Owner Ludivine Grégoire showcases of-the-moment Gallic (and a few Italian) designers like Vanessa Bruno, Jerome Dreyfuss, and Carvin. ✉ *1216 Lexington Ave., between 82nd and 83rd Sts., Upper East Side* ☎ *212/249–4053* ⊕ *www.boutiqueludivine.com* Ⓜ *4, 5, 6 to 86th St.*

Marina Rinaldi. If you are a curvy gal and want to celebrate your figure rather than hide it, shop here. A branch of Milanese fashion house Max Mara, Marina Rinaldi sells form-flattering knit dresses, wool trousers, and coats that are tasteful and luxurious. ✉ *815 Madison Ave., at 69th St., Upper East Side* ☎ *212/734–4333* ⊕ *www.marinarinaldi.com* Ⓜ *6 to 68th St.–Hunter College.*

Max Mara. Think subtle colors and classics in plush fabrics—pencil skirts in heathered wool, tuxedo-style evening jackets, and wool and cashmere overcoats. The suits are exquisitely tailored. ✉ *813 Madison Ave., at 68th St., Upper East Side* ☎ *212/879–6100* ⊕ *www.maxmara. com* Ⓜ *6 to 68th St.–Hunter College.*

Milly. These bright, cheerfully patterned clothes look as at home on the Upper East Side as they would in Palm Beach or Marrakech. At designer Michelle Smith's U.S. flagship, find flirty cocktail dresses, beach-ready maxis, and boldly patterned bathing suits. ✉ *900 Madison Ave., at 73rd St., Upper East Side* ☎ *212/395–9100* ⊕ *www.milly.com* Ⓜ *6 to 77th St.*

Morgane Le Fay. The clothes here have a dreamy, ethereal quality that is decidedly feminine. Silk gowns are fluid and soft, while blazers and coats are more tailored. Her wedding dresses are also popular with brides who want a dreamy but understated look. ✉ *980 Madison Ave., between 76th and 77th Sts., Upper East Side* ☎ *212/879–9700* ⊕ *www. morganelefay.com* Ⓜ *6 to 77th St.*

Oscar de la Renta. Come here for the ladylike but bold runway designs of this upper-crust favorite. Skirts swing, ruffles billow, embroidery brightens up tweed, and even a tennis dress looks like something you could go dancing in. ✉ *772 Madison Ave., at 66th St., Upper East Side* ☎ *212/288–5810* ⊕ *www.oscardelarenta.com* Ⓜ *6 to 68th St.–Hunter College.*

Otte. This stylish mini chain has outposts around the city, but the Upper East Side location has the biggest selection of clothing from on-trend designers such as Rachel Comey and Band of Outsiders, as well as its own line. If you want that nonchalant-chic look, like an oversize velvet jacket thrown over skinny jeans, this is your place. ✉ *1281 Madison Ave., between 91st and 92nd Sts., Upper East Side* ☎ *212/289–2644* ⊕ *otteny.com* Ⓜ *6 to 96th St.*

Ralph Lauren. Even if you can't afford the clothes here, come just to soak up the luxe lifestyle. The designer's women's flagship is housed in a 22,000-square-foot building inspired by the avenue's historic Beaux Arts mansions, complete with its own curving marble staircase and

17

stone floors. In addition to the complete women's collection, the brand's lingerie, housewares, and fine-jewelry and watch salon are here. ✉ *888 Madison Ave., at 72nd St., Upper East Side* ☎ *212/434–8000* ⊕ *www.ralphlauren.com* Ⓜ *6 to 68th St.–Hunter College.*

Roberto Cavalli. Rock-star style (at rock-star prices) means clothing decked out with fur, feathers, and lots of sparkle. Animal prints are big in this temple to the over-the-top. ✉ *711 Madison Ave., at 63rd St., Upper East Side* ☎ *212/755–7722* ⊕ *www.robertocavalli.com* Ⓜ *N, R, W to 5th Ave./59th St.; F, Q to Lexington Ave.–63rd St.*

Sachin & Babi. Sachin and Babi Ahluwalia used to source textiles for luxury designers like Oscar de la Renta. Now, they use that same design sensibility to produce a gorgeous line of globally inspired women's formal wear and accessories. The embroidery is exquisite, the colors vibrant. ✉ *1200 Madison Ave., between 87th and 88th Sts., Upper East Side* ☎ *212/996–5200* ⊕ *www.sachinandbabi.com* Ⓜ *4, 5, 6 to 86th St.*

Tom Ford. Famous for revamping Gucci, Ford does not disappoint with either his eponymous line or his new Madison Avenue flagship, a sleek, gradiose temple to glamorous fashion. Women's stilettos and clutches are unabashedly sexy, while men's selections veer toward the traditional and are impeccably tailored. Shirts come in more than 300 hues, and off-the-rack suits start around $3,000. His Black Orchid unisex fragrance is a cult favorite. ✉ *672 Madison Ave., at 61st St., Upper East Side* ☎ *212/359–0300* ⊕ *www.tomford.com* Ⓜ *F, Q to Lexington Ave.–63rd St.; N, R, W to Lexington Ave./59th St.*

Tomas Maier. The creative director of luxury Italian company Bottega Veneta now has an eponymous store in Manhattan. The elegant, wood-floored space showcases Tomas Maier's understated clothing for men and women as well as jewelry and home goods, such as candles. Best bets include classic black dresses and structured handbags. ✉ *956 Madison Ave., between 75th and 76th Sts., Upper East Side* ☎ *212/988–8686* ⊕ *www.tomasmaier.com* Ⓜ *6 to 77th St.*

Tory Burch. The global flagship of this preppy boho label is housed in an elegantly restored town house. The five-story space features Tory Burch's signature orange-lacquer walls, purple curtains, and gold hardware. If you already own her iconic ballet flats, browse through the ready-to-wear collection, handbags, shoes, and jewelry. Her new Tory Sport line is sometimes available as well. ✉ *797 Madison Ave., between 67th and 68th Sts., Upper East Side* ☎ *212/510–8371* ⊕ *www.toryburch.com* Ⓜ *6 to 68th St.–Hunter College.*

Valentino. No one does a better red than Valentino, and the mix here at this four-story town house is at once audacious and beautifully cut; the fur or feather trimmings, low necklines, and opulent fabrics are about as close as you can get to celluloid glamour. Big spenders can request the VIP suite. ✉ *821 Madison Ave., between 68th and 69th Sts., Upper East Side* ☎ *212/772–6969* ⊕ *www.valentino.com* Ⓜ *6 to 68th St.–Hunter College.*

Vera Wang. This celebrity wedding-dress designer churns out dreamy dresses that are sophisticated without being over-the-top. Choose from A-line and princess styles, as well as slinky sheaths. If money is no object, bespoke wedding dresses are available. An appointment is essential. ⊠ *991 Madison Ave., at 77th St., Upper East Side* ☎ *212/628–3400* ⊕ *www.verawang.com* Ⓜ *6 to 77th St.*

Vilebrequin. Allow St-Tropez to influence your summer style. This iconic French swimwear designer began by making classic striped, floral, and solid-color trunks in sunny hues for both men and boys. Nowadays, it's expanded to include a women's line, resort wear, and summery accessories. ⊠ *1007 Madison Ave., between 77th and 78th Sts., Upper East Side* ☎ *212/650–0353* ⊕ *us.vilebrequin.com* Ⓜ *6 to 77th St.*

DEPARTMENT STORES

Barneys New York. This luxury boutique-style department store continues to provide fashion-conscious and big-budget shoppers with irresistible, must-have items at its uptown flagship store. The extensive menswear selection has a handful of edgier designers, though made-to-measure is always an option. The women's department showcases posh designers of all stripes, from the subdued lines of Armani and rag & bone to the irrepressible Alaïa and Isabel Marant. The shoe selection trots out Prada boots and Loeffler Randall mules; the cosmetics department keeps you in Kiehl's, La Mer, and Chantecaille; jewelry runs from the whimsical (Jennifer Meyer) to the classic (Ileana Makri). The store also has a blow dry bar, a brow bar, several restaurants, and more. ⊠ *660 Madison Ave., between 60th and 61st Sts., Upper East Side* ☎ *212/826–8900* ⊕ *www.barneys.com* Ⓜ *4, 5, 6 to 59th St.; N, R, W to Lexington Ave./59th St.*

Fodor's Choice ★ **Fivestory.** Located inside an Upper East Side town house, this luxurious mini department store carries clothing, accessories, shoes, and home decor for men, women, and children in an elegant setting (think marble floors and lots of velvet and silk). It specializes in independent designers but also showcases designs from heavy hitters such as Proenza Schouler and Dior. ⊠ *18 E. 69th St., at Madison Ave., Upper East Side* ☎ *212/288–1338* ⊕ *www.fivestoryny.com* Ⓜ *6 to 68th St.–Hunter College.*

FOOD AND TREATS

Fodor's Choice ★ **La Maison du Chocolat.** Stop in at this artisan chocolatier's small tea salon to dive into a cup of thick, heavenly hot chocolate. The Paris-based outfit sells handmade truffles, chocolates, and pastries that could lull you into a chocolate stupor. ⊠ *1018 Madison Ave., between 78th and 79th Sts., Upper East Side* ☎ *212/744–7117* ⊕ *www.lamaisonduchocolat.us* Ⓜ *6 to 77th St.*

JEWELRY AND ACCESSORIES

Asprey. This luxury retailer's claim to fame is jewelry; its own eponymous diamond cut has A-shape facets, but the British brand caters to all tastes. Everything from leather goods and rare books to polo equipment and scarves is available. ⊠ *853 Madison Ave., between 70th and 71st Sts., Upper East Side* ☎ *212/688–1811* ⊕ *www.asprey.com* Ⓜ *6 to 68th St.–Hunter College.*

MUSEUM STORES

Metropolitan Museum of Art Store. Highlights of the museum's sprawling shop are a phenomenal book selection, as well as posters, Japanese print note cards, and decorative pillows covered in William Morris prints. Reproductions of statuettes and other objets d'art fill the gleaming cases. Don't miss the jewelry selection, with its Byzantine- and Egyptian-inspired baubles. ⊠ *1000 5th Ave., at 82nd St., Upper East Side* ☎ *212/570–3894* ⊕ *store.metmuseum.org* Ⓜ *4, 5, 6 to 86th St.*

Museum of the City of New York. Satisfy your curiosity about New York City's past, present, or future with the terrific selection of books, cards, toys, and photography posters. ⊠ *1220 5th Ave., at 103rd St., Upper East Side* ☎ *917/492–3330* ⊕ *shop.mcny.org* Ⓜ *6 to 103rd St.*

Neue Galerie. Like the museum, the in-house bookshop and design store focus on German, Austrian, and Central European art. Everything from children's toys to accessories and home decor is available here. ⊠ *1048 5th Ave., at 86th St., Upper East Side* ☎ *212/994–9496* ⊕ *shop.neuegalerie.org* Ⓜ *4, 5, 6 to 86th St.*

Fodor's Choice ★ **Shop Cooper Hewitt, Smithsonian Design Museum.** Prowl the shelves at this well-stocked museum shop for intriguing urban oddments and ornaments, like sculptural tableware, Alexander Girard dolls, housewares by Alessi, and Japanese notebooks by Postalco. ⊠ *Cooper Hewitt, Smithsonian Design Museum, 2 E. 91st St., at 5th Ave., Upper East Side* ☎ *212/849–8355* ⊕ *shop.cooperhewitt.org* Ⓜ *4, 5, 6 to 86th St.*

SHOES, HANDBAGS, AND LEATHER GOODS

Anya Hindmarch. Although arguably most famous for her "I'm Not a Plastic Bag" tote, Hindmarch's real standouts are buttery leather shoulder bags and satchels, which are decidedly understated. Her designs run the gamut from cheeky to ladylike. Leather goods can be embossed with monograms, entire sentences, or a sketch. ⊠ *795 Madison Ave., between 67th and 68th Sts., Upper East Side* ☎ *646/852–6233* ⊕ *www.anyahindmarch.com* Ⓜ *6 to 68th St.–Hunter College.*

Bally. If you want to channel your inner princess, you can't go wrong with the ladylike pumps and high-heeled boots here. The mostly leather accessories and clothing are equally tasteful. ⊠ *689 Madison Ave., at 62nd St., Upper East Side* ☎ *212/751–9082* ⊕ *www.bally.com* Ⓜ *F, Q to Lexington Ave.–63rd St.*

Charlotte Olympia. The Art Deco–inspired space at this British shoe store showcases very sexy and expensive stilettos, pumps, and flats. Accessories such as shoulder bags and clutches are also available. ⊠ *22 E. 65th St., at Madison Ave., Upper East Side* ☎ *212/744–1842* ⊕ *www.charlotteolympia.com* Ⓜ *6 to 68th St.–Hunter College.*

Christian Louboutin. Lipstick-red soles are the signature of Louboutin's delicately sexy couture slippers and stilettos, and his pointy-toe creations come trimmed with beads, buttons, or "tattoos." ⊠ *967 Madison Ave., between 75th and 76th Sts., Upper East Side* ☎ *212/396–1884* ⊕ *www.christianlouboutin.com* Ⓜ *6 to 77th St.*

Devi Kroell. You may have spotted her snakeskin hobo on celebs such as Halle Berry and Ashley Olsen. This serene space is a perfect backdrop for the designer's luxury handbags and shoes, which are crafted from premium leather. Roomy shoulder bags come in python and calf leather, and evening bags have a touch of sparkle. There's also a selection of jewelry and scarves. ⊠ *717 Madison Ave., between 63rd and 64th Sts.,*

Upper East Side ☎ *212/888–7755* ⊕ *www.devikroell.com* Ⓜ *F, Q to Lexington Ave./63rd St.*

Hermès. The legendary French retailer is best known for its iconic handbags, the Kelly and the Birkin, named for Grace Kelly and Jane Birkin, as well as its silk scarves and neckties. True to its roots, Hermès still stocks saddles and other equestrian items in addition to a line of beautifully simple separates. A men's store is located across the street. ⊠ *691 Madison Ave., at 62nd St., Upper East Side* ☎ *212/751–3181* ⊕ *www.hermes.com* Ⓜ *N, R, W to 5th Ave./59th St.; F, Q to Lexington Ave./63rd St.*

Jack Rogers. Beloved by prepsters everywhere, this brand is most famous for its Navajo sandal, worn by Jackie Onassis. You can still buy the Navajo at the Jack Rogers flagship store, as well as other footwear like loafers, boots, and wedges. ⊠ *1198 Madison Ave., between 87th and 88th Sts., Upper East Side* ☎ *212/259–0588* ⊕ *www.jackrogersusa.com* Ⓜ *4, 5, 6 to 86th St.*

Jimmy Choo. Pointy toes, low vamps, narrow heels, ankle-wrapping straps—these British-made shoes are sometimes more comfortable than they look. ⊠ *699 Madison Ave., between 62nd and 63rd Sts., Upper East Side* ☎ *212/759–7078* ⊕ *www.jimmychoo.com* Ⓜ *F, Q to Lexington Ave./63rd St.*

John Lobb. If you truly want to be well-heeled, pick up a pair of these luxury shoes, whose prices start at around $1,200. Owned by Hermès, John Lobb offers classic styles for men, such as oxfords, loafers, boots, and slippers. They've recently expanded to offer similar cuts in women's styles. Bespoke shoes are also an option. ⊠ *800 Madison Ave., between 67th and 68th Sts., Upper East Side* ☎ *212/888–9797* ⊕ *www.johnlobb. com* Ⓜ *6 to 68th St.–Hunter College.*

Robert Clergerie. Although best known for its chunky, comfy wedges, this French brand is not without its sense of fun. The sandal selection includes beaded starfish shapes, and for winter, the ankle boots have killer heels with padded soles. ⊠ *19 E. 62nd St., between 5th and Madison Aves., Upper East Side* ☎ *212/207–8600* ⊕ *www.robertclergerie. com* Ⓜ *N, R, W to 5th Ave./59th St.; F, Q to Lexington Ave./63rd St.*

Fodor's Choice ★ **Smythson of Bond Street.** Although Smythson still sells stationery fit for a queen—check out the royal warrant from England's HRH—it is also a place to scoop up on-trend handbags, iPad cases, and wallets. The hues range from sedate brown and black to eye-popping tangerine. The softbound leather diaries, address books, and travel accessories make ideal gifts. ⊠ *667 Madison Ave., between 60th and 61st Sts., Upper East Side* ☎ *212/265–4573* ⊕ *www.smythson.com* Ⓜ *F to 57th St.; N, R, W to 5th Ave./59th St.*

Tod's. These coveted driving moccasins, loafers, and boots are the top choice for jet-setters who prefer low-key, logo-free luxury goods. Though most of the women's selection is made up of low-heel or flat styles, an increasing number of high heels have been driving up sales. The leather handbags feature the same fine craftsmanship. ⊠ *650 Madison Ave., at 60th St., Upper East Side* ☎ *212/644–5945* ⊕ *www.tods. com* Ⓜ *N, R, W to 5th Ave./59th St.*

17

THE UPPER WEST SIDE

Although largely a residential neighborhood, the Upper West Side has some excellent food (including Zabar's) as well as smaller boutiques.

BOOKS AND STATIONERY

Westsider Books & Westsider Records. This wonderfully crammed space is a lifesaver on the Upper West Side. Squeeze in among the stacks of art books and fiction, or pop outside for the $1 bargains. Don't miss the rare-book collection. Nearby, at 233 West 72nd Street, the record shop has an equally impressive collection of vinyl and CDs. ⊠ *2246 Broadway, between 80th and 81st Sts., Upper West Side* ☎ *212/362–0706* ⊕ *www.westsiderbooks.com* Ⓜ *1 to 79th St.*

CHILDREN'S CLOTHING

FAMILY **Felix and Fanny.** When you shop at this funky boutique (formerly known as A Time for Children), you'll also be doing some good, as 100% of the profits go to the Children's Aid Society. Choose from toys, books, and clothing, which include classic brands such as Petit Bateau as well as more whimsical choices like graphic-print footed PJs. ⊠ *2868 Broadway, between 111th and 112th Sts., Upper West Side* ☎ *212/580–8202* ⊕ *www.felixandfanny.org* Ⓜ *1 to Cathedral Pwky.–110th St.*

CLOTHING

Fodor's Choice **bocnyc.** Who needs to go downtown for cutting-edge designers? This
★ store stocks sleek designs from the likes of Ulla Johnson, Loeffler Randall, and A.L.C. The selection of bags, shoes, and jewelry is just as stylish. ⊠ *410 Columbus Ave., between 79th and 80th Sts., Upper West Side* ☎ *212/799–1567* ⊕ *www.bocnyc.com* Ⓜ *1 to 79th St.; B, C, to 81st St.–Museum of Natural History.*

Intermix. Whether you're looking for the perfect daytime dress, a pair of J Brand jeans, or a puffer coat that doesn't make you look like the Michelin man, Intermix sells a well-curated assortment of emerging and established designers. Expect to see designs from DVF, rag & bone, and Missoni. There are a number of locations in the city. ⊠ *210 Columbus Ave., between 69th and 70th Sts., Upper West Side* ☎ *212/769–9116* ⊕ *www.intermixonline.com* Ⓜ *1, 2, 3, B, C to 72nd St.*

Pachute. This cozy boutique, which means "simple" in Hebrew, specializes in stylish casual wear. If your weekend uniform consists of button-down shirts, understated jewelry, and espadrilles, then make a beeline here. There's also a location on the Upper East Side. ⊠ *57 W. 84th St. , between Columbus Ave. and Central Park W, Upper West Side* ☎ *212/501–9400* ⊕ *www.pachute.com* Ⓜ *B, C to 86th St.*

FOOD AND TREATS

Fodor's Choice **Zabar's.** When it comes to authentic New York food, it's hard to beat
★ rugelach, bagels, or lox from this iconic, local-favorite specialty food emporium. ⊠ *2245 Broadway, at 80th St., Upper West Side* ☎ *212/787–2000* ⊕ *www.zabars.com* Ⓜ *1 to 79th St.*

SHOES, HANDBAGS, AND LEATHER GOODS

Tani. Fashionable Upper West Side ladies love this shoe store for its huge selection and patient staff. Tani's selection is mostly classic-with-a-twist, and shoppers find brands that are more cool than sexy, such as Dolce Vita and Camper. ⊠ *131 W 72nd St., between Columbus and Amsterdam Aves., Upper West Side* ☎ *917/265–8835* ⊕ *www.taninyc. com/* Ⓜ *1, 2, 3, B, C to 72nd St.*

BROOKLYN

BOERUM HILL

BEAUTY

Fodor's Choice

★

Twisted Lily. One of the most comprehensive collections of independent and natural fragrances hides behind this elegant storefront on busy Atlantic Avenue. The knowledgeable staff know their way around hundreds of scents and will happily help you find your favorite, but be prepared to want to take more than a few home. The boutique also carries candles and skincare, grooming and beauty products. ⊠ *360 Atlantic Ave., between Hoyt and Bond Sts., Boerum Hill* ☎ *347/529–4681* ⊕ *twistedlily.com* Ⓜ *A, C, G to Hoyt–Schermerhorn.*

GIFTS AND SOUVENIRS

Regular Visitors. Part homewares store (see: Kinto mugs and Fog Linen towels), part luxe apothecary (i.e. Marvis toothpaste and French Girl dry shampoo), part artisan grocer (peruse local honeys and Mexican hot sauces), and then some, this bright, thoughtfully designed neighborhood shop has everything you didn't know you needed. There's also a wall of magazines (many independent and hard-to-find), and the store doubles as a coffee shop, with just a few counter seats in the window for laptop-toting creatives and friends catching up. ⊠ *149 Smith St., at Bergen St., Boerum Hill* ☎ *646/766–0484* ⊕ *www.regularvisitors.com* Ⓜ *F, G to Bergen St.*

HOME DECOR

The Primary Essentials. Stock up on handcrafted ceramics, textiles made by artisans in India, candles and perfumes from Mexico, desk accessories from Japan, and artwork fit for a renovated loft at this Brooklyn design store from former stylist Lauren Snyder. The boutique is pleasant and relaxed—the shop is nearly as elegant as the products it stocks—and carries designers found nowhere else in New York. A new location just opened in NoLIta, too. ⊠ *372 Atlantic Ave., between Hoyt and Bond Sts., Boerum Hill* ☎ *718/522–1804* ⊕ *theprimaryessentials.com* Ⓜ *A, C, G to Hoyt–Schermerhorn.*

BROOKLYN HEIGHTS

FOOD AND TREATS

Fodor's Choice

★

Sahadi's. Inhale the aromas of spices and dark-roast coffee beans as you enter this Middle Eastern trading post that's been selling bulk foods in Brooklyn since 1948. Bins, jars, and barrels hold everything from nuts, dried fruit, olives, and pickled vegetables to cheeses, chocolate, candy, those intoxicating coffees, and all manner of spices. There's a large selection of prepared food and groceries as well. ⊠ *187 Atlantic Ave., between Clinton and Court Sts., Brooklyn Heights* ☎ *718/624–4550* ⊕ *www.sahadis.com* Ⓜ *2, 3, 4, 5 to Borough Hall; R to Court St.; A, C, F, R to Jay St.–MetroTech.*

17

DUMBO
BOOKS AND STATIONERY

FAMILY **Powerhouse Arena.** Edgy art-book publisher powerHouse is a vision in concrete and steel at this bright showroom that sells illustrated titles, children's books, and works by authors from Joseph Mitchell to Gary Shteyngart. The space also hosts publishing parties, book launches, readings, and discussion groups. ⊠ *28 Adams St., between Front and Water Sts., DUMBO* ☎ *718/666–3049* ⊕ *www.powerhousearena.com* Ⓜ *A, C to High St.; F to York St.*

CLOTHING

Front General Store. Outfitting DUMBO's cool kids since 2011, this shop sells his-and-hers vintage Ralph Lauren blazers, 1940s Royal Stetson hats, and other well-chosen odds 'n' ends, including antique Mexican glassware and Chesterfield-esque leather armchairs. ⊠ *143 Front St., between Pearl and Jay Sts., DUMBO* ☎ *646/573–0123* ⊕ *frontgeneralstore.com* Ⓜ *A, C to High St.; F to York St.*

CARROLL GARDENS
FOOD AND TREATS

Fodor's Choice ★ **G. Esposito & Sons Jersey Pork Store.** The epitome of an old-school Italian butcher and specialty shop, Esposito's has been serving the area once known as South Brooklyn for almost 100 years. Brothers and co-owners John and George Esposito run the store their grandfather opened in 1922 and are still producing homemade sausages, dry-aged soppressata, and hero sandwiches made on Caputo's bread. Order up an Italian Combo with the works, or the habit-forming Santino's "Fluffy" Combo, stuffed with chicken cutlets, sweet peppers, Asiago cheese, pesto, and oil and vinegar, and grab a seat in neighboring Carroll Park to chow down. ⊠ *357 Court St., between Union and President Sts., Carroll Gardens* ☎ *718/875–6863* Ⓜ *F, G to Carroll St.*

GIFTS AND SOUVENIRS

Swallow. If you're looking for a gift or a special trinket for that hard-to-shop-for friend or family member who has exquisite taste and an appreciation for the fine designs of nature, head to Swallow. Anatomy- and nature-inspired jewelry, vases, painted gold-leaf mirrors, chimes made of obsidian shards and dried eucalyptus, and other objets d'art and curiosities are just some of the offerings. Browsing here is a bit like traveling down the rabbit hole into a grown-up's housewares wonderland. ⊠ *361 Smith St., Carroll Gardens* ✛ *between Carroll and 2nd Sts.* ☎ *718/222–8201* ⊕ *www.dearswallow.com* Ⓜ *F, G to Carroll St.*

COBBLE HILL
BOOKS AND STATIONERY

FAMILY **Books Are Magic.** Author Emma Straub opened this spacious and well-stocked bookstore after neighborhood landmark BookCourt closed, and even used her predecessor's tall wooden bookshelves in creating the new space. Books Are Magic hosts author events—many with celebrated writers who happen to live in Brooklyn—several days a week. Don't miss the excellent kids' area in the back. ⊠ *225 Smith St., at Butler St., Cobble Hill* ☎ *718/246–2665* ⊕ *www.booksaremagic.net* Ⓜ *F, G to Bergen St.*

CLOTHING

Bird. Looking for the chicest women's wear in Brooklyn? You'll find it at this beloved boutique known for its high prices attached to enviable items from Tsumori Chisato, Marni, and Ulla Johnson, to name a few of the indie designers. Everything from knit sweater dresses and cardigans to statement shoes and delicate gold jewelry share the cozy space. There are a few items for men as well. ⊠ *220 Smith St. at Butler St., Cobble Hill* ☎ *718/797–3774* ⊕ *www.birdbrooklyn.com* Ⓜ *F, G to Bergen St.*

PARK SLOPE

GIFTS AND SOUVENIRS

FAMILY **Annie's Blue Ribbon General Store.** The perfectly giftable, Brooklyn-made products at this variety store include Apotheke candles and diffusers, Bellocq teas, Claudia Pearson's hand-drawn tea towels, Brooklyn Slate, and Bocce's Bakery birthday-cake treats for your favorite canine. Brooklyn-themed tchotchkes, ecofriendly cleaning supplies (including a Common Good Refill station), stationery, and toys round out the selection. ⊠ *232 5th Ave., between President and Carroll Sts., Park Slope* ☎ *718/522–9848* ⊕ *www.blueribbongeneralstore.com* Ⓜ *R to Union St.*

TOYS

FAMILY **Brooklyn Superhero Supply Co.** If you can't crack a smile in this store— where all proceeds from superhero costumes, gear, and secret identity kits benefit 826NYC's writing and tutoring programs for kids—step immediately into its Devillainizer cage. Once cleansed, browse the invisibility, dark matter, and cloning tools sold in plastic jugs and fake paint cans. The clever labels listing "ingredients" and "warnings" are worth every ounce of the tongue-in-cheek superpower products. Hours are daily 11–5 but the volunteer staff must sometimes answer the call of duty elsewhere; call ahead when making a special visit. ⊠ *372 5th Ave., between 5th and 6th Sts., Park Slope* ☎ *718/499–9884* ⊕ *www. superherosupplies.com* Ⓜ *F, G, R to 4th Ave.–9th St.*

CONEY ISLAND

FOOD AND TREATS

FAMILY **Williams Candy.** Selling homemade candy apples, marshmallow sticks, popcorn, nuts, and giant lollipops for more than 75 years, this old-school corner candy shop with the yellow awning is a Coney Island mainstay. Owner Peter Agrapides used to visit the store with his mother when he was a kid; he's been the proud owner for 30 years. ⊠ *1318 Surf Ave., between W. 15th St. and Stillwell Ave., Coney Island* ☎ *718/372–0302* ⊕ *www.candytreats.com* Ⓜ *D, F, N, Q to Coney Island–Stillwell Ave.*

WILLIAMSBURG

CLOTHING

Fodor'sChoice
★ **Brooklyn Tailors.** The husband-wife team behind this men's tailor has been crafting bespoke, made-to-measure, and off-the-rack suits, shirts, and overcoats for the well-dressed gents of New York since 2007. The store also carries a curated range of shoes, sweaters, grooming products, and other accessories from brands like Filippo de Laurentis and the British Belt Company. ⊠ *327 Grand St., between Havemeyer St. and Marcy Ave., Williamsburg* ☎ *347/799–1646* ⊕ *www.brooklyn-tailors.com* Ⓜ *L to Lorimer St.; G to Metropolitan Ave.*

17

In God We Trust. This NYC-based brand is as popular for its simple, classic jewelry as it is for clean-lined clothes. The womenswear tends to be boxy and menswear-inspired, and the store also carries a curated selection of bags, accessories, and home decor from other designers. Jewelry pieces like signet rings and heart pendant necklaces can be engraved; some are sold already engraved with whimsical phrases. ✉ *129 Bedford Ave., between N. 9th and 10th Sts., Williamsburg* ☎ *718/384–0700* ⊕ *ingodwetrustnyc.com* Ⓜ *L to Bedford Ave.*

HOME DECOR

Leif. A lifestyle store that embodies the, well, Brooklyn lifestyle, this bright little boutique has a curated collection of homewares, jewelry, beauty products, and prints by local artists. Find geometric rugs and pillows, linen tableclothes, hand-painted ceramics pitchers, tassel earrings, colorful knit accessories, fragrant candles, and more. ✉ *99 Grand St., between Wythe Ave. and Berry St., Williamsburg* ☎ *718/302–5343* ⊕ *www.leifshop.com* Ⓜ *L to Bedford Ave.*

NIGHTLIFE

Updated by
Kelsy Chauvin

New Yorkers are fond of the "work hard, play hard" maxim, but the truth is, Gothamites don't need much of an excuse to hit the town. Any day of the week could easily be mistaken for a Friday or Saturday; the bottom line is that when the the the mood strikes, there are always plenty of choices in this 24-hour city. Whether it's raising a glass in a historic saloon, a dimly lit cocktail den, or a swanky rooftop lounge; checking out the latest band; or laughing it up at a comedy show, it isn't hard for visitors to get a piece of the action.

The nightlife scene still resides largely downtown—in the dives and speakeasies of the East Village and Lower East Side, the classic jazz joints and piano bars of the West Village, and the Meatpacking District's and Chelsea's "see-and-be-seen" clubs. Midtown, especially around Hell's Kitchen, has developed a vibrant scene, too, and plenty of upscale hangouts dot the Upper East and Upper West Sides. Brooklyn and Harlem are go-to destinations for in-the-know locals.

Keep in mind that *when* you go is just as important as *where* you go. A club that is packed at 11 pm might empty out by midnight, and a bar that raged last night may be completely empty tonight. *Time Out New York* magazine has a good list of roving parties (⊕ *www.timeout.com/newyork*), as does *Urban Daddy* (⊕ *www.urbandaddy.com/new-york*). Scour industry-centric websites, too, like *Eater* and *Grub Street*, which catalog the comings and goings of many a nightlife impresario. *New York* magazine and the *New York Times* have listings of cabaret and jazz shows, the latter mainly in its Friday and Sunday Arts sections. Bear in mind that a venue's life span is often measured in months, not years. Phone ahead or check online to make sure your target hasn't closed or turned into a polka hall (although, you never know—that could be fun, too).

LOWER MANHATTAN

FINANCIAL DISTRICT

BARS

The Bar Room. The same year that the Brooklyn Bridge opened (1883), the Temple Court building welcomed its first visitors—though back then it was an office tower, not the lushly restored hotel (The Beekman) it became in 2016. The Bar Room is among the neighborhood's highlights, a splendid ground-floor lounge where libations are arguably priced more for the landmark setting and gorgeous furnishings than for their quality. Nevertheless, there's no other hotel bar in New York where you can gaze up a nine-story atrium lined with ornate ironwork while sipping a glass of bubbles; just reserve prime seats in advance. ⊠ *The Beekman, 5 Beekman St., at Park Row, Financial District* ☎ *212/658–1848* ⊕ *www.thebeekman.com* Ⓜ *R, W to City Hall; 4, 5, 6 to Brooklyn Bridge; 2, 3, A, C, J, Z to Fulton St.*

Fodor's Choice
★
The Dead Rabbit. For exquisite cocktails without the dress code or pretentious door policy typical of some New York cocktail dens, venture to the tip of Manhattan for a night of Irish hospitality in a 19th-century-inspired saloon. The ground-floor taproom serves craft beers and whiskeys of the world, while the upstairs parlor shakes and stirs craft cocktails, many utilizing Irish whiskey—accompanied by ragtime music played live on the piano. ⊠ *30 Water St., Financial District* ☎ *646/422–7906* ⊕ *www.deadrabbitnyc.com* Ⓜ *1 to South Ferry; R, W to Whitehall St.*

Fodor's Choice
★
Pier A Harbor House. Jutting out from Battery Park, this national landmark served both the harbor police and fire departments, but since 2014 it has been a uniquely restored public complex. Enjoy the nautical details and refurbished original decor across its four main areas, each serving a selection of seafood and pub food. The Long Bar and the Oyster Bar occupy the main floor and outdoor deck—which gets crowded on summer evenings for the mesmerizing views. The teak-lined, upstairs Commissioner's Bar is more compact, with a balcony perfect for sipping from the champagne and aperitif menu. The pier's finest cocktails are served in the speakeasy-style Blacktail, pouring Cuban-inspired libations concocted by experts from the Dead Rabbit. ⊠ *22 Battery Pl., on west side of Battery Park, Financial District* ☎ *212/785–0153* ⊕ *www. piera.com* Ⓜ *4, 5 to Bowling Green.*

The Wooly Public. Despite the elephant- and woolly mammoth–themed art decorating the walls, the Wooly Public takes its name from the magnificent Woolworth Building in which it's housed. The atmosphere invites both after-work socializing or everyday imbibing of fine cocktails, wine, and beer in the spacious, classically styled bar area. There are weekday happy hour specials (for both drinks and oysters), and DJs and live musicians provide jazz and other mostly mellow tunes on Thursday, Friday, and Saturday evenings. ⊠ *9 Barclay St., between Broadway and Church St., Financial District* ☎ *212/571–2930* ⊕ *www. thewoolypublic.com* Ⓜ *R, W to City Hall; 2, 3 to Park Pl.; A, C to Chambers St.; E to World Trade Center.*

18

TRIBECA

BARS

B Flat. The design is red-on-red here, and the Asian-style cocktails are particularly groovy (literally—one, with citrusy Japanese yuzu juice and vodka, has been dubbed the Groovy) at this Japan-meets-'50s-America lounge. Listen to live jazz while nibbling on American and Japanese-inflected treats. ✉ *277 Church St., between Franklin and White Sts., TriBeCa* ☎ *212/219–2970* ⊕ *www.bflat.info* Ⓜ *1 to Franklin St.; A, C, E, J, N, Q, R, W, Z, 6 to Canal St.*

Brandy Library. The most important book in this exquisite, wood-paneled "library" is the leather-bound menu listing hundreds of brandies and single-malt scotches. The bottles are on handsome backlighted shelves, though, and you can learn what makes each of them special by chatting with the spirit sommelier—or by buying into one of the lounge's sophisticated tasting classes. ✉ *25 N. Moore St., between Varick and Hudson Sts., TriBeCa* ☎ *212/226–5545* ⊕ *www.brandylibrary.com* Ⓜ *1 to Franklin St.; A, C, E to Canal St.*

M1-5. This lipstick-red, high-ceiling spot is a roomy lounge and playground (as in, billiards, shuffleboard, and darts). There are screens for sports, a long bar, and weekend dance parties—all without a cover charge. Extra points, too, for the bar's name, which cites TriBeCa's warehouse zoning law. ✉ *52 Walker St., between Broadway and Church St., TriBeCa* ☎ *212/965–1701* ⊕ *www.m1-5.com* Ⓜ *A, C, E J, N, Q, R, W, Z, 6 to Canal St.*

Smith and Mills. Attractive downtown Manhattanites frolic at this tiny gem of a gin mill, where debonair mixologists dispense elixirs (and oysters) from a bar hung with pots and pans. There are cozy table-nooks for couples, and while the food is worth a visit, many locals come here late when a craft-cocktail craving hits. ✉ *71 N. Moore St., between Hudson and Greenwich Sts., TriBeCa* ☎ *212/226–2515* ⊕ *www.smithandmills.com* Ⓜ *1 to Franklin St.; A, C, E to Canal St.*

Terroir Wine. This fine wine bar is impressive to oenophiles, and welcoming to everyone thanks to the extensive wine list, including options by the glass, bottle, or sizable tasting pours. A neighborhood favorite, the bar is easy to walk right by on charming Harrison Street, but once inside you will find seats at the bar for wine-centric conversations with the sharp staff or more private nooks for a romantic evening of wine and cheese. ✉ *24 Harrison St., between Greenwich and Hudson Sts., TriBeCa* ☎ *212/625–9463* ⊕ *wineisterroir.com* Ⓜ *1 to Franklin St.*

Tiny's and the Bar Upstairs. In the heart of TriBeCa, this diminutive three-story town house dates all the way back to 1810. The ground floor is home to a restaurant with a wood-burning fireplace in the back, and food is served until late; upstairs, a pressed-copper bar provides an intimate place for cocktails and snacks. This is prime date territory, and Tiny's old-fashioned ambience is perfect for a romantic predin-ner cocktail. ✉ *135 West Broadway, between Duane and Thomas St., TriBeCa* ☎ *212/374–1135* ⊕ *tinysnyc.com* Ⓜ *1, 2, 3 to Chambers St.*

Ward III. You can get a solid Negroni or Manhattan at this exposed-brick watering hole, but where the bar really shines is in its bespoke cocktails. Fight for a seat at the bar if possible to watch the sharply clad barkeeps whip up house specialties, or simply give them a few descriptive words ("spirit-forward," "something with bourbon," "light and refreshing") and let them create a cocktail on the spot to match your thirst. ⊠ *111 Reade St., between West Broadway and Church St., TriBeCa* ☎ *212/240–9194* ⊕ *www.ward3.com* Ⓜ *1, 2, 3, A, C to Chambers St.*

CHINATOWN, NOLITA, AND SOHO

CHINATOWN

BARS

Apotheke. Tucked away down a winding lane deep in Chinatown, this cocktail apothecary is a surprising find in a neighborhood known more for soup dumplings than creative tipples. Influenced by the 19th-century absinthe parlors of Paris, this historically inflected spot is all about drama and presentation. Think low-lit chemistry lab more than traditional bar—the results are not only delicious but also a feast for the senses. ⊠ *9 Doyers St., near Pell St., Chinatown* ☎ *212/406–0400* ⊕ *www.apothekenyc.com* Ⓜ *6, J, N, Q, R, W, Z to Canal St.; 4, 5, 6 to Brooklyn Bridge–City Hall.*

NOLITA

BARS

Sweet & Vicious. This unpretentious lounge is high on the sweet factor and luckily low on the vicious attitudes. There's a lovely back garden that's more private than the sceney bars you might otherwise hit in SoHo and NoLIta. ⊠ *5 Spring St., between the Bowery and Elizabeth St., NoLIta* ☎ *212/334–7915* ⊕ *www.sweetandvicious.nyc* Ⓜ *6 to Spring St.; J, Z to Bowery.*

SOHO

BARS

City Winery. Is it the city's most creative wine bar? Or its most impressive concert space? Both, actually. Pairing killer music (Nick Lowe, Shawn Colvin, War, Los Lobos) with unique events (Klezmer Breakfast, Cheese Brunch, tours of its in-house winery, special "Vinofile" memberships, and a Twitter–wine-tasting party called Spit and Twit), the City Winery has ample room for customers with "good taste" in every sense of the term. ⊠ *155 Varick St., at Vandam St., SoHo* ☎ *212/608–0555* ⊕ *www. citywinery.com/newyork* Ⓜ *1 to Houston St.*

Ear Inn. Since the early 1800s, this watering hole (at one time also a bordello) has been a sturdy New York landmark in a rapidly changing downtown. For those imbibers who prefer a pint of Guinness over the latest cocktail fads, the long wooden bar offers a cozy, unhurried place to raise a glass and rub elbows with New Yorkers. The benches outside are also a perfect spot to relax in the warmer weather, and live music and readings three times a week evoke the bar's artistic heritage. ⊠ *326 Spring St., between Greenwich and Washington Sts., SoHo* ☎ *212/226–9060* ⊕ *www.earinn.com* Ⓜ *1 to Houston St.; C, E to Spring St.*

18

Fanelli's. Linger over the *New York Times* at this well-worn neighborhood bar and restaurant, a down-to-earth SoHo landmark that's been serving drinks (and solid cuisine—dig those burgers!) since 1847. The old-timey photos on the walls add to the vintage atmosphere, as do the no-nonsense bartenders. ⊠ *94 Prince St., at Mercer St., SoHo* ☎ *212/226–9412* Ⓜ *R, W to Prince St.; B, D, F, M to Broadway–Lafayette St.*

Jimmy. Located on the 18th floor of the trendy James Hotel, Jimmy is an all-season rooftop bar with stellar views and a cozy fireplace. Sit in a corner nook for Empire State Building vistas, or head toward the outdoor pool area to survey the bridges over the East River. Cocktails are a highlight, featuring seasonal ingredients and novelties like ice cubes made from cinnamon water. ⊠ *James Hotel, 15 Thompson St., at Grand St., SoHo* ☎ *212/201–9118* ⊕ *www.jimmysoho.com* Ⓜ *C, E to Spring St.; A, C, E, 1 to Canal St.*

La Compagnie des Vins Surnaturels. Cheese, charcuterie, and chocolate are all temptations at this cozy wine bar, lined with exposed-brick walls and shelves stocked with wine (the complete list is over 600 bottles). This is the dimly lit sister property of a bar of the same name in Paris; the bottles on the wine list lean heavily toward French options, though by-the-glass options are more varied. ⊠ *249 Centre St., between Broome and Grand Sts., SoHo* ☎ *212/343–3660* ⊕ *www.compagnienyc.com* Ⓜ *6 to Spring St.*

Pegu Club. Modeled after an officers' club in Myanmar, the Pegu manages to feel expansive and calm even when packed. The well-dressed and flirtatious come here partly for the exotic surroundings, but primarily for the cocktails, which are innovative, prepared with superlative ingredients, and predictably pricey. ⊠ *77 W. Houston St., 2nd fl., between West Broadway and Wooster St., SoHo* ☎ *212/473–7348* ⊕ *www.pegu-club.com* Ⓜ *B, D, F, M to Broadway–Lafayette St.; 6 to Bleecker St.*

EAST VILLAGE AND LOWER EAST SIDE

EAST VILLAGE

BARS

Beauty Bar. Grab a seat in a barber chair or under a dryer at this made-over hair salon where, during happy hour, the manicurist will do your nails for a fee that includes a drink. (How's that for multitasking?) The DJ spins everything from new wave to soul—a great soundtrack for primping. ⊠ *231 E. 14th St., between 2nd and 3rd Aves., East Village* ☎ *212/539–1389* ⊕ *www.thebeautybar.com* Ⓜ *4, 5, 6, L, N, Q, R, W to 14th St.–Union Sq.*

Blind Barber. Stand outside this address and you may wonder why you've been sent for cocktails in an active barber shop. But wait, what's that secret door in back? It's your portal to the spacious Backroom speakeasy where the vintage style, diamond-tufted booths, and both classic and custom cocktails make patrons feel as if they've been transported back to Prohibition (minus the glowing smartphones). ⊠ *339 E. 10th St., between Aves. A and B, East Village* ☎ *212/228–2123* ⊕ *blindbarber.com* Ⓜ *L to 1st Ave.*

CLOSE UP

Kickin' Karaoke

If you're looking for a venue other than your shower to bust out your own vocal stylings, you're in good company. Otherwise-jaded New Yorkers are hooked on the goofy, addictive pleasure of karaoke. The K-word means "empty orchestra" in Japanese, and seems to delight both downtown hipsters (who dig the irony of kitsch) and uptown financiers (who need a good rebel yell at the end of a workday), and everybody in between who loves to flex the golden pipes—especially after a few drinks.

There are three ways of getting your lead-vocalist groove on: doing it for the whole bar at a karaoke night or specialty bar programmed for singing (usually about $1.50 per song); reserving a private room at a dedicated karaoke venue, where only your friends get the pleasure of your wondrous warbles; and bounding up onstage in front of a live band.

The hard-core karaoke places tend to be either grungy or glitzy, sometimes with more than a dozen available rooms for rent by the hour or night (each one includes a music machine, microphones, and bar service), along with tens of thousands of songs filling beat-up binders. Those catalogs include everything from "Sweet Caroline" and "I Will Survive" to pop hits by Adele, Garth Brooks, and Madonna—and, of course, many a Broadway show tune (this is New York, after all). A few top venues are the two downtown locations of **Sing-Sing** (✉ *9 St. Marks Pl.* ☎ *212/387–7800* and ✉ *81 Ave. A* ☎ *212/674–0700*); Midtown's slick **Pulse** (✉ *135 W. 41st St., between Broadway and 6th Ave.* ☎ *212/278–0090*); and just about anywhere else in the unofficial Koreatown that sprawls around Herald Square, like **Karaoke Duet 35** (✉ *53 W. 35th St., 2nd fl., between 5th and 6th Aves.* ☎ *646/473–0826*).

For live-band karaoke, head to the Lower East Side's hottest songfest: Monday-night rock 'n' roll karaoke at **Arlene's Grocery** (✉ *95 Stanton St.* ☎ *212/995–1652*).

18

Death & Company. Theater behind the bar, inventive cocktails, and decadent bar bites attract a steady stream of New Yorkers with a thirst for craft drinks. There are staple tipples and a new slate of concoctions twice yearly, each of them priced to savor rather than chug, and all of them built by expert bartenders. Seating is first-come, first-served, but the host outside this dimly lit, mysteriously windowless bar will log your name and text when your sexy seats are available. ✉ *433 E. 6th St., between 1st Ave. and Ave. A, East Village* ☎ *212/388–0882* ⊕ *www. deathandcompany.com* Ⓜ *F to 2nd Ave., 6 to Astor Pl.*

Karma. At the top of the "hookah bar" heap that has taken this neighborhood by storm, Karma provides a stylish sprawl with Indian decor (dig that wrought-metal statue of Kali) for local scenesters to fill their bowls and suck in the various aromatic tobaccos available. It's also one of the rare NYC venues that still allows cigarette smoking, its permits grandfathered in before the 2003 indoor-smoking ban (heavy-duty ventilation helps clear the air). Daily happy hours start early at 3 pm, and there are live comedy and music shows and DJs nearly every night.

✉ *51 1st Ave., between 2nd and 3rd Sts., East Village* ☎ *212/677–3160* ⊕ *www.karmanyc.com* Ⓜ *F to 2nd Ave.; 6 to Bleecker or Spring Sts.*

McSorley's Old Ale House. One of New York's oldest saloons (established in 1854) and immortalized by *New Yorker* writer Joseph Mitchell, McSorley's is a must-visit for beer lovers, even if only two kinds of brew are served: McSorley's Light and McSorley's Dark (each served two per order in small glass mugs). It's also essential for history lovers, and though it's usually filled with bros, the bar is friendlier to women than it once was. (The surly motto here once was "Good ale, raw onions, and no ladies.") Go early to avoid the down-the-block lines on Friday and Saturday nights. ✉ *15 E. 7th St., between 2nd and 3rd Aves., East Village* ☎ *212/473–9148* Ⓜ *6 to Astor Pl.*

Fodor's Choice ★ **Mother of Pearl.** Downstairs from Cuban restaurant Cienfuegos, this bright and inviting corner bar may catch your eye for its vivid nouveau-tiki style, but once inside, you'll be glad to stay for the innovative concoctions tucked within the pearlescent menu. Besides the expected rum-forward cocktails—including boozy-fruity punch bowls for groups—co-owner and head bartender Jane Danger employs an array of spirits, along with zingy bar snacks. You're unlikely to find better, friendlier service anywhere in the neighborhood, which merrily reinforces the happy-go-lucky tropical vibe. ✉ *95 Ave. A, at E. 6th St., East Village* ☎ *212/614–6818* ⊕ *www.motherofpearlnyc.com* Ⓜ *6 to Astor Pl.; R, W to 8th St.–NYU; F to 2nd Ave.*

Otto's Shrunken Head Tiki Bar & Lounge. It's a tiki bar that's long been a neighborhood go-to for its easy-breezy attitude, affordable drinks, and hula-crazy eye candy. Drop in to enjoy the bamboo bar, fish lamps, cute banquettes, drinks served in shrunken-head mugs, a tattooed, punk-rock crowd, and beef jerky for sale. There are live music and spoken-word shows in the back room, and DJs prone to spinning anything from '50s rock to "Soul Gidget" surf music. ✉ *538 E. 14th St., between Aves. A and B, East Village* ☎ *212/228–2240* ⊕ *www.ottosshrunkenhead. com* Ⓜ *L to 1st Ave.*

Fodor's Choice ★ **Pouring Ribbons.** This polished, spacious second-floor cocktail bar is named after the way a drink forms iridescent liquid ribbons when it is expertly poured. Career bartenders shake or stir your concoction of choice from seasonal menus, each libation with a sliding scale that allows you to visualize just how "spiritous" or "refreshing" you want your drink to be. Elaborate cocktail garnishes on the bar look tempting enough to eat, but order some cheese and charcuterie to accompany your drinks instead. ✉ *225 Ave. B, 2nd fl., between 13th and 14th Sts., East Village* ☎ *917/656–6788* ⊕ *www.pouringribbons.com* Ⓜ *L to 1st Ave.*

Temple Bar. Unmarked and famous for its classic cocktails and romantic atmosphere, Temple is prime date territory, especially once you drift past the sleek bar to the back, where, swathed in almost complete darkness, you can lounge on a comfy banquette, order an old-fashioned or other sophisticated cocktail, and invest in some fine conversation. ✉ *332 Lafayette St., near Bleecker St., East Village* ☎ *212/925–4242* ⊕ *www.templebarnyc.com* Ⓜ *B, D, F, M to Broadway–Lafayette St.; 6 to Bleecker St.*

CABARET AND PIANO BARS

Club Cumming. When multitalented actor Alan Cumming opened his namesake club in 2017, the East Village saw a welcome return of queer cabaret culture in a former gay-nightclub space. The club hosts nightly musical and spoken-word shows (sometimes multiple per night; usually free) by cutting-edge artists. While they're worth a peek, the compact space is often too popular (i.e.—crowded) to view the stage—so if you'd like a little elbow room, aim to catch an early show on a weeknight. ✉ *505 E. 6th St., at Ave. A, East Village* ☎ *917/265–8006* ⊕ *clubcummingnyc.com* Ⓜ *F to 2nd Ave.; 6 to Astor Pl.; L to 1st Ave.*

Fodor's Choice ★ **Joe's Pub.** Named for the Public Theater's near-mythic impresario Joe Papp, and located inside the renovated, historic Public Theater, Joe's is the ultimate cabaret lounge for A-list and longtime-favorite downtown performers who revel in the intimate setting—and for New Yorkers keen to discover marvelous, innovative shows and artists rarely enjoyed elsewhere. The venue serves good food and solid cocktails, and has nary a bad seat, be it at a table, booth, or bar—but if you want to occupy one, buy tickets and/or reserve your spot beforehand and make a night of it. ✉ *425 Lafayette St., between 4th St. and Astor Pl., East Village* ☎ *212/539–8778* ⊕ *www.publictheater.org/Joes-Pub-at-The-Public* Ⓜ *6 to Astor Pl.*

LOWER EAST SIDE

BARS

Fodor's Choice ★ **Back Room.** The Prohibition-era atmospheric touches here include tin ceilings, chandeliers, velvet wallpaper, mirrored bars, an amply sized fireplace, and a "hidden" outdoor entrance (which you can find easily enough, through the back alley). The music consists of rock CDs rather than a live spinmeister, and the drinks come in old-fashioned teacups or wrapped in paper bags. These and other quirks attract a slightly older clientele than many of its rowdier neighbors. ✉ *102 Norfolk St., between Delancey and Rivington Sts., Lower East Side* ☎ *212/228–5098* ⊕ *www.backroomnyc.com* Ⓜ *F to Delancey St.; J, M, Z to Essex St.*

Fodor's Choice ★ **Nitecap.** Drift down a few stairs into this cozy LES bar perfect for catching up with friends in its polished nooks; going solo from one of the cushy bar seats; or flirting with a date, thanks to its two-seat booths. You'll find fine, friendly service and drinks (no food) here, with a seasonally changing menu sure to surprise and delight with uncommon infusions, flavor combinations, punches, mocktails, and a handful of inventive cocktails on tap. ✉ *151 Rivington St., between Suffolk and Clinton Sts., Lower East Side* ☎ *212/466–3361* ⊕ *www.nitecapnyc.com* Ⓜ *F to Delancey St.; J, M, Z to Essex St.*

Spitzer's Corner. No, you won't rub shoulders with New York's infamous ex-governor Eliot Spitzer here, but you can find 40 types of craft beer on tap plus a selection of the bottled variety, good gastropub food, ample bar and communal-table seating, giant windows that open in warm weather, and wooden walls supposedly taken from pickle barrels. ✉ *101 Rivington St., at Ludlow St., Lower East Side* ☎ *212/228–0027* ⊕ *www.spitzerscorner.com* Ⓜ *F to Delancey St.; J, M, Z to Essex St.*

18

LIVE MUSIC VENUES

Arlene's Grocery. On Monday nights, crowds pack into this former Puerto Rican bodega for Rock 'n' Roll Karaoke, where they live out their rock-star dreams by singing favorite anthems onstage with a live band. The other six nights of the week are for local bands, variety shows, burlesque, the occasional murder-mystery party, and seasonal specialty acts. ⊠ *95 Stanton St., between Ludlow and Orchard Sts., Lower East Side* ☎ *212/358–1633* ⊕ *www.arlenesgrocery.net* Ⓜ *F to 2nd Ave.*

Fodor's Choice
★

Bowery Ballroom. This legendary theater with Art Deco accents is probably the city's top midsize concert venue. Packing in the crowds here is a rite of passage for musicians (some already big; some on the cusp of stardom), including the Gossip, Yo La Tengo, and the exuberant Go! Team. Grab one of the tables on the balcony (if you can), stand (and get sandwiched) on the main floor, or retreat to the comfortable bar in the basement, which fills up after each show. ⊠ *6 Delancey St., between the Bowery and Chrystie St., Lower East Side* ☎ *212/533–2111* ⊕ *www. boweryballroom.com* Ⓜ *J, Z to Bowery.*

The Delancey. From the palm-studded rooftop deck (heated in winter, breezy in summer), to the posh ground-floor lounge, and down to the programmed basement venue where DJs and rock bands hold court, the multifaceted Delancey, at the foot of the Williamsburg Bridge, is a versatile spot for thirsty lounge lizards. ⊠ *168 Delancey St., between Clinton and Attorney Sts., Lower East Side* ☎ *212/254–9920* ⊕ *www. thedelancey.com* Ⓜ *F to Delancey St.; J, M, Z to Essex St.*

Mercury Lounge. You have to squeeze past all the sardine-packed hipsters in the front bar to reach the stage, but it's worth it. Not only does this top-quality venue specialize in cool bands on the indie scene, but it was also where the late, great Jeff Buckley used to stop by to do spontaneous solo shows. Other big-name musicians follow in his footsteps with occasional pop-up shows of their own. ⊠ *217 E. Houston St., at Ave. A, Lower East Side* ☎ *212/260–4700* ⊕ *www.mercuryloungenyc.com* Ⓜ *F to 2nd Ave.*

Pianos. With two venues for live music and DJs—the Showroom downstairs and the Upstairs Lounge—as well as a full bar that serves food downstairs, there's something for everyone at this Lower East Side staple. It's especially fun late nights and weekends. ⊠ *158 Ludlow St., near Stanton St., Lower East Side* ☎ *212/505–3733* ⊕ *www.pianosnyc. com* Ⓜ *F to Delancey St.; J, M, Z to Essex St.*

Rockwood Music Hall. Musicians and DJs rev up the crowd seven days a week at this intimate, multistage venue. Performances start as early as 3 pm on the weekends and 6 pm during the week—meaning you can get your live music fix and catch up on your sleep, too. Many shows are free, making Rockwood a top spot to catch budding talent. ⊠ *196 Allen St., between Houston and Stanton Sts., Lower East Side* ☎ *212/477–4155* ⊕ *www.rockwoodmusichall.com* Ⓜ *F to 2nd Ave.; J, Z to Bowery.*

GREENWICH VILLAGE AND WEST VILLAGE

GREENWICH VILLAGE

BARS

124 Rabbit Club. Named for a 19th-century bar on, or near, its current site, this tiny/charming/divey craft-beer bar is often passed by unnoticed. But ring the bell to enter a hushed, low-lit subterranean bar with funky decor and rabbit images, where the menu dazzles with exotic and seasonal brews on tap and by the bottle (along with a few nice wines). ✉ *124 MacDougal St., between W. 3rd and Bleecker Sts., Greenwich Village* ☎ *646/781–0575* Ⓜ *A, B, C, D, E, F, M to W. 4th St.*

Vol de Nuit. Tucked away from the street, the "Belgian Beer Bar" (as everybody calls it) features a European-style, enclosed outdoor courtyard and a cozy interior, all red light and shadows. NYU grad-student types come for the mammoth selection of beers on tap as well as the fries, which are served with Belgian flair in a paper cone, with an array of sauces on the side. ✉ *148 W. 4th St., at 6th Ave., Greenwich Village* ☎ *212/982–3388* ⊕ *www.voldenuitbar.com* Ⓜ *A, B, C, D, E, F, M to W. 4th St.*

GAY NIGHTLIFE

Fodor's Choice
★

Stonewall Inn. Drink in history—literally. The Stonewall Inn is the bar made famous as the site of the June 1969 Stonewall Riots, when lesbian, gay, bisexual, and transgender patrons fought back against one of the police department's routine raids, ultimately galvanizing America's homosexual civil-rights movement. Today, the crowd is a fabulous mix of friendly bar goers who show their pride of place every day in this legendary (and gay-owned) Village tavern. Drop by to drink anytime from happy hour through late night, to play a round of pool, or to catch a show or dance party upstairs. Just don't miss the new plaque out front marking Stonewall as a National Historic Landmark. ✉ *53 Christopher St., between 7th and Greenwich Aves., Greenwich Village* ☎ *212/488–2705* ⊕ *thestonewallinnnyc.com* Ⓜ *1 to Christopher St.–Sheridan Sq.*

JAZZ VENUES

Fodor's Choice
★

Blue Note. Considered by many (not least its current owners) to be "the jazz capital of the world," the Blue Note was once the stomping ground for such legends as Dizzy Gillespie, and still hosts a variety of acts, from Chris Botti to jazz and Latin orchestras to Maceo Parker. Expect a steep cover charge except for late shows on weekends, when the music goes from less jazzy to more funky. ✉ *131 W. 3rd St., near 6th Ave., Greenwich Village* ☎ *212/475–8592* ⊕ *www.bluenote.net* Ⓜ *A, B, C, D, E, F, M to W. 4th St.*

The 55 Bar. Duck into this slim, Prohibition-era jazz club to catch small ensembles of jazz, blues, and funk players nightly, and channel the Village's groovy legacy while sipping stiff drinks. There are early and late shows (at either 6 or 7 pm, or 10 pm), and shows are free or have a nominal cover charge of around $10. ✉ *55 Christopher St., between 7th Ave. and Waverly Pl., Greenwich Village* ☎ *212/929–9883* ⊕ *www.55bar.com* Ⓜ *1 to Christopher St.–Sheridan Sq.*

18

LIVE MUSIC VENUES

(Le) Poisson Rouge. Head into the street-level or underground entrances to behold this cutting-edge, multipurpose entertainment and dance emporium, whose name means "the Red Fish" (and whose parentheses around "Le" remain a mystery). Blending just the right mix of posh notes (lush decor, fine dining), party nights, reasonable pricing, and brave music programming (retro-pop, jazz, electronic, cabaret, rock, folk—even rollicking drag-queen bingo), the Poisson is an essential NYC fixture. ✉ *158 Bleecker St., at Thompson St., Greenwich Village* ☎ *212/505–3474* ⊕ *www.lepoissonrouge.com* Ⓜ *A, B, C, D, E, F, M to W. 4th St.*

WEST VILLAGE

BARS

Corner Bistro. Opened in 1961, this lovable neighborhood saloon serves what many think are some of the best (and most affordable) burgers in town. Once you actually get a seat, the space feels nice and cozy, but until then, be prepared to drink a beer amid hungry, sociable patrons. ✉ *331 W. 4th St., at 8th Ave., West Village* ☎ *212/242–9502* ⊕ *www. cornerbistrony.com* Ⓜ *1, 2, 3, A, C, E to 14th St.; L to 8th Ave.*

Fodor's Choice
★

Employees Only. The dapper, white-coated bartenders at this cocktail bar mix delicious, well-thought-out tipples with debonair aplomb and freshly squeezed mixers. Sip one in the dimly lit bar area and you might feel like you've stepped back in time—if it weren't for the crush of trendy West Village locals and visitors at your back. Look for the green awning that says "EO" and the neon "Psychic" sign out front. Tasty, if pricey, fare is served in the restaurant at the back. ✉ *510 Hudson St., between Christopher and 10th Sts., West Village* ☎ *212/242–3021* ⊕ *www.employeesonlynyc.com* Ⓜ *1 to Christopher St.–Sheridan Sq.; A, B, C, D, E, F, M to W. 4th St.*

Hudson Bar and Books. Along with its sister branch—Lexington Bar and Books—uptown, the Hudson reflects a literary bent with handsome cigar-bar flare. It's hardly a hushed library; the atmosphere here is more about book decor than serious literature. It's seriously clubby, with wood paneling and leather banquettes. And this is one of the few lounges in NYC where you can still smoke with your classic, seasonal, and signature cocktails. ✉ *636 Hudson St., at Horatio St., West Village* ☎ *212/229–2642* ⊕ *www.barandbooks.cz/hudson* Ⓜ *A, C, E to 14th St.; L to 8th Ave.*

Fodor's Choice
★

Little Branch. Top-quality cocktails, dim lighting, and snug booths make this the ideal spot for a conversation with friends (that you can actually hear) or an intimate date. In true speakeasy fashion, despite its sweet location on a busy corner of the West Village, you could wander by never knowing the charm and expert concoctions being stirred up just downstairs. ✉ *22 7th Ave. S, at Leroy St., West Village* ☎ *212/929–4360* Ⓜ *1 to Houston St.*

The Otheroom. Head to the far west Otheroom for a flight of fancy drinking in good company. The menu is reliable and creative, with dozens of microbrews and international wines available by the glass— though choices change weekly, just to keep it interesting. ✉ *143 Perry St., between Greenwich and Washington Sts., West Village* ☎ *212/645– 9758* ⊕ *theotheroomnyc.com* Ⓜ *1 to Christopher St.–Sheridan Sq.*

White Horse Tavern. According to New York legend, writer Dylan Thomas drank himself to death in this historic West Village tavern founded in 1880. When the weather's nice, try to snag a seat at one of the sidewalk tables for breezy people-watching, and do enjoy the bar's reasonable prices—just don't overdo it like Thomas. ☒ *567 Hudson St., at 11th St., West Village* ☎ *212/989–3956* Ⓜ *1 to Christopher St.–Sheridan Sq.*

Wilfie & Nell. Combine the cozy atmosphere and frothy pints standard at Irish pubs with a well-heeled West Village crowd and you get Wilfie & Nell, a candlelit bar full of communal tables for making new friends. This perpetually crowded neighborhood go-to, with its low ceilings and locally sourced food, is a popular singles spot as well as a good match for night owls: food and brews are served into the wee hours. ☒ *228 W. 4th St., between 10th St. and 7th Ave. S, West Village* ☎ *212/242–2990* ⊕ *www.wilfieandnell.com* Ⓜ *1 to Christopher St.–Sheridan Sq.; A, B, C, D, E, F, M to W. 4th St.*

CABARET AND PIANO BARS

The Duplex. No matter who's performing, the big, gay audience hoots and hollers in support of the often kitschy performers at this music-scene staple on busy Sheridan Square, open since 1951. Singers and comedians hold court in the cabaret theater, while those itching to take a shot at open mic head downstairs to the lively piano bar. Warmer seasons bring a most welcome outdoor seating area, offering some of the neighborhood's best people-watching. ☒ *61 Christopher St., at 7th Ave. S, West Village* ☎ *212/255–5438* ⊕ *www.theduplex.com* Ⓜ *1 to Christopher St.–Sheridan Sq.*

GAY NIGHTLIFE

Henrietta Hudson. The nightly parties at this laid-back West Village HQ for the Sapphic set attract young professional women, out-of-town-ers, and longtime regulars. Because the DJ and pool table quickly create a crowd, though, lesbians arrive early to stake their claim to a spot, especially on weekends. ☒ *438 Hudson St., at Morton St., West Village* ☎ *212/924–3347* ⊕ *www.henriettahudson.com* Ⓜ *1 to Christopher St.–Sheridan Sq.*

The Monster. This "Monster" is a friendly one. This locals'-favorite gay bar has anchored its prime corner spot since 1970 and still serves as a lively piano bar and watering hole at street level, with an energetic disco downstairs programmed with a variety of nightly events, including Sunday tea dances. ☒ *80 Grove St., between W. 4th St. and 7th Ave. S, West Village* ☎ *212/924–3558* ⊕ *www.manhattan-monster.com* Ⓜ *1 to Christopher St.–Sheridan Sq.*

JAZZ VENUES

Fodor'sChoice
★

Village Vanguard. This prototypical jazz club, tucked into a cellar in the Village since the 1940s, has been the haunt of legends like Thelonious Monk and Barbra Streisand. Today you can hear jams from the likes of Bill Charlap and Ravi Coltrane, and on Monday night the sizable resident Vanguard Jazz Orchestra blows its collective heart out. ☒ *178 7th Ave. S, between 11th and Perry Sts., West Village* ☎ *212/255–4037* ⊕ *www.villagevanguard.com* Ⓜ *1, 2, 3 to 14th St.*

18

LIVE MUSIC VENUES

SOB's. The initials stand for "Sounds of Brazil" (no, not what you—and everybody else—might think), and this is *the* place for reggae, African, and Latin music, with some jazz gigs sprinkled in. Tito Puente Jr. sometimes holds court here, as does calypso's Mighty Sparrow when he's up north. Don't miss the Haitian dance parties, the after-work Latin-groove happy hour, or the bossa-nova brunches. There's usually about a $20 cover charge, and while there is a food menu, it's better to just come for the music. ✉ *204 Varick St., near Houston St., West Village* ☎ *212/243–4940* ⊕ *www.sobs.com* Ⓜ *1 to Houston St.*

CHELSEA AND THE MEATPACKING DISTRICT

CHELSEA

BARS

The Half King. Writer Sebastian Junger (*The Perfect Storm*) is one of the owners of this would-be literary mecca, though the ambience is more publike than writerly. And that's fine, since the King draws such a friendly crowd. Enjoy its frequent readings, gallery exhibits, and comfort-food menu. ✉ *505 W. 23rd St., between 10th and 11th Aves., Chelsea* ☎ *212/462–4300* ⊕ *www.thehalfking.com* Ⓜ *C, E to 23rd St.*

Porchlight. At this southern-inflected bar you can have your cocktails and eat your fried oysters and smoked cheddar biscuits, too. Located in far West Chelsea (a short hike from the subway), this relaxed watering hole from New York restaurateur and hospitality king Danny Meyer is an intimate space to quaff and nibble the night away. ✉ *271 11th Ave., between 27th and 28th Sts., Chelsea* ☎ *212/981–6188* ⊕ *porchlightbar. com* Ⓜ *C, E to 23rd St.; 1 to 28th St.*

COMEDY CLUBS

Gotham Comedy Club. This 10,000-square-foot club—complete with a chandelier and roomy downstairs lounge—showcases popular headliners such as Roy Wood Jr. and Kate Clinton, and the occasional pop-in by big-name funny folks like Dave Chappelle and Lewis Black. ✉ *208 W. 23rd St., between 7th and 8th Aves., Chelsea* ☎ *212/367–9000* ⊕ *go-thamcomedyclub.com* Ⓜ *1 to 23rd St.*

GAY NIGHTLIFE

Barracuda. The drag shows and freewheeling, flirty dance nights are what lure a mostly male crowd to this cute, casual neighborhood hangout, far less pretentious (some might say it's adorably divey) than some of its grander Chelsea neighbors. ✉ *275 W. 22nd St., between 7th and 8th Aves., Chelsea* ☎ *212/645–8613* Ⓜ *C, E, 1 to 23rd St.*

Gym Sports Bar. At New York's first gay sports bar, the plentiful flat-screen TVs and cheap Budweisers draw athletic enthusiasts of every stripe, from athlete to armchair. The bar sponsors—and frequently hosts parties for—a number of local gay sports teams. ✉ *167 8th Ave., at 18th St., Chelsea* ☎ *212/337–2439* ⊕ *www.gymsportsbar.com* Ⓜ *A, C, E to 14th St.; L to 8th Ave.; 1 to 18th St.*

THE MEATPACKING DISTRICT

BARS

Plunge. The Gansevoort Hotel's slick rooftop bar would be worth visiting even without its sweeping Hudson River and Manhattan views. Sleek and glossy, Plunge has soft lighting, cool furnishings, and sexy servers. The music isn't too loud and there is ample space—indoors as well as out. Cocktails are predictably pricey, but there are weekday happy-hour specials from 5 to 7 pm. ⊠ *Gansevoort Hotel, 18 9th Ave., at 13th St., Meatpacking District* ☎ *212/660–6736* ⊕ *www.plunge.nyc* Ⓜ *A, C, E to 14th St.; L to 8th Ave.*

The Standard Hotel Biergarten. Practically the official bar of the High Line park, the Standard Biergarten is a sprawling, bustling space complete with Ping-Pong, bench tables, and big steins of beer. For food, there's a grill bar and the indoor Living Room lounge. It's unlikely that you'll be able to enter the chic, multivenue hotel rooftop without an advance reservation, so plan accordingly. ⊠ *The Standard, High Line, 848 Washington St., at 13th St., Meatpacking District* ☎ *212/645–4646* ⊕ *www. standardhotels.com* Ⓜ *A, C, E to 14th St.; L to 8th Ave.*

DANCE CLUBS AND DJ VENUES

Cielo. Avid clubgoers gravitate to this Meatpacking District music-pumping mecca to guzzle cocktails, groove to top-flight DJs spinning soulful Latin beats, funk, and techno, boogie on the sunken dance floor, and smoke in the no-frills garden outside. Sunday night is home to the award-winning Deep Space parties, where resident and guest DJs rev up the faithful. ⊠ *18 Little W. 12th St., between 9th Ave. and Washington St., Meatpacking District* ☎ *212/645–5700* ⊕ *www.cieloclub.com* Ⓜ *A, C, E to 14th St.; L to 8th Ave.*

UNION SQUARE, GRAMERCY, AND THE FLATIRON DISTRICT

UNION SQUARE

BARS

Rye House. A welcoming bar with slick cocktails and a clever take on comfort food, the Rye House beckons just steps from the chain-store overload of Union Square. Whether you sample the white-truffle popcorn and fried pickles or their own take on a Sazerac, this place is a welcome respite from the hustle and bustle outside. ⊠ *11 W. 17th St., between Broadway and 5th Ave., Union Square* ☎ *212/255–7260* ⊕ *www.ryehousenyc.com* Ⓜ *4, 5, 6, L, N, Q, R, W to 14th St.–Union Sq.*

GRAMERCY

BARS

Fodor'sChoice ★ **Dear Irving.** This cocktail parlor invites guests inside with its name, the beginning of an imaginary love letter to Irving Place, on which the bar resides. Interiors themed for different eras are chic and refined, and just as at sister property Raines Law Room, there are private sections of tables and couches for intimate conversations. Reservations are recommended, especially during prime weekend hours, but must be made online. ⊠ *55 Irving Pl., between 17th and 18th Sts., Gramercy* ⊕ *www. dearirving.com* Ⓜ *4, 5, 6, L, N, Q, R ,W to 14th St.–Union Sq.*

18

Old Town Bar. The proudly unpretentious bi-level Old Town is redolent of old New York, and why not? It's been around since 1892. Tavern-style grub, mahogany everywhere, and atmosphere galore make this a must for anyone hankering to drink in vintage NYC. ✉ *45 E. 18th St., between Broadway and Park Ave. S, Gramercy* ☎ *212/529–6732* ⊕ *www.oldtownbar.com* Ⓜ *4, 5, 6, L, N, Q, R, W to 14th St.–Union Sq.*

Pete's Tavern. A historic landmark (where O. Henry was a loyal customer), this is one of the bars that claims—with its 1864 date—to be the oldest continuously operating watering hole in the city. Pete's has charm to spare, with its long wooden bar and cozy booths, where locals crowd in for a beer or a fantastic burger. When weather warms up, sidewalk tables with red-and-white-checkered tablecloths on scenic Irving Place are a neighborhood favorite. ✉ *129 E. 18th St., at Irving Pl., Gramercy* ☎ *212/473–7676* ⊕ *www.petestavern.com* Ⓜ *4, 5, 6, L, N, Q, R, W to 14th St.–Union Sq.*

JAZZ VENUES

Fodor's Choice
★
Jazz Standard. The Standard's sizable underground room draws top names in the business. As a part of Danny Meyer's southern-food restaurant Blue Smoke, it's one of the few spots where you can get dry-rubbed ribs to go with your bebop. Bring the kids for the Jazz Standard Youth Orchestra concerts every Sunday afternoon. ✉ *116 E. 27th St., between Park and Lexington Aves., Gramercy* ☎ *212/576–2232* ⊕ *www.jazzstandard.com* Ⓜ *6 to 28th St.*

LIVE MUSIC VENUES

Fodor's Choice
★
Irving Plaza. This two-story venue is known for its solid rock performances, both indie (DJ Shadow and Sleater-Kinney) and more mainstream (Lenny Kravitz)—even if they can get a little pricey. Red walls and chandeliers add a Gothic touch. If the main floor gets too cramped, seek sanctuary in the chill bar upstairs. ✉ *17 Irving Pl., at 15th St., Gramercy* ☎ *212/777–6817* ⊕ *www.irvingplaza.com* Ⓜ *4, 5, 6, L, N, Q, R, W to 14th St.–Union Sq.*

FLATIRON DISTRICT

BARS

Flatiron Lounge. Here, resident mixologists rely on the freshest (and sometimes most exotic) ingredients available. The cocktail menu at this Jazz Age–style lounge changes often, but if you're stumped, tell the bartenders what you like and they'll happily invent a bespoke concoction on the spot. ✉ *37 W. 19th St., between 5th and 6th Aves., Flatiron District* ☎ *212/727–7741* ⊕ *www.flatironlounge.com* Ⓜ *1 to 18th St.; F, M to 14th St.; L to 6th Ave.; 6 to 23rd St.*

The Lobby Bar at Ace Hotel. A hot spot for the digital set, this hotel's lobby and adjoining restaurant spaces—the Breslin and the John Dory—have been packed since they opened in 2009 at this Pacific Northwest import. If your bearded hipster friend came into some cash, his place would look like the lobby here, with reclaimed-wood tables, beer signs, and beautiful people in oversize eyeglasses drinking coffee by day or craft drinks by night (while a DJ spins in the background). ✉ *20 W. 29th St., between Broadway and 5th Ave., Flatiron District* ☎ *212/679–2222* ⊕ *www.acehotel.com/newyork* Ⓜ *R, W to 28th St.*

Fodor's Choice
★ **The NoMad Bar.** A sultry space from the team behind the NoMad Hotel, this bi-level bar impresses with its inviting leather banquettes, extensive golden-lit bar, and tempting list of craft cocktails. The food leans toward upscale classics, such as chicken potpie with foie gras and bacon-wrapped hot dogs with black truffle, and the setting is pure sophistication. ✉ *1170 Broadway, at W. 28th St., Flatiron District* ☎ *212/796–1500* ⊕ *www.thenomadhotel.com* Ⓜ *R, W, 6 to 28th St.*

Fodor's Choice
★ **Oscar Wilde.** If the life-size statue of Oscar Wilde out front doesn't catch your eye, the flamboyant interior surely will. Step inside to behold Manhattan's longest bar (at 118½ feet), and one of the city's most visually striking establishments. It seems like every inch is occupied by art and objects that blend busy Victorian and baroque styles, colors, and materials—from antique clocks and stained glass to a giant carved-marble fireplace, as well as vintage lamps and statuettes (and colorful Wilde quotes). The building was once home to the 1920s Prohibition Enforcement HQ, but now the bar serves expertly concocted, authentic Prohibition- and Victorian-era tipples. A relatively basic food menu is available, but the spotlight is on the cocktails and atmosphere. ✉ *45 W. 27th St., between Broadway and 6th Ave., Flatiron District* ☎ *212/213–3066* ⊕ *www.oscarwildenyc.com* Ⓜ *R, W to 28th St.*

Raines Law Room. There's no phone number or big sign for this speakeasy; just ring the bell to enter. Wood-burning fireplaces, deep banquettes, and curtains for privacy all contribute to the comfortable, living room–like vibe—perfect for a date or intimate group gathering. An outdoor, candlelit garden is functional, too: herbs grown here are used in the carefully crafted cocktails. ✉ *48 W. 17th St., between 5th and 6th Aves., Flatiron District* ⊕ *www.raineslawroom.com* Ⓜ *F, M to 14th St.; 4, 5, 6, L, N, Q, R, W to 14th St.–Union Sq.*

18

MIDTOWN EAST AND MURRAY HILL

MIDTOWN EAST

BARS

The Bar Downstairs. The bar without a name in the basement of the Andaz 5th Avenue hotel may lack a moniker, but it certainly has pedigree. Alchemy Consulting, a joint venture from Chicago's Violet Hour and New York's Death & Co., designed the cocktails here; look for spins on the Negroni and Manhattan in the sleek subterranean space. The food menu is similarly upmarket, with a variety of nebulously Spanish small plates. ✉ *Andaz 5th Avenue, 485 5th Ave., at 41st St., Midtown East* ☎ *212/601–1234* ⊕ *newyork5thavenue.andaz.hyatt.com* Ⓜ *B, D, F, M to 42nd St.–Bryant Park; 7 to 5th Ave.; 4, 5, 6, S to Grand Central–42nd St.*

Fodor's Choice
★ **The Campbell.** Classy tipplers and well-dressed commuters pack into this Grand Central Terminal bar (especially during the evening rush), but don't let the crush of humanity scare you away—you can have a romantic time here in one of Manhattan's more beautiful rooms. The restored space dates to the 1920s, when it was the private office of an executive named John W. Campbell, who impressed his friends and colleagues by entertaining them in this exquisite space. Sample the good life as you sip

cocktails from club chairs and banquettes. The proprietor also offers the smaller Campbell Palm Court and enclosed, outdoor Campbell Terrace; the latter is just outside in the former taxi driveway. ⊠ *Grand Central Terminal, 15 Vanderbilt Ave. entrance, Midtown East* ☎ *212/297–1781* ⊕ *www.thecampbellnyc.com* Ⓜ *4, 5, 6, 7, S to Grand Central–42nd St.*

King Cole Bar. A justly beloved Maxfield Parrish mural of "Old King Cole" himself, as well as his artful court, adds to the already considerable elegance at this romantic and essential Midtown meeting place. Try a Bloody Mary—this is where the drink was introduced to Americans, and be ready to pay for the privilege of drinking in this legendary establishment. ⊠ *St. Regis Hotel, 2 E. 55th St., between 5th and Madison Aves., Midtown East* ☎ *212/339–6857* ⊕ *www.kingcolebar.com* Ⓜ *E, M to 5th Ave./53rd St.*

P. J. Clarke's. Mirrors and polished wood and other old-time flair adorn New York's most famous Irish bar, which poured its first whiskey in 1884 (at the first location in what's now a regional chain). Steeped in Hollywood lore—Steve McQueen was once a regular, Buddy Holly proposed to his wife here, and it's the setting for scenes from the 1945 movie *Lost Weekend*—Clarke's draws in the after-work crowd that appreciates drinking beer, slurping oysters, and eating exceptionally juicy burgers while immersed in the place's history. ⊠ *915 3rd Ave., at 55th St., Midtown East* ☎ *212/317–1616* ⊕ *www.pjclarkes.com* Ⓜ *6 to 51st St.; E, M to Lexington Ave./53rd St.; 4, 5, 6 to 59th St.; N, R, W to Lexington Ave./59th St.*

GAY NIGHTLIFE

Evolve Bar and Lounge. Filling out a space that's long been the site of a gay establishment, Evolve is a go-to for mostly men to mingle after work and on weekends. The long bar is a watering hole for many regulars, and the smoke-friendly back patio is an added incentive to unwind in a bar unlike others in the neighborhood. Check the bar's social-media pages to see what go-go shows and open-mic lineups are planned. ⊠ *221 E. 58th St., between 2nd and 3rd Aves., Midtown East* ☎ *212/355–3395* Ⓜ *4, 5, 6 to 59th St.; N, R, W to Lexington Ave./59th St.*

Townhouse Bar. It's the elegant yin to the casual yang of **Evolve,** which is just across the block at East 58th Street. Distinguished mature men from the Upper East Side meet younger would-be versions of themselves at this "gentlemen's club," which looks like the home of a blueblood with superb taste. The attire is "uptown casual" if not fancier, and there are daily happy hours plus weekly special events. ⊠ *236 E. 58th St., between 2nd and 3rd Aves., Midtown East* ☎ *212/754–4649* ⊕ *www.townhouseny.com* Ⓜ *4, 5, 6 to 59th St.; N, R, W to Lexington Ave./59th St.*

MURRAY HILL

BARS

Middle Branch. This enticing, two-story speakeasy-style bar in Murray Hill is located inside a former antiques store—and, like its West Village sibling, Little Branch, there's no sign outside to announce its presence. Cocktail lovers find the brick town house anyway, and inside, linger over small plates, live jazz, and a long list of sophisticated drinks. ⊠ *154 E. 33rd St., between 3rd and Lexington Aves., Murray Hill* ☎ *212/213–1350* Ⓜ *6 to 33rd St.*

MIDTOWN WEST

BARS

Célon Lounge. Underneath the Bryant Park Hotel—and dramatic arched ceilings—is one of the more unexpected and spectacular spaces in Midtown, thanks to its Moroccan decor and Mediterranean-inspired cocktail and light-fare menus. Expect to sip herbally aromatic craft drinks while international pop music plays, and fashionistas and media types unwind in style. ⊠ *Bryant Park Hotel, 40 W. 40th St., between 5th and 6th Aves., Midtown West* ☎ *212/642–2257* ⊕ *www.celonlounge.com* Ⓜ *B, D, F, M to 42nd St.–Bryant Park; 7 to 5th Ave.*

Joe Allen. Everybody's en route either to or from a show at this "old reliable" on boisterous Restaurant Row, celebrated in the musical version of *All About Eve.* Chances are you'll even spot a Broadway star at the classic bar—with its robust scotch and whiskey menus—or in the dining room. Still, our favorite thing about Joe's is not the show crowd but the hilarious "flop wall," adorned with posters from musicals that bombed, sometimes spectacularly. (Check out the ones for *Paradox Lust, Got Tu Go Disco,* and *Dude,* the unfortunate sequel to *Hair.*) ⊠ *326 W. 46th St., between 8th and 9th Aves., Midtown West* ☎ *212/581–6464* ⊕ *www.joeallenrestaurant.com* Ⓜ *A, C, E to 42nd St.–Port Authority; N, R, W to 49th St.*

Lantern's Keep. The elegance of cocktail culture from another era is alive and well at Lantern's Keep, an intimate lounge tucked behind the lobby of the Iroquois Hotel. Reservations are recommended for this romantic lounge, where plush seats are huddled around a fireplace. There is no standing room here, resulting in a luxurious, leisurely vibe. Cocktails are works of art and bartenders are helpful at identifying your perfect poison. ⊠ *Iroquois Hotel, 49 W. 44th St., between 5th and 6th Aves., Midtown West* ☎ *212/453–4287* ⊕ *www.iroquoisny.com/lanternskeep* Ⓜ *B, D, F, M to 42nd St.–Bryant Park.*

Fodor's Choice ★ **The Rum House.** Among the glittering lights of Broadway theaters, Rum House is a destination bar thanks to its attention to the craft of mixing cocktails. The sister property to downtown favorite Ward III, this bar has nightly live piano music and creative libations in addition to all the classic cocktails. See if you can figure out where Michael Keaton sat during scenes from 2015's *Birdman.* ⊠ *228 W. 47th St., between 7th and 8th Aves., Midtown West* ☎ *646/490–6924* ⊕ *therumhousenyc.com* Ⓜ *N, R, W to 49th St.; A, C, E to 42nd St.–Port Authority.*

Russian Vodka Room. Forget **Russian Samovar** across the block—here's where the serious vodka drinking goes down. The Vodka Room features a glowing, sophisticated front room with nightly piano player, a more sumptuous back room, a generous attitude-adjustment hour (that's Russki for happy hour), and an impressive variety of infused vodkas from horseradish to ginger to pepper. For those who crave variety, a vodka tasting menu is available, as are culinary standards like caviar and borscht. ⊠ *265 W. 52nd St., between Broadway and 8th Ave., Midtown West* ☎ *212/307–5835* ⊕ *www.russianvodkaroom.com* Ⓜ *1, C, E to 50th St.*

18

Fodor's Choice
★

Salon de Ning. Take a break from 5th Avenue shopping at this glass-lined penthouse bar on the 23rd floor of the ritzy Peninsula Hotel, where the sumptuous decor is inspired by the historic tale of Shanghai socialite Madame Ning. Drinks are pricey, of course, but what isn't in this neighborhood? The views are worth it, especially from the rooftop terraces. ⊠ *Peninsula Hotel, 700 5th Ave., at 55th St., Midtown West* ☎ *212/903–3097* ⊕ *newyork.peninsula.com* Ⓜ *E, M to 5th Ave./53rd St.*

CABARET AND PIANO BARS

Don't Tell Mama. Composer-lyricist hopefuls and established talents show their stuff until 3 am nightly at this convivial Theater District cabaret. Extroverts will be tempted by the piano bar's open-mic policy as well as by the other showroom's singers, comedians, and drag acts. Those needing a break from the above can find it in the quieter exposed-brick lounge. ⊠ *343 W. 46th St., between 8th and 9th Aves., Midtown West* ☎ *212/757–0788* ⊕ *www.donttellmamanyc.com* Ⓜ *A, C, E to 42nd St./ Port Authority; C, E, to 50th St.*

COMEDY CLUBS

Caroline's on Broadway. This high-gloss club presents established names as well as comedians on the edge of stardom. Janeane Garofalo, David Alan Grier, Colin Quinn, and Gilbert Gottfried have all headlined. ⊠ *1626 Broadway, between 49th and 50th Sts., Midtown West* ☎ *212/757–4100* ⊕ *www.carolines.com* Ⓜ *N, R, W to 49th St.; 1 to 50th St.*

Upright Citizens Brigade. Raucous sketch comedy, audience-initiated improv, and classic stand-up take turns onstage here at the city's absolute capital for alternative comedy. There are classes available, too. UCB relocated to Hell's Kitchen from its familiar Chelsea venue in 2017 and now offers ADA accessibility; the troupe also has an outpost in the East Village. ⊠ *555 W. 42nd St., Midtown West* ☎ *212/366–9176* ⊕ *hellskitchen.ucbtheatre.com* Ⓜ *A, C, E to 42nd St.–Port Authority; 1, 2, 3, 7, N, Q, R, S to Times Sq.–42nd St.*

GAY NIGHTLIFE

Posh. Lest you think that Hell's Kitchen has no good gay lounges, Posh has walls covered in fine work by local artists, drag shows and special party nights, trophies over the bar, ample room for kibitzing and dancing, plenty of neon decor, and long hours to suit any schedule, from 2 pm to 4 am. ⊠ *405 W. 51st St., at 9th Ave., Midtown West* ☎ *212/957–2222* ⊕ *www.poshbarnyc.com* Ⓜ *C, E to 50th St.*

JAZZ VENUES

Birdland. This place gets its name from saxophone great Charlie "Yardbird" (or just "Bird") Parker, so expect serious musicians such as John Pizzarelli, the Dave Holland Sextet, and Arturo O'Farrill's Afro-Cuban Jazz Orchestra (on Sunday night). The dining room serves moderately priced American fare with a Cajun accent. ⊠ *315 W. 44th St., between 8th and 9th Aves., Midtown West* ☎ *212/581–3080* ⊕ *www.birdland-jazz.com* Ⓜ *A, C, E to 42nd St.–Port Authority.*

Fodor's Choice ★ **Dizzy's Club Coca-Cola.** For a night of jazz with big names and talent but without the pretension, turn to Dizzy's, an intimate club with Manhattan-skyline and Central Park views and southern-inflected cuisine (gumbo, blackened fish dishes) and cocktails. Late-night sessions are ideal for an after-dinner nightcap; some of the drinks, such as the Dizzy Gillespie, are named after jazz legends. ⊠ *Jazz at Lincoln Center, 10 Columbus Circle, inside the Time Warner Center, 5th fl., Midtown West* ☎ *212/258–9595* ⊕ *www.jazz.org/dizzys* Ⓜ *1, A, B, C, D to 59th St.–Columbus Circle.*

Iridium. This cozy, top jazz venue is a sure bet for big-name talent like the David Murray Black Saint Quartet and Michael Wolff. The sight lines are good, and the sound system was designed with the help of Les Paul, inventor of the solid-body electric guitar, who used to play here every Monday night. The rest of the week sees a mix of artists like Chuck Mangione and the Eddie Daniels Band. ⊠ *1650 Broadway, at 51st St., Midtown West* ☎ *212/582–2121* ⊕ *www.theiridium.com* Ⓜ *1 to 50th St.; N, R, W to 49th St.*

LIVE MUSIC VENUES

B. B. King Blues Club & Grill. This lavish Times Square club is vast, shiny, and hosts a range of musicians, from the Harlem Gospel Choir to George Clinton and the P-Funk All-Stars. It's also where you can occasionally catch rock legends like Aaron Neville or the Pointer Sisters, though some folks prefer the weekly Beatles Brunch (every Saturday at noon) or other tribute jams. ⊠ *237 W. 42nd St., between 7th and 8th Aves., Midtown West* ☎ *212/997–4144* ⊕ *www.bbkingblues.com* Ⓜ *A, C, E to 42nd St.–Port Authority; 1, 2, 3, 7, N, Q, R, S, W to Times Sq.–42nd St.*

UPPER EAST SIDE

BARS

American Trash. You might tell from the name that this isn't your granddad's UES drinking establishment. Bicycle tires, golf clubs, and other castoffs cover the walls and ceiling, ensuring that the Trash, a sanctum of sleaze, merits its descriptive name. Eight plasma TVs, three video games, a defiantly rock 'n' roll jukebox, and a pool table keep the neighborhood crowd (as well as stray bikers who hate them) busy. Some nights local bands play classic rock. ⊠ *1471 1st Ave., between 76th and 77th Sts., Upper East Side* ☎ *212/988–9008* Ⓜ *6 to 77th St., Q to 72nd St.*

Fodor's Choice ★ **The Auction House.** This Victorian-style lounge brings a touch of downtown chic to the sometimes suburban-feeling UES with candlelit tables, high tin ceilings, and velvet couches. Rap and hip-hop fans should look elsewhere (the only tunes coming out of this joint are alternative and rock), and baseball caps and sneakers are strictly forbidden, as are—at the other end of the spectrum—fur coats. ⊠ *300 E. 89th St., between 1st and 2nd Aves., Upper East Side* ☎ *212/427–4458* ⊕ *theauctionhousenyc.com* Ⓜ *4, 5, 6, Q to 86th St.*

Bar Pleiades. The cocktail bar companion to Café Boulud, also in the Surrey hotel, Bar Pleiades is a livelier alternative to the more staid

18

atmosphere at the Carlyle's Bemelmans Bar. The design is classic to a fault, employing a black-and-white theme that's positively Audrey Hepburn–esque. Drinks rotate seasonally, there are tasty nibbles from the café kitchen, and Fridays bring live jazz from 9 pm to midnight. Though it doesn't have the same drink menu, the rooftop bar is a cozy aerie good for people- and skyscraper-watching. ⊠ *The Surrey, 20 E. 76th St., between 5th and Madison Aves., Upper East Side* ☎ *212/772–2600* ⊕ *www.barpleiades.com* Ⓜ *6 to 77th St.*

Seamstress NY. This dedicated cocktail den—complete with low lighting, exposed brick walls, and cozy booth seating—elevated the drinking options in what can feel like a quiet neighborhood. Cocktails (and the creative bartenders who invented them) may be the main draw here, but the food menu is worth a look, too, including weekday oyster happy hours, 5:30–7 pm. ⊠ *339 E. 75th St., between 1st and 2nd Sts., Upper East Side* ☎ *212/288–8033* ⊕ *www.seamstressny.com* Ⓜ *6 to 77th St., Q to 72nd St.*

Subway Inn. Okay, so it's not *exactly* the original Subway Inn, which stood as an all-time favorite Manhattan dive bar for more than 70 years, until rising rents forced it out of business in 2014. But wander just two avenues east to behold the same iconic neon sign and a few other interior keepsakes at the new location, now a friendly local haunt run by the family of a bartender who spent years slinging drinks at the old watering hole. ⊠ *1140 2nd Ave., at E. 60th St., Upper East Side* ☎ *212/758–0900* Ⓜ *4, 5, 6, N, R, W to Lexington Ave./59th St.*

CABARET AND PIANO BARS

Fodor's Choice ★　**The Carlyle.** The hotel's discreetly sophisticated **Café Carlyle** hosts such top cabaret and jazz performers as Christine Ebersole, Judy Collins, John Pizzarelli, Steve Tyrell, and Woody Allen, who swings on the clarinet with the Eddy Davis New Orleans Jazz Band. The less fancyschmancy (though still pricey) **Bemelmans Bar,** with a mural by the author of the *Madeline* books, features a rotating cast of pianist-singers. ⊠ *35 E. 76th St., between Madison and Park Aves., Upper East Side* ☎ *212/744–1600* ⊕ *www.thecarlyle.com* Ⓜ *6 to 77th St.*

COMEDY CLUBS

The Comic Strip. The atmosphere here is strictly corner bar, belying its storied history: Eddie Murphy is said to have discovered Chris Rock here, for example. The famous stage also helped launch the careers of funnymen Paul Reiser and Jerry Seinfeld, though these days you're more likely to see fresh faces still trying to find their humorous groove. ⊠ *1568 2nd Ave., between E. 81st and 82nd Sts., Upper East Side* ☎ *212/861–9386* ⊕ *www.comicstriplive.com* Ⓜ *4, 5, 6, Q to 86th St.*

GAY NIGHTLIFE

Fodor's Choice ★　**Brandy's Piano Bar.** A singing waitstaff warm up the mixed crowd at this delightful and intimate uptown saloon and piano bar, getting everyone in the mood to belt out their favorite tunes. In fact, the Brandy's scene is so cheerful that some patrons call it musical Prozac, keeping depression at bay. ⊠ *235 E. 84th St., between 2nd and 3rd Aves., Upper East Side* ☎ *212/744–4949* ⊕ *www.brandyspianobar.com* Ⓜ *4, 5, 6, Q to 86th St.*

UPPER WEST SIDE

BARS

The Empire Hotel Rooftop Bar. The only thing better than hanging out in Lincoln Center on a lovely night is hanging out a dozen stories above Lincoln Center and taking in city views. Thanks to the Empire Hotel's sprawling rooftop bar—most of it outdoors, covered by a retractable roof, and heated in winter—you can enjoy that pleasure even on nights that are less than lovely. ⊠ *44 W. 63rd St., between Broadway and Columbus Ave., Upper West Side* ☎ *212/265–2600* ⊕ *www.empire-hotelnyc.com* Ⓜ *1 to 66th St.–Lincoln Center.*

Hi-Life NYC. The fantastic neon signs, padded black walls, large round mirrors, and L-shape bar here make you think you've wandered onto a 1940s movie set. Settle into a banquette and watch the neighborhood bons vivants (and bon-vivant wannabes) leap into action nightly, be it early for the daily happy hour or late nights till 3 am. ⊠ *477 Amsterdam Ave., at W. 83rd St., Upper West Side* ☎ *212/787–7199* ⊕ *www.hi-life.com* Ⓜ *1 to 86th St.*

Fodor'sChoice
★
Maison Pickle. From the same father-son team who made Jacob's Pickle a neighborhood fave, this pleasant restaurant is deservedly famous for its French-dip sandwich and other filling dishes. But its "old-school but progressive" cocktails, wine, and beer menus keep both of its separate bars busy. This is the sort of place where one visit will make you a regular. ⊠ *2315 Broadway, near W. 84th St., Upper West Side* ☎ *212/496–9100* ⊕ *www.maisonpickle.com* Ⓜ *1 to 86th St.*

Manhattan Cricket Club. Paying homage to the gentlemen's clubs of yore, this intimate UWS speakeasy welcomes everyone, provided you're in appropriate attire (no sneakers or baseball caps) and possess an appreciation for sophisticated cocktails elegantly served. Delicate bar snacks complement boutique bottled beverages and, more importantly, the club's fine spirits made into classic or creative (and notably named) concoctions. Reservations are recommended. ⊠ *226 W. 79th St., between Broadway and Amsterdam Ave., Upper West Side* ☎ *646/823–9252* ⊕ *www.mccnewyork.com* Ⓜ *1 to 79th St.*

COMEDY CLUBS

Stand Up NY. Head to this low-key club that lends a stage to both aspiring comedians and veteran comics who pop in to polish their material. Catch a pre-show drink in the front bar, then join the laughter in the back room for the price of a $15–$20 ticket, plus an $18 drink minimum. FYI to parents: the comedy showroom is open to guests 16 and up, as long as those under 18 are with a guardian. ⊠ *236 W. 78th St., between Broadway and Amsterdam Ave., Upper West Side* ☎ *212/595–0850* ⊕ *standupny.com* Ⓜ *1 to 79th St.*

JAZZ VENUES

Smoke. If you can't wait to get your riffs on, head uptown to this lounge near Columbia University, where the music starts at 7 pm and continues with one or two more shows nightly, plus a Sunday jazz brunch at 11:30 am. Performers include some of the top names in the business, including turban-wearing organist Dr. Lonnie Smith and the drummer Jimmy Cobb (who kept time on Miles Davis's seminal album *Kind of*

18

Blue). ✉ *2751 Broadway, between 105th and 106th Sts., Upper West Side* ☎ *212/864–6662* ⊕ *www.smokejazz.com* Ⓜ *1 to 103rd St.*

HARLEM

BARS

Corner Social. With nearly 20 beers on tap, sports on big screens, and bar food that's anything but boring, it's no surprise that this neighborhood favorite is packed on weekends. In warm weather an outdoor patio gives you a front-row seat to the scene on Lenox Avenue. ✉ *321 Lenox Ave., at 126th St., Harlem* ☎ *212/510–8552* ⊕ *www.cornersocialnyc. com* Ⓜ *2, 3 to 125th St.*

Ginny's Supperclub. Head downstairs from Marcus Samuelsson's renowned Red Rooster restaurant and find yourself in a glamorous lounge that seems right out of the 1920s. The cocktails are classic with a modern flair, and there is live music and/or DJs most Saturday evenings and some weeknights, as well as a gospel brunch. Advance reservations are recommended. ✉ *310 Lenox Ave., at 125th St., Harlem* ☎ *212/421–3821* ⊕ *www.ginnyssupperclub.com* Ⓜ *2, 3 to 125th St.*

Harlem Public. A juicy burger, live music, and more than a dozen craft beers on tap make this the type of neighborhood watering hole every New Yorker wants on their corner. Plenty of stools fill the sprawling space, along with a scattering of tables on the sidewalk during warm weather. It's an unfussy spot to raise a glass after a day of exploring vibrant Harlem. ✉ *3612 Broadway, at 149th St., Harlem* ☎ *212/939–9404* ⊕ *www.harlempublic.com* Ⓜ *1, A, B, C, D to 145th St.*

Shrine. It doesn't look like much from the outside, but this small performance venue with a global slant hosts multiple events each night, including live music, DJs, spoken word, and dance. These days there's usually a crush of out-of-towners during showtimes, but the music remains stellar and the establishment itself is the stuff of legend. ✉ *2271 Adam Clayton Powell Jr. Blvd., between 133rd and 134th Sts., Harlem* ☎ *212/690–7807* ⊕ *www.shrinenyc.com* Ⓜ *2, 3 to 135th St.*

JAZZ VENUES

Minton's Playhouse. The jazz institution that once featured big-name performers such as Dizzy Gillespie and Duke Ellington is now a sophisticated supper club with a roster of house-band jazz performers and featured musicians. The southern-revival food is garnering acclaim (the kitchen is shared with the Cecil restaurant next door). It's not a cheap night out (or weekend brunch), but worth the splurge. Jackets are required for men; reservations are recommended. ✉ *206 W. 118 St., near Adam Clayton Powell Jr. Blvd., Harlem* ☎ *212/243–2222* ⊕ *www. mintonsharlem.com* Ⓜ *2, 3, B, C to 116th St.*

BROOKLYN

BOERUM HILL AND COBBLE HILL

BARS

Clover Club. Long recognized for excellent drinks—both classic and inspired by the classics—and a cozy vibe, this is one of the best cocktail bars in Brooklyn. Passionate mixologists cook up seasonal cocktail menus and tasty bites to pair with them. Weekends get busy so better to head there on weeknights when you can sit at the bar and call bartender's choice. ⊠ *210 Smith St., Boerum Hill* ☎ *718/855–7939* ⊕ *www.cloverclubny.com* Ⓜ *F, G to Bergen St.*

Fodor'sChoice **Grand Army.** Housed in a former corner market, this easygoing neigh-
★ borhood bar may not appear to take its craft cocktails and quality beer list seriously. But the staff, led by master bartender and co-owner Damon Boelte, know precisely how to mix a classic libation or one from the sophisticated, themed menu that changes each fall and spring. ⊠ *336 State St., at Hoyt St., Boerum Hill* ☎ *718/422–7867* ⊕ *www.grandarmybar.com* Ⓜ *A, C, G to Hoyt–Schermerhorn St.*

DUMBO

BARS

Cecconi's Dumbo. The latest addition to the brand's upscale eateries, Cecconi's made a splash joining the polished DUMBO culinary and cultural scene in 2017. The Italian menu and stunning, East River–facing outdoor terrace are enough to warrant a visit; but no matter the season or weather, the roomy bar, outstanding service, and inviting furnishings make this a hot spot well worth a trip to this historic district. ⊠ *55 Water St., DUMBO* ☎ *718/650–3900* ⊕ *cecconisdumbo.com* Ⓜ *A, C to High St.; F to York St.*

Superfine. The narrow, bi-level floor plan might seem a little odd, but friendly service and convivial, colorful crowds transform this renovated warehouse into a welcoming, quirky neighborhood spot. The kitchen's organic menu changes seasonally, but the real action is at the bar, where stiff concoctions are poured near the orange-felt pool table. ⊠ *126 Front St., DUMBO* ☎ *718/243–9005* ⊕ *www.superfine.nyc* Ⓜ *A, C to High St.; F to York St.*

WILLIAMSBURG

BARS

Barcade. Stop reminiscing about your arcade-loving youth and start playing the more than 30 vintage video games (most cost a mere quarter) lining the walls of this high-spirited bar-arcade. Challenge yourself with favorites like Ms. Pac-Man or rarities like Rampage. Barcade isn't just about the games, though: there's a good selection of microbrews, as well as snacks. ⊠ *388 Union Ave., Williamsburg* ☎ *718/302–6464* ⊕ *www.barcadebrooklyn.com* Ⓜ *G to Metropolitan Ave.; L to Lorimer St.*

Fodor'sChoice **Ides Bar.** One of the buzziest bars in Williamsburg, the Ides benefits
★ from its privileged position on the Wythe Hotel's rooftop. Well-heeled patrons from all over the world line up for entry ($10 on Fridays and Saturdays after 6 pm) and the jaw-dropping views of the Manhattan

18

skyline. It's a hot spot on weekends, and crowded—it's more than worth it to go early and have that memorable view all to yourself. This is one of NYC's rare gratuity-free bars, and the only slightly higher menu prices reflect it. ⊠ *Wythe Hotel, 80 Wythe Ave., 6th fl., Williamsburg* 🕾 *718/460–8006* ⊕ *www.wythehotel.com/the-ides* Ⓜ *L to Bedford Ave.*

Fodor'sChoice **Maison Premiere.** Step inside this buzzy bar and restaurant, marked only
★ by a small "Bar, Oysters" sign, and you'll instantly feel whisked away to New Orleans. Sip expertly made cocktails at the horseshoe-shaped bar, or dine on platters of oysters at one of the café tables (there are full dinner and brunch menus as well). In spring and summer, the back garden is a lush oasis with cast-iron tables amid wisteria and palms. ⊠ *298 Bedford Ave., Williamsburg* 🕾 *347/335–0446* ⊕ *www.maison-premiere.com* Ⓜ *L to Bedford Ave.*

Radegast Hall & Biergarten. The vibe is boisterous at this sprawling beer garden, with plenty of communal tables that foster a convivial atmosphere. The Central European beers on tap and in bottles pair well with hearty foods like schnitzel, goulash, and delicious hot pretzels. There's free live music most nights. ⊠ *113 N. 3rd St., Williamsburg* 🕾 *718/963–3973* ⊕ *www.radegasthall.com* Ⓜ *L to Bedford Ave.*

Spuyten Duyvil. You might need to be a beer geek to recognize the obscure names of the more than 100 imported microbrews available here, but the connoisseurs behind the bar are more than happy to offer detailed descriptions and make recommendations. They'll also help you choose cheese and charcuterie platters to match your beverages. The space is narrow, with limited seating: all the more reason to take advantage of the huge backyard in summer. ⊠ *359 Metropolitan Ave., Williamsburg* 🕾 *718/963–4140* ⊕ *www.spuytenduyvilnyc.com* Ⓜ *L to Lorimer St.; G to Metropolitan Ave.*

BREWERIES

Brooklyn Brewery. This brewery put the borough's once-active craft beer scene back on the map when it opened in this former matzo factory in Williamsburg in 1996. Free 15-minute guided tours are offered on weekend afternoons, and there are always at least 8 or 10 offerings in the convivial taproom: the signature lager is popular, as is the Belgian-inspired Local 1, or try one of the seasonal options. Note that no open-toed shoes are allowed on the tours. ⊠ *79 N. 11th St., Williamsburg* 🕾 *718/486–7422* ⊕ *www.brooklynbrewery.com* Ⓜ *L to Bedford Ave.; G to Nassau Ave.*

LIVE MUSIC VENUES

Bembe. This steamy, bi-level lounge is Williamsburg's answer to Miami clubbing, though decorated with salvaged items including an old redwood front door from a New York State winery. The crowd is as eclectic as the DJ-spun beats that range from reggae to Brazilian—often accompanied by live drumming. The tropical bar menu adds to the place's Latin cred. ⊠ *81 S. 6th St., Williamsburg* 🕾 *718/387–5389* ⊕ *www. bembe.us* Ⓜ *J, M, Z to Marcy Ave.*

Music Hall of Williamsburg. This intimate, trilevel music venue in a former mayonnaise factory has excellent acoustics, so it's no surprise that it draws die-hard fans of rock and indie music. There's balcony seating and an additional bar upstairs. If you love Manhattan's Bowery Ballroom, you'll feel the same way about this venue; it's run by the bookers at Bowery Presents, so you can expect the same quality lineups. ⊠ *66 N. 6th St., Williamsburg* ☎ *718/486–5400* ⊕ *www.musichallofwilliamsburg.com* Ⓜ *L to Bedford Ave.*

Union Pool. A former pool-supply store now serves as a funky multipurpose venue, complete with a corrugated tin–backed bar, a photo booth, a small stage for live music, and cheap PBR. It's a popular spot on the Friday-night circuit, especially for late-night dancing. The back patio has a taco truck and a fire pit. ⊠ *484 Union Ave., Williamsburg* ☎ *718/609–0484* ⊕ *www.union-pool.com* Ⓜ *G to Metropolitan Ave.; L to Lorimer St.*

GREENPOINT
BARS
Diamond Lil. This understated yet outstanding neighborhood bar—which takes its name from Brooklyn native Mae West—mixes fantastic cocktails in a refined, art nouveau setting enhanced by a lovely custom artwork behind the bar. Settle into the two-person booths with a friend and catch up in style with a finely crafted cocktail or one of the other well-priced beverages. ⊠ *179 Nassau Ave., Greenpoint* ⊕ *diamondlilbar.com* Ⓜ *G to Nassau Ave.*

BUSHWICK AND EAST WILLIAMSBURG
BARS
Fodor'sChoice ★ **Featherweight.** The cocktail list at this small spot is full of the hits you'd expect at a bar run by the experts behind the two Weather Up spaces in Manhattan and Prospect Heights. Part of the allure, though, is that bartenders will mix a cocktail to your precise specifications. Prime time here is late night. Finding the entrance is part of the fun: look for the painted feather and the three-story-tall mural of a boxer. ⊠ *135 Graham Ave., Brooklyn* ☎ *202/907–3372* ⊕ *www.featherweightbk.com* Ⓜ *J, M to Lorimer St.; L to Montrose Ave.*

PARK SLOPE
BARS
Fodor'sChoice ★ **Union Hall.** This neighborhood standby has something going on just about every night. On the main floor, two bocce courts and a library nook with couches and fireplace are popular hangouts; downstairs, there are smart comedy shows featuring *Daily Show* and *Saturday Night Live* regulars, eclectic talks, or DJs spinning. The outdoor patio is open in good weather. The menu of perfectly tasty burgers, sandwiches, and bar snacks (beer cheese is a highlight) means the patrons tend to settle in for the evening. Events are either free or have a modest cover ($5 to $20). ⊠ *702 Union St., Park Slope* ☎ *718/638–4400* ⊕ *www. unionhallny.com* Ⓜ *R to Union St.*

LIVE MUSIC VENUES
Fodor'sChoice ★ **Barbès.** Outstanding regulars like the Django Reinhardt mantle-bearer Stephane Wrembel, western-swingers Brain Cloud, and Slavic Soul Party spin threads of folk and "ethnic" into 21st-century music, while the Erik Satie Quartet keeps Satie, Britten, and other classical composers relevant. Performances take place in the back room, where a pitcher

18

is passed to collect the $10 suggested cover. Up front, the somewhat musty, Parisian-like bar has a laid-back vibe and a full cocktail menu. ✉ *376 9th St., Park Slope* ☎ *347/422–0248* ⊕ *www.barbesbrooklyn. com* Ⓜ *F, G to 7th Ave.*

QUEENS

ASTORIA
BARS
Bohemian Hall & Beer Garden. Warm summer nights and cold, frothy beers have been savored by locals for over 100 years at the Bohemian Hall & Beer Garden. With pitchers of beer, picnic tables, live music, and Czech dishes from the kitchen, this sunny garden is an ideal spot for getting together with old friends—or making new ones over big mugs of Staropramen and Pilsner Urquell. While some of the outdoor seating is covered, in the event of rain, the well-worn indoor bar is just as inviting, though comparatively tiny. ✉ *29-19 24th Ave., Astoria* ☎ *718/274–4925* ⊕ *www.bohemianhall.com* Ⓜ *N, W to Astoria–Ditmars Blvd.*

LONG ISLAND CITY
BARS
Dutch Kills. The dark bar and cozy wooden booths at Dutch Kills—a cocktail den with a nod to the neighborhood's historic roots—serves up finely crafted drinks at a couple of dollars cheaper than similar Manhattan watering holes. Expect precisely chiseled chunks of ice and skilled bartenders who, with a few queries into your preferences and curiosities, can create a concoction just to your taste. (As the former industrial zone that is Long Island City continues to gentrify and turn residential, expect to see more and more craft bars around the neighborhood.) ✉ *27-24 Jackson Ave., Long Island City* ☎ *718/383–2724* ⊕ *www.dutchkillsbar.com* Ⓜ *E, M, R to Queens Plaza; G to Court Sq.; 7, N, Q to Queensboro Plaza.*

PERFORMING ARTS

Updated
by Sarah
Amandolare

The streets of New York alone are stageworthy. With so many people faking it 'til they make it, daily life can take on the feeling of performance—to exhausting, and inspiring, effect. No wonder that the city draws a constant influx of actors, singers, dancers, and musicians from around the globe, all striving for their big break and infusing the city with a crackling creative energy. This fiercely competitive scene produces an unrivaled wealth of culture and art that many New Yorkers cite as the reason they're here, and that millions more are determined to travel for.

Although costly ticket prices can make attending a Broadway show a less common outing for even the most devout theater-loving New Yorkers, that's not true of many other kinds of more affordable performances. Whether the audiences are primarily local or not, it's their discernment that helps drive the arts scene, whether they are flocking to a concert hall to hear a world-class soprano deliver a flawless performance, or crowding into a cramped café to support fledgling writers reading from their own work.

New York has upward of 200 "legitimate" theaters (meaning those with theatrical performances, not movies), and many more ad hoc venues— parks, churches, lofts, galleries, rooftops, even parking lots. The city is also a revolving door of special events: summer jazz, one-act-play marathons, film festivals, and music and dance celebrations from the classical to the avant-garde, to name just a few.

PLANNING

ARTS PLANNER
BROADWAY AND OFF-BROADWAY — WHAT'S THE DIFFERENCE?

There are just over 40 Broadway theaters in New York, and although you might expect their shows to be the best ones in town, the designation depends on theater capacity (which must count at least 500 seats), not quality. Nearly all are within a few blocks of Times Square. A show must be performed in a Broadway theater as part of the eligibility requirements for a Tony Award. Off-Broadway theaters, which are scattered throughout the city, have 100 to 499 seats; Off-Off-Broadway venues seat fewer than 100.

DANCE, OPERA, MUSIC, AND MORE

Besides being home to outstanding theater, New York is one of the premier cities in the world for ballet and contemporary dance, opera, and classical music. Start your search with a visit to the websites of three of the city's biggest performing arts centers: Lincoln Center (⊕ *www. lincolncenter.org*), Carnegie Hall (⊕ *www.carnegiehall.org*), and the Brooklyn Academy of Music (⊕ *www.bam.org*). They all have detailed events calendars, and the listings demonstrate the sheer depth and range of great performances available in New York. It's also helpful to consider the time you're visiting. Many arts groups schedule the bulk of their performances from September through May, with special holiday events planned in November and December. Although the number of performances in many venues tapers off in the dog days of summer, the season also brings lots of festivals and outdoor performances, many of them inexpensive or free. Finally, it's smart to also check out the websites of any museums you think you might want to visit while in town. The Frick, for instance, has been hosting world-class classical-music concerts in its 165-seat Music Room since 1938, while the Metropolitan Museum of Art periodically stages concerts and other performing arts events in locations like the Egyptian Temple of Dendur, or in its enviable gallery of musical instruments.

19

WHAT'S ON?

The *New York Times* (⊕ *www.nytimes.com/events*) listings are probably the single best place to find out what's happening in the city. The *New Yorker*'s Goings On About Town listings (⊕ *www.newyorker.com*) are more selective, while *New York* magazine (⊕ *www.nymag.com*) gives a slightly more opinionated spin on the performing arts. The theater sites ⊕ *www.playbill.com*, ⊕ *www.theatermania.com*, and ⊕ *www.offoffonline.com* (for Off-Off-Broadway) provide information like synopses, accessibility info, run times, seating charts, and links to buy tickets. Sites like ⊕ *www.broadway.org*, run by The Broadway League; ⊕ *www. offbroadway.com*, run by the League of Off-Broadway Theatres and Producers; and ⊕ *www.broadwaycollection.com*, geared toward the travel trade, but with information in multiple languages, are each a wealth of information.

BUYING TICKETS AT FULL PRICE

How much do tickets sell for, anyway? The average price paid for a Broadway show runs about $110; not counting the limited "premium seat" category (or discount deals), the low end for musicals is in the $30–$75 range. Nonmusical comedies and dramas start at about $30 and top out at about $175. Off-Broadway show tickets run $30–$125, and Off-Off-Broadway shows can run as low as $15–$25, or even less if you find a deal. Tickets to an opera start at about $25 for nosebleed seats and can soar to more than $400 for prime locations. Classical music concerts go for $25 to $100 or more, depending on the venue and the performers. Dance performances are usually in the $15 to $70 range, but expect choice seats for the ballet to cost more, especially around the holidays.

Scoring tickets is fairly easy, especially if you have some flexibility. Always start with the website of the venue or theater company to see what going rates are (and if any deals are available). If timing or cost is critical, the only way to ensure the seats you want is to make your purchase in advance—and that might be months ahead for a hit show. In general, tickets for Saturday evening and for weekend matinees, or for Broadway shows featuring big-name stars for limited runs, are the toughest to secure, and the priciest.

For smaller performing arts companies, and especially for Off-Broadway shows, try **Ticket Central,** on Theater Row; service charges are nominal here. **SmartTix** is a reliable resource for (usually) smaller performing arts companies, including dance and music; their service charges are nominal as well.

Sure bets for Broadway (and some other big-hall events) are the box office or either **Telecharge** or **Ticketmaster.** Virtually all larger shows are listed with one service or the other, but never both; specifying "premium" helps get elusive—and expensive—seats. A broker or your hotel concierge should be able to procure last-minute tickets, but many regard brokers as legal scalpers, and their prices may even exceed "premium" rates. Be prepared to pay steep add-on service fees for all ticketing services.

■TIP→ Although online ticket services provide seating maps to help you choose, the advantage of going to the box office is twofold: there are no add-on service fees, and a ticket seller can personally advise you about sight lines—and knee room—for the seat location you are considering. Broadway box offices do not usually have direct phone lines; their walk-in hours are generally 10 am until curtain.

BUYING DISCOUNT TICKETS

The cheapest—though chanciest—ticket opportunities are found at participating theater box offices on the day of the performance. These rush tickets, usually about $25–$40, may be distributed by lottery and are usually for front-row (possibly neck-craning) seats, though it can vary by theater; there are also standing-room-only seats available on occasion (usually for under $30). Check the comprehensive planner on ⊕ *www.nytix.com,* or go to the box office of the show you are interested in to discover whether they make such an offer and how to pursue it. Obstructed-view seats or those in the very rear balcony are sometimes available at deeply discounted rates, for advance purchase.

For advanced discount purchases, the best seating is likely available by using a discount code. Procure these codes, good for an average of 20% to 50% off, online. (You need to register on each website.) The excellent no-subscription-required ⊕ *www.broadwaybox.com* posts nearly all discount codes currently available for Broadway shows. As with the discount codes provided through online subscriber services—**TheaterMania, Playbill,** and **Your Broadway Genius** (the last is for groups only) among them—to avoid service charges, you must bring the printout to the box office, and make your purchase there. You can also download mobile ticketing apps, such as **TodayTix,** which offer discounted last-minute and advance tickets.

For seats at up to 50% off the usual price, get same-day discount tickets by going to one of the **TKTS booths** (⊕ *www.tdf.org*): there's one in Times Square, others at Lincoln Center and South Street Seaport, and a fourth in downtown Brooklyn. Although they do tack on a $5-per-ticket service charge, and not all shows are predictably available, the broad choices and ease of selection—and, of course, the solid discount—make TKTS the go-to source for the flexible theatergoer. You can browse available shows for that day online or via a TKTS app (⊕ *www.tdf.org/tktsapp*), or check the electronic listings board near the ticket windows to mull over your options while you're in line. At the Times Square location (under the red glass staircase), there is a separate "Play Express" window (for nonmusical events) to further simplify (and expedite) things; they also offer a 7-Day Fast Pass, meaning if you buy tickets today, you can come back within the next seven days to make another purchase without having to wait on line. Times Square hours are Monday and Wednesday–Saturday 3–8, and Tuesday 2–8 for evening performances; for Wednesday and Saturday matinees 10–2; for Sunday matinees 11–3; and for Sunday evening shows, from 3–7. The South Street Seaport location, at the corner of Front and John Streets, is open Monday–Saturday 11–6, and Sunday 11–4, except in winter. Brooklyn hours are Tuesday–Saturday 11–3 and 3:30–6. The Lincoln Center location, in the David Rubenstein Atrium, is open Tuesday–Saturday noon–3 and 3:30–7, and Sunday noon–3 and 3:30–5. All ticket sales are for shows on that same day (one exception: the Brooklyn location's matinee tickets are for next-day performances only). Credit cards and cash are accepted at all locations. ■ TIP➔ **Ticket-booth hours may vary over holiday periods; also note that the longest lines are generally within the first hour of the booths' opening.**

Contacts Playbill. ⊕ *www.playbill.com.* **SmartTix.** ☎ *212/868–4444* ⊕ *www. smarttix.com.* **Telecharge.** ☎ *212/239–6200, 800/447–7400* ⊕ *www.telecharge. com.* **TheaterMania.** ☎ *212/352–3101, 866/811–4111* ⊕ *www.theatermania. com.* **Ticket Central.** ✉ *Playwrights Horizon, 416 W. 42nd St., between 9th and 10th Aves., Midtown West* ☎ *212/279–4200* ⊕ *www.ticketcentral.com* Ⓜ *A, C, E to 42nd St.–Port Authority.* **Ticketmaster.** ☎ *866/448–7849 for automated service, 800/745–3000* ⊕ *www.ticketmaster.com.* **TKTS Times Square.** ✉ *Duffy Sq., 47th St. and Broadway, Midtown West* ☎ *212/912–9770* ⊕ *www.tdf.org/ tkts* Ⓜ *1, 2, 3, 7, N, Q, R, S to Times Sq.–42nd St.* **TodayTix.** ☎ *855/464–9778* ⊕ *www.todaytix.com.* **Your Broadway Genius.** ☎ *877/943-2929* ⊕ *www. yourbroadwaygenius.com.*

19

Best Tips for Broadway

Whether forking over hundreds of dollars for a top seat or shoestringing it with a standing-room ticket, you'll have better Broadway experiences to brag about if you take our advice.

Do your homework. Remember— your friend's must-see may not be yours. Subscribe to online newsletters ahead of your trip for access to show reviews, special ticket offers, and more. If it's a classic play or opera, you may enjoy it more if you've read a synopsis before you go.

Reserve and plan ahead. The TKTS booth is great if you're up for what the fates make available, but for must-sees, book early. While you're at it, ask whether the regular cast is expected. (An in-person stop at the box office is the most reliable way to score this information, but don't hold them to it unless it's the day of the performance. If there is a change then—and the replacement cast is not acceptable to you—you may get a refund.) For musicals, live music often adds a special zing; confirm when ticketing to avoid surprises on the rare occasion when recorded music is used.

Check theater seating charts. Front mezzanine is a great option; with seats that overhang the orchestra section, they can be better (though not always less expensive) than many orchestra seats. Book with a seating chart at hand (available online and at the box office). Check accessibility, especially at older theaters with multiple flights of stairs and few elevators.

Know when to go. Typically, Broadway shows give eight performances a week. There are nightly performances from Tuesday through Saturday night,

and matinees at 2 pm on Wednesday and Saturday and at 3 pm on Sunday (on Monday most theaters are closed, or "dark"). Weekend shows, especially Saturday night, are the most difficult tickets to get. Tuesday is especially promising, and typically an earlier curtain—7 instead of the usual 8 pm— helps ensure a good night's sleep for your next day of touring.

Dress right. You can throw on jeans to go to the theater these days, but personally we feel shorts and sneakers have no place on Broadway (at least in the audience). Bring binoculars if your seats are up high, check bulky coats if a coat check is available, and drop bags and packages off at your hotel room in advance— theater seats tend to be narrow, with little leg room.

Travel smart. Trying to get to the show on time? Unless you don't mind watching the meter run up while you're stuck in traffic, avoid cabs into or out of Times Square. Walk, especially if you're within 10 blocks of the theater. Otherwise, take the subway; many train lines converge in the area.

Dine off Broadway. Dining well on a budget and doing Broadway right are not mutually exclusive. The key is to avoid eating in Times Square itself—even the national chains are overpriced. Consider eating earlier instead, in whatever neighborhood you're visiting that day. If you're already in Midtown, head west to 9th or 10th Avenue, where prix-fixe deals and ethnic eateries are plentiful and many actors and theater folk live. You never know whom you'll see on the street or at the next table.

LOWER MANHATTAN

FINANCIAL DISTRICT
READINGS AND LECTURES

Poets House. Situated in a bright and airy building in the residential area of Battery Park City and near the Hudson River, this reading room is an open resource for all ages, with a 70,000-volume library, readings, and other poetry-centric events. ⊠ *Battery Park City, 10 River Terr., at Murray St., Financial District* ☎ *212/431–7920* ⊕ *www.poetshouse.org* Ⓜ *1, 2, 3, A, C to Chambers St.*

TRIBECA
MUSIC

FAMILY **Tribeca Performing Arts Center.** This center celebrates theater (with a clever children's series) and dance but is primarily known for jazz. Highlights in Jazz and Lost Jazz Shrines are two of its special series. ⊠ *199 Chambers St., between Greenwich and West Sts., TriBeCa* ☎ *212/220–1460 for tickets* ⊕ *www.tribecapac.org* Ⓜ *1, 2, 3, A, C to Chambers St.*

SOHO

READINGS AND LECTURES

Fodor's Choice ★ **The Greene Space** (*Jerome L. Greene Performance Space*). The local public radio stations WNYC and WQXR invite the public into their intimate (125 seats) studio for live shows featuring classical, rock, jazz, and new music; audio theater; conversation; and interviews. It's a great place to get up-close with writers and newsmakers, as well as musicians and actors who might be playing Carnegie Hall, Broadway, or the Met Opera a few days later. ⊠ *44 Charlton St., at Varick St., SoHo* ☎ *646/829–4000* ⊕ *www.thegreenespace.org* Ⓜ *C, E to Spring St.; 1 to Houston St.*

Housing Works Bookstore Cafe. Amid roughly 25,000 books and CDs for sale, Housing Works hosts a wide range of literary and cultural events, including quirky readings, sometimes with unannounced surprise guests; journal and book launches; and storytelling or music nights. This cozy store is staffed largely by volunteers, and all profits go toward fighting homelessness and HIV/AIDS. ⊠ *126 Crosby St., between Houston and Prince Sts., SoHo* ☎ *212/334–3324* ⊕ *www. housingworks.org/locations/bookstore-cafe* Ⓜ *N, R, W to Prince St.; B, D, F, M to Broadway–Lafayette St.*

Fodor's Choice ★ **The Moth.** Dedicated to first-person storytelling, this roving series has spread far beyond New York, where it was founded in 1997 by the writer George Dawes Green. But it's still going strong here: the curated Mainstage shows feature celebrities and everyday people alike who've worked with The Moth directors to shape their stories. At the much looser, open-mic StorySLAMs, competitors are randomly selected and given just five minutes to tell their story, which must tie in with the night's theme. These tales get told at Housing Works and other venues downtown and throughout the city. ⊠ *Housing Works Bookstore Cafe, 126 Crosby St., between Houston and Prince Sts., SoHo* ☎ *212/742–0551* ⊕ *themoth. org/events* Ⓜ *N, R, W to Prince St.; B, D, F, M to Broadway–Lafayette St.*

19

THEATER

HERE. Celebrating all manner of contemporary, genre-bending productions, the original home of Eve Ensler's *The Vagina Monologues* and Basil Twist's *Symphonie Fantastique* also houses art exhibitions and a café. ✉ *145 6th Ave., between Spring and Dominick Sts., SoHo* ☎ *212/647–0202, 212/352–3101 for tickets* ⊕ *www.here.org* Ⓜ *C, E to Spring St.*

EAST VILLAGE AND LOWER EAST SIDE

EAST VILLAGE

Danspace Project. Founded to foster the work of independent choreographers such as Lucinda Childs and David Gordon, Danspace Project sponsors performances that are as fresh—and idiosyncratic—as the historic church space they occupy. Performance series curated by guest artists are also a regular part of the calendar. ✉ *St. Mark's Church in-the-Bowery, 131 E. 10th St., at 2nd Ave., East Village* ☎ *212/674–8112, 866/811–4111 for tickets* ⊕ *www.danspaceproject.org* Ⓜ *6 to Astor Pl.; N, R to 8th St.–NYU; L to 3rd Ave.*

FILM

Fodor's Choice
★ **Anthology Film Archives.** Dedicated to preserving and exhibiting independent and avant-garde film, Anthology Film Archives is made up of two screening rooms that seat 187 and 72 as well as a film repository and a library, all inside a renovated redbrick courthouse. Cofounded in 1970 by the downtown legend and filmmaker Jonas Mekas, Anthology remains a major destination for adventurous and unusual movies, new as well as old. The Essential Cinema series delves into the works of canonized, groundbreaking directors; the frequent festivals are more eclectic and may cover under-recognized auteurs, as well as hard-to-see films of all types. This is an experience for film lovers, not casual moviegoers, so don't expect the amenities you'd find at a multiplex. ✉ *32 2nd Ave., at 2nd St., East Village* ☎ *212/505–5181* ⊕ *www.anthologyfilmarchives.org* Ⓜ *F to 2nd Ave.*

MUSIC

SubCulture. With its exposed brick, structural pillars, theater-style seating, and industrial-chic bar, this intimate subterranean concert hall could just as easily be a cool lounge as a venue for musical theater and Broadway concerts, and occasional classical and jazz performances. Series here have included in-the-round performances of all of Beethoven's string quartets; the piano music of Debussy and Ravel; and concerts from Tony Award–winning composers, featuring guest appearances by various Broadway stars. ✉ *45 Bleecker St., between the Bowery and Lafayette St., East Village* ☎ *212/533–5470* ⊕ *www.subculturenewyork.com* Ⓜ *6 to Bleecker St.; B, D, F, M to Broadway–Lafayette St.*

READINGS AND LECTURES

KGB Bar. A nexus of the downtown literary scene, KGB keeps a busy calendar of readings and discussions: start with Sunday Night Fiction or KGB Poetry on Monday night. The name and the Soviet kitsch are a nod to the bar's history as a speakeasy for leftist Ukrainians. The Red Room, an additional performance space one floor above the bar, hosts varied nightly events and late-night live jazz on Friday and Saturday. ✉ *85 E. 4th St., between the Bowery and 2nd Ave., East Village* ☎ *212/505–3360* ⊕ *www.kgbbar.com* Ⓜ *F to 2nd Ave.; 6 to Bleecker St.*

Nuyorican Poets Cafe. The reigning arbiter of poetry slams, the Nuyorican Poets Cafe hosts open-mic events and the influential granddaddy (b. 1989) of the spoken-word scene, the Friday Night Poetry Slam. Other performances, including hip-hop open mics, jazz acts, and theatrical performances, round out the schedule. Although tickets for many of the popular shows like the Friday Night Poetry Slam and the Monday-night open mics can be purchased in advance online, it's still a good idea to line up early; the small venue can get packed to the point of standing-room only. ✉ *236 E. 3rd St., between Aves. B and C, East Village* ☎ *212/780–9386* ⊕ *www.nuyorican.org* Ⓜ *F to 2nd Ave.; J, M, Z to Essex St.*

The Poetry Project. Launched in 1966, the Poetry Project has been a source of sustenance for poets (and their audiences) ever since. This place has seen performances by Allen Ginsberg, Amiri Baraka, Sam Shepard, Patti Smith, Anne Waldman, and many others. At current readings you might find artists of the same caliber. Prime times are Monday, Wednesday, and Friday. ✉ *St. Mark's Church in-the-Bowery, 131 E. 10th St., at 2nd Ave., East Village* ☎ *212/674–0910* ⊕ *www.poetryproject.org* Ⓜ *N, R, W to 8th St.–NYU; 6 to Astor Pl.; L to 3rd Ave.*

THEATER

Classic Stage Company. At the CSC's cozy 199-seat theater you can see excellent revivals—such as Chekhov's *Three Sisters,* Shakespeare's *Romeo and Juliet,* or several plays of Euripides—often with a modern spin, reigning theatrical stars, and new scores. ✉ *136 E. 13th St., between 3rd and 4th Aves., East Village* ☎ *212/677–4210* ⊕ *www.classicstage.org* Ⓜ *4, 5, 6, N, Q, R to 14th St.–Union Sq.; L to 3rd Ave.*

La MaMa E.T.C. Ellen Stewart (1919–2011) founded La MaMa E.T.C. in 1961 in a small Manhattan basement. Since that time, the Experimental Theatre Club has grown continuously, all the while taking risks on unknown works that cross cultures and performance disciplines (of note, Blue Man Group got its start here). In an effort to keep theater accessible, tickets are a bargain across the theater's four venues, ranging from just $10 to $31. ✉ *66 and 74A E. 4th St., between the Bowery and 2nd Ave., East Village* ☎ *212/352-3101* ⊕ *www.lamama.org* Ⓜ *F to 2nd Ave.; 6 to Bleecker St.*

New York Theatre Workshop. Works by new and established playwrights anchor this theater's repertoire. Jonathan Larson's *Rent* got its start here before going to Broadway, as did the hit musical *Once.* Works by Tony Kushner (*Homebody/Kabul*), Caryl Churchill, Amy Herzog, and Paul Rudnick have also been staged here. Hit the box office for day-of CheapTix rush tickets; those seats are $25—in cash—as available, and are only on offer to young people (under 25), seniors (over 65), artists, and residents of the Lower East Side, with proper ID. ✉ *79 E. 4th St., between the Bowery and 2nd Ave., East Village* ☎ *212/460–5475* ⊕ *www.nytw.org* Ⓜ *F to 2nd Ave.; 6 to Astor Pl.*

19

Performance Space 122 (PS122). Founded in 1980 inside a 19th-century public school building, Performance Space 122 has helped launch the careers of many downtown musicians and artists, both on the fringe and otherwise. After a renovation, it reopened in 2018 with two new theaters and a modernized interior. A new semiannual themed series, the first of which focused on the changing face of the East Village, presents hybrid and interdisciplinary works that blend performance with installations and readings by different artists with varied visions. ⊠ *150 1st Ave., at 9th St., East Village* ☎ *212/477–5829* ⊕ *www.ps122.org* Ⓜ *6 to Astor Pl.; L to 1st Ave.*

Fodor's Choice **The Public Theater.** Fresh theater, such as Lin-Manuel Miranda's current
★ Broadway sensation *Hamilton,* and *Here Lies Love,* David Byrne and Fatboy Slim's "poperetta" about Imelda Marcos, keep people talking about the Public Theater, which was founded in 1954. Many more noted productions that began here (*Hair, A Chorus Line*) went on to Broadway and beyond. Main stage productions release $20 mobile lottery tickets through the TodayTix app. Check online for available performances. ⊠ *425 Lafayette St., south of Astor Pl., East Village* ☎ *212/539–8500, 212/967–7555 for tickets* ⊕ *www.publictheater.org* Ⓜ *6 to Astor Pl.; N, R, W to 8th St.–NYU.*

Theater for the New City. This four-theater cultural complex stages three- or four-week-long runs of new shows by emerging and mid-career American playwrights. The socially conscious group also runs a free arts festival every Memorial Day weekend and a free summer program of street theater, performed in all five boroughs. ⊠ *155 1st Ave., between 9th and 10th Sts., East Village* ☎ *212/254–1109* ⊕ *www.theaterforthenewcity.net* Ⓜ *6 to Astor Pl.; L to 1st Ave.*

LOWER EAST SIDE
THEATER
Dixon Place. Founded back in the 1980s, this small, nonprofit theater continues to host worthy, and frequently unconventional and hilarious, performances of theater, music, dance, and more, with a focus on new works. Its popular HOT! Festival of Queer Performance, held in July, is the longest-running LGBTQ festival in the world. Whatever you're seeing of the some 1,000 shows held here each year, the Lounge, Dixon Place's cheerful bar, is a great place to meet up before the show and connect with artists after. ⊠ *161A Chrystie St., between Rivington and Delancey Sts., Lower East Side* ☎ *212/219–0736* ⊕ *www.dixonplace.org* Ⓜ *J, Z to Bowery; B, D to Grand St.*

GREENWICH VILLAGE AND WEST VILLAGE

GREENWICH VILLAGE
FILM
Angelika Film Center. Foreign, independent, and specialty films are screened here. Despite its (six) tunnel-like theaters, small screens, and the occasionally audible subway rumble below, it's usually packed with cinephiles; get a snack at the café while you wait for your movie to be called. ⊠ *18 W. Houston St., between Mercer St. and Broadway, Greenwich Village* ☎ *212/995–2570* ⊕ *www.angelikafilmcenter.com/nyc* Ⓜ *B, D, F, M to Broadway–Lafayette St.; 6 to Bleecker St.; N, R, W to Prince St.*

IFC Center. The IFC Center shows a mix of repertory and first-run independent, art-house, shorts (including cartoons), and foreign movies. Despite the modern wire-mesh facade, there are still clues that this was once the much-beloved Waverly Theater. ⊠ *323 6th Ave., at 3rd St., Greenwich Village* ☎ *212/924–7771* ⊕ *www.ifccenter.com* Ⓜ *A, B, C, D, E, F, M to W. 4th St.–Washington Sq.*

PERFORMANCE CENTERS

FAMILY **NYU Skirball.** This pristine, wood-lined theater on the NYU campus supports emerging artists, with interesting dance, music, and theater events, often in collaboration with international companies. Conferences and a speaker series featuring prominent cultural figures such as writer Ta-Nehisi Coates and philosopher Judith Butler round out the calendar, which also includes many family-friendly events. ⊠ *566 LaGuardia Pl., at Washington Sq. S, Greenwich Village* ☎ *212/992–8484, 888/611–8183 for tickets* ⊕ *www.nyuskirball.org* Ⓜ *A, B, C, D, E, F, M to W. 4th St.; N, R, W to 8th St.–NYU.*

READINGS AND LECTURES

Center for Architecture. This contemporary glass-faced gallery near Washington Square hosts lively discussions (which may be accompanied by films or other visuals) on topics like modernist architecture in Africa or what to expect when you renovate an apartment. ⊠ *536 LaGuardia Pl., between 3rd and Bleecker Sts., Greenwich Village* ☎ *212/683–0023* ⊕ *cfa.aiany.org* Ⓜ *A, B, C, D, E, F, M to W. 4th St.*

THEATER

FAMILY **Monday Night Magic.** Since 1997, Michael Chaut and three other magi-
Fodor's Choice cian producers have been running these weekly performances in and
★ around Greenwich Village (they've been a permanent fixture at the Players Theatre since 2011). The acts, usually four per night on stage, come from all over the world and often include performers you'd see in much bigger theaters and clubs on other nights. The mind reading and sleight of hand with birds, cards, balls, and handkerchiefs come at a fast pace. The magic continues even during intermission, when at least two additional magicians mingle with guests in the lobby and in the theater to perform card tricks and other "close-up magic." Although the acts are tailored for an adult audience, they're also suitable for younger viewers, ages 12 and older, especially on special family nights. ⊠ *Players Theatre, 115 MacDougal St., between 3rd and Bleecker Sts., Greenwich Village* ☎ *718/575-1349, 800/838–3006 for tickets* ⊕ *www.mondaynightmagic.com* Ⓜ *A, B, C, D, E, F, M to W. 4th St.*

WEST VILLAGE

FILM

Fodor's Choice **Film Forum.** In addition to premiering new international features and
★ documentaries that are otherwise hard to catch on the big screen, this nonprofit with four theaters hosts movies by canonized directors such as Hitchcock, Godard, and Bertolucci; in-depth film series devoted to particular actors or genres; and newly restored prints of classic works. The small concession stand in the lobby serves tasty cakes and freshly popped popcorn. This is no megaplex, but updates in 2018 included new seats with more legroom and a higher slope

19

FILM SERIES AND REVIVALS

Although many of the screens listed here show first-run releases, old favorites and rarities are the heart of their programing. These gems—which include just about every kind of film, from silent and noir to the most au courant experimental work—are frequently screened at museums, cultural societies, and other institutions, such as the **French Institute Alliance Française** (☎ 212/355–6100 ⊕ www.fiaf.org), **Scandinavia House** (☎ 212/779–3587 ⊕ www.scandinaviahouse.org), and major branches of the **New York Public Library** (☎ 917/275–6975 ⊕ www. nypl.org). A reliably creative range of repertory screenings can always be found at **Anthology Film Archives** (☎ 212/505–5181 ⊕ www.anthologyfilmarchives.org), **Film Forum** (☎ 212/727–8110 ⊕ www.filmforum.org), the **Museum of Modern Art (MoMA)** (☎ 212/708–9400 ⊕ www.moma.org), the **Museum of the Moving Image** (☎ 718/777–6888 ⊕ www.movingimage.us), the **Brooklyn Academy of Music** (☎ 718/636–4100 ⊕ www.bam.org), and the **Film Society of Lincoln Center** (☎ 212/875–5601 ⊕ www.filmlinc.com).

for better views. ⊠ 209 W. Houston St., between 6th Ave. and Varick St., West Village ☎ 212/727–8110 ⊕ www.filmforum.org Ⓜ 1 to Houston St.; C, E to Spring St.

CHELSEA

DANCE

FodorsChoice **Joyce Theater.** Set within a former Art Deco movie house in Chelsea, the
★ 472-seat Joyce Theater has superb sight lines and presents a wide range of classical and contemporary dance. Its 48-week season includes a rotating roster of diverse international, national, and New York–based companies. ⊠ 175 8th Ave., at 19th St., Chelsea ☎ 212/691–9740, 212/242–0800 for tickets ⊕ www.joyce.org Ⓜ A, C, E to 14th St.; L to 8th Ave.; 1 to 18th St.

New York Live Arts. This Chelsea space serves as the home stage for the innovative Bill T. Jones/Arnie Zane Dance Company. It's also a laboratory for new choreographers and artists in residence, and hosts nonchoreographed events such as panel discussions. ⊠ 219 W. 19th St., between 7th and 8th Aves., Chelsea ☎ 212/691–6500, 212/924–0077 for tickets ⊕ www.newyorklivearts.org Ⓜ 1 to 18th St.; A, C, E, to 23rd St.

THEATER

FAMILY **TADA!** Vibrant original musicals for family audiences are performed by a cast of talented kids (ages 8 to 18). Most shows are on weekends, and children's tickets start at $15. ⊠ 15 W. 28th St., 2nd fl., between Broadway and 5th Ave., Chelsea ☎ 212/252–1619 ⊕ www.tadatheater.com Ⓜ 1, 6, N, R, W to 28th St.

MIDTOWN WEST

FILM

Fodor's Choice ★ **Museum of Modern Art (MoMA) films.** You'll find some of the most engaging international film repertory around at Roy and Niuta Titus Theaters 1 and 2, in MoMA's lower level, and at the Celeste Bartos Theater, in the lower level of the Cullman Education and Research Building on the museum campus. Sometimes the films tie in with current art exhibitions; the Contenders series, which starts each fall, is a chance to catch up on the past year's releases that are likely to win awards, or at least stand the test of time. Movie tickets are available at the museum for same-day screenings (a limited number are released up to one week in advance). They're free if you have purchased museum admission ($25); otherwise they cost $12. ⊠ *11 W. 53rd St., between 5th and 6th Aves., Midtown West* 🕾 *212/708–9400* ⊕ *www.moma.org/calendar/film* Ⓜ *E, M to 5th Ave./53rd St.; B, D, F, M to 47th–50th Sts./Rockefeller Center.*

The Paris Theatre. Across from the Plaza Hotel stands The Paris Theatre—a rare, stately remnant of the single-screen era. Opened in 1948, it retains its wide screen (and balcony) and is a fine showcase for new movies, often foreign and with a limited release. Tickets can only be reserved online through the theater's website. ⊠ *4 W. 58th St., between 5th and 6th Aves., Midtown West* 🕾 *212/823–8945,* ⊕ *www.theparis-theatre.com* Ⓜ *N, R, W to 5th Ave./59th St.; F to 57th St.*

MUSIC

FAMILY
Fodor's Choice ★ **Carnegie Hall.** Internationally renowned Carnegie Hall has incomparable acoustics that make it one of the best venues in the world to hear classical music, but it's also strong in jazz, pop, cabaret, and folk music. Since the opening-night concert on May 5, 1891, which Tchaikovsky conducted, virtually every important musician the world has known has performed in this Italian Renaissance–style building. Leonard Bernstein had his debut here; Vladimir Horowitz made his historic return to the concert stage here. The world's top orchestras perform in the grand and fabulously steep 2,804-seat **Isaac Stern Auditorium**; the 268-seat **Weill Recital Hall** often features young talents making their New York debuts; and the subterranean 599-seat **Judy and Arthur Zankel Hall** attracts big-name artists such as the Kronos Quartet and Milton Nascimento to its stylish modern space. A noted roster of family concerts is also part of Carnegie's programming. The Carnegie box office releases $10 rush tickets for some shows on the day of performance, or you may buy partial-view seating in advance at 50% off the full ticket price. ⊠ *881 7th Ave., at 57th St., Midtown West* 🕾 *212/247–7800* ⊕ *www.carnegiehall.org* Ⓜ *N, Q, R, W to 57th St.–7th Ave.; B, D, E to 7th Ave.; F to 57th St.*

19

PERFORMANCE CENTERS

Baryshnikov Arts Center. Famed dancer and actor Mikhail Baryshnikov's longtime vision came to fruition in this modern performing arts venue for contemporary dance, theater, music, and film. The center, set within the Hudson Yards neighborhood, hosts a range of resident artists, including dancers and musical groups, as well as productions by boundary-breaking international choreographers, playwrights, filmmakers,

and musicians. The vibrant programming is presented in the center's 238-seat Jerome Robbins Theater and the 136-seat Howard Gilman Performance Space. ⊠ *450 W. 37 St., between 9th and 10th Aves., Midtown West* ☎ *646/731–3200* ⊕ *www.bacnyc.org* Ⓜ *A, C, E to 34th St.–Penn Station; 7 to 34th St.–Hudson Yards.*

FAMILY **The New Victory Theater.** In a magnificently restored space from 1900, The

Fodor's Choice New Victory Theater presents an international roster of supremely kid-

★ pleasing plays, music, dance, opera, puppetry, and circus performances. Through the organization's workshops and arts activities, children and their parents can also learn more about other parts of theater (writing, for instance) and kinds of performance, such as break dancing. Count on reasonable ticket prices, high-energy and high-class productions, and the opportunity for kids to chat with the artists after many performances. ⊠ *209 W. 42nd St., between 7th and 8th Aves., Midtown West* ☎ *646/223–3010* ⊕ *www.newvictory.org* Ⓜ *1, 2, 3, 7, N, Q, R, S, W to Times Sq.–42nd St.; A, C, E to 42nd St.–Port Authority.*

Fodor's Choice **New York City Center.** Pause as you enter this neo-Moorish building, built

★ in 1923 for the Shriners (cousins of the Freemasons), and admire the ornate decorative details in the lobby and theater. City Center's 2,200-seat main stage is perfectly suited for dance and special theatrical events. The Tony Award–honored Encores! series, generally held in spring, revisits musicals of the past in a concert format—an event that has led to shows returning to Broadway, with the long-running *Chicago* among them. During summer, Encores! Off-Center features concert versions of Off-Broadway musicals. Tickets for City Center's annual Fall for Dance festival sell out quickly. ⊠ *131 W. 55th St., between 6th and 7th Aves., Midtown West* ☎ *212/581–1212 for tickets* ⊕ *www.nycitycenter.org* Ⓜ *N, Q, R, W to 57th St.–7th Ave.; F to 57th St.*

Fodor's Choice **Radio City Music Hall.** This landmark was built shortly after the stock

★ market crash of 1929; John D. Rockefeller wanted to create a symbol of hope in what was a sad, broke city. When it opened, some said Radio City Music Hall was so grand that there was no need for performances, because people would get more than their money's worth simply by sitting there and enjoying the space. Despite being the largest indoor theater in the world with its city-block-long marquee, it feels warm and intimate. Seventy-five-minute "Stage Door" walking tours ($26.95) run year-round, but access is limited during show times. Day-of-tour tickets are sold at the Radio City Avenue Store, or at the 51st Street tour entrance during the Christmas Spectacular season; advance tickets are available by phone, at the box office, or through the website.

Although there are concerts and other events here year-round, the biggest draw is the Radio City Christmas Spectacular: more than a million visitors every year come to see the iconic Rockettes dance. Make reservations as early as possible, especially if you want to attend near Christmas or on a weekend. Certain dates and times tend to sell out, but you can usually find tickets for all shows until mid-October. Tickets start at $49 per person for the 90-minute show, although there are often promotions and deals available, especially for nonpeak times. ⊠ *1260 6th Ave., between 50th and 51st Sts., Midtown West* ☎ *212/247–4777,*

19

New York's Film Festivals

New York's extreme diversity is what makes it a cinephile's heaven: you'll find dozens of festivals for niche interests and for those just wanting to be at the front end of what's out there. New releases and premieres dominate the festival scene, but the city has its share of retrospective events, especially in summer.

The city's preeminent film event is the annual **New York Film Festival** (⊕ www.filmlinc.com), presented by the Film Society of Lincoln Center, from late September into October. The lineup is announced about a month in advance, and screenings often sell out quickly (though standby tickets are available for most events). Film venues include Lincoln Center's Alice Tully Hall, Walter Reade Theater, and Elinor Bunin Munroe Film Center. In January, the Film Society join forces with the Jewish Museum to produce the **New York Jewish Film Festival** (⊕ www.nyjff.org); in March it joins MoMA to present **New Directors/ New Films** (⊕ www.newdirectors. org), and June brings the society's collaboration on the **Human Rights Watch Film Festival** (⊕ ff.hrw.org), among other festivals and repertory programming throughout the year.

The **Tribeca Film Festival** (⊕ www. tribecafilm.com/festival) takes place in mostly downtown venues for about two weeks starting mid-April and shows mainstream premieres along with indie flicks, television debuts, a conversation series, and more.

Fans also flock to other noteworthy annuals like the **New York Asian Film Festival** (⊕ www.asiancinevision.

org) from late June to early July; and the **Margaret Mead Film Festival** (⊕ www.amnh.org/explore/margaret-mead-film-festival) in October or November and **DOC NYC** (⊕ www. docnyc.net) in November, two fall festivals that focus on documentaries from all over.

For kids, the year-round programs of the **New York International Children's Film Festival** (NYICFF ⊕ www.gkids.com) peak in March with an extravaganza of about 100 new films for ages 3–18.

Summer in New York sees a bonanza of alfresco film; screenings are usually free (but arrive early to secure a space; screenings begin at dusk). The **HBO Bryant Park Summer Film Festival** (⊕ www.bryantpark.org) shows classic films at sundown on Monday, June–August. The **Hudson RiverFlicks** (⊕ www.riverflicks.org) series in July and August has movies for grown-ups on Wednesday evening on Pier 63; Hudson RiverFlicks also has Family Fridays for kids at Pier 46. The Upper West Side has **Summer on the Hudson** (⊕ www.nycgovparks. org) with Wednesday-night screenings on Pier 1, near West 70th Street. **Rooftop Films'** (⊕ www.rooftopfilms. com) Underground Movies Outdoors is more eclectic than most other film series, with shows outdoors in summer on rooftops in all five boroughs. Check the schedule for off-season screenings as well. On Thursday evenings in July and August, check out **Movies with a View in Brooklyn Bridge Park** (⊕ www. brooklynbridgepark.org).

866/858–0007 for tickets ⊕ www.radiocity.com Ⓜ B, D, F, M to 47th–50th Sts./Rockefeller Center; N, Q, R, W to 49th St.

The Town Hall. Founded by suffragists and built in 1921 by famed architectural firm McKim, Mead & White, The Town Hall has been part of NYC's cultural fabric for almost 100 years. Notable Town Hall claims include: Strauss, Stravinsky, and Isaac Stern's U.S. debuts; Marian Anderson's first NYC recital; Dizzy Gillespie and Charlie Parker's introduction of bebop to the world; and Bob Dylan's first major concert. More recently, the stage has welcomed musicians like Gilberto Gil, Joan Baez, Patti Smith, and David Byrne; comedians like Stephen Colbert and Larry David; the only East Coast staging of Hunter S. Thompson's "The Kentucky Derby Is Decadent and Depraved"; TED Talks Live; and more. ⊠ *123 W. 43rd St., between 6th Ave. and Broadway, Midtown West* ☎ *212/997–6661, 800/982–2787 for tickets ⊕ www.thetownhall.org* Ⓜ *1, 2, 3, 7, N, Q, R, S, W to Times Sq.–42nd St.; B, D, F, M to 42nd St.–Bryant Park.*

READINGS AND LECTURES

LIVE from the NYPL. The New York Public Library's discussion series includes a rich program of lectures and reading events from the biggest names in books and culture in general. Most programs are held at the famous main library. ⊠ *Stephen A. Schwarzman Bldg., 5th Ave. at 42nd St., Midtown West* ☎ *917/275–6975, 888/718–4253 for tickets ⊕ www.nypl.org/live* Ⓜ *B, D, F, M to 42nd St.–Bryant Park; 7 to 5th Ave.*

THEATER

FAMILY **New Amsterdam Theatre.** In 1997 Disney refurbished the elaborate 1903 Art Nouveau New Amsterdam Theatre, where Bob Hope, Jack Benny, Fred Astaire, and the *Ziegfeld Follies* once drew crowds. *The Lion King* ruled here for the first nine years of its run, followed by *Mary Poppins* and then *Aladdin,*which opened in 2014. *Frozen* debuts in 2018. ⊠ *214 W. 42nd St., between 7th and 8th Aves., Midtown West* ☎ *866/870–2717 for tickets ⊕ www.disneyonbroadway.com* Ⓜ *1, 2, 3, 7, N, Q, R, S, W to Times Sq.–42nd St.; A, C, E to 42nd St.–Port Authority.*

Playwrights Horizons. Known for its support of new work by American playwrights, this Off-Broadway theater was the first home for eventual Broadway hits such as *Grey Gardens* and Wendy Wasserstein's *Heidi Chronicles.* ⊠ *416 W. 42nd St., between 9th and 10th Aves., Midtown West* ☎ *212/564–1235, 212/279–4200 for tickets ⊕ www.phnyc.org* Ⓜ *A, C, E to 42nd St.–Port Authority.*

Roundabout Theatre Company. This nonprofit theatrical company is known for its revivals of classic musicals and plays, including *Anything Goes* and *The Importance of Being Earnest.* Its main stage, the American Airlines Theatre, is the former Selwyn—the venerable home to the works of Noël Coward, George S. Kaufman, and Cole Porter in their heyday. The Roundabout's other Broadway venues are Studio 54, which was the longtime home of its successful *Cabaret* revival, and the Stephen Sondheim Theatre. The two Off-Broadway stages at the Harold and Miriam Steinberg Center for Theatre on West 46th Street show a mix of classics and works from up-and-coming playwrights.

19

✉ *American Airlines Theatre, 227 W. 42nd St., between 7th and 8th Aves., Midtown West* ☎ *212/719–1300* ⊕ *www.roundabouttheatre. org* Ⓜ *1, 2, 3, 7, N, Q, R, S, W to Times Sq.–42nd St.; A, C, E to 42nd St.–Port Authority.*

Signature Theatre Company. Designed by the architect Frank Gehry, the company's Pershing Square Signature Center houses three theater spaces. The Tony Award–winning theater company provides a platform for both New York and world premieres, as well as revivals. All tickets are $30 for a show's initially announced run. A central space with a café and bookstore connects the theaters, so come early, or stay late; the café is open until midnight Tuesday through Sunday. ✉ *Pershing Square Signature Center, 480 W. 42nd St., between 9th and 10th Aves., Midtown West* ☎ *212/967–1913, 212/244–7529 for tickets* ⊕ *www. signaturetheatre.org* Ⓜ *A, C, E to 42nd St.–Port Authority.*

UPPER EAST SIDE

PERFORMANCE CENTERS

FAMILY **92nd Street Y.** Well-known soloists, jazz musicians, show-tune stylists, and chamber music groups perform in 92Y's 905-seat **Kaufmann Concert Hall.** But the programming is hardly limited to music—its online calendar bristles with popular lectures and readings series featuring big-name film and TV stars, authors, poets, playwrights, political pundits, and media bigwigs (many events are live streamed or archived online). Also worth the Upper East Side trek are the Harkness Dance Festival, film programs, and many family-friendly events. ✉ *1395 Lexington Ave., at 92nd St., Upper East Side* ☎ *212/415–5500 for tickets* ⊕ *www.92y.org* Ⓜ *6 to 96th St.; 4, 5, 6 to 86th St.*

Fodor's Choice **Park Avenue Armory.** Completed in 1881 and occupying an entire city
★ block, this handsome Gothic-style brick building now serves as a splendid arts center but was originally the headquarters, drill hall, and social club for the Seventh Regiment, a National Guard unit called the "Silk Stocking" regiment because its members were mainly drawn from wealthy Gilded Age families. The sumptuous reception rooms on the first floor and Company Rooms on the second floor were designed by Louis Comfort Tiffany, Stanford White, and other fashionable designers of the time. The armory eventually fell into disrepair; in 2007, help came in the form of a major restoration that is ongoing, and the armory was put into the service of art. The huge installations, plays, and immersive concerts here take advantage of the massive space its 55,000-square-foot drill hall provides. Intimate artist conversations, recitals, and experimental performances are held in the smaller first- and second-floor spaces, including the stunning Veterans Room that reopened in 2016 and features red-glass Tiffany windows that take on a blue glow when sunlight hits. ✉ *643 Park Ave., between 66th and 67th Sts., Upper East Side* ☎ *212/616–3930, 212/933–5812 for tickets* ⊕ *www.armoryonpark.org* Ⓜ *6 to 68th St.–Hunter College, F, Q to Lexington Ave./63rd St.*

Jazz at Lincoln Center performs at Frederick P. Rose Hall next to Columbus Circle.

READINGS AND LECTURES

Works & Process. Insight into the creative process is what the Works & Process program at the Guggenheim is all about. Often drawing on dance and theater works in progress, the live performances are complemented by illuminating discussions with their choreographers, playwrights, and directors. There are very popular holiday concerts, too. ⊠ *Guggenheim Museum, 1071 5th Ave., between 88th and 89th Sts., Upper East Side* ☎ *212/423–3575* ⊕ *www.worksandprocess.org* Ⓜ *4, 5, 6 to 86th St.*

UPPER WEST SIDE

MUSIC

Great Music in a Great Space. This aptly named series of public concerts is inspired by a wide range of musical traditions and performed in St. John the Divine's massive, atmospheric, Gothic-style space. The program showcases composers and performers of choral and instrumental music, often to sold-out crowds. ⊠ *Cathedral Church of St. John the Divine, 1047 Amsterdam Ave., at 112th St., Upper West Side* ☎ *212/316–7540* ⊕ *www.stjohndivine.org* Ⓜ *1, B, C to Cathedral Pkwy.–110th St.*

FAMILY **Jazz at Lincoln Center.** A few blocks south of Lincoln Center itself, this Columbus Circle venue is almost completely devoted to jazz, with a sprinkling of other genres mixed in. Stages in Rafael Viñoly's crisply modern **Frederick P. Rose Hall** include the 1,200-seat **Rose Theater,** where a worthy Jazz for Young People series joins buoyant adult programming a few times each year. Also here is **The Appel Room,** an elegant theater with a glass wall overlooking Columbus Circle. In the smaller **Dizzy's Club Coca-Cola,** there are two sets nightly, plus late-night sessions Tuesday–Saturday, all accompanied by a full bar and restaurant with a New Orleans–inspired menu. ⊠ *Time Warner Center, 10 Columbus Circle, 5th fl., Broadway at 60th St., Upper West Side* ☎ *212/258–9800, 212/721–6500 for tickets* ⊕ *www.jazz.org* Ⓜ *1, A, B, C, D to 59th St.–Columbus Circle.*

Merkin Concert Hall at Kaufman Music Center. A destination for both old-school and cutting-edge musical performances, this concert hall around the corner from Lincoln Center is a lovely, acoustically advanced 450-seater that presents chamber pieces. It's also known for jazz, world, new music, and especially its Ecstatic Music Festival (from January through March), when an eclectic group of indie-classical artists more than lives up to its billing. ⊠ *129 W. 67th St., between Broadway and Amsterdam Ave., Upper West Side* ☎ *212/501–3330* ⊕ *www.kaufman-musiccenter.org/mch* Ⓜ *1 to 66th St.–Lincoln Center.*

Miller Theatre. Adventurous programming of jazz, classical, early and modern music, and dance makes up the calendar at this Columbia University theater, founded in 1988. A well-designed 688-seater, this is a hall that rewards serious listeners. ⊠ *Columbia University, 2960 Broadway, at 116th St., Upper West Side* ☎ *212/854–1633, 212/854–7799 for tickets* ⊕ *www.millertheatre.com* Ⓜ *1 to 116th St.–Columbia University.*

PERFORMANCE CENTERS

Fodor's Choice ★ **Lincoln Center.** A major cultural destination, attracting more than 5 million visitors annually, the Lincoln Center complex is one of the most concentrated places for the performing arts in the nation, as home to 11 resident organizations, including the Chamber Music Society of Lincoln Center, Film Society of Lincoln Center, Jazz at Lincoln Center, The Juilliard School, Lincoln Center for the Performing Arts, Lincoln Center Theater, Metropolitan Opera, New York City Ballet, New York Philharmonic, New York Public Library for the Performing Arts, and the School of American Ballet.

This massive, white-travertine-clad complex contains 30 venues in all, part of a 16-acre campus that was planned by prolific New York architect Wallace Harrison, and built as part of an urban-renewal effort from 1962 to 1969; some 40 years later, it was given a thorough remodeling to better integrate it into the neighborhood. Visitors today can enjoy improvements such as expanded public and green spaces, free Wi-Fi, and various dining options.

To get oriented, start across the street, on Broadway between 62nd and 63rd Streets, at the David Rubenstein Atrium. There you'll find free Wi-Fi, tables, a café, and that rarest of NYC commodities: a public restroom. Free musical and dance performances, as well as discussions and spoken-word programs, are held throughout the week. Day-of-show discounted tickets for many Lincoln Center venues may be purchased in person here; there is a limit of four tickets per customer. Because the box office is closed on Monday, any available tickets for Monday performances are sold on Sunday.

The acoustics in **Alice Tully Hall** are top-notch; the hall's home to the Chamber Music Society of Lincoln Center (*www.chambermusicsociety. org*). **David Geffen Hall** is the residence of the New York Philharmonic (*www.nyphil.org*); its season is September to June. Orchestra rehearsals are open to the public on selected weekday mornings ($20, plus fees; usually Wednesday or Thursday). A popular Young People's Concert series takes place Saturday afternoon, four times throughout the season. Lincoln Center presents its well-attended Great Performers, Mostly Mozart Festival, and White Light Festival in these halls, too.

The largest hall, the **Metropolitan Opera House** is notable for its dramatic arched entrance, as well as its lobby's immense Swarovski crystal chandeliers and Marc Chagall paintings. The titan of American opera companies and an institution since its founding in 1883, the Metropolitan Opera (*www.metopera.org*) brings the world's leading singers to the vast stage here from September to May. All performances, including those sung in English, are subtitled on small screens on the back of the seat in front of you. A frequent resident of the Met (and sometimes, of the David H. Koch Theater) is the American Ballet Theatre (*www.abt. org*), renowned for its gorgeous full-program renditions of the 19th-century classics (*Swan Lake, Giselle, The Sleeping Beauty*) with choreography re-envisioned by 20th-century or contemporary masters. A limited number of same-day $25 rush orchestra seats are available at the Met's website. These tickets go on sale for Monday through Friday evening performances at noon, for matinees four hours before curtain, and for Saturday evenings at 2 pm.

The **David H. Koch Theater,** designed by master architect Philip Johnson and considered one of the world's top theaters for dance, is the home of the formidable New York City Ballet (*www.nycballet.com*), which has a roster of more than 90 dancers, a 62-piece orchestra, and an unmatched repertory of modern masterpieces, including landmark works by George Balanchine, Jerome Robbins, and Peter Martins. NYCB performs at the theater for 21 weeks each year, including fall, winter, and spring repertory seasons, with Thanksgiving through New Year's devoted to the beloved annual production of Balanchine's *The Nutcracker.* The theater also hosts a mix of other internationally famous dance troupes throughout the year, as well as White Light Festival performances.

19

The **Lincoln Center Theater** complex houses the Vivian Beaumont Theater, the smaller Mitzi E. Newhouse Theater, and the rooftop Claire Tow Theater, which has 112 seats and a small outdoor terrace.

The **Film Society of Lincoln Center** (*www.filmlinc.com*) presents film series devoted to "the best in world cinema," including silents, documentaries, retrospectives, and recent releases, at the 267-seat Walter Reade Theater and the Elinor Bunin Munroe Film Center, which features two auditoriums, a café, and an amphitheater that hosts talks and panel discussions.

In addition to extensive musical and theatrical holdings, the **New York Public Library for the Performing Arts** mounts periodic exhibitions related to major artists and composers. At the library's free year-round

Silent Clowns series (*www.silentclowns.com*), held Saturday afternoons each month in its auditorium, rarely seen prints of the silent era's comedy masters are paired with live piano music.

Tours of Lincoln Center, including the Met, take place daily and leave from the atrium; reservations are recommended and can be made from the website (*atrium.lincolncenter.org*) or in person. Tours do not include backstage areas, but sometimes do visit parts of the auditoriums. Backstage tours of the Met ($30) are held during the performance season. ✉ *From 62nd to 66th St., between Broadway/ Columbus and Amsterdam Aves., Upper West Side* ☎ *212/875–5000 for main switchboard, 212/721–6500 for tickets* ⊕ *www.lincolncenter. org* Ⓜ *1 to 66th St.–Lincoln Center.*

FAMILY **Symphony Space.** Although Symphony Space runs an energetic roster of classical, jazz, international, and other kinds of music, it also excels with many other kinds of art programming. On the literary front, its two halls—the **Peter Jay Sharp Theatre** and the **Leonard Nimoy Thalia**— host a celebrated roster of literary events, including Bloomsday on Broadway, the Thalia Book Club, and the famed Selected Shorts series (stories read by prominent actors and produced as a podcast and radio show on National Public Radio). There's also a popular comedy series, Uptown Showdown, as well as Performance in HD screenings from the National Theatre Live, Royal Shakespeare Company, and Royal Opera House, and Secret Science Club North science talks. Plays, films, and "Thalia Docs" on Sunday (usually true-to-their-roots art-house screenings) round out the adult programming. For the family, turn to the hugely popular **Just Kidding** lineup for a nonstop parade of zany plays, sing-alongs, puppetry, and dance midday Saturday (and sometimes Sunday). ✉ *2537 Broadway, at 95th St., Upper West Side* ☎ *212/864–5400* ⊕ *www.symphonyspace.org* Ⓜ *1, 2, 3 to 96th St.*

THEATER

Fodor's Choice **Shakespeare in the Park.** Some of the best things in New York are, indeed,
★ free—including this summer festival presented by the Public Theater and performed at an open-air stage in Central Park. Many notable performers have appeared here, including Meryl Streep, Michelle Pfeiffer, Christopher Walken, Helen Hunt, Morgan Freeman, Al Pacino, Anne Hathaway, and Kevin Kline. The tickets are given out (limit two per person) starting at noon on the day of each show, and always sell out. What you save in money, you make up for in time and tedium—lines are usually *long*. Plan to line up by midmorning or earlier if there have been good reviews. (A limited number of tickets for that night's performance are also distributed via an in-person lottery at The Public Theater, 425 Lafayette Street, at Astor Place.) The easiest way to score these scarce tickets is to register via a mobile lottery using the TodayTix app between midnight and noon on the day you'd like to attend; an email response after noon confirms (or denies) success. Making a tax-deductible donation to the Public Theater is one way to avoid the lines and be sure you get a ticket. ✉ *Delacorte Theater, Central Park, Midpark, use 81st St. entrance at Central Park W, Upper West Side* ☎ *212/967–7555* ⊕ *www. publictheater.org* Ⓜ *B, C to 81st St.–Museum of Natural History.*

HARLEM

MUSIC

Apollo Theater. Michael Jackson, Ella Fitzgerald, and James Brown are just a few of the world-class performers who have appeared on this equally famed stage, which first opened back in 1934. If the Apollo's Amateur Night doesn't get you up to 125th Street on Wednesdays, consider the theater's intimate late-night music series, Apollo Music Café, on select Friday and Saturday nights, featuring a variety of jazz, pop, hip-hop, and rock performers. ✉ *253 W. 125th St., between Frederick Douglass and Adam Clayton Powell Jr. Blvds., Harlem* ☎ *212/531–5300, 800/745–3000 for tickets* ⊕ *www.apollotheater.org* Ⓜ *2, 3, A, B, C, D to 125th St.*

PERFORMANCE CENTERS

Harlem Stage. Set in a perfectly restored 1890 former Croton Aqueduct facility, Harlem Stage is a cozy 200-seat uptown venue for jazz, world music, and dance. ✉ *The Gatehouse, 150 Convent Ave., at 135th St., Harlem* ☎ *212/281–9240* ⊕ *www.harlemstage.org* Ⓜ *B, C to 135th St.; 1 to 137th St.–City College.*

BROOKLYN

WILLIAMSBURG
FILM

Fodor's Choice ★ **Nitehawk Cinema.** The only movie theater of its kind in the New York City area, Nitehawk shows first-run and repertory films in three theater spaces and serves a full menu in-theater, as well as popcorn and snacks. Themed dining specials are paired with each indie film. Movies often sell out on weekends, so buy tickets in advance. After the film, bring your ticket stub down to the ground-level bar for $4 beers and well drinks. ✉ *136 Metropolitan Ave., Brooklyn* ☎ *718/782–8370* ⊕ *www.nitehawkcinema.com* ✎ *Tickets $12* Ⓜ *L to Bedford Ave.*

FORT GREENE
PERFORMANCE CENTERS

Fodor's Choice ★ **Brooklyn Academy of Music** (*BAM*). Founded in 1861 and operating at its current location since 1908, BAM is a multidisciplinary performing arts center that has grown to span three edifices, including the Beaux Arts, seven-story Peter Jay Sharp building. It's known for innovative performances of many types, and the facilities include an unadorned "black box" theater, dance venues, a four-screen movie theater, an opera house, and an open-plan performance and restaurant space. ✉ *Peter Jay Sharp Bldg., 30 Lafayette Ave., Fort Greene* ☎ *718/636–4100* ⊕ *www.bam.org* Ⓜ *2, 3, 4, 5, B, D, N, Q, R, W at Atlantic Ave.–Barclays Ctr.; G to Fulton St.; C to Lafayette Ave.*

PARK SLOPE
THEATER

FAMILY **Puppetworks.** Marionette puppets have been enacting classic fairy tales like *Beauty and the Beast*, *Goldilocks and the Three Bears*, *Jack and the Beanstalk*, and *Pinocchio* for children at this storefront theater since 1990. A friendly puppeteer preps the young audience on theater

19

etiquette before each performance. Afterward, theater education continues with a Q&A. Public performances are given on weekends only; call or email for reservations. ⊠ *338 6th Ave.* ☏ *718/965–3391* ⊕ *www. puppetworks.org* ⊴ *$11* Ⓜ *F, G to 7th Ave.*

DUMBO
THEATER

Fodor'sChoice **St. Ann's Warehouse.** The latest iteration of this cutting-edge arts institu-
★ tion (originally launched in the East Village in 1980) occupies a stunningly refurbished tobacco warehouse from 1860 that sits beneath the Brooklyn Bridge in Brooklyn Bridge Park. The 24,000-square-foot space features original brick archways, an elegant outdoor courtyard, an exhibition space, and a theater hosting such performances as an all-female production of *Henry IV* and the American premiere of Irish playwright Edna Walsh's first opera. ⊠ *45 Water St., DUMBO* ☏ *718/254–8779* ⊕ *stannswarehouse.org* Ⓜ *A, C to High St.; F to York St.*

QUEENS

ASTORIA
FILM

Museum of the Moving Image films. This museum touts two theaters, including both a show palace and an intimate screening room, where classic Hollywood and foreign titles share the screen with experimental works, new films from the international festival circuit, live musical collaborations, and in-person appearances by moviemaker luminaries. Daily short films are screened in Tut's Fever Movie Palace, a fab Red Grooms and Lysiane Luong–designed installation. ⊠ *36–01 35th Ave., between 36th and 37th Sts., Astoria* ☏ *718/777–6888* ⊕ *www.movingimage.us/films* Ⓜ *M, R to Steinway St.; N, Q to 36th Ave.*

TRAVEL SMART
NEW YORK CITY

GETTING HERE AND AROUND

New York City packs a staggering range of sights and activities into the 301 square miles of its five boroughs. You probably want to focus most of your visit in Manhattan, but with more time, taking a trip to Brooklyn or one of the other three boroughs (Queens, the Bronx, or Staten Island) is worthwhile.

If flying into one of the three major airports that service New York—John F. Kennedy (JFK), LaGuardia (LGA), or New Jersey's Newark Liberty (EWR)—pick your mode of transportation for getting to Manhattan before your plane lands. Tourists typically either take a car service or head to the taxi line, but those aren't necessarily the best choices, especially during rush hour. Public transportation, especially if you're traveling light and without young children, is an inexpensive option.

Once you're in Manhattan, getting around can be a breeze when you get the hang of the subway system. Better yet, if you're not in a rush and the weather's cooperating, just walk—it's the best way to discover the true New York. Not quite sure where you are or how to get where you're headed? Ask a local. You may be surprised at how friendly the city's inhabitants are, debunking their reputation for rudeness. In the same getting-there-is-half-the-fun spirit, there are also boat and bus journeys that let you see the city from a whole new perspective.

■ AIR TRAVEL

Generally, international flights go in and out of John F. Kennedy or Newark Liberty airport, while domestic flights go in and out of both of these, as well as LaGuardia Airport.

AIRLINE SECURITY ISSUES

Transportation Security Administration (*TSA*). The TSA offers travel tips and has answers for almost every question about travel safety and security procedures. ⊕ *www.tsa.gov.*

AIRPORTS

The major air gateways to New York City are LaGuardia Airport (LGA) and John F. Kennedy International Airport (JFK) in the borough of Queens, and Newark Liberty International Airport (EWR) in the state of New Jersey.

Airport Information JFK International Airport (*JFK*). ☎ 718/244–4444 ⊕ *www.jfkairport.com.* **LaGuardia Airport** (*LGA*). ✉ Flushing ☎ 718/533–3400 ⊕ *www.laguardiaairport.com.* **Newark Liberty International Airport** (*EWR*). ☎ 973/961–6000 ⊕ *www.newarkairport.com.*

TRANSFERS—CAR SERVICES

Car services can be a great convenience, because the driver often meets you in the baggage-claim area and helps with your luggage. The flat rates are often comparable to taxi fares, but some car services charge for parking and wait time at the airport. To eliminate these expenses, other car services require you to telephone their dispatcher (or order a car through their app) when you land so they can send the next available car to pick you up. The New York City Taxi and Limousine Commission rules require all car services to be licensed and pick up riders only by prior arrangement; if possible, call 24 hours in advance for reservations or at least a half day before your flight's departure. Drivers of nonlicensed vehicles ("gypsy cabs") often solicit fares outside the terminal in baggage-claim areas. Don't take them: you run the risk of an unsafe ride in a vehicle that may not be properly insured and will almost certainly pay more than the going rate. Getting a car via the Uber or Lyft ride-sharing services or one of their competitors is another option.

For phone numbers, see Taxi Travel.

TRANSFERS—TAXIS AND SHUTTLES

Outside the baggage-claim area at each of New York's major airports are taxi stands where a uniformed dispatcher helps passengers find taxis (*see Taxi Travel*). Cabs are not permitted to pick up fares anywhere else in the arrivals area, so if you want a taxi, take your place in line. Shuttle services generally pick up passengers from a designated spot along the curb.

GO Airlink NYC, NYC Airporter, and SuperShuttle run vans and some buses from JFK, LaGuardia, and Newark (NYC Airporter does not run to Manhattan from Newark) airports to popular spots like Grand Central Terminal, the Port Authority Bus Terminal, Penn Station, and hotels in Manhattan. Fares on NYC Airporter, for instance, cost about $15–$18 one way and $28–$34 round-trip per person to or from JFK or LGA. Those rates are significantly cheaper than taking a taxi if you're on your own, but probably not if there are two or more of you traveling together. If you choose to use such services, keep in mind that customers' satisfaction with them is very mixed; online reviews often complain of rude employees and significant waits for vans to both arrive and reach their destinations. In any case, allow lots of time for the shuttle's other pickups and drop-offs along the way.

Shuttle Service GO Airlink NYC.
☎ 212/812-9000, 877/599-8200 ⊕ www. goairlinkshuttle.com. **NYC Airporter.** ☎ 718/777-5111 ⊕ www.nycairporter.com. **SuperShuttle.** ☎ 800/258-3826 ⊕ www. supershuttle.com.

TRANSFERS FROM JFK INTERNATIONAL AIRPORT
The rate for traveling between JFK and Manhattan by yellow cab in either direction is a flat fee of $52.80 plus surcharges and tolls (which average about $6). The trip takes 40–60 minutes. Prices are roughly $25–$55 for trips to most other locations in New York City. You should also tip the driver for safe driving and good service.

JFK's AirTrain ($5) connects JFK Airport to the New York City Subway (A, E, J, and Z trains) and the Long Island Railroad (LIRR)—both of which take you to

Manhattan or Brooklyn. The monorail system runs 24 hours. ■TIP➔ Not sure which train to take? Check ⊕ *citymapper. com/nyc*, ⊕ *www.iridenyc.com*, or ⊕ *tripplanner.mta.info* (or their corresponding apps) for the best route to your destination. Subway travel between JFK and Manhattan takes less than an hour and costs $3.75 in subway fare (including $1 to buy a refillable MetroCard) plus $5 for the AirTrain. The LIRR travels between JFK's AirTrain stop (Jamaica Station) and Penn Station in around 30 minutes, for about $17, including the AirTrain fee. When traveling *from* Manhattan to JFK via subway, take the E train to Sutphin Boulevard or take the A train to the Howard Beach station; then, in either case, transfer to the AirTrain. If you are riding the A train, be sure to take an A train marked "Far Rockaway" or "Rockaway Park," not an A train bound for "Lefferts Boulevard."

JFK Transfer Information AirTrain JFK.
☎ 877/535-2478 ⊕ www.airtrainjfk.com. **Long Island Railroad.** ☎ 511 ⊕ www.mta.info/lirr.

TRANSFERS FROM LAGUARDIA AIRPORT
Taxis cost $30–$50 (plus tip and tolls) to most destinations in New York City, and take at least 20–40 minutes.

For $2.75 (pay with a MetroCard or exact change in coins, no pennies) you can ride the Q70 bus to the Woodside–61st Street subway station in Queens (with connections to the 7 train, or to the LIRR, with service to Penn Station) or to the Jackson Heights–Roosevelt Avenue subway stop, where you can transfer to the E, F, M, R, and 7 trains and reach many points in Manhattan and Brooklyn. Another option is to take the M60 bus to its end point at 106th Street and Broadway on Manhattan's Upper West Side, with connections en route to several New York City Subway lines (2, 3, 4, 5, 6, A, B, C, D, N, and Q trains). Allow at least 60 minutes for the entire trip to Midtown, and perhaps a bit more during heavy traffic or rain.

TRANSFERS FROM NEWARK AIRPORT

Taxis to Manhattan cost $50–$70 plus tolls and tip and take 20–45 minutes in light traffic; inquire with the airport's taxi dispatcher about shared group rates, too. If you're heading to the airport from Manhattan, there's a $17.50 surcharge on top of the normal taxi rate, plus tolls and a customary tip.

AirTrain Newark, an elevated light-rail system, can take you from the airline terminal to the Newark Liberty International Airport Station. From here you can take New Jersey Transit (or, for a much higher price, Amtrak) trains heading to New York Penn Station. It's an efficient and low-cost way to get to New York City, particularly if you don't have many in your group and aren't carrying massive amounts of luggage. Total travel time to New York Penn Station via New Jersey Transit is approximately 30 minutes and costs $13. By contrast, a similar, slightly faster trip (about 25 minutes) via Amtrak costs roughly $28. The AirTrain runs every three minutes from 5 am to midnight and every 15 minutes from midnight to 5 am. Note that New Jersey Transit trains first make a stop at the confusingly named Newark Penn Station before they reach New York Penn Station, their final stop. If you're not sure when to get off the train, ask a conductor or fellow passenger.

Coach USA, with Olympia Trails, runs Newark Airport Express buses that leave for Manhattan and stop at Port Authority, Bryant Park (at 42nd Street and 5th Avenue), and Grand Central Terminal about every 15 to 30 minutes until midnight. The trip takes roughly 45 minutes, and the fare is $16 (plus a $1 administrative fee). Buses headed to Newark Airport depart at the same intervals, from the same Manhattan locations.

Newark Airport Transfer Information
AirTrain Newark. ☎ 888/397–4636 ⊕ www.airtrainnewark.com. **Coach USA—Newark Airport Express.** ☎ 908/354–3330, 877/863–9275 ⊕ newarkairportexpress.com.

TRANSFERS BETWEEN AIRPORTS

There are several transportation options for connecting to and from area airports, including shuttles, AirTrain and mass transit, and car service or taxi. SuperShuttle and NYC Airporter run vans and buses between Newark, JFK, and LaGuardia airports. AirTrain provides information on how to reach your destination from any of New York's airports. Note that if you arrive after midnight at any airport, you may wait a long time for a taxi. There is also no shuttle service on NYC Airporter at that time.

Contacts AirTrain. ☎ 800/247–7433 ⊕ www.panynj.gov/airtrain.

▌BOAT TRAVEL

The Staten Island Ferry runs across New York Harbor between Whitehall Street (next to Battery Park in Lower Manhattan) and St. George terminal in Staten Island. The free 25-minute ride gives you a view of the Financial District skyscrapers, the Statue of Liberty, and Ellis Island.

New York Water Taxi shuttles passengers to the city's many waterfront attractions between the Hudson River (on Manhattan's west side) and East River (on its east side), including stops in Lower Manhattan (for access to the 9/11 Memorial Museum) and the South Street Seaport, as well as two locations in Brooklyn.

An all-day pass on the water taxi is $35; a similar pass that also allows passengers to visit the 9/11 Memorial Museum as part of their sightseeing package is $59. Another package includes a visit to One World Observatory for $62.

Also consider NY Waterway, which runs ferry service across the Hudson River between Manhattan and ports in New Jersey and upstate New York. In addition, the NYC Ferry operates along the East River, connecting Manhattan with Brooklyn, Queens, and, seasonally, with Governors Island (the ferries also connect several locations within Brooklyn and in Long Island City, Queens).

NY Waterway ferries offer single-trip ($1.75–$21.50) and monthly passes ($196–$642.50); the price varies greatly based on the the length of the trip. The NYC Ferry has one-way tickets for $2.75, or you can buy a 30-day pass for $121.

Information New York Water Taxi (*NYWT*). ☏ *212/742–1969* ⊕ *www.nywatertaxi.com.* **NY Waterway.** ☏ *800/533–3779* ⊕ *www.nyway-way.com.* **NYC Ferry.** ⊕ *www.ferry.nyc.* **Staten Island Ferry.** ☏ *311, 212/639–9675 outside NYC* ⊕ *www.siferry.com.*

▌ BUS TRAVEL

Most city buses in Manhattan follow easy-to-understand routes along the island's street grid. Routes go north and south on the avenues and east and west on the major two-way crosstown streets: 96th, 86th, 79th, 72nd, 66th, 57th, 42nd, 34th, 23rd, and 14th. Bus routes usually operate 24 hours a day, but service is infrequent late at night. Traffic jams can make rides maddeningly slow, especially along 5th Avenue in Midtown and on the Upper East Side. Certain bus routes provide "limited-stop service" during weekday rush hours, which saves travel time by stopping only at major cross streets and transfer points. A sign posted at the front of the bus indicates limited service; ask the driver whether the bus stops near where you want to go before boarding.

To find a bus stop, look for a light-blue sign (green for a "limited" bus, which skips more stops) on a green pole; bus numbers and routes are listed, with the stop's name underneath.

Bus fare is the same as subway fare: $2.75. Pay when you board with exact change in coins (no pennies, and no change is given) or with a MetroCard.

MetroCards *(see Public Transportation)* allow you one free transfer between buses or from bus to subway; when using coins on the bus, you can ask the driver for a free transfer coupon, good for one change to an intersecting route. Legal transfer points are listed on the back of the slip. Transfers generally have time limits of two hours.

Several routes in the city now have so-called Select Bus Service (SBS) rather than limited-stop service. These routes include those along 1st and 2nd Avenues and 34th Street in Manhattan, as well as the M60, which travels between LaGuardia Airport and 125th Street in Harlem. The buses, which are distinguished from normal city buses by signs identifying the bus as SBS on the front, make fewer stops. In addition, riders must pay for their rides before boarding with either a MetroCard or coins at a machine mounted on the street. The machine prints out a receipt. This receipt is the only proof of payment, so be sure to hold onto it for your entire SBS trip or risk a fine for fare evasion.

Bus route maps and schedules are posted at many bus stops in Manhattan, major stops throughout the other boroughs, and ⊕ *MTA.info.* Each of the five boroughs of New York has a separate bus map; they're available from some station booths, but rarely on buses. The best places to obtain them are the information kiosks in Grand Central Terminal and Penn Station, and the MTA's website. Additionally, the MTA Bus Time app ⊕ *bustime.mta.info* provides riders with real-time bus arrival information citywide.

Most buses that travel outside the city depart from the Port Authority Bus Terminal, on 8th Avenue between 40th and 42nd Streets. You must purchase your ticket at a ticket counter, not from the bus driver, so give yourself enough time to wait in line. The terminal is connected to the subway (A, C, E, N, Q, R, S, W, 1, 2, 3, and 7 lines), which offers direct travel on to Penn Station, Grand Central Terminal, and more. Several bus lines serving northern New Jersey and Rockland County, New York, make daily stops at the George Washington Bridge Bus Station from 5 am to 1 am. The station is connected to the 175th Street station on the A line of the subway, which travels down the west side of Manhattan.

A variety of discount bus services, including BoltBus and Megabus, run direct routes to and from cities such as Philadelphia, Boston, and Washington, D.C., with the majority of destinations along the East Coast. These budget options, priced from as little as $10 one way (sometimes even less, if you snag a deal), depart from locations throughout the city and can be more convenient than traditional bus services.

Buses in New York Metropolitan Transportation Authority (MTA) Travel Information Line. ☎ 511 ⊕ www.mta.info.

Buses to New York BoltBus. ☎ 877/265–8287 ⊕ www.boltbus.com. **Coach USA.** ☎ 800/877–1888 ⊕ www.coachusa.com. **Go Buses (by Academy Bus).** ☎ 855/888–7160 ⊕ www.gobuses.com. **Greyhound.** ☎ 800/231–2222 ⊕ www.greyhound.com. **Megabus.** ☎ 877/462–6342 ⊕ us.megabus.com. **New Jersey Transit.** ☎ 973/275–5555 ⊕ www.njtransit.com. **Trailways.** ☎ 800/225–6815 ⊕ www.trailways.com.

Bus Stations George Washington Bridge Bus Station. ✉ 4211 Broadway, between 178th and 179th Sts., Washington Heights ☎ 800/221–9903 ⊕ www.panynj.gov. **Port Authority Bus Terminal.** ✉ 625 8th Ave., at 42nd St., Midtown West ☎ 212/564–8484 ⊕ www.panynj.gov.

▪ CAR TRAVEL

If you plan to drive into Manhattan, try to avoid the morning and evening rush hours and lunch hour. Tune in to traffic reports online or on the radio (e.g., WCBS 880 or 1010 WINS on the AM radio dial) before you set off, and don't be surprised if a bridge is partially closed or entirely blocked with traffic.

Driving within Manhattan can be a nightmare of gridlocked streets, obnoxious drivers, and seemingly suicidal jaywalkers and bicyclists. Narrow and one-way streets are common, particularly downtown, and can make driving even more

difficult. The most congested streets of the city generally lie between 14th and 59th Streets and 3rd and 8th Avenues. In addition, portions of Broadway near Times Square (from 42nd to 47th Street) and Herald Square (33rd to 35th) are closed to motorized traffic. This can create gridlock and confusion in nearby streets.

GASOLINE

Gas stations are few and far between in Manhattan. If you can, fill up at stations outside Manhattan, where prices are generally cheaper. In Manhattan, you can refuel at stations along 10th and 11th Avenue south of West 57th Street, and in other locations scattered throughout the island. Some gas stations in New York require you to pump your own gas; others provide attendants.

PARKING

Free parking is difficult to find in Midtown, and on weekday evenings and weekends in other neighborhoods. If you find a spot on the street, check parking signs carefully, and scour the curb for a faded yellow line indicating a no-parking zone, the bane of every driver's existence. Violators may be towed away or ticketed literally within minutes. If you do drive, use your car sparingly in Manhattan. If you can't find public parking, pull into a guarded parking garage; note that hourly rates (which can be $40 or more for just two hours) decrease somewhat if a car is left for a significant amount of time.
▪ TIP➜ BestParking (⊕ nyc.bestparking.com) helps you find the cheapest parking-lot options for your visit; search by neighborhood, address, or attraction.

ROAD CONDITIONS

New York City streets are generally in good condition, although there are enough potholes and bad patch jobs to make driving a little rough in some areas, as on sections of 2nd and 3rd Avenues, and along Broadway. Road and bridge repair seem to go on constantly, so you may encounter the occasional detour or a bottleneck where a three-lane street narrows to one lane. Many drivers don't slow down for yellow lights here—they (foolishly) speed up to make it through the intersection. Heavy rains can cause street flooding in some areas, most notoriously on the Franklin D. Roosevelt Drive (known as the FDR Drive and sometimes as East River Drive), where the heavy traffic can grind to a halt when little lakes suddenly appear on the road.

RULES OF THE ROAD

On city streets the speed limit is 25 mph, unless otherwise posted. No right turns on red are allowed within city limits, unless otherwise posted. Be alert for one-way streets and "no left turn" intersections.

The law requires that front-seat passengers wear seat belts at all times. Children under 16 must wear seat belts in both the front and back seats. Always strap children under age four into approved child-safety seats. It is illegal to use a handheld cell phone while driving in New York State. Police have the right to seize the car of anyone arrested for DWI (driving while intoxicated) in New York City.

CAR RENTALS

When you reserve a car, ask about cancellation penalties, taxes, drop-off charges (if you're planning to pick up the car in one destination and leave it in another), and surcharges (for being under or over a certain age, additional drivers, or driving across state or country borders or beyond a specific distance from your point of rental). All these things can add substantially to your costs. Request car seats and extras such as GPS when you book.

Rates are sometimes—but not always— better if you book in advance or reserve through a rental agency's website. There are other reasons to book ahead, though: for popular destinations (like NYC), during busy times of the year, or to ensure that you get certain types of cars (vans, SUVs, exotic sports cars).

■TIP➜ Make sure that a confirmed reservation guarantees you a car. Agencies sometimes overbook, particularly for busy weekends and holiday periods.

Rates in New York City average $70–$120 a day and $300–$500 a week (plus tax) for an economy car with air-conditioning, automatic transmission, and unlimited mileage. Rental costs are lower outside New York City, specifically in such places like Hoboken, New Jersey, and Yonkers, New York. If you already have a membership with a short-term car-rental service like Zipcar, consider using them for your car needs in the city.

CAR-RENTAL INSURANCE

If you own a car and carry comprehensive car insurance for both collision and liability, your personal auto insurance probably covers a rental, but read your policy's fine print to be sure. If you don't have auto insurance, you should probably buy the collision- or loss-damage waiver (CDW or LDW) from the rental company. This eliminates your liability for damage to the car. Some credit cards offer CDW coverage, but it's usually supplemental to your own insurance and may not cover special vehicles (SUVs, minivans, luxury models, and the like). If your coverage is secondary, you may still be liable for loss-of-use costs from the car-rental company (again, read the fine print). If you're planning on using credit-card insurance, use that card for *all* transactions, from reserving to paying the final bill.

You may also be offered supplemental liability coverage. The car-rental company is required to carry a minimal level of liability coverage insuring all renters, but it may not be enough to cover claims in a really serious accident if you're at fault. Your own auto-insurance policy should also protect you if you own a car; if you don't, you have to decide whether you are willing to take the risk.

U.S. rental companies sell CDWs and LDWs for about $9 a day; supplemental liability is usually more than $10 a day. The car-rental company may offer you all sorts of other policies, but they're rarely worth the cost. Personal accident insurance, which is basic hospitalization coverage, is an especially egregious rip-off if you already have health insurance.

■ TIP→ You can decline insurance from the rental company and purchase it through a third-party provider such as AIG's Travel Guard (⊕ *www.travelguard. com*)—$9 per day for $35,000 of coverage.

▌ PUBLIC TRANSPORTATION

When it comes to getting around New York, you have your pick of transportation in almost any neighborhood you're likely to visit. The subway and bus networks are extensive, especially in Manhattan, although getting across town can take some extra maneuvering. If you're not pressed for time, consider taking a public bus *(see Bus Travel)*; they generally are slower than subways, but you can also see the city as you travel. Yellow cabs *(see Taxi Travel)* are abundant, except during the evening rush hour, when many drivers' shifts change, and in bad weather, when they get snapped up quickly. If it's late at night or you're outside Manhattan, using a ride-sharing service such as Lyft or Uber may be a good idea. Like a taxi ride, the subway *(see Subway Travel)* is a true New York City experience; it's also often the quickest way to get around. However, New York (especially Manhattan) is really a walking town, and depending on the time of day, the weather, and your destination, hoofing it could be the easiest and most enjoyable option.

During the height of weekday rush hours (especially from 7:30 am to 9:30 am and 5 pm to 7 pm), avoid Midtown if you can—subways and streets are jammed, and travel time on buses and taxis can easily double.

Subway and bus fares are $2.75 per ride. Reduced fares are available for senior citizens and people with disabilities; there are some restrictions during rush hours on express buses and the Long Island and Metro-North railroads.

You pay for mass transit with a Metro-Card, a plastic card with a magnetic strip. (The MTA is also planning to introduce electronic contactless payment options beginning in 2019). There is a $1 fee for any new MetroCard purchase but there is an 11% bonus added to the card if you put $5.50 or more on the card. (There is a $5.50 minimum card purchase at station booths; this minimum does not apply at vending machines.) A Single Ride Ticket (sold only at MetroCard vending machines) is $3. To help calculate the exact number of rides you need without having a balance left over, note that putting $9.91 on an existing MetroCard will get you $11 value, equal to four rides (add $1 for any new MetroCard purchase). As you swipe the card through a subway turnstile or insert it in a bus's card reader, the cost of the fare is automatically deducted. With the MetroCard, you can transfer free from bus to subway, subway to bus, or bus to bus, within a two-hour period.

MetroCards are sold at most (but not all) subway stations and some stores—look for an "Authorized Sales Agent" sign. The MTA sells two kinds of MetroCards: unlimited-ride and pay-per-ride. Seven-day unlimited-ride MetroCards ($31) allow bus and subway travel for a week. If you expect to ride more than 11 times in one week, this is the card to get.

Unlike unlimited-ride cards, pay-per-ride MetroCards can be shared between riders. (Unlimited-ride MetroCards can be used only once at the same station or bus route in an 18-minute period.)

You can buy or add money to an existing MetroCard at a MetroCard vending machine, available at most subway station entrances (usually near the station booth). The machines accept major credit cards and ATM or debit cards. Many also accept cash, but note that the maximum amount of change they return is $6, which is doled out in dollar coins.

SUBWAY TRAVEL

The subway system operates on more than 840 miles of track 24 hours a day and serves nearly all the places you're likely to visit. It's cheaper than a cab, and during the workweek it's often faster than either taxis or buses. The trains are well lighted and air-conditioned. Still, the New York subway is hardly problem-free. Many trains are crowded, the older ones are noisy, the air-conditioning can break, and platforms can be dingy and damp. Homeless people sometimes take refuge from the elements by riding the trains, and panhandlers and buskers head there for a captive audience. Although trains usually run frequently, especially during rush hours, you never know when some incident somewhere on the line may stall traffic. In addition, subway construction sometimes causes delays or limitation of service, especially on weekends and after 10 pm on weekdays.

You can transfer between subway lines an unlimited number of times at any of the numerous stations where lines intersect. If you use a MetroCard (see *Public Transportation*) to pay your fare, you can also transfer to intersecting MTA bus routes for free. Such transfers generally have a time limit of two hours.

Most subway entrances are at street corners and marked by lampposts with an illuminated Metropolitan Transportation Authority (MTA) logo or globe-shape green or red lights—green means the station is open 24 hours and red means the station closes at night (though the colors don't always correspond to reality). Subway lines are designated by numbers and letters, such as the 3 line or the A line. Some lines run "express" and skip stops, and others are "local" and make all stops. Each station entrance has a sign indicating the lines that run through the station. Some entrances are also marked "uptown only" or "downtown only." Before entering subway stations, read the signs carefully. One of the most frequent mistakes visitors make is taking the train in the wrong direction. Maps of the full subway system are posted in every train car and usually on the subway platform (though these are sometimes out of date). You can usually pick up free maps at station booths.

For the most up-to-date information on subway lines, call the MTA's Travel Information line or visit its website. The MTA Weekender, MTA TripPlanner, and Citymapper apps and websites are a good source for figuring out the best line to take to reach your destination, as is Google Maps. Alternatively, ask a station agent.

Schedule and Route Information Metropolitan Transportation Authority (MTA) Travel Information Line. ☎ 511 ⊕ *www.mta.info.*

Subway Information Citymapper. ⊕ *www. citymapper.com.* **MTA The Weekender.** ⊕ *web. mta.info/weekender.* **MTA Trip Planner.** ☎ *511* ⊕ *tripplanner.mta.info.*

▌ TAXI TRAVEL

Yellow cabs are almost everywhere in Manhattan, cruising the streets looking for fares. They are usually easy to hail on the street or from a cabstand in front of major hotels, though finding one at rush hour or in the rain can take some time (and assertiveness). Even if you're stuck in a downpour or at the airport, do not accept a ride from a "gypsy cab." If a cab is not yellow and does not have a numbered aqua-color aluminum medallion bolted to the hood, you could be putting yourself (or at least your wallet) in danger by getting into the car.

You can see whether a taxi is available by checking its rooftop light. If the numbers are lit, the cab is available, and the driver is ready to take passengers—he or she is required to take passengers to any location in New York City as well as Newark Airport and two adjoining counties, although only NYC and Newark locations are metered. Once the meter is engaged (off-meter rates are prohibited; even JFK and out-of-town flat fares must be recorded by the meter for the passenger's protection), the fare is $2.50 just for entering the vehicle, which includes the first.3 mile, and 50¢ for each unit thereafter. A unit is defined as either.3 mile when the cab's cruising at 6 mph or faster or as 60 seconds when the cab is either not moving or moving at less than 6 mph. New York State adds 50¢ to each cab ride. There's also a 50¢ night surcharge added between 8 pm and 6 am, and a much-maligned $1 peak-hour surcharge is tacked on between 4 pm and 8 pm. Lastly, there is also a 30¢ "improvement surcharge" for all rides. All taxi drivers are required to accept credit cards as payment. On rare occasions, some who prefer cash claim their machines are broken when that isn't actually the case. If a driver waits until the end of the ride to mention a broken machine and you want to pay by credit card, you may wish to ask the driver to turn off the meter and drive you to an ATM to see if this extra hassle is worth it.

One taxi can hold a maximum of four passengers (an additional passenger under the age of seven is allowed if the child sits on someone's lap). You must pay any bridge or tunnel tolls incurred during your trip. In order to keep things moving quickly, all taxi drivers are required to use an E-ZPass in their cabs to automatically pay tolls, and they must pass the discounted toll rate along to the passenger; the total toll amount is added to the final fare. Taxi drivers expect a 10% to 20% tip, which should be awarded for safe driving and good service.

To avoid unhappy taxi experiences, try to know where you want to go and how to get there before you hail a cab. ■TIP→ **Know the cross streets of your destination (for instance, "5th Avenue and 42nd Street") before you enter a cab; a quick call to your destination will give you cross-street information, as will a glance at a map.** Also, speak simply and clearly to make sure the driver has heard you correctly—few are native English

speakers, so it never hurts to make sure you've been understood. If headed for a far-flung location in Brooklyn or Queens, it can be helpful to pull up the location using Google Maps or a similar app, especially if the driver doesn't have GPS of his own. When you leave the cab, remember to take your receipt. It includes the cab's medallion number, which can help you track the cabbie down in the event that you've left your possessions in the cab or if you want to report an unpleasant ride (or even to compliment your driver for a great experience). Any charges, such as those for bridges, are itemized on the receipt; you can double-check to make sure you were charged correctly.

Yellow taxis can be difficult to find in parts of Brooklyn, Queens, the Bronx, and Staten Island. To help with this issue, in 2013 the city of New York created a brand-new class of taxi service: apple-green Boro Taxis, which act like yellow taxis: they charge the same metered rates, accept credit cards, and must take you to any location within the city of New York. The difference is that green taxis are only allowed to pick up fares in non-Manhattan boroughs and in Manhattan locations above 96th Street.

If you're outside Manhattan and can't find a yellow or green taxi, it may be more convenient and less expensive to call a car service. Locals and staff at restaurants and other public places can often recommend a reliable company that services a particular neighborhood or borough. For example, Arecibo Car Service offers low rates from Brooklyn to any of NYC's airports. Most services offer flat-rate fares, but always confirm the fee beforehand; a 10%–20% tip is customary.

Another increasingly popular option is booking a car through one of the car service apps like Uber, Lyft, Juno, or SheRides, which match passengers with potential car-service drivers. After booking a car through one of their respective apps, you can trace its journey to you via GPS, and you get a notification once it has arrived. These services are sometimes cheaper than a taxi (especially if the service has a carpool option that allows passengers to share rides at a discounted fare), but sometimes more, especially if "surge pricing" is in effect (when it's raining or at other high-demand times). The apps do let you get an estimate on rates before you book, but Juno is the only one that offers fixed "surge-free" rates regardless of demand, weather, or traffic. Payment and tipping (if applicable) are also done via the apps.

Car-Service Companies Arecibo Car Service. ☎ ⊕ *www.arecibocc.com.* **Carey.** ☎ *800/336–4646* ⊕ *www.carey.com.* **London Towncars.** ⊠ *Long Island City* ☎ *212/988–9700, 800/221–4009* ⊕ *www.londontowncars. com.*

Ride-Share and App-Based Car Services Juno (by Gett). ⊕ *gojuno.com.* **Lyft.** ⊕ *www. lyft.com.* **Uber.** ⊕ *www.uber.com.*

▌ TRAIN TRAVEL

For information about the subway, see Subway Travel.

Metro-North Railroad trains take passengers from Grand Central Terminal to points north of New York City, both in New York State and Connecticut. Amtrak trains arrive at Penn Station. For trains from New York City to Long Island and New Jersey, take the Long Island Rail Road and New Jersey Transit, respectively; both operate from Penn Station.

Although Penn Station does not have a telephone contact or website, the train services provide information. The PATH trains to New Jersey offer service to Newark, Jersey City, Harrison, and Hoboken; the main PATH stations are located at 33rd Street and the World Trade Center.

Information Amtrak. ⊠ *Penn Station, Midtown West* ☎ *800/872–7245* ⊕ *www. amtrak.com.* **Long Island Rail Road.** ⊠ *Penn Station, Midtown West* ☎ *511* ⊕ *www.mta.info/ lirr.* **Metro-North Railroad.** ⊠ *Grand Central Terminal, Midtown East* ☎ *212/532–4900, 511* ⊕ *www.mta.info/mnr.* **New Jersey Transit.** ⊠ *Penn Station, Midtown West* ☎ *973/275– 5555* ⊕ *www.njtransit.com.* **PATH.** ☎ *800/234– 7284* ⊕ *www.panynj.gov/path.*

Train Stations Grand Central Terminal. ⊠ *89 E. 42nd St., at Park Ave., Midtown East* ⊕ *www.grandcentralterminal.com.* **Penn Station.** ⊠ *From 31st to 33rd St., between 7th and 8th Aves., Midtown West* ☎ *511.*

ESSENTIALS

▮ COMMUNICATIONS

INTERNET

You can check your email or surf the Internet at all public libraries, many cafés and public parks, and most hotels. In addition, most of New York's subway stations have both Wi-Fi and mobile service. LinkNYC has also started to replace pay phones with kiosks that provide free high-speed Wi-Fi. The goal over the next several years is to provide more than 7,500 for use in all five boroughs. NYC & Company (the city's official visitor information website; ⊕ *www.nycgo.com*) and Google Maps offer online maps that outline free Wi-Fi hot spots in the New York area; the app WiFi Finder can also help you track down hot spots.

Contacts LinkNYC. ⊕ *www.link.nyc.*

▮ DISABILITIES AND ACCESSIBILITY

New York has come a long way in making life easier for people with disabilities. At most street corners, curb cuts allow wheelchairs to roll along unimpeded. Many restaurants, shops, and movie theaters with step-up entrances have wheelchair ramps. Though some New Yorkers may rush past those in need of assistance, you'll find plenty of people who are more than happy to help you get around.

NYC & Company's website, ⊕ *www.nycgo.com/accessibility*, has information on the accessibility of many landmarks and attractions in their free downloadable guide. The NYC Mayor's Office for People with Disabilities is another great resource outlining accessibility throughout the city. If you need to rent a wheelchair or scooter while in New York, Scootaround will deliver it to your hotel (or wherever you're staying); reservations can be made up to a year in advance.

Local Resources NYC Mayor's Office for People with Disabilities (*MOPD*). ☎ *311* ⊕ *www.nyc.gov/mopd.* **Scootaround.** ☎ *888/441–7575* ⊕ *locations.scootaround.com/nyc.*

LODGING

Despite the Americans with Disabilities Act (ADA), the level of accessibility seems to differ from hotel to hotel. Some properties may be accessible by ADA standards for people with mobility disabilities, but not for people with hearing or vision impairments, for example.

If you have a hearing impairment, check whether the hotel has devices to alert you visually to the ring of the telephone, a knock at the door, and a fire/emergency alarm.

If you're bringing a service dog, you're not required to let the hotel staff know ahead of time (they must accommodate your service dog regardless); however, you may wish to notify them in advance as a courtesy.

SIGHTS AND ATTRACTIONS

Most public facilities in New York City, whether museums, parks, or theaters, are wheelchair-accessible. Some attractions have special programs for people with mobility, sight, hearing, or cognitive disabilities.

TRANSPORTATION

Although the city is working to retrofit stations to comply with the ADA, not all stations, including many major ones, are accessible, and they are unlikely to be so in the near future. Accessible stations are clearly marked on subway and rail maps. Visitors in wheelchairs have better success with public buses, all of which have wheelchair lifts and "kneelers" at the front to facilitate getting on and off. Bus drivers provide assistance.

Reduced fares are available to disabled passengers; if paying with cash, you need to present a Medicare card or Paratransit card. You may also apply for a Temporary Reduced-Fare MetroCard in advance of your visit. Visitors to the city are also eligible for the same Access-a-Ride program benefits as New York City residents. Drivers with disabilities may use windshield cards from their own state or Canadian province to park in designated handicapped spaces.

Information Reduced-Fare MetroCard.
🖅 511 ⊕ www.mta.info/accessibility/transit. htm.

GAY AND LESBIAN TRAVEL

Attitudes toward same-sex couples are very tolerant in Manhattan and most other parts of the city. Hell's Kitchen, Chelsea, and Greenwich Village are some of the most prominently gay neighborhoods, but gays and lesbians feel at home almost everywhere. One of the world's oldest and largest gay-pride parades takes place on 5th Avenue the last Sunday in June.

The Center offers wellness programs, health and support services, and arts and entertainment events for the LGBT community. It is in Greenwich Village and is open to visitors 365 days a year.

PUBLICATIONS
For listings of gay events and places, check out *Time Out New York* magazine, which includes a gay-friendly take on what's happening in the city.

Gay Publications Gay City News. ⊕ gaycitynews.nyc. **TimeOut NY LGBT.** ⊕ www.timeout.com/newyork/lgbt.

Local Information The Center (*Lesbian, Gay, Bisexual & Transgender Community Center*). ✉ 208 W. 13th St., between 7th and 8th Aves., Greenwich Village 🖅 212/620–7310 ⊕ www. gaycenter.org.

KIDS IN NEW YORK

For listings of children's events, consult *Time Out New York* (⊕ www.timeout. com/new-york-kids), *New York* magazine (⊕ nymag.com/family/kids/), and other local media. The Friday *New York Times* arts section (⊕ www.nytimes.com/section/ arts) also includes children's activities. Other good sources on happenings for youngsters are the websites NYMetroParents (⊕ www.nymetroparents.com) and New York Family (⊕ www.newyorkfamily.com), and their respective magazines. If you have access to Spectrum cable television, check the local all-news channel NY1, where you'll find a spot aired several times daily that covers current and noteworthy children's events. *Fodor's Around New York City with Kids* (available in most bookstores) can help you plan your days together.

LODGING
Before you consider using a cot or fold-out couch for your child, ask how large your hotel room is—New York City rooms are usually small. Many hotels in New York allow children under a certain age to stay in their parents' room at no extra charge, but others may charge for them; be sure to find out the cutoff age for children's comps or discounts before booking.

PUBLIC TRANSPORTATION
Up to four children shorter than 44 inches who are traveling with a paying adult ride for free on MTA buses and subways. If pushing a stroller, don't struggle through a subway turnstile; ask the station agent to buzz you through the gate (the attendant will ask you to swipe your MetroCard through the turnstile nearest the gate). Keep a sharp eye on your kids while in the subway; at some stations there is a gap between the train doors and the platform.

MEDIA

NEWSPAPERS AND MAGAZINES

The major daily newspapers in New York are the *New York Times* and *Wall Street Journal,* both broadsheets, and the *Daily News* and *New York Post,* which are tabloids. Local magazines and websites include the *New Yorker* and *New York*. All of these are widely available online (although some require paid subscriptions) and at newsstands and shops around town.

MONEY

In New York, it's easy to get swept up in a debt-inducing cyclone of $60-per-person dinners, $120 theater tickets, $20 nightclub covers, and $300 hotel rooms. But one of the good things about the city is that you can spend in some areas and save in others. Within Manhattan, a cup of coffee can cost from $2 to $4, a pint of beer from $5 to $9, and a sandwich from $6 to $14. Generally, prices in the other four boroughs are slightly lower than those in Manhattan.

The most generously bequeathed treasure of the city is the arts. The stated admission fee of $25 at the Metropolitan Museum of Art is a suggestion for New York State residents and is mandatory for outside visitors. Admission is valid for three days and also includes the Met Breuer and the Cloisters. Many other museums in town have special times during which admission is free. The Museum of Modern Art, for instance, is free on Friday from 4 to 8. In summer a handful of free music, theater, and dance performances, as well as films (usually screened outdoors), fill the calendar each day.

Prices in this guide are given for adults. Reduced fees are typically available for children, students, and senior citizens.

CREDIT CARDS

Record all your credit card numbers—as well as the phone numbers to call if your cards are lost or stolen (there's a contact number typically listed on the back of the card)—in a safe place, so you're prepared should something go wrong.

Reporting Lost Cards American Express. ☎ 800/528-4800 ⊕ www.americanexpress. com. **Diners Club.** ☎ 800/234-6377 ⊕ www. dinersclub.com. **Discover.** ☎ 800/347-2683 ⊕ www.discover.com. **MasterCard.** ☎ 800/627-8372 ⊕ www.mastercard.com. **Visa.** ☎ 800/847-2911 ⊕ www.visa.com.

RESTROOMS

Public restrooms in New York are few and far between. If you find yourself in need of a restroom, head for Midtown department stores, museums, or the lobbies of large hotels to find the cleanest bathrooms. Public atriums, such as those at the Citicorp Center and The Shops at Columbus Circle, also provide good public facilities, as do Bryant Park and the many Starbucks coffee shops in the city.

Restaurants usually allow only patrons to use their restrooms, but if you're dressed well and look as if you belong, you can often just sail right in. If too self-conscious for this brand of nonchalance, just ask the host or hostess nicely. Be aware that cinemas, Broadway theaters, and concert halls have limited amenities, and there are often long lines before performances/screenings and during intermissions.

SAFETY

New York City is one of the safest large cities in the country. However, do not let yourself be lulled into a false sense of security. As with visitors in any large city, unsuspecting travelers in New York remain particularly easy marks for pickpockets and hustlers.

After the September 11, 2001, terrorist attacks, security was heightened throughout the city. Never leave any bags unattended, and expect to have yourself and your possessions inspected thoroughly in such places as airports, sports stadiums, city buildings, and sometimes even subway stations or museums.

Ignore the panhandlers on the streets and subways, people who offer to hail you a cab (they sometimes appear at transit hubs like Penn Station, the Port Authority, and Grand Central), and limousine and gypsy-cab drivers who (illegally) offer you a ride.

Keep jewelry out of sight on the street; better yet, leave valuables at home. Don't carry wallets, smartphones, or other gadgets in your back pockets, and make sure bags and purses stay closed.

Avoid deserted blocks in unfamiliar neighborhoods. A brisk, purposeful pace helps deter trouble wherever you go.

The subway runs around the clock and is generally well trafficked until midnight (and until at least 2 am on Friday and Saturday nights), and overall it is very safe. If you do take the subway late at night, ride in the center car, with the conductor. Watch out for unsavory characters lurking around the inside or outside of stations.

When waiting for a train, head to the center of the platform, and stand far away from its edge, especially when trains are entering or leaving the station. Once the train pulls into the station, avoid empty cars. While on the train, don't engage in verbal exchanges with aggressive riders. If a fellow passenger makes you nervous while on the train, trust your instincts and change cars. When disembarking, stick with the crowd until you reach the street.

Travelers Aid International helps stranded travelers, airport passengers, and unaccompanied children, and works closely with the police and other social service agencies.

■ TIP➔ **Distribute your cash, credit cards, IDs, and other valuables between a deep front pocket, an inside jacket or vest pocket, and a hidden money pouch.**

Information Travelers Aid International (JFK). ✉ *JFK International Airport; Terminals 1, 4, 5, 7, 8, Queens* ☎ *718/656–4870* ⊕ *www. travelersaid.org/jfk.*

■ SENIOR-CITIZEN TRAVEL

The Metropolitan Transportation Authority (MTA) charges lower fares for passengers 65 and over.

Senior citizens can apply for reduced-fare metro cards by mail or in person; for more information, visit ⊕ *web.mta.info/nyct/ fare/rfapply.htm.*

To qualify for age-related discounts, mention your senior-citizen status up front when booking hotel reservations (not when checking out). Be sure to have identification on hand. When renting a car, ask about promotional car-rental discounts, too, which can be cheaper than senior-citizen rates.

■ SPORTS AND THE OUTDOORS

The New York City Department of Parks & Recreation lists all of the recreational facilities and activities available throughout NYC's parks.

Contact Information NYC Department of Parks & Recreation. ☎ *311* ⊕ *www.nycgov-parks.org.*

BASEBALL

The subway gets you directly to the stadiums of both New York–area major-league teams: the New York Mets play at Citi Field, at the next-to-last stop on the 7 train in Queens, while the Yankees defend their turf at Yankee Stadium in the Bronx, accessible via the B, D, and 4 trains. The Mets-affiliated minor-league Brooklyn Cyclones are named for Coney Island's famous wooden roller coaster. They play 38 home games at MCU Park, next to the boardwalk, with views of the

Atlantic over the right-field wall and Luna Park amusement park over the left-field wall. Most people make a day of it, with time at the beach and amusement rides before an evening game. Take the D, F, N, or Q subway to the Coney Island–Stillwell Avenue Station, and walk one block to the right of the original Nathan's Famous hot dog stand.

For another fun, family-oriented experience, check out the Staten Island Yankees, one of New York's minor-league teams, which warms up many future New York Yankees players. The stadium, a five-minute walk from the Staten Island Ferry terminal, has magnificent views of Lower Manhattan and the Statue of Liberty.

Contact Information Brooklyn Cyclones. ✉ *MCU Park, 1904 Surf Ave., at 19th St., Coney Island* ☎ *718/372–5596* ⊕ *www.brooklyncyclones.com* Ⓜ *D, F, N, Q to Coney Island–Stillwell Ave.* **New York Mets.** ✉ *123-01 Roosevelt Ave., at 126th St. and Roosevelt Ave., Flushing* ☎ *718/507–8499* ⊕ *www.mets.com* Ⓜ *7 to Mets–Willets Point.* **New York Yankees.** ✉ *Yankee Stadium, 1 E. 161st St., at River Ave., Bronx* ☎ *718/293–6000* ⊕ *www.mlb.com/yankees* Ⓜ *4, B, D to 161st St.–Yankee Stadium.* **Staten Island Yankees.** ✉ *Richmond County Bank Ballpark, 75 Richmond Terr., St. George* ☎ *718/720–9265* ⊕ *www.siyanks.com* Ⓜ *Staten Island Ferry.*

BASKETBALL

The New York Knicks arouse intense hometown passions, which means tickets for home games at Madison Square Garden are hard to come by. Try StubHub to score tickets. The Brooklyn Nets are across the river, in the swanky Barclays Center. The stadium is easily reachable by 11 different subway lines (9 at the center, but 2 more are nearby) and the LIRR. The men's basketball season runs from late October through April. The New York Liberty, a member of the WNBA (Women's National Basketball Association), had its first season in 1997. The season runs from May through September, with home games played at Madison Square Garden.

Contact Information Brooklyn Nets. ✉ *Barclays Center, 620 Atlantic Ave., at Flatbush Ave., Prospect Heights* ☎ *917/618–6700 for box office* ⊕ *www.nba.com/nets* Ⓜ *2, 3, 4, 5, B, D, N, Q, R to Atlantic Ave.–Barclays Center.* **Madison Square Garden.** ✉ *4 Pennsylvania Plaza, between 31st and 33rd Sts. and between 7th and 8th Aves.New York* ☎ *212/465–6741* ⊕ *www.msg.com* Ⓜ *1, 2, 3, A, C, E to 34th St.–Penn Station.* **New York Knicks.** ☎ *212/465–5867* ⊕ *www.nba.com/knicks.* **New York Liberty.** ☎ *212/465–6073 for tickets* ⊕ *liberty.wnba.com.*

BICYCLING

In recent years, bicycling the streets of Manhattan and many parts of Brooklyn and Queens has become more mainstream and much less the sole province of bike messengers and zealots. The city government and biking organizations have both helped make it safer, and drivers and pedestrians are more aware that bikes are likely to be on the road, too. Check the NYC Department of Transportation's website for a cycling map that shows the best routes and roads with designated bike lanes, as well as local road rules, including for taking a bike on public transit.

For biking under more controlled conditions, head to New York's major parks. Central Park has a 6-mile circular drive with a couple of decent climbs. North of 72nd Street, its roadways are permanently closed to car traffic, making cycling here particularly appealing; other sections are open to vehicular traffic on weekdays from 8 am to 10 am (the Central Drive/East Drive is open to cars from 7 am to 7 pm on weekdays).

Beware of renting a bike from the many illegal vendors that hang out on the streets near Central Park, especially by Columbus Circle. It's usually better to rent from a business with an actual storefront; there are a number of reputable bike shops within a few blocks of the park. Most bike-rental stores have copies of the very handy official NYC Bike Map, which is published annually and shows traffic flow and bike lanes for all of New York City. The map and other bicycling resources can also be found at the Department of Transportation's website, ⊕ *www.nyc.gov/bikes*.

The busy bike lane along the Hudson River Park's esplanade parallels the waterfront from West 59th Street south to the esplanade of Battery Park City. Rentals are available within the park. The lane also heads north, connecting with the bike path in Riverside Park and the esplanade between West 72nd and West 100th Streets, continuing all the way to the George Washington Bridge. From Battery Park it's a quick ride up to the Wall Street area, which is relatively deserted on weekends, and over to the bike lane along the East River.

As of 2017, the 3.3-mile circular drive in Brooklyn's Prospect Park is closed to cars year-round. It has a long, gradual hill that tops off near the Grand Army Plaza entrance.

Bike Rentals and Information **Bike and Roll NYC.** ⊠ *451 Columbus Ave., between 81st and 82nd Sts., Upper West Side* ☎ *212/260–0400* ⊕ *bikeandrollnyc.com* Ⓜ *1 to 79th St.; B, C to 81st St.-Museum of Natural History.* **Get Up and Ride.** ⊠ *330 S. 3rd St., near Keap St., Williamsburg* ☎ *646/801–2453* ⊕ *www. getupandride.com.* **New York City Department of Transportation.** ☎ *311* ⊕ *www. nyc.gov/bikes.* **Pedal Pusher Bike Shop.** ⊠ *1306 2nd Ave., at 69th St., Upper East Side* ☎ *212/288–5592* ⊕ *www.pedalpusherbike-shop.com* Ⓜ *6 to 68th St.-Hunter College; Q to 72nd St.* **Toga Bike Shop.** ⊠ *110 West End Ave., at 64th St., Upper West Side* ☎ *212/799–9625* ⊕ *www.togabikes.com* Ⓜ *1 to 66th St.-Lincoln Center.* **Waterfront Bicycle Shop.** ⊠ *391 West St., between Christopher and W. 10th Sts., West Village* ☎ *212/414–2453* ⊕ *www.bikeshopny.com* Ⓜ *1 to Christopher St.-Sheridan Sq.*

CITI BIKE BICYCLING SHARE

New York's bike-sharing program debuted in 2013 with hundreds of stations, the majority in Manhattan south of Central Park and northern Brooklyn; hundreds more have been rolled out through 2017, with expansions covering most of Manhattan, deeper into Brooklyn, into Long Island City and Astoria in Queens, and across the Hudson River to Jersey City. The three-speed, 40-pound, bright-blue bikes, which are either charming or clunky depending on your perspective, are outfitted with lights and bungee cords to secure small bags and other items. They don't come with helmets, though: wearing one is recommended but not mandatory.

After buying a Citi Bike pass, you are able to borrow an unlimited number of the bikes for either 24 hours ($12) or three days ($24). What is limited is your time with a particular bike: the time between unlocking a bike at one station and returning it to another must be 30 minutes or under, or you face additional charges, and these overtime charges add up quickly (all the way to $1,200 for never returning a bike at all). As soon as you return one bike, you're free to get another—even one from the same location.

Before you pull a bike from one of the bays and start the 30-minute clock running, spend a little time planning your route. Citi Bike's website, ⊕ *www. citibikenyc.com*, and apps are helpful with this, because they show the best routes to destinations and which of the computerized outdoor stations have bikes available, and—just as important—which have empty bays available for when it's time to return your bike.

Contact Information **Citi Bike.** ☎ *855/245–3311 for customer service* ⊕ *www.citibikenyc. com.*

GROUP BIKE RIDES

Bike New York runs a 40-mile, five-borough bike ride the first Sunday in May. The Five Borough Bicycle Club organizes day and weekend rides. The New York Cycle Club sponsors regular rides for every level of ability. Time's Up!, a non-profit advocacy group, leads free recreational rides and workshops for cyclists;

the Central Park Moonlight Ride, departing from Columbus Circle at 10 pm the first Friday of every month, is a favorite.

Contact Information Bike New York. ☏ 212/870-2080 ⊕ www.bike.nyc. **Five Borough Bicycle Club.** ☏ 347/688-2925 ⊕ www.5bbc.org. **New York Cycle Club.** ⊕ www.nycc.org. **Time's Up!** ☏ 212/802-8222 ⊕ www.times-up.org.

BOATING, KAYAKING, AND PADDLEBOARDING

Central Park has rowboats (plus a Venetian gondola for evening glides) on the 22-acre Central Park Lake. Rent your rowboat, which holds up to four people, at Loeb Boathouse, near East 74th Street, from April through November ($15 an hour). Gondola rides (complete with gondolier) are available during the same period and can be reserved ($45 per half hour); the gondola hold up to six people.

Operated by Manhattan Community Boathouse is the Pier 96 Boathouse in Midtown West, where you can take a sturdy kayak out for a paddle for free on weekends from late May through early October and on Monday, Tuesday, and Wednesday evenings from June through the end of August. This walk-up kayaking program is offered on a first-come, first-served basis (no reservations are taken in advance) and is suitable for people of all ages and abilities. Kayaks, paddles, life jackets, and basic instructions are provided. All participants must sign a liability waiver and know how to swim. The Downtown Boathouse, at Pier 26 in TriBeCa, has a similar season and services. Manhattan Kayak + SUP gives kayak and stand-up paddleboard (SUP) lessons for all levels and runs trips on the Hudson River between May and late September, including a fun New York After Dark tour for $65.

Contact Information Downtown Boathouse. ⊠ Pier 26 Boathouse, near N. Moore St. at the Hudson River, TriBeCa ⊕ www.downtownboathouse.org Ⓜ 1 to Franklin St.; A, C, E to Canal St. **Loeb Boathouse.** ⊠ East side of Central Park between 74th and 75th Sts., Central Park ☏ 212/517-2233 ⊕ www.thecentralparkboathouse.com/boats.php Ⓜ 6 to 77th St.; Q to 72nd St. **Manhattan Community Boathouse.** ⊠ 56th St. at the Hudson River, Midtown West ⊕ www.manhattancommunityboathouse.org Ⓜ 1, A, B, C, D to 59th St.–Columbus Circle. **Manhattan Kayak + SUP.** ⊠ Pier 84, 555 12th Ave., at 44th St., Midtown West ☏ 212/924-1788 ⊕ www.manhattankayak.com Ⓜ A, C, E to 42nd St.–Port Authority.

FOOTBALL

The football season runs from August through December. The enormously popular New York Giants play at MetLife Stadium in East Rutherford, New Jersey. Most seats for Giants games are sold on a season-ticket basis. However, single tickets are occasionally available at Giants.com or on ticket resale sites like the NFL Ticket Exchange (by Ticketmaster) or StubHub. The New York Jets also play at MetLife Stadium. Jets tickets are likewise hard to come by, with most snapped up by fans before the season opener.

Contact Information MetLife Stadium. ⊠ One MetLife Stadium Dr. ☏ 201/559-1515, 201/559-1300 for box office ⊕ www.metlifestadium.com. **New York Giants.** ☏ 201/935-8222 for tickets ⊕ www.giants.com. **New York Jets.** ☏ 800/469-5387 for tickets ⊕ www.newyorkjets.com.

HOCKEY

The New York Rangers, one of the oldest teams in the National Hockey League, operate out of Madison Square Garden. The New York Islanders hockey team plays in the Barclays Center in Brooklyn. The New Jersey Devils take the ice at the Prudential Center—aka The Rock—in Newark, New Jersey. The regular season for hockey runs from October through early April, and the playoffs go through June.

Contact Information New Jersey Devils. ⊠ Prudential Center, 25 Lafayette St., Newark ☏ 973/757-6600 box office ⊕ www.nhl.com/devils Ⓜ NJ Transit or PATH to Newark Penn

Station. **New York Islanders.** ⊠ *Barclays Center, 620 Atlantic Ave., at Flatbush Ave., Prospect Heights* ☎ *917/618–6700* ⊕ *islanders.nhl.com* Ⓜ *2, 3, 4, 5, B, D, N, Q, R to Atlantic Ave.–Barclays Center.* **New York Rangers.** ⊠ *Madison Square Garden, 4 Pennsylvania Plaza, between 31st and 33rd Sts. and between 7th and 8th Aves.New York* ☎ *212/465–6000* ⊕ *rangers.nhl.com* Ⓜ *1, 2, 3, A, C, E to 34th St.–Penn Station.*

ICE-SKATING

The outdoor rink in Rockefeller Center, open from October through mid-April, is much smaller in real life than it appears on TV and in movies, with only 150 skaters permitted at a time—though it *is* as beautiful, especially when Rock Center's enormous Christmas tree towers above it. Reservations can be booked in advance via the website and are recommended—especially around the holidays. Otherwise, tickets are first-come, first-served, so be prepared to wait (early morning is the best time to get on the ice quickly). Be prepared to pay, too: skating rates are $25–$32 for adults, which doesn't include skate rental ($12). Central Park has two rinks, also open from late October through early April, including the beautifully situated Wollman Rink, which has skating until long after dark beneath the lights of the city. Be prepared for daytime crowds on weekends. The Lasker Rink, at the north end of Central Park, is usually less crowded than Wollman. Chelsea Piers' Sky Rink has two year-round indoor rinks overlooking the Hudson. Skate rentals are available at all rinks. The skating rink at the Winter Village at Bryant Park has "free" skating, although this doesn't include skate rental ($15–$19) or the likely fee to either buy a lock for a locker or have bags checked ($10–$15). Winter Village's rink is open from November through early March, daily from 8 am to 10 pm. A FastPass (available online, includes skate rental and bag check) allows you to skip the line; it costs $30. In Brooklyn, the beautiful LeFrak Center at Lakeside Prospect Park, which opened in 2013, also offers seasonal skating. ■ TIP➔ **Every winter the trendy Standard Hotel, in the Meatpacking District near the High Line, makes its own tiny ice rink. The rink, at 848 Washington Street at West 13th Street, is usually open late into the evenings. When you're done skating under the lights, hot toddies and Alpine-inspired snacks are ready to take the edge off any chill.**

Contact Information **Lasker Rink.** ⊠ *Midpark near 106th St., Upper West Side* ⚓ *Park entrance at 110th St. and Lenox Ave.* ☎ *917/492–3856* ⊕ *www.laskerrink.com* Ⓜ *B, C to Cathedral Parkway–110th St.; 2, 3 to Central Park North–110th St.* **LeFrak Center at Lakeside Prospect Park.** ⊠ *171 East Dr., southeast corner of Prospect Park, Prospect Park* ☎ ⊕ *lakesidebrooklyn.com* Ⓜ *Q to Parkside Av.; B, S to Prospect Park.* **The Rink at Rockefeller Center.** ⊠ *5th Ave., between 49th and 50th Sts., lower plaza, Midtown West* ☎ *212/332–7654* ⊕ *www.therinkatrockcenter. com* Ⓜ *B, D, F, M to 47th–50th Sts./Rockefeller Center.* **The Rink at Winter Village at Bryant Park.** ⊠ *476 5th Ave., between 40th and 42nd Sts. (closer to 6th Ave.), Midtown West* ☎ *917/438–5170* ⊕ *wintervillage.org/skate* Ⓜ *B, D, F, M to 42nd St.–Bryant Park.* **Sky Rink at Chelsea Piers.** ⊠ *Pier 61, W. 21st St., at the Hudson River, Chelsea* ☎ *212/336–6100* ⊕ *www.chelseapiers.com/sr* Ⓜ *C, E to 23rd St.* **Wollman Skating Rink.** ⊠ *North of 6th Ave. and Central Park S. entrance, between 62nd and 63rd Sts., Central Park* ☎ *212/439–6900* ⊕ *www.wollmanskatingrink.com* Ⓜ *1, A, B, C, D to 59th St.–Columbus Circle; N, R, W to 5th Ave.–59th St.; F to 57th St.*

JOGGING

All kinds of New Yorkers jog, some with dogs or babies in tow, so you always have company on the regular jogging routes. What's not recommended is setting out on a lonely park path at dusk. Go running when and where everybody else does. On Manhattan streets, roughly 20 north–south blocks make a mile.

In Manhattan, Central Park is the busiest spot, specifically along the nearly

1.6-mile path circling the Jacqueline Kennedy Onassis Reservoir. A runners' lane has been designated along park roads; the entire loop road is a hilly 6 miles. A good 1.75-mile route starts at the Tavern on the Green along the West Drive, heads south around the bottom of the park to the East Drive, and circles back west on the 72nd Street park road to your starting point. Riverside Park, along the Hudson River bank in Manhattan, is glorious at sunset. You can cover 3 miles by running from West 72nd to West 100th Streets and back, and the Greenbelt trail extends roughly 4 more miles north to the George Washington Bridge at 181st Street. Other favorite Manhattan circuits are the Battery Park City esplanade (just over a mile), which connects to 4 more miles of jogging paths in Hudson River Park, as well as to sections of the East River Esplanade.

The New York Road Runners (NYRR) organizes the annual New York City Marathon the first Sunday in November and hosts a variety of other races and running activities throughout the year.

Contact Information New York Road Runners (*NYRR*). ☎ ⊕ *www.nyrr.org.*

▮ STUDENTS IN NEW YORK

New York is home to Columbia University, New York University, Fordham University, the City College of New York, and other educational institutions. With colleges scattered throughout the five boroughs, and a huge population of public and private high-schoolers, it's no wonder the city is rife with student discounts. Wherever you go, especially museums, sightseeing attractions, and performances, identify yourself as a student and ask if a discount is available, but be prepared to show your ID.

ArtsConnection Teen Programs/High 5 Tickets to the Arts is a great program for teens (or anyone in middle or high school). Tickets to a wide variety of performances (though only rarely Broadway shows) and museum passes are sold for $5 online or by phone. And, for every student ticket, an adult can get a $5 ticket, too. Check the website to find out about upcoming events and offerings.

Contact Information ArtsConnection.
✉ *520 8th Ave., Suite 321, at 36th St., Midtown West* ☎ *212/302–7433* ⊕ *teens.artsconnection.org/faq-high5* Ⓜ *A, C, E to 34th St.–Penn Station.*

▮ TAXES

A sales tax of 8.875% applies to almost everything you can buy retail, including restaurant meals. However, prescription drugs and nonprepared food bought in grocery stores are exempt. Clothing and footwear costing less than $110 are also exempt.

▮ TIPPING

The customary tipping rate for taxi drivers is 10%–20%; bellhops are usually given $2 per bag in luxury hotels, $1 per bag elsewhere. Hotel maids should be tipped $2 per day of your stay. A doorman who hails or helps you into a cab can be tipped $1–$2. You should also tip your hotel concierge for services rendered; the size of the tip depends on the difficulty of your request, as well as the quality of the concierge's work. Tour guides should be tipped 15%–20% if you enjoyed the tour. Waiters should also be tipped 15%–20%, though at higher-end restaurants, a solid 20% is more the norm. Tip $1 or $2 per drink you order at the bar, or possibly more if you're ordering something especially time-consuming to make.

▮ VISITOR INFORMATION

The Grand Central Partnership (a business-improvement district) operates a number of information kiosks in and around Grand Central Terminal and also offers free tours of the neighborhood. The kiosks are loaded with maps and helpful brochures on attractions throughout the city and are staffed by friendly, knowledgeable, multilingual New Yorkers.

NYC & Company is the city's official tourism and visitor information resource. Via its website, ⊕ *www.nycgo.com*, and official NYC Information Centers (located in Midtown West at Macy's Herald Square as well as in Lower Manhattan at City Hall Park and the South Street Seaport), NYC & Co. offers recommendations on attractions and accommodations, descriptions of neighborhoods and noteworthy sites, and bundled sightseeing passes that feature a variety of attractions at a discounted price. Its official visitor guide and map, both downloadable from NYC & Company's website as well as in hard copies available around town, are very useful.

The Downtown Alliance has information on the area encompassing City Hall south to Battery Park, and from the East River to West Street; the Times Square Alliance covers the Times Square area. For a free booklet listing New York State and New York City attractions and tour packages, contact the New York State Division of Tourism.

CONTACTS

City Information Downtown Alliance. ☎ 212/566-6700 ⊕ www.downtownny.com. **Grand Central Partnership.** ☎ 212/883-2420 ⊕ www.grandcentralpartnership.nyc. **NYC & Company.** ⊕ www.nycgo.com. **Times Square Alliance.** ✉ Midtown West ☎ 212/768-1560 ⊕ www.timessquarenyc.org.

Statewide Information New York State Division of Tourism. ☎ 800/225-5697 ⊕ www.iloveny.com.

INDEX

PHOTO CREDITS

Front cover: Stu99 | Dreamstime.com [Description: Statue of Liberty, Liberty Island, New York City]. 1, Songquan Deng/Shutterstock. 2, Kord.com/age fotostock. 4, Alexpro9500 | Dreamstime.com. 5 (top), Tiraspr | Dreamstime.com. 5 (bottom), Flavijus | Dreamstime.com. 6 (top left), Spirit of America/Shutterstock. 6 (top right), Deidre Schoo. 6 (bottom left), Leungphotography | Dreamstime.com. 6 (bottom right), Friday | Dreamstime.com. 7 (top), Diegograndi | Dreamstime.com. 7 (bottom), Sepavo | Dreamstime.com. 8 (top left), Hannoonnes | Dreamstime.com. 8 (top right), Look Die Bildagentur der Fotografen GmbH / Alamy Stock Photo. 8 (bottom left), Brandon P Davis - BPD Photography. 8 (bottom right), Palinchak | Dreamstime.com. 9, Leesniderphotoimages | Dreamstime.com. 10 (top left), PitK / Shutterstock. 10 (top right), Javenlin1018 | Dreamstime.com. 10 (bottom left), Zhukovsky | Dreamstime.com. 10 (bottom right), ali sinan köksal/Flickr, [CC BY 2.0]. 11 (top), V0v | Dreamstime.com. 11 (bottom), Stu99 | Dreamstime.com. **Chapter 1: Experience New York City:** 16-17, Sean Pavone / Shutterstock. 45, Photodisc. 47 (top), Liberty Helicopters, Inc. 47 (bottom), Joshua Haviv/ shutterstock. 49 (top) and 49 (bottom), Library of Congress Prints and Photographs Division. **Chapter 2: Lower Manhattan:** 51, Sepavo | Dreamstime.com. 53, Cpenler | Dreamstime.com. 54, Chuck Pefley/Alamy. 59, Almaz 888 | Dreamstime.com. 63, Estormiz/Wikimedia Commons. **Chapter 3: SoHo, NoLIta, Little Italy, and Chinatown:** 65, Littleny | Dreamstime.com. 67, Kmiragaya | Dreamstime.com. 68, Adeliepenguin | Dreamstime.com. 70, Getty Images/iStockphoto. 73, Philip Lange/Shutterstock. **Chapter 4: The East Village and the Lower East Side:** 75, Robert K. Chin / Alamy. 77, Bruce Monroe/Flickr, [CC BY-SA 2.0]. 78, Tomás Fano/Flickr, [CC BY-SA 2.0]. 82, wdstock / iStockphoto. **Chapter 5: Greenwich Village and the West Village:** 85, Almaz888 | Dreamstime.com. 87, Evelyn Proimos/Flickr, [CC BY 2.0]. 88, wdstock/iStockphoto. 89, Ambient Images Inc./Alamy. 92, Jennifer Arnow. **Chapter 6: Chelsea and the Meatpacking District:** 95, Marco Rubino / Shutterstock. 97 and 98, Jennifer Arnow. 105, Nicolas McComber/iStockphoto. **Chapter 7: Union Square, the Flatiron District, and Gramercy Park:** 107, Sean Pavone / Shutterstock. 109, Kord.com/age fotostock. 110, Littleny | Dreamstime.com. 112, Natursports | Dreamstime.com. 114, Marco Rubino / Shutterstock. **Chapter 8: Midtown East:** 117, Kord.com/age Fotostock. 119, Jaap Hart/iStockphoto. 120, svlumagraphica/iStockphoto. 122, Jewelite | Dreamstime.com. 127, Stuart Monk/iStockphoto/Thinkstock. 128, Stuart Monk/Shutterstock. **Chapter 9: Midtown West:** 131, Dibrova | Dreamstime.com. 133, Ahavelaar | Dreamstime.com. 134, Alexpro9500 | Dreamstime.com. 135, Andykazie | Dreamstime. com. 138, oversnap/iStockphoto. 141, Berniephillips | Dreamstime.com. **Chapter 10: The Upper East Side:** 145, Nicholas Pitt/Alamy. 147, Kmiragaya | Dreamstime.com. 148, Superbo | Dreamstime. com. 154, Sampete | Dreamstime.com. 155, Renaud Visage/age fotostock. 156 (top), Renaud Visage/ age fotostock. 156 (center), Metropolitan Museum of Art. 156 (bottom), Ancient Art & Numismatics/Flickr. 158 (top), Kristen Bonardi Rapp/Flickr. 158 (bottom), Metropolitan Museum of Art. 159, Wild Bill Studio/Metropolitan Museum of Art. 160 (top and bottom), Metropolitan Museum of Art. **Chapter 11: The Upper West Side:** 163, Mary Robnett. 165, Momos/Wikimedia Commons. 166, Kord.com/age fotostock. 170 and 171, Jennifer Arnow. 172 (top left), Sepavo | Dreamstime.com. 172 (top right), Craig Chesek/AMNH. 172 (bottom), Dennis Finnin/AMNH. 174, American Museum of Natural History. 175 and 176, Denis Finnin/AMNH. 177 (top), C. Chesek/AMNH. 177 (bottom), D. Finnin/C. Chesek/AMNH. 179, Rabbit75 | Dreamstime.com. 183, Kmiragaya | Dreamstime.com. **Chapter 12: Harlem:** 185, Aijadream | Dreamstime.com. 187, Joe Malone/Agency Jon Arnold Images/ age fotostock. 188, SuperStock/age fotostock. 191, Adam Reich. **Chapter 13: Brooklyn:** 193, Olga Bogatyrenko/Shutterstock. 195, Jennifer Arnow. 196, Ace Stock Limited/Alamy. 199, Stocksnapper | Dreamstime.com. 205, Mary Robnett. 208, Littleny | Dreamstime.com. 210, pio3 / Shutterstock. **Chapter 14: Queens, the Bronx, and Staten Island:** 213, Sylvain Grandadam/age fotostock. 215, Michel Friang/Alamy. 216, Terry Robinson/Flickr, [CC BY-SA 3.0]. 221, Elizabeth Beller, via Wikimedia Commons [CC BY-SA 3.0]. 225, Ffooter | Dreamstime.com. 227, littleny / Shutterstock. 232, Jennifer Arnow. **Chapter 15: Where to Eat:** 235, Nick Solares. 236, The Spotted Pig. 238, Ace Stock Limited/ Alamy. **Chapter 16: Where to Stay:** 321, Adrian Gaut. 322, Park Hyatt New York. **Chapter 17: Shopping:** 353, Mary Robnett. 354, Richard Levine/Alamy. 359, Piero Ribelli. **Chapter 18: Nightlife:** 405, Michael Belardo/Alamy. 406, Jazz Guy /Flickr, [CC BY 2.0]. **Chapter 19: The Performing Arts:** 433, Brian Stanton. 434, Evan Joseph. 446, Jiawangkun | Dreamstime.com. 451, Jazz at Lincoln Center. **Back cover, from left to right:** Kan1234 | Dreamstime.com; Littleny | Dreamstime.com; scriptingnews/ Flickr. **Spine:** Rabbit75 | Dreamstime.com.

NOTES

NOTES

NOTES

NOTES

NOTES

ABOUT OUR WRITERS

 Sarah Amandolare is a New York-based freelance journalist covering travel and science. Her writing has appeared in The *New York Times*, The *Guardian*, *High Country News*, and *Undark*, among other publications. She is also the blog editor for New Women New Yorkers, a nonprofit that offers free workforce development programs for young immigrant women in New York City. For this edition, she updated the Performing Arts chapter.

 Since 2001, **Kelsy Chauvin** has lived among the brownstones of Fort Greene, Brooklyn. She's a writer and photographer who's explored travel, nightlife, food, LGBT culture, and more for *Fodor's*, *Condé Nast Traveler*, *Passport*, *Rand McNally*, and other publications. No matter where she's at, you can always follow her travels on Instagram and Twitter, @kelsycc.

 West Village resident **David Farley** has been writing and updating the Where to Eat chapter since 2012. He is the author of the travel books *An Irreverent Curiosity* and *Underground Worlds*. His food and travel writing regularly appear in *The New York Times*, *The Wall Street Journal*, *AFAR*, and *National Geographic Traveler*, among other publications. Find him on Instagram at @davidfarley7.

 Laura Itzkowitz is a Greenpoint-based freelance writer with a passion for travel, arts and culture, lifestyle, design, and food and wine. She co-wrote *New York: Hidden Bars & Restaurants*, the award-winning guide to New York's speakeasy scene published by Jonglez Editions. When not globetrotting, you can probably find her sipping a dirty Martini at one of the city's best bars. Laura updated the Where to Stay Chapter.

 Christina Knight has lived in Park Slope since 1995 and is a senior multimedia producer at WNET/Thirteen where she works with *American Masters*, *Great Performances*, and NYC-ARTS.org.

 Joshua Rogol, a native of Stamford, Connecticut, now calls the Boerum Hill neighborhood of Brooklyn home. He is a licensed New York City Tour guide and freelance travel writer. The most likely place to find Josh is on the city's streets, leading groups of hungry visitors and locals to the best hot spots that New York's culinary and craft beer scene have to offer. In addition to updating Harlem, Queens, the Bronx, Staten Island, and Travel Smart, Josh has also contributed to Fodor's New England.

 Emily Saladino lives in Brooklyn's Clinton Hill neighborhood. She contributes food, culture, and travel stories to BBC, *Condé Nast Traveler*, *USA Today*, *Travel + Leisure*, and others.

 Kate Thorman is a freelance writer and editor who divides her time between New York and London. Her food and travel writing can be found in such publications as *Afar* and *Bon Appétit*. For this edition Kate updated the Shopping chapter.

Caroline Trefler is a writer and world traveler who still gets excited exploring the nooks and crannies of New York City, where she's lived for the past 20 years. For this edition of Fodor's New York City, she updated the Experience chapter and all the Exploring chapters below 34th Street.

Manhattan Subway Lines